I0799487

Inuit Shamanism and Christianity

McGill-Queen's Indigenous and Northern Studies
(In memory of Bruce G. Trigger)

Sarah Carter and Arthur J. Ray, Editors

1 *When the Whalers Were Up North*
Inuit Memories from the Eastern Arctic
Dorothy Harley Eber

2 *The Challenge of Arctic Shipping*
Science, Environmental Assessment, and Human Values
Edited by David L. VanderZwaag and Cynthia Lamson

3 *Lost Harvests*
Prairie Indian Reserve Farmers and Government Policy
Sarah Carter

4 *Native Liberty, Crown Sovereignty*
The Existing Aboriginal Right of Self-Government in Canada
Bruce Clark

5 *Unravelling the Franklin Mystery*
Inuit Testimony
David C. Woodman

6 *Otter Skins, Boston Ships, and China Goods*
The Maritime Fur Trade of the Northwest Coast, 1785–1841
James R. Gibson

7 *From Wooden Ploughs to Welfare*
The Story of the Western Reserves
Helen Buckley

8 *In Business for Ourselves*
Northern Entrepreneurs
Wanda A. Wuttunee

9 *For an Amerindian Autohistory*
An Essay on the Foundations of a Social Ethic
Georges E. Sioui

10 *Strangers Among Us*
David Woodman

11 *When the North Was Red*
Aboriginal Education in Soviet Siberia
Dennis A. Bartels and Alice L. Bartels

12 *From Talking Chiefs to a Native Corporate Elite*
The Birth of Class and Nationalism among Canadian Inuit
Marybelle Mitchell

13 *Cold Comfort*
My Love Affair with the Arctic
Graham W. Rowley

14 *The True Spirit and Original Intent of Treaty 7*
Treaty 7 Elders and Tribal Council with Walter Hildebrandt, Dorothy First Rider, and Sarah Carter

15 *This Distant and Unsurveyed Country*
A Woman's Winter at Baffin Island, 1857–1858
W. Gillies Ross

16 *Images of Justice*
Dorothy Harley Eber

17 *Capturing Women*
The Manipulation of Cultural Imagery in Canada's Prairie West
Sarah A. Carter

18 *Social and Environmental Impacts of the James Bay Hydroelectric Project*
Edited by James F. Hornig

19 *Saqiyuq*
Stories from the Lives of Three Inuit Women
Nancy Wachowich in collaboration with Apphia Agalakti Awa, Rhoda Kaukjak Katsak, and Sandra Pikujak Katsak

20 *Justice in Paradise*
Bruce Clark

21 *Aboriginal Rights and Self-Government*
The Canadian and Mexican Experience in North American Perspective
Edited by Curtis Cook and Juan D. Lindau

22 *Harvest of Souls*
The Jesuit Missions and Colonialism in North America, 1632–1650
Carole Blackburn

23 *Bounty and Benevolence*
A History of Saskatchewan Treaties
Arthur J. Ray, Jim Miller, and Frank Tough

24 *The People of Denendeh*
Ethnohistory of the Indians of Canada's Northwest Territories
June Helm

25 *The Marshall Decision and Native Rights*
Ken Coates

26 *The Flying Tiger*
Women Shamans and Storytellers of the Amur
Kira Van Deusen

27 *Alone in Silence*
European Women in the Canadian North before 1940
Barbara E. Kelcey

28 *The Arctic Voyages of Martin Frobisher*
An Elizabethan Adventure
Robert McGhee

29 *Northern Experience and the Myths of Canadian Culture*
Renée Hulan

30 *The White Man's Gonna Getcha*
The Colonial Challenge to the Crees in Quebec
Toby Morantz

31 *The Heavens Are Changing*
Nineteenth-Century Protestant Missions and Tsimshian Christianity
Susan Neylan

32 *Arctic Migrants/Arctic Villagers*
The Transformation of Inuit Settlement in the Central Arctic
David Damas

33 *Arctic Justice*
On Trial for Murder – Pond Inlet, 1923
Shelagh D. Grant

34 *Eighteenth-Century Naturalists of Hudson Bay*
Stuart Houston, Tim Ball, and Mary Houston

35 *The American Empire and the Fourth World*
Anthony J. Hall

36 *Uqalurait*
An Oral History of Nunavut
Compiled and edited by John Bennett and Susan Rowley

37 *Living Rhythms*
Lessons in Aboriginal Economic Resilience and Vision
Wanda Wuttunee

38 *The Making of an Explorer*
George Hubert Wilkins and the Canadian Arctic Expedition, 1913–1916
Stuart E. Jenness

39 *Chee Chee*
A Study of Aboriginal Suicide
Alvin Evans

40 *Strange Things Done*
Murder in Yukon History
Ken S. Coates and William R. Morrison

41 *Healing through Art*
Ritualized Space and Cree Identity
Nadia Ferrara

42 *Coyote and Raven Go Canoeing*
Coming Home to the Village
Peter Cole

43 *Something New in the Air*
The Story of First Peoples Television Broadcasting in Canada
Lorna Roth

44 *Listening to Old Woman Speak*
Natives and Alternatives in Canadian Literature
Laura Smyth Groening

45 *Robert and Francis Flaherty*
A Documentary Life, 1883–1922
Robert J. Christopher

46 *Talking in Context*
Language and Identity in Kwakwaka'wakw Society
Anne Marie Goodfellow

47 *Tecumseh's Bones*
Guy St-Denis

48 *Constructing Colonial Discourse*
Captain Cook at Nootka Sound
Noel Elizabeth Currie

49 *The Hollow Tree*
Fighting Addiction with Traditional Healing
Herb Nabigon

50 *The Return of Caribou to Ungava*
A.T. Bergerud, Stuart Luttich, and Lodewijk Camps

51 *Firekeepers of the Twenty-First Century*
First Nations Women Chiefs
Cora J. Voyageur

52 *Isuma*
Inuit Video Art
Michael Robert Evans

53 *Outside Looking In*
Viewing First Nations Peoples in Canadian Dramatic Television Series
Mary Jane Miller

54 *Kiviuq*
An Inuit Hero and His Siberian Cousins
Kira Van Deusen

55 *Native Peoples and Water Rights*
Irrigation, Dams, and the Law in Western Canada
Kenichi Matsui

56 *The Rediscovered Self*
Indigenous Identity and Cultural Justice
Ronald Niezen

57 *As affecting the fate of my absent husband*
Selected Letters of Lady Franklin Concerning the Search for the Lost Franklin Expedition, 1848–1860
Edited by Erika Behrisch Elce

58 *The Language of the Inuit*
Syntax, Semantics, and Society in the Arctic
Louis-Jacques Dorais

59 *Inuit Shamanism and Christianity*
Transitions and Transformations in the Twentieth Century
Frédéric B. Laugrand and Jarich G. Oosten

Inuit Shamanism and Christianity

Transitions and Transformations in the Twentieth Century

FRÉDÉRIC B. LAUGRAND AND JARICH G. OOSTEN

McGill-Queen's University Press
Montreal & Kingston | London | Chicago

ISBN 978-0-7735-3589-3 (cloth)
ISBN 978-0-7735-3590-9 (paper)
ISBN 978-0-7735-7636-0 (ePDF)

Legal deposit first quarter 2010
Bibliothèque nationale du Québec

Reprinted 2012, 2022

Printed in Canada on acid-free paper that is 100% ancient forest free (100% post-consumer recycled), processed chlorine free

This book was first published with the help of a grant from the Canadian Federation for the Humanities and Social Sciences, through the Aid to Scholarly Publications Programme, using funds provided by the Social Sciences and Humanities Research Council of Canada. Funding was also received through the Fonds Gérard-Dion, Université Laval.

Funded by the Government of Canada | Financé par le gouvernement du Canada | Canada

Canada Council for the Arts | Conseil des arts du Canada

We acknowledge the support of the Canada Council for the Arts.
Nous remercions le Conseil des arts du Canada de son soutien.

Library and Archives Canada Cataloguing in Publication

Laugrand, Frédéric
Inuit shamanism and Christianity : transitions and transformations in the twentieth century / Frédéric B. Laugrand and Jarich G. Oosten.
(McGill-Queen's Indigenous and northern studies ; 59)
Includes bibliographical references and index.
ISBN 978-0-7735-3589-3 (bnd)
ISBN 978-0-7735-3590-9 (pbk)
ISBN 978-0-7735-7636-0 (ePDF)

1. Inuit – Religion. 2. Inuit – Social life and customs. 3. Inuit mythology. 4. Inuit – Missions. 5. Shamanism – Canada, Northern – History – 20th century. 6. Christianity – Canada, Northern – History – 20th century. I. Oosten, Jarich II. Title. III. Series: McGill-Queen's Indigenous and northern studies 59

E99.E7L3895 2010 299.7'812 C2009-904078-6

Frontispiece: *Marble Island* by Ruth Annaqtuusi Tulurialik. Linocut and stencil on mulberry paper. Winnipeg Art Gallery Collection. Courtesy Inuit Art Foundation.

Set in 10.2/12.5 Minion Pro with Myriad Pro
Book design & typesetting by Garet Markvoort, zijn digital

We dedicate this book to the elders who shared their knowledge with us in our workshops, especially those elders who passed away before this project could be completed: Gino Akkaq, Luke Anautalik, George Kappianaq, Felix Kupak, Luke Nuliajuk, and Felix Pisuk.

Contents

Part Four | Connecting to Ancestors and Land

Illustrations

Acknowledgments

Many helped us with this book. First of all, we wish to thank the elders who contributed so extensively to this project. We particularly thank Ollie and Lizzie Itinnuaq, Peter Suvaksiuq, Josie Angutinngurniq, and Job and Eva Muqyunniq for organizing and hosting the elders workshops in Kangiq&iniq (2000 and 2002), Arviat (2003), Kugaaruk (2004), and Arviat (2005). We thank all the elders who participated in these workshops and shared their recollections and knowledge with us.

We wish to express our special gratitude to Susan Sammons of Nunavut Arctic College for her continuous support of our work. Many Inuit helped us in organizing the workshops, in translating the recorded material, and in giving support to our project. We thank Henry Kablalik, Noa Tiktak, Atuat, and Alexina Kublu. We also thank John MacDonald for granting us access to the interviews of the Iglulik Oral History Project as well as for his hospitality during our research in Iglulik. We are grateful as well to Bishop Reynald Rouleau and the Oblate Fathers for supporting and facilitating our research. We express our gratitude to the many colleagues, friends, and graduate students whose stimulating ideas enriched classes, conferences, and the writing of many papers.

Finally, we wish to thank the Dutch Research Council (NWO) and the Netherlands Institute for Advanced Study in the Humanities and Social Sciences (NIAS) in Wassenaar for providing us with their support and facilities during the preparation of this book in 2005. Our research activities in the field were financed by the Social Sciences and Humanities Research Council of Canada (SSHRC), the Fonds québécois de la recherche sur la société et la culture (FQRSC), the Fonds Gérard-Dion, the Department of Justice of Canada, and the Department of Culture, Language, Elders and Youth of Nunavut.

Frédéric Laugrand
Jarich Oosten

Arviat, June 2009

Introduction

In this book, we will explore the complex transitions and transformations of Inuit religious beliefs and practices in northeastern Canada, in the territory now called Nunavut, in the nineteenth century and twentieth century. In the nineteenth century, Inuit *angakkuuniq* (shamanism) was at the core of Inuit beliefs and practices, but when the Inuit adopted Christianity, it receded into the background. Although many Inuit think of *angakkuuniq* as a feature of the past, it continues to fascinate them and many elders are convinced that it is still very much alive.

Inuit *angakkuuniq* is generally considered to be a form of shamanism. Some scholars think of shamanism as a universal phenomenon, whereas others view it as a characteristic feature of peoples inhabiting northern Eurasia and North America. Many of the distinctive features of shamanism in Eurasia can also be found in Inuit *angakkuuniq*. The *angakkuq* (shaman) is supported by helping spirits acquired in an initiation, possesses special skills and knowledge, and fulfils a wide range of functions in society, such as procuring game, healing the sick, and correcting the weather. He possesses special paraphernalia – a shamanic belt, for example.

Shamanism is embedded in a framework of cosmological beliefs and practices. Not only human beings but also animals are sentient beings that have to be respected. Rules of respect also pertain to places, objects, and their non-human owners. The deceased watch over their descendants and namesakes. A wide range of ritual rules control the interactions among these agencies. For Inuit, shamanism is not a separate tradition, but part of a wider cosmology. They consider the introduction of Christianity as a break with the past. Ritual rules were no longer observed, and the missionaries taught that only human beings had souls. Christianity had no space for the countless non-human beings that were supposed to inhabit the earth, the sky, and the sea. However, people continued to observe some rules of respect, and meetings with non-human beings remained a regular feature of hunting experiences. Even today, Inuit observe shamanic features in some forms of Christianity. Victor Tungilik, an elder from Naujaat who had practised as an *angakkuq* in his younger days, made this observation with respect to the Pentecostal Church: "When I went and listened to them it was very enjoyable, but on the other hand they seemed to be chanting like the *angakkuit* [shamans]." And he added, "I don't know why they say they are truer believers. They too go out hunting on Sunday."[1] The fact that the Pentecostals sound like *angakkuit* is a minor point, but that they do not observe the Sundays is a serious matter. Thus, the difference between Christianity and *angakkuuniq* is subordinated to more general principles associated with observing the cosmological order. According to Felix Kupak, an elder from Naujaat, the *angakkuq* Qimuksiraaq once said that shamanism would disappear, but would come back through Christianity.

In this book, we will explore how in the nineteenth and twentieth centuries the Inuit of northeastern Canada integrated the traditions of Inuit and Qallunaat (white people), especially shamanism and Christianity, into their society. The revival of Inuit culture can be witnessed today in the promotion of Inuit Qaujimajatuqangit (Inuit knowledge that is still useful), and the revival of traditional techniques such as igloo building, drum dancing, and sewing does not constitute an invention of tradition but represents a stage in a complex process of cultural transformation, one that testifies to the resilience of Inuit culture and its capacity to integrate external influences.

In Part 1, "*Angakkuuniq* and Christianity," we will examine various aspects of the transition from shamanism to Christianity. In chapter 1, we will discuss how Inuit and Qallunaat shared conceptions of the decline of Inuit culture. These notions exist in both cultural traditions but are embedded in quite different ideologies. We will explore the ideological and theoretical perspectives that inform the debates on religious change in Nunavut. In chapter 2, we will discuss the complex relationship between missionaries and *angakkuit*, showing that missionaries to some extent replaced *angakkuit* and were well aware of it. Yet a shamanic tradition continued, and *angakkuit* continued to practise. Relations between missionaries and *angakkuit* remained ambiguous and strained. We will examine various attempts that were made to integrate Christianity and shamanism in the first half of the twentieth century. These were opposed by the Roman Catholic and Anglican missionaries as well as by the Royal Canadian Mounted Police (RCMP). When it became clear that this option was not feasible, the attempts to reconcile Christianity and shamanism were apparently relinquished. The replacement of the Sedna feast by Christmas celebrations, discussed in chapter 3, was a relatively smooth process, since missionaries were often unaware of the extent to which Christmas celebrations integrated traditional beliefs and practices. Part 1 shows how Christianity and shamanism merged in many respects and were integrated in the wider framework of Inuit culture.

In Part 2, "Animals, Owners, and Non-human Beings," we will focus on beings outside human society. In Inuit culture, religious beliefs and practices were always part and parcel of a hunting existence. The relations to prey constituted the core of this hunting existence. Survival depended on correct relationships with animals, which were considered as sentient and conscious beings. We will examine how the relationship between human beings and non-human beings took shape in a dynamic process of transformation. In chapter 4, we will examine the relations between animals and human beings and the concepts of *tarniq* (miniature image) and *atiq* (name or namesake) that connect and differentiate the relations between Inuit, ancestors, and animals. Relations to animals were organized by rules of respect. With the adoption of Christianity, these rules were gradually replaced by moral principles. In the ethnographic literature, great importance is attached to the owners of the sea, the sky, and the moon. In chapter 5, we will show that although these owners receded to the background and were replaced by God, the weather and the earth have retained their importance and must still be treated with great respect. In chapter 6, we will explore the significance of other non-human beings, showing that they continue to play an important part in the discourse of the elders.

In Part 3, "Encounters, Healing, and Power," we will move to the dynamics of cultural experiences and practises. In chapter 7, we will explain how the experiences of shamanic initiation were preserved and transformed in conversions, visions, and dreams. In chapter 8, we will discuss the significance of helping spirits and explore their significance in healing and exorcism. In chapter 9, we will discuss the importance of words and objects and show how prayer and hymns replaced the old *irinaliutiit* (powerful words).

In Part 4, "Connecting to Ancestors and Land," we will focus on continuity in the relations to ancestors and land. In chapter 10 we will examine the development of *qilaniq*, the divination technique of head lifting, and drum dancing, practices that seem to be related. Particularly drum dancing has become an important marker of the identification with the tradition establishing a connection with the ancestors. In chapter 11, we will show how Pentecostal movements and healing-the-land rituals integrate traditional notions into a modern framework that easily fits within modern political and religious ideologies. In our final chapter (12), we will analyse the processes of transition and transformation and summarize the conclusions of the book.

A NOTE ON ORTHOGRAPHY AND SOURCES

In our text and glossary, we have followed the rules of the standard Roman orthography in use in Nunavut today. The older sources, such as Boas, Peck, and Rasmussen, use older orthographies, often based on Greenlandic traditions. We have retained those specific orthographies in the quotations.

Courses in oral tradition and elders workshops have been important sources of information. The results of the workshops in Arviat (2003, 2006, 2007), Kugaaruk (2004), Baker Lake (2005), and Churchill (2008) have not yet been published. Therefore, we cannot indicate page numbers for these workshops, but instead refer to them by place name and year: Arviat workshop, 2003; Kugaaruk workshop, 2004; and so on. We have also included interviews with elders who participated in the Iglulik Oral History Project preserved in Iglulik; these have been referred to by "IE" (Inuit elders) plus the number of the interview in the project. Unpublished individual interviews are referred to by the year of the interview.

We follow standard orthography in spelling the names of the elders, unless the elders have indicated a preference for another spelling (e.g., Kupak instead of Kupaq or Etanguat instead of Itanguat). A list of elders and their place of residence can be found in Appendix 2.

We usually use Inuktitut place names, and we refer to the inhabitants of a place by the place name with the suffix *-miut* (e.g., Iglulingmiut, people from Iglulik) or the suffix *-miutaq* (e.g., Aivilingmiutaq, inhabitant of Aivilik).

In quotations, the original spelling of the authors is retained. Whenever necessary, punctuation has been inserted or modified to facilitate reading.

Part One | *Angakkuuniq* and Christianity

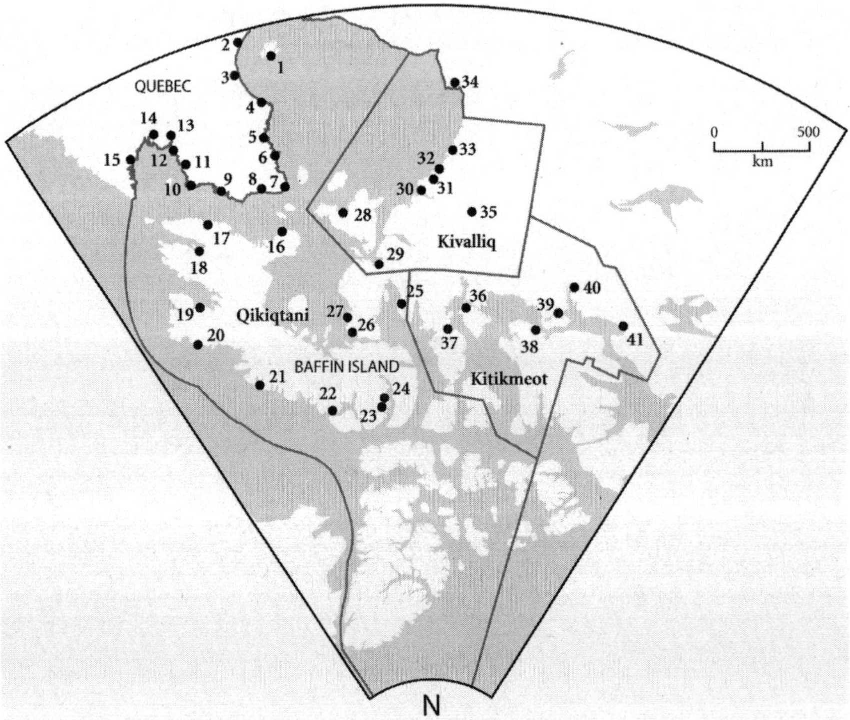

Map of Nunavut communities. Map by F. Laugrand.

1 Sanikiluaq
2 Kuujjuarapik
3 Umiujaq
4 Inukjuak
5 Puvirnituq
6 Akulivik
7 Ivujivik
8 Salluit
9 Kangiqsujuaq
10 Quaqtaq
11 Kangirsuk
12 Aupaluk
13 Tasiujaq
14 Kuujjuaq
15 Kangiqsuyalujjuaq
16 Kinngait/Cape Dorset
17 Kimmirut
18 Iqaluit
19 Panniqtuuq/Pangnirtung
20 Qikiqtarjuaq
21 Kangiqtugaapik/Clyde River
22 Mittimatalik/Pond Inlet
23 Nanisivik
24 Tununirusiq/Arctic Bay/Ikpiarjuk
25 Kugaaruk/Pelly Bay
26 Igloolik
27 Sanirajak/Hall Beach
28 Salliq/Coral Harbour
29 Naujaat/Repulse Bay
30 Igluligaarjuk/Chesterfield Inlet
31 Kangiq&iniq/Rankin Inlet
32 Tikirajuaq/Whale Cove
33 Arviat
34 Churchill
35 Qamanittuaq/Baker Lake
36 Uqsuqtuuq/Gjoa Haven
37 Taloyoak
38 Iqaluktuuttiaq/Cambridge Bay
39 Umingmaktuuq/Bay Chimo
40 Kingauk/Bathurst Inlet
41 Qurluqtuq/Kugluktuk

1

Continuity and Decline

PERCEPTIONS OF DECLINE

Qallunaat Perceptions of Decline

In the sixteenth century, European ships began to visit the Inuit of northeastern Canada. Encounters between Inuit and Qallunaat usually took place in the summer, as Europeans ships were not designed or equipped to survive the harsh arctic winters, but in the early nineteenth century, a British expedition searching for the Northwest Passage spent two winters at Lyon Inlet (1821–22) and Iglulik (1822–23). The British naval officers Parry (1824) and Lyon (1824) provided extensive descriptions of Inuit life. At that time the British Empire was almost at its zenith, and the expansion of Western civilization at the expense of so-called savage and primitive societies was taken for granted. The decline of these societies was considered a natural phenomenon, only to be expected, owing to the unavoidable progress caused by increasing contact with civilized society. The demise of Inuit culture was considered to be only a matter of time.

John Ross, the first European to reach the Inuit of Boothia Peninsula, spent three winters (1829–32) in the area. When he made contact with the Inuit, he provided them with brandy. He would later write:

> [O]ur brandy was as odious as our pudding (n.b., plumpudding); and they have yet, therefore, to acquire the taste which has, in ruining the morals, hastened the extermination of their American neighbours to the southward. If, however, these tribes must finally disappear, as seems their fate, it is at least better, that they should die gradually by the force of rum, than that they should be exterminated in masses by the fire and the sword of Spanish conquest; since there is at least some pleasure, such as it is, in the mean time, while there is also a voluntary, if slow suicide, in exchange for murder and misery. Is it not the fate of the savage and the uncivilized on this earth to give way to the more cunning and the better informed,

to knowledge and society? It is the order of the world, and the right one: nor will all lamentations of a mawkish philanthropy, with its more absurd or censurable efforts avail one jot against an order of things as wise as it is, assuredly established. All which it is our duty to provide for, is, that this event be not hastened by oppression and wrong, that it may not be attended by the suffering of individuals.[1]

Inuit would either disappear or be absorbed by Western civilization. The disappearance of the Inuit was considered a moral issue, and it was the responsibility of the white man to make it bearable for them.

Integration of natives into Western civilization, according to many, was not necessarily a good thing. In 1858, the Moravian missionary Mathias Warmow wrote about the Inuit of South Baffin Island: "I am always sorry to see the Esquimaux … imitating the Europeans in all respects. They were undoubtedly better off in their original state and more likely to be gained for the kingdom of God. But when they begin to copy our mode of life they are neither properly Europeans or Esquimaux and will speedily die out, in consequence of the change."[2] The assessment that Inuit were already too much acculturated and might be on the road to extinction may have played a part in Warmow's recommendation to his society that it not open a mission on Baffin Island.[3]

In the nineteenth century, Inuit were increasingly employed by whalers and greatly contributed to the success of whaling in the area.[4] Western observers considered the impact of whaling as detrimental to the persistence of Inuit culture. The German scientist Kumlien (1879, 13) observes, "It is certain that since the whalers have begun coming among the Cumberland Eskimo, and introduced venereal diseases, they have deteriorated very much. They now almost depend upon ships coming, and as a consequence are becoming less expert hunters, and more careless in the construction of their habitations, which are merely rude temporary shelters made at a few minutes' notice. Great suffering often ensues from living in these miserable huts."

The whalers brought new goods and prosperity to the Inuit, but also new diseases and new customs. In the course of the nineteenth century, the Inuit population was greatly reduced, mainly through the illnesses introduced by the whalers.[5] Sexual intercourse between the whalers and Inuit women was frequent. The first Anglican missionaries in Cumberland Sound tried to protect the Inuit from the influence of the whalers. In a letter to the Church Missionary Society (CMS) in 1897, Peck emphasized "[t]he absolute necessity of counteracting as soon as possible the terrible influences of the crews of whaling ships."[6]

Demographic decline and cultural decline were perceived as closely connected. The adoption of Western technology, clothing, and housing was considered the very proof of the decline of Inuit culture. Western observers did not consider the possibility that Inuit were incorporating and integrating Western technology, even Western religion, into their own cultural traditions.

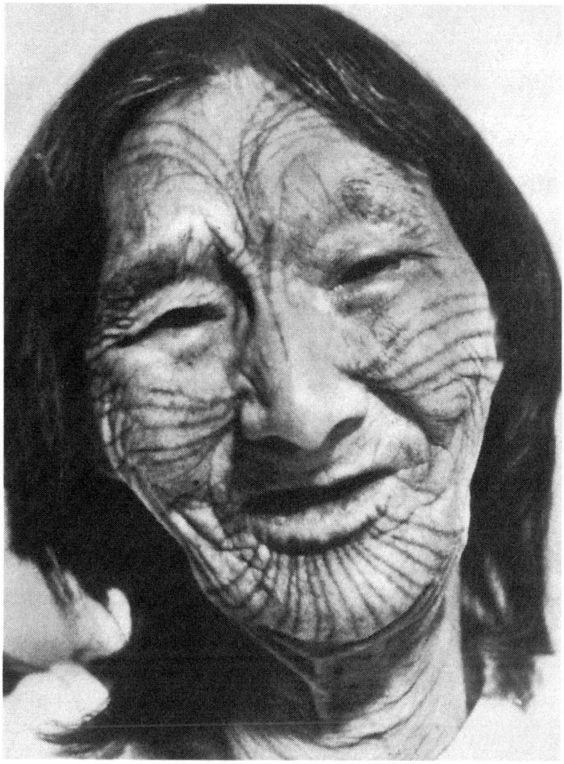

Woman elder with tattoos. Courtesy of Archives Deschâtelets.

In the second half of the nineteenth century, the decline of whaling brought hardship to the Inuit, and the missionaries did their best to relieve their needs.[7] Kumlien (1879, 43) suggests that many religious beliefs and practices were already on the decline because of the arrival of the whalers: "It seems very probable that before the advent of whalemen they practiced a great many rites and ceremonies, many of which are now obsolete, or exist only in tradition. Sometimes one of these old customs will be repeated, but, as a general thing, not in the presence of a white man, if they can help it."

Traditional beliefs and customs were disappearing even before the first missionaries became active in Cumberland Sound at the end of the nineteenth century. The Anglican missionaries Bilby and Peck reported that the Sedna feast was already declining before the first Inuit were converted. Many ethnographic reports refer to the disappearance of traditional customs. Hunting rules changed, as many of the old prohibitions no longer applied to game animals killed by rifles. The tradition of tattooing women was already disappearing at the end of the nineteenth century.[8] Therefore, ethnographers of Inuit culture such as Boas and Rasmussen focused on recording "traditional" Inuit culture before it disappeared, "hoping to save what can yet be saved."[9] Sometimes they deliberately

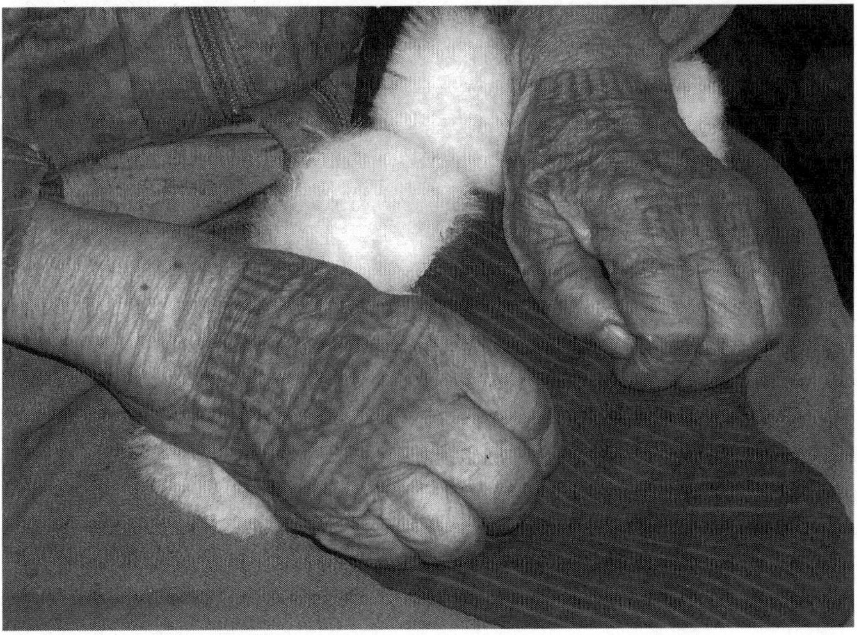

Tattoos on the hands of Niviuvaq from Talurjuaq. Photograph by C. Remie.

omitted references to innovations in their ethnographies.[10] Like many later ethnographers, they paid little attention to the impact of the whalers.[11] Reflecting upon the future of the Iglulingmiut, the Danish archaeologist Mathiassen (1928, 240), a member of the Fifth Thule expedition (1921–24) led by Knud Rasmussen, states, "What the future of the Iglulik Eskimos will be is difficult to say. Will it be possible for this little tribe, five hundred people, spread over an enormous area of land, to continue being able to hold its own in the struggle for existence, or will it, like so many other primitive peoples, be swallowed up in the fight against European civilisation?"

The members of the Fifth Thule expedition focused on the anthropological and archaeological reconstruction of traditional Inuit culture and paid much less attention to changes occurring in Inuit societies in that period, notably the adoption of Christianity. Mathiassen did not consider it worthwhile to collect detailed information on the Inuit conversion rituals that were spreading at a great speed through many camps on Baffin Island and the Melville Peninsula. In Iglulik he met Umik and his followers,[12] who were promoting Christianity in the area, but he was not impressed: "[I]t will presumably disappear just as quickly as it came when it no longer has the interest of novelty."[13]

After the establishment of the first Anglican mission post in Uumanarjuaq (Blacklead Island) in 1894 and the first Roman Catholic mission post in Igluligaarjuk (Chesterfield Inlet) in 1912, the adoption of Christianity by Inuit increased rapidly. Inuit often requested missionaries to found mission posts in communities that had already adopted the new religion. Thus, Father Henry, an Oblate missionary, founded a Catholic mission post at Kugaaruk (Pelly Bay) in 1935 at the request of the Nattilingmiut. The success of the mission contributed to the conviction that traditional Inuit culture was gone. Missionaries who stayed in the mission posts for many years were aware that traditional practices sometimes continued in secret,[14] but they assumed this would not go on for long. Already in the 1940s, Oblate missionaries were recording myths and stories in order to preserve Inuit traditions. Inuit oral traditions were recorded and collected by G. Mary-Rousselière, F. Van de Velde, A. Thibert, and M. Métayer. As well, missionaries urged the Inuit to record their own traditions in diaries and other written records.[15]

While missionaries were recording Inuit traditions, anthropological attention from the 1950s to the 1970s shifted to law and community studies. The Canadian government began to pursue a policy of settling Inuit in permanent communities, and quite a number of acculturation and community studies of the period focused on the modernization of Inuit culture (Brody 1979; Crowe 1969; Damas 1969; Mathiasson 1967; Van den Steenhoven 1959). This shift in focus was thought to contribute to a process that would see Inuit become full participants in modern Canadian society.

As it came to be assumed that shamanism and other traditional beliefs and practices had disappeared, the recording or preservation of the old traditions was no longer considered a priority, and the emphasis, especially in American and Canadian anthropology, shifted to studies of change and modernization. In Europe, traditional Inuit culture was still considered more important, but it tended to be delegated to the domain of the history of religion, as it was taken for granted that these traditions now belonged to the past (Gabus 1940, 1944; Michéa 1949; Frederiksen 1964).

In the late 1960s, a new anthropological interest in shamanic traditions arose. Anthropologists working in this field often developed their research in close collaboration with missionaries. A. Balikci (1970) conducted research in Kugaaruk in cooperation with Father F. Van de Velde, and R. Savard cooperated with Father M. Métayer, who at the end of the 1950s recorded many drum dances and collected many stories from the elders (see Métayer 1973). But the topic of shamanism was still difficult to discuss. J. Briggs (1970) attempted a study of shamanism among the Utkuhikjalingmiut but failed to get any response from her informants, who clearly preferred not to discuss the matter with an outsider.

It was only when Inuit elders themselves were ready to discuss the traditions of the past with outsiders that anthropologists became aware of the tenacity and resilience of Inuit culture. By the mid-1970s, the traditions of Inuit elders were gradually being recorded. Notably, B. Saladin d'Anglure and his co-researchers from Laval University, such as F. Thérien (1978, on shamanism) and R. Dufour

(1977, on names; 1987, on traditional birth), successfully collected new information on traditional beliefs and practices. The first Inuit authors emphasized the impact of change and transformation.[16] With the emergence of a pan-Inuit ideology (see the creation of the Inuit Tapirisat of Canada in 1971), as well as various political journals (e.g., *Inuit Today* and *Taqralik*), Inuit began to regain an appreciation for the richness of their traditions. The foundation of the Inuit Cultural Institute in 1975 and especially the organization of various elders conferences made it clear that Inuit traditions needed to be recorded and thus preserved.[17] This need soon became a political issue, but the preservation of Inuit traditions was never seen as incompatible with Inuit adoption of modernity.

In the 1980s the land claims issue, which ultimately led to the foundation of Nunavut in 1999, dominated political debate. Inuit leaders who had been trained in residential schools argued that Inuit were perfectly capable of dealing with the modern political and economic order. In social sciences and the humanities, the study of oral traditions became a central topic, leading to the development of new research projects in the 1980s and 1990s. In cooperation with Inuit elders such as Noah Piugaattuk and Rose Iqallijuq and Inuit researchers such as Louis Tapardjuk, George Qulaut, and Leah Otak, J. MacDonald of the Iglulik Research Center and Dutch anthropologist W. Rasing started a project that involved interviewing elders about oral traditions in Iglulik; the project resulted in an impressive collection of recordings of the recollections of elders.[18]

In the mid-1990s, we started a project on oral traditions with Susan Sammons and Alexina Kublu of Nunavut Arctic College, our purpose being to develop new teaching tools and materials.[19] As Inuit began to take pride in their own cultural traditions, their inhibitions over communicating about sensitive issues like shamanism lessened, and in the late 1990s elders such as Victor Tungilik from Naujaat or Felix Pisuk from Kangiq&iniq admitted that they had been trained as shamans or had been involved in shamanic practices. When the Nunavut government was established in April 1999, it supported research on Inuit knowledge and traditions. A special department, the Department of Culture, Language, Elders and Youth (CLEY), was founded to promote the transfer of knowledge from elders to youths. The department coined the concept of Inuit Qaujimajatuqangit (Inuit knowledge that is still useful). Recent books like MacDonald's excellent work on Inuit astronomy (1998), Bennett and Rowley's impressive study *Uqalurait* (2004), and Mannik's comprehensive *Inland Nunamiut* (1998) present Inuit perspectives of the past and are almost entirely based on Inuit elder testimony. Political leaders such as Peter Irniq support the transfer of knowledge and the preservation of Inuit traditions. In a few Inuit communities, new associations have begun to produce books and movies. Isuma Productions in Iglulik, for example, produces films on Inuit traditions and has earned worldwide renown with *Atanarjuat*. Today, with the rapid disappearance of the generation of elders who were raised before Inuit settled in modern communities, the preservation of traditional knowledge, as well as traditional skills and techniques, has been assigned a high priority.[20]

Inuit Perceptions of Decline

Notions of decline held by ethnographers were reinforced by Inuit traditions relating to the decline of their culture. Rasmussen (1931, 481) reported, "There are ancient traditions that the Utkuhikjalingmiut once were a great nation, so numerous that all the hills looking over Lake Franklin were sometimes enveloped in smoke from the many camp fires round the lake." With respect to the Ukjulingmiut, he related that they were

> once a numerous people, who spent the summer on King William's Land and Adelaide Peninsula, or at Ualiq further west. In winter time they hunted the seal on the ice in Queen Maud's Sea. Once, however, the winter was a very severe one, blizzards blowing incessantly over Queen Maud's Sea; famine broke out and the Ukjulingmiut tried to escape from death by starvation by moving to Simpson Strait to fish for arctic cod. A great many people died, however; some froze to death, others starved, and the bodies of the dead were eaten by the living – in fact many were killed to provide food, for these poor people were driven almost mad by their sufferings that winter.
>
> The Ukjulingmiut never forgot that year of horror. The few survivors determined to go in to the mouth of Back River, where there never was any scarcity of food; there was always game, caribou and musk oxen in the interior, seals in Elliot Bay, and trout abounded in Back River. The Ukjulingmiut mixed with the Utkuhikjalingmiut and now live together with them.[21]

Mathiassen (1928, 21) also relates that the Iglulingmiut assumed they had been much more numerous in the past: "According to their own traditions, they have previously been much more numerous, which indeed seems to be confirmed by the enormous number of ruins of habitations spread over the country." Inuit assumed not only that their numbers had dwindled, but also that the powers of shamanism had greatly diminished. According to Rasmussen (1929, 131), many of the great séances of the past were no longer practised among the people of Iglulik. He writes, "But now all is mediocrity: the practise, the theories of all that one should know may still be remembered, but the great and dizzying flights to heaven and to the bottom of the sea, these are forgotten. And therefore I was never able to witness a spirit séance which was really impressive in its effect." Some Inuit might even view white people as superior *angakkuit*. Rose Iqallijuq, for example, one of the first Inuit converts to Catholicism, recalled a shamanic competition between Rasmussen, known by Inuit as Kunut, and Ingniruniq, Joe Haulli's father.

> At that time Kunut and Joe Haulli's father were both shamans. They were living in a cabin. There were white people and Inuit living in there. As

both of them were shamans, they wanted to make a competition to know who was the best. So at first, Joe Haulli's father using his ritual said: "I am going out and I will be back inside." As he went outside, a very, very small *qamutik* [dog sledge] was made and very, very small wooden persons were made too. There were also three very nice lemmings for dogs. Those three were tied to the sledge by a hair. As he was doing this, his wife said: "These are his *tuurngait* [helping spirits]." After he finished, Kunut was next. Kunut just said: "I am not going to go out, I am just going to listen what my *tuurngait* will do." So, as Kunut was in there and as he was performing, he closed his eyes, moved his arms around. As he was doing that, the cabin started shaking, the cupboard started opening so it was shaking. As the cupboard opened, we could see these fingernails. As it was still shaking, we didn't see the *tuurngait*, but the *tuurngait* were shaking the cabin, and we saw fingernails. As the cabin was shaking, Inannerunasuaq told Ingniruniq to stop doing this, that they had experienced it so that he could now stop. It was really scary at that time, maybe because the cabin was shaking. That's why Kunut was so powerful a shaman and Ingniruniq was not so powerful. When he was a little boy and when this happened, Joe Haulli, also called Tasiuq, peed into his pants.[22]

Clearly, some Inuit did think of some Qallunaat as *angakkuit* and questioned the superiority of their own shamans.

Rasmussen (1931, 295–6) found the Nattilingmiut even more critical of their shamans:

> The Netsilingmiut themselves are very emphatic in pointing out that they no longer have great shamans among them. The whole art rests upon traditions from olden times, and the respect for shamanizing is really only created by what people know from the old tales a shaman should be able to perform, if only he is sufficiently well up in his art. I took very great pains in order to penetrate the people's own views of their relations with the supernatural. But although great trust was placed in me, it was difficult to obtain satisfactory answers. Naturally, the shamans themselves were interested in respect being preserved for their art, and those who were not shamans were often afraid that, if they were too candid in what they said, they might be punished by an offended shaman.

Dwelling upon the topic of decline, Rasmussen (1931, 296) refers to his informant Ugpik: "He asserted as his opinion that the art of shamanizing was in a state of complete decay. As the shamans were now, he declared, they only satisfied timid and pliant natures who felt a yearning for help from others. The only shaman who in his opinion was of any importance was the "exiled" Iksivalitaq … That man had a remarkable power over others, and in fact had for a time been a teacher to his young son. The latter had quickly become a "visionary," had had many dreams and lived long in a dual world as real shamans must do; as the boy was no longer in company with Iksivalitaq he had lost this faculty."

Ikilinik, an Utkuhikjalingmiutaq Rasmussen had met in the Back River area, expressed these thoughts:

> Here at Utkuhikjalik there are no shamans now. The shamans of our day do not even serve an apprenticeship, and they claim that they get their powers from dreams, visions, or sickness. For myself, I am not a shaman, as I have neither had dreams nor been ill. Now that we have firearms it is almost as if we no longer need shamans, or taboo, for now it is not so difficult to procure food as in the old days. Then we had to laboriously hunt the caribou at the sacred crossing places, and there the only thing that helped was strictly observed taboo in combination with magic words and amulets. Now we can shoot caribou everywhere with our guns, and the result is that we have lived ourselves out of the old customs. We forget our magic words, and we scarcely use any amulets now. The young people don't. See, my chest is bare; I haven't got all the bones and grave-goods that the Netsilingmiut hang about them. We forget what we no longer have use for. Even the ancient spirit songs that the great shamans sing together with all the men and women of the village we forget, all the old invocations for bringing Nuliajuk up to earth so that the beasts can be wrested from her – we remember them no more.[23]

Perceptions of decline were shared by ethnographers as well as by participants, but for different reasons. Iglulingmiut, Nattilingmiut, and Utkuhikjalingmiut all assured Rasmussen that their ancestors were vastly superior to themselves. The *angakkuit* of the old days were said to be able to kill animals by just looking at them. However, whereas for outsiders the decline of shamanism was a natural phenomenon, caused by contact with civilized society, for the Inuit it was part of an ideological framework that emphasized the superiority of ancestors over descendants, of *inummariit* (true Inuit) over modern Inuit.

In 1946 Svend Frederiksen collected much information from the *angakkuq* Qimuksiraaq in Igluligaarjuk, Chesterfield Inlet. At that time Qimuksiraaq was not yet considered an exceptionally important *angakkuq*,[24] and many people thought that his brother Nagjuk was much stronger. But today elders who witnessed Qimuksiraaq's activities in their youth believe he was a very powerful shaman, and they enjoy telling stories about his performances. Even today the *angakkuit* of the past acquire mythical proportions in the perceptions of their descendants. When Iqallijuq died at the age of ninety-five in Iglulik, the distance she had taken from shamanism over her lifetime did not diminish rumours that she probably had been a shaman herself. Many elders are considered to have been *angakkuit* in the past. Today they represent the *inummariit*, the people who lived the true Inuit life. The elders themselves view their own grandparents in this way. Thus, the notion of *inummariit* is a relative one, always referring to preceding generations.

The discourse on decline continues today. It may refer to the future of Inuit culture, changes in the climate, or social problems. Apparently, it is hard not to perceive change in moral terms.

A THEORETICAL PERSPECTIVE AND METHODOLOGICAL APPROACH

Continuity and Transformation

In the social sciences, the notion of transformation has obtained a central place through the work of C. Lévi-Strauss and other structuralist scholars. It was crucial to Lévi-Strauss's conviction that social reality can be formalized and explained in terms of mathematical operations. He applied this approach especially to mythology, arguing that in this domain, where everything seems to be allowed, logical formulas can be demonstrated and the categories of human thinking revealed. His famous canonical formula is an example. But the fact that myths can be organized in mathematical formulas does not explain very much if there is no theory of interpretation that allows us to understand the relevance or significance of these formulas. Later structuralist anthropologists tried to develop such a theory, but they failed to develop one that was either satisfactory or convincing (see Maranda 2001).

Lévi-Strauss's basic intuition that myths are usually transformations of each other in time as well as in space has proved to be influential. New approaches inspired by him have been developed by such scholars as E. Désveaux (2001, 2007), who applied the notion of quadrants as a framework of transformation in the study of Amerindian myths and rituals. B. Saladin d'Anglure (1986) applied a structuralist perspective to Inuit cosmology, showing that the fetus in the womb, a person in an igloo, and Sila in the sky can be seen as transformations of each other. Oosten (1976) also adopted a structuralist perspective to analyse Nattilik and Iglulik religious traditions. Yet the question arises, to what extent can these structuralist interpretations be verified of falsified. How do the complex structures and models developed by scholars in the description and analysis of other cultures relate to the variations in perspectives that can be found in each society? Scholars employ notions such as mental grids (Wachtel 1971; see also Douglas 1970), habitus (Bourdieu 1985), interiorization and externalization (Berger and Luckmann 1966), and structuration (Giddens 1984) to try to bridge the gap between general models and individual variation. The structural tension between the models of scholars and the views of the participants has always been one of the central theoretical issues in the social sciences (see de Josselin de Jong

1956). Today it has become a political and ethical issue, as anthropology is often conceived by aboriginal people as an attempt to subordinate aboriginal society to the cognitive and moral categories of Western society.

This structural tension between scholars and participants can never be satisfactorily resolved, since the cognitive and moral frameworks of different cultures will always vary. It is essential to the anthropological endeavour that anthropologists acknowledge that they are caught in a cognitive and ideological framework just as their informants are. While there may be much common ground, there will always be points where cultural perspectives are incompatible (Descola 2005). Even though anthropology seeks to explain, it will usually only interpret. It is essentially a hermeneutic discipline, implying translation and interpretation. But how do we translate? Do we present another culture in such a way that it becomes easily accessible to a broad public, or do we wish to show the importance and complexity of cultural differences? Author Peter Freuchen (1939, 1961), a member of the Fifth Thule expedition and well-known author on Inuit, opts for the former approach. He shows in an admirable way that Inuit are human beings just like we are, and he provides anecdotes that are immediately instructive to a general public and that convey the illusion that Inuit are not that difficult to understand. At the other end of the spectrum, we find his friend Knud Rasmussen exposing the richness and complexity of Inuit culture in terms of the perspectives of the participants themselves. In his introduction to his study of the Iglulik Eskimos, he states, "[I]t has always been one of my main objects, in the portrayal of primitive culture, to get the natives' own views of life and its problems, their own ideas expressed in their own fashion. This was often quite as important to me as eliciting new elements in their religious and spiritual life" (1929, 11). In his valorization of the views of the participants, Rasmussen was exceptional, and his approach probably contributed significantly to his success as an ethnographer. In a few months he amassed vast collections of tales, rituals, and rules. He published many of these collections almost verbatim, risking losing his readers at an early stage. But as a result, his ethnographies are a rich treasure trove of ethnographic information. In contrast to most contemporary ethnographers, he carefully specified the names of his informants, preserving local and individual variation in the data.

Whereas anthropologists tend to focus on the differences between their own culture and that of an aboriginal people, Inuit are far more interested in the differences within their own culture. Thus, Inuit valorize local differences that an anthropologist would often consider of minor importance compared to the great differences he or she perceives between different cultures. In this book we try to do justice to the complexity and richness of Inuit culture as it takes shape in the testimony of the elders and in ever-changing rituals and practices, but we also attempt to understand and analyse the processes of change and continuity. We present extensive ethnographic data organized in a framework intended to show the patterns that give structure to these processes. Instead of immediately imposing our categories of interpretation on the participants, we will first explore how Inuit themselves shape the relationship between the individual and society, the past and the present.[25]

Inuit make a sharp distinction between shamans and Christians, Inuit and Qallunaat, although in practice these categories may merge. Anthropologists and historians cannot escape the need to interpret these disjunctions in terms of continuity and transformation. Here, we do not use the word "transformation" to refer to a logical operation in the way Lévi-Strauss did in his study of Amerindian mythology, but to refer to subtle changes and alterations, changes that are often deceptive in that they suggest fundamental changes and obscure the strong resilience of Inuit culture. The notion of transformation emphasizes the subtle dialectics of change and continuity that are central to the dynamics of Inuit culture and especially evident in the dynamism of shamanism and Christianity.

In examining processes of transition and transformation among the Inuit of northeastern Canada over the last two hundred years, we look at Inuit culture in a synchronic as well as a diachronic perspective. As early as 1950, Evans-Pritchard (1962, 152) stated, "The thesis I have put before you, that social anthropology is a kind of historiography, and therefore ultimately of philosophy or art, implies that it studies societies as moral systems and not as natural systems, that it is interested in design, rather than in process, and that it therefore seeks patterns and not scientific laws, and interprets rather than explains."

In his Marrett lecture, Evans-Pritchard challenged Radcliffe Brown's vision of social anthropology as a natural science. The necessity to study societies as moral systems had already been pointed out by the French Année sociologique school at the beginning of the twentieth century, notably by Durkheim and Mauss. They saw society not just as set of social relationships, but also as a set of representations comprising morals, ideas, and values that have to be grasped. Durkheim argues as follows:

> A society can neither create nor recreate itself without at the same time creating ideal(s). This creation is not a sort of work of supererogation for it, by which it would complete itself, being already formed; it is the act by which it is periodically made and remade. Therefore when some oppose the ideal society to real society, like two antagonists, which would lead us in opposite directions, they materialize and oppose abstractions. The ideal society is not outside of the real society: it is part of it. Although we are divided between them as between two poles which mutually repel each other, we cannot hold to one without holding to the other; for a society is not made up merely of the mass of individuals who compose it, the ground which they occupy, the things which they use, and the movements which they perform but above all is the idea which it forms of itself.[26]

Thus, we are not only confronted with empirical data that can be observed but also with ideas and values. An anthropologist is necessarily involved in the ideas and values of his own society and can never escape the epistemological and ideological debates concerning the categories of interpretation.

Anthropology has a long history of interpreting other societies in terms of pejoratives, such as savages, primitives, non-literate people, underdeveloped countries, traditional cultures, and non-Western peoples. When these terms came into fashion, they were considered to be descriptive categories and not perceived as pejoratives, but gradually scholars became aware of the negative connotations of these terms and replaced them with other terms that unavoidably turned into pejoratives again. These terms derive their significance from an ideological temporal framework with evolutionist connotations that is still attractive. Even though nineteenth-century evolutionism is rejected in anthropology today, many scholars still presume that other cultures gradually give way to modern society. This ideological historical perspective is a modern transformation of the old evolutionist ideology, and it often serves to legitimize strategies designed to enforce the modernization of native peoples.

As societies can be perceived as different moral systems, it is only to be expected that these moral systems will turn out to be incompatible in some respects. One such case is the fur boycott. Trapping used to be a vital feature of economic life in the North; it was an important source of income for the aboriginal people. In the past several decades, the fur market has almost completely collapsed owing to economic as well as ideological reasons. Today Inuit do not accept that the protection of animals should take supremacy over their own well-being, and they experience the fur boycott as an action directed against their cultural identity as hunters. The poster "SAVE THE BABY VEAL: AVOID CULTURAL PREJUDICE" turns the tables on the Americans and Europeans, but fails to change their attitudes. Most Europeans and Americans think that Inuit should not cling to a hunting way of life that belongs to the past. They should adapt to modern society and realize that the preservation of nature is more important than the preservation of a hunting mode of existence. For Inuit, giving up a hunting means giving up their culture; for Europeans and Americans, it is a necessary step in a process leading to full participation in a global civilization.

Today these conflicting views affect every dimension of the complex relationships between federal agencies and aboriginal people. The Canadian government wishes to integrate aboriginal people into a modern Canadian society, where aboriginal people would have the same rights and obligations as other Canadian citizens. Aboriginal people wish to participate in Canadian society without giving up their cultural identity. A new political and cultural consciousness has been growing among aboriginal peoples. They have mastered the political and ideological discourses of modern society and use them to defend themselves in political and legal struggles to maintain their cultural and political autonomy. Aboriginal people feel that they have been studied from an outsiders' perspective, and they wonder to what extent anthropology reflects the morality, ideas, and values of the colonial powers and the oppression they represented. Many people believe that anthropologists are steeped in the morality of Western soci-

"SAVE THE BABY VEAL." This poster was designed to turn the tables on anti-seal hunt activists. Source: http://photos1.blogger.com/blogger/4708/191/1600/babyveal.0.jpg.

ety and are incapable of grasping the morals, ideas, and values of another society. In a guide for researchers titled *Negotiating Research Relationships with Inuit Communities* (Nickels et al. 2006, 2), it is stated, "Inuit often feel that scientists do not make enough effort to consider Inuit knowledge and perspectives when framing research questions and designing studies. Inuit occasionally dismiss as unnecessary and irrelevant studies (especially those on harvested wildlife species) that they believe Inuit already possess. A common perspective is that Inuit have the answers to many of the questions scientists propose to investigate."

Inuit often feel that they are better qualified to do research on their own culture but lack the training and resources to do so. *Uqalurait* (Bennett and Rowley 2006) presents an oral history of Nunavut that gives precedence to the aboriginal perspective in presenting the recollections of Inuit elders. Anthropologists and historians are becoming increasingly aware of the need to give scope to aboriginal perspectives. Today researchers in Nunavut require a research permit granted by the Nunavut Research Institute and approved by the local community where the research is to be conducted. The Nunavut government plays an important part in the development of research agendas, particularly in research on Inuit Qaujimajatuqangit.

Inuit Qaujimajatuqangit

The phrase Inuit Qaujimajatuqangit was coined in the 1990s when Inuit decided to replace the modern notion of "Inuit traditional knowledge."[27] It refers to Inuit knowledge that had been handed down from the ancestors and embodied fundamental ideas and values that distinguished Inuit from Qallunaat. The development of the concept demonstrated a new valorization of the Inuit cultural heritage and a rejection of the notion that modernization implied an unconditional acceptance of Qallunaat ideas and values.

From the start, the notion of *qaujimajatuqangit* raised intensive debates among Inuit. Did it refer specifically to the knowledge held by the elders, or did it encompass the knowledge of all Inuit? The question has never been resolved completely. Because Inuit elders are held in high esteem because of their experience and knowledge, they are usually considered to be the ones who should be consulted on questions concerning Inuit knowledge. But people are well aware that the elders have more experience with the life out on the land than with specific problems of modern society. Thus, while their recollections of shamanic beliefs and practices will not be challenged, their views on the modern schooling system or on women's shelters may be subjected to intensive debate in Inuit society.

Elders, as well as youths, acknowledge Inuit Qaujimajatuqangit as an important part of the Inuit cultural heritage that should be preserved. Nunavut government also hold this position. It supports the recording of Inuit Qaujimajatuqangit and hopes that the wisdom of the elders will help solve pressing social problems in modern Inuit communities. The Nunavut Social Development Council (NSDC) (n.d., 12) recommends the following: "Traditional Inuit laws, practices and beliefs, including those pertaining to spirituality and shamanism, need to be researched, recorded and shared." *Towards Justice That Brings Peace* (1998, 12), an NSDC report of a meeting in Kangiq&iniq in 1998, notes, "In the old days when the Elders were not able to help an individual they sent them to a Shaman. The Shaman used 'positive messages' to help individuals. Shamans could counter mystical beings who had bad intentions. Once the Church arrived, it asked Inuit to get rid of such positive inner values, but Inuit still used them as a last resort." Clearly, a political discourse is developing that sketches an idealized image of shamans conforming to modern values. The shaman is depicted as representing true Inuit wisdom, in contrast to Qallunaat traditions, including the church. The loss of a shamanic tradition is perceived as part of the decline of Inuit culture, and researching Inuit Qaujimajatuqangit is perceived as a way to recover a cultural heritage that will enable Inuit to create a modern society based on their own traditions and values.

In modern Nunavut, elders play an important role in the preservation of Inuit Qaujimajatuqangit. In the past, they probably played a similar role as authorities on knowledge. The *isumataq* (the one with *isuma*, thought, intelligence), the

(left) Eva Muqyunniq from Arviat, one of the Ahiarmiut elders who survived the relocations to Nueltin Lake and Henik Lake. She is very knowledgeable about Ahiarmiut cultural traditions; (right) her husband, Job Muqyunniq, also an Ahiarmiut elder who survived the relocations to Nueltin Lake and Henik Lake. Joe hosted the workshop on the Ennadai Lake relocations in 2005 and demonstrated the *qilaniq* technique in Arviat. Photographs by F. Laugrand.

leader of the camp, was usually an elder hunter with much experience. In the small hunting camps of the past, elders did not constitute a special category as they do in the present, but they played their part as grandparents in the daily life of the camp and its families. Age was always an important factor in the distribution of knowledge. Knowledge was precious; it was not shared with everyone, but was only passed on to close relatives or sold at a good price. Rasmussen (1929, 165) reported that the Aivilik *angakkuq* Ava bought powerful words from an old woman named Qiqertainaq: "In return for this valuable information, Aua had provided Qiqertainaq with food and clothing for the rest of her life."

In the present, as in the past, knowledge is unevenly distributed. The modern idea that knowledge should be shared and that elders should pass on their knowledge to youth does not always agree with the elders' conviction that they should only pass on important sensitive knowledge to their own relatives.[28] Knowledge is not valued for its own sake, but for its efficacy. It is passed on because it will help people to survive and prosper. In this respect, there is a correlation between knowledge and success. Knowledge results in prosperity, and prosperity allows one to obtain more knowledge. Whereas there is a moral obligation to share food, there is no such obligation with respect to knowledge. On the contrary, sharing

(left) Jose Angutinngurniq from Kugaaruk. Angutinngurniq's father, Niptayok, and his grandfather Allakannuak were important leaders in Kugaaruk. Angutinngurniq himself is very much respected for his knowledge and leadership. He participated in the workshops we facilitated in Kangiq&iniq and Arviat and hosted a workshop in Kugaaruk. When performing *qilaniq* in Pelly Bay, he demonstrated his skills in this old Inuit practice; (right) Peter Suvaksiuq from Arviat. Suvaksiuq is a son of Pinngiqqaajuk, and his grandmother Kikpaq was an *angakkuq*. In Kangiq&iniq, Suvaksiuq demonstrated the immersion in water method of shamanic initiation, a Padlirmiut technique. He shared many recollections with us, including his near death experiences. He hosted a workshop on shamanism in Arviat in 2003. Photographs by F. Laugrand.

knowledge may imply losing an advantage that may be important in the future. Elders point out that prosperous or wealthy people are often envied and targeted by evil shamans or sorcerers.

Because the elders are the ones thought to be the authorities on the knowledge of the past, we have focused on their perceptions of the past. We are well aware that their views are not representative of those of the majority of Inuit people, but their position as elders invests them with the authority to advise, council, and direct younger generations.

In this study, we will focus on the Inuit traditions involving shamanism and Christianity that have played a central part in the discourse of the Inuit elders who have been our main informants. They still remember life on the land before Inuit began to live in permanent settlements. Many of them witnessed shamanic performances or received some shamanic training. This knowledge is not always

(left) Felix Pisuk from Kangiq&iniq. Pisuk was a son of the *angakkuq* Inuksuk. As a boy, Pisuk was trained as an *angakkuq*, but his father's brother intervened to stop his initiation. Pisuk had an extensive and detailed knowledge of shamanic traditions. In the workshops we often enjoyed his detailed knowledge and his experiences. He died in 2004; (right) Felix Kupak from Naujaat. Kupak had a difficult childhood and endured severe starvation. He survived and founded a large family. He told us that *angakkuit* were never able to perform when he was present. He possessed an extensive knowledge of shamanism as well as Christianity. He shared his near-death experiences with us as well as his recollections of Tirisikuluk. He died in 2005. Photographs by F. Laugrand.

passed on. Modern Inuit society finds it hard to provide a suitable framework for the transfer of knowledge from elders to youths. Elders and youths both complain about the loss of traditional knowledge in modern society.

Traditions of Inuit Qaujimajatuqangit vary in different areas, and this variation is acknowledged by the elders. Each elder has his or her own knowledge, and it is absolutely essential that this knowledge be seen as related only to that particular elder. Once the source, more specifically the name of the elder, is lost, the knowledge loses its roots and becomes devoid of much value to most Inuit.

Each elder is prepared to acknowledge the value of the different opinions and experiences related by others. In a course on oral traditions in 1996,[29] Pauloosie Angmalik and Saullu Nakasuk from the South Baffin Island presented their views on passing on their knowledge. Saullu Nakasuk, an elder from Pannirtuuq, said, "I'm only telling you about what I've experienced. I'm not going to

(left) Luke Anautalik from Arviat. Anautalik was an excellent carver and well versed in Ahiarmiut shamanic traditions. Originally from the Churchill area, he moved to Ennadai Lake and went through the relocations initiated by the Canadian government in the 1950s. He showed his great skills in various demonstrations of shamanic techniques. He died in 2006; (right) Levi Iluittuq from Kugaaruk. Iluittuq described in detail how he had been called to become an *angakkuq* (shaman) but had decided not to be one. In Kangiq&iniq he played an important part in setting up the of *qilaniq* (head lifting) demonstration, and in Kugaaruk he shared some Christian visions and dreams with us. Photographs by F. Laugrand.

tell you about anything I haven't experienced ... Even if it's something I know about, if I haven't experienced it, I'm not going to tell about it." Saullu Nakasuk and Pauloosie Angmalik stressed the point repeatedly in an exchange with Julia Shamaiyuk, one of the students, in the same course:

JULIA: One is not to talk about something without having experienced it?

SAULLU: Yes. One is not to talk about something just from hearsay, because it is too easy to speak a falsehood. It is not desirable to tell untruths.

JULIA: Yes.

PAULOOSIE: The lie would come out later, or if the true story were told, the apparent lie.

SAULLU: Yes. That's the way it was.

PAULOOSIE: Having heard about it just once, knowing … I have already stated that I can say that I don't know anything about it if I have only heard about it just once. If at a later time someone were to tell about it like it really is, and though I did not intentionally lie, I would be like someone who had lied. Thinking about my own reputation, I have continued this as a practice.

Thus, elders have to be very careful in their public statements. They often prefer not to discuss a subject if they think they might make a mistake or suspect doing so could negatively affect a social relationship. We have heard elders discuss a subject at length and then on another occasion deny any knowledge of it. Clearly, denying knowledge is considered far less serious than making mistakes or providing correct information in the wrong context.

The elders emphasized the value of the traditions. Saullu Nakasuk stated, "It is not possible to forget the words of our elders, when we had our elders as the ones who gave us instructions. Even so, what one heard as a child keeps on coming back even though it is not always on your mind."

Sources

Ethnographies as well as archival sources provide detailed information on Inuit culture and society in the past. Unfortunately, this information is usually organized in categories of Western thought classifying non-human beings as gods and spirits, or aspects of human beings as souls. Early ethnographers such as Boas and Peck were more interested in establishing the true meaning of key concepts such as *inua* and *tuurngaq* than in charting the debates, variations, overlaps, and changes of these concepts over time.[30] In the older sources, traditional Inuit culture was firmly identified with the past. The study of modern Inuit culture, or cultural transformations in Inuit culture, only became a topic much later. The dichotomy between a past identified with traditional culture and a present identified with modern culture obscures the continuity and dynamics of Inuit culture. In this study, we will avoid such an essentialist approach and focus on the continuous reshaping and reconstructing of ideas and values in the past as well as in the present. Whereas archival and ethnographic sources usually provide outsider perspectives of Inuit culture embedded in Western ideas and values, oral traditions provide insider perspectives embedded in Inuit ideas and values. In the interplay of these various perspectives, a better understanding of the dynamics of Inuit culture can be achieved.

Oral Traditions

Between 1996 and 2008, we set up a serious of courses and workshops in close cooperation with the Inuit Studies Program of Nunavut Arctic College in Iqaluit. The purpose of these courses and workshops was to facilitate the transfer of knowledge from elders to younger generations and to record the knowledge of the elders. As a format for the courses, we opted for a dialogue between elders and youths, and thus the elders were interviewed by young Inuit students. This format ensured that the questions posed to the elders sprang from the context of modern Inuit society. The students usually wanted to hear about Inuit life of the past, but sometimes they asked questions directly relating to their own situation. One student asked Mariano Aupilaarjuk, an elder from Kangiq&iniq, this question:[31] "I was told as a small child that if my ancestors had committed a wrongdoing, that we their descendants would have to pay for their mistakes. I'd like to know if this is true." Aupilaarjuk answered, "This is exactly what happened to my wife and me. Our ancestors did something that was very wrong, and because of that several of our children passed away at a young age. Our great-grandfather was an *angakkuq* who had killed another *angakkuq*. He told us about this. He did not want the consequences to fall upon us because it was he who had broken the *maligaq* [a rule or principle to be observed or followed]. It was a *maligaq* that pertained to him. Even after I am dead, my descendants will still continue to be affected. This is very unfair, but that's the way it works." In his answer, Aupilaarjuk took into account that this form of retaliation is considered unfair today.

In another course, a student asked Tungilik from Naujaat,[32] "Is it true what they say, that people who have sex with animals shorten their lives?" Tungilik answered:

> It is true if they do not want to tell about it. I have heard that this kind of action shortens their life. It's very dangerous. I would be told that it is not dangerous to have sex with a person. If one woman did not accept, there would be other women. One should never have sex with a woman during her menstruation. This too causes illness. All these things have been told to me. If a woman enticed a man to have sex with her while she was menstruating, then she too was cutting short her life. Those are the sorts of things that the *tuurngait* did not like. These are the sorts of things that would make a *tuurngaq* angry. This was back then, not now.

Tungilik was implying that the *tuurngait* (helping spirits) were responsible for shortening one's life, but he immediately added that this was the case in the past, but not today. A temporal perspective is thus always present in the accounts of the elders.

The interviews provided a framework for questions on issues that had fascinated young people since childhood. One student addressed George Kappianaq from Iglulik: "There were a lot of *aqsarniit* [northern lights] in Kinngait for about two years. At that time they were so close that although I was an adult, I fled from them. They were very bright and although I found them beautiful, I was afraid of them." Kappianaq answered, "What the elders say about being cautious so your head isn't decapitated is very true. They say this because it happened in the past. There would be incidents of people who had their heads lopped off when they were whistling at them to get them to come closer. The *aqsarniit* rushed by the person who was standing there and knocked their head off. They say that they play kickball using a walrus head for their *aqsaq*, their kickball."[33]

The elders' answers reflect a deep conviction that people have to answer for their deeds and are sanctioned by agencies outside human society. The elders often emphasized this perspective. In a workshop in Kugaaruk in 2004, Ollie Itinnuaq from Kangiq&iniq related this incident: "I was a taxi driver one time in Kangiq&iniq. This woman, a nun, had a suitcase with a small chip. They went into a plane. We put the suitcase in the plane in the front. It kept opening. The pilot closed it. He looked away. As soon as it took off, the plane crashed because he was mistreating the nun's suitcase. It's clear because the pilot wasn't treating the nun right, the plane crashed. We had a meeting after that and I tried to tell people who were investigating that crash that something had happened just after take-off." The crash is viewed as a result of a lack of respect.

In the oral tradition courses in Iqaluit, a wide range of topics were discussed, ranging from life-stories, traditional law, medicine, cosmology, the environment, dreams to childrearing. The discussions were published verbatim by Nunavut Arctic College.[34] These courses at the college made it clear how much knowledge on shamanism the elders had retained; yet the elders did not consider a school to be a suitable context for the transfer of sensitive knowledge. They prefer to discuss these issues out on the land or in the privacy of their homes and with close relatives.

In the past, Inuit knowledge was passed on in the context of daily life. Young people learned from their elders by observing, listening, and supporting them. The introduction of the modern school system resulted in a dichotomy between modern and traditional knowledge.[35] Children acquired new knowledge that was not shared with their elders, and at the same time they had less opportunity to learn from their elders, as they had to spend their days at school. Many elders expressed their dissatisfaction with this situation. Elisapee Ootoova from Mittimatalik stated:

> In our community, school started in 1963. It seemed to be good then. Not all of my children attended school. The younger of the two older ones was in school. It turns out it was wrong of us to agree to send them to school when the teaching material was irrelevant to the North. We were wrong in some ways and right in other ways. It is good to learn to read and write in English to be able to understand the language. But they were not taught about the lifestyle in the North. All our children in Mittimatalik have been taught as though they were to continue on to Ottawa. They are not taught the way of life in our community. They are not taught what to do when food becomes scarce.[36]

Both elders and youngsters are concerned about the generation gap, and new roads to facilitate the transfer of knowledge from elders to youths are being explored. Recognition of the connection between the land and animals on one side and mental and physical health on the other has led to programs that take young Inuit out on the land. There they can be taught by elders and can recover from the strain of community life.[37]

Elders Workshops on Inuit Qaujimajatuqangit and Shamanism

A different format was developed for the workshops that explored shamanism. A series of workshops with elders was set up in Kangiq&iniq (2000, 2002, 2003), Arviat (2003, 2006, 2007), Kugaaruk (2004), Qamanittuaq (2005), and Churchill (2008) to record the richness of the traditions preserved by elders. The first elders workshop, in Kangiq&iniq in 2000, was organized out on the land in a cabin specially adapted for the purpose by Itinnuaq from Kangiq&iniq. The workshop was financed by the Department of Justice, and it was intended to explore how traditional knowledge could contribute to solving social problems in modern Inuit society. As the subject of shamanism was considered delicate and controversial by the elders, it was decided that no young people should be present and that no outsiders should be present during the meetings. The workshop proved quite successful, as the elders not only shared their views on the past and the present but also gave recommendations on how to deal with some of the acute problems plaguing modern Inuit communities.[38] An agreement was made with the Pulaarvik Friendship Centre in Kangiq&iniq to organize another workshop that would involve more youths in the transfer of knowledge processes. Two further workshops were organized in Kangiq&iniq in 2002 and 2003, these ones involving youngsters as well as elders, and in subsequent workshops in Arviat, Kugaaruk, Qamanittuaq, and Churchill, youngsters were also invited to participate. Although the elders were initially uncomfortable discussing shamanism in the presence of youths, they gradually became accustomed to it and were prepared to give information and direction to the young people.

In the workshops in Kangiq&iniq, the participating elders all stated that they believed in shamanism, but insisted that they were not *angakkuit* themselves. Many had been in close contact with *angakkuit,* and some had been trained for some time to become *angakkuit.* They were convinced that shamanism still exists and that in each community you can find *angakkuit.* In the oral tradition courses taught at Nunavut Arctic College in the 1990s, elders had already emphasized the continuity of shamanism. Lucassie Nutaraaluk from Iqaluit remembered, "Then I was told that every community has *angakkuit* and would always have *angakkuit.* That is what I was told. There are probably *angakkuit* here in Iqaluit, too."[39] Kappianaq from Iglulik thought the same: "Yes. For sure. There will always be *angakkuit* until the end of time. I think there are numerous *angakkuit* in parts of the Qitirmiut."[40]

In the Kangiq&iniq workshops in 2000 and 2002, each day began with prayer. The elders emphatically stated that they believed in Christianity as well as in shamanism. They wanted to preserve the good things of shamanism and use them to solve the social problems of modern society. Aupilaarjuk, a member of the choir in the Catholic church in Kangiq&iniq, said, "We don't want to bring back everything from the past, but we should bring back some things. We need to bring back the things that were good. I'm not trying to eradicate Christianity, but we need to put it together with the good aspects of *angakkuuniq* if we are to really follow the Inuit way of life."[41]

Itinnuaq from Kangiq&iniq, an adopted son of the *angakkuq* Anarqaq, expressed this view: "Being an *angakkuq* can be helpful, just as prayer can be helpful. Both have their usefulness, both can work. The *angakkuit* and the ministers both pursue good. The missionaries think only of the soul, they do not think about life. An *angakkuq* knows that life is short and therefore he wants people to have good lives. I think that *angakkuit* are useful spiritually because they take away all wrongdoings. If only ministers and priests deal with a person, the person will die with wrongdoings still not confessed. It was not like that with an *angakkuq*."[42] Itinnuaq recognizes an additional value of shamanism. It involves not only the spirit but also the body, enabling people to die with their transgressions confessed. He apparently reasons that the Catholic confession alone does not take care of this completely. His sister, Qalasiq, a woman elder from Kangiq&iniq, had a similar view: "We have to put shamanism and Christianity together if we are really to follow the Inuit way of life. We believe in both systems."[43]

Today there is much speculation in the various Inuit communities over who might be *angakkuit*. It is therefore not surprising that the elders participating in the workshops stated emphatically that they were Christians and not *angakkuit*. Only rarely will an Inuk come forward and admit that he or she is a shaman or has been a shaman. An exception in this respect is Victor Tungilik from Naujaat, who admitted during a course in Iqaluit that he had practised as a shaman for several years.[44]

The data collected in the various workshops testify to the richness and vitality of the shamanic tradition in Inuit society. As the elders grew more comfortable with the presence of young people and other members of the community, they became willing to demonstrate traditional techniques, such as *qilaniq*, a technique of divination by head lifting, and instruct young people on the correct performance of these techniques. But the boundaries between play and seriousness are volatile, and during the *qilaniq* demonstrations, serious questions began to be asked. In 2002 in Kangiq&iniq, the elders organized a series of demonstrations of shamanic practices and techniques, allowing the people of the community to attend. Luke Anautalik from Arviat gave such a convincing demonstration of a shamanic trance that many people wondered whether this was the real thing. Because the demonstrations and performances were recorded on video, many small details of the elders' performances have been preserved that would otherwise have been lost.

The workshop discussions and demonstrations expressed the great respect in which these traditions are still held by elders as well as young people. By connecting the testimony of the elders to ethnographic records and archival sources, we can better understand the nature and dynamics of Inuit traditions and knowledge. However, this is not always easy. The elders were usually reluctant to comment on archival sources. In many cases, the Inuk who had provided the information was not clearly identified, and even when his name was known, the elders often had no knowledge of that person and thus felt unable to assess the value of the information provided.

Regional Variation

The elders who participated in the workshops and courses came from various communities. They were well aware of the importance of regional differences and greatly interested in these variations, acknowledging that each community – and even each family – has its own traditions. Many elders had lived in other communities or knew that their parents originated from other communities. Even though dialectal variation is still an important issue in the North, strict boundaries between different communities are hard to maintain.

In the nineteenth century, Boas (1964 [1888], 425) already recognized that Inuit could not be easily divided into tribes or other distinct groupings: "In my opinion a great difference between these tribes never existed. Undoubtedly they were groups of families confined to a certain district and connected by a common life." Relations between areas varied. Mathiassen (1928, 23) writes, "My old friend Takornaq, who accompanied me on my journey to Ponds Inlet, expressed it in this manner: that if she were to have a new husband, it was all the same to her whether he was an Aivilingmio, an Iglulingmio or a Tununermio; if need be, a Qaernermio or an Akudnermio might to do; but a Netsilingmio; never!" Although the Aivilingmiut feared the Nattilingmiut, this did not prevent the two groups from mixing, and today a community such as Naujaat has a mixed population of Nattilingmiut and Aivilingmiut. Although Nattilingmiut were feared by Iglulingmiut and Aivilingmiut, Nattilingmiut in turn feared Kitlinermiut. Rasmussen reports, "I had not been there very long before they began to talk about their neighbours to the west, the Kitlinermiut, whom they all seemed to fear. They were dangerous people, they told me, and they believed we would never again see Qʃvigarssuaq and his companion; they had been murdered."[45]

Fear of other groups did not imply organized warfare.[46] Boas (1964 [1888], 465) writes:

> Real wars or fights between settlements, I believe, have never happened, but contests have always been confined to single families. The last instance of a feud which has come to my knowledge occurred about seventy years ago. At that time a great number of Eskimo lived at Niutang, in Kingnait Fjord, and many men of this settlement had been murdered by a Qinguamio of Anarnitung. For this reason the men of Niutang united in a sledge journey to Anarnitung to revenge the death of their companions. They hid

themselves behind the ground ice and killed the returning hunter with their arrows. All hostilities have probably been of a similar character.[47]

Inuit emphasize the importance of the cultural differences between different areas. When Rasmussen (1930, 111) told Kibkarjut (Padlirmiutaq) that he had heard another version of a story she had related, she explained:

> I had heard this story related somewhat differently among the Harvaqtôrmiut where the woman who cuts off part of her face forms an item in the fantastic adventures of Kivioq, and when I asked whether the version here given might not be correctly remembered, the answer, given very energetically, was as follows: "We tell you only that which we know ourselves, and that which has been told throughout the ages in our tribe. You, who come from other peoples, and speak the tongue of other villages (dialect), and understand other Inuit besides ourselves, must know that human beings differ. The Harvaqtôrmiut know many things we do not know and we know many things they do not. Therefore you must not compare the Harvaqtôrmiut with us, for their knowledge is not our knowledge as our knowledge is not theirs. Therefore we tell you only what we know from our own villages."

In 1997 Nutaraaluk from Iqaluit commented, "I think our stories vary from community to community even though they are the same *unikkaaqtuat*."[48] Inuit elders profess great interest in the regional variation of their stories and traditions. In our projects on oral traditions, we attempt to record the richness of these traditions as they have taken shape in different areas, communities, and families. In charting the variation in the elders' testimony, we acknowledge regional differences, family traditions, and personal experiences. Interactions between areas were frequent and intense, as people used to travel far and wide and communities were continuously exposed to new influences from elsewhere. It was in this way that Christianity rapidly spread from one camp to the next in the early stages of its development. In tracing regional differences, we do not focus on identifying specific traditions with particular areas or groups, but instead focus on the dynamics and variations of these traditions as they followed different patterns of development in various areas. We apply the "field of anthropological study" approach as it was developed by Marcel Mauss and the Leiden anthropologists.

The Field of Anthropological Study Approach

In his 1935 inaugural lecture to the chair of ethnology at Leiden University, J.P.B. de Josselin de Jong (1977, 166–7) developed the notion of a field of anthropological study. He opened his lecture with a statement of the problem: "All attempts at classifying mankind into smaller or clearly delimited groups according to race or culture have been utterly fruitless." Classifications and typologies of cultures had only resulted in a "growing aversion to this kind of characterization and description of culture … in modern ethnology for the past twenty years." De Josselin de Jong argued that ethnological research on "individual groups is conducted with a hitherto unknown accuracy and intensiveness, while at the same time there is a concern with wider areas of ethnological research, perhaps best designated for the moment as 'fields of ethnological study.'" He defined the field of ethnological study as "certain areas of the earth's surface with a population whose culture appears to be sufficiently homogeneous and unique to form a separate object of ethnological study, and which at the same time apparently reveals sufficient local shades of differences to make internal comparative research worth while." Jos D.M. Platenkamp (1991) quite correctly pointed out that the definition of the field of ethnological study was clearly derived from Mauss, who was such an inspiration to the Leiden structuralists in the 1920s and 1930s.

In his famous 1904 paper *Seasonal Variations of the Eskimo*, Mauss (1979, 19) notes, "But we must not lose sight of the fact that the Eskimo occupy an extensive coastal area. There exist, not one, but many Eskimo societies whose culture is sufficiently homogeneous that they may be usefully compared, and sufficiently diverse that these comparisons may be fruitful." He argued, "The Eskimo offer such a privileged field of study because their morphology is not the same throughout the year." By focusing on social morphology, Mauss is questioning the anthropogeographical approach proposed by Ratzel, with its main emphasis on geography: "By this term, social morphology, we refer to the science whose investigations are intended not just to describe but also to elucidate the material substratum of societies. This includes the form that societies assume in their patterns of residence, the volume and density of their population, the way in which the population is distributed, as well as the entire range of objects that serve as a focus for collective life."

Mauss (1979, 27) argues that the settlement, not the tribe, is "the true territorial unit" in this field of study. In his view, the settlement is not just a territorial unit: "The settlement has more than just a name and a territory; it also possesses a linguistic unity as well as a moral and religious one. Although these two categories may appear initially to be unrelated, we have purposely linked them because the linguistic unity to which we wish to call attention has a religious basis and is related to ideas about the dead and their reincarnation." The settlement thus constitutes the basis of Eskimo morphology. Mauss tries in his article to demonstrate how the life of the settlement is decided by a seasonal rhythm of intensive social life in winter, when families shelter together in one settlement, and a much more individualist life in summer, when individual families disperse out on the land. In his conclusions, he pointed out that such a pattern could be found among many cultures, suggesting a relative autonomy in the seasonal rhythm of society with respect to climatic and geographic conditions.

In his 1935 inaugural lecture, J.P.B. de Josselin de Jong (1977, 168) attempted to define the Malay Archipelago as a field of ethnological study in terms of its social features, arguing that they form part of an integrated whole or system: "The deeper we delve into this system the clearer it shows itself to be the structural core of numerous ancient Indonesian cultures in many parts of the Archipelago." He described this structural core in terms of four distinctive features: asymmetric connubium, double descent, socio-cosmic dualism, and a special kind of resilience in reacting to cultural influences from outside. The concept of the structural core was connected with a research program focusing on the relationship between the social and cosmic organization of society and the temporal framework of continuity and transformation in Indonesian societies.

The research issues at stake in Mauss's study of "Eskimo" society were obviously quite different from those involved in de Josselin de Jong's study of Indonesia. In his study, Mauss referred to an area of linguistically and culturally closely related people. In contrast, the Malay Archipelago had great linguistic and cultural variety, and the unity of the field of ethnological study was largely determined by the Dutch colonial context. The wide range of cultures and languages in the archipelago had in different degrees been shaped by great traditions, such as Buddhism, Hinduism, and Islam. De Josselin de Jong's conception of the field of ethnological study implied a temporal framework emphasizing traditions that were originally shared by all Indonesian cultures. He was not so much concerned with the definition of the area, which was already given by the colonial situation, but with the development of a research program that would allow the researcher to deal with the problem of cultural variation in that area.

For Mauss, the notion of a privileged field of study served to solve one of the most difficult problems in Eskimo society – the lack of discrete social units that could be clearly distinguished from each other as the constituting units of social life. Neither the house nor the hunting camp nor any grouping of hunting camps plays that part in Inuit society. Mauss tried to solve this problem, but he was well aware that his solution was not satisfactory and still required a broader framework in a field of privileged study. The notion of a field of privileged study provided the foundation for J.P.B de Josselin de Jong's concept of the field of ethnological study, renamed a field of anthropological study by his nephew and successor P.E. de Josselin de Jong in the early 1980s. Mauss was looking for distinct units in an apparently linguistically and culturally homogeneous area, whereas J.P.B. and P.E. de Josselin de Jong were looking for unity in a highly diverse area.[49]

Mauss's attempt to define the winter settlement as the basic social unit of Inuit society did not do justice to the inherent flexibility and dynamics of Inuit society, but his notion of a field of study was to prove very fruitful. In a field of anthropological study, local variations are examined as cultural variants linked by transformations in time and space. Only by charting the cultural diversity and richness of local traditions can we do justice to the complexity of a field of anthropological study. In our comparison of local traditions, we thus do not assume that different groupings can be clearly distinguished from each other; instead we examine the variations and patterns, the diversity and richness, of the cultural variation in the whole area under study.

Our area of interest encompasses the Kivalliq (including the Nattilik area), the North Baffin area (including Iglulik), and the South Baffin area, from Kinngait (Cape Dorset) to Kangiqtugaapik (Clyde River).[50] The close cultural relationships between the Kivalliq and the North and South Baffin areas (see map of Nunavut communities, p. 2) are well known. The Kivalliq and North Baffin areas are also closely connected. In his description of Iglulik shamanism, Rasmussen (1929) relied to a large extent on *angakkuit* who came from the Nattilik area, such as Anarqaq and Unaliq. He referred to them as immigrant Nattilingmiut. There is little point in searching for an original Iglulik shamanism without any Nattilik influences, since Nattilingmiut were clearly active as shamans in Iglulik. Nattilingmiut also intensively interacted with other groups, such as Padlirmiut and Aivilingmiut (see Remie 1988; Csonka 1995). In concentrating on these three areas, we may give less attention to relevant connections to related areas (Inuinnait [Copper], Nunavik, or West Greenland). However, we chose the three areas on the basis of the intensive interaction within the whole region and the availability of a rich corpus of ethnographic data and missionary archives. Moreover, most of the elders participating in our workshops came from these three areas.

Inuit traditions of knowledge are in important respects locally oriented. Knowledge of the land plays a central part in Inuit life. It is important to know how the animals move, where to hunt at which season, at which dangerous places one should not camp or hunt, or which specific rituals must be carried out before entering a particular area (e.g., Marble Island). One has to know where to go for trade or what trade goods are required at a particular place and time. Such knowledge largely determines where people will reside and how they will organize their travels. Obviously, it is historically embedded. When whaling declined and the missionaries and the Hudson's Bay Company (HBC) trading posts took over the trading role, knowledge and practices had to change and adapt.

Inuit have always moved over large areas, taking their family traditions with them. Their knowledge depends not only on family tradition but also on local knowledge. Knowledge traditions cannot be identified with a particular local group, since groups as well as traditions are continuously changing. Thus, knowledge is often more strongly associated with a particular place than with a particular group – for example, people from other regions have to know what rules to follow when they hunt caribou in Piling or visit Marble Island.

Historical Perspective

To facilitate discussion, we distinguish between different historical periods in our field of historical study:

1. *Pre-contact.* For this period, our knowledge depends almost completely on archaeological evidence. In many areas, the pre-contact period extended into the nineteenth century, although at Frobisher Bay, contact had already

been made between Frobisher and the Inuit by the end of the sixteenth century. Information on beliefs and practices, however, remained scarce until the period of first contacts.

2. *First contacts with Qallunaat.* In this period, aboriginal people had their first interactions with explorers, traders, and missionaries. Although this period began in the eighteenth century, in most areas it extended from the early nineteenth century until the coming of the missionaries and anthropologists at the end of the nineteenth century. Inuit life was seriously affected by diseases imported by Qallunaat during this period. Inuit began to use Western technologies and material goods. They were also attracted by Christian notions and rules. Extensive ethnographic records by Parry, Lyon, Hall, Warmow, Kumlien, Boas, and other nineteenth-century ethnographers provide us information on the rapidly changing life of the Inuit.
3. *Adoption of Christianity.* This started at the end of the nineteenth century on South Baffin Island and the beginning of the twentieth century on North Baffin Island and the Kivalliq, when Inuit began to adopt Christianity, and it lasted until the middle of the twentieth century, when the modern settlements took shape.
4. *Post–Second World War.* Many settlements that were to become permanent communities had already developed in the first half of the twentieth century, but only in the second half of the twentieth century did the old nomadic ways of life disappear as Inuit moved, or were moved, into permanent settlements under the sway of the Canadian government.
5. *The present times of modern Nunavut.* The foundation of Nunavut in 1999 not only brought Inuit some degree of political autonomy, but also stimulated a revalorization of Inuit culture. Inuit culture has begun to be shaped by the political ideology of modern Nunavut, and this ongoing process has important implications for Inuit perceptions of traditional beliefs and practices and for the development of new forms of Christianity in modern Nunavut.

The above periodization should be handled with caution, for any periodization very much depends on the perspective. Inuit, for example, do not attach any special value to the first contacts period. This might explain why the whaling era is not seen as a relevant period when Inuit discuss shamanism.

In *Arctic Migrants,* Damas (2002) used another periodization, as he correctly pointed out that the settlement of Inuit in permanent settlements was a gradual process, starting long before the 1950s and 1960s. He suggested that the term nomadic may fit aboriginal society but that Inuit life during the fur trade and contact-traditional period is better described as semi-nomadic.[51] Inuit themselves tend to experience life in the settlements as an important break with the past. The problem was not that they were going to live in permanent settlements –

they were already used to that – but that they had lost control over their rhythm of life, which ensured a healthy balance between life out on the land and life in a camp or settlement, and were being forced to adopt the Qallunaat ideology and way of life.

Similarly, the establishment of modern Nunavut is not experienced as a break with the past by all the generations. The younger people tend to see it as a new opening to the future, but many elders feel that it has not changed much in their daily life. While elders acknowledge that they have now incorporated many aspects of Western life into their lives – rules, habits, technology, food, and so on – they often emphasize that they will never become Qallunaat.

We will use the historical periods we identified with restraint and only consider these markers as heuristic tools. Our periodization helps to integrate the development of Inuit culture and society into a Western historical perspective, but it does not necessarily help us understand Inuit perspectives of their past. We will return to these historical periods in the final chapter, when we summarize our results.

In analysing the Inuit perspective, we mainly rely on the information provided by different generations of elders. We do not assume that the views of elders accurately represent Inuit perceptions of the past, but even in modern Inuit society, the elders are considered to be the ones who can speak with authority about those perceptions. Younger generations prefer not to speak about the past in detail, as they cannot base their assessments on personal recollections. They prefer to refer anthropologists and historians to knowledgeable elders.

ANGAKKUUNIQ (SHAMANISM) AND CHRISTIANITY

Today the word *angakkuq* is translated as shaman, and words such as sorcerer, conjuror, and magician are no longer used. The derivation of the word *angakkuq* is unclear. It may be related to the word *angak* (mother's brother) as suggested by Thalbitzer (1930). The term "shaman," derived from the Tungus word *saman*, has become a central theoretical concept in the study of religion.[52] Some scholars considered a shaman to be a type of functionary marked by a capacity to go into a trance and that could be found anywhere in the world;[53] others conceived of the shaman as a functionary who was typical of a cultural area extending over northern Europe, northern Asia, and the Americas.[54] They speculated that in this area this functionary may have already existed in the Palaeolithic period and represents one of the oldest expressions of human religion. Obviously, considerable variation exists in this huge area, and it is thus risky to develop a general model to cover the wide range of features.

Inuit shamanism extends over more than ten thousand kilometres along the Arctic coast. Haase (1987) and Merkur (1985, 1991) published comparative studies on the subject.[55] Their studies were based on literary sources that assumed a clear distinction could be made between shamans and the other members of the community. Merkur even suggested a distinction between shamans and laypeople, arguing that shamanism represented an esoteric tradition in Inuit religion. This point of view was also shared by Williamson (1974, 26): "[Angatqut are] usually older people of recognized wisdom, experience and intellect ... Many of the inland angatqut considered themselves only capable of undertaking physical healing, advising their group on taboos, warding off baleful spirits, and divining the sources of misfortune. Even so, they were very important people, and some who used their esoteric knowledge and magical power in malevolent ways were greatly feared. Among the coastal Eskimo the art of shamanism occasionally reached great philosophical and metaphysical heights."

Saladin d'Anglure (1986, 1988b, 2006) views shamans as a separate category and adopts Czaplicka's term of "a third sex" to do justice to the sexual ambiguity he attributes to *angakkuit*. He blames the collapse of Inuit ideas and values, as well as the disappearance of the shamans, for the social problems of modern Inuit society.

> Why has there been such an increase in the number of suicides among youth? Why ... an increase of interpersonal and domestic violence? Why ... an increase in alcohol and drug abuse and mental illnesses? Why ... a high percentage of babies born to very young single mothers? Why ... a high rate of obesity and deterioration in the state of health? Why ... such a social crisis ...? May I propose a tentative answer?
>
> Perhaps it is because the Inuit have been losing their value system, their ideology, their traditional religion, and their last shamans ... I will finish with a call for help to the spirits of the numerous Inuit shamans of the past who still live among us through the people bearing their names.[56]

But the distinction between shamans and other members of a community raises considerable problems. The early ethnographers met many people who professed they were shamans. Early in the nineteenth century, Lyon (1824) received much information from the shaman Tulimaq, but this does not mean that Tulimaq was the most important shaman at the time. Today elders often emphasize the value of not coming forward as a shaman. Elders participating in the Kangiq&iniq workshop observed that Qimuksiraaq's wife was a more powerful shaman that he was because she managed to hide from him that she was a shaman.[57] It has often been observed in stories about shamanic feats that someone is asked to perform as a shaman even though he has never made public that he is a shaman. In the winter of 1921–22 on Southampton Island, almost all of the adults seemed to be able to perform as shamans.[58] Apparently, the most important shamans performed rarely, whereas the less important *angakkuit* seemed to be far more active.

There appears to be an inherent ambiguity in the shamanic complex. On the one hand, shamans are expected to perform, to show off, and to compete with their rivals, whereas on the other the powerful shamans are expected to keep a low profile and only perform in cases of real need. Rasmussen provides descriptions of performances by Anarqaq and Unaliq, who at the time were thought to be less important *angakkuit*, but not performances by Ava, who was his main informant on shamanic matters, or by Ivaluardjuk, who was his main informant on stories and practised only rarely,[59] or by Orulo, the wife of Ava, who according to their son Ujaraq was also an *angakkuq*. Clearly, we are dealing with a pattern where lesser *angakkuit* were expected to show off and the more powerful *angakkuit* were reluctant to reveal their powers. A denial of shamanic skills would then be consistent with the behaviour of a powerful *angakkuq* who does not want his powers to be exposed. Victor Tungilik related this incident: "There was one man who was trying to get me. This person started to put me down and said, 'You are an *angakkuq*. You are a very powerful *angakkuq*, and you are enviable because you are going to be capable all your life.' This was at the Co-op store. A lot of people were gathered at the Co-op store and this person said this to me very loudly. I knew I was protected. As I said, my *tuurngait* protect me from bad things and as a result I am still alive today. I was protected because they didn't want me to die. I do pray. I do go to church, but at that time I used my powers."[60] Exposing a person as a powerful *angakkuq* is considered to be an attack. It is also a risky action, as powerful *angakkuit* know how to defend themselves.

Elders often stress that everyone has powers, and they are convinced that many people are in fact *angakkuit* but will not admit it. Thus, it is never clear who is an *angakkuq* and who is not. In the past, there were people who performed frequently and emphasized their status as *angakkuit*, people who were supposed to be *angakkuit* but did not admit it, and people who unexpectedly might turn out to be *angakkuit*. When, in Williamson's words, shamanism went underground, the position of the shaman became even more complex. Christianity and shamanism were supposed to be incompatible, but shamanic activities continued, although people were less and less prepared to acknowledge they were shamans. Qimuksiraaq confided in Frederiksen in 1946, and in 1999 Tungilik spoke of his own shamanic activities; but these individuals were exceptions.[61] We were fortunate to participate in a series of workshops with elders who were very knowledgeable about shamanism, several of them having had at least some training in shamanism. Obviously, it is pointless to pursue the question whether some of them were shamans, since they emphatically denied that they were.

Today a new interest in shamanism is expressed in films made by Inuit, such as *Atanarjuat* (2001), *Angakkuit* (2003), and *The Journals of Rasmussen* (2006). Shamanism is a key feature of *Atanarjuat*, contrasting bad and good shamans. In the *Journals of Knud Rasmussen*, the transition from shamanism to Christianity is the central theme. The revival of an interest in shamanism is not without controversy. Some Inuit Christians take a strong position against any interest in shamanism, associating it with the works of the devil or the practices of the past. They are afraid of a revival of shamanism. The ambiguity around shamanism is part of

Inuit traditions. Shamans were respected as well as feared, and elders consistently point out that there were always good and bad shamans. Because of their skills and abilities, shamans were able to help people, but they could also to hurt them. The border between aggression and protection was not always clear, and an important problem was the question of revenge.

CONCLUSION

In the past, the beliefs and practices relating to shamanism were embedded in a framework of traditions that connected people to the land and its human and non-human inhabitants – the animals, the deceased, and the wide variety of other beings that populated the universe. People required expert knowledge to deal with different beings and dangerous times and places. Shamans might have been the experts in this knowledge, but much knowledge was shared. When Christianity was adopted, shamanism was no longer publicly performed, but many beliefs and practices continued. Inuit showed amazing creativity in integrating new beliefs and practices into their culture and, conversely, in integrating Inuit traditions into Christian beliefs and practices. The period from the transition to Christianity until the establishment of modern Nunavut was not just a time of cultural loss, but also a time of great cultural innovation. *Angakkuit* were not just defending the traditions of the past, but also adopting new beliefs and practices. They played a key role in the transition to Christianity, some opposing and others supporting the new religion. The interaction between missionaries and *angakkuit* helped shape the new religion.

2

Missionaries and *Angakkuit*

INTRODUCTION

The adoption of Christianity by the Inuit is still not well understood. Missionary sources usually ascribe the success of the mission to the work of the missionaries, but provide little insight into the decision-making process among the Inuit themselves. In this chapter, we explore the role of Inuit leaders and shamans in the adoption of Christianity. We show that they played a crucial role in this process of religious transformation. We also explore the role of the missionaries who facilitated conversion by accepting that they were considered to be *angakkuit* by the Inuit.

In 1771 the Moravian Brethren began their missionary activities among the Canadian Inuit in Labrador. It took the missionaries some time to make their first conversions, but over the course of the nineteenth century most Inuit in the area were converted to Christianity. In the second half of the nineteenth century, the Anglican Church Missionary Society became active in Nunavik. Edmund James Peck, "the Apostle to the Inuit," worked between 1876 and 1893 in Nunavik and then moved to South Baffin Island, where an Anglican mission was founded in Uumanarjuaq (Blacklead Island) in 1894. It took the missionaries at Uumanarjuaq about seven years to make the first conversions, in 1901. A few years later, in 1905, Peck left Baffin Island. In 1912 the mission was left completely in the hands of the Inuit lay preachers, and by that time the process of Christianization had become irreversible.

In 1912 a Catholic mission was established in Igluligaarjuk (Chesterfield Inlet). The first conversions were made in 1916, and after that Christianity spread rapidly in the Kivalliq.[1] There was fierce competition between Roman Catholic and Anglican missionaries. Inuit often tried to integrate both Anglican and Catholic, or Christian and shamanic, perspectives. Today the rivalry between the two churches no longer dominates the debates. Inuit have completely incorporated Christianity into their cultural traditions and consider it as part of their cultural heritage.

In this chapter, we first briefly discuss the development of the Anglican Church in the South and North Baffin regions and examine in more detail some of the religious movements in that area. We then discuss the development of Roman Catholicism in the Kivalliq. Finally, we discuss the development of these two churches from a comparative perspective, focusing on the recollections of the elders.[2]

THE ADOPTION OF CHRISTIANITY ON SOUTH BAFFIN ISLAND

The Anglican missionaries Edmund James Peck and Joseph Parker arrived in Uumanarjuaq in 1894. As Inuit men were out hunting or whaling most of the time, the missionaries concentrated their efforts on teaching women and children, a long-term strategy that proved to be highly effective.[3] The first Inuit to show some interest in Peck's preaching were women and sick people, but there were no conversions. During his stay at Qikiqtat in 1896, Peck related that Singak, who was suffering from consumption, had decided not to follow the shamans,[4] but this did not lead to his conversion. While the missionaries were wondering about the efficacy of their mission, Inuit began to adapt the new religion to their own traditions.[5]

A RELIGIOUS MOVEMENT AT KINNGAIT

Peter Pitseolak described a religious movement in Kinngait in 1901. The Anglican missionaries made no reference to it in their journals and were apparently unaware of the events. Pitseolak described it as "the first religious time," indicating that it happened one year before his birth. His father had been closely involved in the events.

> Simigak was out hunting one night, sitting by the seal hole waiting for a seal to come up. All of a sudden he saw Jesus coming down to watch him. He thought it was Jesus but he was mistaken; it was Satan. When he returned home he told the people he had seen Jesus. Then Simigak said, "We must get together, everybody must get together," and they all went to a place near Cape Dorset called Tooneen. There they built a giant igloo for a church. It had no roof so they could see the Heavens. Simigak was the chief in the Etidliajuk area ... But when they gathered in the big new church, Simigak's cousin, Keegak, was outdoing everyone with the ceremony.
> In that church, the leadership passed to Keegak, "the messenger" – that was the meaning of his name. He became the leader because he strongly believed that Simigak had seen Jesus. He thought of a Keegak as a person who was looking after all the people like a God. Keegak was the God in the first religious time. In the giant igloo the people gathered to worship. Keegak was dancing and singing. He led the dances and he sang:

I am, I am, I am
I am the big God,
God thinks of me
I am
There in Sugluk,
There in Padlee …

Once he danced naked. He was a saint now and he no longer had any sins. He was dancing wildly. His male organs were swinging all over the place. His belly had red marks from dancing so wildly. He danced and danced. But the igloo had no roof and finally he began to get cold. Then he said, "I am going to Heaven! I am going up; I am going up." He told everyone to get out of the igloo. "Everybody out; everybody out." People were confused about what was going on. They began to get out. Inukjuarjuk was the last person to start to leave but when he was going Keegak stopped him. "We are both going up," he said. He said this because he had borrowed Annie, Inukjuarjuk's daughter.

But Simigak didn't like the idea that only two people should go to Heaven and he said, "You are not the only ones who are going up … We are all going up." Of course nobody got up. Finally Keegak had to go home because he got too cold. His penis had goose pimples.

After this, whenever Evitah, Keegak's daughter, went to visit people they used to ask her, "Has you father gone up yet?" She used to answer, "No. Because the Eskimo people have too many sins."

Keegak was singing in the igloo all the time. He sang that the same things were happening in other places. He saw that Sugluk people in Arctic Quebec and Padluk people around Pangnirtung had the same things going on. People thought Keegak had become a shaman because he could see what was happening in other places.

While the people were like this, they appointed a special person to cut the women's hair and shave the beards. Too much hair would drag the people back when they were going up. The women had cold heads! And Martha, Keegak's wife, would chew on the blubber and put the blubber oil all over the clothing, especially on the new clothing. She'd say, "You're too neat; you're too neat." Pretty soon Martha and Keegak were the only people who had good clothing.

This happened after Okhamuk – Reverend Peck – had preached to the people that they should not be so possessive of their things … So the people threw away all their good clothing and anything they had – rifles and beads. They kept their bad clothing and tried to have good hearts.

People threw away their food. Anything Keegak asked for he would get … People said Keegak was just like a white man – bossing everybody. All the other camps would bring him meat and he had even women who were not married to him making him clothes. He was a big boss now and he had white man's jacket made out of sealskin.

Martha and Keegak had never been powerful, but all of a sudden, power was waiting for them. They grabbed it.

In the first religious time when Keegak became a Christian nobody was killed in our land although around Pangnirtung there was a killing at this time. There were no killings here, but I think Keegak and Martha may have been trying to kill someone. In that giant igloo where they used to sing Keegak and Martha beat up two people. They were out of their minds, like white or Eskimo people when they are drunk. Keegak was jumping on the front side of a man who was lying on the ground. Martha was doing the same to a woman. The man's son told Keegak to stop jumping on his father so the man didn't die. The man was on the ground because he wasn't supposed to refuse if Keegak told him to do something. People were thinking that when Jesus was crucified he wasn't fighting back. So this man didn't fight back. No doubt he was trying to copy Jesus.

But even then they knew they were making mistakes. Simigak, Keegak's cousin, told him that only my father, Inuarjuak, and Simigak himself would be going to heaven because everyone else was making too many mistakes to get up. Keegak realized then he was wrong and said: "We're going to go along with you."

So Keegak wasn't a Keegak – the leader – any more. When he realized his name was wrong he wanted to go back to his old Inuit name, Annoyak. Then he took his baptized name Jayko. He was really a friendly person. Most of the people liked him. He wasn't good looking but he had a good personality. He did some wrong but he was really a good person at the time he died … always trying to help with food. He died in 1923 and he is buried down in Etidliajuk in one of the two big barrels left by a ship.[6]

Simigak's religious experience occurred at an *aglu* (breathing hole of a seal), a privileged point of communication between the world of men and that of the game and spirits in Inuit cosmology.[7] The name of Jesus was probably known to the Inuit in Kinngait at the time. His appearance in a shamanic vision at a breathing hole provided a way to integrate him in Inuit cosmology. Apparently, Jesus' message was that the Inuit had to build a church, a giant igloo without a roof. It is not clear what Simigak expected to happen in this new church. Here the initiative was taken over by Keegak, "the messenger." Some shamanic competition may have been involved, and Keegak may have outdone Simigak in claiming that he was God. Pitseolak noted that at this point Keegak took over the leadership from Simigak.

Keegak claimed he was everywhere, a concept not altogether foreign to the idea that a shaman was able to see and visit all places in the world. People assumed that Keegak had become a shaman. He took off all of his clothes and danced wildly in the half-open igloo. Clearly, he intended to ascend to the sky, but his failure to do so does not seem to have affected his position, as it was attributed to the sins of the other members of the community.

Pitseolak referred to the cutting of the beards of the men and the hair of the women and to the spoiling of the clothes with blubber, and he observed ironically that only Martha and Keegak were left with clean clothes. He did not relate how the religious movement ended. People prepared themselves to go up in the sky by cutting their hair, spoiling their clothes, discarding their possessions, and even throwing away their food. The coming of the end of the world apparently required that people discard their means of survival. Thus, there would only remain the choice between Parousia and death. Keegak and Martha received all the goods they had asked for. In many respects, Keegak adopted the behaviour of a white man: he dressed himself like a white man and behaved like a white boss. He seems to have required absolute obeisance from his followers. The violent trampling of one of his followers is startling. Absolute commitment was required, and no hesitation was tolerated.

Pitseolak pointed out that Keegak and Martha grabbed power when they had the opportunity. He also observed, "At that time, when people were changing, they believed the wrong things. They were so mixed up they overdid their religion ... When you tell a story about these people who were overdoing their religion it sounds as if they were all drunk. They were blind to what they were doing."[8] But he still considered Keegak a good man. He noted that he was always prepared to share food. Pitseolak's respect for the cult leader reflects the respect that elders usually had for these people. Even though they made mistakes, they were good people. Keegak himself decided to relinquish the name Keegak – the 'apostle', the 'messenger' – which he had adopted.

THE FIRST CONVERTS

In 1901 a general change in the attitude of Inuit became apparent, notably in the Cumberland Sound area. Peck observes this change: "There is a reality about prayer here which the writer has never experienced elsewhere ... God becomes a reality; faith is strengthened and hope is brightened."[9] On 4 May 1901, Atterngouyak, an old woman suffering from consumption, expressed the wish to be baptized. Worried by her state of health and weakness, Peck agreed to baptise her the next morning, on 5 May 1901. On 7 May, Atterngouyak was unable to come to the church,[10] and she again asked Peck to baptise her but this time in public.[11] That year, 1901, the number of baptism candidates increased greatly. Peck reports, "Monday and Tuesday January 14 and 15: Two wonderful days. No less than twenty four women and two men (26 in all) came to me during the above days wishing to confess their faith in Jesus. I had conversation and prayer with each person, and I was indeed thankful to notice in not a few cases a real desire to cast in their lot with God's people."[12]

On 26 May 1901, the three most promising candidates – Arane, Immukke, and Nooeyout – were finally baptized before a large and most-attentive congregation.[13] The missionaries were grateful that their hard work had at last yielded results. But what made the Inuit decide to accept Christianity? Clearly, something had changed. A letter from Peck's fellow missionary Bilby to Baring Gould, secretary of the Church Missionary Society, sheds light on what had happened: "A great spirit of Revival was beginning amongst the Eskimo. Unknown to Mr. Peck, meetings were held by the people and the question of following Christian teaching was discussed by the heathen leaders, visits were also paid to other bands of Eskimo for the same purpose. The outcome of these meetings was that they would favour Christianity and during the following months they came to the service and diligently [to] learn and also to follow … the teaching."[14] Evidently, the Inuit leaders themselves had made a decision in their meetings. The missionaries had not participated in these meetings, and Inuit had made their decision on their own terms. Inuit women and some of the men were allowed to adopt Christianity, but the important leaders did not yet commit themselves.

THE REVELATION OF ANGMALIK

Angmalik was a highly competent hunter, a famous leader, and probably a shaman. His attempt to come up with his own version of Christianity in 1902 was a critical event in the brief history of the mission of Uumanarjuaq. Angmalik claimed to have received a revelation from Sedna, the sea woman who owned the sea mammals. The missionaries Peck and Greenshield were adamant in rejecting his version of Christianity. With some apprehension, they awaited word of how the people responded to Angmalik and were greatly relieved when their perspective prevailed. Peck reported the events of the day in his diary.

> A wonderful day. The Church was packed morning and evening. Hardly any of the men had gone hunting, and the attention and reverent behaviour of the people was quite remarkable. I naturally inquired what these things meant. This is the answer which I received, an answer which gave me great joy … they told me that having considered the new doctrine propounded by Angmalik, and having also considered the words they heard and read, viz., the words of Jesus, they had come to the conclusion that His words were in every way preferable, and therefore they had determined to cast away their heathen customs and come to the place of prayer.[15]

The defeat must have been hard on Angmalik, and it took a long time before he was prepared to accept Christianity on the missionaries' terms. His wife, Ashivak, played an important role in the transition to Christianity, publicly rejecting the old beliefs and practices. Her daughter Eevik gave this account:

> Later, when my parents returned to Kikitaet from Oomanayoak, they saw that the people had changed from their old ways of life into bad and evil ways and worshipped a false god they called Sanah. My mother wanted the people to turn back. So in the summer my mother got some women together to make caribou clothes. The clothes were at least two times as big as the ones Eskimos wore, or maybe bigger than anybody could use on earth. They made everything, the parkas, the kamik, the mittens, the pants, in fact the whole works. After they finished, everything was thrown into the water because that is what my mother wanted them to do. They made these clothes so that they could throw them into the water and no longer be followers of this God.[16]

After that, the authority of missionaries was no longer openly challenged in Cumberland Sound. In the areas outside the direct influence of the missionaries, the incorporation and integration of Christian ideas and practices into the wider context of Inuit culture could go on unchecked. It was particularly in those areas that a wide range of religious movements developed and flourished. Local leaders and shamans played key roles in the adoption of new ideas and practices.[17]

PETER TULUGARJUAQ

In 1901, Peck (1922, 21) observed that an early group of Inuit proselytes constituted "a goodly band [that] became what we may call chief readers, or leaders in the congregation." The most important leader, Peter Tulugarjuaq, was first mentioned by Peck in his journal entry of 23 November 1903. Peck writes that he had invited Tulugarjuaq to become the first native Christian teacher on Baffin Island: "I spoke to him of the necessity of confessing Christ in every possible way and invited him out of love to Jesus, to become a teacher. To this proposal he readily consented, so we then read together a portion of Scripture. This he will read next Sunday in church and he will, I trust, be led on, through the help of the Holy Spirit to take an active part in this Arctic work. Tooloakjuak, for this is the name of our friend, is one of the most promising candidates for baptism, has a good report amongst the Eskimo, and is in many ways, a very reliable man."[18]

Peter Tulugarjuaq's transition to Christianity may have triggered a series of conversions in Cumberland Sound and especially at Uumanarjuaq.[19] Apparently, Tulugarjuaq had been invited to become a lay reader even before he was baptized. It may well have been a condition he set for his baptism. We do not know whether he was an *angakkuq* before his conversion, but it is quite possible. In his journals, Peck avoided references to shamanism and never identified a convert as a former shaman. German explorer B. Hantzsch's (1977, 30) description of Tulugarjuaq as "[o]ne of the most experienced men in those parts … , one of the most intelligent persons of the region," suggests that Tulugarjuaq had a suitable profile and some power. We may assume that had Peck known that

Tulugarjuaq had been an *angakkuq*, he would not have made it public, but shamans often played a key role in conversions.

In a letter to Baring-Gould, Peck's colleague Bilby writes of one such shaman in 1902: "One of the chief conjurors who has been greatly against the mission in the past seemed very much changed last winter. On one occasion, when Mr. Peck was coming back from Frobisher Bay, he took shelter in a house belonging to the traders. This conjuror and his companions were sailors on board and at once requested a service from Mr. Peck. The request was granted gladly and a very hearty service followed."[20] Bilby does not does not provide the name of this shaman. In Uumanarjuaq, Peck (1922, 23) perceived the decay of shamanism as early as 1903, noting that "the influence of the magicians is almost overcome."

The missionaries fiercely opposed shamanic practices, especially the practice of spouse exchange associated with shamanism and the Sedna feast.[21] Yet they exhibited considerably interest in shamanic knowledge. Between 1897 and 1905, Peck collected a wealth of ethnographic data on shamanism, one example being a list of 457 helping spirits.[22] The missionaries' ambiguous attitude towards shamanism, on one side rejecting its practice and on the other recording its knowledge, may have puzzled the Inuit. It seems that many Inuit considered the missionaries to be shamans, and this may have been the case at Uumanarjuaq. In 1896, shortly before he boarded ship and left the mission, Peck wrote, "Some of them had suggested that I should cut them with knives so that the marks of wounds would be a continual reminder of our sojourn amongst them."[23] The shamans may have been challenging him in order to find out whether he was a shaman or to show their own shamanic powers. They may also have seen the Christian religion as a superior form of shamanism.

Kudlu Pitsiulak (1995 interview) indicated that some of the people at Uumanarjuaq at that time still rejected Christianity and ridiculed Tulugarjuaq and the first converts. "People who do not believe in Christianity would make fun of the Christians (*ukpirtuit*) and with Tulugarjuaq's wife, the people were saying 'angalik tingilik.' To make fun of them, they would also say that God too is a shaman, singing 'angalik tingilik.'"

After his conversion Tulugarjuaq rapidly took charge of matters, and soon the whole community at Uumanarjuaq became Christian. When the last missionaries departed from Uumanarjuaq in 1910, the religious community was left in the safe hands of Tulugarjuaq. After leaving for England on 10 September, the Anglican missionary Greenshield noted, "It was very hard saying good-bye, especially to Tooloogakjuak, and we both felt it much."[24]

Greenshield returned to Uumanarjuaq in 1911, and his assessment of the religious situation was very positive: "On going ashore I found everything in excellent order, all having been taken care of by Tooloogakjuak." There had been a difficult winter and some of the women and children were so weak they could hardly walk. Yet they had saved biscuit for him at his return.[25] In a letter to Mr Baring Gould he wrote: "I found the church, house, hospital and store all in per-

Reverend Peck conducts a church service on Uumanarjuaq (Blacklead Island). The Inuit in the service are shown wearing their Sunday clothes. Source: Anglican Church of Canada, General Synod Archives (A ANG P 7502.12B).

Sanctuary at Chesterfield Inlet representing the revelation of Maria at Lourdes. Photograph by J. Oosten.

Reverend Armand Tagoona's church as seen today in Qamanittuaq. It evokes the traditional feasting house, the big igloo. Photograph by J. Oosten.

Qulliq (oil lamp) in front of the pulpit in the new Roman Catholic church in Kugaaruk (Pelly Bay). Photograph by J. Oosten.

Statue of the Virgin Mary in front of a wall hanging depicting Inuit kneeling before the cross, in the new Roman Catholic church in Kugaaruk. Photograph by F. Laugrand.

fect order, they having been again taken care of by our Senior Native Teacher, Peter Tooloogakjuak."[26]

Once the leaders had made the transition, the shamans no longer practised openly. Lucaasie Nutaraaluk from Iqaluit recalled, "My father stopped being an *angakkuq* when he began working for the ministers. It seemed that those who worked for the ministers tended to be leaders."[27] And Etuangat Aksaajuq from Panniqtuuq (1995 interview), born in Uumanarjuaq in 1901, remembered, "When I was a child, shamanism was evil in a way and everybody would know. The shamans would hide by that time and still be doing some of their rituals … As I start to remember, not a lot of people but a few of them were still shamans. But they were scared … they hid themselves because they did not want that Christians could see them, they would be too shy."

Shamanism did not disappear, but it began to be practised only outside of the sphere of the missionaries. Only after the 1910s did shamanic practises disappear in Cumberland Sound and shamanic knowledge cease to be passed on to the younger generations. Pitsiulak (1995 interview), born in Uumanarjuaq in 1910, recalled, "I did not know too much about shamanism because it was not going on when it was my time. My parents and my mother would not allow it because they

The old church in Kugaaruk was founded by Father Henry, who arrived in the area in 1935. Photograph by F. Laugrand.

were converted, they were Christians, and so they didn't want me to hear anything about shamanism." Pauloosie Angmalik (1995 interview), born in Uumanarjuaq in 1911, confirmed that perception: "I can hardly say anything about the time before Christianity, about the shamans, because my parents and especially my adopted mother would never talk about shamanism in front of me. My mother was really shy with shamanism because she knew that I would learn it very quickly and she wanted that I went to the right way following Christianity. So even when there were people around, she would say that she would not talk about shamanism in front of me. That's the way it was."

As a consequence, little of the richness of shamanic traditions is preserved in the recollections of the elders from South Baffin Island. From Uumanarjuaq the Anglican religion rapidly spread to the south and to the north. Anglican missionaries were very successful in both directions, thanks to the initial proselytism organized by the early catechists or by local families that had been exposed to Christian ideas when they had visited Cumberland Sound.

NORTH BAFFIN ISLAND

By the early 1920s, missionaries had not yet travelled to Iglulik, but Bibles and hymn books put in circulation by the Anglican missionaries had already arrived up north (Mathiassen 1928, 235; Ross 1984a, 141) and hymns recorded by Peck were available in the Hudson's Bay Company trading posts. The books written in the syllabic orthography[28] developed by the Anglican missionaries were avidly read, and various religious movements and rituals developed as a result.

At that time, a shaman from North Baffin Island named Umik began to preach the Gospel together with his son Nuqallaq, who was known to have killed the trading officer Robert Janes (Sakirmia). Just after this killing, which took place north of Mittimatalik in 1920, the two men left Baffin Island for the Iglulik area and founded a new Christian cult. During the winter of 1921–22, more than thirty-five Inuit families from the camps of Ingnertoq, Pingerqalik, and Iglulik were converted "in a flash" to Umik's religious movement.[29] According to Emile Imaruittuq from Iglulik (interview), "Inuit started following him, then his relatives came and then people from the whole community." The new religion spread quickly, reaching the Aivilingmiut camps of Ava and Apaq in Itibdjeriang in the spring of 1922.[30] Mathiassen's companion, Freuchen (1939, 394), provided a few details on the movement, describing "Umiling" as a Christian preacher who, with his son, tried to elevate the morality of Inuit sexual mores by forbidding the trading of wives, even though they also stipulated that he and his son were allowed to borrow anyone's wife. Mathiassen's (1928, 235) more detailed description of Umik's movement does not agree in every respect with Freuchen's information.

> When we came to Ingnertoq, the most southerly settlement of the Iglulingmiut in the winter of 1921–22 we saw a white rag on a pole outside the snow house and, when we arrived at the place we were surprised by the inhabitants shaking hands with us; even the tiniest child had to do it. Inside the snowhouse the crucifix ... was hanging ... We wished to buy it, but they were unwilling as they said it was a very powerful amulet. We met the same white flag and the same handshake at the more northerly places, Pingerqalik and Iglulik, signs that the inhabitants belonged to Uming's congregation. At Iglulik we met the prophet Uming himself, an elderly, intelligent man, who ruled there absolutely. Besides the hand-shake and the flag, his religion included abstention from work on Sundays, gathering now and then in his snow house and singing hymns which he had taught them, and, what is more, the hunters were to bring their booty to him and he would distribute it. His son, the murderer Noqatdlaq, acted as a sort of assistant priest and did not lift a finger in hunting either. When people arrived at the settlement or departed from it, all the inhabitants gathered and sang a hymn, after which the hand-shaking commenced; even the dog's paws were taken. Uming was also a liberal man, permitted polygamy, offered to "lend" us his wife during our stay at Iglulik and continued to exchange wives for a year at a time with another man.

Apparently Umik exercised some control on the exchange of goods as well as of women.[31] Corporal McInnes of the Royal Canadian Mounted Police obtained additional information during his fifty-eight-day trip to Iglulik in 1923:

> The Iglulik tribe of Eskimos consists approximately of 35 families … They are very enthusiastic over religion, which they follow in their own crude style, singing hymns and reading from their Testament several times a day. The most attractive pastime, however, is trying to count the number of the pages and the hymns. They demonstrate the fact that they are christianized by carrying a flag, generally white, attached to the komitik [dogsled] when traveling, and while at the village they greet all arrivals by the grown population lining up side by side in the most prominent place in front of the igloos, when the arrival is within hearing distance they all join in singing a hymn. The arrival approaches the line-up within a few yards, then stops his komitik and remains standing until the hymn is finished. The singers then advance in single file and greet him with three shakes of the hand … The same formalities are gone through on the return of a resident of the village if he leaves only for a few hours.[32]

Hubert Amarualik (1995 interview), an elder from Iglulik, recalled the shamanic powers of Umik: "I heard about Umik when he was travelling here by ship. He had to go through Akaniqjuaq to come here and he was supposed to be here for at least a year. But as there was much ice up there, the ship couldn't come here, so Umik returned the ship to Pond Inlet by using his spirits and his shaman's power."

Rose Iqallijuq (2000 interview) from Iglulik stated that Umik was an *angakkuq*. Michel Kupaaq (1995 interview) from Iglulik also referred to the special capacities of Umik, notably his ability to change words: "You know these writings from the Bible, Umik would cover them up and show them to the other people. But after he had covered them on his body, there would be a different writing." Samuel Arnakallak (1995 interview) from Mittimattalik related, "Umik was one of the first persons who heard about Christianity in Iglulik. He originated from the Iglulik area. So when he came back in Iglulik from Pond Inlet, he started to talk about baptism and about Christianity. He had a son, Nuqallak. Umik used to talk a lot about Christianity, saying that if you died you can come back to life. He used to talk about the baptism too and say that through baptism, you could even see the dead people again … even their loved friends who might have been in graves for a long time, for more than a month."

Iqallijuq (1995 interview) related that Umik saw the relation between himself and his son as that between God and Jesus:

> Umik was Qiugaqjjuk's father. At that time Umik was part shaman, part Christian, but maybe his mind was a little bit mixed-up. At that time, we were living in a very small island, my in-laws, Ittuksarjuat, Uttak, and his wife … We were living in a very small camp. I was outside the tent with a baby. As we heard something, we knew that somebody was coming over by dog-team. Later we knew that it was Umik. As they were coming, Umik used to say "awa a, awa a." I was so scared that I started running to my

> camp, leaving my kid behind. The little kid was crying but I was still running to my in-law. As I went in their tent I said that some stranger was coming. My in-law asked me then, "What do you mean?" and I told him that I heard "awa a, awa a." Then my mother in-law told me that it was Umik. When Umik arrived, he said, *"Gutiu irninga, Qadlunaaq nunanut angijaqaumat"* meaning "God's son has been taken away by White men to [the] south." On the moment, I didn't understand, but after a while, I realized that his son had been arrested. A year later Umik came back but his lungs had decayed. He was working too hard, being a slave too much, and he died early. We didn't know Umik for a long time, because we used to live in a different camp. But I heard about him. Umik used to say that he was a very religious person, being himself a God. "God's son has been taken down south," that's what he used to say. Umik was a shaman and he was a Christian too. When somebody was coming from very far, he would know and tell you their names. He was probably all mixed-up, so his mind was probably not good. As Umik drew that ivory crucifix and carved it, he started praying for that ... As Umik told me, "Pray this and then never change your religion again." I said, "Yes," but I only said yes through here [pointing to her forehead]. I didn't wanted to pray to that ivory stone, so I only said yes here and not inside. Umik was like that, he used to pray for this.

Mathiassen describes Umik as an "elderly, intelligent man" but only refers to Nuqallaq as a murderer. Clearly, the ethnographers found it difficult to reconcile Nuqallaq the murderer with Nuqallaq the preacher; they suspected he was exploiting other Inuit for his own purposes, acquiring the control of goods as well as of women. The elders did not doubt the shamanic powers of Nuqallaq, and we hear no comments about exploitation. The comments of Iqallijuq are particularly insightful, as they confirm that religious leaders were sometimes identified as God or Jesus.

In Umik's Christian movement, traditional patterns and new symbols were integrated. The crucifix, for example, was seen as a powerful amulet that could not be sold. Traditional patterns of wife exchange were continued. Parts of the New Testament were read and hymns were frequently sung. The religious leader exercised great authority, but Iqallijuq was not prepared to follow him. She handled the problem skilfully and did not confront him. The distinction between Christians and non-Christians was stressed in the handshaking ritual, which included the tiniest child and even the dogs. The combined use of handshaking and flags seems to have represented the creation of a new community. Iglulik elders have continued to speak of Umik with great respect. Iqallijuq said that Umik was a shaman as well as a Christian. His movement was apparently an attempt to transcend the dilemma of having to be either a shaman or a Christian. Like Keegak, Umik was both. Aipilik Innuksuk (1995 interview) commented with respect to Umik, "I only heard how Umik became a religious person. But his religion was besides Roman Catholic and besides Anglicanism. It was something else. Uming and Qallutiaq started this kind of religion but there was also another person, I forgot his name. These people used to see a person, very light, shining around his head. Their religion was really overdone."

Kupaaq said that Umik was "neither Catholic, nor Anglican, but something else, a religious person [*ukpirtuujuviniq*], who had his own beliefs." Piugaattuq (1995 interview) from Iglulik added, "Umik knew many things about religion. That's why he became a religious person." Martha Nasook (1995 interview), wife of a famous Anglican minister whose parents used to live with Umik, confirmed that he was neither Catholic nor Anglican but had "his own beliefs." George Kappianaq (1995 interview) described Umik as "a very religious person" [*ukpirtummarialaursimajuq*] but also "kind of mixed-up." He had always been "a powerful man," but "when he got sick, his power was getting away and he had no more power when he died." Kappianaq concluded, "If he hadn't called himself a God, he probably would have lived longer."

In 1921 Rasmussen visited the North Baffin area and became acquainted with the *angakkuq* Ava, who converted to Christianity in that same year: "Already at that time it had made a great impression on Aua that all his kinsmen and friends had become adherents of the belief in heaven. And yet it took almost a year before himself turned his back on his helping spirits. His conversion only took place in the last fall, when he met some families of the Aivilik tribe during his residence at Repulse Bay who held prayer meetings in an igloo."[33]

Freuchen (1939, 389–90) reports that Ava told him he had seen the Trinity: "Awa told us that only last summer he had had a remarkable experience … He was sitting outside his tent carving a walrus tusk when he saw three men approaching the settlement. He did not know who they might be, but suddenly recognized them as the new gods of the Trinity, the Father, the Son and the Holy Ghost. Awa shouted for everyone to come out and receive the dignified guests. And then, when a certain little girl discovered they wore pants of rabbit skin and very tall caps, she had to laugh. This made the Trinity angry, and, while they smiled forgivingly, they altered their course so that they passed by without stopping or even speaking a word in greeting. The natives had been greatly disappointed, but they said the Holy Ghost presented such a laughable aspect from the rear that they all gave way to their mirth. His posteriors curved in instead of out. The Trinity had never been seen again."

After Ava had been converted, Rasmussen worried about how he would continue his research.

> I had heard a little about this conversion and was now very anxious to find out whether he had so profoundly abjured his belief that he no longer upheld the old traditions and customs of his tribe. Therefore I told him immediately the reason for my arrival and expressed the hope that his transition to another belief would not impede our cooperation. To my

great joy he answered that this would not be the case. He explained that he indeed had sent away his helping spirits, as he had no more use for them, but that this was exactly the reason why he could now tell all the secrets, which had been too sacred for him to communicate in the past. A faithful spirit conjuror cannot disclose the secrets of his life without weakening his relationship to the supernatural. And this was the reason that he had been so reticent in the past. Now, on the contrary, all his knowledge was available to me, and he even looked forward to the many evening conversations that lay in store for us. Then I spent several weeks as the guest of Aua and Orulo and in this time I could write down extensive material on the spiritual culture of the Eskimos that later on also lay the foundation for my work among other tribes.[34]

Thus, Ava's conversion to Christianity allowed him to transfer his shamanic knowledge to Rasmussen. Similar processes may have occurred in Uumanarjuaq, allowing Peck to collect his ethnographic data on shamanism. The conversion to Christianity of *angakkuit* implied that they could freely discuss their knowledge and practice without having to fear that they would lose their power by disclosing these things. Their adoption of Christianity, however, did not imply that their belief in *angakkuuniq* had disappeared. It only implied that they no longer practised it, many shamans having decided to send their *tuurngait* away. Ava told Rasmussen that he had sent all his helping spirits to his sister on Baffin Island.[35] Some a*ngakkuit* decided to continue their shamanic practices. Kappianaq mentioned the case of Sauri: "I heard of a shaman who refused religion when Christianity started. He used to say that when he prayed, he could not see for whom he was praying. But through shamanism instead, he could see his spirits, so he wanted to be a shaman. He was refusing Christianity."[36]

The elder Qanguq told the Catholic missionary Guy Mary-Rousselière the story of his father, Qaunnaq, who had tried to become an *angakkuq* in vain:

When my adoptive father was young, he had played at being an *angakkuq* like other children, but he had never become a real *angakkuq*. While others converted, he envied the *angakkuit* and was jealous of them. While they abandoned their spirits, he, on the contrary, did his best to devote himself to shamanic practises and tried to steal the abandoned spirits … It was his idea to convert after he had become an *angakkuq* and not before. That is why he tried to practise shamanism in secret. I will sing the song that he used in his attempts to master shamanic practises, as he did his best to obtain the spirits of the old *angakkuit* and to become an *angakkuq* himself. This is the song:

Where to find (it)? Nothing can be done.
The spirit of the past, is it perhaps dead?

> Impossible to find it. Where is it?
> Are we not the most knowledgeable because of the small signs in the shape of hooks?
> Nothing can be done. Impossible to find it.
> Ai, i, u, a, pai, pi, pu, pa, etc.

> This is what he chanted when he began to understand the books and to convert. Those books that came from the white men, that is what he is referring to, when he wanted to become an *angakkuq* as well as know the books ... He could well set out on a spirit quest, but he never managed to discover them.[37]

In 1921 another religious movement was instigated, this one by Neakuteuk at Home Bay. Neakuteuk (Niaquttiaq) was employed by the Sabellum Trading Company, which had a small trading post at the Bay of Kivituq.[38] At that time, Inuit in the area had been in regular contact with Christianity for several years. Various people coming from Cumberland Sound had settled there, but no missionary had yet arrived. According to Peneloo, Neakuteuk had difficulty reading and understanding the Bible. He asked people to hit him on the head whenever he left the igloo so that his understanding would improve. Although Neakuteuk lost a lot of blood, he claimed that from then on he was able to understand what he read. During the Christmas celebrations, Neakuteuk announced that he was Christ.[39] According to Wallis (1943, 115), he simulated the crucifixion of Jesus. People clustered about him, knelt, and kissed the hem of his robe. He appointed two disciples and selected three messengers, to whom he gave biblical names, to carry the doctrine to all peoples.

The momentum of the movement increased when Neakuteuk began to make prophecies. He claimed that the end of the world was near and people had to prepare for it. "You are all to love one another for so it is written." There would be no more wives and husbands: "the women have to take off all their clothes and jump around ... and the men must have sexual intercourse with their mothers."[40] He ordered his people to go without food and sleep and threatened them frequently with a knife and a gun. He forced them to kill several of their dogs.[41] Returning to his igloo, he fired his gun at the walls, shot in the air to kill angels, and finally declared he was God creating thunder. Anticipating his approaching death, Neakuteuk decided to baptize the whole world with his blood. He inflicted a wound on his head and declared, "You are baptized in my blood." When a blind man named Munyeuk went "to him asking to have some wind inside so that he can go up to Jesus," Neakuteuk declared that it was time to kill Munyeuk, for he was now "full of God's spirit and later might be bad." Then Kautak and Kedluk killed the blind man. After the murder, Neakuteuk demanded that the two men kill three of their dogs.[42] Neakuteuk did not stop there, but now insisted that Lemik be killed because he could not read or copy the Bible. When Neakuteuk was about to kill Lemik's wife with a hammer, one of his own cousins, Kidlapik, wounded him mortally with his gun. In agony, Neakuteuk continued to claim he was Jesus and therefore immortal. According to the reports of the RCMP, who questioned the people who had witnessed Neakuteuk's death, his remains were buried with exceptional care. Sergeant Joy reported that Neakuteuk's body was washed and the water was sprinkled over the lamps. One of the lamps started to sing "to the effect that its flame was everlasting and could not be extinguished," and at the same moment the corpse of the deceased began to breathe again, laughed, and placed its hands on its head. A man named Takoshaga then sprinkled three drops of this water mixed with blood on the head of all adults and children. Today those who remember these happenings remind each other of the words written on the tomb of Neakuteuk: "It is not good for man to take the place of God."[43]

Neakuteuk is depicted in many sources as an illiterate and simple guy who went from bad to worse and finally fell victim to the consequences of his own misguided actions.[44] But when we read between the lines, it becomes clear that Neakuteuk was a powerful leader held in esteem by those who survived him. The reports related that people believed that to some extent he came to life again as he had predicted he would. During his life, his followers were prepared to obey him and to perform the executions he demanded. As in the case of Umik, not everybody followed him. Murder was not taken lightly in Inuit society, and it is clear that Kidlapik felt that Neakuteuk had gone too far, leaving him with no alternative but to shoot him.

Various features of Neakuteuk's movement frequently occurred in parousial movements in the Canadian Arctic.[45] There is the identification with Jesus, the killing of the dogs, the concept of the messenger, the expectation of the imminent end of the world, the baptism, and the dancing or running around naked. As in the case of Umik we find a complex and creative integration of traditional and Christian elements. An interesting feature is the wounding of the head, which occurs twice. The first time it provides Neakuteuk with a better understanding of the Bible; the second time it serves to baptize others with blood. The wounding of oneself recalls shamanic practices, and the first wounding may well have had the connotation of a shamanic initiation. Lucassie Nutaraaluk from Iqaluit recalled that some *angakkuit* made people into *angakkuit* by bumping heads.[46] The image of Neakuteuk hanging on the cross like Christ recalls the crucifix of Umik. The image of the crucified Christ, sacrificed for the salvation of humankind, seems to have appealed to the Inuit. It may have evoked the symbolism of shamanic initiation, where symbolic death and revival often occur.[47] In choosing messengers, Neakuteuk clearly conformed to a Christian model.

There have been various practices involving the exchange of spouses in Inuit culture (*nuliijaut* – wife sharing; *uilijauti* – husband sharing), particularly in shamanic contexts. Relationships between sons and mothers were a different matter. In these cases, a transgression and inversion of social norms seems to have been required to establish a state of perfection in anticipation of the coming of the end of the world. This need for perfection may also have been the motive for murdering two imperfect people, one blind and another who was presumed to be unable to read or copy the Bible. Here, Neakuteuk's movement met its end, as some of the people present realized that things were getting out of hand.

The ritual procedures following Neakuteuk's death were of utmost interest. According to traditional beliefs, there was a close association between soul and lamp, and a mother could hide the soul of her son under the lamp to make him invulnerable.[48] The relationship between lamp and soul was evoked when the lamp became immortal and Neakuteuk came to life again. Moreover, the water that had effected this miracle was mixed with blood and sprinkled on everyone. In this way everybody benefited from the powers of immortality associated with the water in which the corpse was washed. In this way, the prophecies of Neakuteuk were validated and his reputation and memory honoured. But Timothy Kadloo (1995 interview) concludes that Neakuteuk became crazy: "Niaqutsiaq (Neakuteuk) was my father's uncle son. He was working for a trading company but he had another job. He was one of the helpers, like a priest. He was becoming crazy. He was really mixed-up so he was really sinning, doing bad stuff and he got crazy. He was going to be so crazy that someone didn't agree with him and he was killed. All the others were so afraid of him, of what he was doing, so they killed him."

Religious upheavals continued for some time. One of the last instances was a movement in Siuralik (Moffet Inlet) in 1946–47. As soon as he heard about it, the Reverend J.H. Turner left Mittimatalik, where he had been established since 1929, for Ikpiarjuk to save his flock According to a member of the RCMP who had travelled in the area,[49] there had been exceptionally high tides, and the people had interpreted this in different ways. One woman, Eekoma, said that she had gone up to the sky and had seen Jesus and other deceased persons. She now possessed the "power to look down into the hearts of men to discern which were bad and which, good." Her husband, Alooloo, became her disciple and announced that he had received some of her powers. Other members of her family joined in; for example, Evalak and Kepilk adopted the role of evangelists. According to the RCMP report, "certain aspects of the old shaman religion were incorporated, apparently, into the ritual, principally the practice of one revealing to the rest all the evil thoughts and intentions which he possessed." At the beginning of the winter of 1946–47, the movement gained momentum and spread to three other camps situated between Arctic Bay and the trading post of Admiralty Inlet. Kongasuretook, Oolayoo, and Ameemeeakjuk joined Eekoma as leaders of the movement. The report relates that strange phenomena were observed. "Spirits walked on the roof, various utensils in the igloo moved by themselves." After being warned by two Inuit,[50] the Reverend Turner sent letters to the new prophets and then travelled to the area himself. Flint (1949, 49–51) quotes Turner from a circular letter the reverend had sent to his supporters in England:

> Alooloo's wife began acting strangely last fall. She set herself up as a teacher and to give authority to her words, pretended to be able to perform

> ridiculous little miracles ... Some visitors from Fury and Hecla Straits ... became influenced, so much that they all became abnormal ... The false prophets had mixed a little Scripture in with their teaching with the result that a number of the Eskimo were half inclined to believe them. The whole affair was obviously the work of evil spirits, and one fellow under their influence claimed to be God. When he arrived, however, at Christmas, he immediately confessed his wickedness ... He found much comfort in Psalm 51. Alooloo and his wife ... seemed sorry for what they had done.

Father Mary-Rousselière (1949, 11), who arrived in Mittimatalik after the events, was told that a woman had died and come to life again. She had obtained disciples and began teaching that the end of the world was near. Trott (1988, 40) gives a brief description of the movement:

> One of the women in this camp claimed to have heard the voice of Jesus giving her a special mission to call the people to repentance. She attempted to establish a rigorous moral code, and is said to have demonstrated her powers by having people shoot at her through the tent canvas (this was the claim of contemporary informants in Arctic Bay). Her messages were promulgated throughout the district by her father and brother, and attracted a great deal of attention from the other Inuit. Inquiries during the fieldwork period were deflected by a reluctance ... most informants claimed that everybody was involved except for themselves. This would suggest that the movement was indeed widespread and the RCMP and HBC reports indicate that hunting and trapping throughout the area virtually stopped.

Elsewhere Trott (1997) examines various features of the movement, some continuous with and others breaking away from Inuit shamanic tradition. The shamanic elements of the movement were obvious, as was noted in the RCMP report: the ascent to the sky, the visit to the dead, the spirits walking on the roof, the utensils flying through the air, and the capacity to observe the true intentions of people. Being shot through the canvas of a tent is another well-known shamanic feat. The movement followed a pattern similar to other movements: relatives joined in and claimed a share of the power of the prophet; the belief in the imminent end of the world was accompanied by an abstention from hunting and trapping, and one person claimed to be God. Like some of the other recent movements, it was stopped in its tracks by the intervention of a minister and the RCMP.

THE ADOPTION OF CHRISTIANITY IN KIVALLIQ

In the Kivalliq region, Anglican and Roman Catholic missionaries had been active in the second half of the nineteenth century but it took until 1912 before a permanent Roman Catholic mission was founded in Igluligaarjuk (Chesterfield Inlet) by the Oblate missionaries Turquetil and Leblanc. The missionaries targeted the *angakkuit* as their main opponents, viewing them as sorcerers or cheats. They considered their work to be dangerous and risky. The murder of the missionaries Rouvière and Leroux by two Inuit, Uluksuk and Sinniksiak, in the Coppermine area in 1913 gave substance to their apprehensions. The two Inuit not only killed the missionaries, but also ate part of their liver, allegedly to prevent them from coming back to life. Schneider (n.d., 114) suggests that a sorcerer, Korsek, had advised the murderers to commit their deed. The missionaries themselves were seen as martyrs. On the occasion of the baptism of six converts in 1921, their replacement, Father Fallaize, wrote: "Sprinkled by the sweat and blood of our martyrs, the good seed has germinated, flourished."[51]

Joseph Tuni

As in Uumanarjuaq, it took several years for the church to make its first converts at the Igluligaarjuk mission. In 1916 the missionary Turquetil (1954, 318) was informed that the mission would be closed if no conversions were expected. The situation changed that same year through the conversion of Joseph Tuni and what the Oblates called "the miracle of Saint Therese." The missionaries referred to Tuni as a patriarch, a man of influence, and Father Rio's[52] unpublished field notes show that he was indeed an *angakkuq*.[53] According to the missionaries, his conversion was preceded by a miracle. Apparently, Turquetil had received an envelope containing a small booklet of six to eight pages on Thérèse de Lisieux[54] entitled *La Petite Fleur de Lisieux*, the Little Flower of Lisieux. The envelope also contained a bit of earth and an inscription specifying that this earth had been taken from soil under the first coffin of the Little Flower of Lisieux and that she performed miracles with it. The next evening, Brother Girard approached a few Inuit visitors from behind and furtively scattered some earth on their hair. The next Sunday, Inuit came to the mass in great numbers, and Tuni announced that he and two other men wished to be baptized with their wives and children.[55] More baptisms followed. Tuni became a catechist and copied some of the prayer books himself. He became, effectively, the leader of a small community of Christians.[56] In the 1920s and 1930s the mission rapidly expanded. Other Catholic mission posts were soon opened, first in Arviat (Eskimo Point, 1924), where the missionaries relied on the family of John Ajaruaq, and then in Salliq (Southampton Island, 1926), Qamanittuaq (Baker Lake, 1927), Mittimatalik (Pond Inlet, 1929), and Iglulik (1933). As in Iglulik, missions were often founded in areas where there were already Catholic communities through the presence of a few Catholic families. In 1935 a mission was founded in Kugaaruk (Pelly Bay) by Father Henry at the request of Catholic Inuit in the area.[57]

By 1930 more than half the population of Igluligaarjuk (96 out of 161) had been baptized.[58] But old customs and new traditions had to be accommodated. Rasmussen (1929, 97) relates an interesting example:

I myself came in to Chesterfield somewhat later, immediately after an old man named Qalaseq had hanged himself. Both Qalaseq and his wife Qalalaq belonged to the local Catholic Mission, and since the missionary had often impressed on them that human life is God's and that it was therefore unlawful for us human beings to kill ourselves, Qalalaq was now very eager to explain to me that her husband had not died of hanging. He had been ill for a year, and since there was no prospect of his recovery, he had grown tired of life, and had asked his wife to lend death a helping hand, but in such a fashion that he should not die during the hanging itself, but should he released from the hide thong that was to strangle him before he finally expired. Qalalaq accordingly assured me most earnestly that she had strangled him with the thong, but before he was quite dead, she had removed it, and at the same time held up before him a little crucifix, which had been given them by the missionary. Therefore, according to her view, Qalaseq had really died a natural death; they had only "hurried death up a little, as it is apt to be so very slow at times."

In Igluligaarjuk, one of the main opponents of the new religion was the *angakkuq* Taliriktuq. In 1916 he opposed Tuni when he made fun of the missionaries.[59] Rose Iqallijuq from Iglulik (1995 interview) recalled: "Before Christianity, Taliriktuq was a powerful shaman. He had a walrus, a wolf and a polar bear as *tuurngait*. When Christianity came, he was really against Christian people. After his son married a woman called Tirisikuluk (also known as Niaqurluq) who was already Roman Catholic, he was still against those Christians. But Tirisikuluk prayed a lot for her father-in-law, not to be spiteful because he was really against religion then. But when she started praying for him, he became Christian after all and he died as a Christian."

In a workshop in Arviat (2003), Felix Kupak from Naujaat remembered Tirisukuluk:

I knew my stepsister well. She was known as Tirisikuluk. Her name was Niaqurluq. When she became ill, we were living at Usutarnaq near Qamanittuaq. She became ill while we were inland. Taliriktuq was an *angakkuq*. He wanted her as a daughter-in-law. He really wanted her to live. He tried very hard to heal her, but he was unable to do so. Her mother, my adopted mother, was trying to heal her through prayer. Both of them were trying their best but neither of them could heal my stepsister Niaqurluq. Taliriktuq didn't want to be inland so we went down to the sea ice. It was when we were down at the sea ice that she became more ill.

During a walk inland, Tirisukuluk appeared to Kupak and told him she wished to convert Taliriktuq and his relatives. Kupak continued his reminiscence: "I myself walked inland and I was on my way home after being out for a walk. My stepsister was so ill she wasn't able to walk and she walked behind me and she asked me, 'Anitasiraq, where are you going?' I knew she was in the *iglu* but when she asked me this I said, 'I am on my way home.' Then she said that she wanted her new in-laws and her husband to become Christian and that I was to aid her in this."

Kupak spent much time with Tirisikuluk during the night when she was unable to sleep, and she asked him to write down what she said. She explained that she wanted to convert her relatives.

> Our *igluit* were not that close because of the lack of snow. My adopted mother took her and she said that she wanted her in-laws and her husband to see her before she died so I went to go and tell them … It was dark and there was no moon. When my adopted mother told me to go I went to her in-laws. The land was flat so I was going to run there. I went out. From high above me right down to the ground there was a bright mist. It was about this wide. When the brightness touched the ground there was brightness all around us. It was even brighter than it is today; I could see a great distance. I had no difficulty running to the other *iglu*. Her in-laws and her husband started coming to our *iglu*. They had no difficulty walking because it was so bright. There was no moon. When they came in, Kingaq who was her husband started crying right away. He took her hand. It was spread out like this. She tried to take his hand. She wasn't aware of what was going on because she was dying. She said to her husband, "Your *irinaliuti* are too numerous. I don't want to touch you." She was dying so my adopted mother wanted her to touch his hand so she allowed him to touch her hand. She died shortly after that. Her in-laws Taliriktuq and Kingaktuq, and her whole family, she would make them Christians. That's what she said. It was shortly afterwards that they became Christians. Her father-in-law wanted it known that he was no longer able to be an *angakkuq* because he had left it behind.[60]

Kupak remembered that a relic was taken to Igluligaarjuk, and he added that shortly after Tirisikuluk's death in 1934, he performed *siqqitirniq*, a conversion ritual involving the eating forbidden meat:[61] "There was a watch like this that would open. Her hair was put in this and taken to the church in Igluligaarjuk. This was kept in the church there. You can see that in the book that was written. Shortly before she died, they came to go and get her. The one who baptized her was Father Fafard. Inuksaq, her son, was the only one who had been baptized at that point. Shortly after she died I was eating heart. That was another occasion for them to become Christian. I don't remember when they were baptized because I moved on. Her in-laws were baptized later."

These events had a great impact, and more families were then converted. Ollie Itinnuaq from Kangiq&iniq recalled, "It was the next year that we were baptized. I was baptized at the same time as Taliriktuq." Taliriktuq asked to have his hair cut to show that he abandoned shamanism. But reputations die hard. Itinnuaq continued: "When Taliriktuq died I was entering my youth. He was a real *angakkuq*. He died just in front of Qamanittuaq. We found his footprints at his grave. He was an old man when he died. He had a cane before he died but there was no cane in his tracks. People recognized the tracks to be his. We don't know where he went. He was heading towards the south. He had not been headed to the Nattilingmiut area where he was from. He was heading eastward towards the beginning of the day."[62]

The missionaries were jubilant to hear about the conversions, and Turquetil writes: "At Chesterfield Inlet a wonderful event has happened that brought the conversion of Talleriktok and his whole family. Even Papak has come to tell me on the spot, 'Now we are only three, me, my wife, and my son,' implying 'We are the only three heathens left' ... For me who has seen the beginning of the mission, the land has completely changed."[63]

PRIESTS AND *ANGAKKUIT*

The missionaries were obviously intent on converting the *angakkuit,* and they sometimes engaged in competitions with them and defeated them with their own weapons. They soon became aware that Inuit considered them to be *angakkuit* of a new kind. Father Turquetil observes: "These poor people take us for sorcerers and believe that we can kill them if we are not satisfied. When they see the illuminated altar, the ornaments, the priest who prays, chants, sprinkles or censes, the small lamp that is always alight in the chapel, when they hear us say the rosary, recite the litanies ... they think we are casting spells and they are afraid, not knowing which spirit we address."[64]

Later, some missionaries began to exploit their reputation as *angakkuit.* Father Ducharme (1954, 7–10) tried to impress an *angakkuq* by using magnesium as a flashlight and thus prove that his tricks were superior to those of the *angakkuit.* Father Rio outran an *angakkuq* in a running contest to show that the amulets of the *angakkuq* did not avail against him. Kupak from Naujaat (2001 interview) related: "Taliriktuq and Father Papion were competing. He would use the abundance of caribou to challenge Father Papion. 'I can find caribou? Can you?' Father Papion said, 'All I have to do is pray and there will be more than you can give me.'"

These competitions convinced Inuit that priests could be powerful *angakkuit.* Rachel Uyarasuk from Iglulik related that when she met the priest at Mittimatalik, she expected him to be able to discern all her faults and transgressions just as an *angakkuq* could.[65] Once people discovered that the priests could not see their transgressions, they tended to hide them. Mariano Aupilaarjuk from Kangiq&iniq observed: "Before that, we had *angakkuit* who could see if we had done something wrong. Even if we didn't want to talk about it, it was impossible to keep a wrong-doing hidden. We had to confess it. If I only confessed part of it he would know there was still some left, and I had to tell everything until there was nothing left. This would not be brought up again. This is how we were. That is how an *angakkuq* would *iqqaqtui,* question, you. Now we keep things hidden. Only God knows. These things will all come out on Judgment Day."[66]

The missionaries were aware of the problem. Van de Velde (1956b, 8) argues that the Inuit accepted the sacrament of penance with ease, not only because they were accustomed to making confessions, but also because under Catholicism the element of fear, intrinsic to the shamanic confession, was absent. "Now that he knows that the priest is unaware as to whether or not his confession is good or bad, he may make an incomplete confession, because he is no longer incited to confess through fear and because he does not clearly understand the consequences of an incomplete confession."

Even though the missionaries could not always match the abilities of the *angakkuit,* Inuit still saw them in the same light. Van de Velde (1956, 8) observes:

> In the Eskimo mind, the priest occupies the eminent place formerly held by the sorcerer. Is not the Catholic priest an "alter Christus" and, for this reason, is he not a mediator between God and men? Was not the sorcerer also a similar link between the spirits on one side and the Eskimos on the other? I think that to the Eskimo mentality there is a very close link between their conception of the sorcerer and the priest … and that the acceptation of the priest in place of the sorcerer is usually easily accomplished, either consciously or unconsciously. A missionary, an expert on the Eskimo language, one day said that the true translation of the word priest should be "angakok," that is, sorcerer, and not "iksirardjuar," the expression actually used and which, when literally translated, means "the great writer."

Swiss ethnologist Jean Michéa (1949, 99, 101) and later Asen Balikci (1962) also concluded that the missionaries replaced the *angakkuit*.

Christian symbols and rituals often replaced traditional symbols and practices. Christian prayer came to be considered as more powerful than *irinaliutiit,* the traditional words of power, but as serving the same main purposes. The Anglican missionary Peck[67] as well as the Roman Catholic bishop Turquetil (1954, 322) emphasized the use of prayer for hunting. The missionaries did not object to being seen as *angakkuit,* and they knew very well that prayers were used as *irinaliutiit*. They adopted Inuit terms such as Anirnialuk (big breath) and Nunaliuqti (maker of the earth) for God. In this way, they linked the concept of God with fundamental Inuit concepts such as *sila* (reason, sky weather) and *nuna* (earth, land), facilitating a shamanic interpretation of Christianity. Thus, the conversion to Christianity did not necessarily imply fundamental changes in the worldview of Inuit. Many shamanic traditions were retained.

Even though Christianity could accommodate shamanic traditions, many *angakkuit* continued their shamanic practices after converting to Christianity. Kupak (2001 interview) recalled, "After I moved to Naujaat, people still became shamans after baptism. I heard that they were dying out very quickly. My belief now is that you cannot serve two gods, only one God." He told how Nagjuk, one of the last *angakkuit*, saw that most of the shamans were dying out quickly and had said, "Whoever is killing the shamans we have, I will put an end to it, including myself." Then he had died.

Itinnuaq, too, gave an account of Nagjuk's death, saying there had been a sickness in Igluligaarjuk and many people had been dying. "Then Nagjuk said that the thing that was causing the deaths was at Qimmirjuaq and was coming closer. He said he would stop it because it was coming closer … Nagjuk was living in the last house. His grandchild had died the day before. There was also another person who had become sick. Nagjuk was not sick at all. He was recalling what he had said. He said, 'I am not able to do anything, because I was told not to. My whole family is going to die. It is only if I die that they can survive.'"[68] Not much later Nagjuk died. Itinnuaq and Kablalik removed the body. Once Nagjuk had died, people began to recover. Itinnuaq recalled, "We started going on our rounds again but nobody else had died. People had begun to heal. I believe it when Nagjuk said that the only way he could prevent more deaths was through his own death. He had been told not to prevent the deaths while still alive."[69] The accounts of the death of Nagjuk testify to the great respect accorded to an *angakkuq* who was prepared to save his fellow men through his own death.

In 1944 the famous Nattilik *angakkuq* Allakannuaq was killed by his sons at his own request. He was killed by hanging in the traditional Inuit way. When Father Henry learned about Allakannuaq's death, he exclaimed somewhat desperately, "But what kind of Christians are we raising?" In a conversation with Remie in the summer of 2001, Father Van de Velde emphasized that from an Inuit point of view Allakannuaq had sacrificed himself. He wanted to end his days so that the younger generation could move inland to hunt caribou and survive. "His deed was in fact an altruistic one," said Van de Velde. "Therefore, we should not judge too harshly." And pointing his finger to heaven, he added, "You will be surprised whom you will see up there."[70]

A few entries in various Codices Historici and other missionary accounts show that the missionaries knew that some *angakkuit* were still practising.[71] Remie (1983) provides ample evidence that the shamanic ideology was still very much alive among the Arviligjuarmiut in Kugaaruk in the 1950s and 1960s. Recourse to old beliefs and practices occurred frequently, particularly in crisis situations (sickness and death, bad hunting, and serious conflicts in social relations).

Inuit often combined Catholicism and shamanism. A good example can be found in the Codex Historicus of the Kugaaruk Mission of 26 October 1959. That day, the resident missionary, Father Van de Velde, wrote:

> Beautiful day, clear, cold. Jose arrives with Lucien just after the departure of Dominique to the river. He transported the cask for the pedestal and the small chapel for the Virgin to be placed at Kunguardjuk. Jose and Lucien will bring the other to be placed at Matjok. Sivorak and her daugh-

ter will accompany them to Matjok. It seems that Niptajok and Illuitok want to see Sivorak. Why … ? Nobody is fooled! She is protestant and a reputed sorcerer with hysterical crises. Just see the four of them on the sled – Jose, Lucien, Sivorak and her daughter – intending to get the sorcerer for Niptajok. They are seated on the cask and carry the chest for the small chapel in Matjok. Nice contrast.

For Father Van de Velde, the female shaman Sivorak was a sorcerer; for the Inuit, she was a healer. The fact that Sivorak was a Protestant probably made it easier for Father Van de Velde to expose her in the Codex.

The missionaries avoided public conflict with *angakkuit*, but it did sometimes occur. In one such case, the shaman Iksivalitaq, the son of the shaman Allakannuaq, wore the *kigluraq*, a little tattoo between the eyebrows, which signified that he had slain a *tupilaq*, an evil spirit. He constantly challenged the religious authority of Father Henry (called Kajoaluk by the Nattilingmiut because of his big red beard) and finally renounced the Catholic faith, saying he didn't want to be reprimanded by Father Henry and Father Papion.[72]

In the Kivalliq, as well, the transition from shamanism to Christianity was by no means a clear-cut break. Donald Suluk, a famous preacher born around 1925 in Igluligaarjuk, gained a great reputation as a musician and preacher. He also became a figure of some controversy in the Kivalliq, since the Roman Catholic Church opposed his teachings and practices. In Kangirsludjuar in 1945, according to Father Choque (1985, 117–18), Suluk was considered a shaman by some and a Christian preacher by others. He would ask people to pray, would use a crucifix and bibles, and would perform shamanic rituals, claiming to be an agent sent by God. Some Inuit families in Kangirsludjuar began to follow his teachings and put a Christian crucifix in front of their igloo. During his trip in the area from 31 October to 14 November 1946, Father Buliard noted the success of Suluk's movement, which he found difficult to oppose.[73] In a letter dated 20 November 1949, he seems depressed about the situation, describing the movement as a mixture of Protestantism and shamanism and Suluk's followers as "enlightened" people.[74]

Dominic Qasaluaq from Igluligaarjuk (2006 interview) remembered Suluk as a preacher who taught people to keep away from evil:

I know he would perform by making something visible. As a young person I saw something I tried to run away from. I have learnt from him that there is a good way of living and a bad way of living. Although the people would often say that he is not an *angakkuq*, I have seen him teaching people about the good and the bad path. He told us that there is Satan, the evil, and he would show us what evil looks like if we do evil things. For him, Satan was the master of people who do evil things.

He explained to the people who were at the drum dances that if we do evil, the master who makes us do bad things would come in so the people would see how it looked like. It was a big *tuurngaq*, *tuurngaqjuaq*. When

I saw this being, I jumped to the back of the bed right at the edge of the igloo. He told us never to get involved with this being. Seeing this being the way it looked made you wish to have a good life. That being had a tail and hands. I could see it, it was very close from me. Then he called other good helpers that cast this evil spirit out. These spirits tied something around his neck and sucked it out, cast it away of the igloo.

Suluk faced strong resistance from both Inuit and missionaries, but today many elders speak about him with respect and emphasize his deep involvement in Christianity. In a 2006 interview, Pelagie Nanauk from Arviat, who became a nun in Igluligaarjuk, remembered attaching an object to his belt so that her wish to become a nun would be fulfilled.

The late Victor Tungilik from Naujaat practised as a healer and *angakkuq* for several years. His parents were Anglicans but wanted him to be raised as a Roman Catholic. His father was an *angakkuq* as well as a Christian, and after he died, Tungilik also became an *angakkuq:* "I don't know how I became an *angakkuq*. It was not that somebody made me into an *angakkuq*. I don't know how it happened. In the evenings there would be a brightness on the ground behind me and it would follow me. It turned out that this was my *ikajuqti* ['helper']. When I mentioned to someone that I would see this when I was alone, I was told that it had been my father's *ikajuqti*. I wasn't scared of it. I didn't think about being scared of it. It was given to me by someone. It would come to me whenever anyone was sick. I would heal people who were ill."[75]

Tungilik said that his *tuurngait* did not oblige him to observe the ritual rules: "When my *tuurngait* would help me they did not have me observe any time of abstaining. They did not have me abstain from eating or doing any type of work. Because of this, I felt I was different from others. It seemed like my *tuurngait* were similar to the Christian religion, they did not make me abstain from anything. When I was given an item to help someone, then it was up to me to heal the person."[76]

Tungilik practised for several years but finally decided to stop. As a child he had heard a priest say in a sermon that sinners would be thrown into a great fire. This warning had impressed him and later contributed to his decision to give up his shamanic practices, even though he was quite effective as an *angakkuq:* "After I had got rid of them [helping spirits], there was a time that I regretted it for my two in-laws died at the same time … That was the only time I felt regret. I thought that maybe if I had not sent away my *tuurngait*, one of them might have remained alive, and I would continue to see him … If I continued to be an *angakkuq,* I would end up in Hell in the great fire. Because I didn't want this to happen, I let my *tuurngait* go."[77]

The missionary perspective that shamanism and Christianity were incompatible was clearly at work here. Later on, Tungilik discovered that not all priests rejected his shamanic activities out of hand: "I told a priest that I had been an *angakkuq* in my past. I told him that I had sent away my *tuurngait* even though they were there to help me. The priest told me that what I had done was wrong because they were there to help me heal people, and that any way of assisting and healing people was a gift from God. When the priest told me this, I believed him. But, as I had already sent my *tuurngait* away, I was not going to request their return."[78]

Tungilik himself never doubted the power of shamanism, but he acknowledged that the power of God was greater: "As I understood more about religion, I let go of my *tuurngait* who were really powerful and really helpful, because I knew there was someone who was even more powerful and even stronger than my *tuurngait*. That made me decide to follow religion."[79] But Tungilik was sure that the *tuurngait* had protected him and that because of them he was still alive.

Tungilik's accounts suggest that shamanism has not been rejected by Christian Inuit, but has been subordinated to a Christian framework. Thus, Tungilik argued that the good *tuurngait* come from God and the bad *tuurngait* from Satan.[80] The continuity of shamanism is to some extent based on a continuing belief in its efficacy. People have felt that without it they would be helpless. Uyarasuk from Iglulik said, "I heard one person who went through the *siqqitirniq* ritual say that he was going to let go of all his healing powers that he used when he was an *angakkuq*. Someone else said we would be helpless, because there would no longer be anyone to find out the causes of illness. I remember someone saying this."[81]

Today many elders take the position that both shamanism and Christianity should receive their due. They feel that *angakkuit* contributed to the well-being of Inuit society and that their role was only partially taken over by ministers and missionaries. They indicate that although in the past some shamans were truly frightening, many of them were very helpful.

CONCLUSION

In the Eastern Arctic, various religious movements emerged within the sphere of influence of the Anglican mission at Uumanarjuaq, but outside its direct control. The Anglican mission had cultivated the strategy of spreading religious texts – notably bibles – gramophone records, and hymnbooks among Inuit. Furthermore, Peck made the gospels available in Inuktitut and syllabic orthography to the Inuit of South Baffin Island.[82] These texts, often studied without the direct guidance of the missionaries, stimulated the development of Inuit forms of Christianity, especially in areas far from Uumanarjuaq. Such a development close to Uumanarjuaq was hardly possible, as its success would immediately have led to a confrontation with the missionaries – as was illustrated by Angmalik's abortive attempt at the very beginning of the conversion process. In the case of Angmalik, the community was caught in a dilemma and opted for the version of Christianity represented by the Anglican missionaries. This choice may have implied more than choosing between the missionaries' version of Christianity and that of Angmalik. It also implied decisions about leadership and authority in religious matters. By accepting the spiritual authority of the missionaries, the community seriously limited the options of their own leaders, who had to accept the authority of the missionaries. Within that framework, Inuit leaders were encouraged to take responsibility and become lay preachers. Well-known examples are Peter Tulugarjuaq and Luke Qillaapik, who as lay preachers had great autonomy and replaced the Anglican missionaries after their departure in 1913.[83]

The Catholic missionaries attributed the development of the new religious movements among the Inuit to the indiscriminate spread of religious texts by the Anglicans. The Oblate missionaries tried to prevent the development of new religious movements by controlling the information provided to the Inuit. They did not spread biblical texts, and they were only prepared to preach Christianity when they had a presence in a community and could thus keep an eye on the results.[84] They were not inclined to delegate religious authority to Inuit leaders and thus tried to visit their flock as often as possible. In many respects, Catholic missionaries were closer to the Inuit people and more prepared to adopt their lifestyles than the Anglicans were. The correlation between conversion and the adoption of a Western lifestyle was less obvious to them than to the Anglican missionaries, who assumed that Christianity and civilization were intimately connected.[85] The Anglicans' strategy of seeking the rapid spread of their ideas proved successful as far as the divulgence of Christian ideas was concerned, but it clearly had consequences with which the Anglicans had not reckoned.

These differences in strategy explain why religious movements developed in areas under the influence but outside the direct control of the Anglican mission, but did not develop in the Keewatin and Nattilik areas, which were predominantly within the sphere of influence of the Catholic mission but, the Igluligaarjuk area excepted, outside its direct control. The rituals of the new movements exhibited various combinations of Christian and shamanic elements, the strands of which are difficult to disentangle. The new movements sought to integrate Christianity within existing patterns of Inuit culture. The church built by Keegak, for example, combines features of a church with those of a traditional *qaggiq* (feast house). In several cases, close cooperation developed between a recognized shaman and a camp leader.

The idea of the imminent end of the world seems to have appealed to the Inuit and was clearly one of the notions most easily adopted in the new religious movements.[86] Existing beliefs about the end of the world may have contributed to the acceptance of Christian eschatological ideas in Inuit culture. Rasmussen (1929, 252) refers to the destruction of the world by Sila (the spirit of the universe). Father Gasté (1869) notes that in 1869 the "savages" feared that the earth would open and vomit flames. In 1941 the Inuit at Orki and Kubvuk, near Iglulik, feared that the earth would devour them.[87] It is difficult to asses to what extent these ideas developed under Christian influence, but they provided a fertile ground for the belief in the imminent end of the world.[88] In most of these movements, the focus was on preparing for this end, and that meant living according to a new morality. The authority of the religious leader had to be accepted; material goods and interests were forsaken or handed over to the religious leader, who took care of their distribution. New rituals and symbols emerged that identified the believers as a new community. These dynamics are still at work today in some evangelical and Pentecostal movements, and the end of the world continues to be a popular subject for discussion on local radio stations.

The new religious movements provided little information on the new world that was expected. The coming of the end of the world might imply that all regular hunting activities would stop or decrease, that dogs would be killed, or hunting implements destroyed. The believers abandoned their earthly possessions and worldly activities in preparation for the new world. Going up to the sky or even death might have meant a shift from the present imperfect world to the new one. Shamans used to travel to the land of the dead or up to the spirits. In some movements (such as Keegak's), it was believed that the religious leaders and the whole community were about to enter a new world. Many leaders claimed to be Christ or God, and those who contested this claim risked their lives.

The elders of today say that one of the main advantages of conversion to Christianity was that women no longer had to cope with the many ritual injunctions regarding food and game.[89] The ritual of *siqqitiq* (discussed in chapter 4) conveys this idea of conversion as a transition to an easier way of life, one with new rules and without the dangers inherent in spiritual relationships with the spirits of game and the dead. The coming of the end of the world required an absolute commitment that might result in violence and disaster. In the fifty years that these religious movements developed in different areas, the attempts to combine shamanism and Christianity gradually lost momentum. Most accounts by Qallunaat suggest that it was the presence and intervention of white people that stopped the movements, but in most cases, especially in the earlier period, Inuit stopped them themselves. The last movements were ended with relative ease largely because the established religions had become firmly rooted in Inuit culture and most Inuit believed that combining shamanism and Christianity was no longer a viable option. More cautious adaptation and negotiation were required to preserve Inuit cultural traditions.[90]

A remarkable feature of many religious movements is the intensity of the religious life. Direct experiences of spirits and non-human beings were an important part of the shamanic tradition. Many of the founders of the new religious movements had visions of Jesus and God and sometimes even identified with them. In this respect, the new movements gave scope to religious experiences embedded in the shamanic traditions of the past. Today Pentecostal and evangelical movements (e.g., the Glad Tidings Church) seem to respond to the need for intense religious experiences in Inuit society, but the Roman Catholic Church and the Anglican Church, in emphasizing the confession of sins and direct experiences of the Holy Ghost, also provide scope more and more for an intense religious life.[91]

3

Inuit Winter Feasts

INTRODUCTION

Feasting was an important part of Inuit social life. When Qallunaat introduced the celebration of Christmas, Inuit were quite willing to participate in it if given the chance. The Christmas celebrations organized by the missionaries took account of the interests of Inuit, notably their enthusiasm for games and various forms of competition and play. Christmas soon evolved into the most important annual festivity, replacing the traditional winter feasts, which apparently had already been in decline when the missionaries arrived in the North. In this chapter, we explore those traditional winter feasts and their replacement by Christmas. We first discuss the traditional winter feasts (notably the Sedna feast and the *tivajuut*) and the crucial role of games in these feasts. Then we discuss the introduction of Christmas and show how various customs, such as Christmas dinner and gift giving, were adopted by Inuit. We examine how distinctive features of the winter feasts, notably games, were integrated into the Christmas context. We argue that the Christmas celebration was in many respects a transformation of the Inuit winter feasts.

THE SEDNA FEAST AND *TIVAJUUT*

Charles F. Hall (1864, 1:528) provides one of the earliest accounts of the Sedna feast as celebrated by the Nugumiut on South Baffin Island:

> At a time of the year apparently answering to our Christmas, they have a general meeting in a large igdlu … on a certain evening. There the angakoq … prays on behalf of the people for the public prosperity through the subsequent year. Then follows something like a feast. The next day all go out into the open air and form in a circle; in the centre is placed a vessel of water, and each member of the company brings a piece of meat, the kind being immaterial. The circle being formed, each person eats his or her meat

> in silence, thinking of Sedna, and wishing for good things. Then one in the circle takes a cup, dips up some of the water, all the time thinking of Sedna, and drinks it; and then, before passing the cup to another, states audibly the time and the place of his or her birth. This ceremony is performed by all in succession. Finally, presents of various articles are thrown from one another, with the idea that each will receive of Sedna good things in proportion to the liberality here shown. Soon after this occasion, at a time which answers to our New Year's day, two men start out, one of them being dressed to represent a woman, and go to every house in the village, blowing out the light in each. The lights are afterwards rekindled from a fresh fire. When Taqulitu was asked the meaning of this, she replied, "New sun – new light," implying a belief that the sun was at that time renewed for the year.

Unfortunately, Hall himself did not witness these meetings, and his account of the feast is therefore based on hearsay: "When one of these meetings and outdoor ceremonies took place, I was absent from the village where most of my Innuit friends were living. Koojesse, Sharkey, and others wished to have me sent for, thinking I would like to be present; but old Artarkparu objected, fearing that I should grow weary before the ceremony was complete, and, retiring from the circle, break the charm. So I was not sent for, but was obliged to gain my information from the natives."

Earlier, Ludvig Kumlien (1879, 29) had related that Inuit were not too keen on outsiders participating in their festivities and ceremonials. Boas suspected that Hall had added Christian connotations to his description,[1] although they may also have been added by Tookoolitoo, who was probably his main informant and had spent quite some time in England. According to Hall, the feast comprised one evening and the next day. The evening was marked by the activities of the *angakkuit*, who prayed on behalf of the community. The next day the focus shifted to the feast for the community at large, everyone sharing in the food and drinks. Each one had to bring a piece of meat. Whereas the participants consumed the meat simultaneously, each individual concentrating on Sedna (the sea woman, the owner of the sea game), they drank the water in succession, each one in turn specifying the time and place of his birth. Depending on whether one was born in summer or winter, one belonged either to the ducks (the summer people) or the ptarmigans (the winter people). Then they exchanged presents. The generosity shown was reciprocated by Sedna. Subsequently, two men, one dressed up as a woman, visited all the houses and extinguished the lights. The conclusion of the feast was marked by the rekindling of the lamps from a fresh fire. Taqulitu's explanation for the rekindling suggests a close relationship between the new sun and the new light.

Kumlien (1879, 19) describes a ceremony that took place at the end of the winter or the beginning of the spring:

> They have an interesting custom or superstition, namely, the killing of the evil spirit of the deer; some time during the winter or early in spring, at any rate before they can go deer-hunting, they congregate together and dispose of this imaginary evil. The chief ancoot, angekok, or medicine-man, is the main performer. He goes through a number of gyrations and contortions, constantly hallooing and calling, till suddenly the imaginary deer is among them. Now begins a lively time. Every one is screaming, running, jumping, spearing, and stabbing at the imaginary deer, till one would think a whole mad-house was let loose. Often this deer proves very agile, and must be hard to kill, for I have known them to keep this performance up for days; in fact, till they were completely exhausted.
>
> During one of these performances an old man speared the deer, another knocked out an eye, a third stabbed him, and so till he was dead. Those who are able or fortunate enough to inflict some injury on this bad deer, especially he who inflicts the death-blow, is considered extremely lucky, as he will have no difficulty in procuring as many deer as he wants, for there is no longer an evil spirit to turn his bullets or arrows from their course.
>
> They seldom kill a deer after the regular hunting season is over, till this performance has been gone through with, even though a very good opportunity presents itself.

The "evil" caribou was represented by an *angakkuq*, who was symbolically killed. The killing of the evil caribou made caribou available to the hunters. This ceremony may have been equivalent to the killing of Sedna at the start of sea mammal hunting season as described by Boas, who assumed that Kumlien was describing the Sedna feast here.[2] However, the description also evokes another ritual performance, recorded by Captain Mutch.[3]

> The angakok takes a ground-seal spear and a line down to the ground-ice and sets it up, with the harpoon-point upward. When the performance opens in the house, the angakok stands up, and near him are his assistant spirits. Then he goes down to the ground-ice, and soon he sees a walrus-spirit, which enters him. As soon as this spirit enters his body, he loses all knowledge of himself. Then his spirit assistants discover him, and harpoon him in the same way as a hunter harpoons a walrus. The angakok believes he dives. As soon as he dives, he sees the snow-houses of the village, which his spirit assistants have so far not noticed. The walrus rises, and moves in the direction of the snow-houses. It enters one of them, and then goes from house to house, frightening all the people. They see the harpoon-heads of the spirit assistants protruding from its body, and blow on them. Finally the walrus goes back to the ground-ice where it was first seen. The people take a little water and pour it over their feet, which is symbolic of drinking water. This helps them to recover from their fright. When the angakok gets

> back to the water, it appears to the spirit assistants as though the walrus had just risen again, and they throw it with a lance. When the spirit assistants have killed the walrus, they drag it out to the ice and pull out the harpoon – not, however, like human beings, who turn the harpoon-point between the splices of the warp, but by pulling it out through the body with all their strength. Then the spirits cut up the body. As soon as they gather the meat, the walrus revives, and becomes a man again. The spirits are particularly careful to put those parts together properly where the harpoon-point has been pulled out. Then the angakok goes back to the house, and his spirit assistants stay outside, ready to do his bidding any time during the following year.

In this description, a walrus spirit enters the *angakkuq;* the *angakkuq* is transformed into a walrus and is harpooned by his helping spirits; and then the helping spirits cut the *angakkuq* into pieces and he revives. Whereas in the feast described by Kumlien the *angakkuq* is killed by other Inuit, in this ritual the *angakkuq* is killed by his helping spirits. The text may well refer to an opening of the winter hunting season. Unfortunately, neither Mutch nor Boas provides an explanation of this performance.

Boas (1964, 606–7) concludes that Kumlien misunderstood the true nature of the proceedings: "I could not learn anything about this ceremony, though I asked all the persons with whom Kumlien had had intercourse. Probably there was some misunderstanding as to the meaning of their feast during the autumn which induced him to give this report." The matter could not be resolved easily, since Boas was unable to trace the figure of Pukimna, the mother of the caribou. It may well be that the ritual cycle around the hunting of caribou was more complex than is usually assumed today. Boas had considerable trouble with Inuit *angakkuit* during his residence in Cumberland Sound. He was accused of causing sickness among the Inuit, and they may have tried to keep information from him.[4]

Kumlien (1879, 43–4) presents an account of the general exchange of women, one of the central features of the Inuit winter feasts:

> Another custom, which was once very popular, is the following: An ancoot dresses himself up in the most hideous manner, having several pairs of pants on, among the rest, and a horrid-looking mask of skins. The men and women now range themselves in separate and opposite ranks, and the ancoot takes his place between them. He then picks out a man and conducts him to a woman in the opposite ranks. This couple then go to the woman's hut and have a grand spree for a day or two. This manner of proceeding is kept up till all the women but one are disposed of. This one is always the ancoot's choice, and her he reserves for himself. The people thus assembled are, of course, all well known to him, and he understands pretty well how to mate them so as to meet general approbation.

The features that Kumlien describes seem to be at the heart of the winter feasts. They can be found in the winter feasts on North Baffin as well as in the Sedna feasts on South Baffin as described by Boas and Bilby.

Boas (1964, 195ff.) describes in detail an Inuit winter feast he witnessed in Qiqirtat (Kekerten Island), Cumberland Sound, on 10 November 1883. The feast was celebrated late in the fall. *Tupilait* (evil spirits of the dead) who had not arrived at their final destiny in the land of the dead attacked the community, people as well as dogs. These evil spirits brought sickness, death, and bad weather. To protect the people, the *angakkuit* were intensively performing their practices inside a large hut. They conducted the ritual of harpooning Sedna, the sea woman. She was lured up by a magic song and harpooned with a seal spear. She freed herself from the harpoon and descended to the underworld again. The *angakkuit* showed the blood-sprinkled harpoon to the audience. The next day a great festival for young and old was celebrated. All wore protective amulets (such as the garments they wore after birth) to protect themselves against Sedna, who was still enraged. Boas describes what happened next:

> The men assemble early in the morning in the middle of the settlement. As soon as they have all got together they run screaming and jumping around the houses, following the course of the sun (nunajisartung or kaivitijung). A few, dressed in women's jackets, run in the opposite direction. These are those who were born in abnormal presentations. The circuit made, they visit every hut, and the woman of the house must always be in waiting for them. When she hears the noise of the band she comes out and throws a dish containing little gifts of meat, ivory trinkets, and articles of sealskin into the yelling crowd, of which each one helps himself to what he can get. No hut is omitted in this round (irqatatung).
>
> The crowd next divides itself into two parties, the ptarmigans (axigirn), those who were born in the winter, and the ducks (aggirn), the children of the summer. A large rope of sealskin is stretched out. One party takes one end of it and tries with all its might to drag the opposite party over to its side. The others hold fast to the rope and try as hard to make ground for themselves. If the ptarmigans give way the summer has won the game and fine weather may be expected to prevail through the winter (nussueraqtung).
>
> The contest of the seasons having been decided, the women bring out of a hut a large kettle of water and each person takes his drinking cup. They all stand as near to the kettle as possible, while the oldest man among them steps out first. He dips a cup of water from the vessel, sprinkles a few drops on the ground, turns his face toward the home of his youth, and tells his name and the place of his birth (oxsoaxsavepunga – me, I was born in –). He is followed by an aged woman, who announces her name and home, and then all the others do the same, down to the young children, who are represented by their mothers. Only the parents of children born during

the last year are forbidden to partake in this ceremony. As the words of the old are listened to respectfully, so those of the distinguished hunters are received with demonstrative applause and those of the others with varying degrees of attention, in some cases even with joking and raillery (imitijung).

Now arises a cry of surprise and all eyes are turned toward a hut out of which stalk two gigantic figures. They wear heavy boots; their legs are swelled out to a wonderful thickness with several pairs of breeches; the shoulders of each are covered by a woman's overjacket and the faces by tattooed masks of sealskins. In the right hand each carries the seal spear, on the back of each is an inflated buoy of sealskin, and in the left hand the scraper. Silently, with long strides, the qailertetang ... approach the assembly, who, screaming, press back from them. The pair solemnly leads the men to a suitable spot and set them in a row, and the women in another opposite them. They match the men and women in pairs and these pairs run, pursued by the qailertetang, to the hut of the woman, where they are for the following day and night man and wife (nulianititijung). Having performed this duty, the qailertetang stride down to the shore and invoke the good north wind, which brings fair weather, while they warn off the unfavourable south wind.

As soon as the incantation is over, all the men attack the qailertetang with great noise. They act as if they had weapons in their hands and would kill both spirits. One pretends to probe them with a spear, another to stab them with a knife, one to cut off their arms and legs, another to beat them unmercifully on the head. The buoys which they carry on their backs are ripped open and collapse and soon they both lie as if dead beside their broken weapons (pilekting). The Eskimo leave them to get their drinking cups and the qailertetang awake to new life. Each man fills his sealskin with water, passes a cup to them and inquires about the future, about the fortunes of the hunt and the events of life. The qailertetang answer in murmurs which the questioner must interpret for himself. The evening is spent in playing ball, which is whipped all around the settlement (ajuktaqtung).[5]

This description of the winter feast, which Boas provided in his first monograph, differs significantly on some points from the data collected in his field notebook as published by L. Müller-Wille (1998). For example, Boas's reference to men running around the settlement in the early morning wearing their best pants is not retained in his description of the feast. Various details that suggest direct influence or contact with the whalers are also omitted. In his notebook, for instance, Boas relates that the men visited the house of Captain Mutch and the cooper. He notes that after the participants stated their name and origin, "a snowman with coal for eyes was built down below and the men shot at it."[6] Boas no longer refers to having thrown beads out among the people himself, his intervention resulting in a fine struggle for the beads. It seems that Boas was intent on describing the winter feast as a "traditional Inuit feast," and did not want to distort that picture by making unnecessary references to Western influences or participation. However, some of the features omitted – for example, the wearing of best clothes and the shooting – became important features of later Christmas celebrations. It may well be that Boas's description of a crucial stage of the ritual, the harpooning of Sedna on the eve of the feast, is based entirely on reconstruction, as no reference is made to it in his notebook entries for 10 and 11 November. Apparently, Boas spent the night of 10–11 November reading three books. Despite these reservations, Boas's description of the feast remains the most detailed and instructive account of a winter feast available.[7]

At the beginning of the winter feast, the evil spirits of the dead attacked the communities. During the feast the antagonistic relationship between the *tupilait* and the Inuit was gradually transformed into a positive relationship between the Inuit and their deceased ancestors, allowing them to represent the Ullurmiut (deceased people from the land of the day) in their favourite play.[8] In the course of the ritual, the success of the hunt was determined in various divinatory games, such as the tug-of-war between the ptarmigans and the ducks.

The exchanges in the feast that Boas describes involved small gifts – "meat, ivory trinkets, and articles of sealskin" – and their distribution resulted in a general scramble. The distribution of Boas's own beads followed the same pattern. The distribution of the women was quite another matter. Here, representatives of the spirits intervened to organize the adults into pairs. The feast included a ritual form of drinking that related the Inuit to their origins. Exchange of food played only a minor role of importance.

Captain Mutch explained that the participants in the feast should wear the pieces of skin their mothers had used to clean them when they were born. If they did not do so, "[t]heir souls would become light, and would leave the body. It is said, that if they wear this piece of skin, they are 'made new.'"[9]

The Qailertetang were probably equivalent to the *qiluktelãk* referred to by Peck in his description of the Sedna feast.[10] Boas (1901, 40) describes the Qailertetang as "a servant of Sedna": "She is represented by a man dressed in a woman's costume and wearing a mask made of seal-skin … She is believed to be a large woman of very heavy limbs, who comes to make good weather and 'to make the soul of men calm like the sea.' She carries harpoon-line, harpoon, and drag, because she is a seal-hunter, but she also carries a skin-scraper. She is dumb, but she sees everything the people do. She likes to see them enjoy themselves, and at her advent a festival is celebrated."

The notion of "servant" may relate to the Inuit concept of the *ikajuqti* (helping spirit), upon whom *angakkuit* often called. Elsewhere, Boas (1907, 491) described the Ekkos, two spirits who played a role in the feast at Akuliaq, on the north shore of Hudson Strait, much like that played by the Qailertetang in Cumberland Sound. They made people confess their transgressions.

> The *Ekkos* are one male and one female. The man has his clothing turned inside out. He wears his hood over his head. It is tied up by thongs wrapped around it to form a horn. His eyes are covered with goggles made of seal-skin to prevent him from seeing from the sides. He also wears a conical mouthpiece. Straps pass from the shoulders down his sides and between his legs, and his long penis is tied up.
>
> The female *Ekko* also has her clothing turned inside out, but no strappings are attached to it. It is supposed that the performers, while in this dress, are possessed by the spirit of the *Ekko*.

In Captain Mutch's account of the feast among the Nuqumiut, we find a third figure besides the Ekko and the Ekkotow who clearly corresponded to the Ekkos at Akuliaq:[11]

> The third of these beings is called "*Noonagekshown*" … He carries a spear in his hand and a drag on his back, and is bound all over with ground-seal lashings. A great many objects are hanging down from his dress. His face is covered with dog-skin. He appears in the spring and in the autumn, and, like *Ekko*, brings health to the sick, and fair weather, and consequently plenty of food to the people. He also distributes the women among the men. The *Ekko* and the *Noonagekshown* do not speak, but they make signs to the people to indicate what they wish to say. At the end of the performance *Noonagekshown* points his sharp-pointed hood at the people, as though he were going to butt, and they run away from him.

Both Ekkos and the Noonagekshown were masked. While the Ekko and Ekkotow appear to have been equivalents of the Qailertetang, the Noonagekshown evokes the Noonageksaktut described by Peck: "The conjurors … are said to be Noonageksaktut, and it is their custom to make such conjurors … And the Noonageksaktut has a cap made of large seal (okjuk) skin which has also a beautiful point going upward. And he has bound on his feet sticks which are used to beat off the snow from garments. And he moves his great feet about making them to appear like the feet of a crow … The conjuror also who absolves from guilt, who clears away the sins (causes of evil) of the Eskimo as often as they do, (so) they go down to the beach (to tell Sedna the transgression)."[12]

The Noonageksaktut also appear to have been *angakkuit*. Peck compares their feet to those of a crow, but probably they resembled raven claws. The Noonageksaktut operated as mediators between Sedna and the community. Aksaajuq from Panniqtuuq (1995 interview) said that this ritual was performed so that Inuit hunters would have a good hunting area: "*Nunagiqsaqtuq* is when the shamans would try to perform a ritual in order that people in the land and in the camps could have good weather and good hunting area. They would try to make the area nice for the hunters so that people could get food. When food and animals were needed and when they would get it, they would also perform *nunagiqsaqtuq*."[13] The name

Noonageksaktut refers to *nuna*, the land, and the Noonageksaktut probably prepared the land by communicating the transgressions of the people to Sedna.

In Peck's description of the Sedna feast, the *qiluktelãk* were not indispensable to the feast and the tug-of-war was between men and women, not between ptarmigans and ducks.

> When there is a Sedna feast, they generally have Qiluktelãk (Qiluktelãk are two men – sometimes however only one ... who are dressed up, in a peculiar fashion like women, and who call the men and women together, and make them for a time man and wife). But sometimes they do not have the Qiluktelãk. When they have a regular Sedna celebration (generally in the autumn), they have a tug of war, the women hauling on one end of the line (rope) and the men on the other. (Now) the Eskimo gather together and while they are assembled, they [fetch] drinking water (which they place in a skin which is fixed on the front part of the Qiluktelãk's dress). The person that drinks from this, mentions the name of the place where he was born, and when the drinking ceremony is over, they have also a distribution of presents (they go from dwelling to dwelling and various things are thrown out to them by the inmates). This they also do for they are so commanded by the conjuror. And when they do not work on account of the Sedna ceremony, the conjurors sometimes go on with their (other) performances of making men good hunters. The Eskimo generally have the Sedna feast when – on account of stormy weather – they are very hungry, as often it is said as Sedna is not willing ... to give the animals.[14]

Peck's text suggests that the Sedna feast was not celebrated on an annual basis, but only when bad weather or scarcity of game required it. Thus the feast was celebrated when the camp was under pressure from *tupilait* or famine. Its purpose was a renewal of the relations among human beings, the deceased, the animals, the land, and (the representatives) of Sedna. The exchange of women was at the core of the feast. Bilby (1923, 213) observes that pregnant women and the elderly were not included in the feast: "These women are *Kooveayootiksatyonerktoot*, i.e., 'no-longer-the material-for-a-rejoicing.'" Non-human representatives of Sedna organized the pairing and made fun of the pairs, who had to restrain their laughter. It is an open question whether the rejoicing that Bilby speaks of pertained only to human beings or also involved non-human agencies. The fact that Bilby refers to the temporary husbands as "Sedna mates" and to the children of such unions as the "offspring of Sedna" suggests the joyous participation of non-human agencies.

TIVAJUUT[15]

In North Baffin variants of the feast, the sea woman played no part and the feast focused mainly on the masked dancers and the wife exchange. It was celebrated in a feast house after an ordinary song feast. The platform was removed, and two men would dress up, one in female and the other in masculine attire. Both wore masks of skin. According to Rasmussen (1929, 241–3),

> The woman's dress would be drawn in tight wherever it should ordinarily be loose and full, as for instance the large baggy kamiks, the big hood and the broad shoulder pieces; the dress in itself should also be too small. The same principle was observed in the case of the man's costume, which was barely large enough for him to get it on at all. The man dressed as a woman should have an anautAq, or snowbeating stick, in his hand, that is, a stick used for beating or brushing snow from one's garments; the male figure should carry a te·ᵍarut, or short dog whip. Finally, the "man" should have fastened in the crutch a huge penis, grotesque in its effect, fashioned either of wood or of stuffed intestines.

Two blocks of snow were placed in the feast house – the jumping block, half the height of a man, and the lamp block, the same height as a man. Then,

> [a]ll the men and women assemble in the qag·e, and now the two masked dancers, who are called tivaju·t, come bounding in. They are dumb performers, and may only endeaveour to make themselves understood by signs, and only puff out breath between the lips and ejaculate "pust, pust" exactly as if they were trying to blow something out. They come bounding in, taking great leaps through the entrance hole, and must jump over the aterartarwik, this also to be done whenever they re-enter after an exit. The first thing the tivaju·t now do is to chase out all the men with blows, the woman striking with her anautaq, the man with his *te·ᵍarut*, the women of the audience being suffered to remain behind. They then caper about, with light, adroit movements, among the women, peering everywhere to see if any man has concealed himself in their ranks.
>
> Should a man be so discovered, he is recklessly and mercilessly thrashed out of the house. As soon as the tivaju·t are sure all the men have gone, they themselves must dash out of the qag·e, to where the men are assembled in a group outside. One of these men then steps up to the tivaju·t, and with his face close to the mask, whispers with a smile the name of the woman inside the qag·e, with whom he wishes to lie the coming night. The two tivaju·t then at once rush back, gaily into the qag·e, go up to the woman whose name has been whispered to them outside, and touch the soles of her feet with anautAq and te·ᵍarut respectively. This is called ikuƒ.iƒut: the ones who hack out something for themselves with an axe or a big, sharp knife. Great rejoicing is now apparent among all the women, and the one woman chosen: ikut·aujəq, goes out and comes in again with the man who has asked for her. Both are expected to look very serious; all the women in the

qag·e however, must be quite the reverse, laughing and joking and making fun, and trying all they can to make the couple laugh; should they succeed, however, it means a short life for the pair. The women in the qag·e make faces, and murmur, in all kinds of surprising tones: unununununununun, unununununun, unununununun! The two who are to lie together must then solemnly and slowly and without moving a muscle of their faces, walk round the lamp block twice, while the following song is sung ...

The words of this song are difficult to translate literally, but the following rather free rendering comes nearest to the sense as given by Orulo:

Masquerader,
teasing, capering Dancer-in-a-mask,
Twist yourself round and kiss yourself behind,
you will find it very sweet.
Give him gifts,
dried moss for lamp wicks,
masquerader, masquerader,
teasing, capering Dancer-in-a-mask!

While this song is being sung, the two maskers stand facing each other and making all manner of lascivious and grotesque gestures; now and again the man strikes his great penis with his te·^{g}arut, and the woman strikes it with her anautAq, and then they pretend to effect a coition standing up. This is intended partly to demonstrate the joys of sexual intercourse, and partly also to elicit a laugh from the couple walking round the lamp block. The game is carried on throughout the evening until all the men and woman have been paired off, the party then dispersing, each man leading home to his own house the woman he has chosen.

In her description of the *tivajuut* as it was celebrated in Iglulik, Rose Iqallijuq referred to an abundance of food at the feast. The *tivajuut* was celebrated in the *qaggiq*, a big igloo specially built for a feast. According to Kappianaq from Iglulik, the celebration was made to strengthen the land.[16]

The contest between the *aggiqiq* (ptarmigans) and *aggiarjuit* (ducks) was an important part of the *tivajuut*.[17] Another was the formation of new couples who would sleep together. This was done by two masked *angakkuit*. When the pairs were formed, the other participants tried to make them laugh, but the couples had to restrain themselves. According to Rasmussen (1929, 231–2, 241–3), this part of the celebration was followed by a copious meal of *igunaq* (aged walrus meat). Saladin d'Anglure (1989, 165n29) points out that the word for the distribution of women by the two masked *angakkuit* was the same as the word for the distribution of frozen meat – *ikujijut*. The woman was referred to as an *ikuktaq*, a part separated from a whole by a violent act. The term evokes the origin myth of the sea woman; according to the myth, sea mammals originated from the finger joints cut off from the sea woman's hands (see chapter 4), suggesting a homology between the women and the sea mammals.

Wife exchange was a widespread phenomenon in Inuit culture. It seems everywhere to have been a basic shamanic practice. Boas (1901, 158) reports that each shamanic séance was followed by an exchange of wives. Ethnographic sources indicate that sexual intercourse with a shaman was often part of the healing practice,[18] and the missionaries always associated shamanic practices with wife exchange. Bilby and Rasmussen suggest that the men chose the women they wanted, but they say little about the rules for selection. Saladin d'Anglure interprets these exchanges at the *tivajuut* more in terms of a restricted exchange between *illuriik* (song partners) than in terms of a general exchange entailing the random sharing of women in the community. A consequence of these exchanges would be that men would have children with different women, and their children would be distributed in the community more broadly than just within the nuclear family. In this respect, the wife exchanges may have had effects not unlike those of procedures for contemporary adoptions, which ensure the wider distribution of children in the community and the strengthening of family ties outside the nuclear family. It would be interesting to explore to what extent the decline of wife exchange practices has stimulated adoption in Inuit culture. However that may be, at the *tivajuut,* husband-wife relations were transcended and sexual intercourse was ordained by non-human agencies and publicly acknowledged by all participants. In this way, the feast became a social as well as a cosmological event, connecting the members of the camp and the non-human agencies involved in the ritual.

The dating of the feast is unclear and may have varied in different areas. Hall connects it to Christmas. In Ikpiarjuk, Trott[19] recorded a song referring to the rising of Akkuktujut (Orion's shoulder stars).[20] He was told by Inuit that in the darkest period, when both the sun and the moon were below the horizon, the rising of these stars told the Inuit that daylight was about to return and was thus an occasion for celebration. More recently, Kappianaq connected the feast to the appearance of the Aagjuuk.[21] This suggests that the *tivajuut* was celebrated in December. However, Boas witnessed a winter feast on 10 November 1883 and Bilby (1922, 210) connects the feast to the tempestuous weather that follows the arctic summer. The feast, then, could also have been celebrated much earlier than December on South Baffin Island. The feast, it seems, was not connected to the winter solstice, but to hunting preparations in the winter season. Both the Sedna feast and the *tivajuut* appear to have prepared the community as well as the land for the hunting season by establishing correct relationships between human beings and the non-human agencies that controlled the success of hunting. The symbolism of identification expressed in Boas's account of the game involving *ullurmiut* (deceased ancestors) may also have played an important part in the sexual intercourse practices that were so detested by the missionaries.

INUIT WINTER FEASTS AND CHRISTMAS

As early as the nineteenth century, European and American Christmas traditions may have begun to shape Inuit winter feasts.[22] Inuit had various opportunities to witness Christmas celebrations and other feasts on the ships of explorers and whalers. Parry and Lyon organized theatres and farces on their ships to keep their men occupied. Lyon (1824, 88–9) reports:

> A liberal subscription having been made amongst the officers prior to leaving England, by which a stock of theatrical clothes, &c. was purchased, it was now proposed by Captain Parry that, as our active operations had ceased for a time, we should make arrangements for performing plays once a fortnight throughout the winter, as a means of amusing the seamen, and in some degree to break the tedious monotony of our confinement. As there could be no desire or hope of excelling, every officer's name was readily entered on the first of dramatis personae. Those ladies who had cherished the growth of their beards and whiskers, as a defence against the inclemency of the climate, now generously agreed to do away with such unfeminine ornaments, and every thing bade fair for a most stylish theatre.

Cross-dressing clearly was an important feature of these plays. The *Illustrated Arctic News* of 1852 published "a sketch of Parry himself transformed into a one-legged fiddler, accompanied by his purser William H. Hooper, disguised as the buxom landlady who liberally dispensed spiked punch throughout the evening."[23] Lyon (1824, 97–8) describes a Christmas celebration in 1821:

> On Christmas Eve, in order to keep the people quiet and sober, we performed two farces, and exhibited phantasmagoria so that the night passed merrily. Christmas Day was very fine, and we all attended church on board the *Fury* as we had been accustomed to do every Sunday since we were frozen in. The people then returned to their dinners at which English roast beef that had been kept untainted since the transport left us, was the principal luxury. To these were added cranberry pies and puddings of every shape and size, with full allowance of spirits. I never indeed saw more general good humour and merriment on a Christmas day since I went to sea. A pretty compliment was paid to all the officers by a well meaning, but certainly not very sober crew, by absolutely forcing each in his turn, beginning with myself, to go out on the lower deck and have his health drank with three hearty cheers.
>
> On the 26th, we sent all the people for a run on the ice, in order to put them to rights, but thick weather coming on, it became necessary to recall them, and, postponing the dinner hour, they were all danced sober by

> 1 PM, the fiddler being, fortunately, quite as he should be. During this curious ball, a witty fellow attended as an old cake woman, with lumps of frozen snow in a bucket; and such was the demand for his pies on this occasion, that he was obliged to replenish pretty frequently.

Each of the officers, in hierarchical order starting with the captain, received a toast.

Inuit were not admitted to religious services but still witnessed the Qallunaat going to church. Lyon (1824, 145) reports, "The 17th being Sunday, our visitors were refused admittance in the early part of the day, and when we all left the Hecla to attend church on board the Fury, their astonishment was unbounded; never having seen us in regular uniform, but generally in thick great coats, they could scarcely recognize even their particular friends. The gay appearance of the marines, such, even in this climate, is the attractive influence of a red coat, so delighted the ladies, that they all danced and shouted in an ecstasy of pleasure as each soldier passed before them."

Inuit were sometimes involved in festivities organized by the crew. According to Lyon (1824, 25–6),

> In order to amuse our new acquaintances as much as possible the fiddler was sent on the ice, where he instantly found a most delightful set of dancers, of whom some of the women kept pretty good time. Their only figure consisted in stamping and jumping with all their might. Our musician, who was a lively fellow, soon caught the infection, and began cutting capers also. In a short time every one on the floe, officers, men, and savages, were dancing together, and exhibited one of the most extraordinary sights I ever witnessed. One of our seamen, of a fresh ruddy complexion, excited the admiration of all the young females, who patted his face and danced round him wherever he went. I was half inclined to suppose they fancied him a woman, although he was nearly six feet high, and stout in proportion. I am sorry to give but a bad account of the morals of our visitors, some of whom were very importunate in offering their wives in exchange for a knife, and the women as anxiously pressing the bargain.

To what extent the Qallunaat customs influenced the Inuit winter feasts is hard to say. Hall and Boas both record that in the winter feasts everyone received a drink of water and then solemnly pronounced his name and place of origin. This type of ritual may have been inspired by the European Christmas tradition – no doubt followed on European ships – of drinking to the health of important people and friends in the homeland.[24]

Was the custom of drinking in turn, following a hierarchical order, observed by the Inuit and integrated into their own rituals? We do not know. But a hundred years earlier, Egede (1818, 283–384) noted with respect to the Greenlanders,

"When they come at a water from which they have not drunken before, an old man, if they have one with them, should drink first, in order to isolate the Tornarssuk, that is the evil in the water that would make the young men ill and die." The importance of first acts in Inuit culture is well attested, and it seems to be the task of the old men to mediate the drinking of water. Therefore, the drinking of water in hierarchical order as described by Boas may well be an old Inuit custom. The comparison of the harpooning to the gift of water constitutes an interesting problem. Sea mammals were supposed to be thirsty because they lived in salt water. A few drops of water were sprinkled in the mouth of the catch. Lucassie Nutaraaluk from Iqaluit told the story of a hunter who met a walrus that said to him, "I'm so thirsty. Please harpoon me."[25] According to Boas, the harpooning of Sedna was compared to the offering of a drink of water. It would be tempting to interpret the gift of water as an act of hospitality, but clearly it also evokes the act of wounding or killing. Moreover, the deceased person who wishes to be renamed and appears in a dream often asks for a drink of water. The drink of water appears to establish a connection, but the nature of that connection may vary.

Cross-dressing continued to be part of Qallunaat Christmas celebrations. A photograph taken by Moodie on Captain Low's ship, the *Neptune,* at Cape Fullerton on Christmas 1903 shows a group of Inuit and Qallunaat around two masked figures, one wearing skirts and the other sporting an excessively long beard.[26] Cross-dressing was also important in the winter feasts in Greenland. Various studies of Christmas celebrations in Labrador (Ben-Dor 1969; Richling 1983; Szala-Meneok 1994) attribute masquerading rituals to Western influence. Unfortunately, we have too little data to make an assessment of the complex interactions between various traditions.[27] Inuit and Qallunaat traditions influenced each other from the start. Therefore, we will focus on the emergence of new forms of rituals combining features of different cultural traditions. We will examine celebrations of Christmas in northeastern Canada, notably the Baffin Island area between 1890 and 1960. We will first consider testimonies from Qallunaat observers and then those of Inuit elders.

CHRISTMAS CELEBRATIONS, 1860–1930S

The first explorers might have used Christmas as an opportunity to acquaint Inuit with the Christian tradition. In 1860 several Inuit witnessed Christmas on the ship on which the American explorer Hall was sailing. Hall gave a Bible to Tookoolito, who had spent two years in England.

> Among the other incidents to be mentioned … I must not forget to say that Christmas and New Year's Day were celebrated by us in our winter quarters with all the honours it was in our power to show. A few of the natives were on board to dine on Christmas Day, and I took the opportunity to

> give Tookoolitoo a Bible that had been placed in my hands by the Young Men's Christian's Union of Cincinnati, and which I thought could not be devoted to a better purpose. I inscribed upon it the following: "Presented to Tookoolito, Tuesday, December 25th, 1860." Her first act was to read the title, "Holy Bible," then to try and read some of its pages, which she still longs to understand.[28]

Inuit who had travelled abroad on Qallunaat ships, had served as interpreters, or had worked with whalers may have learnt much about Christian celebrations such as Christmas before the missionaries arrived. As soon as the missionaries opened a permanent mission in Uumanarjuaq in 1894, however, they instituted the celebration of Christmas. Peck recorded brief descriptions of these celebrations in his diary.

> Had quite a number of our Eskimo friends along today. Several brought presents of gloves, caps, etc., which they had knitted, and some of which they desired us to use for our own comfort, and also to show to the kind ladies in England who had sent them the wool, and knitting pins. After friendly greetings, we entertained our visitors with coffee and cake, and pointed out to them the true reason why we should rejoice on this day … The great events of the season, viz. distribution of prizes and illumination of Christmas tree, the latter made by Mr. Parker, proved a great success … After singing a hymn and engaging in prayer the distribution of prizes took place. These were, first for the most regular attendants at school, second, for the most cleanly. One girl who had not missed a day at school, received the first prize, another girl had only missed one, while another had only been absent twice. Fourteen prizes were given to those who had shown some love, at least for soaps and water, and had made their appearance at school with clean faces and hands … After distribution of prizes … each member of our little flock was presented with some article.[29]

Peck thought the giving of prizes and the illumination of the Christmas tree were the highlights of the day. The Inuit arrived with gifts, some of them intended for the English ladies who had sent gifts to them. Reciprocally, at the end of the feast, the missionaries gave gifts to all of the members of their flock. They offered the Inuit food and drink and used the opportunity to preach the gospel. This became a tradition in Uumanarjuaq. Each Christmas the missionaries provided Western-style food and drink and awarded prizes for certain accomplishments. In 1895 there were prizes for school attendance, and two years later for memorizing the Scriptures. Thus, the aspect of competition, so essential to Inuit festivities, was preserved in Christmas celebrations. In contrast, the Christmas tree did not gain an important place in Inuit Christmas celebrations for a long time.

The Christmas celebrations organized by the missionaries continued to follow the same pattern after Peck left the mission in 1905.[30] The missionaries offered the Inuit special food and used the opportunity to teach them some Christian values. They also gave them a small gift with a reminder of God's great gift to humankind.[31] Among the Oblates in charge of the Roman Catholic mission, similar traditions can be found. Father Ducharme notes that in Igluligaarjuk, where the first Catholic mission in Hudson Bay opened in 1912, Christmas was the most joyful time of the year. People would come from afar. Besides providing a big meal, the missionaries and the Grey Nuns used to organize a fishing party and give out all kinds of small gifts – clothes, biscuits, candies, tobacco, pipes, matches, dolls, and the like.[32]

Christmas celebrations were also held on board visiting ships. An early twentieth-century description by Captain J.E. Bernier documents how Inuit were invited on his ship at North Baffin Island and participated in the European celebrations of Christmas in 1906:

> On December 24 the ship was washed and cleaned and the officers had their state rooms decorated for Christmas with flags and family photos.
>
> Our native Kanaka was instructed to tell the other natives that they were invited to spend Christmas day on board with their families. I gave orders to the steward to have dinner ready for about one hundred natives. Preparations were made to receive them; I also sent an invitation to Captain Mutch to celebrate Christmas with us.
>
> *December 25th, Christmas Day* – There was Sunday service in the forenoon; it was well attended by the members of the expedition and some of the natives who had already arrived for the dinner. At 1 P.M. all the natives had arrived on board with their families; about one hundred and twenty persons, they sat down to a good Canadian dinner. After dinner I addressed them a few words; telling them again that they were Canadians and would be treated as such as long as they would do what was right. At 7 P.M. tea and coffee were served to all the invited, and some candy was given to the children. A deputation of natives and some members of the crew came and asked my permission to dance on board. Knowing the pleasure it would afford them, I could not refuse the request and was glad to accede to their wishes and see that they would amuse themselves. The natives behaved very well and there were no disturbances of any sort, but perfect good order reigned throughout. During the evening there were different tricks and acts done by the members of the expedition and natives. There were wrestling matches between Canadians and other matches of the same style between Eskimos; the men also performed acrobatic feats, juggling and other acts. Music selections from the pianola and the gramophone were given during the evening. The Eskimos danced to the music of

> the accordion. It was well on to twelve o'clock before the dance ceased and the natives left for their homes. Everybody seemed to have enjoyed himself immensely and was glad of the celebration.

The Christmas celebration is described as a Canadian banquet to which Inuit were invited. Small gifts were often added.[33] On Bernier's ship, the element of dancing was added at the request of Inuit and members of the crew. The first missionaries used a gramophone to provide music, but there are no references to dancing in descriptions of the celebrations they organized. Competitive games joined in by Canadians and Inuit alike were a striking feature of all such celebrations. An abundance of food was a recurrent feature of the Christmas celebrations organized by Qallunaat for Inuit, as Bernier describes:

> Christmas day was fine and calm and all preparations for celebrating the day were completed. Forty natives from the Eskimo village, including those from Fury and Hecla strait and Agoo, went on board the ship and amused and interested themselves, in various ways. Some of them attended the religious service which formed part of the day's engagements. Although silent and well-behaved, they seemed to be endeavouring to comprehend the meaning of the service and its purpose. Others of the natives roamed about the ship asking questions of those of the crew who did not attend the religious service, about each article that they did not know the use of nor value. A temporary table of some planed boards was arranged at which the natives sat down and food in sufficient quantity and of a kind to satisfy their simple tastes was served. They ate their Christmas dinner with relish and seemed, in their love for those things that appeal to hungry people accustomed to live on raw fish or flesh, to regret that "Christmas comes but once a year."[34]

CHRISTMAS CELEBRATIONS IN THE 1920S AND 1930S

In 1920s and 1930s, after many Inuit had already been converted on South Baffin Island, Christianity was also adopted by most of the Inuit in the North Baffin area. Missionaries as well as traders contributed significantly to the development of the Christmas celebrations.[35]

Richard Finnie remembers the Christmas celebrations at the Kugluktuk trading post in 1930.[36] The missions and the store took care to have sufficient supplies for the event. By the 24th of December almost 140 Inuit had assembled at the settlement. After building their igloos, Inuit "started according to a custom they had developed to go the rounds of all the white men's dwellings, staying at each one long enough to enjoy some refreshments, mainly hardtack and tea." On Christmas Day the trading post apprentice paraded outside as Santa Claus. The impersonation lasted for only a few minutes. His beard fell off and he was recognized. Then he handed out gifts to the children. Later the white men danced with the Eskimo women to the latest Broadway tune. At five o'clock a dinner was served at the wireless station. After dinner the Qallunaat heard that there was going to be a native dance. They joined the Inuit in an enormous igloo where a drum dance was performed for several hours.

The Christmas celebration was an occasion for intense interaction between Inuit and Qallunaat. Qallunaat hosted Inuit at their houses when the Inuit came to receive treats, but the white people were also guests of the Inuit in the great igloo, where they witnessed dancing and feasting. The great igloo clearly had the function of the traditional feast house (*qaggiq*), where the great winter feasts used to be celebrated. Whereas Qallunaat and Inuit danced together at a party given by the doctor, Qallunaat did not participate in the drum dances and the songs of the Inuit. The impersonation of Santa Claus was unusual. Only much later did Santa Claus become an important figure in Christmas celebrations.

In 1935 in Mittimatalik, Pond Inlet, a similar pattern emerges from an account of Christmas provided by Alex Stevenson (1965). Several days before Christmas, baking supplies from the Hudson's Bay Company store were turned over to several Inuit women so that they could make preparations for Christmas dinner. On Christmas Day, the Inuit took over a warehouse for the feast. They served a special dinner to their guests (two policemen and the missionaries). After dinner, races and games were held, notably dog team races. In the evening, a dance was organized, accompanied by accordion and fiddle: "Although the old Eskimo drum dances were still held in some Arctic settlements, the people of Pond Inlet preferred reels and jigs from the early Scottish whalers."[37]

Graham Rowley (2007, 179–80) describes a celebration of Christmas in Lyon Inlet in 1938 at which no priest was present:

> Next day was Christmas Eve and it brought much larger, longer, and more crowded dances. At one time there were eight couples on the floor and six were common. It was the first Inuit square dance I had attended when somebody was calling. This was usually Cleveland's Johny and he used a mixture of Inuit and English. "Pissukpose" for Promenade, followed by "Swing you a partner." After two or three hours there was an interval, not because the dancers were tired but because the ice floor was beginning to melt. It soon refroze and the dancers returned for two more hours …
>
> On Christmas Day the custom was to shake hands with everybody one met and say, "Christmassy." Qaunnaq had a long service in his igloo which I did not attend because nobody told me about it. While it was in progress I made little packages for each igloo, containing a plug of tobacco, a number of cigarettes, a bar or two of chocolate, chewing-gum, and some candies, with a rather larger package for Qaunnaq's igloo.
>
> The Church service was followed by a feast for everybody. We started with a traditional dish which I had read about but never seen before, con-

> sisting of caribou fat already chewed up with berries by the women. It was followed by boiled rice and bannock. Then came tea and ship's biscuits, which were my contributions. After a short pause, frozen caribou appeared in large quantities, and then frozen char and more tea. We finished with a salad – the contents, mainly lichen of the stomachs of several caribous. They may have been other dishes, but these were the only ones I ate. During the meal Evalak passed me a piece of paper on which he had written INOOET 45, the number of people present, which I am sure was everybody in the camp ...
>
> We returned to our igloo after the feast, and the exchange of presents began. So far as I could make out everybody in the camp gave everybody else a present. The children from each family would arrive carrying something for everyone in the igloo, and they would be given something to take back to distribute to their families. I know that I received four dog harnesses, some dog traces, the promise of a dog, some lines made of bearded sealskin, a pair of caribou-skin moccasins, a pair of kamiks, a cigarette holder, a whip, sealskin for replacing worn-out boot bottoms, a lamp trimmer, and many objects collected from old houses. I had great difficulty in finding suitable and adequate presents in return. Tea and plug tobacco were a great help. The Inuit often had the same problem and many presents changed hands several times during the day. I saw Kutjek, faced with having to find too presents at short notice, divide a packet of cards he had been given into two and gave half to each.

According to Rowley, the days between Christmas and New Year's were devoted to feasting, dancing, visiting, and many meals. His description gives emphasis to the significance of Christmas and gift giving, and shows that he was deeply involved in the celebration, even though he missed the service held in Qaunnaq's igloo.

Qallunaat testimonies indicate that white people played a central role in the organizing of Christmas celebrations in the North. Qallunaat provided Inuit with the means to celebrate Christmas. Their influence manifested itself in many ways, in the food, clothing, dances, and so on. Traditional Inuit dances were giving way to the new forms of dancing introduced by the whites. The main emphasis in Qallunaat accounts is on food, games, music, and dancing. Rowley's particular emphasis on gifts can also be found in Inuit testimonies referring to the same period; these testimonies allow a better understanding of Inuit perceptions of Christmas celebrations.

TESTIMONIES OF INUIT ELDERS

Inuit elders have vivid memories of the Christmas celebrations of their youth. While these celebrations cannot be dated precisely, most of the elders' recollections seem to refer to the 1930s and early 1940s. In this section, we will begin by presenting a few of their narratives, taking note of regional variations as well as the differences and similarities between Catholics and Anglicans. An account provided by a white observer will illustrate the merging of Inuit and Christian traditions in the celebration of Christmas that took place in Kugaaruk (Pelly Bay).

Emile Imaruittuq (1995 interview) remembered his first Christmas in the Iglulik area. Games were organized by the Oblate missionary.

> While the light was briefly on the priest would have a line tied to the string. He used to shoot at the string and that was the game. There would be three chances to cut this little string with a bullet. Whoever shoots the string would have the prize. It was just a 22 gun that would be used. In the olden days when I started remembering, we used to exchange gifts, we actually would give to ourselves. Even to the standard it was not much, in those days it was very precious. That is how we used to give each other. As the years went by, that giving and receiving attitude start disappearing. The whole feeling of Christmas has more and more faded away. To our grandchildren we still give when we are able, when we have the money. In the olden days we also used to have a feast. It was the Roman Catholics that introduced to us the celebration of Christmas. First, we would go to the service and in the same place we would have a feast: pilot biscuits, beans, etc. We used to make beans and that was part of the feast. It used to be so delicious! In the olden days they started celebrating Christmas as well within the homes, eating country food … My grandmother would take out flour and make pancakes during Christmas. That was very special. Many elders and adults used to save special food, special diet, for Christmas and that's how it was in the Iglulik area.

In Imaruittuq's account, the gifts, the food, and the games organized by the priest all had a central place. The game he referred to was often played at Christmas time. Country food, as well as Western-style food, was frequently served, according to the elders. The act of giving was emphasized. The gifts might have been small, as it was the act of giving that counted.

An account by Michel Kupaaq from Iglulik (1995 interview) shows that the gift could even be completely symbolic:

> People would gather for the feast. In the Christmas time (Quviasukvik), people would go to church for the midnight mass. But after twelve hours, we would go back to the church. Nowadays, Christmas is longer. We play games all the week long, until the New Year's day comes. At that time, when Christmas was coming closer, I would get happy because it would be Christmas. But nowadays, we have to make gifts, wrap them and then

(above) Ollie and Lizzie Itinnuaq at their marriage in 1949. Courtesy of Archives Deschâtelets; (left) Ollie Itinnuaq from Kangiq&iniq. Ollie is a son of Peter Freuchen, a member of the Fifth Thule expedition. He was raised by his adoptive father, the *angakkuq* Anaqqaq. He played an important part in the preservation of Inuit traditions as head of the Inuit Cultural Institute. He has an extensive knowledge of the land, shamanic traditions, and local history. He hosted the elders workshops on shamanism in Kangiq&iniq in 2000 and 2002. Photograph by F. Laugrand.

The late Victor Tungilik from Naujaat and Rachel Ujarasuk from Iglulik discussing shamanism and Christianity at Nunavik Arctic College, Iqaluit. Tungilik practised actively as an *angakkuq* for some years. Ujarasuk, originally from the Kangiqtugaapik area, shared many recollections on the transition to Christianity. Photograph by F. Laugrand.

> put a name on them. At that time, we didn't have to do that. We would just give a present to someone. There were exchange gifts with the people who wanted to do that. Then, we would shake hands. Then we would say: "This gift for you is part of an angel."
>
> I remember that once somebody gave me a long big knife as an exchange gift. I was happy to get a knife that long. I kept the knife during the week and after Christmas, as we would go out hunting to get food to survive, I was happy because I thought I could use the knife for carving and making an igloo. But just after Christmas, my parents told me to give the knife back to the person who gave it to me. I did not want to do it, but as I had to, I did it.

Thus the gifts that were exchanged might be returned after some time. Theresi Ijjangiaq from Iglulik (1995 interview) contrasted the presents of today with the exchange gifts of the past: "After the midnight mass, when the service was over, we used to exchange gifts but not like right now, in the old way instead. There were no presents but just exchange gifts: needles and so on."

In the descriptions of Imaruittuq, Kupaaq, and Ijjangiaq, all Catholics from Iglulik, priests had an important role in the celebration of Christmas. In Angli-

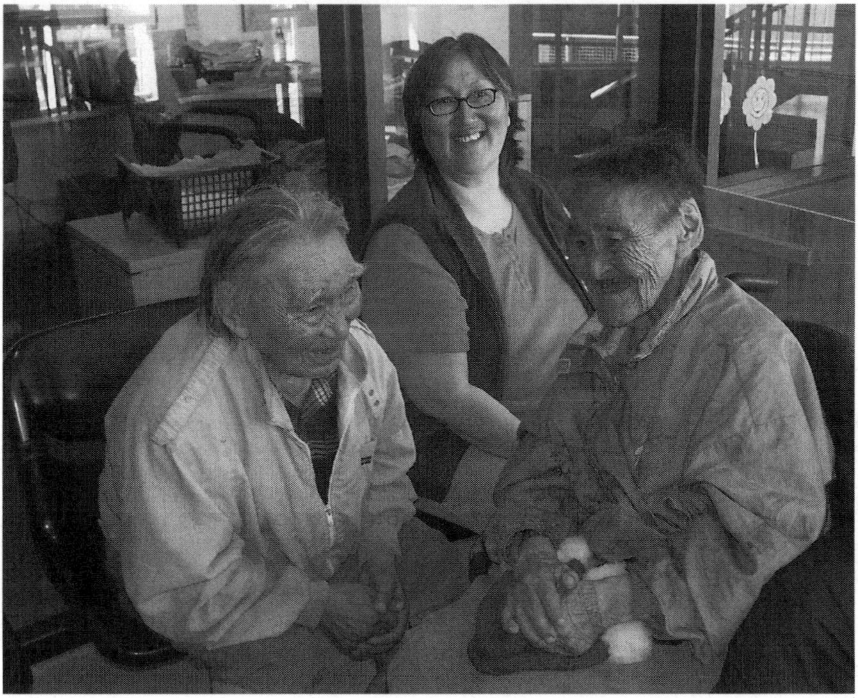

(left) Niviuvaq from Talurjuaq, (right) Kupak from Naujaat, and (in the middle) Amaya from Kugaaruk at the workshop in Kugaaruk in 2004. Photograph by C. Remie.

can testimonies as well, ministers were often seen as having had a central place. Tategat Akpaliapik (1995 interview) remembered how Christmas was celebrated in Mittimatalik: "During Christmas time (Quviasukvik), Mikiniqsaq (Reverend J.H. Turner) would visit us in the camps. When we were sleeping, Mikiniqsaq would wake us up and we would receive presents under our pillows. Then we would have a big feast in there." Saullu Nakasuk (1995 interview), an elder from Panniqtuuq, did not mention the role of the Anglican minister but emphasized that even if gifts were small, they were crucial to the festivities: "We really enjoyed the gifts even if they were not big. Sometimes, we could even get a dog for Christmas. We were thankful to have Christmas." The gift of a dog is interesting, especially since dogs, through their names, were often very closely associated with their owner.[38] It was perceived here as a small gift.

The elders also remembered many Christmas celebrations where there had been no missionaries present. Elise Qulaut (1995 interview), a Catholic from Iglulik, recalled: "When I was a little girl, on Christmas, we used to gather in a big igloo. Then I remember that there was a feast (*nirivijjuaq*) and dancing in Avvajja.

Before the feast started, people would go out and shoot in the air. I was scared and I thought people were shooting the moon. It was Christmas or Happy New Year, I don't know … Back then, Christmas was during only one day, today, it's all the week. I remember that people, mostly the closest camps, they used to gather in this *qarmaq* [house covered with skins] and say a prayer or the midnight mass, even when the missionary was not around." Like Kupaaq, she emphasized that Christmas celebrations had been much shorter in the past.

Rachel Uyarasuk, an Anglican elder from Iglulik, grew up in the Kangiqtugaapik area. She remembered how the feast was celebrated in outpost camps when *ulluriaqjuaq* (Venus) could be seen and there were no ministers around.[39]

> I can tell a bit about the first Christmas I remember. We all had *igluit* and we were going to be celebrating Christmas. As children we were told that we were going to be celebrating Christmas. We would be told how many days it would be until Christmas. We started counting the days. We were told that we would be using our personal effects to celebrate, but it was probably because we wanted to get new things so by word of mouth. We knew we would be celebrating [and] we started anticipating the day. In the morning I was woken up and told today is going to be Christmas so I should wake up. I put on my caribou clothing but we tried to put on our best for that day. Those that had additional clothing did this. I was woken up by my father. We went out for a bit and came back and we started shaking hands with each other because we heard that is what we had to do. Just before we went out people started rushing around and my father took a rifle and went out and shot the rifle. We heard the rifle shot and we all rushed out. I had clothing with a hat that was separate. We were told that after we went out we were going to say "hurray." I took my hat that was not attached to my clothing and my mother gave it to me and said that was what I was going to use … to say "hurray." Our neighbors also shot their rifles. This was going on while it was still dark. We could hear rifle shots and people would go hurray. I was holding on to my hat and then we'd go hurray. We were celebrating and were very happy. Later on that day we would go and pray and sing hymns. We went to someone else's *iglu* and it was cold. Even though it was light it was still winter. We all went in. The women took off their *kamiik* and went up on the bed platform. The bed platform was totally full, there was hardly any place to sit. There were people sitting all over the place because we were going to pray. And we prayed and there was a hymn sung. It turns out that the hymn that was sung was not a Christmas hymn, but that's the song we sang. We sang that hymn. People sat down on the floor because the *iglu* was so full. After this hymn was sung, somebody would read a prayer. Then another hymn would be sung. This is the first Christmas I remember. I remember the first

> hymn but I don't remember the other hymns that were sung. After we had sung hymns and prayed and were about to go out we all shook hands with each other. Those women who had sat on the bed platform put on their *kamiik* and we all went home. We also knew that we would be feasting. We would have a feast where we prayed, so all the meat we would be feasting on was brought there. We feasted on meat. We did not have tea. [There] was *tunuq* [caribou fat] that was prepared as *aluq*, we ate *quaq* [frozen fish] and *uujuq* [cooked meat], and we ate meat that we did not normally eat such as polar bear and caribou. It probably was kept for this occasion. It was a joyous time because we were celebrating. That is the first Christmas I can remember. After we had feasted we then started exchanging gifts. These were our own personal things that we exchanged. We did it when the day was over. It was already dark. We would go over to another place to exchange gifts. The gifts [that] were exchanged were not that big. It could be a caribou skin or a sealskin or any other personal effects. It was still a very happy occasion.[40]

The handshakes and rifle shots constituted the start of the feast. The practice of shaking hands was a custom adopted from Qallunaat; it played an important role in the adoption of Christianity, as it expressed acknowledgment of a new relationship.[41] People came together in an igloo, sang hymns, and prayed. They feasted on country food and exchanged gifts. Uyarasuk, too, emphasized that the gifts were small and consisted of personal belongings.

Hannah Ujaraq from Iglulik (1995 interview) recalled how the feast was celebrated at Qikiqtaarjuak before priests had come to the area: "[W]hen Christmas was coming, we used to build a big igloo and we had dances in there for Christmas (*Quviaksukvik*). At that time, we used to have a feast in this big igloo, eating caribou meat, *maktaaq* (whale blubber) … only country food because there was no white man food at that time. After having a feast, we used to have dances and say prayers. Even though there was no ministers the whole camp used to say prayers. Aloloo, Anguilainuk's son, used to preach in our camp." The building of a big igloo is a recurrent feature of Christmas celebrations. Ujaraq's description conforms in many respects to Uyarasuk's account of celebrations on North Baffin Island. In Qikiqtaarjuak, Qallunaat food was not yet available.

Victor Tungilik remembered how Christmas used to be celebrated in Naujaat among the Catholics:

> During Christmas, the Catholic mission would get items from the Hudson's Bay Company. Also, the Bay Manager would climb up on top of the house and we would have a candy scramble. There would be other items in this *parlaniq*, scramble. It was very enjoyable. While we were at the Catholic mission, we would *nugluktaq* and try to get a stick into a hole.

> We would wrestle two at a time, and people would get prizes. The prizes were things like tea and tobacco. I was scared when somebody wanted to wrestle with me. It turned out that the person who wanted to wrestle with me wanted to do so because he wanted me to win. When I lifted that person I could not even feel his weight. It turned out that he wanted me to win a prize. I couldn't feel his weight at all when I threw him on the ground. So at first, here I was scared of him and it turned out he just wanted me to win tea or tobacco. I knew he wasn't trying hard to win at all. I was really happy to win.[42]

The importance of the game is quite clear in Tungilik's account. Christmas provided an opportunity for Tungilik's opponent to give Tungilik a gift.

Nugluktaq was another popular game. It involved putting a stick into a hole and always had sexual connotations. The Oblate priest Philippe (1948, 6–7), for instance, notes that before Christianity, the winner of that game would be allowed to choose one of the women as a sexual partner. Interestingly, the *nugluktaq* became part of Inuit Christmas celebrations and remained so even within the Catholic missions.[43]

Leah d'Argencourt (1976, 28–40) relates her childhood memories of Christmas celebrations in Mittimatalik: "The most important part was to rejoice and celebrate the birthday of our Lord Jesus Christ." In the weeks preceding Christmas, community activities focused increasingly on trapping arctic foxes and preparing the furs. These were to be sold at the Hudson's Bay store so that presents could be bought. The men bought presents such as special Qallunaat food and machine-made clothing. There were not yet Christmas trees, according to Leah. Children had to go to bed before their parents "so we would be bright and early getting up." Leah, too, emphasizes the importance of gifts. Prunes and candies were found in duffel socks. She makes special note of the ritual of handshaking between relatives but does not describe the games extensively. The Christmas dinner consisted of a mix of Western and Qallunaat food – "cooked meat, and home-made beans and rice with raisins and powdered milk."

The old style of celebrating was also remembered by Atsainak Akeeshoo from Iqaluit (1974, 8), who recalled a Christmas at a hunting camp, probably in the 1950s.

> On Christmas morning, we would all get up very early in the morning, go to our neighbors' houses and shake everybody's hands.
>
> Then we would wait all day for it to get dark so we could start exchanging gifts with friend and adults. We would give away needles, pieces of rope, perhaps five bullets for father, marbles, thread and even our clothing that we've been wearing for years Each of these things became treasures, like a multi-million dollar diamond would be to rich people.

Dog teams would come to our camps bearing gifts from the other camps and we would return their visit in the same way. There was no feasting but everyone got into gift-giving as if it was going to be the last Christmas ever.

Our mothers would receive bags, donated by churches, each containing thread, thimble, needles, face cloth or towel, and a bar of face soap. It was so exciting to see all those nice-smelling things come out of the bags one by one! Each piece was looked at and felt by all the members of the household before we went on with the rest.

If we were lucky, we would each get two pieces of candy or gum and maybe even a hard biscuit. Sometimes the RCMP used to come, by dog team, just before Christmas and they would leave a whole box of biscuits and that would be saved till Christmas night.

Christmas was not at all commercialized then. We celebrated the birth of Christ and followed what the three wise men did on Christmas night. Christmas was not for Santa Claus and toys and free candies. There was a form of a Santa Claus, a gift-giver, but we weren't taught to believe in him. I wonder how many children know about our old Christmas days and how much fun they can be without all kinds of treats in schools, big community parties for children with cartoons and free gifts from the government?

Today, the children rely on Santa Claus to make their Christmas a happy time with tinsel and gifts. We still have a gift-giving or exchanging but it doesn't get into a fever-pitch like it used to.

Why not try to bring the old spirit of Christmas back this year so we can overflow with happiness ... Inuit and Whites exchanging gifts and going into each other's homes to wish each other a Merry Christmas!

Akeeshoo contrasted the old celebrations with modern festivities. There was a Santa Claus, but no one had to believe in him. Schools and government did not yet play an important part in the celebrations. Gifts were small, and Christmas had not yet become commercialized.

The following account of Christmas illustrates the merging of a new tradition with many of the old practices. In Kugaaruk the missionaries took an active part in organizing the Christmas celebrations. From the moment he arrived in Kugaaruk, Father Van de Velde played a central role in the organization of games and competitions.[44] The missionaries also took care of the prizes that would be awarded. The festivities were held in a big igloo, with food and competitive games as the main ingredients. Frank Gonda (1963, 28–9) describes how Christmas was celebrated in Kugaaruk in the early 1960s.

The igloo about twenty-five feet in diameter and fifteen feet in height was built in a few days.

At eight o'clock Christmas Eve, one hundred and five gaily attired men, women and children assembled in the igloo for what was to be three nights and two days of games, contests, feasting and prayers.

Christmas Eve was highlighted by ancient Eskimo games and target shooting. Firing from about twenty-five feet with a .22 at strings from which dangled various prizes was quite a feat of marksmanship. A few of the contestants miraculously hit a string and thus claimed a prize. A special moment of Christmas Eve was the opening of presents. These gifts were sent to Father Van de Velde from his sister in Belgium. There was a gift for everyone. Such practical objects as cloth, wool, knives and even chess sets were the most frequent items. The Eskimos here are avid chess players.

Midnight Mass, said by Father Van de Velde, was solemn and beautiful, and somehow, having this service in an igloo seemed to bring the message that is Christmas so vividly to everyone.

After Mass, we enjoyed a lunch prepared by the mission and consisting of tea, porridge and biscuits. Candies were distributed to the children.

Christmas day was extremely cold. The thermometer read 48 degrees below zero when everyone came to the igloo at eleven-thirty for Mass. After Mass everyone went home for awhile to wait for the big Christmas dinner at three o'clock. The stew had been cooking slowly all night, and needed last-minute attention before serving up.

At three o'clock everyone converged on the igloo again bringing mugs with them. Dinner was ready. The first course was sixty frozen arctic char, previously sliced. After this was put away, the two huge kettles of caribou stew were brought in. Mugs were dipped in and soon this too disappeared. Then the steaming kettles of tea were brought in. Each family brought its kettle; there were about twenty-five gallon kettles full of lovely, strong, hot tea. Needless to say each was drained.

After dinners there were more games, contests prizes and candy. The archery contest was performed with an ancient bow of musk-ox horn. Each contestant shot four arrows from about fifteen feet. The target was an iron ring about two inches in diameter stuck in the igloo wall.

Practically everyone had a turn, beginning with the oldest hunter. The last to try were the small children, and even the women took part in it.

In some ways the day after Christmas was the most exciting. We moved out of the igloo for some of the events. The feature event was the dog team race. Twenty-seven drivers and one hundred and sixty-two howling dogs took part; each driver was allowed six dogs. It was very cold and the course was long; many of the Eskimos had donned their caribou parkas.

The start was furious. Many teams got tangled, momentarily, but everyone was straightened away, and soon disappeared into the gloom across Pelly Bay. The winner Otto Apsauqtaun, returned over the course in about forty minutes, closely followed by Augustin Annartok. The rest soon returned to claim their prizes. Each was eligible. Twenty-seven prizes were placed on a table, and each in turn, according to his position in the race, stepped up to claim a prize. The prizes were good, but, of course, the big prize was winning the race, for this would be remembered, and would be the topic of conversation until the next race.

Other outdoor events included the foot races, and one marvelled at the endurance of the Eskimos in being able to run in such extreme cold. One was for the young men, who ran to the top of a hill about one and one half miles from the Mission and back. The hill is about one thousand feet high and there is a huge cross on top. Every contestant was awarded a prize – with winners getting first choice.

At five o'clock it was back in the *kaget* for the drum dance. One seemed to be transported back to ancient times listening to the aged ladies chanting their weird songs and hearing the boom of the drum and watching the dancer gyrate to the rhythm of the beat. The dancer would emit an occasional "*Iy-hi*" which added more strangeness to the atmosphere. In each of the alcoves there were five or six chanters, and these ladies would sing the song of the dancer, whatever it was. It might be the Song-of-my-Father or the Song-of-my-Grandfather. The drumming and chanting stopped at 10 p.m., and soon everyone went home. That is how we celebrate Christmas in Pelly Bay.

The word *qaggiq* refers to a feast or celebration as well as to the big igloo where the feast and the games were held. In his book *Christmas in the Big Igloo* (1983), Kenn Harper, an independent researcher from Iqaluit, rightly identifies the *qaggiq* as one of the striking features of Inuit Christmas celebrations.

THE TRANSFORMATIONS OF THE INUIT WINTER FEASTS

Christmas was celebrated on the ships commanded by Parry and Lyon in the early 1820s, but Inuit were not allowed on the ships on Sundays or holidays. Neither did the Qallunaat participate in Inuit winter feasts. But there was frequent contact between Qallunaat and Inuit, and Inuit were able to observe what went on during the Christmas celebrations. Thus, European Christmas celebrations may have influenced the winter feasts that Hall, Boas, and Bilby described. The rifle shooting, recorded in the diary of Boas, later became a striking feature of the Inuit Christmas celebrations. The ritual drinking of water, described by both Hall and Boas, disappeared. The practices of donning of one's best clothes,[45] gift giving, and games continued in the Christmas celebrations. When the missionaries arrived, Christmas celebrations gradually replaced the Inuit winter feasts. In most places the traditional winter feasts vanished quickly. In 1899 Bilby noted that shamanism and the winter feasts were already disappearing from South Baffin Island,[46] although no Inuit had yet been converted. That year no winter feast was held. In 1901 he noted that the feast was still celebrated, but only by old people. The *tivajuut* probably disappeared from North Baffin Island when the Inuit adopted their own version of Christianity, long before the missionaries arrived. In the winter of 1921–22, Rasmussen himself did not witness a *tivajuut*, but relied on Ava and Ivaluardjuk for information about the feast. In recent years, only a few elders – Atuat (born in 1894), Ujaraq (born in 1901), and Iqallijuq (born in 1905), for example – were able to give accounts of the *tivajuut* based on personal experience.

On South Baffin Island the missionaries provided Western-style food and drink to the Inuit. The disappearance of wife exchange and the increasing importance of food were the most striking changes in the transition from winter feasts to Christmas celebrations. Anglican as well as Catholic missionaries had no objections to games, and as noted above, they played leading roles in organizing them and awarding prizes.

The missionaries' tradition of hosting the Inuit was adopted by other Qallunaat, such as Hudson's Bay Company traders and captains of visiting ships. Not infrequently, the Inuit would not be served the same Christmas meal that their Qallunaat hosts would enjoy. According to Fleming's account of Christmas 1913, the Anglican missionaries had their own Western-style Christmas dinner before serving food "likely to be enjoyed by our guests. Two large steaming puddings, something like our Christmas pudding but not nearly so rich were served with molasses for sauce."[47]

The missionaries gave small gifts to the Inuit, in this respect continuing an old tradition. As early as 1883 Boas and Mutch had presented gifts at the winter feast. The role of the Qallunaat in organizing the feast remained central. They provided small presents, candy scrambles, dance, and music. Christmas became a feast that brought Inuit and Qallunaat together, but both also kept to their own traditions. Apart from the communal celebrations, Qallunaat might still dine on their own together, and Inuit had their own festive rituals, notably handshaking and exchanging gifts with relatives. The elders emphasized that the gifts could be small, and as Kupaaq remembered, they might even be returned after Christmas. It was the act of giving, not the gift itself, that was most valued. The idea of sharing gifts as well as food was thus central to the new rituals.

It is striking how religious boundaries could be crossed at Christmas. In a few of the accounts, the Inuit practice of visiting people was mentioned as an important aspect of the events leading up to Christmas. Father Schneider (1983, 14) recollects that in Tavani in the 1940s, when there was still intense rivalry between Catholics and Anglicans, his Catholic mission was completely full of Anglicans at Christmas.[48]

Games were central to the traditional winter feasts. They gave structure to the festivities and allowed tensions to dissolve. It is significant that the games have not decreased in importance at all since the disappearance of the old Inuit winter feasts. In fact, the extension today of the celebrations over many days is to a large extent due to the games in which Inuit participate with great enthusiasm.[49] Many of the games that were played during the old winter feasts – tug-of-war, for example – have been preserved in new forms, and new games have been added and invented. In this respect, the ideology of the community has not changed at all. In Inuit society, games have always served to dissolve the tensions and transform potentially dangerous and hostile relationships into friendly competitive ones (recall Tungilik's friendly wrestling match).

Today, elders complain that Christmas has become too commercial. Leah d'Argencourt looks back nostalgically to a time when shops and government had not yet meddled with the feast. However, missionaries, whalers, ship captains, and Hudson's Bay Company agents always played important parts in the preparations for the Christmas celebrations. The current commercialization and increasing scale of the feast appears to be a continuation of an old tradition.

The various names for the feast elucidate its important features. "*Nirivigjuaq*" (place/time of the great meal) gives emphasis to the importance of food in the feast. Many missionaries objected to this term, thinking that it did not express the essence of Christmas. They preferred "*pivijuaq*" (the big event) or, like Father Schneider (1983, 14), "*Jisusi anivvia*" (the birth of Jesus). The terms "*nuqqavik*" (the time when we stop) and "*qitinguq*" (in the middle) reflect the contrast between the time of the feast and ordinary time. The word "Quviasukvik" (the place/time of joy) emphasizes that Christmas is above all a time of rejoicing. This also seems to have been the connotation with "winter feast" and *tivajuut,* with their great emphasis on fun and laughter. In the shamanic tradition, the notions of joy and light were closely related. Laughter expressed the acceptance of a social relationship, and refraining from laughter, which was often important in meetings with non-human beings, implied a denial of such a relationship. As the Inuit winter feasts and the Christmas celebrations connected people to one another through their relationship to the land and its non-human beings, the sharing of joy and laughter remained an indispensable feature of these feasts.

The Inuit winter feasts transformed hostile relationships between the living and the dead into new alliances, allowing people to identify with their deceased ancestors and namesakes. The feasts renewed the community's relationships with the land, the game, and its owners.[50] While the traditional winter feast initially emphasized the danger of *tupilait* attacking the community, the Christmas celebration emphasized the coming of light, connecting the birth of the Saviour with the return of the light. The celebration of the New Year at the winter solstice is therefore highly significant. The transition to Christianity also implied a shift from sexual symbolism to alimentary symbolism. Some of the basic patterns in the Christian rituals and traditions may have seemed familiar to Inuit, and this may have facilitated their adoption by the Inuit. Thus, Quviasukvik connects the past and the present, articulating the central values of Inuit and Christian traditions.

Part Two | Animals, Owners, and Non-human Beings

4

Hunters and Prey

INTRODUCTION

Inuit identify themselves as hunters, and they perceive hunting as the foundation of their existence. Inuit and animals have always been connected in a cosmic cycle maintained by hunting and the rules that pertain to it. In this chapter, we will examine the complex relations between animals and human beings in the past and in the present. We will begin by discussing the origin of human beings and animals and will then examine the sexual discourse with respect to animals and hunting. We will explore the notion of the *tarniq* (the miniature image of a being), a feature of animals as well as of human beings and which the missionaries identified with the soul. We will describe the fate of the *tarniq* after death and the danger that it may be transformed into an evil spirit or *tupilaq*. Respect for *tarniit* motivated the complex system of rules that organized relationships between animals and human beings.

We will show that although the complex system of ritual rules that once existed has largely disappeared, respect for prey is still considered a core value in modern Inuit society. Finally, we will discuss the *atiq* (name, namesake), a feature that distinguishes human beings from animals and connects them to their ancestors.

HUMAN ORIGINS

Rasmussen recorded various myths about the origin of human beings when he travelled among the Iglulingmiut and Nattilingmiut.[1] The first human beings came from the earth. The old *angakkuq* Unaliq gave this story to Rasmussen (1929, 252):

> It is said that once upon a time the world fell to pieces, and every living thing was destroyed. There came mighty downpours of rain from the heavens, and the earth itself was destroyed. Afterwards, two men appeared

on earth. They came from hummocks of earth; they were born so. They were already fully grown when they emerged from the ground. They lived together as man and wife, and soon one of them was with child. Then the one who had been husband sang a magic song:

A human being here
A penis here.
May its opening be wide
And roomy.
Opening, opening, opening!

When these words were sung, the man's penis split with a loud noise and he became a woman, and gave birth to a child. From these three mankind grew to be many.[2]

In Iglulik the first pair were named Aakulugjuusi and Uumaarniittuq; it was the latter who became a woman.[3] According to Alexina Kublu from Iglulik, "Aakulugjuusi and Uumaarniittuq did not die, they just returned to the soil from which they had come into being."[4] Today, the primeval pair are identified as Adam and Eve.[5]

The Nattilik woman Nalungiaq told Rasmussen (1931, 208) that at first the world was dark: "In the very first times there was no light on earth. Everything was in darkness, the lands could not be seen, the animals could not be seen. And still, both people and animals lived on the earth, but there was no difference between them. They lived promiscuously. A person could become an animal, and an animal could become a human being. There were wolves, bears, and foxes, but as soon as they turned into humans they were all the same. They may have had different habits, but all spoke the same tongue, lived in the same kind of house, and spoke and hunted in the same way." Thus, in the darkness there was no difference between human beings and animals in terms of human appearance, language, and habits. Their relationship was marked by promiscuity. The animals that Nalungiaq specified were all land animals and predators.

Light was created by magic words. The distinction between day and night was made when the fox called for darkness and the hare for daylight. The hare gained the upper hand, and since that time, day and night alternate.[6] In these mythic times, men as well as animals used magic words to shape the world.[7]

According to an Iglulik myth, the first human beings lived on an island. They became so numerous that the island could not support them and began to slope down to the sea. Then an old woman shouted, "Let [it] be so ordered that human beings can die, for there will no longer be room for us on earth."[8] Thus death came to mankind as a necessity for survival.

The earliest human beings lived under difficult conditions. Everything was scarce. The Nattilingmiutaq Inugpasugjuk told Rasmussen that in the earliest days people had very little to eat. Earth was their principal food. It was very difficult to kill caribou, and people had to make a single animal last for the whole winter. In summer, they had to satisfy themselves with one little unborn seal. Men did not yet have warm caribou skins, and they had to use the skins of birds and foxes.[9] Even children were scarce.

The Aivilingmiutaq Ivaluardjuk, a storyteller and an important informant of Rasmussen's, told this story:

> In the earliest ages, women were often unable to have children. And when people were out on a journey and settled at a place, one might see them going round about the camping ground, bending down and searching about in the earth. It is said that in that way they sought for children from the earth; the children of earth. And with the children they found on the ground it was in this wise: a long search was needed to find boys, but one had not to go far to find girls. Not all however, were equally lucky. Some found only girls, perhaps because they would not take the trouble to go far, being lazy, but those who were not afraid of walking, those who were not lazy, they had sons.[10]

The women put the children in their *amauti* (hood) and observed the same rituals they would have if they had given birth to the children themselves. Boas (1901, 483) relates that according to the Inuit of Cumberland Sound,

> Akkolookjo and his wife Omerneeto established the laws which the Eskimo have to obey now. Omerneeto used to wear her husband's boots. She did not fasten the upper strings properly, but allowed the boot-leg to sag down and the boot-strings to drag over the ground. One day the soul of an infant that was on the ground crept up the boot-string and up into her womb. Up to that time, children had been found in the snow. The child grew in the womb, and finally was born. It began to cry, and gradually became old enough to speak. One day it told its parents how it had crawled into Omerneeto's womb. It continued, "There I was as in a small house. Every night when you cohabited, a dog would come in and vomit food for me to make me grow. Finally I longed to get outside; and when I got out, I wanted to speak, but all I could do was to cry. When I wanted other food than milk, I could only say 'papa;' and when I wanted to say 'I am thirsty,' I could only say 'oo, oo.'"

The tale confirms a strong association between the penis and a dog, which plays a central part in several versions of the myth of the sea woman and was later corroborated by Rose Iqallijuq from Iglulik.[11] Sexual intercourse was thought to provide food for the child. In the myth the child is not the result of intercourse between man and woman. The "soul" of the child comes of its own free will to the woman just as game is thought to come of its own free will to the hunter.[12] Once the child is in the womb, the father feeds the child with his seed just as he will feed the child after its birth with the meat he obtains. The mother is mainly responsible for the growth and the strength of the child, while the father provides the meat for its body to grow.

According to Boas (1901, 143), "Akkolookjo and Omerneeto gave advice to the people saying, that when they should become numerous they would have to obey certain customs." Rules of observance (*piqujait*, something that was requested to be done) and of abstention (*tirigususiit*, refraining from something that was forbidden) were important in Inuit perceptions of correct human behaviour. The observance of such customs was explicitly connected to the concept of "being numerous" (in contrast to the scarcity that was emphasized with respect to a mythical past).[13] Akkoloojo and Omerneeto provided a list of rules:

> When a woman is with child, she shall wear the teeth of the wolf as amulets. She shall attach them to the back of her inner shirt, and after the child is born she shall place them on the edge of the hood to prevent harm from coming to the child's soul. A woman who has a young child has a string which is fastened to the front part of her shirt, and passes under the lower part of her jacket. The other end has a clasp made of a bear's tooth, which serves to fasten it, and at the same time to protect the child's soul until it grows stronger. When the child is able to walk about alone, that string must be sewed to its jacket or shirt, and the tooth must be sewed to the back of the shirt. Care must be taken that the tooth shall not be lost because it keeps the soul from danger.[14]

Thus, the tooth of the bear protects the *tarniq* of the child. The mother has to observe many *pitailiniit* (rules of refraining) with respect to food. It is usually assumed that she may only eat meat from game provided by her husband and from this meat she should refrain from eating specific parts. Boas (1901, 143) reports that she should not eat "any part of the seal except the kidneys, because they make it dark for the child in the womb." Similar restrictions continued to be observed after the adoption of Christianity. Helen Konek from Arviat reported that one of her children died because she had eaten the head of a caribou that was still attached to its neck.[15] Rules also served to prevent complications with the umbilical cord. According to Boas (1901, 143), a woman "fastens her front hair at the sides with rings of thread, else it may strangle the child." Martha Okutak from Arviat said that pregnant women should not play the string game because otherwise the umbilical cord might strangle the infant.[16] Using objects derived from animals and observing the rules pertaining to animals would make a person a good and effective hunter.

Rasmussen (1929, 171) reports that "if the child is a boy, he must have the stump [of the umbilical cord], and the little flint knife used to cut it with, as amulets. They are sewn into his inner jacket on either side of the chest." A similar custom is still respected. Okutak reported that even today if you want a child to be wise in life, part of the umbilical cord has to be preserved by the mother. Matthew Akaralak from Arviat confirmed this tradition, saying he had respected it himself at the birth of one of his daughters.[17]

It took time to build a relationship between hunter and prey, and the mother played an important part in its construction. Rasmussen (1929, 173–4) describes rituals that were observed in the *kinirvik* (birth hut):

> Hanging beside her lamp, the mother must have a small skin bag (miŋulertequteqarfia). Whenever she is about to eat, she must cut off a small piece of meat, rub it on the child's mouth, and place it in the bag, before commencing her meal. This is called miŋulerterivəq, and is regarded as a sacred rite – a sacrifice in effigy to the spirits, the dead, and the holy meat. This act protects the child against hunger, and renders it skillful in hunting later on, bringing abundance of game. Another interpretation says that it is nutAra.lu.p ati.e nererqublugit: in order that the child's namesake soul may have something to eat …
>
> The miŋulerterivəq ceremony comes to an end when the stay in the kinervik is over, and the woman then takes the skin bag, filled with tiny fragments of meat, and carries it to the blowhole of a seal. Into this she throws all the scraps of meat, the first meat which has touched the boy's lips, and in a way served as his first flesh food. They are thus thrown back into the sea whence they came, and some people believe that by miŋulerterineq the separate pieces receive souls and become seals once more, which can be caught again by the boy when he grows up. If the child is a girl, the scraps of meat are merely thrown out on the edge of the beach at the expiration of the kinervik period. The empty skin bag is flung out on the ice.

Thus, the deceased – especially the deceased namesakes – and the future prey are connected to the child by the mother. This is also clearly the case in another practice related by Rasmussen (1929, 174), which shows how women were involved in making a good hunter from the start: "A woman in the kinervik … must never eat her fill … In the evening, after the last meal, a small piece of meat is placed in the diaper, also intended for the child's ateq, or name-soul. If it is a boy, and the mother wishes him to be especially fortunate in hunting, she eats not twice, but three times a day, but never eating her fill; for the mother's hunger renders the child light, i.e. swift in hunting."

After giving birth, a woman had to cover her hair with her hood, a tradition that has continued in the context of Christianity.[18] The mother's work bore fruit when the young boy made his first catch. First catches were celebrated in the past and are still a cause of joy today. In making his first catch, the young hunter was taking an important step towards establishing a relationship with the animal. The *angakkuq* Ava related to Rasmussen (1929, 117): "At last I was big enough to go out with the grown up men to the blowholes after seal. The day I harpooned my first seal, my father had to lie down on the ice with the upper part of his body naked, and the seal I had caught was dragged across his back while it was still alive. Only men were allowed to eat of my first catch, and nothing must be left. The skin and the head were set out on the ice, in order that I might be able later on to catch the same seal again. For three days and nights, none of the men who had eaten of it might go out hunting or do any kind of work."

Among the Nattilingmiut, a drum dance was held at the occasion of a first catch.[19] The first catch is still celebrated today, and usually the young hunter has to abstain eating from it. Emile Imaruittuq from Iglulik related:

> When a person catches an animal for the first time it must be distributed and consumed completely. If any of the meat is saved it will stall the catching of more animals in the future. For this reason a first kill should be eaten as soon as possible. If you are named after a person and that person's wife is still alive you are obligated to give some of that meat to your wife through your name. This is a strong *maligaq* that should be followed.
>
> If the parents of the person you were named after were still alive, you were obligated to give them meat also. If you didn't give meat to the people who should be receiving it, they would feel hurt. This is why you have to distribute a first kill in the community.[20]

The prey was shared by the hunters as well as the community. After a seal was killed, part of its liver was eaten by all the participating hunters. Then the animal was brought into the community, where the wife of the hunter would take care of its distribution. The consumption of the liver suggests an intimate connection between the hunters and their prey, one that had a human origin, as related in Inuit mythology.

HUMAN ORIGINS AND APPEARANCES

Many Inuit narratives relate how animals originated from human beings: the sea mammals grew out of the fingers of a young woman, the narwhal out of an old woman, the ptarmigan out of a child, and the black bear out of a girl. The transformation of mistreated human beings into animals is a dominant feature in many narratives.

In the story of the origin of sea mammals, a man threw his daughter out of his *umiaq* (woman's boat) into the water. When she clung to the side of the boat, he cut off her finger joints. They fell into the water and changed into sea mammals – usually whales, walruses, bearded seals, or seals. The girl herself sank to the bottom of the sea and became the owner of the sea mammals.[21] This famous story attributes a human origin to the animals that humans hunt and eat. In the story of the narwhal, a hunter (usually the moon man) was hunting beluga with an old woman (usually his mother or grandmother). When she tied the harpoon line around her waist, he harpooned a big beluga that pulled her into the water. The old woman changed into a narwhal. Boas (1901, 307–8)[22] relates the story of the origin of the black bear. A brother and a sister had no parents. The girl had not observed the rules of the community and she lived by herself in an old hut. Her brother visited her because he was fond of her, and she warned him that she was going to transform into a black bear that would devour other people. She told him to put sticks around his house. He did so, and when she had changed into a bear, she devoured all people except her brother.

When a human being transforms into an animal, the process is usually irreversible. Only *angakkuit* can transform into animals and then return to their original human state. Animals can adopt a human appearance but their transformations are never permanent. They can never become fully human, and sooner or later they must return to their animal condition. There are many stories about encounters between human beings and animals in human appearance. People might be deceived at first by the human appearance of an animal, but after a while they would usually discover that they were not dealing with an *inuk*, but with an *inua*, the human person of an animal.

Animals in human appearance might visit communities. The Aivilik storyteller Ivaluardjuk told Rasmussen (1929, 276–7) about such an occurrence:

> There were once a bear and its wife and their two children that came in human form to visit a village. After they had got there, they set about building a snow hut. While their parents were building the house, the children, a brother and a sister, went visiting about the village. In the course of their visits there was a man who asked them:
>
> "What is the name of your father?"
>
> "Bear," answered the boy.
>
> "And what is your mother's name?"
>
> "Mouth."
>
> "What then is your brother called?"
>
> "Hide."
>
> "And you yourself?"
>
> "I am called Miserly."
>
> During the night, the bears felt anxious lest the human beings should attack them, now they had learned who they were, and so they fled away before the people of the village were awake.

In this story, it was not the animal, but its *inua*, its person, who was perceived by human beings. The story illustrates the element of trickery. Animals do not have names, *atiit*, like human beings, and by asking their names the man established their true nature. The bears were aware of this and fled. The element of trickery is important in these stories, and capable *angakkuit*, such as Kiviuq, could discern the true nature of animals in human appearance. The Kiviuq story relates how Kiviuq married various animals in human appearance, such as a fox and a snow goose, but these relationships could not last.[23]

THE DISCOURSE ON SEXUAL RELATIONSHIPS BETWEEN PEOPLE AND ANIMALS

Whereas marriage with an animal in human appearance is a recurring topic in stories, bestiality was another matter. It was strictly prohibited but remained a subject of speculation. Rasmussen (1931, 197–8) heard about several people who were supposed to have had sexual intercourse with animals, notably dogs:

> For instance it is told of a woman Qubliusaq who once when out gathering fuel had intercourse with a dog that she had taken with her. She had told of it herself and had said that it had been very painful. This had happened recently. The story is told of another woman who once in years gone by had had relations with her dog, the result being that she had become pregnant and had given birth to young, some of which were dogs with human hands and hairless bodies. She had been confined in the open air in the shelter of some stones, but her fellow-villagers had been ashamed of her and pushed the stones down over her so that she and her young were killed.

Iglulik elders emphasized the dangers of bestiality. According to Kappianaq (IE 334), "When a man engages in sexual conducts other than a woman, they are referred to as *sunarlluk*. If a person had some sexual engagements with other things than a woman, then death is within his domain. The act of engaging in bestiality is forbidden by Takatumaaluup, indeed it is absolutely forbidden, this act is also forbidden by God."

Piugaattuk (IE 59) emphasized that bestiality with wildlife is far more dangerous than intercourse with dogs: "Soon he will start to experience health problems and soon his physical condition will start to get damaged while he is still early in his adulthood. This is because he is not engaged only with a dog but with wildlife. When they are engaged only with dogs which are domesticated animals by people, they did not start to get physical deterioration immediately. I know this from what I have seen. It tends to shorten the life of the individual." Piugaattuk (IE 22) described how shame often prevented people from confessing: "On more than one occasion I have witnessed the slow agonizing death of certain individuals who have been engaged in bestiality. A shaman would have made all possible effort for them to confess to their secret but they will not disclose it because of the embarrassment they would endure by disclosing their habit. When they finally confess at a stage where they are beyond help they will not be cured and died as a result."

Imaruittuq from Iglulik stated that he knew people who had seen the offspring of the union of people and dogs.[24] Whereas bestiality itself, especially with wildlife, is strictly prohibited, the symbolism of the hunt has definite erotic connotations. This is illustrated by Tungilik's account of his first successful seal hunt at a breathing hole:

> When he finally started telling me about how to hunt, he told me to recall the first time that I had had sex, and to remember what my breathing was like. I was to remember my breathing. He said that's the kind of breathing that the seal would have when it was approaching the *aglu* [breathing hole]. I had never had sex with a woman, so I didn't know anything about the kind of breathing he was talking about. Then one day, the *qiviutaq* [piece of feather] moved. You had to just wet the very tip of it and not the rest, because if it was completely wet, it would be unable to move. I was told that this piece of down was used so you would know when there was a seal approaching. When it was moving, I started holding my breath. When the feather started going up, it fluttered a bit, and I was finally aware of the seal's breathing. I was shaking because I knew there was a seal there. Before that time I never knew about this. I never knew what it was going to be like. My breathing became laboured. The *qiviutaq* would move depending on the inhaling and exhaling of the seal. I started using the seal's breathing to help me know when to harpoon it. When I thought the seal was coming up, I thought it was time for me to harpoon it. I went to harpoon it when the seal was very close. This is how I learned to successfully harpoon a seal, through becoming aware of its breathing. My knee joints seemed very loud because I was shaking so much. That's the way it was. I finally understood how this piece of bird down was used. It started moving because of the movement of the water. It seemed to stop, and then it started fluttering again. When it went down a bit, that's when the seal was coming up and it was time to harpoon it.[25]

The act of harpooning evokes the act of sexual intercourse, but such an act should never take place with the animal itself. When a hunter dreamt of having sex with a beautiful woman, it often meant a successful hunt. Jose Angutinngurniq from Kugaaruk remarked, "If I dream I am next to a woman, when I wake up the next morning I know I will have a good hunt."[26] The woman may well represent the *inua* of the animal.[27]

TARNIQ

Rasmussen (1929, 58–9) states that the soul and the name make people particularly sensitive to the rules of life:

> The soul, tarniŋa or inu·sia, is that which gives to all living things their particular appearance. In the case of human beings it is really a tiny human being, in the case of the caribou a tiny caribou, and so on with all animals; an image, but very much smaller than the creature itself.
>
> The *inu·sia* (meaning "appearance as a human being") is situated in a bubble of air in the groin; from it issue appearance, thoughts, strength, and life. It is that which makes the man a man, the caribou a caribou, the walrus a walrus, the dog a dog, etc.

Life depends on this miniature image inside the *pullaq* (bubble of air). According to Felix Pisuk from Kangiq&iniq, "When I die my *tarniq* will no longer be a bubble. It will become the way you see me."[28] According to the Inuktitut-English dictionary by Lucien Schneider (1985, 270), *pullaq* means "bubble of the air rising from the depths of the water" and is etymologically related to *puijiit*, sea mammals that pop their head out of the water to breathe.[29]

Rasmussen (1931, 217) identifies *tarninga* (his or her *tarniq*) with *inusia* among the Iglulingmiut and *tarniq* with *inoseq* (*inusiq*) among the Nattilingmiut. "The soul is the being and appearance of the living, and therefore is called not only tarneq, but also ino·seq." Rasmussen firmly places the *tarniq* or *inusiq* in a visual perspective: it determined the appearance of a being. Thus, we will refer to the *tarniq* as an "image," denoting a person's appearance as associated with his or her health and well-being. The *tarniq* differentiated the appearance of a being. The *tarniq* of a human being was a miniature human being, and that of a caribou a miniature caribou. The health and vitality of a being depended on its *tarniq*. It might leave the body temporarily, but if it did not return, the separation between body and *tarniq* would become final and that being would die.

Ethnographers such as Boas translate *tarniq* as "soul," and after the transition to Christianity, *tarniq* became the Inuktitut translation of the Christian concept of soul. The terms *tarniq* and *tarninga* (his or her *tarniq*) are frequently found in ethnographic literature and testimonies by elders. But the words *inusia* and *inusiq* are only provided by Rasmussen. They may have been used as glosses to explain that one's appearance as a human being was determined by the *tarniq*. The *tarniq*, the miniature image of a being, was usually located in a vital organ, such as the liver, the kidneys, or the groin. The word is derived from the root *tar*-, "shadow." In the *tuurngait* language that was used in communications between *angakkuit* and their helping spirits, this root can be found in the words *tarejumaq* ("shadowmaker") for *angakkuq* and *ṭau* ("shade") for a deceased person. As the origin of strength and vitality of a being, the *tarniq* was also vulnerable to attacks by evil *angakkuit*. It could be strengthened and protected in a variety of ways. Rasmussen (1931, 215) related that when Qaqortingneq was born, "his soul was taken out of his body and placed beside his mother's lamp. The shaman who did it was named Qaqortingneq like himself. Now his mother had long been dead, but it was still assumed that his soul lay under her old lamp; he was therefore invulnerable."

Tarniit could be perceived in other ways. Some of the elders said that when a person was asleep, a shaman would see his *tarniq* upside down.[30] According to Ollie Itinnuaq from Kangiq&iniq (1999 interview), the proportion of light and dark indicates whether a *tarniq* is good or bad: "I have seen *tarniit.* There is a brightness to them. We've seen pictures of saints and religious pictures. Pictures of saints are always depicted with brightness around the head or around the body. *Angakkuit,* too, used to see brightness. There is an aura. If a person has a bright aura, it is all around them. If you aren't an *angakkuq,* it is hard to look at it. If someone is said to be bad, even though they have a *qaumaniq,* it is not as bright, as there is darkness in the centre. When a person is really good, the centre is bright also."

The *tarniq* survived at death. According to Kappianaq, "If the body were to die the *tarniq* would take on the appearance of the body and would be recognizable as that person."[31] It was usually assumed that the *tarniq* departed for one of the lands of the dead, either the land of the moon man or that of the sea woman. Rasmussen (1929, 94) writes: "After death, there are two different places to which one may pass either up into heaven to the Udlormiut, or People of Day; their land lies in the direction of dawn, and is the same as the Land of the Moon Spirit. The other place to which the dead may come lies down under the sea. It is a narrow strip of land, with sea on either side; and the inhabitants are therefore called Qimiujarmiut: 'the dwellers in the narrow land.' The immigrant Netsilingmiut call them Atlet: 'those lowest down,' for they live in a world below the world in which we live."

People who suffered a violent death went to the land of the *ullurmiut,* the others joined the *qimiujarmiut* (people from the narrow land). According to Rasmussen (1929, 99), "Dead people live on just in the same way as while on earth, and store up food for the winter as they did when alive." Moreover, those going to the narrow land had to pass through a purgatory: "Those whose offenses against taboo are not wiped out by a violent death, and who have therefore to go to the Sea Spirit for purification before they can pass to the company of the 'blessed' in the Narrow Land, have then to pass through a period of purgatory, under the guardianship of Isarrataitsoq, the length of time varying, according to the magnitude of the offenses, from one to two years, or even several years. Exceptionally good people may, however, get off with less than a year."[32]

The father of the sea woman was particularly associated with the punishment of those who had committed bestiality. On South Baffin Island, there were similar traditions. Peck relates, "It is said that old people who made a full confession of their sins go to the place of bliss when they die, but those who die in pain being supposed to retain their sins (e.g. not full confession) go to Sedna."[33] According to Boas (1964 [1888], 588), "The dead, who are seized by Sedna's father, Anguta, are carried to this dwelling. The dog moves aside only a little, just enough to allow the souls to pass. They have to stay in this dismal abode during a whole year, lying by the side of Anguta, who pinches them. The happy land is heaven and is called Qudlivun (the uppermost ones). It abounds with deer, which are easily caught, and no ice or snow ever visits it."

The sea woman had the power to transform the *tarniit* of the deceased into animals. In various accounts, the *tarniq* might incarnate into an animal or human being.[34] Boas (1901, 234) tells the story of a hunter who recognized the soul of his deceased mother in a fox and therefore could not kill it. In the famous story of Arnaqtaaqtuq told by Celestine Iqijjuk from Kivalliq, a rejected fetus reincarnated time and again in different beings, such as dogs, seals, and caribou, until it was finally reborn as a human being.[35] Boas (1901, 321ff.) provides an interesting version, describing how a *tarniq* might enter the being that ate its corpse: "Once upon a time an old woman who had died was buried, and then a raven came and began to eat her. Her soul entered the body of the raven, and she became a raven. The raven laid its eggs; but a man came and shot the bird, took it into his house, and gave it to a dog to eat. Then the woman's soul entered the dog." After many modes of existence, it entered a seal. Finally the soul of this seal entered the harpoon of the hunter that killed it. From there it entered the womb of the wife of the hunter, and thus the old woman was finally reborn as a human being.[36] The distinction between animals and human beings was precarious, and the boundary between people and animals could be easily crossed when the *tarniq* passed from one existence to the next.

The transgression of rules had a profound effect on a *tarniq* and might cause it to transform into an evil spirit and take revenge on the transgressor. Rasmussen (1929, 58) explains:

> Where any act of violence is committed against this soul, or any offense by breach of taboo, it becomes an evil spirit, wreaking harm and death in return. But it must not be supposed that all animals are angered when they are killed. Animals have in reality no objection to being killed by human beings, as long as the rules of life are observed by the latter. It may even happen, and not infrequently, that an animal will approach a human being, actually desiring to be killed by that particular person. An animal may perhaps be tired of being what it is; and since its soul cannot change its envelope until the body has been killed, it is natural that animals should sometimes wish to die. The great danger in killing animals commonly hunted lies in the fact that there is hardly a single human being who has kept the rules of life and lived throughout in accordance with the laws laid down by the wisdom of his forefathers. Therefore it is said that the greatest danger lies in the fact that unclean and often guilty human beings have to depend entirely on the souls of other beings for food.

If an animal or human being died, people had to observe many *tirigusiit.* If they broke these rules, the offended *tarniq* might change into a *tonraq hiqloriqtuq,* an evil spirit, intent on avenging itself on the people who did not respect it.[37] According to Rasmussen (1929, 144), "It may happen that a village is haunted by evil spirits. Such are called nunaluit or tupilait. By evil spirits is understood not only fabulous beasts and the mountain spirits here referred to, which live out in the wilds on earth, but also the ghosts of dead souls which have become hostile to mankind and dangerous owing to failure to observe precisely the rules of taboo after their death. A shaman setting out to fight such beings and render them harmless must arm himself with a walrus knife or that particular kind of snow knife which is made from walrus tusk with no iron edge inserted, and which is called havu·jaq."

Whereas normally *tarniit* were not supposed to have bones or blood, *tupilait* had blood, and after killing a *tupilaq,* the shamans showed the blood on their hands to other people. According to Boas (1901, 130), the *tupilaq* changed back into a soul when it was killed. Death effected a separation between the body and the *tarniq.* The nature of the *tarniq* was a topic of discussion in Inuit society.[38] Oosotapik, one of Peck's informants in Cumberland Sound, told Peck that many *tuurngait* (helping spirits of the shamans) were able to kill the souls of the animals, so that they could be easily killed by the hunters. However, another of Peck's main informants, Qoojessie, emphatically denied that this was possible, explaining that souls were immortal and could not be killed.[39] Another difference of opinion existed with respect to the trips of the *angakkuit* to the lands of the deceased in the nether world and the upper world. Rasmussen (1929, 124) notes that some people assumed that the *angakkuq* himself made the trip, while others assumed that only his *tarniq* made it.

PITAILINIIT

The animals that were hunted and killed were sentient beings endowed with a *tarniq.* This was why it was important for people to respect the game. Ivaluardjuk stated: "The greatest peril of life lies in the fact that human food consists entirely of souls. All the creatures that we have to kill and eat, all those that we have to strike down and destroy to make clothes for ourselves, have souls, like we have, souls that do not perish with the body, and which must therefore be propitiated lest they should revenge themselves on us for taking away their bodies."[40]

In the past, the situation was even more precarious, as explained by the *angakkuq* Anarqaq.

> "In the old days, it was far worse than it is now," put in Anarqaq, "Everything was more difficult, and our customs accordingly much more strict. In those days, men hunted only with bow and arrow and knew noth-

ing of the white men's firearms. It was far more difficult to live then, and often men could not get food enough. The caribou were hunted in kayaks at the crossing of rivers and lakes, being driven out into the water where they could be easily overtaken in a kayak. But it was hard to make them run the way one wished, and therefore rules were very strict about those places. No woman was allowed to work there, no bone of any animal might be broken, no brain or marrow eaten. To do so would be an insult to the souls of the caribou and was punished by death or disaster."[41]

Respect towards wildlife took shape in a wide variety of principles, customs, and rules. These were often referred to as taboos by anthropologists such as Boas and Rasmussen. Hoebel (1964, 60) observes, "[A] people more tabu-ridden would be difficult to find." Boas and Rasmussen made long lists of taboos, treating them as if they were part of a generally acknowledged Inuit system of rules. But rules varied greatly in different areas. For example, there were many rules governing the caribou hunt for Inuit living inland. They had to follow the strict rules associated with the caribou crossing places[42] and also those concerning the treatment and eating of caribou meat. Barnabas Peryouar from Qamanittuaq recalled that they were not allowed to break the leg bones of caribou with any metal tool, nor to use any small metal thing to scoop out marrow; Julie Tulugaq related that her mother was only allowed to eat the tip of the caribou tongue;[43] And Silas Kalluk remembered "that some people were not allowed to eat hearts of animals or kidneys. They were rules that people followed and that is how it was. If they didn't follow rules they would be neglected or a shaman may lose his helping spirit."[44]

The Iglulingmiut had a reputation for being very strict in the application of rules, particularly with respect to the sea mammals. There was great variation in the rules to be observed, not only in different areas, but also by families and even individuals. Inuit used various terms to refer to these rules: for example, *pitailiniq*, refraining from doing something; *tirigusuusiit*, specific injunctions imposed on a person; *tiringnaqtuq*, anything that is a cause of one needing to observe *tirigusuusiq*; and *maligait*, accepted guidelines for doing things that need to be followed. Today the word *maligaq* is used as a translation for "Canadian Law."[45]

Rules of respect governed a wide range of cultural behaviour. Some rules concerned the earth, others the relationships between human beings. Most rules had to do with the different parts of animals – the skins, bones, meat, sinews, and so forth. They specified how different categories of people should or should not handle these parts in specific contexts. Women who were menstruating or had just delivered a child were particularly at risk in this regard. Rasmussen (1929, 98) reports: "The worst offense against taboo which any woman can commit is concealment of menstruation or abortion. Women during the menstrual period are especially unclean in relation to all animals hunted, and may thus expose the entire community to the greatest danger and disaster if they endeavour to conceal their impurity."

There are many stories about hunters who failed to kill any prey because a woman had hidden her miscarriage. Animals were always aware of the transgressions of human beings. Herve Paniaq from Iglulik told a story about a hidden miscarriage and the consequent retaliation.

> I will tell a story about the hunters of the camp who caught walrus. The hunters came back with their catch. One of the hunters' wives went to help her husband when he arrived as he didn't really have anyone to help him when he was trying to go up a slope. She was pregnant at this time and when she was helping him carry the meat she felt something come out between her legs. She thought she had started menstruating so she went behind the tent to urinate and she passed a very small but fully formed stillborn child. She put the dead child on a flat stone, and she was about to go tell her husband about it but she got scared and changed her mind. They had flat stones they used for a bed platform and there was gravel beneath it so she dug a small hole and put the dead child there and buried it. Once she had done that she went back to her husband to help him with the work. Then hunger came to the camp and there were no animals around. The hunters even gave up looking for animals and just stayed around the camp. Even people in other camps were experiencing the same thing. There was a young adult shaman in another camp who was starting to ask questions about why they were going hungry. Once he found out why, he went in his *qajaq* [kayak] to the camp where the woman was. The couple had moved their tents away from the main camp as the husband wanted to be in a quiet place. The shaman had the people gather from the main camp and he started asking them what they thought could be the reason that they were struggling. The people started talking about possible reasons and they all admitted all the wrongs they had done. When he was finished with them, he went to the couple's tent, and the couple were adults by now. He said to the woman, "You are the reason why we are going through hard times. You hid a dead baby under your bed platform and you buried it." Her husband picked up a knife as he was quite depressed from losing children. He took his wife by the shoulder and slapped her. She admitted that she had been scared to tell him the truth as he was the type who was abusive. She then told the story of what happened, that she was helping him when he returned from hunting and she felt something come out and she delivered a very small stillborn baby. She was scared to tell her husband so she buried the baby instead. She said she had nothing more to say. The shaman returned to the other camp members and made them go through confessions again. When he finished, he left as he had arrived, by *qajaq*. After his departure, they could hear ice creaking throughout the night, and they could hardly wait for daylight. Next day, sure enough, there was this big sheet of ice with an abundance of walrus. The walrus were bellowing and

the hunters got their catch that day and they didn't go hungry again after that.[46]

Boas (1901, 120) explains that animals could actually see the transgressions of human beings:

> The souls of the sea-animals are endowed with greater powers than those of ordinary beings. They can see the effect of the contact with a corpse, which causes objects touched by it to appear dark in color; and they can see the effect of flowing human blood from which a vapor arises that surrounds the bleeding person and is communicated to every one and everything that comes in contact with such a person. The vapor and the dark color of death are exceedingly unpleasant to the souls of sea-animals that will not come near a hunter thus affected. The hunter must therefore avoid contact with people who have touched a body, or with those who are bleeding, more particularly with menstruating women or with those who have recently given birth. The hands of menstruating women appear red to sea-animals. If any one who has touched a body or who is bleeding should allow others to come into contact with him, he would cause them to be distasteful to seals, and therefore to Sedna as well. For this reason custom demands that every person must at once announce if he has touched a body, and that women must make known when they have had a miscarriage. If they do not do so they will bring ill luck to all the hunters.

Rasmussen (1929, 172–3) relates that menstruating women or women who had just delivered a child had to refrain from contact with animals and their products, especially raw and fresh meat. In the past, a woman was required to give birth in a special birth hut, the *kinirvik*, and she remained there for one or two, sometimes even three, months. Special rules applied to her: she should only eat meat of prey killed by her own husband, she was not allowed to cut her own meat, she should not go out visiting, she should not have intercourse with her husband, she should not eat the entrails or heart of any animal or egg, and so on. The new mother should avoid being seen by wildlife and keep her direct contact with animals and hunters to a minimum. These rules were only gradually lifted.

It was likely because of the severity of these rules that women sometimes hid a miscarriage despite the dire consequences such an act might have for the community. In fact, elders frequently mentioned that a hidden miscarriage was the most obvious reason why hunters failed in their task.

Death was also a cause of great concern, especially for the relatives and companions of the deceased. A period of strict rules followed upon a death:

> The period of na·ce·vəq, i.e. maintaining the strict death taboo for men is three days, for women four days; during these days the persons concerned

must do no work, must not wash, comb their hair or cut their nails; the lamp must not be cleaned, the dogs must not be fed, and the persons are not allowed to cut up their own meat for cooking. Sexual intercourse is forbidden, as also dancing or song festivals. The brother or sister of the deceased must during these days leave his or her own house and stay in that of the deceased, so that they may be together until the soul of the deceased passes away.

Sledges must not be driven during the days of strict death taboo. Should it be absolutely necessary to go out hunting, it must be done on foot. The noise of the sledge is offensive to the dead.[47]

After the period of strict rules, people still had to refrain from many social activities and from hunting, and they were only allowed to resume their normal tasks gradually. To refer to the observance of funerary rules, Rasmussen uses the word *nasivik,* which, according to Schneider (1985, 97), means "place that is raised above the surrounding country from which one can look out for game." Thus, the word refers to a time and place for observing game. It evokes Inuit burial places and cemeteries, which Inuit preferred to place on hills or at the coast so that they would provide a vantage point from which the deceased, as well as living, could observe the game of the land or the sea.

After the killing of an animal, various rules had to be observed. Some of these evoked the rules of respect for the dead that applied to a human's death. Rasmussen (1929, 184) states that the following rules were fundamental:

When a whale, a bearded seal or a bear is killed, no man's or woman's work must be done for three days. It is also strictly forbidden during these three days to cut turf or gather fuel from the earth. Clothing may, however, be mended; and distinction is here to be observed between ordinary needlework and actual mending.

If a man comes home with an animal which he has killed out at the edge of the ice, he must not enter the house on his return until he has removed his outer clothing.

He drew up extensive lists of the rules that had to be observed for each animal when killed. For example:

When a seal is brought into a house, no woman in the house may sew or do any other work until the seal has been cut up. This applies, however, only to winter hunting, in snow huts, not in tents during summer.

As long as a newly captured seal has not been cut up, the following things are taboo:

Rime must not be wiped from the window pane.

Skins from the sleeping place must not be shaken out over the floor.

The mats of plaited willow twigs must not be straightened or rearranged.
No oil must be spilled from the lamp.
No work must be done with stone, wood or iron.
Women must not comb their hair, wash their faces or dry any footwear.[48]

Special rules obtained for various types of seal, such as bearded seals. Different categories of game had to be kept apart, especially land game and sea game.[49] Only by observing all these rules could human beings maintain an order where animals would allow themselves to be killed and to be reborn.

Animals were thought to reincarnate continuously, and the same prey was always expected to return to a hunter who had shown it due respect. Peter Arnatsiaq from Iglulik explained that an old bear was full of scars because it "would return to his being after his meat was all eaten up following his capture by the hunters. In those days any animal used to return after they had served their purpose to the human kind; this was known as *angiraaliniq*."[50] Thus hunter and prey were connected in a cycle of exchange. The hunter depended on the animal for survival, and the animal was brought to life again by the rules of respect that the hunter and his wife observed. Inuit often emphasize that if the animals are not hunted, their numbers will dwindle and they will gradually disappear.

SIQQITIQ

The introduction of Christianity implied that most prohibitions were lifted. In the North Baffin area, the ritual of *siqqitiq* evolved to mark the transition. A meeting would be held, and the heart of an animal, usually a fresh seal, would be divided into pieces and eaten by all participants. As the eating of a heart was prohibited by traditional customs, especially to women, the ritual marked the transition to a new way of life, free of the restrictions of the old ways.[51] Noah Piugaattuk from Iglulik (1997 interview) recalled:

> Shamans were losing their power through *siqqitiq*. Before Christianity, they could not eat certain things from certain animals, but after eating [heart in the *siqqitiq* ritual] they can now do anything they want to. That's how they started Christianity. Back then I went through *siqqitiq* too. Somebody went bearded seal hunting. The man came back with a seal. He brought us a heart, they cut it into pieces. Those people who wanted to go through *siqqitiq* confessed what they did and what they didn't like from the past. Some even cried while they were confessing. Then, these people were given this cut meat. Umik, Anguliainuk and Umik's son were religious persons giving food. Qadlutsiaq could not do it. Only those who knew about religion could give that food. Back then, hearts of some animals were not supposed to be eaten by some people. So, when they were

> going to eat it, through *siqqitiq* they would forget their past. Before *siqqitiq* some people could eat heart, but other people, mostly women, were not allowed to eat heart. If a woman's relatives died, she couldn't eat some meat for about a year. After *siqqitiq*, hunters would stop to give water to the seal they shot, because that would be Satan's rules. At that time we did not know what baptizing was.

Iqallijuq from Iglulik (1997 interview) recalled how she celebrated *siqqitiq* with her in-laws in Ittusardjuat's camp:

> As we went inside, the tent was full of people. The whole camp was in there and I saw a plate with walrus meat, like heart, guts, liver and brain. There were very small pieces on the plate. First somebody ate, then all ate, and we finished it. Then we said a prayer to God, that we wanted a new life and that we wanted the good spirit to come down. We were all Inuit there. There was no Anglican minister and no Catholic priest. We were all together, we were using *siqqitiq*. I was baptized later on … A lot of people did *siqqitiq* at that time. The plate was really full of meat such as heart, liver, intestines, tongue and a lot of people gathered in there. They all ate and they finished the whole plate. They just took the meat together and ate it by themselves. Before, the women could not eat some parts of meat, like tongue, head, or some parts of seal. But when they did *siqqitiq*, they ate this forbidden meat from the plate saying, "Let me eat a piece of the body of Christ," and then somebody gave them religion. Now they could eat everything they wanted. After they did this, they said a prayer to God.

Rachel Uyarasuk from Iglulik also participated in the ritual and recalled how it was intended to end the rules for the observance of rituals "after they heard of religion, when they wanted to turn towards Christianity":

> When they decided they were going to *siqqitiq*, they went to the windbreak. It was nice outside. The sun was shining since it was spring. They brought a seal to the wind break. They cut the seal open and took out the intestines, the liver, heart, the eyes, the tongue and they were all cut to small pieces. They did not have plates in those days, so they placed them on the seal. They were cut into tiny pieces and put together. In the end, the people were in a line, and each was given a piece of meat to put into the mouth. People were asked why they wanted to go through this ceremony. Everyone of them replied, "We are going through this because we want to take Christianity." My mother told me, if I were asked, to say, "I want to go to Jesus." When the person giving the meat came to me, that person gave me an eye and a piece of intestine. It was cut small enough to chew. I was asked why I wanted to take religion. Here I was, just a child. I was old

enough to speak. I replied as my mother instructed me "Because I want to go to Jesus when I die." Everyone of us was given a piece of meat. The meaning of this was that all these parts of a seal, the meat, the heart, the intestine were all parts of the *pittailiniq*, the taboos. And they were no longer going to be used or observed. There would be no part of the seal that people would have to refrain from eating. This was not just the case for seal, but for all other animals as well. There were not going to be any more refrainings from eating any parts of any animal. This is why we were given bits and pieces of everything.[52]

The foods especially favoured in the *siqqitiq* were the heart and the other parts of the animal that had often been forbidden. Such parts were also emphasized in the *ariserpoq* practice that Rasmussen describes (1929, 175): "On the first occasion of eating raw meat after childbirth the woman must, if her child is a boy, ariserpoq, i.e. a piece of intestine about 1.½ metres long, and a piece of liver, are placed in her cooking pot, taken out again quickly, so as to be hardly more than dipped in the boiling water, and the women must then swallow the intestine whole, without cutting it, and immediately after eat the liver, which must likewise not be masticated, but swallowed rapidly (she must not cut either one or the other)."

The pattern of *siqqitiq* evokes early Christian traditions where the rejection of Mosaic law was expressed by the eating of non-kosher food.[53] The old rules were rejected, but new ones were introduced, such as the obligation to respect Sundays. Rachel Uyarasuk recalled, "We would be told that we were not to sew on Sunday. Nobody should do any kind of work on Sunday. It was written in the Bible. People did not go out hunting if they had meat. If we were in need of food, people would go hunting even on Sunday, but if an animal was killed, we were to finish it right away. Because not all of us were present, we were unable to finish the whole animal. We only ate part of it. These days, when a person kills an animal on Sunday they don't try to finish it."[54]

But many elders continued to follow specific rules. And today some believe that the basic principle of observing rules to have good life has been preserved. Ollie Itinnuaq from Kangiq&iniq observed:

People would follow *tirigusuusiit*. There were a lot of them to follow. Whenever there was a death, there were things people were not allowed to do. When they were trying to heal someone through *qilaniq* [head lifting] or through *irinaliutiit* [powerful words], or through shamanic rituals, there were things people had to refrain from. *Tirigusungniq* had so many purposes. There were things that people had to do and things they had to refrain from doing. When we became Christian, we were told not to *tirigusuktuq* any more. We still have things we have to refrain from. As Catholics, if we have not gone to confession, we are not to go to communion. That is *tirigusuktuq*. There is *tirigusungniq* even within the church. When we say that we don't *tirigusuktuq* any more, we are lying, because there are still things we have to refrain from doing.[55]

Otto Apsauqtaun from Kugaaruk recalled:

> I have *tiringnaqtuq*. I have something in me. I will be talking about my older brother. I was to be *tiringnaqtuq*, but I was born a little bit later. I was born around the time when *tiringnaqtuq* was starting not to be practised. My older brother didn't have any *tiringnaqtuq* to follow. He could put on a woman's clothing. He could wear any kind of clothing. Because I had *tiringnaqtuq* before, people tried to remove that thing, but nobody wanted to wear my clothing. They were afraid to wear my clothing in the past. Only today it has changed. I was not to eat the heart of certain animals. Later on I was able to eat the heart from any animal. *Tiringnaqtuq* has stopped being practised. In the past, nobody was allowed to wear my clothing. I was not allowed to wear anyone else's clothing. Today this has been broken. I'm living just like everybody else. In the past, I was not allowed to wear women's clothing, and women were not allowed to wear my clothing. It doesn't make much sense today.[56]

According to Mary Anguti from Kugaaruk these rules are still very much alive: "I have heard and seen people follow *tirigusungniq*. Some people were very careful following these rules. People would tell me not to wear somebody else's clothing when I was young; not boots, or socks, or anything. I was not to wear somebody else's clothing. People told me to take care of myself. *Tirigusungniq* is still out there. It's a living thing. They would give *tirigusungniq* a certain name. When you got older the *tirigusungniit* got weaker and weaker. Because I was not allowed to wear other people's clothing, it was necessary to make new clothing for me."[57]

Although the elders said that the rules are a tradition of the past, they still quite frequently observe some of them themselves. Felix Pisuk recalled: "When I was about to turn sixteen, she (the *angakkuq* Qaviajak) told me I was never to eat a caribou heart or a caribou liver. To this day I have never eaten caribou heart or liver. She told me that if someone more powerful than me gave me a heart on a plate, I was to eat part of it but not finish it. When I was in Arviat that happened to me. I was given a heart to eat by a powerful *angakkuq*, but I remembered being told not to finish it. If I had finished the heart, I would have died. After I returned to Kangiq&iniq the person who had given me this food died, not even a month later."[58]

Today, in the context of Christianity, the rules about respecting animals are often still observed. In the Arviat workshop in 2007, Thomas Ubluriak from Arviat said that his father had taught him that a hunter should not have sex with his wife or quarrel with her when he was going to hunt sea mammals the next day. He had always observed these rules. In the same workshop, Martha Okutak from Arviat noted that a woman should not make herself up when her husband was going out on such a hunt.

The missionaries taught that only human beings had souls, and thus, when the word *tarniq* was accepted as a translation of the Christian concept of soul, most *pitailiniit* were no longer observed. But even today Inuit are convinced that animals have to be respected. If a person doesn't show respect, the animals will retaliate. In a workshop in Iqaluit, Imaruittuq from Iglulik recalled:

> From the time we were small we were taught to have the highest respect for all wildlife, even for the smallest bird. We were told to treat all wildlife with respect, even baby birds and animals. If we didn't do this they could take revenge on us. If we abused a certain part of an animal, that same part within us would be affected. I heard a story about a man that mistreated an eider duck. There is a *piqujaq* to respect even the smallest bird. We have to ensure that the younger generation is aware of this as well. Wildlife has to be given the highest respect. This is another story about a man who shot a caribou in the leg. The wounded caribou was still alive when he cut off its nose because he wanted to eat it. As a result of this, later in his life his nose became decayed and it fell off. This is what happens if you mistreat wildlife.

Imaruittuq believed that even insects would retaliate: "Even insects should be treated with respect. We were taught not to mistreat black flies and mosquitoes because they could take revenge on us as well. There was a hunter who used his scope to burn mosquitoes. The next thing he knew he was being swarmed by them. When they swarm around you it can be suffocating, it can be that bad. You shouldn't mistreat insects. You can squash them, but you can't mistreat them."[59]

Inuit assumed that animals had to be hunted and were created for that purpose. Imaruittuq explained: "If you legitimately hunt wildlife and don't cause them to suffer, if you respect them, then it is fine. There will be suffering on occasion but you have to try and minimize this out of respect for the animal. We should not even make nasty comments about wildlife. We shouldn't quarrel about them amongst ourselves. Wildlife has been placed on this earth for us to use, but we must treat them with respect."

Imaruittuq pointed out that Qallunaat are not always aware that Inuit consider animals as cosmological agencies that will take action whenever people break the rules, the *piqujait*, relating to them: "When we started dealing with land claims we had to talk a lot about wildlife. This created a lot of fear amongst the elders. They used to tell us not to quarrel about wildlife because this was a very dangerous thing to do. We explained to them that we had to quarrel about the wildlife because we were negotiating with the *qallunaat* and this was a *qallunaat* process.

We explained that we were legitimately negotiating over the wildlife. This is a *piqujaq* that we must adhere to. We should not quarrel about wildlife or it will take revenge on us."[60]

Inuit perceive the relationship between themselves and animals as one between hunters and prey. With the sole exception of dogs, animals are not seen as part of human society. Yet because Inuit assume that animals and human beings share a common origin, they believe that animals have human features. Elders think that animals are no longer respected sufficiently. They complain about the caribou carcasses left on the land and the bones found around the houses in the communities. Mariano Aupilaarjuk from Kangiq&iniq stated:

> There are times you would come across bones. For instance, bones from a caribou that had been killed by wolves. We were told if we came across bones on the ground we were to turn them around and then leave them. I still follow this practice today. I'll explain the reason for turning the bones. If I am in bed sleeping, I would become very tired if I just slept on one side. I would feel better if I were to move. In the same way, bones become tired from just lying in one way. It is in order for them to feel better that we have to turn them the other way. That is the *maligaq* concerning bones. I still follow this because I want to take away their tiredness.[61]

Aupilaarjuk prefers the old rules over the new laws.

> We just shouldn't be killing our wildlife without reason. We should only be killing them for food. There is no need to have new laws about wildlife for Inuit had their *maligait* about wildlife even though they were not written. The present laws about wildlife are not our *maligait*. The *maligait* that we follow are not seen because the Inuit *piusiq* is not visible. What I told you about the bones is a *maligaq* although it doesn't require a licence. It is a *maligaq* where respect is shown through wanting the bones of the caribou to feel rested. That way we show our gratitude to the animal. This is an Inuit *piusiq* [custom] that is not being practiced anymore. In the past, all bones were carefully gathered together for this was one of the greater *tirigusuusiit*.[62]

He feels that Inuit should be in charge of wildlife themselves.

> It is the Inuit who should be in charge of their land because we do not try to hunt caribou until they are extinct. We have always tried to be careful with our hunting. This is what I think. There has been a quota placed on polar bears. In the past we had no quotas. Because there is a quota system in place in the communities today, it seems that the number of bears killed has increased because the people keep hunting them until the quota has

been met. I believe if Inuit were free to hunt polar bear they would be killing fewer bears than they actually are. In the past I remember that we wouldn't even get five polar bears over the winter. Now because of the quotas they hunt them until they reach that number.[63]

Today the management of wildlife is one of the central political issues in Nunavut. It is still conceived as the foundation of the relationship between Inuit and land. Many Inuit, and particularly the elders, do not trust biologists.[64] Barnabas Peryouar from Qamanittuaq explained, "Biologists don't believe us when we tell them that they are making the caribou change their routes by bothering them. Biologists never grew up on the land with caribou, they never learned about caribou all their lives like the Inuit. People who grew up with caribou and lived by the rules of the seasons know more about them, they know what to do to keep caribou from turning back from the crossing, but they are not heard from."[65]

Animals – like human beings – were believed to have a *tarniq*, an image or shade, that survived after death. Animals might be able to adopt the appearance of a human being, they might even have *isuma* (reason), but they lacked an important feature that distinguished human beings from them. Animals did not have a name that connected them to deceased ancestors. Only dogs received a name, but that name connected them not to their ancestors, but to their human owners.[66]

ATIQ, THE NAME

A child only became a complete person when it received an *atiq*, a name, usually from a deceased relative. The word *atiq* means "name" as well as "namesake" and therefore refers to a relation, not to an essence. According to Rasmussen (1929, 172), "A child cries for a name, and when the one whose name-soul is to take up its dwellings in the newly born infant is summoned, care must be taken that all qualities that soul possessed are communicated to the child." When a child was born it received a name in order to become a human being and food in order to grow. A child could be killed before, but not after, it had received a name.[67]

Some Nattilingmiut thought that people who had died wanted to go on living on earth and would choose the newborn person in whom they wanted to live again.[68] During the naming process, the people would try to determine which deceased person wanted to be reborn. When the child was not satisfied with its name and continued crying, a new name had to be given. Janet Uqayuituq described a slightly different procedure in Qamanittuaq: "Naming children our parents' way is like this: we are in labour and the baby wants to be born but can't, so the people attending the birth start saying names and when a name that the baby wants to be named is said, then the baby would be born. Even when people are saying different names, if they don't say a name of someone that the baby wants to be named after, it won't be born for a while."[69]

According to Boas (1901, 32), the Inuit at Cumberland Sound assumed that the soul of a deceased person entered the body of its namesake and remained there for about four months. "It is believed that its presence strengthens the child's soul, which is very light, and apt to escape from the body. After leaving the body of the infant, the soul of the departed stays near by, that it may re-enter the infant in case of need."

The Iglulingmiut believed that the deceased gave constant support to their living namesakes: "We obtain aid from our namesakes when we strive with all our strength against any peril," and "Our namesakes and the namesakes of our namesakes are near us all."[70] The Iglulik *angakkuit* said that on their spirit flights, they could see behind each human being a procession of spirits aiding and guiding as long as the rules of life were observed, but when the rules were not observed and a man was tempted to act in a way that the dead disapproved of, then all the invisible guardians turned against him as enemies and he was lost beyond hope.[71]

People inherited their strength and skill from their namesake. The namesake relationship enabled people to share in the qualities of their ancestors and thus to become strong and successful as human beings. When people became ill, they were often given a new name to support them.[72] It was advantageous to have more than one name. Among the Nattilingmiut, it was common to have five to ten names. The old woman Maniilaq told Rasmussen (1931, 221): "I am named Manelaq because when that name was mentioned I came out of my mother's womb. Taqalekitaq was a name I once got while I was ill, and it mended me … I was held up solely by names. It is because of names that we breathe, and it is also because of them that we can walk on our legs. Through all these names I have grown old. I have withstood the attacks of shamans and all the dangers that would otherwise have uprooted me from the dwelling places of man.

The name played a central part in maintaining the continuity of society, connecting the Inuit to their deceased namesakes. Among the Iglulingmiut, children were not allowed to address old people by name, only by terms of relationship.[73] Francois Quassa related: "You should never call an older person by name. To this day, if I call someone by name and he is older, I feel very uncomfortable. We were always told to respect our elders and never to use their names. If for some reason, just by a slip of the tongue, we called an elder by his or her name, we were scolded. It was forbidden."[74] Names were not gender specific, and a person might receive the name of a deceased person of the opposite sex. Alexina Kublu from Iglulik, for example, was named after her grandfather, Kublu.

It was especially the name that made a human being a social person and distinguished him or her from animals and other beings that did not have names that defined their social identity. The continuity of a community was maintained through the transfer of the names of the deceased to their descendants. The name did not refer to an essence or intrinsic quality of the individual being named, but rather to an ancestor of the living namesake. It was a relational identity. The namesake relationship also implied that the social relationships of a deceased person could be transferred to his or her namesake.[75] Today, some people still have many names, as described by Alexina Kublu:

> My sister Michelline holds numerous names. She calls me *inurlak* (almost a person). I call her *angak* (maternal uncle). I don't know the reason for either *tuq&urausiq* (way of referring to someone). I refer to her as Michelline because both Ataguttaaluk and Ukumaaluk are equally important. By using the name Michelline a choice between the two is avoided. My mother called her by her name Ataguttaaluk because she was named as such after my father's young brother. She is also named Ukumaaluk after my mother's father. Often my mother would say to her: "*Kinagigakkit*?" (What do I have you as?) Michelline would reply: "*Ataatagigavinga*" (You have me as a father). One of her names, Aakuainnuk, had been an exceptionally tall man. While he was still alive, he used to say that he was going to be wonderfully short when he would return in his *atiqs*. I know of four people named after him and they are not even five feet tall.[76]

Whereas the dead continued an anonymous existence in the lands of the dead, their individual skills, abilities, and appearance were passed on by their names. The deceased wished to be reborn.[77] They might inform a pregnant woman or her relatives about their wishes. Fanny Arngnasungaaq from Qamanittuaq explained, "If that person has been dreamt of more than once … and if you know the person well … the person in your dreams is letting you know that she wants you to be her [parents]."[78]

Kublu herself had experienced how the deceased may claim a child as an *atiq*:

> A few days after my daughter was born I dreamt that Andre (Nattiq, Attaarjuat, Utuqqaq) Aqatsiaq came to visit me and my new-born baby in the hospital. Just then, the hospital registrar came along to register my daughter's birth. I filled out everything but kept the space for the father blank. Andre told the registrar to write his name in the blank. I told him that I did not want his name on the paper, that I did not want him with me, that I did not want him to be named in my daughter. He then said: "If you just use my church name Andre and my government name Aqatsiaq,[79] then your child doesn't have to use any of my names." I again said to him that I did not want him with my daughter at all, that she was not going to be named after him. At that point I was woken up by my daughter crying. A few day later after, I got out of the hospital. Andre's father Aqaattiaq held my daughter in his arms and said: "Angutiq atigijumajarauna" (I want her to be my *angutiqati*, paternal cousin). His son had been named Nattiq after his paternal uncle Qutittalik/Arraq's son. My daughter does not carry Andre's name Utuqqaq, but she did call his mother *nuliarainnuk* (wonder-

ful wife) because he had been named after her first husband Attaarjuat also.[80]

The meaning of the dream could not be ignored when Andre's father addressed the child as his *angutiqati*. It is better for the child if a parent complies with the wishes of the deceased and the elders.

When people do not want to choose between two names, they may take recourse to a Christian name to solve the problem. Kublu referred to one of her sisters as Michelline in order to avoid choosing between the names Ataguttaaluk and Ukumaaluk. Similarly, her sister Qunngaatalluriktuq addressed Kublu's daughter as Papatsi to avoid having to choose between Amak&ak and Akittiq.

The introduction of Christian names did not really affect the old system, as Inuit continued to identify with their ancestors through names and integrated the old traditions into the new naming system. According to the Oblate missionary Turquetil, Inuit were familiar with the idea that the spirits of the deceased in heaven wished to help their descendants, and when everyone had received a Christian name, they felt happy: "I asked someone whether he liked his name. Oh yes, he said, Joseph was good and his name will live in me and he will help me."[81] Some Catholic missionaries, such as Father Daniélo (1949, 14), emphasized the values of the old traditions: "One should not suppress the beautiful custom of nominal kinship that preserves the memory of the elders and, purified by the church, becomes the cult of our deceased." Stevenson (1993, 154) emphasizes the enduring importance of the naming system in Panniqtuuq as "one of the cornerstones of Central Inuit ideology."

There was some opposition to the old system, however, especially among Anglican missionaries. Samuel Arnakallak from Mittimatalik (1993 interview) recalled: "I remember that one of the first missionary here [Mittimatalik] didn't want that we have our Inuit names anymore because those names were from the dead (I mean to be named after a dead person). But when he left, we got our names back again. Mr Daulby used to say that dead people were calling dead people. But as we didn't like the idea, Inuit took their names again." And Trott (1988, 71) observes with respect to the community of Ikpiarjuk, "There has been intense pressure on the part of missionaries to eliminate the naming practices as it requires "pagan" beliefs to continue. The naming system as a system of relating to other people, has remained in place."

According to Kublu, new and modern naming traditions have become integrated:

> The fact that the tradition of giving sickly children a name is still being practised was illustrated by my niece Stella's newborn son. As he was born, people were aware that there were one or two people for him to be named after. He has since ended up with seven *atiit* in addition to his church name and his government identity. As he was only four months old when his last

name was given and also because he was such a sickly baby, his identity among the people had not yet solidified. Stella informed me of the names that were given him. He started off being Akittiq X 3, meaning he was named Akittiq after the husband of my father's cousin who died of cancer, Akittiq for the son of my father's nephew who had committed suicide, and Akittiq for the son of my father's brother who was hit by a car. He was also given the name Mainu/Siqujjut of his paternal grandmother's father whose *atiit* are now in their forties. Moreover, he received the name of his paternal grandfather's father, Ujarak, whose *atiit* are around six years old. He also carries the names of Nasuk and his wife Killaq. Killaq is a name that fits the proper time frame (around a year or so) but Nasuk died about six years earlier. At the time his paternal grandfather said that maybe Maliki/Qamaniq would help to make the child strong. Stella brought him to the church and had him baptized Jeremy Tyrone for good measure. These two names were the church names of the two young Akittiqs.[82]

Each name carries a history as well as a network of relationships. Through the names passed down, society reproduces itself and connects to its past. A complex system of terms of address ensures that the relationships embedded in the names are acknowledged. Kublu describes her own naming:

> I am named Kublu/Nuqallaq after my maternal step-great-grandfather. This name was given to me even before my birth, because he had died while my mother was pregnant with me. There was no other person before him to hold the name Kublu, "thumb," because this name was given to him as a child to deter him from the habit of sucking his thumb.
>
> The names Aapak/Imaruittuq were given to me at birth by my mother's midwife Qajugasukkaaq. She held me and said "una irnira" (this is my son). Therefore I bear the name of her son. I called her *akkak* (father's brother) as her son had done, and her husband was my *ataata* (father). They both called me *irniq*, son. Her eldest daughter Ingnirjuk was my *arnaqati* (maternal cousin of the same sex) and her second daughter Panikpakuttuk is my *aliqannaaksaq* (older sister). I carry only those two names of my mother's midwife's son. He carried numerous other names such as Uttuttiaq, Sigalaakuluk, and Imaruittuq's names Paniaq and Ukaliannuk.
>
> The name Alexina was given to me by the Catholic church when my *panik* (daughter; in this case my maternal grandmother) brought me to the church when I was three hours old, and had me baptized.
>
> I called my own father Kupaaq *ningauruluk* (horrible son-in-law) because no man would have been good enough for my *atiq*'s first grandchild, and my mother Arnainnuk my *irngutaq* (grandchild) …

> My mother's mother Iqallijuq, calls me *ataatakuluk* (fatherkuluk). She is my *panik*. Her two step-sisters Uriuqtuq and Nattiq, Kublu's actual daughters, both called me *ataata*. Kublu's oldest son Maktaaq from his second marriage to Ataguttiaq calls me *ataata*, and I call him *irniq*. His wife Kupaaq is my *ukuaq* (daughter-in-law). She does not have the same name as my father. I have been able to find out that Kublu's mother's name had been Quliit, because I called one of "my" (i.e. my grandfather Kublu's) children *anaanakuluk* (motherkuluk). I don't remember my mother's father Ukumaaluk, but his *atiqs* call me *ningaukuttuk* (brother/cousin-in-law), because of Kublu's marriage to Ataguttiaq.[83]

Today young Inuit have to rely on elders to explain to them the meaning of names and the terms of address they imply. A reconstruction of the past reveals a person's relationship to those whose names she or he was given. Still, the importance of ancestors has by no means been properly recognized. Inuit emphasize that they owe their survival to their ancestors. The ancestors not only live on in the lands of the dead but also in the land where they are buried and in the children who are named after them.

CONCLUSION

Over centuries, Inuit have received the names of their deceased ancestors. After death, their *tarniq* would go to a land of the dead while their name would be passed on in the community. Animals that were killed did not go to a land of the dead, but their *tarniit* reincarnated in other animals. The *tarniq* of a human being could reincarnate in an animal, as the story of Arnaqtaaqtuq illustrates, but it was usually assumed that it travelled to a land of the dead.

The distinction between animals and Inuit was especially articulated in the practice of naming. Even though dogs or pets could receive a name, animals were essentially anonymous, caught in a cycle of continuous rebirth in which they would become prey to hunters.[84] Inuit were connected through ancestors by names, and in the names the continuity of society took shape.

As hunters, Inuit were responsible for the cycle of the game, and they used to assume that animals had to be hunted in order to remain numerous. In modern Inuit society, people easily integrate this responsibility into the modern ideology of sustainable development. The rules of the past are transformed into respect for the land and nature, and it is recognized that the task of human beings is to protect the animals.[85] However, most Inuit do not accept the idea that animals would be protected if hunting were restricted. Many remain convinced that only by hunting animals can the game be protected. In a paper on the seal as part of Inuit culture, six students from Arctic College write: "Inuit spirituality is not just shamanism or Christianity. An important aspect of spirituality is to be able to provide for your family."[86] For the students, the hunting life lies at the core of

Inuit cosmology. They state emphatically: “The seal, however, provides us with more than just food and clothes. It provides us with our identity. It is through sharing and having a seal communion that we regain our strength, physically and mentally.”[87]

Animals and human beings may share a common origin, but they have a different position in the cycle of the hunt. Even though some animals, such as bears[88] and wolves, are recognized as hunters, they are not supposed to kill and eat people. Human beings should only be eaten after death, whereas animals can be killed to be served as food. In this normative perspective, Inuit are viewed as hunters and animals as prey. This distinction takes shape through the name: human beings are connected to the ancestors through their names, whereas animals lack such a connection and are subject to a continuous circle of reincarnation. The traditional naming system has been combined with the Canadian naming system, and today Inuit continue to believe that people are closely connected to their deceased namesakes. They derive important qualities from their namesakes, who watch over them and protect them as long as they observe the moral rules that maintain society. Ancestors live on in names. The continuity of society takes shape in those names just as cultural continuity takes shape in the naming system.

The notion of *tarniq* was integrated into Christianity in the concept of soul. The missionaries assumed that only human beings had a soul and that animals did not have one. Inuit accepted this view, but they continued to respect animals and the land. Today, the ritual rules have been replaced by the moral obligation to respect animals. But the relations human beings have with the land and prey are still perceived as the foundation of Inuit culture and society.

5

The Owners of the Sky, the Land, and the Sea

INTRODUCTION

In this chapter we will examine the non-human agencies connected to the sky, the land, and the sea. These agencies would sanction human beings if they transgressed the rules of life. The sea and the sky each had an *inua*, its person or owner. We will explore the place of these owners in Inuit beliefs and practices. The earth, *nuna*, could not be associated with one particular *inua*, but was inhabited by many non-human beings and held the graves of the deceased. The importance of the land and the deceased has often been overlooked in studies of Inuit religion and cosmology.[1] We will explore how the land has retained its central importance in Inuit cosmology. The animals of the land usually had an *inua*, and *angakkuit* were able to see them and communicate with them.

With the adoption of Christianity, the notion of *inua* disappeared almost completely and God replaced the sea woman as the owner of the animals. Respect for the land and the weather continues to be a marked feature of Inuit culture. While the stories about the sun and the moon and the sea woman are almost forgotten, many features of the shamanic complex – particularly the sea woman – now re-emerge to take shape in the context of the arts.

THE MORAL ORDER OF THE WORLD

In their perceptions of the world, Inuit have emphasized a close connection between the weather, the land, the animals, and human behaviour. If human beings misbehave, the weather, the land, or the animals will retaliate. Lucaasie Nutaraaluk from Iqaluit observed, "I believe we are disciplined for our actions through the weather. Ottawa and Montreal are perfect examples [this interview was conducted right after the ice storm of 1997]. I believe a lot of people just see that as an act of nature or a scientifically explainable act, but to my mind they are being disciplined for what we have done. Anytime there is too much wrongdoing being committed we get disciplined in various ways such as earthquakes. Even here in Iqaluit if we start fighting too much there could be an earthquake or really bad weather could come upon us."[2]

The land is shaped by the thoughts of people, and when the land is good to you, you have to reciprocate with a gift. Margaret Uyauperk Aniksak from Arviat stated, "If people are careless and the earth is damaged, then surely, healthy growth will not occur. The earth is shaped by people's thoughts … Any land you have been to previously must be given something as a token of receiving something good in return."[3] In the workshop in Arviat in 2007, Thomas Ubluriak from Arviat said that when you enter a new land, you should give a token, and Margaret Hannah from Arviat stated that even as Christians you should give a token at certain places, probably out of respect for the hardships suffered by the people who had lived there. At a meeting in Churchill in 2008, Henri I&luarnik from Arviat suggested that an elder who was not feeling well should give a token to the earth if she had just returned to the place where she had grown up.

The relationship between people and the world is embedded in a moral order according to which all actions are reciprocated by agencies such as the sky and the weather, the land and the animals. Missionaries, explorers, and ethnographers assumed that the belief in one or more gods constituted the core of a religion. They tried to assess which non-human beings constituted the most important deities or even the supreme being of the Inuit. Sila, the sky, and Sedna, the sea woman, have both been considered as the supreme deity. Rasmussen (1929, 62) suggests that the sea woman was the highest deity and that others were subordinated to her, "both Sila and Tarqeq … acting as agents to see that her will is obeyed."

But the Inuit did not have a concept that corresponded to the white people's notion of deity. Inuk author Rachel Qitsualik (1999, 12) observes with respect to the sea woman, "Unfortunately they assumed that this aquatic female character was a goddess which Inuit did not have." Rasmussen (1929, 62) was well aware of the problem:

> It will now be clearly apparent, from the statements of the Eskimos themselves, as above quoted, that the idea of a God, or group of gods, to be worshipped, is altogether alien to their minds. They know only powers or personifications of natural forces, acting upon human life in various ways, and affecting all that lives through fair and foul weather, disease and perils of all kinds. These powers are not evil in themselves, they do not wreak harm of evil intent, but they are nevertheless dangerous owing to their unmerciful severity where men fail to live in accordance with the wise rules of life decreed by their forefathers … The term used by the Hudson Bay Eskimos for the guiding powers is *Ersigiʃavut*, "those we fear," or *mianeriʃavut*, "those we keep away from and regard with caution."

In his writings about the Inuit, Rasmussen took recourse to concepts such as "powers" and "personifications of natural forces," since the concept of God seemed inappropriate. Obviously these solutions raised new problems, as the concept of nature was as foreign to Inuit as that of God. Today the Inuktitut word *Guti* does not refer to a category of supernatural beings, but specifically to the Christian God.

Most researchers continued to use terms such as "deity" or "god" (e.g., Thalbitzer 1926, 1928; Savard 1970) for the owners of the sea, the moon, and the sky.[4] Merkur (1991, 37) observes, "Certainly the Inuit have no term corresponding precisely to 'deity' or 'god.'" But he thinks this should not prevent us from using these terms. He continues: "What we, as Westerners, mean by the terms 'deity' and 'god' remains vague; but a de facto consensus applies the terms as honorifics to the greater *inue*, while denying them to the greatest of spirits. For this reason I see no reason to object to their continued use."

Unfortunately, the plural *inue* (used by Merkur) makes little sense in Inuktitut. The word *inua* is composed of the root *inu* and a suffix *possessivum "–a"* referring to the third person singular. It is best translated as "its person," with the connotations of "its inhabitant" or "its owner." The words *inua* and *inuk* (pl. *inuit*) are closely connected. The word *inuk* refers to a person and *inuit* to people, but they are by no means universal terms that can be applied to all people. Indians (*allait*) and white people (Qallunaat) are not Inuit. They do not speak Inuktitut (like an Inuk), and they do not hunt like Inuit. *Inua* is a relational term. Thus, one may speak of *tariup inua* ("of the sea, its person," i.e., the person of the sea), but there is no point in speaking of an *inua* or *inuat* (pl.) as a general concept. The concept can only be used when the being or object it refers to is specified. Moreover, terms such as "deity" or "god" may be honorific concepts in a cultural tradition that attributes gods and deities to great civilizations and spirits to primitive cultures, but this tradition does not contribute to a better understanding of Inuit culture.

Terms such as "sea mother" (used in Merkur 1991) and "sea woman" (Sonne 1990) have the advantage that they reflect this relational quality of the concept, but they specify the gender of the person, and this is not done in Inuktitut. In this book, we opt for the terms "sea woman" and "moon man," which emphasize the human origin of the *inua* of the sea and the *inua* of the moon. Takanakapsaluk, the sea woman, and Tatqiq, the moon man, were originally human beings. Sila, the *inua* of the sky and the weather, was originally a giant. The sea woman, the moon man, and Sila were transformed because of evil actions. The Nattilik woman Nalungiag explained this to Rasmussen (1931, 209–10): "But sun and moon and stars, thunder and lightning, are all people who once have gone out into space ... Evil actions and taboo-breakings have populated the air with spirits. The sun and the moon murdered their mother, and, though they were brother and sister, they loved each other. For that reason they ceased to be humans."

Whereas the sea woman and the moon man have a name and human origin, *nuna* (the land) and Sila (the sky) preceded human beings.

NUNA, THE LAND

Inuit myths of the origin of human beings tell us that in the past the first human beings were created from the earth, from *niaqutait* – hummocks of earth.[5] The first children were produced by the earth, and originally people ate earth.[6] Earth was a source of life, and the first two people did not die, but returned to the soil.[7] The reproductive and alimentary cycles were encompassed by earth until human beings learned to reproduce themselves and to hunt for game. Some animals were produced by the earth. The caribou, for instance, came from the earth and were referred to as "lice of the earth" in the language of the *tuurngait* (helping spirits).[8]

The earth must be respected, for if it wasn't, it might take action against human beings. Rasmussen (1929, 19) relates, "The earth grew angry if men out hunting worked too much with stones and turf in the building of their meat stores and hunting depots." Among the Nattilingmiut, "[t]he earth, and everything belonging to it – stones, grass, turf, etc. – are sacred throughout the whole of the summer, both at the salmon places and at nablut; for this reason alone stone huts must never be built, nor must one break stones, pluck grass, or wipe the hands on grass."[9] It was also forbidden to have sex with the earth "by making hollows in hummocks of earth and committing onanism there."[10] This prohibition may refer to the origin myth of the first human beings, who originated from hummocks of earth.

The Iglulingmiut believed that if people stayed in a place too long, the earth became hot and this would affect their well-being. Eugene Amarualik (IE 287) from Iglulik told how people would leave their old home after three years of occupation so that the land would not "get hot" (*uunarsiqunagu*). For this reason, his community had been moved from Avvajja to Iglulik. Amarualik described how the camp leader Ittusardjuat had made the decision: "Before his death he (Ittusardjuat) made it known that he wanted the place to be abandoned for three years so that the land will get a chance to cool down. It was because of that [that] the rest of the family members never returned. It might be unfair bad for him because the rest of the family did not return. He had requested that Avvajja be allowed to cool for three years and my father heard him say that."[11]

Living within a community is associated with hotness, and it is generally assumed that living on the land outside the community is healthy and refreshes and invigorates a person. Traditionally, it was thought that places where no human traces could be found in the snow were especially appropriate for making contact with spirits and other non-human beings. People in the North Baffin area would go to such places and pray by shouting words (*qinngaq*) or the name of a person to seek help in a dangerous situation, to locate wildlife, or to improve the weather.[12] According to Rose Iqallijuq from Iglulik, every adult could *qinngaq* in a situation of need, but not children. A person who wanted to *qinngaq* should go away from the camp to an area with fresh snow. This would help the person reach the deceased. Ujaraq from Iglulik recalled: "We were shouting to the air asking that these men be brought in safety. When my father first started to *qinngaq* he let out a long piercing cry. That is how my father started the *qinngaq* when he asked [that] Nataaq and Kublu [be] brought back in safety. He shouted that if there was anything around to help, he wanted them brought back. He first said their names."[13] Nowadays, elders advocate bringing young offenders or people in trouble out onto the land to restore their mental and physical health.

The earth also holds the deceased. The dead were traditionally deposited out on the land, but today they are buried in burial places, which preferably overlook the land or the sea. Thus, the land is covered with graves that are visited by relatives of the deceased and have to be respected. The land is also covered with traces of previous inhabitants: tent rings, remains of sod houses, objects, graves, and *inuksuit*.

The land and the sky cannot be owned by people. They are shared by those who live there. Inuit still consider themselves to be *nunaqqatigiit*, those who share land, or *silaqqatigiit*, those who share the air, the wind, the weather.

RESPECTING PLACES

When travelling on the land, people need to know where the good hunting areas can be found and which places are dangerous and should be avoided. Some places are only safe if certain rules are observed. Boas (1901, 150) reports, "When travellers approach a hill in Tununirn, they must turn a somersault. Only old people are exempt from this custom." As burial grounds are often located on high places, these places are likely to be associated with deceased people. Marble Island is well known for the rules that apply to visitors. Takornaq told Rasmussen (1929, 26–7) that she saw an old Qairnirmiut woman from Qamanittuaq (Baker Lake).

> I was told that this old woman was the first who ever saw Oqshoriaq. Before that time, it was nothing but a heap of pressure ridges in the ice. It was not until later that the ice turned to the white stone we call Oqshoriaq. I remember the first time we came to that island, we had to crawl up on to the land, and were not allowed to stand upright until we reached the top. That was done then, and it is done to this day, for the Island is a sacred place; magic words made it, and if we do not show respect for it by crawling it will change to ice again, and all the people on it will fall through and drown.

Rasmussen (1929, 76) reports that Marble Island was a special place where no woman was allowed to work, and Boas (1901, 151) notes, "In olden times Marble Island was a low black rock on which the ice used to be piled up. One day a widow was looking out to sea. When she gazed at the piles of ice, the ice became displeased, and was turned into stone." Since then, people have crawled up on their knees and elbows. Saladin d'Anglure (2006, 74–6) connects this crawling practice to the *ukpikarniq* jump, which in the very first days of humanity, when death did not yet exist, allowed Inuit to rejuvenate themselves. He also compares it to a similar practice described by Moses Nuvalingaq from Sanikiluaq, who said that when a person arrives at a place for the first time, he or she has to crawl like a baby and say, "Ungaa! Ungaa! Ungaa!"[14]

On Marble Island, the custom of crawling is still practised today. Felix Kupak from Naujaat related:

> The reason why they do things there is because it was formed from ice that was breaking up. It used to be ice. Uqsuriak became a rock. Even today, people of my age, when we go there by boat, we don't walk to the land. There is some earth on that island, but it's mostly rock. When you crawl onto it you have great joy getting onto the island, crawling toward the land from the sea. Another thing I heard, the story must have been from around here, was about these people who went there by boat, a peterhead. Once you get to Uqsuriak you have to crawl, not walk, but just a short distance. You don't have to crawl all the way. I heard that this person said, "Why do I have to crawl? It is just land." As soon as he got off the boat, he started walking. He died right there because he didn't obey the traditional law … There are strange places like this, where something happened a long time ago; they have been touched by something.[15]

Other islands also had to be approached with care. Margaret Uyauperk Aniksak from Arviat remembered "a custom where Inuit would imitate a person almost falling over as they stepped onto the shore of Sentry Island as they arrived to spend the summer hunting. They would park the bow of their boat on the shore, step off and pretend to almost fall over. There was a special custom where Inuit would turn their heads in the direction of the land when they approached Uhuganarnaat (Maguse River), Akuq (mouth of Maguse River) and Arviaqjuaq (Sentry Island). This custom has long been abandoned."[16]

Andy Mamgark from Arviat spoke of "an island called Tuurngaqtialaaq. There have been numerous cases where the objects disappeared on people and this is for real. Uqaqtialaaq … wanted to prove this myth by staying overnight at the spot on his way to Baker Lake. He spent the night there deliberately. That very night his lead dog died."[17]

George Agiaq Kappianaq recalled various places near Iglulik that were considered dangerous:

> I have heard of such places near Iglulik where I am from. On the mainland we did not go to the central area often, especially towards the west, where

> there is a place called Isiriaq. Even when you are close to this hill, it looks as though it is far away. It seems to be shimmering. When people were out caribou hunting, they never camped nearby. They did not even climb up on it to search for caribou. You would hear voices of people that were not part of the group you were with at that place.
>
> In the inlets there is another place called Pingurjuaq. There is an *inuksugaq* up on top of it. People rarely went on top of that hill. People did occasionally climb it whereas they never climbed Isiriaq on the west side. Further south there is a place called Kaaksaq. If you had a tent near the top, you would hear the sound of laughter all night long, even more than at Isiriaq. It was said that when my father and people his age were growing up, before we started living in Maniituq, they went fishing around there, when the fish were spawning up river at a place called Ikiq. They could hear the sound of people all night long. Fish do not always run in that river. Maybe there were *tarriassuit* [invisible or shadow people] who did not want people to come around.
>
> To the south of Iglulik there are also two little hills that people never climbed because if they did, they would experience danger. Even recently, a few years ago, someone put a fox trap there, and that person lost his strength there guiding his dogs. I went hunting around Kaaksaq with my father, and we set up a tent. I could hear noises. We stayed up quite late. The adults did not seem to notice it, but you could hear the sound of laughter. We set up a tent near Kaaksaq, because my father wanted to know more about it. Those were the main places that I have heard about or experienced personally that were known to be dangerous.[18]

Kappianaq added that people should still respect these places, for "[e]ven though we have become Christians, the land hasn't changed." He emphasized that one should not challenge the wisdom of the elders: "When people, through experience, have learned about these places, they caution others about them. If a person knowingly decides to challenge this knowledge and goes there, he will lose his strength. It is usually hills and high places that are dangerous."

Lakes are also places that sometimes have to be approached with caution. Boas (1901, 150) reports, "No woman is allowed to look at a large pond near Iglulik while it is open. Should she do so, she would become blind. The men like to hunt caribou in this pond. While they are staying there, their huts are put up behind a hill, out of sight of the pond. When a caribou is killed, they take it ashore and break off one antler, which is pushed into the ground with the foot. When a man who is hunting alone has killed a caribou in this pond, he must not eat of it until he finds some company."

At the workshop in Kugaaruk in 2004, Kupak from Naujaat related, "Close to Aivilik, there is a lake. We were told never to camp near that lake for some reason. We can't camp there. We Inuit believe in these things. Some places can be scary and dangerous." Reverend Armand Tagoona (1975) from Qamanittuaq gives the example of Dubawnt Lake: "The Inuit are afraid of that lake, because, they say, it has big fishes, fishes that swallow human beings and even whole caribou. When I told the Qablunaat the story they just laughed and said, 'There is no fish that big that could swallow men. But there could be something else, not fish.' Is there anybody who would like to go and see if there's any big fishes in Dubawnt Lake? There are stories too about the Inuit who used to make their camps and live around Dubawnt Lake. The Inuit call it Tulimaalugyuaq, that is, the place where there are big ribs. I think it would be interesting to take a look around Tulimaalugyuaq." Andy Mamgark from Arviat recalled, "Qablunaarurgvik (place where Qablunaat originated) is a place we are not allowed to talk about … It is just off the point on the edge of the lake. People are not to approach it directly."[19]

These lakes were places where special rules apply. Not respecting a place might result in a dog dying or a person losing his strength. Neory Aniksak from Arviat recalled, "At this lake in the old days, people were told that they were not allowed to take the legs off the caribou that they had killed, when they skinned them. If a person were to cut the legs off a caribou he would surely die. They were not even allowed to make holes in sealskins in this place. I have heard of one man who snapped his line (made of bearded sealskin) by accident, and threw it to the dogs so he would not have bad luck. The dog died that day."[20]

Places where *inuksuit* were built also had their own traditions. Monique Kopanuak from Arviat recalled "a place [Avvarii'juak] where no man could go because long ago there was a kayak accident. The two statues [stone pillars] there are of girls who were left behind by their parents, and who did not know where to go. They turned into statues, so from then on no man could even go near the place. They are absolutely not allowed to go there. These two girls were barefoot or naked when they landed, so they were shy of men. From that time on no man could go near them."[21] At the Arviat workshop in 2003, Peter Suvaksiuq from Arviat spoke of what happened to his uncle named Anikkak: "He didn't really believe in stories like that so he went over to see where those two women had turned to stone. He looked down and he saw those two rocks. After that incident he went home and got very sick."

Stones also had healing properties. Philip Kigusiutnak from Arviat recalled, "At Uhuganarnaat there is a sacred stone where people slurp the small hole in the stone. In so doing it is supposed to protect us from sickness."[22] According to Luke Suluk from Arviat, "Any person requiring healing was taken to Kattaujaq, whose name means an entrance: just wide enough for a person to go through with a flat stone at the top forming an arch. The camp healer would have the person pass underneath, and if the stone did not fall, the person would be healed."[23]

Old campsites have to be treated with respect. Jose Angutinngurniq from Kugaaruk talked about this at the Kugaaruk workshop in 2004:

> Old campsites are called *maturniit*. If something sad happened in those places, we should not return there. This is what I heard. I heard this all the time, even up to today. Still today, out of respect, I try not to camp in those places. There are tent rings; they are not to be used again. They are there to stay. You should try not to use the rocks that were used to pitch a tent, whether caribou or seal skin. Rocks were used to tie the skins down. They are not to be used again, because the spirit of that rock might come to you. They are there to stay. You have to put something around the rock, and not touch it. If you are going to use it, you have to move it.

Demanding special respect were places where people were buried. In the same workshop, Ollie Itinnuaq from Kangiq&iniq recalled one such place, called Qatiktalik:

> When I used to work for the RCMP, I would take trips to Aivilik with the officers and we would go through Qatiktalik and other places. Sometimes we would leave some food and belongings there. There are five *qallunaat* graves at Qatiktalik. You can still hear their spirits. They are not there anymore, but their sprits are still there. We can hear them. Even the *qallunaat* would hear them. So the RCMP finally told us not to go through there anymore. I travelled there with a person who was part Inuk and part *qallunaat*. His mother was an Inuk and his father was a *qallunaaq*. He didn't believe in traditional beliefs very much. We camped there and even though he didn't believe in those traditional beliefs, he didn't want to be alone. He was afraid to be alone. He wasn't easily scared, but there was something in Qatiktalik.

Itinnuaq added that his parents maintained their traditional beliefs even after they started going to church. Even today many elders still emphasize the need to respect certain places.

The land was scattered with graves, and people would know where the graves of their relatives were and visit those places. A visit to the grave of a dead person was considered beneficial for the living person. Iqallijuq from Iglulik related, "Whenever we went to the land where my namesake was buried, my mother would always take me to the grave … Now you can see me as an old lady: there were times when I almost died but I was able to recover because of visiting that grave. As a matter of fact, I was given the sacrament of last rites on two occasions when I was comatose. Both times I was able to recover, and so I know that it helps to visit the grave of your namesake."[24]

Graves could be found all over the land, and people had to know the places where the deceased were buried so they could observe the rules pertaining to those places. Margaret Uyauperk Aniksak remembered how one elder wanted to be treated after death: "Even though he died a very old man his desire for people to be happy never ended. He left a wish that whenever people passed by his place of death that they should make jokes to make him laugh. This would bring luck to the hunter. He wanted to live a happy life on earth while he lived, so he left a wish for people to stretch the rim of their eyes wide open as a joke, to make him laugh and for good luck in hunting. He wanted people to laugh at him or joke about him ... The people just followed his wish, since he was a very old man. Some Inuit were very respectful to elders, so his wish naturally became a custom."[25]

In the 2003 workshop in Arviat, Suvaksiuq from Arviat related how he was cured by honouring the wishes of the deceased and visiting their graves: "On an island there is a grave there. He used to tell people to stop there for tea. Three years ago while I was alone I went down there for tea. I wanted to find out what it was like. I took a thermos. The grave was exposed. You could see the bones. They weren't covered at all, at Qikiqtarjuat, just a little way from here. I had tea and I said I was tired of being sick. The next day I got rid of my sickness. When you test something sometimes it will really happen."

In the past, a corpse was deposited out on the land. Stones were placed around it, but it was not covered and thus it would be devoured by dogs or wild animals. Burial deposits, usually personal belongings and miniatures, were placed beside the body. After the corpse had been devoured by animals, only the bones and the objects remained.

The bones and the objects should be respected and left alone. Human bones are scattered over the earth and bleached by Sila.[26] There was an old custom to turn the bones found on the land,[27] but they should not be taken away. Their removal by archaeologists caused great concern among Inuit and is still a matter of controversy. At a conference in Quebec in November 2007, former Nunavut commissioner Peter Irniq (2008) asked for the return to Nunavut of the human remains and burial deposits that were removed by Qallunaat.

SILA, THE SKY

Sila is a concept that embraces a wide range of related categories, such as the sky, the weather, and the outside.[28] The direction of Sila is the direction in which the sun moves, and this is the direction that normally has to be followed. During an elders' conference in Rankin in 2002, the direction of Sila was not respected at the start of an introductory round, and the elders were greatly perturbed. Sila is associated with reason, and a person without Sila is a person without reason. Sila refers to the world and its order as it is represented by the movements of the constellations in the sky.

To what extent Sila can be considered a person is unclear. In the South Baffin sources (notably Boas and Peck), little attention is given to that concept. Rasmussen in particular emphasizes the significance of Sila as the *inua* or owner of the sky in the Nattilik and Iglulik area. Here Sila seems to have been identified with Nârssuk (Nattilik), Narshuk, or Nartsuk (Iglulik), the child of a giant often represented as a baby. This identification apparently also existed in the South Baffin area. Nutaraaluk from Iqaluit remembered, "My father used to tell me about this. *Naarjuk* is the name of the weather spirit, *silaup inua*. According to my father the spirit is said to be female and is very strong."[29] Today, elders have few recollections about Sila as a person. Aupilaarjuk from Kangiq&iniq observed, "Naarjuk is the name of the *silaup inua* but I rarely heard of that spirit. But I often heard how powerful that spirit was ... Naarjuk is said to be very powerful. In Kangiq&iniq there is one person I talked to, who told me that the weather had a very powerful spirit. This person I talked with, heard this from Qimuksiraaq. Qimuksiraaq said that the weather had a very powerful spirit."[30]

Tagoona (1975) wondered whether *silaup inua* was a distinct entity: "Are they not the Silaup inungit, that is, 'people of the air'? Inuit used to believe that there is a silaup inua, or "Man of the air," who controls everything and watches the Inuit. When he comes in sight you must not stand on your feet or you might get hit on the head because your head might be a little too high."

According to Rasmussen (1929, 71), "Among the Iglulingmiut and the Aivilingmiut this spirit is regarded more than all else as a personification of the weather, and therefore, instead of Sila, the term persəq is used, meaning snowstorm, or even anəre, the wind."

In the Nattilik and Iglulik areas, some mythical traditions are connected with Sila or Narsuk. Rasmussen (1929, 72) writes:

> Nartsuk, also pronounced Narshuk, was originally the child of a giant and his wife, both of whom were murdered, first the father, then the mother killed. This evil-doing turned the child into a spirit, which flew up into the sky and became the lord of the weather. It is always dressed in a full costume of caribou skin – a dress with tunic and breeches made in one piece, and very wide, as worn by children generally. When Nartsuk shakes his dress, air rushes out from all the loose space in his clothing, and the winds begin to blow.
>
> When the spirit of the winds keeps on blowing and there is no peace for men to go out hunting by land or sea, then a shaman has to go up into the sky and beat him, thrash him with a whip, until he calms down and the storms subside.[31]

Nakasuk from Iglulik told Rasmussen that the "wickedness of mankind turned him [the spirit of the wind] into a tonraq [helping spirit]."[32] Rasmussen (1929, 72) adds, "The Spirit of the Wind has a face almost like that of a human being, but shamans relate that it has a very thin covering of hair, rather like that of a bear; this hair, however, is found only on the face and hands." His size and force are recurrent topics in stories about Sila. His penis was enormous. Four women could sit on it.[33] Rasmussen (1929, 71–2) tells an Iglulik story illustrating the power of Sila. A man found a little child on a great plain. When he thought of killing him, a voice said, "If you kill me, then the world will perish" (sila imiktukƒAra·luk· – literally, "then Sila, the expanse of heaven, will collapse"). According to the Nattilingmiut, one day Sila will destroy the pillars of the world.[34]

Felix Pisuk from Kangiq&iniq related this story:

> There was a giant named Naarjuk from Mittimatalik. When it would fly around, there would be a blizzard. This very nice looking giant was lying down on a skin making noise. Then he started to fly on the skin. When he was in the air, there was a loud noise and a very strong wind, and he would walk in the air. Maybe he's the one who makes the blizzards start. The *angakkuq* would find out what was happening and he would use his long knife to try to scare the wind. He then asked the wind who he was, and he replied he was Naarjuk. That's what they call him in Nattilik. "I think you're the one that makes the weather bad, so I'm going to kill you," the *angakkuq* said. Naarjuk said, "If you kill me the whole world is going to flood." Then Naarjuk got angry that the *angakkuq* was scaring him, and he turned into something else. The *angakkuq* could not strike the wind with his knife. Then the world was surrounded with a rainbow.
>
> He couldn't break through that with his feet. He was going crazy. It was like a *pinguq*, an ice hill. When he touched the ground with his heels, he was walking into the *pinguq*. When he struck the land it made a loud noise, and the *pinguq* was in front of him.
>
> Then he found a way to get out. When he was going out he said, "I will have you as an *ungirlaak*, a bound-up bundle of walrus meat." After the *angakkuq* said that, Naarjuk just nodded his head and felt sorry. The *angakkuq* was furious with him because he had made the wind. When he tied him, he tied him up tightly. Then the weather was very nice with hardly any wind. The people were at sea somewhere up there, either in Ittuaqturvik or in Talurjuaq. When the *angakkuq* was away there were no blizzards, but they had a hard time catching seals. So, the *angakkuq* went back to see the one he had tied up. Naarjuk didn't do anything. He was just standing beside him growing bigger and bigger, and you could hear his teeth chatter because he was very cold. He thought that he was going to freeze, so the *angakkuq* tried to untie him, but he had a hard time taking the rope off. When he loosened the rope, there was snow blowing. You could see the top of the mountains. After that they started catching seals.[35]

The stories emphasize the destructive power of Sila. He is a force to be feared. Ava told Rasmussen (1929, 56), "We fear the weather spirit of earth, that we must fight against to wrest our food from land and sea. We fear Sila." If the weather was bad and the wind continued to blow, *angakkuit* had to calm him down. Boas

(1964 [1888], 593) describes such attempts as carried out on South Baffin: "Storm and bad weather, when lasting a long time and causing want of food, are conjured by making a large whip of seaweed, stepping to the beach, and striking out in the direction whence the wind blows, at the same time crying Taba (It is enough)."

More common in that area was the technique of cutting the wind (*silagiqsaqtuq*). Etuangat Aksaajuq from Panniqtuuq (1995 interview) remembered this practice: "When the weather was pretty bad, windy, the shamans would try to pull it down, using a hook (*niksik*) so they would point that way. Sometimes they would even bleed it, and blood would drop down. Only the shamans would be able to see that, ordinary people could not see it. They would try to tire the wind out, and you could hear it in the air. They would try to cut the wind so that nice weather would come." Nutaraaluk from Iqaluit also described this technique, saying that *angakkuit* "could control the wind. When there were gale force winds, they would get a gaff and a knife to cut the wind. While they were performing this practice with the gaff and a knife, it would be as though they would almost be lifted up. Once they succeeded in cutting the strength of the wind, there would be calm weather."[36]

North Baffin Inuit consider the practice of cutting the tendons of the wind a South Baffin tradition.[37] Rasmussen (1929, 72) describes the Iglulingmiut practice: "When the spirit of the wind keeps blowing and there is no peace for to go out hunting by land or sea, then a shaman has to go up into the sky and beat him, thrash him with a whip, until he calms down and the storms subside."

Storms could also be caused by *silaat*, eggs that were found on the land. Rasmussen (1929, 203) writes, "It is said that they are the children of the earth. Anyone killing such a *silaq* must observe the same taboo as a man who has lost his brother."[38] Today, *silaat* may still be found and careful hunters will leave them alone. From these eggs grew white animals, but if they were prematurely broken, the weather became bad and fierce storms could arise. In similar traditions in the Nattilik area, *silaat* turned into musk oxen.[39] Pisuk from Kangiq&iniq recalled how he had found an earth egg and had told his father about it:

> He said, "Let's go and see what you saw." I took him back there. The narrow part was pointed downwards. He told me it was an earth egg and that if I broke it, [it] would become very windy. He said if we were to cook it whole and eat it, then nothing would happen to the weather, but that the weather would really be aware of it if we broke it. When my father told me you were not supposed to break them, he seemed afraid. He said that if it was really an earth egg, then it would be fresh. It was as fresh as a newly laid egg. My mother cooked it and cut it into pieces, and my brothers and sisters and I all ate it. It was in the Saagluk area near Qamanittuaq.[40]

Silaat will turn into large animals. Angutinngurniq from Kugaaruk commented: "*Silaat* is what they are called after they hatch. I have heard that the eggs are not all the same colour, but they all become *silaat*. They become different animals depending on the colour of the eggs."[41]

The notions of Sila (wind, reason, outside, and weather) and *silaat* are rather abstract categories, devoid of personal features. In the narratives about the giant's child, more personal features emerge in the Nattilik and Iglulik areas, but these cannot be found in other areas. Researchers have ascribed a central position to Sila in Inuit cosmology,[42] but in the older sources the notion of *silaup inua* was already ambiguous.[43]

THE SUN AND THE MOON[44]

Knud Rasmussen (1929, 74) observes that the Iglulingmiut consider the moon spirit to be a friendly one, whereas the Nattilingmiut see him to be a big, strong, and bad-tempered man, often perceived as angry and dangerous: "It may fail to give hunting luck, and even before a man has to die it may carry him away from earth and take him up to the land of the dead."[45]

Regardless of the positive or negative images people have of him, the structural features and characteristics of the moon man as they emerge in myths and shamanic stories are very similar in Iglulik and Nattilik. The famous story of the origin of the sun and moon, though in different versions, can be found in both areas. The Iglulik version collected by Rasmussen (1929, 77-81)[46] relates how a blind boy, Aninga, who lived with his sister, Siqiniq, and his (grand)mother regained his eyesight through the help of a loon. Then he avenged himself on his (grand)mother because she kept the meat of a bear he had killed from him. She turned in a narwhal, and the boy and his sister travelled over the world until they settled down in a camp where they married. While Siqiniq was in the birth hut, people had many song feasts. Her brother often visited her secretly to have sexual intercourse with her. As the girl did not know who her lover was, she blackened his face with soot and followed him into the feasting house. When she found out it was her brother, she was so ashamed that she cut off one of her breasts and offered it to her brother as food. Then she ran out of the feasting house with a torch. Her brother took another torch and pursued her. When they ran around the house, Aninga stumbled and his torch was extinguished. As Aninga continued to pursue her, they began to rise into the sky, and circling around in the sky, they became sun and moon. Siqiniq with her burning torch became the sun and Aninga the moon.

This story exists in many variants. Parts of it can be told separately as isolated stories. A recurrent feature is the connection between the brother-sister incest and the origin of the sun and moon, constellations that regulate time. The brother-sister incest takes place inside the dark *kinirvik*, the birth hut, where the brother cannot be recognized, and he is exposed in the *qaggiq*, the feast house, where the soot markings are noticed by everyone. Once the sister finds out that she had had intercourse with her brother, she cuts off a breast, offering herself as food for her brother. The actions of brother and sister result in a loss of humanity, and they rise to the sky, where they regulate the temporal patterns of the tides, menstruation, the seasons, and the light.

The moon seems to be particularly associated with temporality and transformation.[47] The moon spirit effected the transformation of Kaugjagiuk, who was mistreated as an orphan, into a powerful hunter, able to avenge himself on those who had mistreated him.[48] Rasmussen (1929, 75–6) relates that little boys wishing to become great hunters practised the following ritual:

> At every new moon, they run out to a spot where the snow is clean and free from footmarks. From here they take a lump of snow, and call up to the moon:
>
> "Give me luck in hunting!" Then they run into the house and put the snow into a water vessel. The reason for this is that the seals, who live in salt water, are always thirsty.
>
> And the snow water thus offered is given by the moon to the seals that are to be captured in the future. On the same principle, their mother must sprinkle water out in the direction of the moon, the first time the baby boy in her amaut sees the moon.

The moon is closely associated with the land of the deceased in the sky, Udlormiut. Rasmussen (1929, 73–4) writes, "Human beings who perish by drowning in the sea or in a lake, go to dwell with the moon; so also those who are killed by their fellows openly or unawares, those who take their own lives out of weariness or because they are old, and finally, all women dying in childbirth." The land of the dead in the sky is thus inhabited by those whose life was shortened and who died by violence or by their own choice. The moon seems even to favour the shortening of one's life:

> People in danger can often hear him calling out:
>
> "Come, come to me! It is not painful to die. It is only a brief moment of dizziness. It does not hurt to kill yourself."
>
> Thus the moon sometimes calls, and it is thus also regarded more particularly as the protector of those perishing by accident or suicide.[49]

The Nattilingmiut and Iglulingmiut thought of the moon as a great walrus hunter.[50] Its influence on the sea and the tides was recognized by the Iglulingmiut and explains why he alone in the sky can hunt marine mammals. The moon predicts the success of the hunt. Among the Iglulingmiut, "[t]here is a saying, that if the moon appears to be leaning backwards while it is growing, Inuit weren't happy about it because it's not carrying animals. But if it appears to be leaning forward, people were happier because they believed it is carrying wildlife."[51]

The moon man can help infertile women. Rasmussen (1929, 75) writes:

> When a woman is barren and cannot bear her husband children, it is the moon that helps her. Sometimes this is done simply by letting the full moon shine on her bare lap, but for the most part, the Moon Man himself goes down to earth driving across the Land of the Sky with his team of dogs. He races across the clear sky with great speed; the ground here is smooth ice without snow; through the clouds, progress is slower, for here there is snow underfoot. Thus driving, he comes to visit the village where the barren woman lives; sometimes he will lie with her there, and that is all, but it may also happen that he carries her off to the Land of Heaven and keeps her there, until she is with child. Any human being who visits the Moon Man must never make a secret of the fact; to keep it secret would mean death.

The trip to the moon is a recurrent theme in stories as well as a shamanic feat. It is fraught with danger, as the visitor to the land of the moon runs the risk of being killed by Ululiarnaq, the woman with the *ulu* (a woman's knife) who tries to make visitors laugh about her pranks and cuts out their entrails with her knife when they do so.[52] There are various stories about a woman who was taken to the house of the moon man and had to survive the trial of Ululiarnaq. Usually she returns to the earth, just as the shaman visiting the moon man does. Today the moon spirit is not very significant in Inuit oral traditions, but various themes in the story, such as the transformation of the woman into a narwhal, are still remembered and discussed by elders.[53]

THE SEA WOMAN

The notion of the woman of the sea was widespread along the arctic coast, but her names varied considerably. She was called Sedna by the Uqqumiut on South Baffin Island, Takanakapsaluk (the terrible one down there) or Uinigumasuittuq (the one who did not want to have a husband) by the Iglulingmiut, and Nuliajuk by the Nattilingmiut further to the west.[54] The etymology of the most well known name of the sea woman, Sedna, used on South Baffin, is contested.

Thalbitzer (1928, 401) glossed the meaning of Sedna as "she down there in the sea." He also suggested that the name may be derived from *sanavoq*, "to work, to make," or from East Greenland Sättuma, "the one of the depth of the sea." The Inuk author Rachel Qitsualik (1999) points out that "Sedna is a distortion of the Inuktitut word 'sanna,' meaning 'down there.'" Ken Harper (2004) adopts the same interpretation in his discussion with Inuit leaders Peter Irniq and Jack Anawak, who stated that they did not know the name Sedna. Harper argued that Sedna was "merely a demonstrative pronoun used, as was often the case in Inuktitut, to avoid using a proper name, especially of one feared or deserving respect."

These interpretations are consistent with the references to the sea woman among the Iglulingmiut further north. Rasmussen (1929, 106) reports, "Some indeed are even afraid to utter the name of Nuliajuk, and simply say Takana, 'the one down there.'" According to Tungilik from Naujaat, "She has been given different names. She has been called Sanna. In my dialect she is called Nuliajuk. Among the Iglulingmiut she is called Takannaaluk."[55]

Lyon (1824, 362) reports that the sea woman was one of the helping spirits of his most important informant, the *angakkuq* Toolemak, who provided him with a list of his *tuurngait*. Peck decided not to include the sea woman Sedna in the list of helping spirits he collected in Cumberland Sound.[56]

Later, Sedna was identified with Satanasi, the devil,[57] by missionaries as well as by Inuit. Aksaajuq from Panniqtuuq (1995 interview) related: "From what I know, when religion came, missionaries would say that she is the devil, Satanasi. Even the shaman would say that afterwards." The sea woman was always considered dangerous and ambiguous, but she has also been identified with Jesus(i), as on a tape by Donald Suluk from Arviat.

Rasmussen (1929, 123–4) emphasizes the ambiguity of the sea woman: "But while Takanakapsaluk gives mankind all these good things, created out of her own finger-joints, it is she also who sends nearly all the misfortunes which are regarded by the dwellers on earth as the worst and direst." This ambiguity is still acknowledged by elders today. Felix Pisuk from Rankin Inlet (2002 interview) observed, "She was a person who was deceiving people. We didn't really believe in Nuliajuk, but even the priest and the Anglican ministers were saying that Nuliajuk was a deceiver and evil. But when you understand the techniques of survival, Nuliajuk was the one who could assist us."

Elders today rarely show any particular interest in the sea woman or in the cultic practices surrounding her; they show much more interest in the shamanic skills and knowledge of their ancestors. The sea woman is now viewed as just one of the many non-human beings populating the earth, the sky, and the sea. But among the younger generation, she is receiving more attention and is frequently represented in carvings, drawings, and other forms of modern Inuit art.

THE SEA WOMAN AND THE CARIBOU WOMAN

Ethnographic texts make reference to a powerful woman who created and owned the caribou. Peck makes a distinction between Tikkertserktok, the woman who owned the caribou, and Sedna, the owner of the sea game, and assumed that the former was even more powerful than the latter.[58] Lyon (1824), too, distinguishes between Pukimna, the owner of the caribou, and the sea woman. Boas (1964 [1888], 588), however, "could not find any trace of this tradition that Anautalik, Nuliajoq's father, is the protector of land animals, nor of that of a being to whom he [Lyon] refers by the name of Pukimna (derived from *pukiq*, the white parts of a deerskin), who lives in a fine country far to the west and who is the immediate protectress of deer, which animals roam in immense herds around her dwelling." Pukimna may have been related to the Padlirmiut Pinga. According to Rasmussen (1930, 51), "Even such an outstandingly clever shaman as Igjugârjuk had difficulty in defining the spirit Hila, declaring time after time that Hila was the same as Pinga, and that Pinga corresponded to the Nuliajuk of the coast dwellers. But as soon as we went further into the various functions of these spirits, it was found that Pinga did not quite coincide with Nuliajuk; Pinga had the special care of the caribou, whereas Hila, as among the coast dwellers, represented everything one feared in the air."

The figure of Pinga remains enigmatic. She shows features of Sila as well as of the caribou woman and the sea woman. Rasmussen (1930, 56) writes, "The mistress of the animals of the hunt, Pinga, lives somewhere up in the air or in the sky, and is often named quite indiscriminately with Hila." He notes that the Umingmaktormiut also referred to the sea woman as Arnaq Pinga ("the woman up there"), while usually she was referred to as Hävna ("her down there"), and explains, "Here they simply take the supernatural forces, spirits, the mother of the sea beasts, and the weather spirit all together as one."[59] The figure of Pinga illustrates the inherent flexibility of Inuit categories in organizing and reorganizing the features of non-human beings. Thus, there is little point in looking for clear distinctions between Pinga, Sila, the sea woman, and the caribou woman. We just have to acknowledge that these entities sometimes merge and that particular features are not necessarily restricted to one being. Both the sea woman and Sila, for example, could be held responsible for the weather. Aksaajuq from Panniqtuuq (1995 interview) said that "when there were no more food around and when there were too many days of bad weather, the shamans would ask Sanna why it was like that. They were the only way to know why because the shaman would know from Sanna. It is their power. So the shamans would try to make that end, they would try to convince Sanna to make good weather because without doing it, they would always become hungry ... Then it would be good weather again, and they could go hunting."

The relationship between the sea woman and the owners of the caribou was unclear. Captain Albert Low (1906, 169), who visited the area in the early 1900s, reports, "There is a goddess of the land-animals called Pukimma, who appears to be closely identified with Nuliayok, and may be the same personage under a different name." Rasmussen (1929, 70) argues that most Iglulingmiut tended to identify the mother of the caribou with the mother of the sea game. Boas (1964 [1888], 588) had difficulty establishing a clear distinction between these two figures. He relates that, according to the Akudnirmiut, a woman created the walrus and caribou were made from articles of clothing:

> During a famine a woman (I could not learn whether she was identical with Sedna or not) carried her boots to the hills and transformed them by

> magic into deer, which spread all over the country. Then she carried her breeches to the sea, where they were changed into walrus. The first deer, however, had large tusks and no horns, while the walrus had horns and no tusks. The Eskimo soon found that this was very dangerous for the hunter, as the deer killed pursuers with their tusks, while the walrus upset the boats. Therefore an old man transferred the horns to the deer and the tusks to the walrus.
>
> It is very probable that this woman was Sedna, as the Eskimo affirm that the observances referring to walrus and deer are commanded by Sedna and as the first tradition accounts for her dislike of the deer.[60]

The results are inconclusive. The sea woman may have been identified with the owner of the caribou in some contexts and not in others. The owners of the game required small offerings at the beginning the sea mammal and caribou hunting seasons. The Iglulingmiut followed specific traditions:

> On first setting out for walrus or seal hunting after having hunted summer or autumn caribou up inland, a fire must be lighted in the snow hut, with fuel of dried seaweed, and over this are held clothing, mittens of caribou skins, harpoon with line and head, and the words "*namarmik-mamarmik*" meaning "give us something that tastes nice" are uttered. Then, in leaving the hut to set out on the hunt, one must step across the fire.
>
> As soon as sealing begins after the close of the caribou season, a small narrow strip of *pukeq* (white skin from the belly of a caribou) is set out, and a piece of sinew thread from the short end (sinew thread is made from the back sinews of the caribou, and that part lying nearest the spine gives the longest threads, the outermost being quite short). This is a sacrifice to Takánalûk, and is called *kiversautit*: "that wherewith something is lowered down" meaning presumably that offences are thus lowered down in the deep.[61]

It was also required that gifts be given to the caribou woman at the beginning of the caribou season. Oosotapik, one of Peck's main informants in Cumberland Sound, related that "the land had an owner, a woman possessing a house on a hill in the centre of the land. She owned the deer. She wanted small soles of boots and lines used for carrying loads in the summer from the men. Only then was she prepared to make the caribou appear so that they could be killed."[62]

The Iglulingmiut also had to offer small gifts when they started caribou hunting.[63] Rasmussen (1929, 195) observes that "people hunting caribou in kayaks on a river or lake must, while hunting, lay out a piece of sealskin under a stone as a sacrifice to Tugtut Igfianut, the Mother of the Caribou." Although Rasmussen describes the ritual as a sacrifice to the *inua* of the sea, it is probably more prudent to see it simply as the initial gift preceding the hunting of sea mammals.

The gifts served to create conditions for successful hunting. The *kiversautit* ritual involved the gift of a piece of caribou skin and sinew thread, as well as miniatures of seals, harpoons, and harpoon heads. The value of these initial gifts appears to have been small, but the success of the hunt depended on them. The gifts were intended for the owners of the game animals, who would then give game to the hunters.

People also gave small offerings to the sea woman to obtain her help. Boas (1907, 533–4) tells a story of a woman who invoked Sedna in time of need. She offered a lamp to the sea woman and reached land safely. "They landed at a place where they were able to ascend a hill. While there, they saw a light shining at a distance, and they knew that this was Sedna's light."

The sea woman could act as a helping spirit to an *angakkuq* and provide game to a hunter. Rasmussen (1931, 287) records *irinaliutiit* (powerful words) he had collected from the Nattilingmiutaq Nakasuk, words that invoked the help of the sea spirit in catching a trout or a salmon.

Luke Nuliajuk, an elder from Gjoa Haven, spoke of how the sea woman's name could be given to human beings:

> My name is Nuliajuk. I have never seen the *Nuliajuk* that we are talking about. Someone told me about a *Nuliajuk* who had been a real person and known by everyone. Before he died in Arviligjuaq, he left instructions that were to be followed by his relatives. He said they were not to go down to the sea for a year. When *Nuliajuk* died, they did not listen to him and they went down to the coast. It was deep winter. Suddenly the ice started to break. They were in an *iglu*. The pot started moving back and forth following the flame of the *qulliq* [lamp]. Some *angakkuit* there performed, in order to protect them from the ice. They said if *Nuliajuk* really wanted the ice to break, she could do so. They were able to stop the ice from breaking, because the pot moved following the flame of the *qulliq*. They said if it was going in the opposite direction, they would not have been able to stop the ice from breaking. Inirnaqhiaq told me this story. He had been out with his mother and seen the ice piled up around. He was quite a distance from the *iglu* the others were in.[64]

Nuliayuk's account corroborates the association between the sea woman and the *qulliq*, which was usually tended to by a married woman and could protect the soul of a person.

THE CREATION OF HUMAN BEINGS AND SEA MAMMALS

According to one widespread narrative, humankind originated from the marriage of a woman and a dog. Another narrative describes how the most important sea game originated from the fingers of a woman who did not want to marry. These stories were usually told separately, but among the Iglulingmiut, they were connected in one long narrative. In 1996, Alexina Kublu recorded an extensive version of the myth as told by her father, Kupaaq, an elder from Iglulik:

> There was once a woman of marriageable age who was frequently wooed. She rejected all the suitors.
>
> Then there arrived a man with his hair in a forehead topknot, a qajaqer, wearing caribou clothing. As it turned out, he was a bull caribou, and once again this one too was rejected. So, because she was wooed for a long time but never wanted to get married, they started calling her "She who never wants to get married."
>
> Her father became angry with her because of her unwillingness to get married and told her to take her dog as a husband, taking them off to an island. The woman and the dog were on the island for a long time. Whenever they were out of food, she put a pack on her dog and sent it to get food from her father.
>
> A long time went past; then the woman became pregnant, and gave birth to little pups. Because the dog was now coming so often to get meat, her father came by qajaq to see why they ran out of meat so often.
>
> He was greeted by all the fawning little pups. When he discovered he had pups for grandchildren, he became very angry. When the dog, with a pack on its back, was fetching food again, he filled its pack with rocks. As the dog was slowly returning to the island, he only got as far as the middle before he gradually lost strength because of the heaviness he felt. And so he sank.
>
> Because his daughter and her children no longer had a provider, the old man himself started to bring food to them. His daughter told her many children, "When your grandfather comes ashore, pretend to fawn all over him and chew his *qajaq* to pieces because he made you fatherless." Well, then when their grandfather arrived, his many grandchildren once again fawned over him, because it was their habit to fawn over him whenever they greeted him. They fawned over him, licking at his qajaq and then chewing away at it until they had made it unfit for use. Because their grandfather no longer had a qajaq, he had to spend time with them on the island. He also had no hunting equipment.
>
> The little pups were gradually getting bigger and because the poor things often got hungry their mother prepared to send them off. Dividing them into three groups of three, she told them about their destinations, and she impressed on them what they would have to do. She told the first group she sent away to head down towards the south. They had only bows and arrows, and these became Indians. She made a boat out of an old boot-sole for the next ones she sent away, telling them, "You will come back by ship." These ones became *qallunaat*. The last ones were not told to go away; however, she told them simply that they should be unseen by people. These became *ijirait* (the invisible people who show up as caribou).

Once again, the father and daughter were alone and once again the woman was often courted, but she still rejected those who wanted her as a wife. Then there arrived someone who appeared to be nicely big; the woman also thought that he seemed to be handsome. He was dressed in sealskin, he never took off his goggles and he never got out of his qajaq. Because he seemed to be handsome (so they say) the One-who-didn't-want-to-marry finally did not reject him. And so, when she at last agreed to be taken as a wife, she was taken away.

After they had been gone for a while and they got to an island, her new husband wanted to urinate. When he finally got around to getting out, his ugly tiny legs were disgustingly short; and when at last he bothered to take off his goggles, his lidless eyes ... how red! So there he was, her awful new husband, a wretched fulmar. The woman, in shock, said to her new husband, "But I thought you were a fine big fellow." So then, they say, the ugly fulmar started to sing, " My beautiful wings, ahahahaha, my grand goggles, ahahahaha." And so, because he had been propped up by his tail feathers, he had looked to her eyes as if he was a fine big fellow. Because of her unwillingness to get married, she now had a fulmar husband, for a long time.

She was lonely now, and very regretful of her pickiness in refusing all those who had come courting. After a fairly long time, her father came all the way to visit his daughter. Because he found her to be neglected, he tried to arrange for her to leave. Before they had gone very far, realizing his wife had been taken, the husband followed. Because he couldn't catch up, he made a great wind, and the father and daughter were caught by huge waves. Because they were inevitably going to capsize, the old man threw his daughter into the water. Naturally his daughter grabbed hold of his *qajaq*. He hit her with his paddle, and (when that didn't work) he chopped off her fingers. As the parts that were chopped off fell into the water, they became the sea-mammals. There were seals, and then square-flippers, and then beluga. When the woman sank, she became a dweller of the sea floor.

Even though her father got home he so much regretted the things he had done that, wrapping himself in his bearskin, he went to the tide-edge and waited to be engulfed. These three are now on the sea floor, the woman who was Uinigumasuittuq, her father and her dog.

Since then, until they acquired Christianity, whenever people who had not lived well died, they found themselves inside the horrible bearskin belonging to the nasty father of that ghastly person down there, where he made them go through agonies until finally they were able to go to the land of the Ullurmiut, the people of the day.

Whenever they had done many evil things, they stayed (there) longer. But because the woman whom they called Takannaaluk (the horrible one down there) had no fingers, she wasn't able to (use a) comb, and so her hair became tangled. Whenever her hair got in tangles, sea-mammals became entangled in it. Whenever they became entangled, they could no longer surface, and whenever they could no longer surface people became hungry, no longer able to catch (the sea-mammals). Whenever they couldn't catch anything for a long time at the seal breathing-holes, a shaman would have to go down to the bottom of the sea. Whenever a shaman went to Takannaaluk by going to the sea-floor, he was said to "*nakkaa-*." Because it was so tiring, the shamans were often reluctant to "*nakkaa-*." Whenever they would "*nakkaa-*" all the people would gather in one iglu. The bare-chested shaman was tied up, and put behind a blind made of skin, while the seal-oil lamps were extinguished. The singing shaman would slowly descend to the bottom of the sea as his voice gradually would become distant. When the shaman would get to the sea-bed, he would comb Takannaaluk.

Only when her hair was combed would the sea-mammals be able to surface once again.[65]

Many versions of this myth have been collected.[66] Although the basic features of the story are usually retained, much variation exists in the way the sea mammals originated from the fingers and the descendants of the woman. The sea mammals include seals, whales, and walruses; the descendants of the woman and the dog are usually non-Inuit beings such as *tuniit* (a people preceding the Inuit), *ijirait* (caribou people), *allait* (Indians), and Qallunaat (white people).[67]

In a version of the story that Boas (1964 [1888], 585) presents, the father pierced the eye of his daughter. Boas comments, "She is very large and much taller than the Inuit. In accordance with the second form of the tradition she has only one eye and is scarcely able to move. Her father is also a cripple and appears to the dying, whom he grasps with his right hand, which has only three fingers."

Whereas the variant forms collected by Boas on South Baffin are quite close to the Iglulik versions, Rasmussen (1931, 212–13) recorded quite a different version among the Nattilingmiut.[68] In a distant past, "a little orphan girl was thrown out into the sea when some people were putting over a fjord in kayaks tied together … Nobody cared about the orphan girl and so she was pushed into the sea when she was trying to get unobserved on to the kayak-raft with the others. But that wickedness turned her into a great spirit, the greatest of all the spirits we fear up here. She became Nuliajuk and made the animals that we hunt."

The Iglulingmiut located the small island where the father had brought his daughter close to the island of Iglulik; it was called Pugtulik and later became part of the island Qikiqtaarjuk, which is now part of the main island of Iglulik.[69] The Nattilingmiut located it in their area: "She it was whose name was Putulik, and yet after her death she was called Nuliajuk! The island to which she was taken when about to be confined, is in Ugjulik, not far from Sherman Inlet. There she bore her many children and lived with them, helped by her father who brought meat over to them."[70] Clearly, different versions have local variations in different areas.

Rasmussen (1932, 27) did not collect a version of this myth from the Umingmaktormiut, who told him that "it has been forgotten how ᴀrnakäpˢha·luk originally got to the bottom of the sea. All that is known is that she has always been there."

Geza Roheim (1924) interprets the myth as being about father-daughter incest, concluding that the dog represents the penis of the father. This interpretation is supported by an origin myth provided by Boas (1901, 483) and Saladin d'Anglure (1977, 2006, 150), which suggests that the dog represents the penis inside the womb.

Whereas the theme of the marriage with the dog occurs across the Arctic, the theme of the sea mammals originating from the fingers of the sea woman is confined to a much smaller area, mainly encompassing the eastern Canadian Arctic and Greenland. Sonne (1990, 9–10) suggests that the narrative may only have developed relatively recently and is connected to trade and whaling activities. She sees the fulmar as well as the hands as symbolizing a meat-sharing relationship. She concludes that the fulmar, "in his acknowledged right to the transformed hands of Sea Woman, was for one reason or other conceived of as a meat sharing partner." In her analysis, she focuses on hands or, by substitution, mittens or even flippers.[71] However, the narrative does not focus on hands, but on fingers and, more specifically, finger joints.

The smallness of the finger joints contrasts with the huge size of the sea mammals into which they transform. The transformation suggests a shift of scale. Rasmussen (1908, 113–15) reports a similar shift of scale with respect to the polar Inuit in his discussion of the use of objects deposited at a grave: "If you take a kayak, you must place a tiny model in the place of it; if you take a harpoon, it must be replaced by the model of a harpoon; if you intend to pay with meat, the piece need not be larger than a finger's length, for the soul can magnify it for itself." The fingers are a measure of the scale on which the *tarniit* (shades or images) operate. The symbolism of the fingers, then, indicates the level of the *tarniit*, whose creation necessarily precedes the origin of sea mammals.[72]

The power embedded in the fingers was expressed in various rituals. Rasmussen (1929, 185–6) reports, "If a seal or bearded seal is captured, all the women of the village must touch the meat of it with their first fingers." Among the Iglulingmiut, a woman who had just delivered a boy had to melt ice or snow for drinking water each morning: "Every time she drinks, she must put a drop of water into the child's mouth with her middle finger. This must be done immediately after the child is born, and repeated every time the mother drinks. The finger in question is supposed to possess a peculiar power in regard to infants, so that the water thus dripping into the mouth will prevent the child from ever suffering from thirst."[73]

Even pointing a finger would establish a connection. Rasmussen (1929, 187) documents a practice in Repulse Bay: "If a woman sees a whale, she must point to it with her middle finger." The power of the fingers was emphasized in a tradition described by Ivaluardjuk: "It is said that in the days when the earth was dark, the only creatures men had to hunt were ptarmigan and hare, and these were hunted by wetting the forefinger and holding it out in the air; the finger then became luminous and it was possible to see the animal hunted."[74]

The Iglulik traditions suggest that through the fingers a connection to the animals could be made. Inversely, the flippers of the seals also constituted a means of contact. A shaman visiting the sea woman in times of scarcity had to tell her that "those up above can no longer help the seals up by grasping their forefingers."[75]

THE DESCENT TO THE SEA WOMAN AND HER HOUSE

Nutaraaluk from Iqaluit related that when "the people in the camp were unhappy or abusive towards wildlife, the wildlife used to move away from the camp. When the wildlife felt they were not welcome, they felt useless to the camp. The animals would flee to Sedna's shed where they were so numerous they seemed like maggots. It was because they had gone there that the hunters couldn't catch them anymore. That was when the *angakkuq* had to go and get them."[76] Powerful shamans were able to descend to that place and then return safely. All knowledge of the dwelling of the sea woman and its inhabitants was based on the shamans' accounts. A recording made by the Roman Catholic missionary Mary-Rousselière in the North Baffin area has preserved evidence of the connection between the *angakkuq*'s experience and the description of the house and its inhabitants.[77]

> *Angakkuit* would go to Kannaaluk. When they would do so, this was called *nakkaajuq*. You could hear the *angakkuq* as he was going down underneath. He would leave his clothing behind. After a while you wouldn't hear his voice at all. Then after some time you could hear him underneath the floor of the iglu. It would sound like it was coming from in the ground. You could hear him coming closer and closer. Then his voice would come from the back of the iglu, and the *angakkuq* would be back once more. He would tell about what he had seen. He said that Kannaaluk and her father shared one *iglu*. Their dog, that was made to sink, sits at the doorway. It is always chewing on a bone and it never moves away. The father, who had wrapped himself in a bearskin while on the shore, is still wearing that bearskin. His daughter sits upon the bed. Whenever her father's hands would reach out from under the bearskin to grab the *angakkuq*, his daughter would say to him, "Pullalik," which means he still has air. He is still alive. Then his hands would go back under. Also there would be a lot of movement underneath the bearskin. It would be the father tormenting someone who had recently died. The ones who would be tormented would be men and women who had committed bestiality. When they died, the father would take them under his bearskin and torment them. They would

> be tormented for a full year from the day they had died, and then they would finally be allowed out.

The *angakkuq* established a connection between the house where the séance was conducted and the house of the sea woman and its inhabitants.

Rasmussen (1929, 124–9) received an extensive and rich account of the *angakkuq*'s descent to the sea woman Takanakapsaluk from the Aivilik *angakkuq* Ava, probably shortly after Ava had been converted to Christianity. Ava informed him, however, that these impressive journeys were no longer made. While the *angakkuq* makes his descent, Ava recounted,

> one may hear deep sighs and the breathing of persons long since dead; these are the souls of the shaman's namesakes, who have come to help. But as soon as one calls them by name, the sighs cease, and all is silent in the house until another dead person begins to sigh.
>
> In the darkened house one hears only sighing and groaning from the dead who lived many generations earlier. This sighing and puffing sounds as if the spirits were down under water, in the sea, as marine animals, and in between all the noises one hears the blowing and splashing of creatures coming up to breathe.

An ordinary *angakkuq* had to overcome various obstacles, such as three large rolling stones that threatened to crush him or Takanakapsaluk's dog stretched across the passage, but for a great *angakkuq* a "way opens right from the house whence they invoke their helping spirits; a road down through the earth, if they are in a tent on shore, or down through the sea, if it is in a snow hut on the sea ice, and by this route the shaman is led down without encountering any obstacle. He almost glides as if falling through a tube so fitted to his body that he can check his progress by pressing against the sides, and need not actually fall down with a rush. This tube is kept open for him by all the souls of his namesakes, until he returns on his way back to earth."

The main challenge for the *angakkuq* is to appease the sea woman.

> When the shaman enters the house, he at once sees Takanakapsaluk, who, as a sign of anger, is sitting with her back to the lamp and with her back to all the animals in the pool. Her hair hangs down loose all over one side of her face, a tangled, untidy mass hiding her eyes, so that she cannot see. It is the misdeeds and offenses committed by men which gather in dirt and impurity over her body. All the foul emanations from the sins of mankind nearly suffocate her. As the shaman moves towards her, Isarrataitsoq, her father, tries to grasp hold of him. He thinks it is a dead person come to expiate offenses before passing on to the Land of the Dead, but the shaman must then at once cry out: "I am flesh and blood" and then he will not be hurt, and he must now grasp Takanakapsaluk by one shoulder and turn

her face towards the lamp and towards the animals, and stroke her hair, the hair she has been unable to comb out herself, because she has no fingers; and he must smooth it and comb it, and as soon as she is calmer, he must say: … "those up above can no longer help the seals up by grasping their forefingers."

Then Takanakapsaluk answers in the spirit language: "The secret miscarriages of the women and breaches of taboo in eating boiled meat bar the way for the animals."

The shaman must now use all his efforts to appease her anger, and at last, when she is in a kindlier mood, she takes the animals one by one and drops them on the floor, and then it is as if a whirlpool arose in the passage, the water pours out from the pool and the animals disappear in the sea. This means rich hunting and abundance for mankind.

When the *angakkuq* returned, all transgressions had to be confessed, especially the hidden menstruations and miscarriages. If necessary, young women who were not present were summoned to come for confession. After the confessions were made, people were relieved and even thankful to those who confessed. They were sure that the next day game would be abundant.

Not only the helping spirits, but also the deceased namesakes of the *angakkuit* and of the people who participated in the performance had a role to play in ensuring a safe passage to the sea woman for the *angakkuq*. The deceased namesakes of the *angakkuq* appeared as sea mammals sighing and breathing, and when the spectators called them by name they withdrew. Their assistance was indispensable, as they kept the way open for the shaman. The dialogues between the *angakkuq* and the sea woman took place in the language of the *tuurngait*, the helping spirits. The *angakkuq* had to identify himself as someone of flesh and blood. In other sources the expression *pullaalik* – someone who has a bubble (i.e., the bubble of air that contains the *tarniq)* – is used.

George Kappianaq (IE 358) from Iglulik could still remember how the *angakkuit* used to *nakaajut* (descend to the sea woman) when the people faced hard times. As the *angakkuq* went down, he could see pieces of clothing lined up one after the other all the way up to the entrance of the dwelling. One could not see the end of the line of clothes. These clothes belonged to all the people who had drowned. When he was about to enter, the *angakkuq* would see a huge dog crunching human bones. Kappianaq explained that these were the bones of people who had led a bad life. "A soul cannot have its person when the bones are gone." *The angakkuq* had to enter without touching the top of the entrance or the dog. He would feel relief after passing this obstacle, but then "the hands are going to come out beneath the cover towards the head aimed at the person who had just entered. The hands are all cracked just as one would see on an old caribou antler."[78] But Uinigumassuittuq, sitting on her platform, would tell her father that the visitor is *pullaalik* (one with the bubble); what she means is that the visitor had a bubble of air containing a soul. Kappianaq explained that "this is all happening in the underworld, the place where there are no bodies except for the occupants who now have the power to rule over any breach of taboos." Then the father would not bother the visitor, but if the visitor had just been a soul without a body (i.e., a deceased person), he would have captured him and made him suffer as long as he could feel pain. When the *angakkuq* returned, he would know the reason for the hardships and which rules the person who had caused the hardships would have to observe. Then people would find it much easier to catch animals again.

Rasmussen states that the Inuit themselves debate whether it is the *angakkuq* himself or his soul that descends down into the sea. According to Peck's account, the soul ascends to Sedna. The use of the term "ascend" instead of "descend" suggests that it is not altogether clear whether the sea woman is located in an upper or a lower world (Pinga is similarly ambiguous). The sea woman is usually described as a giant figure, but the Umingmaktormiut believed that she "lives on a rock at the bottom of the sea in a puilän·uᴀq: a little bubble. There she lives with her husband and a small child."[79] In this perspective the sea woman herself is considered a *tarniq*.

The descent to Sedna was fraught with danger, and a safe return was not guaranteed. Qumangaapik, an elder from Mittimatalik, related:

> Sometimes the ice would form at the hole behind the curtain if the shaman was gone too long visiting Takannaaluk, and you could hear the shaman struggling to come back to the surface through the iced-over breathing hole. When that happens they sound like they have something over their mouths and cannot breathe. Even a shaman cannot get to the surface if he has taken too long, and when that happens the only ones who can help are the shaman's grandmother or mother, who have to go behind the curtain to help the shaman come back to the house. It is said by the shaman that that deepest place is very unpleasant and terrifying, and the place is very old. It is a place of no return, and is filled with every wickedness known to mankind.[80]

According to Rasmussen, the sea woman inhabited a house like that of the *tuniit*, a people that preceded the Inuit and had been driven away by them. Lyon (1824, 363) reports that her "house is exceedingly fine, and very like a kabloona looking-glass; and, what is still more attractive to an Eskimaux, it contains plenty of food." According to Boas (1901, 119), it was believed that she lived in a house built of stone and whale ribs and that her dog husband was stationed on the floor of the house, guarding the entrance. People living west of Hudson Bay assumed it was very warm there.[81] The Nattilik woman Nalungiaq told Rasmussen (1931, 226–7) that Nuliajuk lived in a house on the bed of the sea that was arranged in the same way as a human house. Rasmussen writes, "Just inside the entrance to her house passage sits kataum inua, the ruler of the passage, who keeps an exact record of all the breaches of taboo committed by mankind up on earth. Everything he sees and hears he passes on to Nuliajuk, and he tries in every possible way to scare the shamans who want to go in to her, so that they will abandon their intention of mollifying her." We may assume that "kataum inua" is the father of the sea woman. In the house there is also a big black dog[82] and "Isarrataitsoq ('the one with no wings, or the one with no arms') – a woman – but nobody knows who she is. She has the same husband as Nuliajuk, and he is a little sea scorpion." Finally, there is a child called Unga – "the one who screams like a child" – stolen as a baby from a sleeping mother when her husband was out hunting at the breathing holes.[83]

The father of the woman of the sea is referred to by Lyon as Nappa-yook or Annow-ta-lig (the man with the club). He is described as a small being,[84] and many believe that he had only one arm. He seems closely associated with Unga, the small being that accompanies the sea woman.[85] The notion of the theft of Unga recalls the figure of Amajorsuk, a giant cannibal woman smelling of seaweed who puts the people she captures into her *amauti*, which suggests a connection between Amjorsuk and the sea woman.

The house of the sea woman abounded with food and that is probably why she was sometimes referred to as Nerrivik (the place of food) by the polar Eskimos.[86] Rasmussen (1929, 67) reports that in the house of the sea woman, "[a]ll the beasts of the sea have their place on the right of her lamp when she calls them together; that place is called ka.ia, and is on the right of the lamp when one sits on the bench in the housewife's place facing the passage. Here she assembles and keeps the beasts of the sea when they are to be withheld from mankind. Only the sharks have a special place to themselves; they live in her urine vessel, and that is why the flesh of sharks tastes of urine."

According to (Boas 1901, 119),

> The souls of seals, ground-seals, and whales are believed to proceed from her house. After one of these animals has been killed, its soul stays with the body for three days. Then it goes back to Sedna's abode, to be sent forth again by her. If, during the three days that the soul stays with the body, any taboo or proscribed custom is violated, the violation (pitsête) becomes attached to the animal's soul, and causes it pain. The soul strives in vain to free itself of these attachments, but is compelled to take them down to Sedna. The attachments, in some manner not explained, make her hands sore, and she punishes the people who are the cause of her pains by sending to them sickness, bad weather, and starvation. If, on the other hand, all taboos have been observed, the sea-animals will allow themselves to be caught: they will even come to meet the hunter. The object of the innumerable taboos that are in force after the killing of these sea-animals, therefore, is to keep their souls free from attachments that would hurt their souls as well as Sedna.

When the *angakkuit* visited the sea woman, she was usually in a state of physical distress because of the transgressions of human beings. Her hair, for instance, would be covered with filth. In the Greenland tradition, this filth is referred to as *aglerutut*. Thalbitzer (1926, 379–80; 1928, 397–8) glosses *agdlerpoq* as "bearing a still-born child" and points out that the word can also mean "to be abstinent for cultic reasons." The two meanings are closely connected, as bearing a still-born child implies the observance of many ritual injunctions. An absence of game animals has been traditionally thought to be caused by the hiding of a premature birth or still-born child (*angiaq*).[87] Rasmussen (1929, 75) writes: "When unclean women offend against taboo, smoke rises from their bodies. And this foul smoke pours out from the houses where they live, and attracts the notice of the Moon Spirit. This smoke gets into the Sea Spirit's eyes, or falls over her face, hair and body in a mess of dirt." The *angakkuit* therefore had to calm her down and comb and clean her hair. Nutaraaluk from Iqaluit explained that the transgressions could also take shape in caribou hair.

> Whenever someone broke a taboo or caused grief to an animal it made the animals difficult to get and an *angakkuq* would have to go down and visit Sedna. My father used to do this. There was a dog, who probably had been her husband, which guarded the door. There was also a big piece of ice at the door which would revolve outwards if stepped upon. Sedna's ears would become full of caribou hair when a *pittailiniq* was broken. Those who stole meat or broke other *pittailiniq* would cause caribou hair to fall in the water and it would collect in her ears. It was only after removing this hair and by shouting in her ear that she could hear and the *angakkuq* could tell her that he had come to get animals. Even though it seemed at first that she would not be moved at all, she would eventually respond.[88]

According to Rasmussen (1929, 127), the sea woman could not see when the hair covered her eyes. But even though the she had only one eye, she would be aware of all of the transgressions human beings made. According to Boas (1907, 496–7), "Any sins committed by the people give pain to her blind eye, and the angakok has to remove the cause of the pain, otherwise she would withhold the sea-mammals from the upper world."

In 1999 Simon Shamaiyuk from Panniqtuuq made a drawing of a *tuurngaq*, a helping spirit, clearly showing the features of the sea woman. She is represented as a large woman with long hair covering one of her eyes.

LIFE AND DEATH

A wide range of refrainings and abstainings – *pitailiniit* – ensured good hunting. According to the Umingmaktormiut the sea woman was also called "nakorut: a giver of strength, because she gives people sea beasts if only they do not break their taboo."[89] Menstruating and pregnant women in particular had to take great care not to offend the sea woman: "[I]f they should happen to see a wild animal, its soul would be offended, and Nuliayoq would cause the women to become blind. It is also believed that the animal would be transformed into a smaller species."[90]

Lyon (1824, 362–3) reports that Nuliajuk punished transgressors of the rules. The sea woman had to be respected. And in Mittimatalik, according to Boas (1907, 492), "[t]he people are not allowed to smile when referring to her or singing about her; and, when mentioning the name of Sedna, they do so in a reverent manner."[91] When offended, she could retaliate in many ways. Boas (1907, 498) notes that she sends the sisters who make thunder and lightning to punish offenders or cause earthquakes. He adds that dangerous places such as tide-rifts and stormy capes were believed to be favourite haunts of Nuliajuq's. The sea woman might rise from the sea and kill offenders.[92] Felix Pisuk from Kangiq&iniq explained:

> *Nuliajuk* has power over all the sea animals. I am only going to talk about what was told to me. I was told that if my wife and I were going to have an *iglu* on the ice, my wife was never to work on summer skins when we were there because Nuliajuk would be angry and refuse to give us game.
>
> My wife was also not to destroy the skin of a calf that was still suckling from its mother because I would lose my abilities to catch polar bears, as bears are both land and sea animals. If I was out bear hunting, it might hunt me instead. We were told to wash our hands and our faces so we would be successful with animals. When my wife was menstruating, she was not to use old clothing as a menstrual pad, for if she did I would see what would have been animals appear as seaweed. Because I was afraid, I have never tried to test this, as it is dangerous.[93]

Inugpasugjuk, originally from the Nattilik area, stated that Nuliajuk might carry off offenders and turn "the victim into some creature of the sea, so that the man or woman in question would have to live on as a seal or walrus or one of the animals that belonged to her."[94] Then the soul of the stolen person lived on in the animal, while the body or bones remained with Nuliajuk. The sea woman had the power to transform the souls of the deceased into animals if they had committed serious transgressions. Inugpasugjuk said that "[o]nly the so-called aŋerlartukxiaq could in such case return to life, with the aid of a shaman. An aŋerlartukxiaq was a human being who had by means of magic words been given the power to come to life again even after having in some way perished by drowning or having been murdered by an enemy." Only powerful shamans were able to wrest from the sea woman the human beings she had stolen. The story of Anarte[95] tells of how he came to life again and recovered his dead brother from the sea woman.

According to Qumangaapik from Mittimatalik, *angakkuit* might descend to the sea woman to recover the soul of a diseased person. They would receive a gift before descending. Then "the shaman goes to the very back of the house and is tied up with a strong rope, and fresh caribou skin is used as a curtain. The shaman will travel beneath the ground sinking into it as seals do when diving into the sea." Here he finds out that "what the dog is chewing on is in fact the sick person the nature of whose illness the shaman is there to determine." The shaman asks Takannaaluk about the nature of the illness and when he comes back reports his findings:

> The only being that can take the soul away from the dog is Takannaaluk. She will not do this unless the sick person speaks up now about the wrong-doing they committed previously. If the sick person confesses, his soul would be freed by Takannaaluk and recover from the illness. Otherwise Takannaaluk's dog will chew him down, down to nothing. If the sick person starts talking, Takannaaluk will take the person's soul from the dog and will release him but only once the secrets are brought out into the open. Then the person is no longer Takannaaluk's hostage. If the sick person refuses to talk, then even a shaman cannot help him to recover and cannot direct him to a better place.[96]

THE ASCENT OF THE SEA WOMAN

The harpooning of Sedna was not only a feature of the Sedna feast (see chapter 3), but also a shamanic feat that has been frequently reported in the Nattilik and Kivalliq areas. A few elders in the South Baffin area still have recollections of the harpooning of the sea woman. Simon Shamaiyuk (interviewed in 1995) from Panniqtuuq, described the harpooning of Sedna: "From what I know, Sedna (Sanna) had really white guts, she had a big caribou stuff down there. I did a sketch in a printing from the printshop. I heard from my father that when many people were starving in a community, as they were in a qarmaq, they did a kind of ritual. Through a hole on the ice, they hit and harpooned her so she got cut … and from the side, all of the seals were coming up from her gut. That was the way seals could come again."

Neither the Sedna feast nor the *tivajuut* is found among the Umingmaktormiut, but the ascent of the sea woman plays a central part in their shamanic practices. Rasmussen (1932, 24–7) describes how the sea woman was lured to a house where a séance was being held by Umingmaktormiut shamans. He (1931, 226) also describes a shamanic technique used by Nattilingmiut to bring the sea woman up by a hook:

> They do it in this way: they make a hook fast to the end of a long seal thong and throw it out of the entrance passage; the spirits set the hook fast in her, and the shaman hauls her up into the passage. There everybody can

> hear her speaking. But the entrance from the passage into the living room must be closed with a block of snow, and this block, u^{v}kuaq, Nuliajuk keeps on trying to break into pieces in order to get into the house to frighten everybody to death. And there is great fear in the house. But the shaman watches the u^{v}kuaq, and so Nuliajuk never gets into the house. Only when she has promised the shaman to release all the seals into the sea again does he take her off the hook and allow her to go down into the depths again.

Victor Tungilik from Naujaat recounted his experiences: "I have never been to Nuliajuk, but I have had her interfering with me in the winter in an *iglu*. The door was closed tight. It was made of snow. She would push it in, and then pull it back. Whenever it was pulled shut again, it would be slammed so hard it would seem as if it was going to shatter. Although the door was made of snow it didn't break, it didn't shatter. I didn't do anything. I didn't deal with her at all. They say that whenever she would start showing herself, it was because she was going to keep the sea mammals to herself. I didn't do anything when she did this."[97]

The Nattilik *angakkuq* Qaqurtungniq was reported to have harpooned Nuliajuk. Ollie Itinnuaq from Kangiq&iniq told the story:

> My mother's grandfather was one of the many people who saw Nuliajuk. Qakuqtinniq had seen Nuliajuk when she came up through a hole in the ice. He said that he wanted the other people he was with to see Nuliajuk, so they went towards her. They harpooned her in the chest. Then Nuliajuk went down into the water. Because Nuliajuk was very strong, Qakuqtinniq called his son who was named *Nuliajuk* to help him. He had him get the dogteam to help pull. He told him to let go. Then he harpooned Nuliajuk in the arm. When he told his son to let go, he was able to stop her from pulling. He managed to stop Nuliajuk but only for a short time. Then she disappeared. There was a *pisiq* that Qakuqtinniq created about this.[98]

Apsauqtaun from Kugaaruk had heard "that in Nattilik, near Talurjuaq, she [Nuliajuk] came out. Qaquqtinniq was from Nattilik. He saw her. He went there to harpoon her. He could see her. Other people came to help him. They grabbed the rope. Nuliajuk was very, very strong."[99]

In representations of the sea woman, shamanic accounts no longer have the importance they had in the past. Shamans no longer come forward to tell of their trips to the sea woman, describing her appearance, her house, and its inhabitants. The knowledge of the sea woman has changed accordingly. Today the elders mention her, but they may speak as though there were more than one sea woman, referring, for instance, to the harpooning of a Nuliajuk. Still, Nuliajuk can sometimes be seen. Nuviuvak from Spence Bay described one sighting:

> There were people coming into the community along the river by *qajaq*, going towards a *kitingujaak*, a river valley. There were two *qajak*, side-

> by-side crossing the lake. They were narrow *qajak*, just wide enough for a person to get in; that's how they were made. Nuliajuk came to those *qajak*. She was a woman. She came and put her hand on one *qajaq*, and then did the same thing to the other. This is the story I have heard. Two people in their *qajak* saw Nuliajuk when they were travelling on the water.
>
> Another time in the winter, some people down at the floe edge saw a woman come out of the water. There were two women with the same husband. They saw Nuliajuk and then they saw a *kanajuk* [sculpin]. They followed the path they made. They went right after Nuliajuk as she travelled by sea.[100]

Thus, elders still recall encounters with the sea woman.

CONCLUSION

The land was a source of food and the origin of life, but out on the land one would also find the traces of the ancestors, their tent rings, graves, objects, and bones. The land had a history, and knowing the land meant knowing its history and respecting its rules. Out on the land dwelled animals, non-human beings and *tarniit*. Nuna and Sila appeared as encompassing agencies in spatial as well as temporal perspectives. They preceded human beings, and Sila will end the world. Their temporal dimension was emphasized by Peter Suvaksiuq, who stated, "The earth and the sky are changing. They are getting old."[101] The distinction between personal and impersonal does not fit these concepts very well, as they appear to have personal as well as impersonal connotations. The elusiveness and richness of these notions and the uncertainty about Sila and Nuna appear as structural features of these concepts in the wider context of Inuit beliefs and practices.

The sky and the earth continue to play a central part in Inuit perceptions, but as in the past, they are largely conceived as impersonal categories representing the sources of life and the moral order.

Thalbitzer (1926), Merkur (1991), and other scholars have tried to assess the nature of the owners of sky, land, sea, sun, and moon. In particular, they consider the sea woman, the moon man, and the sky as deities. The sea woman and the moon man have a human origin, and elaborate myths explain their origin. The old stories are still told and new stories emerge, but even among elders, confusion about the distinctions between the protagonists of different myths persists. Elders are sometimes unsure about the relations between the sea woman and other beings. In this respect, there is continuity with the past, when distinctions between the sea woman, Pinga, Amajorsuk, and other figures were also not always clear. At an elders conference in Kangiq&iniq in 2002, an elder from Arviat referred to the mother of the moon man as Nuliajuk and another elder commented that in fact this was Atuqtuqarnaq.[102] Thus, the figure of the sea woman and the mother of the moon spirit, who was transformed into a narwhal, would easily merge in the perception of an elder from Arviat, whereas an elder from Rankin Inlet would distinguish between those categories.

It was never easy to distinguish the sea woman from other figures. Thus, the relations between the sea woman, Pinga, Sila, and the mother of the moon spirit were often ambiguous. The earliest sources refer to the sea woman as a powerful *tuurngaq*. Once the missionaries arrived, she was easily identified with the devil. She is now often interpreted in a more positive way. Even though the rules of the past (*pitailiniit*) have been replaced by rules of Christian conduct, Inuit are still keenly aware of the need to respect these non-human beings in the world.

Before the coming of the missionaries, the sea woman had a central place in cosmology as the origin and owner of the sea mammals, and probably as the owner of all mammals, but in this respect she was replaced by God. Rachel Uyarasuk, an elder from Iglulik, recalled, "[T]here was not going to be any more *pittailiniq* after we began to follow Christianity. Because animals were made by God to be food for humans, people were going to be able to eat whatever part of the animal they wanted to. When they started following religion, the *angakkuit* let go of their powers, and people let go of their *pittailiniq*."[103]

The lands of the dead are now replaced by a heaven inhabited by Christian people, in the past called *majulajuit* (those want to go to heaven). The word *majulajuit* has the connotation of climbing, and the image of stairs to heaven can often be found in Inuit stories and art.[104] Whereas the sea woman has lost her central position in ritual as owner of game, she is often represented in art as a woman who combines human and animal features. Whereas a central feature of the origin myth was the sexual union of a woman with animals (a bird or a dog), now the elements of the union are combined in the body of the woman herself – most commonly, a body with a human upper half with an animal lower half.

Modern artists represent the sea woman as a *taliillaajuuq*, a woman with a fishtail,[105] but many other associations are depicted in carvings and drawings.[106] This lack of a clearly defined iconography always seems to have been a structural feature of this enigmatic figure. It has provided the flexibility required for the shamanic experience, allowing shaman to give their own version of their encounter with the sea woman. Today, the same flexibility allows modern Inuit artists to express fundamental features of Inuit life – the human/animal contrast, for example – in complex representations that may involve several sea women in the same art object and complex configurations of heads, animals, and human beings. The shift from a shamanic context to the context of carving and art illustrates the flexible and dynamic nature of Inuit culture and allows for the continuity of ancient notions in new contexts.

6

Inuunngittut, Non-human Beings from the Land and the Sea

INTRODUCTION

Inuit mythology tells us how in a mythical past the categories of time and space were gradually articulated to the point where the present order of the world was realized. This order is by no means eternal. It has a beginning and an end. At the end of time, Sila, the owner of the sky and the weather, will kick the pillars supporting the sky and the world will collapse. Since the beginning of time, the world became populated by human beings, animals, and many other beings. Even though *inuunngittut*, non-human beings, may resemble human beings or even have a human origin, they are usually marked by some significant physical differences that enable Inuit to tell whether or not they are dealing with real Inuit.

In this chapter, we will explore the various categories of non-human beings thought to inhabit the Inuit universe; we will also look at the relationships these non-humans maintain with the Inuit. We will examine the physical and mental characteristics, visibility, alliances, spatiality, and temporality of these non-human beings to assess the nature of these relationships. There is no point in distinguishing between "real" human beings, such as *allait* (Indians) and Qallunaat (white people), and imagined human beings that only exist in the stories and experiences of the Inuit. We can only understand the relationships between Inuit and various categories of non-human beings by considering the latter as part of an encompassing world view. Stories and personal experiences of encounters with non-human beings shape the features and properties of various categories of non-human beings. Most encounters with non-human beings take place outside the community. Some non-human beings, such as *tuurngait* (helping spirits) or *tarniit* (shades or souls), may enter the communities, but most non-human beings do not. But they are still around. Mariano Aupilaarjuk from Kangiq&iniq observed, "I think there are beings amongst us all the time. They are not scary or dangerous. You can hear their footsteps. Sometimes we know they are there … I think these beings still exist today."[1]

In the past, the *angakkuit* were believed to be able to see non-human beings that could not be discerned by other people. Today, when the very existence of shamans has become a controversial issue, there is great uncertainty with respect to such encounters. People may have met caribou behaving in strange ways and suspect they have seen *ijirait* (beings associated with caribou), or perhaps they just saw snowmobiles in the middle of nowhere driven by unknown beings. Inuit often relate such experiences, explicitly admitting that they cannot be sure that they were really dealing with non-human beings. The doubt a person expresses serves to make it clear that he or she is no fool. Sometimes people can be quite outspoken about these experiences. George Kappianaq from Iglulik did not doubt for a moment that *ijirait* attempted to kidnap his wife, even though he never got a clear sight of them.[2]

The accounts of such experiences are considered to be *unikaat* (stories referring to a recent past), not *unikaaqtuat* (stories or myths referring to a distant past). But over time they may increase in authority, and once the people who have related them die, they may come to be held as undisputed proof of the existence of these non-human beings and as evidence of their behaviour.

In Inuit culture we find great variety in the beliefs about non-human beings. Each community and even each family has its own traditions and beliefs. Rasmussen (1929, 204) writes, with respect to the Iglulingmiut, "The Eskimos believe that they are surrounded on all sides by spirits, the same spirits which the angakut enlist in their service as helping spirits, and answering spirits." The most encompassing category is that of the *tuurngait,* since almost everything can function as a helping spirit. It is especially in this category that new spirits are always emerging.[3]

In speaking of the Nattilingmiut, Rasmussen (1931, 239) sketches a gloomy picture of the spirits: "It is the belief that air and sea and earth are full of spirits, mostly evil spirits, very rarely good ones. All these invisible beings are dead people or killed animals who, on account of some breach of taboo, have not obtained peace after death. They are greatly feared, and it sometimes happens that men dare not sleep alone when hunting caribou, even during the light nights of summer. And as autumn draws on, when the nights become dark and stormy, it is all a man dare do to leave tent or snow hut, even to relieve nature." Here Rasmussen is referring to *tupilait,* the evil spirits that played an important part in Nattilik shamanism.[4] The destruction of *tupilait* was one of the most important tasks of the shamans in this area. The antagonistic attitude towards *tupilait* does not imply that Nattilingmiut had the same hostility to other spirits. But *tupilait* were obviously very dangerous. Rasmussen (1931, 239) notes, "It is said that the spirits are particularly partial to children." *Tupilait* were usually either *tuurngait* sent by a shaman to attack someone or the *tarniit* of dead people and animals intent on killing people to avenge some transgression.[5] In contrast to *tupilait, tuurngait* were primarily seen as spirits that help *angakkuit.*

Like the terms *tuurngaq* and *tupilaq,* the word *inurajaq* is a general term that can refer to a wide range of different beings. *Inurajait* is glossed by Kublu as "invisible beings that have footprints. They can be seen by dogs."[6] The Inuit universe of non-human beings is very diverse, and categories may merge in some contexts. For example, the same name may refer to different spirits in different areas, or the same spirits may have different names in different areas. We will first discuss the categories of non-human beings that are still very important in the discourse of the elders and will then, from a comparative perspective, turn our attention to their various features.

THE DESCENDANTS OF UINIGUMASUITTUQ

The story of Uinigumasuittuq, "she who does not want a husband," tells of the origin of various peoples and sea game.[7] Apparently, "mankind did not grow to be many until after a girl had married a dog and later went down to the bottom of the sea and procured game for men."[8] This is an Iglulik version:

> At last she decided to send her children away; she laid all the dog-children in the sole of a kamik, and settling three straws in for masts, said: "... You shall be skilful in the making of weapons."
>
> And then they drifted out to sea.
>
> It is said that the white men are descended from these dog-children. But those of her children that were born in right human form she placed on an alaq: a piece of sole leather that goes under the sole of the kamik proper, and these she sent drifting over to land. From these, it is said, are descended all the itqili't, the Chippeweyan.[9]

In most versions of the myth, the woman put her children on the soles of her *kamiit* and put straws upon them as masts. Then these *kamiit* changed into ships that carried her children away. These boats are clearly modelled on the ships of the Qallunaat. In most versions the Qallunaat are associated with valuable tools, while the *allait* (Indians) are associated with violence. According to a version of the myth related by Kupaaq from Iglulik, the *allait* had only bows and arrows.

Allait, Qallunaat, and *ijirait* were generally thought to have been the offspring of the relationship between the woman and the dog, but there is considerable variation in the myth. In a version collected by Boas (1901, 163–7) in Cumberland Sound, Inuit and *inugarulligait* (dwarves) were included among the children of this union. In an Iglulik version collected by Saladin d'Anglure, *tuniit* were included.

ALLAIT OR *ITQILIIT*

Most Inuit in the North and South Baffin areas had only heard about *allait* – they had never encountered them – and they assumed that these were people who lived somewhere inland, far away. In the south Kivalliq, interactions between Ahiarmiut and Chippeweyan were frequent.

In the Nattilik version of the *allait* origin myth (in which a woman has intercourse with a dog), the woman says, "Avenge me on your grandfather, showing yourselves bloodthirsty as often as you meet with human beings [Inuit]." The Nattilingmiutaq Qaqurtingniq related, "When she had made her dog-young tear her father to pieces and then repented of it, she wanted to send her young ones away, and so she put some of them, the most horrible among them, those that were half man and half dog, on a kamik sole and made them sail over to the mainland; she made magic over them and, as they drifted away, shouted that they were always to be at enmity with people. That is how the Itqilît became wicked people, and there has always been enmity between them and the Inuit."[10]

In his description of *allait*, Qaqurtingniq stressed their doglike features:

> We call them Itqilît (those with many louse eggs) because they are full of lice. They are quick runners and clever hunters, but when they bring down a caribou they do not carry the meat as we do. People say that they carry it in their teeth like a dog does. In fact they have many dog-habits. If an Itqilît is taken by surprise, he will show his teeth and growl like a dog. When they are out hunting they try to smell as dogs do. Inuit who have lain concealed and watched Itqilik hunters that were looking for game, have seen them sniff the air and the ground just like dogs trying to get the scent. People say that like shy dogs they hate the smell of the Inuit.

He added, "When an Itqilît woman gets into the state when she wants to mate with men, she flings out her hair and runs about the village, and then the men fight for her just as dogs do." The association of Indians with dogs is a strong and recurrent feature in Inuit traditions. Indians were not considered as suitable marriage partners. The widespread tale of Navaranaaq, or Navaranaagluk, relates how a marriage alliance between Inuit and *allait* led to mutual destruction and to the death of the woman who was married to the Indian.[11]

A Nattilik story told by Manilaq (Rasmussen 1931, 124–5) hinted that the *allait* might practise cannibalism. Two men were hidden in a tent by an old *itqilik*. When his sons entered they said, "There's a smell of man here. It smells of shin bones in here!" But the old man told them not to harm the two men who were concealed inside the tent. In another story related by Manilaq, some Indians captured Inuit women, raped them, and tried to kill them. Indians are thus also called *unalit*, those who make war (Churchill workshop, 2008). Two Nattilik tales recorded by Rasmussen (1931, 124–6) tell of how Indians attacked Inuit but Inuit managed to survive, once because an Inuk woman blinded the Indian who attacked the Inuit, and another time because a magic song made the Inuit invisible to the Indians. These stories suggest that Inuit can stand up to Indians if they are not seen by them. Negative connotations associated with *allait* are also found in the South Baffin area.[12]

QALLUNAAT

Whereas *allait* were associated with violence, Qallunaat were often associated with useful goods that could be obtained by Inuit.[13] The respect for Qallunaat goods did not imply that Inuit considered Qallunaat a superior form of human being. Rasmussen (1931, 128) quotes the words of the old Nattilingmiutaq Kuvdluitsuq: "It is generally believed that white men have quite the same minds as small children. Therefore one should always give way to them. They are easily angered, and when they cannot get their will they are moody and, like children, have the strangest ideas and fancies."

Qallunaat had visited coasts of the Central Arctic since the end of the sixteenth century, usually in the summer. For Inuit, these regular visits of Qallunaat implied trade. For a long time Qallunaat were temporary visitors, having no connection to the land. They were associated with ships and useful tools but were not thought of as genuine humans.[14] The Nattilik version of the origin myth of Qallunaat advised, "Be skilful in all manner of work you undertake."

The meaning of the term Qallunaat is usually glossed as "those with big eyebrows," suggesting a connection to eyesight or visibility. The Qallunaat may have been associated with the telescopes they used for observing the Inuit. It is interesting to note that in tales about *tuniit* and *ijirait,* much attention is given to the capacity to observe everything through devices that appear to be modelled on telescopes.[15]

We find no mythical accounts of marriages between Qallunaat and Inuit. The almost complete absence of Qallunaat women in the period of early contact, as well as the temporary nature of the contacts between Inuit and Qallunaat, may explain this. Sexual intercourse between whalers and Inuit women was frequent, but these encounters did not create marriage alliances. They did, however, result in gifts of useful goods, such as tobacco, needles, and knives. The children resulting from these unions were raised by the women and their relatives and incorporated into Inuit society. Various white men and women, or spirits clothed like white women, could be found among the *tuurngait.*

TUNIIT

The *tuniit* (or *tunrit*) were a strong people who had inhabited the land before the Inuit but were driven away by them. Rasmussen (1929, 256)[16] described them as a great and strong people who lived in stone houses in winter. According to the Nattilingmiut,

> [I]n the earliest times it was the Tunrit that made the country "inhabitable," which means that they did all the work that made it possible to hunt the caribou and catch the salmon with the gear they had invented themselves and the hunting methods that were used. It was the Tunrit

> that found the places where the caribou crossed the waters, and they built cairns in various parts of the country and thus compelled the animals to follow certain paths so that while on land they could be hunted with the bow and arrow from talut (hides) or pursued in kayaks at nablut (the crossing places) either over lakes or wide rivers. They it was, too, that found the fishes in the rivers and set up the saputit (from sapiva·: stop something on its way), that is to say stone dams and fish weirs built of stones at the places where the salmon run, so that those that were shut in could be speared with the leister … Our country Tunrit made into country, giving it crossing places and for the caribou made paths and the rivers furnished with saputit.[17]

In the Baker Lake area, *tuniit* are still remembered as strong ancestors "who looked like humans" but who "were not real humans." John Makitgaq from Qamanittuaq recalled, "At Ittimnaryuk, there is an ancient weir which was made by Tuniit. The weirs made by Tuniit are made with very large rocks, so large that a mere Inuk couldn't lift them up, that place has one of those weirs. Usually, the river flow at every ice break up washes the smaller rocks away, so people would put the rocks back and build it up again, and keep using that weir … That particular weir is called Tuniqtat."[18]

The Inuit therefore arrived in a land that had already been made habitable. According to the Iglulingmiut, the *tuniit* were effective hunters of sea mammals, but very quarrelsome and easily angered, while according to the Nattilingmiut, they "were so good natured as to be almost timid and therefore easily took flight." The Nattilingmiut told Rasmussen that the "Tunrit always fled north or east, never to the west.[19] One would think their forefathers had believed that everybody to the west was hostile towards them. And they never came back. But one can still see the ruins of their stone houses with the entrance passage overgrown with big, yellow, sappy flowers on thick stalks. 'These flowers make good amulets that have growing power and strength in them,' said old Katsarsuk, who told the story to me."[20]

According to the Aivilingmiutaq elder Ivaluardjuk, the *tuniit* had many villages at Uglit near Iglulik.[21] They were associated with specific places, sometimes with their names. Thus, it is said that at Tasirsuaq, a lake near Tununiq, the Tunaluit lived, a man and a woman of the *tuniit* tribe.[22] The places where the *tuniit* had lived were well known, and Qaqurtingniq provided Rasmussen (1931, 114–15) with a list of the names of these places. According to the Nattilingmiut, "they loved the sea when it was not covered with ice and preferred to choose settlements where there were plenty of whales, walruses and seals, and these they hunted in their kayaks. They were skilled at musk ox hunting, too, and bold bear hunters."[23] The Nattilingmiut said that the *tuniit* spoke the same language they did, though with some dialectical differences. In winter they were mainly dressed in bear furs. Stone was their preferred material to work on, and they also used stones for graves.

> Whereas the Netsilingmiut only used stones for making meat caches, the Tunrit made use of them both for graves and houses. They piled great stones over the dead. This they considered to be most necessary, and to this day they are fond of relating a story showing how reluctant the Tunrit were to neglect this custom. When they were driven from Sherman Inlet there was an old woman, Akusínguaq, who was so feeble that she was unable to go with them. And, as she had to be left behind, they could not bear the thought that she might die among people who simply laid their dead out on the ground, so they buried her alive under great stones. Even to this day her grave is shown to strangers and it is widely known as a place to make offerings that always result in good hunting.[24]

Many stories testify to the strength of the *tuniit*. "A walrus hauled up on the ice was dragged home just like an ordinary fjord seal, by thongs fastened to its body; so strong were those men."[25] They were magnificent swimmers and able to throw their spears with their feet with great efficiency.[26] According to South Baffin traditions, *tuniit* had neither boats nor dogs but walked great distances to kill walruses with harpoons, hauling the carcasses onto the beaches.[27] Nattilik stories relate that the *tuniit* were lazy and did not like to walk. In one story, a lazy *tuniq* rubbed the soles of his feet against a stone at Lake Kangirluk, between the big Nattilik Lake and Itsuarturvik, so that it would appear that he had walked a lot.[28] Another story, about an attack on an Inuk village, is very similar to well-known stories about wars between Indians and Inuit, as pointed out by Rasmussen (1931, 119). According to Hawkes (1916, 143–7), in Nunavik, Inuit and *tuniit* had been able to intermarry up to the time the Inuit were betrayed by a *tuniit* woman (this refers to the Navaranaq myth),[29] which led to the extermination of the *tuniit* by the Inuit.

The main features of the *tuniit*, then, are that they preceded the Inuit; they were strong and slow; they shaped the country and had links with specific places and with the stone houses that can still be found in many places; and they hunted big animals, such as bears and whales.

Tuniit are supposed to be still around. Henry Ivaluarjuk from Iglulik told George Kappianaq that he saw one from a plane.[30] At the elders conference in Kangiq&iniq in 2002, Levi Iluittuq from Kugaaruk talked about having had a dream about a giant figure in bear clothes. The elders immediately identified him as a *tuniq*.

IJIRAIT

Rasmussen (1929, 113)[31] observes that among the Iglulingmiut the *ijirait*, or invisible mountain spirits, are among the *angakkuit*'s most powerful helping spirits. He glossed the meaning of the word as "those who have something about the eyes," explaining that their eyes and their mouth were not set transversely in their faces, but lengthwise, so that they "blink sideways." They have excellent eyesight. They live inside the hills, which they have fitted up like great stone houses, much resembling those inhabited by white men. They are not visible to human beings but only to shamans. One should never show any fright when one hears them, for they only attack the timid and cowardly. Ordinary people become afraid as soon as they hear their whistling in the air. According to Pujuat Tapaqti from Kangiq&iniq, the sound of human whistling indicates that *ijirait* are around.[32] Avaalaqiaq's daughter recalled seeing an *ijiraq* in Baker Lake in 1933, when she was eighteen: "My son and daughter Evelyn went out to hunt. We saw two caribou, and shot the first one, but we couldn't shoot the second. Some caribou just won't die. I asked my son how many more bullets we had and he said six. So I got really scared. This caribou walked all around us in a circle, and then came back where it started. Caribou don't look back to where they came from. So I knew this was one that we shouldn't kill. Some caribou are human. You can tell by their legs. When they grow new fur it is very thin. This one was very thick. So we went back to the camp."[33]

The *ijirait* are fast runners and can overtake caribou easily. When they capture human beings, they turn them into fast runners by having the flesh from their shinbones or toes eaten away by worms in the earth or creatures in the sea. They are anthropomorphic and live like humans, but they can take on the shape of caribou. Their faces look like the muzzles of caribou,[34] they use caribou skins as clothes, and they dislike everything originating from the sea.

The *ijirait* are strong as wolves. They have objects, much like the mirrors of white men, that show all that is happening far way among the dwellings of human beings.[35]

The *ijirait* dislike anything connected to childbirth. "If a woman becomes insane it is either because she has committed some serious breach of taboo, or because she has once seen some ijerqat and thereafter visited a woman in childbirth. The ijerqat will not endure this; they feel such dread of women in childbirth that they deprive any woman who has done this of her wits."[36]

Lucassie Nutaraaluk from Iqaluit and Mariano Aupilaarjuk from Kangiq&iniq discussed *ijirait* in an oral traditions course in Iqaluit in 1998. Nutaraaluk suggested, "Maybe they are the deceased's people's *tarniit* that remain on the land." He added, "Some of those who roam the earth are said to never leave it." Aupilaarjuk stated, "Dead people turn into *ijirait*. That is what I have heard. I have not seen this personally, but I believe it … *ijirait* are said to be deceased people that turn into caribou." He also said that *ijirait* "can go to the store, but no matter how many times they shop, the stock never depletes. Over time they can buy snowmobiles just like we do. When we had dog teams, they had dog teams. When we no longer used dog teams and we used snowmobiles, they used snowmobiles." Thus, the development of *ijirait* was correlated with that of ordinary human beings. Aupilaarjuk said that his wife saw an *ijiraq* and therefore they must be able to come to the community. The distinction between *ijirait* and other categories of non-human beings is not always clear. Nutaraaluk identified the *ijirait* with the *tarriassuit*: "For me *ijirait* and *tariassuit* are the same ... They are just different words for the same thing."[37]

There are many traditions about *ijirait* in Iglulik, but they exist elsewhere as well.[38] In a workshop in Kangiq&iniq in 2002, Peter Suvaksiuq from Arviat observed, "In our area there is a place called Ijiralik. I have never seen an *ijiraq*. They say that they do exist around Arviat. Others have seen them. They look like caribou, but they also have a human form. People say that those who go there often lose things like pocket knives, etc." Other elders at the meeting added their own experiences. Iluittuq from Kugaaruk once met a caribou that had appeared to come out of the ground, and he decided that it was an *ijiraq*. Therefore, he did not eat it. "I wanted to eat it, but my wife told me not to. If we had eaten it, I wonder what would have happened to us." Jose Angutinngurniq from Kugaaruk said that he once followed a caribou that had suddenly disappeared. "The land was very flat. There was nowhere for it to hide. Then I thought that maybe it was an *ijiraq* and that's why it had disappeared. That's what made me believe in them." Ollie Itinnuaq from Kangiq&iniq said that he killed a bull that was probably an *ijiraq*, but then had forgotten about it. Pujuat Tapaqti commented, "I have heard that *ijirait* make you forget what you have seen. You only recall it afterwards."[39]

Aupilaarjuk indicated that whereas *ijirait* could easily retaliate if one of them was killed, people who had a tattoo between their eyes, a *kigjugaq*, were usually protected from their attacks. The marking provided protection.[40]

Kappianaq gave an extensive account of his meetings with *ijirait*:

> I don't think *ijirait* are ever going to die out. The ones closer to shore are as big as humans. The ones that live more inland are larger. If you haven't heard about them and you encounter them, they can be very scary. I have heard that they have a snout like a caribou ... If there was an *ijiraq* close by, I would not be able to feel the ground much. My feelings would be numbed because I was in fear. They are not evil, and therefore they are able to help. They could be scary, or they could be helpful. *Qajaaksaqtuq*, is when the ice is thin and the waves make the ice ripple. An *ijiraq* is able to make the land ripple ... I saw three of them as they were playing on the rocks. Another time I saw those same three in the form of caribou. They were three different sizes. I wanted to catch them, but they would move further away. I got lost for three days because of them. I was lost for three days and three nights. It was very scary, even though I did not see them in their true form. I had left my dogs behind even though I wanted to get home ... They didn't make any sound at all. You could see them in between the ropes of the tent. I think it was because they didn't attempt to scare me that I was not scared. I just watched them, and I talked to my wife about them. The *ijirait* stayed close by. I think those three had been childhood playmates of my wife. My wife knew them and had been taken inland by them. If it had

> been only me, I would have ended up without a wife, but because my father was there this didn't happen. The old woman Qaataniq told me that her father had taken my wife back from the *ijirait* … they had actually taken her home. She had large bruises on her thighs and on her upper arms … The bruises appeared as two thumb and eight finger prints. The *ijirait* can hold you down as though you were a child. Even if I was screaming and kicking, I could be held as though I were a child.
>
> … My wife was not able to talk about what happened to her for a long time. She could not remember. It was only about three years later that she was finally able to talk about this. Whether male or female, the *ijirait* can make a person forget what has happened to them. It can be very scary if you don't know anything about them … There are times when I feel the need to talk about this. Not often, but the need comes upon me to talk about it because I experienced it. Therefore I know that there are *ijirait* even though I am Christian. If I said they didn't exist, I know that I would be lying.[41]

Rasmussen (1929, 205–6) describes an encounter that the *angakkuq* Qingaisilaq (or Oqaminiq), the father of the *angakkuq* Ava, had with the *ijirait*. One *ijiraq* tried to throw him down, but the *angakkuq* withstood the attack. They separated on friendly terms, and the *angakkuq* had a coat made with ornamentations depicting the encounter.[42]

Rose Iqallijuq (IE 91) from Iglulik describes a period when her husband Amarualik, an *angakkuq*, lived for some time with the *ijirait*:

> Amarualik, my late first husband, was approached by them and was immediately surrounded by them. Once he was surrounded they got closer to him and at that moment he was asked if he was dangerous. He replied that since he had never seen them before, he would not intimidate them. At that moment he was asked to join them, so he started to flee from them since he had no intention of joining them. However, he soon was overtaken and held, making it virtually not possible to break free from their grasp. He again was asked to join them, but he continually told them he had no desire to be amongst them. As he was a shaman, he called upon his helping spirits to assist him, so he was let go so he left them and they disappeared at the same time. Then, later, he had another encounter with them but this time he did not flee from their presence but he was stoned until he lost consciousness. He was now living amongst them. Two females were now after him so he submitted to one of them. He started to live with her. She decided that he would surely be missed by his own people, so she suggested that he return to his people as she will be able to see him now on a frequent basis. So he went back to his people. Before he joined his people he had planned to tell about his encounter but he completely forgot about them, including the time he was stoned.

Rasmussen (1929, 206–8) presents stories about two women who were kidnapped by the *ijirait* and two old men who joined them.[43] The stories reflect two recurrent themes associated with the *ijirait*: they kidnap people, and the spirits of the deceased join them.

Iqallijuq (IE 91) explained how hard it was to deal with the experience of encountering an *ijiraq:*

> The period when one started to have maladies, the shamans … used to call upon their helping spirits to find the cause of the ailment. So they were able to get the victims to disclose their experiences when the shamans found out through their shamanistic rituals. The victim will be encouraged to give the details of his experiences with the *ijirait*. The shaman will be persistent so the victim would tell him the whole story. One would feel so compassionate towards the victims when they were relating the story. The victims would agonize so much that they would yell, sing, and brawl even to the point of paralysis and unconsciousness before they could tell about their experience. Some would recover from their malady when they had disclosed their experiences with the *ijirait*. They would recover even when the odds of recovery were very slow before they related their experience. However my late husband Amarualik and Qingaq never recovered as there was no one around to do shamanistic rituals. There was no one amongst our number that would suspect something out of ordinary as there was no shaman amongst us. Amarualik, my late husband opened up when he started to sing just before he was to pass away. His lungs were damaged so puss was coming out but I believe there was an internal damage. On both cases when they were dying they came out only when both were subconscious in their death bed and eventually passed away. From these two experiences I have seen the consequences of people that had made contacts with the *ijirait*. Prior to the introduction of Christianity, the persons that had made contacts with the *ijirait* used to be healed from their ailment when they were made to remember their experiences with *ijirait*.

Iqallijuq (IE 26) said that the *ijirait* continued to pursue her husband: "Every time we went to sleep I could hear rocks moving and it seemed the earth around us was moving. I used to be frightened at first but I got used to it. Afterwards he got sick and he started to chant and that was the time I found out when he confessed to me. He said that the spirits wanted him and when he dies he is not going to heaven, because he is going to go to the spirits that wanted him. He said he will join the spirits now and when the world ends he will go to heaven because he had confessed what had happened to him. That is what happened."

Today, young Inuit tell stories about occasional meetings with *ijirait*, describing them as people who suddenly turn into caribou. Kopak, Ishulutak, and Arnatsiaq, three young Inuit who participated in the cosmology course taught by Saladin d'Anglure in Iqaluit in 1998, told one such story: "There was one case where a young hunter killed an *ijiraq*. The Inuit elders told the young hunter not to go hunting alone and not to go to certain places as the *ijirait* would try to kill him and make it look like an accident. There was one case where a hunter died in a very shallow river ... When a young hunter goes hunting he has to be very careful not to shoot an *ijiraq* caribou. He needs to make sure to look at the antlers to determine that it is not a spirit, as the Inuit have a strong taboo about this."[44] Hunters have to make sure they are not shooting at an *ijiraq*.

THE *TARRIASSUIT*

Rasmussen (1929, 210–11) relates that the *tarriassuit*, or shadow people, are just like ordinary human beings.[45] They have the same kind of houses, weapons, harpoons, and bladder harpoons as the Inuit, but one can only see their shadows. They are not dangerous, and they are good to human beings. *Angakkuit* were happy to have them as helping spirits. They hunt by running, and can only bring down an animal if they are able to overtake it on foot. They only become visible when they die. According to the Aivilingmiutaq elder Ivaluardjuk, one can never catch sight of them, by looking straight at them.

Nattilingmiut refer to *tarriassuit* as *talliqat* or *tallirait*. In a Nattilik story told by the Nattilingmiutaq Nakasuk, an Inuk woman once married one of them. Although he was a good husband to her, the woman could not accept that she never saw him, and finally she thrust a knife at the place where he was sitting. A handsome young man appeared at the moment of his death and then dropped to the floor. When the shadow people wanted to take revenge, nothing happened, for the Inuit could not see them and the shadow people would not attack people who did not defend themselves.[46]

Iqallijuq (IE 091) from Iglulik told of another marriage between Inuit and *tarriassuit*:

> The ones that hunted on the ice were known as *tarriaksuit*. They make their homes in the mountain. There was someone in Pond Inlet that had married a *tarriaksuk* or [taken her as] a girlfriend. He was taken into a mountain right through a cliff by the *tarriaksuit*. It is said that one cannot see them face to face, but you could see them through the corner of your eye without facing them. You can make out their faces or hair built in the same manner as an Inuk. They make their home in the mountains; one enters right through the cliff. It appears there is no entrance but it will open. When he was taken amongst them his sleds were hidden and his dogs turned invisible. They are quite different from *ijirait*. They are land creatures.

Boas (1907, 543) reports that Inuit used to exchange wives with the *tarriassuit*. These traditions are still very much alive. Kopak, Ishulutak, and Arnatsiaq related the experiences of Naujarlaq, an elder from Kangiqtugaapik, who said he had once lived with the *tarriassuit*. According to him, these spirits are in many ways similar to the *ijirait*. They are invisible, they have no footprints, they live in mountains, watch humans, and now own cars, snowmobiles, trucks, and vans. They go to the same shops as Inuit do and share a few characteristics with white people. Naujarlaq said that he even had a *tarriassuit* girlfriend whom he married in a *tarriassuit* church. She gave him a daughter who looked just like his own daughter but a little bit older.[47]

THE *INGNIRIUGJAIT*

Rasmussen (1929, 208–10) glosses the meaning of *ingniriugjait* as "the great fire." He explains, "The name refers to the fact that the windows of the sea spirits, or perhaps more correctly the shore spirits, are sometimes seen lighted up. The spirits of earth, on the other hand, have luminous lard bladders in their huts and take their name from this." The *ingniriugjait* seem to encompass the contrast between land and sea. The shore spirits look like human beings. They are handsome, although some say they have noses like caribou. They live in warm and comfortable houses on small reefs or rocky islets. They only wear sealskin clothes and live entirely on animals from the sea. They are not hostile to people, and shamans often use them as helping spirits. They provide food to the shamans or send up newly killed seals from their dwellings just below the surface under the sea.[48]

The land spirits live far inland and hunt only caribou. They resemble human beings, but their eyes and mouths are like those of the *ijirait*. They have very narrow faces and long noses. They are mighty hunters and always have an abundance of meat and fine caribou skins. Along the walls inside their houses are small shining things that look like intestines filled with suet and entrails, resembling the intestines of both caribou calves and fully grown beasts. People who obtained such an object would become very great shamans, provided they carried the light on their person for the rest of their life. It would become the shaman's *angakkua* or *qaumaniq* (shamanic vision).

Rasmussen classifies spirits of the sea and spirits of the land under one heading. In this context, the contrast between land and sea is not marked, although the sea spirits are clearly associated with seals and the land spirits with caribou that resemble the *ijirait* in many respects. These spirits can give the shaman his *angakkua*.

Rasmussen tells a story about a young man who was killed after harpooning a seal that turned out to be an *ingneriujaq* of the sea. The seal took revenge on him by transforming the seal meat the young hunter had eaten into a harpoon, which killed him. Another story relates that the *ingniriugjait* of the earth cannot bear to see a person sleep. A young man who visited them was woken up continually until he died of exhaustion.[49] Boas (1907, 525, 543–4) presents a variant of the story, describing *ingniriugjait* as "the people without eye-lids," apparently unable to sleep. In this account, it was the shore spirits who kept the unfortunate young man awake.

The *ingniriugjait* resemble the *ijirait* in some respects. Instead of receiving old men into their midst as the *ijirait* do, they kill young men by depriving them of sleep. The lack of sleep suggests that the spirits themselves are always awake and thus, like the *ijirait,* live in a time dimension quite different from that of ordinary human beings.

THE *INUGARULLIGAIT*

Rasmussen (1929, 212) translates *inugarulligait* as "the little people, or dwarfs." He relates that they live in the mountains and look just like human beings. They are no bigger than the lumbar vertebra of a walrus set on end. They are dressed in caribou skins. They are hostile to human beings, and when they meet one, they begin to increase in size. As soon as they have grown as tall as their opponent, they fall upon him and try to throw him down. If they succeed, they hold their victim down until he dies of starvation. If they fail, they feign to die. But if one looks back after leaving them, they have always disappeared without a trace. Boas (1907, 540) writes, with respect to Cumberland Sound, "When a dwarf is thrown by a person, he is unable to arise as long as the person who has thrown him remains in sight."

The *inugarulligait* kill their game by following an animal until they overtake it. They are very swift and can outrun any animal. *Angakkuit* liked to have them as helping spirits because they are very effective. In a story collected by Rasmussen (1929, 13; 1931, 256), some *inugarulligait* ate the hindquarters of a caribou bull and the tail fin of a whale. After they left, the hindquarters of the caribou bull changed into those of a gull and what had been the tail fin of a whale was now no more than the stump of a bird's tail. Thus dwarfs can make things appear as if they are large. The Nattilingmiut explained that the *inugarulligait*'s kayaks and sledges, their dogs, their houses, and their tents all grow. But when no one is there to see these things, they are small. The animals that *inugarulligait* hunt are really quite small and only become big when humans see them. The bears of the *inugarulligait* are only lemmings, but if they meet humans, they become bears. Their walruses are only eider ducks, but if humans come upon them, them they turn into walruses. Boas (1907, 540) relates, "An old Aivilik woman claimed that one day, when she was following a sledge, she saw a dog about as long as her hand carrying a tent on its back, crossing her trail. She did not see any of the dwarfs themselves." There are several stories about Inuit dogs that fight the dogs of dwarves or even come to the assistance of their master when he is fighting a dwarf.[50]

In Cumberland Sound, dwarfs are believed to be related to the wind. According to a story collected by Boas (1907, 540), whenever a dwarf is seen, a gale of wind can be expected. Another story relates that every time people tried to approach fleeing dwarfs, the wind would increase in strength. Sarah Haulli (IE 099) from Iglulik supported this perception, saying that "they are capable of causing heavy winds. It is also said that they have the capacity to grow at will … Once the *inugarulligaajjuk* attains the same height as that of the human kind, he will start to fight him until he is able to suffocate him." Nutaraaluk from Iqaluit reported that *inugarulligait* are little people who use the same skin clothing as Inuit. They are fast runners, very strong –they can tow in a bearded seal – and are quite violent towards people. They jump up, and wrapping themselves around you, they suffocate you with their groin area.[51] Kappianaq related, "I have heard that they are very small and that they are prone to want to fight. Whether I was a man or a woman, if the *inugarulligaq* were to look at me from my feet up, then it would grow to the same height I was and it would start fighting ... I have heard that their footprints are only as big as the butt of a rifle. When they are tracking a fox and they get it, they consider themselves to have gotten a bear."[52]

According to Felix Kupak from Naujaat, the *inugarulligait* are flat-footed. When they ask a person for food because they are hungry, he has to give it to them and then he will become a successful hunter.[53] Anautalik from Arviat related that the pants of the *inugarulligait* have baggy knees and so people are afraid of those who wear trousers with baggy knees. *Inugarulligait* can be beaten by tickling and will only get up when you are out of sight.[54] Eva Muqyunniq from Arviat observed that *inugarulliit* can make people forget. She had met four of them and could only remember meeting them a year later.[55] Suvaksiuq, also from Arviat, recalled that he and Luke Suluk had found the house of an *inugarulligait* family and that Luke had wanted to make a picture of it. Suvaksiuq had told him to put a quarter inside the house as payment and that it would be safe to do so, as people were not supposed to take something just from the ground.[56]

Silas Putumiraqtuq from Qamanittuaq (Baker Lake) recalled how his father had once killed a dwarf:

> My father was cleaning the ice window, but he looked where Kunititaaq was looking and he also saw a dwarf. He was black faced, and even his face was hairy, and he had a long turned up nose. He was standing on the back of the bed, striking pieces of wood together, so my father jumped down and took the snow knife, which was at the edge of the bed and floor, and crawled on the bed to get close to the dwarf. The dwarf realized Uqaut was near him and jumped down between the skins and disappeared. It just limped under him, under the skins on the *iglu* bed, so my father just struck the snow knife down where the dwarf had disappeared. He kept on stabbing down and when he finally pulled it out the snow knife was stained with blood. They were just children and no one believed them. Since they were kids they probably thought that if they just stood there and did nothing the dwarf would kill them both with his wooden clubs.[57]

Today, dwarfs are still around, and they are seen as powerful beings who live close to human beings. Abe Okpik, a well-known Inuit leader originally from the western Canadian Arctic, told an interesting story about *inugarulliit*:

> In Cambridge Bay someone saw some not too long ago. They don't mix with us. One of the stories she told us, and even my father's uncle told me, quite a long time ago, was about a family of *inugarulliit* that came to our Noatak camp. They said, "We want to stay with you. We want to stay with you and raise our family and live among you." There was a male and a female and their little daughter. So there was one family, according to my father's uncle and that old lady, who wanted to live with the common people because they were good providers. Those people always had big Inuit dogs for packing and so on, and they looked after them. After the *inugarulliit* were living there for a while, and after the ground started to freeze a bit, one of the dogs accidentally bit the little girl and she died. They begged the family to stay but they said, "We can't stay, because traditionally we don't do those things. We're going to leave you because we don't trust you; you did something to our girl." They parted and they said, "We'll see you in the region sometime."
>
> But this guy had a little bow and arrow and he shot the dog. When he shot the dog his arrow went through the dog and landed in the ground. They knew it landed in the ground. When they left, the people looked for that arrow. It went through and into the ground. They found it in the permafrost. That's how powerful the arrow was.[58]

Okpik added that they celebrated song feasts, playing the drum, and danced as a group. "Someone who was far from the coastal area would imitate a walrus, another would get up and dance like a bird; someone would dress like a bear. They imitated all these living things. They had their own way of making people understand and communicating their feelings."[59] Clearly, the *inugarulligait* are still very much alive in the discourse today.

INUKPAIT

According to Rasmussen (1929, 214), *inukpait* (giants) look like ordinary human beings. They are harmless and well disposed towards mankind. Boas (1907, 540) records an interesting story about a giant who joined Inuit in fighting the *allait*. Giants often have names (e.g., Inukpasugjuk).[60] A human being cannot have intercourse with an *inukpak* woman because she is so big that he will drop into her vagina and die. If an *inukpak* man has intercourse with a human woman, his penis will split her and kill her.[61]

As in the case of dwarfs, food is often an important feature in stories about *inukpait*. A story collected by Rasmussen (1929, 216) relates that a man survived on the crumbs that a giant dropped. According to the Nattilingmiut, giants hunt giant bears, *nanurluit*, for food.[62]

Suvaksiuq from Arviat related, "Some time ago my father [and I] were out and we saw an *inukpak* by a lake. We were on our way to Arviat when we saw an *inukpak* so I believe they exist." As a child, he saw an *inukpak* trying to enter the igloo, but it got stuck in the entrance.[63] Today, recollections about encounters with *inukpait* are far scarcer than those about *inuragulligait.*

THE SPIRITS OF STONES

Boas (1964 [1888], 591–2) reports that stones serve as helping spirits for *angakkuit*:

> The tornait of the stones live in the large boulders scattered over the country. The Eskimo believe that these rocks are hollow and form a nice house, the entrance of which is only visible to the angakoq whose genius lives in the stone. The tornaq is a woman with only one eye, in the middle of the brow. Another kind of tornaq lives in the stones that roll down the hills in spring when the snow begins to melt.
>
> If a native happens to meet such a stone, which is about to become his tornaq, the latter addresses him: "I jumped down in long leaps from my place on the cliff. As the snow melts, as water is formed on the hills, I jumped down." Then it asks the native whether he is willing to have it for his tornaq, and if he answers in the affirmative it accompanies him, wobbling along, as it has no legs.

Rasmussen's informant Nakasuk told him about the *uvivigtut,* "the fidgety ones," those that move about uneasily and restlessly. They live at Iluileq near the river that the salmon go up in autumn. They look like humans. If one comes upon them unawares, they disappear straight into the flat wall of a big stone. People say that these stone spirits live on stone and that the small, round shiny stones around the big stone are their excrement. Nakasuk related that once an Inuk man married an *uvivigtut* woman and took her away. He was attacked by *uvivigtut,* and they tickled him until he died. When people tried to avenge him, the spirits fled into a stone. The *uvivigtut* had a shaman who slapped the stone with the skin of an ermine that he carried as an amulet on the hood of his inner coat. Every time he hit it, one of the spirits disappeared into the stone. When one of the Inuit pierced the ermine skin with an arrow, the skin lost its power. The spirits could no longer escape into the stone, and all of them were killed. Nakasuk commented that the *uvivigtut* are good helping spirits and would be harmless if only they were not so prone to tickling those they fell in with.[64]

Spirits might be associated with fire stones, stones used for pounding blubber or marrow bones, cooking stones, and the various stones people used out on the land. Rasmussen (1929, 181) notes that "[s]tones which have been used for "kau^{w}arsikʃik"... i.e. for hammering blubber so as to make the oil flow freely when placed in the lamp, or stones which have been used as hammers to crush marrow bones, must always be thrown outside when a house is abandoned." Aupilaarjuk from Kangiq&iniq reported that when people left an igloo, they had to clean it and move all the stones quite a distance from the igloo.[65]

Kappianaq from Iglulik reported that people should not hit a caribou head or heart with a stone; neither should they hit or break a caribou bone: "Whenever people knock on a caribou bone, when they are breaking bones or something, then you would hear *apsait* later on. I believe in this because I've seen it myself. Sometimes the sound of cracking ice is dangerous. I have experienced this twice when we moved to different camps away from that area. If you moved away from that cracking ice sound nothing would happen. I don't really know what it is, but it's very loud. *Apsait* are very loud. Some places are like that."[66]

Apsait are associated with thunder and lightning. Kappianaq spoke of this connection: "They say an *apsaq* could be as bright as a spark from lightning. When they are about to appear, they will come to the entrance. If the *apsaq* hits its shin bones, then it will be as bright as lightning and the ground shudders. If I don't want to flee, I am to urinate on the bottom of the doorway. I also heard that if you were to flee from them, even though they have a human form, they don't have a body. Those who had the ability to see them said they do have a human form. If I were to flee they would catch me unless I was running away sideways. After I fled sideways, I was to stop."[67]

Alain Ijiraq from Iglulik as well as Ollie Itinnuaq from Kangiq&iniq described the sound of *apsait* as a loud banging noise evoking the cracking of the ice.[68] According to Aupilaarjuk, an *apsaq* was "a being that only has a head and legs. They usually travel in family groups and become noisier as they get closer. They are said to live in the rocks that oil lamps are placed on in an *iglu*, if the rocks are not thrown out of the *iglu* when it is permanently vacated. They are considered dangerous as they can create fires in *igluit*."[69] This description evokes South Baffin drawings that depict *tuurngait* with only a head and legs,[70] as well as the representations of *tunnituarruk* common in Nunavik, such as the carvings by the famous artist Davidialuk Alasuaq.

Itinnuaq experienced an encounter with *apsait*:

> They say that there are *apsait* on land. I know they exist and I have heard about them. Up on the land while I set up camp, I was going to feed my dogs. My axe broke while I was going to cut up the meat to feed my dogs so I started using a stone to crush the meat. Our dogs used to be loose back then. I took their harnesses off and I was feeding them. It became night and it was dark. I could hear *apsait* below me. The sound became louder and louder and it was all over. It became uncomfortable so I started thinking I should harness up my dogs and leave. Then I thought, if I do leave I am never going to leave this behind, so I started wondering how I could stop hearing these *apsait*. The noise was very loud. Before I fell asleep, I was frightened so I couldn't sleep. I don't know what happened when the sound started going away. You could hear them go away, and then they were gone. I listened for them and then I fell asleep. I forgot about the sounds of the *apsait*. I woke up and it was late in the day because I had stayed up late because of the *apsait*. It is because they actually exist that you can hear

them. When I was told about this experience, I was asked how I had dealt with this. I said that I fed my dogs using a stone to cut up the meat as I had broken my axe handle. An elder told me that whenever you smash the heart of any animal, then you are calling the *apsait*.[71]

This story illustrates that the appearance of *apsai*t is related to a transgression.

THE PEOPLE IN THE SEA

Various beings in human appearance lived in the sea. Apart from the sea woman, there were *tuutaliit* (often mentioned as being among the helping spirits of the *angakkuit*), *qallupilluit, lumajuut,* and *taliillajut* (the latter are sometimes referred to as mermaids). In Inuit oral traditions, the distinctions between these categories of non-human sea dwellers are often not clear. In particular, the categories *lumajuut* and *taliillaajut* can easily merge with that of the sea woman.

Boas (1964 [1888], 620) describes an individual spirit by the name of Qalupalik. According to an old tradition, when the hunting had been unsuccessful, a poor old woman gave her grandson to Qalupalik, who put the child into his large hood. When the Inuit were successful in hunting again, she regretted her deed and a man and a woman succeeded in getting the boy back. Nowadays, elders still stress that *qallupilluit* really like children. When they catch a child, they carry him away on their back. "*Qallupilluit* are described as having scaly, bumpy skin like a sculpin." As they live in the water and have pouches on their back, children are discouraged from playing too close to the water's edge.[72]

Aalasi Joamie from Iqaluit said that a *qallupalik* once approached their camp at night: "Nobody saw it but the dogs were so scared that they got on top of the *qammaq*. The people started wondering if it was a *qalupalik*. When we were out clam digging, my brother-in-law saw the tail of an *amauti* made of *mitiq*, eider duck skin. He saw the *qalupalik* running very close to us. Every night we heard something saying 'viivi.'"[73]

Haulli (IE 099) from Iglulik believed that *qallupilluit* "for certain are still in our waters." Kappaniaq commented on them:

> I have never seen one, but they say they do exist. They are said to have eyes and mouths that slant downwards. The term for this is *palluqsingajuq*. I have heard that Felix Alaralak has seen one. I have only heard their sounds under the ice in the past, when I spent more time playing on the shore … This is the sound they would make, "aqatututu." You could also hear them jumping under the ice. I have heard them myself, so I know they exist … I have heard of children being taken, and placed in their *amautit*. I have not heard of anyone being taken in an *amauti* since I was born. They say that the *amauti* is so deep that the child would just fall in. The child would be taken down to the shore. This even happened to one child who was no longer a toddler anymore. The *qallupilluk* kept the child. I have also heard

that the *qallupilluit* used seaweed as whips. They used *qiqquat*, the seaweed with the flat leaf and the long tapering stem, not the *kuanniit*.[74]

The image of a *qallupalik* putting people into his hood evokes the figure of Amajurjuk. According to the Nattilingmiut, Amajurjuk, the one who carries something on her back, is a giant woman who steals children. Instead of an *amauti*, she has a big space in her back formed of driftwood that smells of rotten seaweed.[75] Victor Tungilik from Naujaat thought that *amajurjuit* – beings that kidnapped people by putting them in their *amauti* – no longer existed,[76] but Felix Pisuk from Kangiq&iniq (1999 interview) reported that he saw one close to the community. He described it as a big woman wearing a big caribou *amauti*. One should not approach the spirit or run away from it; running away would cause death or great sickness.

According to Rasmussen (1931, 247), *tuutaliit* resemble human beings as well as seals. People call them seal-men. Some people believe that they are descended from the *tuutalik* who avenged his father's death in the story of Kiviuq. *Tuutaliit* are splendid breathing-hole hunters and are not afraid of going down through the breathing hole when game is scarce. They often serve as helping spirits.

Kappianaq remembered his mother telling him about a powerful creature in the waters that could do anything. It had a fluke like a whale and the upper body of a human being with a head. It could penetrate the earth and was known as a *tuutalik*. He heard that one was caught around Kinngait and that the people gave it a human burial because they feared it might take revenge. He related:

> We call them *tuutalit*. I have never experienced one or seen one. I have heard that the top part of their bodies has a human form, and the bottom part is the flipper of a whale … When they come up, they use their right hand and when they submerge they use their left hand. They have the proportions of a human. My younger brother saw one when he was young. What he saw must have been an adult, because it was quite large … I think it was a big male. The chest was quite wide. Those who have seen one say their flesh is quite dark. They have hair similar to a seal because they are sea mammals. I have heard that some *angakkuit* have them as helpers … I have heard that when a *taliillajuuq* was trying to help a person they could come up on land. If an *angakkuq* calls on a *taliillajuuq*, it is able to come right away through the earth. All beings, animals or not, that are used as helpers can come right away, even sea mammals like *ugjuit* [bearded seals] … My grandfather Tulugaarjuk had a *taliillajuuq*, a *tuutalik*, as a *tuurngaq*. It helped him physically. If my grandfather was in need of his helper, the moment he thought of it, it would appear right away.[77]

Kappianaq claimed that *tuutaliit* and *taliillajuut* are the same. According to Peter Pitseolak from Kinngait, the *taliillajuut* are very similar to seals and that hunters might harpoon them by mistake:

> Apalirak told me a story about a man who lost a son at a camp where several men had disappeared. This man was forever hunting, probably looking for his dead son. He was hunting one day with another man when something got hold of the tail of his kayak and tried to pull it down. These men tested. They put their kayaks back to back and watched to see if something came up. Something did. The man harpooned it and while the creature was struggling under the water, trying to get free, there was a lot of crying. Real cries. Then the creature died and got lost. The men didn't even have a chance to see what it looked like. But they heard the cries of a crowd of voices –from the bottom of the sea. All the crying must have been other taliyayus.[78]

Maaki Kakkik from Panniqtuuq had heard stories about the *taliillajuut* from her grandmother, Miali Tuttu: "Myself, I really haven't seen a *Taliillajuuq*. I have heard that Alasi's late husband, Joanasie, when he was a child, was at the low tide and saw a small *Taliillajuuq*. When he saw one that was stuck at low tide, he played with it with a hook and the *Taliillajuuq* had its mouth wide open. He had the *Taliillajuuq* hooked. While he did that, it died. He had made fun of the *Taliillajuuq* all that time. He then gave it to the dogs, but the dogs did not want it. That is what happened. We had heard that we should never make fun of them."

Taliillajuut can help people in need. Miali Tuttu said that they saved her husband when he went through thin ice. Then he was lifted up by a *taliillajuuq*. "When he tried to see what it was, it was something bluish that was going down deeper, and he also saw its hair. They can really help. They are not supposed to be made fun of at all, if we see one at any time. I have told even our children so they can tell their children too, that if they see a living being or if they see an adult that is stuck in the low tide, they are helpless."

If you make fun of the *taliillajuut*, they will not help you when you need them and you will drown. Miali said that this happened to Alasi's husband: "Alasi's husband died in the water down south even though it did not seem dangerous. They have lifeguards down south. He died in the water; he had gone south for medical reasons and never came back. He was swimming in the water but did not come back to the surface. He was the one that made fun of the *Taliillajuuq* and killed it. That is why they should not be made fun of. They are the helpers and they can help."

Miali reported that even though they have arms, they are really fish; they have long hair and a delicate skin, just like fish skin; if they treated cruelly, they can fight back; and their number seems to have diminished: "I think there were a lot more long ago but I do not know where they went. Maybe they ran away. The only one I have heard about, is when Alasi's husband killed one ... The dogs probably see these *taliillajuut* since they walk around the low tide area, because when or where dogs go, they see different animals."[79]

Carvings of *taliillajuut* are frequently featured in art books. A *taliillajuuq* is often represented as a woman with long hair and naked breasts, the lower part of her body a fish tail covered with fish scales. She may be accompanied by a small *taliillajuuq,* evoking the relationship between the sea woman and the infant Unga. A coloured pencil drawing of such a figure by Pitseolak is presented in Pitseolak and Eber 2003 (40) with the words, "Talilayu who keeps the sea animals away from the hunters." According to July Papatsie from Pangnirtuuq, these entities are a species born from Sedna's finger with the other sea mammals. They are benevolent spirits able to save you when you fall in the sea. They are thus to be respected.[80]

Like the *taliillajuut,* the *lumaajuut* combine the features of a human being and a fish. A South Baffin elder told Tapea Keenainak, a student at the Nunavut Arctic College, "I do not really know them, only that it is the person of the sea, a woman. In our dialect we call her Lumaaju; when she is going under she makes the sound *lumaaq.*"[81] In her account of the story of the blind boy and his sister, an elder identified the person of the sea as the woman who gave birth to the blind boy after she turned into a white whale.[82] Pitseolak heard the story from Takeassuk, an Inuk from Nunavik, on the other side of his community: "Takeassuk once told me a story about the half-whale woman. It is a true story. She was shot by Indians. They thought they'd hit a seal. After they shot her they went to look at her and they saw the hair braided. Half of her was some kind of whale or fish – there was a flipper – and the body part was human. The Indians started shouting, 'We're murderers, we're murderers.' They buried her on the land. Probably her bones are still there in Arctic Quebec."[83]

In Nunavik, the widespread myth of the half-woman, half-fish creature also evokes the sea woman. Davidialuk Alasuaq from Povungnituk told a story about a meeting with a sea woman. A poor man was gathering driftwood along the shore when he saw a creature who was half human, half fish. She was huge. After he had helped her, she wanted to show him her gratitude and thus left him a gramophone, a rifle, and a sewing machine.[84] Davidialuk made a carving representing the man and the woman. It is worthwhile to note that in one of Davidialuk's coloured, felt-pen drawings the comparison between the sea woman figure and the half-woman, half-fish creature is even more explicit. Davidialuk wrote the following caption for this drawing, reproduced in Driscoll 1982 (24): "The man is pushing the seamaiden with a tree branch and asking her whether she has a husband. She says she has, and that she even has children. He asks whether she has a house of her own. 'Oh yes,' she said, 'we have a house under water.' The seamaiden asked the man whether there was anything he wanted, but he said he didn't know what he wanted. She said, 'I am going to give you a gun, a sewing machine and a gramophone.' The next day the man returned. The gun, the sewing machine and a gramophone were there!" With respect to another version of this story, Davidialuk commented that "white men are learning [to do as the half-fish did]."[85] Thus, the sea woman has become a mediator, introducing modern culture.

In June 1979 the Montreal Museum of Fine Arts organized an exhibition of fifty-one objects, mainly from the 1960s and 1970s, representing the sea woman and other sea people. Most of these objects were identified as representing "Sedna" or "sea goddess." The exhibition illustrated the lack of boundaries between categories such as the sea woman, *lumaaju*, and *taliillaajuut*. A *taliilajuuq* may be referred to as the sea goddess,[86] and conversely the sea woman may be depicted as a *taliillajuuq*, a woman with a fish tail, often a whale tail.

INGILLIT, ANGELS

With the adoption of Christianity, more non-human beings appeared in the Inuit universe as demons, and Inuit began to have experiences of the Devil, or Satanasi, and angels. Reverend Duncan reported that as soon as he arrived in Pond Inlet, in 1929, Inuit informed him that an angel had visited their camp (Laugrand 2002c, 351). A couple of decades later, in the Kivalliq region (Michéa 1949, 74), a person named Kanaiok asked a shaman to invoke the Devil, and the Devil suddenly appeared in the river as a walrus. Pujuat Tapaqti from Kangiq&iniq saw angels when she was very sick and expecting to die:

> I lay there waiting for my last breath. I saw these stairs. There were two angels on each side of the stairs. One of them had a wreath that was going to be placed on my head. The other one had flowers that I was going to hold. I lay there waiting for my last breath, but it never happened. I was ready to die. I was ready to climb those stairs. I was ready to leave my sons and my husband and go above. Up above the stairs I could hear singing. I had heard that I was going to have to go through a narrow opening, but what I saw were stairs as wide as this room. There were two angels that had come to get me. I tried my utmost to die, but I did not die. I lay there waiting for my last breath. Because it did not happen I took my son back.[87]

Suvaksiuq from Arviat related an experience he had had of angels after being attacked by a wolf: "This happened a long time ago. A wolf bit me on my legs. There are black marks there from its front teeth. My leg was broken on my right. I died in Itiguviak when I had an accident one time. There were angels who grabbed me. They told me when those two spots will disappear I will die."[88]

Luke Anautalik from Arviat described how, at a difficult time, he was guided home by some mysterious lights. He went to see Jimmy Makpah, the Anglican minister, who told him the lights were angels. "There were seven of them. Seven angels came to me to guide me to the settlement back to Arviat. I found out from Jimmy that they were guiding angels."[89]

CATEGORIES

Distinctions between the various categories of non-human beings are sometimes unclear. The *ijirait,* for example, are sometimes hard to distinguish from the inland *ingniriugjait,* and some people confuse the *ijirait* with the *tarriassuit.* Sometimes distinctions are a question of names. Thus, the *taliillajuut* can easily merge with the sea woman or with *lumaajuut.* Distinctions between individual spirits and spirit people are also often unclear, as shown by Amajurjuk/*amajurjuit* or Qalupalik/*qallupilluit.* The use of concepts is often contextual. A being may be referred to as a *tuurngaq* in one context and as a *tupilaq* in another. Elders themselves are not always sure about the differences between the various categories. The distinctions between various kinds of non-human beings are never clear. All sorts of transitions, transformations, mediations, and mergings may occur. The Inuit world is never fixed or permanent, but always open and flexible. The appearance and representations of non-human beings are continuously changing, and people can never be sure about their true form or even about their existence.

The universe of non-human beings is changeable and new categories can emerge, as accounts of non-human beings vary and are based on stories as well as on the idiosyncratic experiences of individual people.

Some categories are mentioned in only one source, and it is hard to assess to what extent their existence is generally acknowledged. Boas (1964 [1888], 621) is the only one to report on the *uissuit,* who apparently lived in the sea and were frequently seen between Iglulik and Nattilik. There were men and women among the *uissuit.* They lived in deep water, never coming up to the surface. Sometimes Inuit tried to catch them by hooks, on which they slowly moved up and down. As soon as Inuit got a bite, they drew in the line, but when *uissuit* approached the surface, they dove down headlong again, only their legs having emerged from the water. Inuit never succeeded in getting one out of the water. As they are only mentioned by Boas, it is hard to judge whether they constitute a separate category or whether they belong to a category known by other names (e.g., *tuutaliit*).

Some categories of non-human beings are mainly known through stories. According to Rasmussen (1930, 114), the *kukilingiattiat* – "those with the great claws" – live far up inland. In winter they dwell in snow huts. They attack human beings with their long claws and keep on scratching them as long as there is any flesh left. They attacked Siqiniq this way in the myth of the sun and moon. Only very bold and skilful shamans have a *kukilingiattiaq* as a helping spirit. On South Baffin Island, meetings with *kukilingiattiat* still occur. Elders report that these beings "are hands with three claws which can emerge unexpectedly from any surface."[90] According to Aqikhivik, many people who disappeared have been attacked and eaten by these people. Inuit were told not to steal, for if they did, they would be scratched by a three-clawed hand.[91]

Another example of a spirit known mainly from a story is the thrashing spirit that brandished a live bearded seal as a whip. It appears in a story told by Ivaluardjuk to Rasmussen.[92] Once, when some people were having a song feast and the children were playing outside, making a lot of noise, this spirit suddenly appeared and killed the children with his whip. Only one little boy managed to hide on the drying rack and survive. The next day the people held a song feast again and some of the men hid in the house. One man hid on the drying frame and poured hot oil on the live bearded seal when the spirit entered the house again. It was killed instantly, and the spirit fled and never returned. Rasmussen explains that the spirit disliked the noise of the feast and the playing children.

According to Rasmussen, there were old tales about the *narajait* among the Iglulingmiut as well as among the Nattilingmiut. He describes the *narajait* as "the ones with the big bellies."[93] They are excellent helping spirits, as their enormous voracity renders them very swift. When a *narajaq* girds up his stomach, there is not a living creature that he cannot outrun. According to a story related by Rasmussen's informant Inugpasugjuk, a *narajaq* once took a human being as a partner.[94] Nakasuk said that they can eat a caribou cow and its calf together. Then they dig a hollow in the ground to lie in at ease – their bellies swollen and distended – and digest what they have eaten. In that position they cannot tolerate anyone in their vicinity, and if someone appears, they shout while he is still a long way off: "Round about! Round about! Go right round about!" They may fear that their bellies will burst at the sound of footsteps close at hand.[95]

The Nattilik woman Manelaq told Rasmussen the story of the *nakasungnaikut*.[96] They have no calves or shin bones on their legs, and therefore they have to creep about instead of walking. They eat their own neighbours, and indeed their own families, if they get the chance. They are active and clever helping spirits, but only very skilful shamans can tame them. Many more non-human beings could be added: thunder and lightning (originally two human beings), the *arnanait*, men carrying children in their *amauti*, the woman who created the caribou, Aukjuk (the eater of entrails), and so on. The world of non-human beings is never closed, as was shown by the appearance of angels and demons with the adoption of Christianity.

The distinction between ordinary animals and animals that are also something else is a popular topic for discussion, and in that respect, the case of *kajait*, or *ka'tut*, is instructive. At the Arviat workshop in 2003, Job Muqjunnik told this story:

> A long time ago before any of us were born, there was a tide in Noah's time. The tide covered the earth and when the land appeared again the ones that died in the flood later became a group of wolves. That's how I heard it. My wife's grandmother was attacked by a group of *kajait*, wolves. The group of wolves were after him and he knew he was going to be attacked so he untied his dogs and let them go. He cut a piece of rope from

> the front of his *qamutik* and turned the *qamutik* upwards. He climbed up there for three days after the wolves attacked him trying to stay away from the wolves. This happened to my wife's grandmother while I was young.

But *kajait* are by no means ordinary wolves. Mary Anautalik stated in the same workshop, "I know all about wolves, not *kajait*. I don't know if there were *kajait*. I think they were ordinary wolves. They came to my camp at Ennadai Lake. It was early summer. There was almost twenty-four hours of daylight. I remember a group of wolves came through our camp. This group was of ordinary wolves."

Barnabas Arngnasungaaq from Qamanittuaq also remembered hearing these beings:

> It was in the middle of the night and I was sleeping, when [I] stirred and woke up. I heard something making sounds outside our tent. It was like when you hear a herd of caribou walking and the sounds they make, but what I heard didn't sound anything like caribou, just a lot of walking sounds was all there was. When I woke up that night I was shaking and getting stiff, trying not to move a muscle, just lying there thinking that there was no way my wife and child and I would get out of this, because I was hearing so much walking beside our tent … Then I thought they must be the wolves that don't have any fur, what we call ka'tut, that had come … The next summer we went back to that camp where we had left our belongings. We also had a meat cache there, and my father's grave was nearby. When we went back to that camp all the dried meat was gone, and the belongings we had left covered were all scattered and broken. My father's grave wasn't torn to pieces, but some of the rocks had been rolled down from where he was buried, and a dead wolf was lying beside the meat cache. So I keep wondering if what I heard that night had been those wolves which I have been terrified of since the time of my birth.[97]

These accounts illustrate that the boundaries between different categories are never clear – one can never be sure whether a caribou is an animal or an *ijiraq*, or wolves ordinary animals or *kajait*. For this reason, we will not focus on the construction of a classification system or taxonomy of non-human beings, but on the features that always recur in different combinations in the descriptions of non-human beings.

Many non-human beings have a language, houses, shamans, song festivals, and so on, but they usually they do not have to observe the abstentions and refrainings that apply to human beings.[98] These rules ensure that human beings will multiply and be successful in hunting. Rules of abstinence, avoidance, or refraining specify what should not be done and which things should be kept apart. These rules apply to crucial stages in human life, such as birth and death, as well as to the separation of specific kinds of game from each other (such as land game from sea game). In the myth of origin, the observance of these rules is connected to the first normal birth and seems to be a precondition for the temporality of human life. It allows human beings to increase in numbers and game to become abundant. Non-human beings do not observe the rules of human society, and they do not multiply the same way as human beings do. *Ijirait* can buy things from warehouses without ever depleting the stocks.

If the Inuit do not observe these rules, they will no longer be successful as hunters and their survival is at risk. The observance of ritual rules implies the maintenance of the correct distance between related processes, such as the distance between the reproduction of human life and the killing of animals. Non-human beings may share the physical features of Inuit, they may be physically superior and have language and shamans, but lacking their system of rules, they are not social beings as Inuit are. They represent different forms of non-sociality that are expressed in various codes, such as visibility, alliance, spatiality, and temporality.

Most non-human beings are rarely seen. Some of them – the *tarriassuit*, for instance – are even invisible. Accounts of meetings with spirits often come from shamans who know how to deal with them (e.g., the story of Oqaminiq and the *ijirait*). For other people, experiences with spirits are frightening (e.g., Kappianaq's encounter with *ijirait*). Most spirits are dangerous even if they are not considered hostile. Giants can easily kill people, but so can dwarfs. Spirits can kill people by depriving them of sleep or tickling them, unaware of the fateful consequences of their actions.

The appearance of non-human beings is often deceptive. *Ijirait* do not want to be seen and so manifest themselves as caribou. Dwarfs can grow to the size of human beings, and their bears are in fact lemmings that appear as bears to human beings. Shamans are able to see the true nature of these spirits because of their *qaumaniq*, their shamanic vision, which enables them to see spirits and shades, but other people can easily be deceived by appearances and risk being killed because of it.

Non-human beings can also be tricked. Zebedee Enoogoo from Arctic Bay related: "The coastal Inuit, when going inland, feared the visit of the *ijirait*. To impress the *ijirait* the Inuit started playing with *avatait*, sealskin floats. The *ijirait* being inlanders don't know what sealskin floats are and think they are boulders."[99] The *ijirait*, believing that the Inuit must be very strong to be able to toss the boulders, flee.[100] While non-human beings are rarely seen by others, they may have excellent eyesight themselves. *Ijirait* and *tuniit*, for example, possess devices that allow them to see well. Inuit are convinced that the spirits and animals observe them and are aware of their actions. If people abuse animals or other non-human beings, non-human beings will retaliate. Thus, non-human beings are often the agents of retaliation in cases where social beings have transgressed social rules. There are many stories about *tarniit* or animals taking vengeance on people (and their relatives) who have not respected them. People are always visible to those non-human agencies that observe whether they are acting as social beings. Retaliation can come from the weather (Sila), from the game, from the *inua* of the game, or from some other agency. In these cases, shamans can perceive the cause of the retaliatory actions. They share with non-human beings the uncanny quality of being able to see everything.

In Inuit culture, every transgression must be confessed, and it can be inferred that it is particularly non-human beings who observe or hear the confessions. As a general principle, people can only be healed through confession, *aniartuq*. Things should not be hidden, but should be brought out in the open for all to hear and see. Visibility – that is, being seen – is a feature of sociality. Conversely, beings that cannot be seen, or can only be seen in a deceptive appearance, are not social.

The visual code is connected to the beginning and the ending of life. People connected with birth or death should not be seen by game animals, and all contact with game should be avoided. These processes are thought to give rise to a vapour, *pujartuq*, emanating from the human body that can be observed by the animals. Visibility can also mark the death of a non-human being. Thus dwarfs appear to die as long as one keeps them in sight, but they disappear as soon as they are no longer watched. A person who harpoons a *qallupalik* must shut his eyes immediately and keep them shut until the *qallupalik* is dead, or else he will capsize the boat and kill the hunters. The death of non-human beings should not be witnessed by human beings. The death of a *tupilak* can only be seen by shamans. Others can only see the blood on his hands.

Visibility is at the core of the shamanic complex. The *qaumaniq* of the shaman allows him to see spirits and souls wherever they are. But too much *qaumaniq* can be dangerous, as observed by Aupilaarjuk from Rankin Inlet (1999 interview). It may shorten a shaman's lifespan. Thus, the notion of visibility, like the observance of social rules, is connected to temporality.

Marriages between Inuit and most non-human beings usually do not work well. In myths, alliances with *allait, tarriassuit, inukpait,* and *uvivigtut,* among other categories, usually lead to disaster. In Iglulik it was assumed that people could have a non-human partner as a spouse. Such a person was called an *uiksaq* (woman who has non-human husband) or a *nuliaksaq* (man who has a non-human wife). Little is known about these relationships. Today they are considered dangerous,[101] but in the past shamans may have been involved with them. The young Inuit Kopak, Ishulutak, and Arnatsiaq observed, "There were some Inuit who had non-humans, such as tarriassuit, tuurngait and ijirait, as spouses. Some say you should never get involved with a non-human as a partner because it is dangerous, but others say that it is not dangerous, it is just like having a normal life but in a different world."[102] Imaruittuq from Iglulik and Nutaraaluk from Iqaluit (both interviewed in 1999) recalled cases where people maintained sexual relationships with non-human beings. In another case of *uiksaq*, the man involved referred to his sexual partner as the devil. Eventually he committed suicide. Clearly there remains some ambiguity about such relationships.

SPATIALITY AND TEMPORALITY

Perceptions of time and space vary. Even today, Inuit elders are easily annoyed by the Qallunaat preoccupation with dates. In 1999, in response to the question "When and where were you born?" Tungilik from Naujaat said, "They say that I was born in the Iglulik area. I wasn't conscious of calendars, dates and years and so I don't know what year I was born because I never thought of years. So I can't talk about it. They say I was born in Iglulik, down where they went to the flow edge, in a place they call Nungiq. It was close to the floe edge and it was a good area to be close to go seal hunting in the winter, because it froze early. I was born on the sea ice, in the early spring at a time of year when the *igluit* started melting. That is when they say I was born."[103]

While Tungilik has no interest in the date of his birth, he is extremely precise in indicating the place as well as the season in which he was born. Not the year, but the season of birth is important. In the pre-Christian winter feasts celebrated on South Baffin, the participants proclaimed the place and season of their birth (see chapter 3). And to determine the success of the hunting season, the men divided into two groups – the ducks, representing the summer, and the ptarmigans, representing the winter – and played a game of tug-of-war. Thus, we are not dealing with a lack of temporal perspective, but a different temporal perspective.

When the Anglican missionaries arrived on Baffin Island at the end of the nineteenth century, they immediately prepared calendars that became very popular among the Inuit. These calendars did not serve to keep track of dates, but to enable Inuit to observe Sundays. Noah Piugaattuq from Iglulik stated this clearly for Anglicans: "The concept of keeping one day a week to observe Sundays was passed from one person to one person, reaching great distance throughout the region. The people knew in advance that there would be a number of days without restrictions or taboos followed by one day that should be observed – a day of full abstention to be fully respected, vital to the Christian belief."[104] Teresi Ijjangiaq from Iglulik indicated that the same practice was followed by Catholic Inuit: "[The priest] made the letter 'I' for each weekday; for Sundays he marked an 'X.' That was the first time I have seen a calendar."[105]

In Inuit culture, spatial and temporal categories take shape in a social context. Outside society, the categories of time and space become problematic. This is illustrated by various features, such as the great speed of the spirits, which enables them to transcend the limits of time and space that apply to human beings. This is a distinctive quality with respect to helping spirits as well as non-human beings like the *ijirait*.

Non-human beings live out on the land, not in the community. Although occasionally evil spirits may enter the community (*tupilait*), they are not supposed to be there. Shamans were able to see *tupilait* and kill them. The majority of spirits live on the land, and Inuit usually know where they live. A place may be called Ijiralik (a place where *ijirait* live), but unlike Inuit, non-human beings do not derive their names from these places. Shamans went to meet the spirits on the land at places without foot tracks. There is a timeless quality about the land and the non-human beings that inhabit it. They make people forget or lose their possessions. These non-human beings can go to stores and buy goods without ever depleting the stores. Even today the land is considered a place where people can be spiritually invigorated and refreshed. Elders take young people out on the land as part of a healing process. But even though the land may have timeless qualities, it can grow old or become hot (see chapter 5 on the move from Avajja to Iglulik). In spring and summer, people like to get out of the communities and spend time in camps and cabins.

Human beings are part of a cycle of life and death. They are born, grow up, become old, and die. Their bodies will be eaten by animals, their shades (*tarniit*) may travel to a land of the dead or incarnate in new beings (animals or human beings), but their names will be passed on to new generations.

The land and its non-human inhabitants are an inexhaustible source of food. As long as Inuit respect the land and its inhabitants, game will be abundant and society will survive. Out on the land, people are invigorated and refreshed. The non-human beings inhabiting the land are not affected in terms of time. The categories of time and place do not apply to them as they do to human beings. The non-human beings are evasive, appearing and disappearing, often invisible, and they unceasingly observe human behaviour and can sanction people if they transgress social rules.

CONCLUSION

Life in the community implies a cycle of life and death. Individuals are born and die, but the continuous incarnation of *tarniit* ensures that animals as well as human beings multiply. Each incarnation of a *tarniq* implies a new cycle of birth and death. The cycle of *tarniit* itself is anonymous and a-temporal. No one knows when and how a *tarniq* incarnates. It is only when the *tarniq* is incarnated that it can be connected to a name. Whereas *tarniit* are anonymous and can incarnate in animals and human beings, names belong to the realm of human beings.[106] Names are not born and they do not die; they are beyond death. They are essentially social. Names transcend the temporality of Inuit kinship relationships, and thus the relations between names takes precedence over kinship relations. Thus, a grandchild can refer to her grandmother as "my daughter," as Kublu did with respect to Iqallijuq.[107] Names can only disappear by being forgotten. Knowledge of the relations between names is knowledge of the social relations of Inuit and the rules of respect and avoidance they imply. The temporal order in the kinship relationship is transcended and sometimes inverted by the a-temporal order of the naming system that expresses the continuity of society.

The name structures a society that is organized in terms of time and space, and at the same time transcends that structure. The system of names has its own logic. Inuit can have names such as Itqilit, or Ijiraq, whereas the beings they are named after usually have no individual names themselves. Non-human beings are not subject to the temporal order of society. They only become part of society through the naming system and in this way bestow some of their qualities on their namesakes. Through names, even the non-human beings inhabiting the land and the sea can participate in society.

Part Three | Encounters, Healing, and Power

7

Initiation, Visions, and Dreams

INTRODUCTION

In the past, shamans were thought to be able to see non-human beings and *tarniit*. They acquired this ability through an initiation that required a first encounter with a helping spirit and the acquisition of *qaumaniq*, shamanic light and vision. Other people did not have this special capability. Today, shamans no longer have an institutionalized role in Inuit society. But encounters with non-human beings are still frequent. They occur mainly out on the land or in visions and dreams. In this chapter we will show that there is great continuity in shamanic initiations as experienced in the past and in visions and dreams today. Initiation, dreams, and visions all connect a person to other beings and open new perspectives and relationships. Dreams and visions have always been important in the shamanic calling, in the initiation of *angakkuit*, and in Inuit conversion to Christianity. In this chapter we will examine classic descriptions of initiation in the ethnographic literature as well as in the recollections of elders who were trained to become *angakkuit*. These show the highly varied nature of initiation experiences. The initiations constituted an important context for the interaction between human beings and non-human agencies. Although *angakkuit* might be the experts in this field, most elders have had experiences and visions that entailed encounters with non-human beings. Today, dreams and visions constitute a privileged platform for the interaction between human beings and non-human agencies. Dreams connect people to the living and the deceased, evoking traditional patterns of shamanic visions and initiations.

INITIATION

Initiation patterns varied widely. The main features of an initiation were that a person acquired *qaumaniq*, shamanic vision, and the assistance of *tuurngait*, helping spirits. *Qaumaniq*, derived from *qau*, "light," provided an *angakkuq* with the shamanic vision that enabled him or her to see with closed eyes and perceive things that were hidden to others.[1] *Tuurngait* might come to a person of their own accord, or a person might seek contact with the *tuurngait*. Shamanic initiation often required a period of instruction and training, and usually an *angakkuq* would receive an *angaluk* or *tapsi*, a belt. Weapons, usually miniatures, were attached to this belt.[2] They were gifts from the community.

Each community had its own traditions of initiation. Ollie Itinnuaq from Kangiq&iniq stated, "Different communities in different regions have different procedures to become an *angakkuq*."[3] Even some families had their own traditions. Our information on shamanic initiation in the North Baffin area comes mainly from Ava and his family, and Rasmussen's information on the Kivalliq from Igjugârjuk and his family.[4]

In a text entitled *Eskimo Heathen Customs*, Peck provides a description of shamanic initiation on South Baffin Island that seems to be based on a verbatim account of an Inuit informant. Men, especially, were initiated after they confessed transgressions. The candidate chosen by the *angakkuq* had to visit the houses of the community and would receive quite a number of charms. Then he had to abstain from many things: he had to eat with his mittens on, let his hair hang down, and not undress when going to bed. He gave many presents to his teacher.[5]

Bilby (1923, 196–209) confirms that a young man or woman would choose a teacher. The duration of the instruction depended on the person's ability to master the various skills of the *angakkuit*. Bilby writes, "the pupil becomes a servant of his teacher and pays for his initiation" (197).

The apprentice had to confess all his or her transgressions to the teacher. Fasting and abstinence, allowing the hair to grow long and hang down, eating with the hands covered, and going to rest without discarding clothes were all part of the training. The candidate had to become familiar with all the traditions and customs and learn the language of the *tuurngait*, "the language in which spirits are to be addressed and in which they express themselves through the initiate,"[6] and the various practises and incantations.

Boas (1907, 133) reports, "When a person becomes an angakok, a light covers his body. He can see supernatural things. The stronger the light is within him, the deeper and farther away he can see, and the greater is his supernatural power." The shamanic vision enabled an *angakkuq* not only to see hidden things such as spirits and shades, but also transgressions of *tirigusuusiit* (things people had to abstain from). *Qaumaniq* was closely associated with joy and was often provided by *tuurngait*. Many of the *tuurngait* on Peck's list of *tuurngait* are described as beings of light or as dwelling in the light or as givers of light.[7]

Boas (1907, 510) relates that, after his initiation, "a young angakok must not whip his dogs for a whole year, as the dogs' spirits might bring injury to him. He must not drink out of a cup that anyone else has used."

Rasmussen (1929, 111–14) gives an extensive description of the training his informant Ava received to become an *angakkuq*. Ava also told Rasmussen about the initiation of his relatives Niviatsian and Uvavnuk. According to Ava, the candidate first gave a valuable present to the *angakkuq* he wished to become his teacher. A tent pole was a customary gift. The wing of a gull was attached to the pole indicating the power to travel to the lands of the dead in the sky and under the sea. The candidate would address the teacher, "I come to you because I desire to see," and the gift would then be placed outside as a present to the future helping spirits of the candidate. The teacher could use the pole later on. That evening the teacher should "invoke and interrogate his helping spirits in order to 'remove all obstacles' ... that is, to eliminate from the pupil's body and mind all that might hinder him from becoming a good shaman." The candidate and his parents should confess all their transgressions. The teacher sat behind a skin on the platform, and after the confession the candidate sat beside him. The period of instruction was not long, especially in the case of men, and five days might be sufficient. During the initial instruction, the candidate was taught at special hours. He was not allowed to sit on ordinary coverings on the platform, and so a pair of men's breeches were laid out under him. He should eat as little as possible. During the training, the teacher and the members of the candidate's household were not allowed to hunt. After the initial instruction, the candidate would have to continue his training on his own outside the camp in solitude.

The first thing the instructor had to do was to withdraw the soul from the eyes, brain, and entrails of the candidate and hand it over to the candidate's future helping spirits. Thus the spirits became familiar with the soul and would not be afraid when the candidate would later invoke them himself. Then the instructor had to procure his *qaumaniq* (or *angakua*). Rasmussen writes, "The first time a young shaman experiences this light, while sitting up on the bench invoking his helping spirits, it is as if the house in which he is suddenly rises; he sees far ahead of him, through mountains, exactly as if the earth were one great plain, and his eyes could reach to the end of the earth. Nothing is hidden from him any longer; not only can he see things far, far away, but he can also discover souls, stolen souls, which are either kept concealed in far, strange lands or have been taken up or down to the Land of the Dead."[8]

The instructor obtained the *angakkua* or *qaumaniq* from the moon spirit, from a deceased person among the Ullurmiut, from Pakitsumang (the mother of the caribou), or from a white lemming.[9] The candidate should acquire the capacity to see himself as a skeleton and then mention every single bone by name in the language of the *tuurngait*, which he had learned from his instructor. Only then he could obtain his *tuurngait*. He had to meet them in person, and they should preferably be animals in human appearance or *ijirait*, spirits of the land. He could not choose them; they would come to him on their own accord.[10]

When the candidate had become an *angakkuq*, he received a shaman's belt.[11] "This consists of a strip of hide to which are attached many fringes of caribou skin, and these are fastened on by all the people he knows, as many as he can get; to the fringes are added small carvings, human figures made of bone, fishes, harpoons; all these must be gifts, and the givers then believe that the shaman's helping spirits will always be able to recognise them by their gifts, and will never do them any harm."[12]

A man who had just become an *angakkuq* should observe various refrainings for a whole year. He should not eat the marrow, breast, entrails, head, or tongue of any animal and the meat he ate should be raw, clean flesh. Women were subject to even more stringent restrictions. Most importantly, they were not allowed to sew throughout that year. The *angakkuq* had to learn *irinaliutiit*, the powerful words and songs that would heal the sick and bring good weather or good hunting.

Rasmussen gives various accounts of shamanic initiation among the Iglulingmiut that do not conform to the pattern described above. He (1929, 115) indicates that the value of training was an issue of debate. Some thought that the best *angakkuit* were those who had never studied under others but went out on the land alone. Others held that one could not become a good *angakkuq* without instruction.

All *angakkuit* had different experiences. Ava told Rasmussen that the preparation for the training of an *angakkuq* should start even before his birth. All the children his mother had given birth to had lain crosswise or were stillborn. When his mother found out she was pregnant again, she said to her housemates, "Now I have again that within me which will turn out no real human being." A woman named Ardjuaq, an *angakkuq*, invoked her helping spirits, but it did no good because Ardjuaq had mended a hole in a mitten on the day after the spirit was called, when she should not have done any work. His mother felt the birth pangs coming, and the unborn child struggled to get out. The spirits were invoked again. All the rules were observed and this helped mother and child. One day his mother assisted his father in harnessing the dogs, although in her condition all work was prohibited. The unborn child again protested and a shaman had to come to the rescue. Elders told his mother that this sensitivity to any transgression was a sign that the child would become a great *angakkuq*, but that dangers and misfortunes would pursue him until that time. Ava was born when his father cut open a walrus with an unborn young one, forgetting that his wife was with child. The infant was born with the umbilical cord twisted around his neck, strangling him. Ardjuaq was sent for, and a special hut was built for his mother. When Ardjuaq arrived, she wiped the blood of Ava's mother from his body with a raven skin and made a little jacket out of it. She said, "He is born to die, but he shall live."

Ardjuaq stayed with his mother until the child showed signs of life. The mother was put on a strict diet and had to observe difficult rules of taboo. No one was allowed to eat meat from any walrus, seal, or caribou that she had eaten from. Only men might visit, and the child was not allowed to wear clothing with the hair of the skins pointing up or down. They lived for a year in that hut. Ava's father was not allowed to sharpen his own knife. When he did, his hand began to swell and the child fell ill. After a year, a woman was allowed to live with them in the hut, but whenever she went out she had to throw her hood over her head, wear boots without stockings, and hold the tail of her fur coat up high in one hand.

When Ava had become a big boy, his mother was allowed to go visiting but only for short visits. When he harpooned his first seal, his father had to lie down on the ice with the upper part of his body naked; then the seal was dragged across his back while it was still alive. Only men were allowed to eat of the catch, and nothing should be left. The skin and the head were set out on the ice, so that Ava would later catch the same seal again. For three days and nights, none of the men who had eaten of it might go out hunting or do any kind of work. Ava had to kill his first caribou with bow and arrow, and only men were allowed to eat it; no woman might touch it. When he harpooned his first walrus, his father shouted at the top of his voice the names of all the villages he knew, and cried, "Now there is food for all!" The walrus was towed in to land while it was still alive, and killed when they reached the shore. His mother, who was to cut it up, had the harpoon line made fast to her body before the harpoon head was withdrawn. After having killed this walrus, Ava was allowed to eat all the delicacies that had formerly been forbidden, such as entrails, and women were now allowed to eat of his catch provided they were not pregnant or had recently delivered.

His mother still had to observe great caution. She had to do her sewing in a special hut that had been built for her, for example. She had to be so careful out of respect for Ava's namesake, a little spirit that became his helping spirit, and so she took great care that Ava should not do anything that was forbidden. He was never allowed to remain in a snow hut where young women were undressing for the night; nor might any woman comb her hair while he was present.

After his marriage, his catch was still to be treated with special care. "If there but lived women with infants near us, my own wife was only allowed to eat meat of my killing, and no other woman was allowed to satisfy her hunger with the meat of any animal of which my wife had eaten."[13] Until he had four children, no woman might eat the entrails of a walrus he killed. Only after Ava had grown old did the rules imposed by Ardjuaq no longer need to be observed.

Despite carefully taking all these precautions, Ava found it difficult to become an *angakkuq*. He visited many famous *angakkuit* and gave them great gifts, but they gave them away at once. If they had kept them, they or their children would have died. Then Ava went into solitude and became melancholy and unhappy. Sometimes he began to weep without knowing why. "Then, for no reason, all would suddenly be changed, and I felt a great, inexplicable joy, a joy so powerful that I could not restrain it, but had to break into song, a mighty song, with only room for the one word: joy, joy! And I had to use the full strength of my voice.

And then in the midst of such a fit of mysterious and overwhelming delight I became a shaman, not knowing myself how it came about. But I was a shaman. I could see and hear in a totally different way."[14]

Ava had acquired *qaumaniq*, and not only could he see in the darkness, but all the spirits of the earth, the sky, and the sea saw his light and came to him as helping spirits. His first *tuurngaq* was his namesake, a little Ava. "When it came to me, it was as if the passage and roof of the house were lifted up, and I felt such a power of vision, that I could see right through the house, in through the earth and up into the sky; it was the little Aua that brought me all this inward light, hovering over me as long as I was singing. Then it placed itself in a corner of the passage, invisible to others, but always ready if I should call it."

Ava was a little spirit (less than half the length of a man's arm), a woman, living at the shore. His second helping spirit was a shark that swam up to him and whispered his name. It helped Ava in his hunting. The little Ava and the shark were his most important *tuurngait*. Rasmussen (1929, 120) records Ava's song of invocation:

Joy, joy,
Joy, joy!
I see a little shore spirit,
A little aua,
I myself am also aua,
The shore spirit's namesake,
Joy, joy!

Ava related, "These words I would keep on repeating, until I burst into tears, overwhelmed by a great dread; then I would tremble all over, crying only: 'Ah-a-a-a-a, joy, joy! Now I will go home, joy, joy!'" Joy was an essential element of the shamanic experience.

Ava also told Rasmussen how some of his relatives were initiated. Once, when his cousin Niviatsian was out hunting walruses with his companions, a great walrus suddenly came up through the ice close beside him and grasped him with his huge fore-flippers, just as a mother picks up her little child. It carried him off to the sea into the deep. It tried to pierce him with its tusk, but finally let him go. Ava's father managed to pull him up. Niviatsian was severely wounded by the walrus tusks and remained unconscious for some time. The old people said the walrus had been sent by the sea woman because Niviatsian's wife had concealed a miscarriage. Niviatsian was able to walk but had to walk a little bit apart from his companions on ice free from footmarks. Close to land the men built him a small igloo, and here they laid him down on a sealskin with his wet clothes still on and shut him in. He stayed in the igloo for three days without food or drink. If he had gone to the houses of his companions, he would have died.

In the meantime a shaman made Niviatsian's wife and mother confess all their transgressions. After three days, Niviatsian had recovered and become a great shaman. The walrus that attacked him became his first *tuurngaq*. A wolverine that fought him ferociously, but was not able to wound him, became his second *tuurngaq*. His third *tuurngaq* was Amajorjuk, who captured him in her *amauti*. He killed her by stabbing his knife into her back. He escaped naked from her *amauti* and found his clothes close to the sea. The smell of rotten seaweed remained with him for half a year. After that he was regarded as the greatest *angakkuq* in the world.[15]

Uvavnuk, Niviatsian's mother, acquired her *qaumaniq* by being hit by a ball of fire. After she had been hit, she sang:

> The great sea
> Has sent me adrift
> It moves me as the weed in a great river
> Earth and the great weather
> Move me
> Have carried me away
> And move my inward parts with joy.[16]

Her song inspired everyone to confess his or her transgressions.

In 1978 Francois Thérien spoke to Ava's son Ujaraq in a series of interviews on shamanism in Iglulik. Ujaraq gave an account of Ava becoming a shaman:

> Long before they used to have guns, my father had gone hunting with other men to the floe edge. While they were hunting, there started to be a current and the ice started to break up. When the ice started to break up, my father was on the ice when it broke up and he was about to drown. Every time he would try to get a hold at the ice, it would sink. When he remembered his great great grandmother he yelled. All of a sudden a raven was flying over him and he was carried to solid ice. When he landed on the ice, he was not freezing at all and that was the time when he became a shaman. He had remembered his great great grandmother, and if he hadn't remembered her, he would have frozen and died. And ever since then he had shamanistic powers.[17]

Ujaraq said that Orulo, Ava's wife, was also an *angakkuq*: "Urulu became a shaman by herself, by the time she was orphan[ed] and her mother had died recently. She didn't know where to live, and she was always worrying. That is how she became a shaman. Nobody was helping her to become a shaman. She did it by herself."[18] Ujaraq thought that she had probably gotten her helping spirits from her late parents. In his accounts, both Ava and Orulo became shamans through the intervention of deceased ancestors. Ujaraq related, "That is how they used to become shamans. When a person that is not a shaman wanted to become a shaman, two shamans would get together and they would put their spirit … into one and give half of their spirit to the person who's trying to become a shaman."[19] His sister Atuat became an *angakkuq* in this way.[20]

George Kappianaq (IE 096) from Iglulik related how his mother almost became an *angakkuq*. Qallunaat played a part in the process.

> First of all I am going to tell you how my mother almost became a shaman. It was during the time when ships used to winter around Qatiktalik … She almost became a shaman, that is, my mother Uviluq, on her own accord. She did not ask anyone's help for her to become a shaman as the family were all alone. She was being approached by the helpers that she wanted.
>
> It happened one evening when she was trying to get some sleep. She saw the daylight coming out from the direction of the north wind. Apparently, it was not a daylight. Later that evening she was made aware of her contacts with her helpers. Afterwards when everyone had gone to sleep, it happened again. This time the brightness extended much more, so much so that it appeared to be daylight.
>
> Again the following day when it was time to sleep – all this time she had not mentioned this phenomenon to my father for she felt apprehensive towards him – when everyone was fast asleep, it happened again. This time the brightness covered the view of vision completely to the other end whence it started from. The actual dawn broke. She let it be as if it never happened. However, she was conscious about it but acted as if it had never happened. The only thing she had in mind was the nightfall. So when the time to sleep came, she was the only one awake. This time the whole scope became bright as a daylight. It must have been about past midnight when she saw a dog team coming in from the direction where the light had originated from. She could identify it quite distinctively as a dog team. They arrived and shortly afterwards they left again. The people were whites.
>
> The following day when everyone was asleep, she saw a ship, this time from the direction where the dog team the previous night had showed up. When the ship got closer, it appeared to anchor. All this time they were staying on the mainland. They used to have a shawl or a scarf in those days known then as *narsiaq*. The captain got out from his cabin, and his *narsiaq* moved around in the wind, which made her inside move as if it was in rhyme with the movement of the *narsiaq*. This was on account that she was overjoyed. The brightness was full despite the fact that this was in the middle of night. After that she was able to see people in other parts or other camps without their knowledge that she was watching them.

In the Kivalliq, Rasmussen collected accounts of initiation from Igjugarjuk, a Padlirmiut *angakkuq* he encountered at Hikoligjuaq.[21] Igjugarjuk explained that one became an *angakkuq* through suffering, by exposing oneself to cold and hunger, to drowning, or to death by shooting. Igjugarjuk himself opted for the first approach:

> One says … Hila must see you and take notice of you, Hila must keep her eye on you … First I hungered five days and was then allowed to drink a mouthful of warm water; the old ones say that only if the water is warm will Pinga and Hila notice the novice and help him. Thereafter I went hungry another fifteen days, and again was given a mouthful of warm water. After that I hungered for ten days, and then could begin to eat, though it only had to be aklernäicut, that is to say the sort of food on which there is never any taboo, preferably fleshy meat, and never intestines, head, heart or other entrails, nor meat that had been touched by wolf or wolverine while it lay in a cache. I was to keep to this diet for five moons, and then the next five moons might eat everything; but after that I was again forced to eat the meat diet that is prescribed for all those who must do penance in order to become clean. The old ones attached great importance to the food that the would-be shamans might eat; thus a novice who wished to possess the ability to kill had never to eat the salmon that we call hiu^{r}lχit. If they eat hiu^{r}lχit, they will, instead of killing others, kill themselves.

Igjugarjuk received his instruction for his initiation from his wife's father, Perqanaq.

> When I was to be exhibited to Pinga and Hila, he dragged me on a little sledge that was no bigger than I could just sit on it; he dragged me far over on the other side of Hikoligjuaq. It was a very long day's journey inland to a place we call Kíngârjuit: the high hills, which are at Tikerarjuaq (by the southeast shore of Hikoligjuaq). It was in winter time and took place at night with the new moon; one could just see the very first streak of the moon; it had just appeared in the sky. I was not fetched again until the next moon was of the same size. Perqánâq built a small snow hut at the place where I was to be, this snow hut being no bigger than that I could just get under cover and sit down. I was given no sleeping skin to protect me against the cold, only a little piece of caribou skin to sit upon. There I was shut in … The entrance was closed with a block, but no soft snow was thrown over the hut to make it warm. When I had sat there five days, Perqánâq came with water, tepid, wrapped in caribou skin, a watertight caribou-skin bag. Not until fifteen days afterwards did he come again and hand me the same, just giving himself time to hand it to me, and then he was gone again, for even the old shaman must not interrupt my solitude. The snow hut in which I sat was built far from the trails of men, and when Perqánâq had found the spot where he thought it ought to be built, he

> stopped the little sledge at a distance, and there I had to remain seated until the snow hut was ready. Not even I, who was after all the one to have to stay there, might set my footprints in the vicinity of the hut, and old Perqánâq had to carry me from the sledge over to the hut so that I could crawl in. As soon as I had become alone, Perqánâq enjoined me to think of one single thing all the time I was to be there, to want only one single thing, and that was to draw Pinga's attention to the fact that there I sat and wished to be a shaman … Pinga should own me. My novitiate took place in the middle of the coldest winter, and I, who never got anything to warm me, and must not move, was very cold, and it was so tiring having to sit without daring to lie down, that sometimes it was as if I died a little. Only towards the end of the thirty days did a helping spirit come to me, a lovely and beautiful helping spirit whom I had never thought of; it was a white woman; she came to me whilst I had collapsed, exhausted, and was sleeping. But still I saw her lifelike, hovering over me, and from that day I could not close my eyes or dream without seeing her. There is this remarkable thing about my helping spirit, that I have never seen her while awake, but only in dreams. She came to me from Pinga and was a sign that Pinga had now noticed me and would give me powers that would make me a shaman.

After a month Perqanaq returned to fetch him.

> But by this time I was not very much alive any more and had not the strength to rise, in fact I could not stand on my feet. Perqánâq pulled me out of the hut and carried me down to the sledge and dragged me home in the same manner as he had dragged me to Kíngârjuit. I was now so completely emaciated that the veins on my hands and body and feet had quite disappeared … For a long time I might only eat very little in order to again get my intestines extended, and later came the diet that was to help to cleanse my body.
>
> For a whole year I was not to lie with my wife, who, however, had to make my food. For a whole year I had to have my own little cooking pot and my own meat dish; no one else was allowed to eat of what had been cooked for me.[22]

After that, Igjugarjuk was acknowledged as a shaman in his own camp as well as other camps.

Peter Suvaksiuq from Arviat related another version of the initiation of Igjugarjuk:

> They made a hole in the ice and Atgaaqtu'nuaq tied him to a piece of wood and put him down through the hole and kept him down there for five days. He did this because whenever something happened, such as a death, they

(above) Ollie Itinnuaq drum dancing in his camp near Kangiq&iniq, 2002. *Left to right:* Felix Kupak, Jose Angutinngurniq, Levi Iluittuq, Bernadette Saumik, Lizzie Itinnuaq, and George Kappianaq; (right) Levi Iluittuq and Peter Suvaksiuq in Kangiq&iniq, 2002. Suvaksiuq, assisted by Iluituq, prepares for a demonstration of a Padlirmiut shamanic initiation. In the past, Padlirmiut *angakkuit* were sometimes initiated by complete immersion in a lake. Photographs by F. Laugrand.

Luke Anautalik demonstrates how an *angakkuq* would kill an evil spirit (*tupilattuq*). Here he is shown coming out his trance, supported by Felix Pisuk on the left and Gino Akkak on the right. Photograph by F. Laugrand.

Ollie Itinnuaq and his *avvaq* (namesake), Jose Angutinngurniq, give a demonstration of fist fighting in Kangiq&iniq in 2002 to show how it was performed in the past. Photograph by F. Laugrand.

had to wait for five days to pass. When my step-mother died, my grandmother waited for five days to pass at the foot of the bed.

When Igjugaarjuk was being made into an *angakkuq* he was tied to a piece of wood and put in a hole in the ice for five days. A lot of people have heard about this. He said that when large trout would start coming near him their mouths would seem huge. The trout were the most fearsome fish that would come by because they had such big mouths. They would make him turn following the path of the sun which is *i&urramut. I&uurait*, trout, always turn following the path of the sun, which is *i&urramut.*[23]

In 2002, Suvaksiuq demonstrated the latter technique of initiation in a workshop on shamanism in Rankin Inlet.

Igjugaarjuk initiated Kinaalik, his sister-in-law, a young woman of about thirty years of age, by shooting her.

Kînâlik had once dreamed about a man in the tribe, dreamed that he would become ill. This was taken as a sign of her disposition for shamanism, the dream having been put into her by spirits. The shaman Igjugârjuk, her brother-in-law, therefore made up his mind to make her a shaman. The people of the village were called together, and Kînâlik's old mother Abggârjuk then asked Igjugârjuk to shoot her. She had previously spent five whole days out, suspended in tent-poles, raised above the ground, in order that Hila might see her and take notice of her. It was winter, cold blizzards were blowing, but she noticed nothing of the cold because her helping spirits were with her. When she was to be shot, she was placed on a skin, sitting by iga, the separate kitchen that is built into the entrance passage; she was placed between iga and the living room itself. She had not to be shot with a lead bullet, but with something from the earth, a little stone. Igjugârjuk therefore shot her with a small round stone in the presence of all the villagers, and she fell over, dead. After that there was a song-feast. Kînâlik lay dead the whole night. She suffered nothing, her future helping spirits protected her. The next morning, just when Igjugârjuk was about to call her to life again, she woke up of her own accord. It now appeared that she had been shot in the heart. Later the stone was taken out and is now preserved by her old mother.

Through this death Kînâlik had become acceptable to helping spirits; Hila had noticed her, and the helping spirits might come to her of themselves. Her principal helping spirit was her dead brother qaluhera^{u}t.

She spoke freely and cheerfully about how her dead brother used to come to her, for among the Caribou Eskimos they are not afraid to mention the dead by name. He used to come to her gliding through the air, legs uppermost, head downwards, but as soon as he had reached the ground he could walk like an ordinary man.

Her other helping spirit was the polar bear hermerzihiut.[24]

Igjugarjuk also initiated Aggiartoq, a young man, to be a shaman. Aggiartoq was tied to a long tent pole and carried to a big lake. "There a hole was hewn in the ice and, clad in caribou-skin frock, mittens and full outfit, Aggiârtoq, bound to the tent pole, was pushed down through the hole so that he stood on the bottom of the lake. There they let him stay five whole days, and when they took him up again he was as dry as if he had never been in water. This young man's helping spirits were the spirit of his dead mother and a human skeleton."[25]

In the workshop in Arviat in 2003, Suvaksiuq spoke of another initiation technique: "If you wanted to become an *angakkuq* you would put the moss that contained all kinds of living things such as insects and caterpillars and whatever else was under the earth on your skin. You had to be able to stand this when it was on your arm. You had to be able to stay still when these living things started sucking on your arm, on your blood."

Shamanic initiation required the acquisition of *qaumaniq* and *tuurngait*. Each *angakuq* had an initiation that was unique to him or her. Later generations might give completely different accounts, but this variation did not seem to bother the elders. The prestige of the shamans of the past appeared only to increase in the stories of the younger generations.

THE SHAMANIC CALLING

Ollie Itinnuaq from Kangiq&iniq (1999 interview) related how people could become shamans through dreams:[26] "Some people were never raised to be shamans and they would start dreaming or when they are in the wilderness, they would experience things. When they would start talking about it openly, unseen forces would start taking over and start following them and they would slowly start becoming shaman. Some would be honed as shamans from the start as their destiny."

Mariano Aupilaarjuk from Kangiq&iniq related how *tuurngait* would appear in dreams or visions during the initiation period. Apparently these *tuurngait* were offering themselves as helping spirits. "Before you become an *angakkuq*, you start dreaming or envisioning something. Some of what you see could be beautiful and some could be scary ... All these things are being made visible to you by your helper. It would be your helper who was making you think these thoughts. You don't know who is going to be your helper; it could be a deceased person, it could be anything. We don't know, it is up to them."[27]

At the workshop in Arviat in 2003, Job Muqyunniq also raised the issue of initiation: "Before the missionaries came, only those with a sound mind would be able to have powers in those days. You can't get powers by yourself. You could never do that. You have to be given a spirit from another person."

One of Rasmussen's informants, the Nattilik *angakkuq* Ugpik, said that a man "became a shaman without desiring it himself. It was the spirits that came to one, especially in dreams." Thus, "[t]he famous woman shaman, Ugtugpagluk, had become visionary once while observing the death taboo over an old uncle. In the days when she lay in the house with the corpse she dreamed that her uncle's soul wanted to get into the house as an evil spirit; but she stopped him every time, and because of her he dared not come in, for she was stronger than the dead man. That dream had made her a shaman, and her dead uncle became her helping spirit from the moment he had felt himself overcome by her."[28]

Victor Tungilik from Naujaat related how he became an *angakkuq*:

> My parents told me not to become an *angakkuq*, but they died by the time I became an adult. I don't know how I became an *angakkuq*. It was not that somebody made me into an *angakkuq*. I don't know how it happened. In the evenings there would be a brightness on the ground behind me and it would follow me. It turned out that this was my *ikajuqti*, helping spirit. When I mentioned to someone that I would see this when I was alone, I was told that it had been my father's *ikajuqti*. I wasn't scared of it. I didn't think about being scared of it. It was given to me by someone. It would come to me whenever anyone was sick. I would heal people who were ill. It was given to me to help heal people. It wasn't through prayer, it was through shamanism. I used what was given to me because I used it to heal people.[29]

Even though Tungilik's parents did not want him to become an *angakkuq*, he had to respond to the call. Refusing it might entail his own death.

> While I was still young, before I was an adult, it started coming to me. I would be given signs. I only found out afterwards that they were for me. My parents had not wanted me to be an *angakkuq*. I was not searching or requesting this for myself, because I knew my parents didn't want this for me. But my parents died when I was young, and it was the *tuurngaq's* wish. My mother's second husband was an old man, and I told him about the things I was seeing. He told me that because I was not requesting them, because they were coming to me, I was going to die if I tried to send them away. Because they were seeking me, I was to listen to them. Because he was an old man, I listened to what he told me.[30]

In the workshop in Kangiq&iniq in 2000, Luke Nuliajuk from Uqsuqtuuq related that it was easier for a child to become an *angakkuq* than for an adult: "I have always known that I did not want to be an *angakkuq*. They say it is very difficult when a child starts becoming an *angakkuq*, but they also say it is all right.

It is much more difficult for a person to become an *angakkuq* as an adult. It is very hard."[31]

Felix Pisuk from Kangiq&iniq described how he was trained as a child to become an *angakkuq*: "Qaaqu's father, Nagjuk, was trying to make me into an *angakkuq*. What we are talking about is really important, so I am not going to keep anything hidden. My mother and father agreed when he told them he wanted to make me into an *angakkuq*. I got to the point where I was able to see what Nagjuk was going to *tupilattuq*.[32] I would see it with him. On the third day, I was told I was to *tupilattuq* on my own. I was to use my hands to kill it. I was able to see it."

Pisuk, however, did not complete the training, as his uncle feared for his life.

> When an *angakkuq* is killed, then his family members start to die as well. My uncle feared for me and did not want me to become an *angakkuq*. After that, I stopped dreaming like a child. I kept dreaming, but not like a child. After my uncle said that to me, I could not see what Nagjuk was going to *tupilattuq* anymore. I could only see his hands. This power was to be given to me. I desired it to be given to me. This is all I can tell you about becoming one. I am not an *angakkuq* and I am happy not to be an *angakkuq*. Maybe if I had become an *angakkuq*, I would have shortened my life. Because of that, I am thankful that I was asked not to become one.[33]

Jose Angutinngurniq from Kugaaruk began to become an *angakkuq* as a child, but as in the case of Pisuk, senior relatives interfered: "I will use myself as an example. I started to become an *angakkuq* as a child but I wasn't aware of it. They say I started levitating when I was inside the *iglu*. When my mother told my grandfather that I was becoming an *angakkuq*, my grandfather who I called my *sanaji*[34] said, 'I don't want my *sanaugaq*[35] to be one.' That was the end of it. I did not become an *angakkuq*. This is what I have been told. I have heard that those who become *angakkuit* as children will be good *angakkuit* but those who become *angakkuit* as adults tend to use their powers for their own personal use."[36]

Simon Inuksaq from Kugaaruk related his experience:

> I almost became a shaman myself. My uncle Iksivalitaq, was a shaman. Right after he died, in early fall, I almost had the spirit come to me from him. Even though I knew I was not meant to become a shaman I almost did. I do not know what happened. I know it is not good when you start to get a spirit within your body. When you are not born with it, it is difficult. I found out it was not a good experience.
>
> My father told me that sleep is very difficult when a spirit is entering your body. Even though everyone is sleeping, sleep is very slow to come. When this happens you start seeing things that [are] not normally there.

When this was happening to me I heard my father, we were in the same dwelling at the time, and I thought he was sleeping. I am named after his younger brother, and he always called me *nukaq*, which means younger brother. I heard him talking to his wife, even though she was already sleeping. He said in a very soft voice, and he called her *nuliaqtaaq*, which means my new wife: "*Nuliaqtaaq*," he said (she of course was an elderly woman), and she answered, "What is it?" very softly my father said, "My *nukaq* is becoming a shaman and he is very young. I am going to drive the spirits away from him." Even when he said that I did not say anything. I thought, "I hope that he can do something to help me." I thought about this because I needed sleep. Right after I had this thought I began to fall into a deep sleep.

Sleep has come very easily to me ever since. These were to be my spirits that were coming to me and my father drove them away. They were good spirits, helping spirits; they sometimes come back to me. There are two kinds of spirits: one is good, and the other is bad. The good ones are called *ikluramut ittut*, and these are the kinds that were coming to me. My namesake was passing them on to me by using my amulets (*aanguat*), and my father, who of course was a shaman himself, drove them away. Even though I did not tell him what was happening to me, he knew.[37]

Even today, shamanic calls may occur. Levi Iluittuq from Kugaaruk gave a rich account of his experience, which was interpreted by the elders as a shamanic calling:

I almost became an *angakkuq*. I fled from it for months because it was not a pleasant experience. One time I was out caribou hunting in deep winter. I had just finished building an *iglu*. I ate and I made some tea. I was all alone. I had caught some caribou and I had butchered them all. I was about to go to bed when I started hearing voices in the *iglu*. There were sounds outside. I could hear footsteps and I started to become frightened. I thought that if I remained there, I was not going to be able to sleep. I felt these voices had come to take me away. When I went out, it was dark because it was winter. What I am telling you is true. I have told this to some other people, but not many.

When I went out, I searched all around the *iglu*. Because it was dark, I could not see very far. I had killed a calf and cut it up. I took that, and I took my stove and things I needed to make tea with, and a ten-gallon gas can that was half-full. I even left my sleeping bag. I filled up my snow machine. I had one of those old Skidoos, one of the first Skidoos that came out. I knew that before I got home, I would need to fill the tank. Because it was dark, I did not search around at all. I started the machine and headed for home. Because it was so dark, I could not tell which direction I was heading. I could only see the snow and what was right in front of me. I took off not really thinking about what direction I was heading. You can feel the machine when you are driving. When I was driving, I could not feel anything underneath me anymore. I usually don't look behind me at my *qamutiik* (sled). I did not even think of it at all. I did not want to look. All I thought about was that I did not want to run out of gas. I could not even feel the ground underneath me anymore. I could see the snow going past my face and my *qulittaq*, my caribou parka. I just looked straight ahead. Sometimes when you are travelling, you can see the red light of a snow machine ahead of you. Even though I could not feel the ground underneath me anymore, I still held on to the throttle. I could see a tail light ahead of me. I could see the light for a while. On each side of the machine there were fairly high hills close together. There was only one path I could take, and it was only wide enough for my snow machine. Even in the winter some of the boulders aren't covered with snow. The smaller ones were farther apart but there were bigger ones you could not go over with a snow machine. They were not snow-covered at all. I went through the only part I could get through even though there was a possibility I could get stuck in-between the rocks. I just continued on. This happened late at night while it was dark. I could feel the air. That was all I could feel as I was driving. I was speeding. Suddenly, it seemed I was back on the ground. When you are landing on a plane, sometimes you land with a jar, and that is the way it was, as if I was suddenly back down on the ground. I could feel the ground again.

There is a part of the river where people go fishing. It seemed as though I landed right there. I had totally forgotten about my *qamutiik* that was behind me. I had had to refuel on my way out, but I had not had to refuel at all on my way back. I recognized where I was and where I had to go. There was another lake where people go fishing. There was a cabin at this other lake and there was a pole there for the radio antennae. It was a pole they got from the old DEW Line site and I passed that by.

I don't like talking about this because I recognized afterwards what it was. There was a fox climbing with its legs around the pole. The tail was black, but it was not dark black, and it was climbing like a person with its legs around the pole. It was not really possible for it to climb, but yet I saw it sit on top of the pole. I was trying to keep my eyes on it, but when I turned away for a moment it was gone. I stopped and searched for it but I could not find it at all.

I started travelling again and I saw this snow machine up ahead. When I caught up to it, it was early morning and people were just waking up. It was the camp of my older brother and my brother-in-law, now deceased. I could not feel my *qamutiik*. Because I was no longer scared and there were people around, I looked back at it. It was not a recognizable *qamutiik* any more. It was so snow-covered. The whole *qamutiik* was covered with snow. Only the front of the runners was visible. The snow should have blown off, but it was completely covered with snow. The snow was very level on the *qamutiik*. I was thinking, "No one is going to believe this." I took my mitts off and started to take the snow off but then I started thinking, "I have to show this to someone." So I went into the *iglu* as no one had come out and I said, "I am going to be leaving now." It was like I did not have all my senses about me. If they had recognized me, they would have said, "Come and have tea with us before you go home," but they did not. I said, "I might become sleepy so I am going to go home now." They agreed to that.

There is a place close to the community where people go fishing in the spring. There were two machines there. When I got close to them, I recognized whose machines they were. Juuti, who used to be from Uqsuqtuuq, was on the second one. Nirlungajuk was up ahead. Juuti stopped behind Nirlungajuk and came towards me. He said, "Have you just gone through a bad experience?" I did not say anything because he seemed to sense something already. Then he said, "Home is close now." The younger man did not say a thing. I had lost all sense of fear. I had forgotten about my *qamutiik* that had been totally covered with snow. When I remembered it, I looked back at it but there was no snow left on it at all. I don't know why there was not any more snow. The only part that had snow was around the runners. This is not really the end but I am going to end it here right now because I don't want to add things that I am not sure about. When I got home I seemed like my normal self again but after this incident, I was told I had been seen at two places at the same time.

I didn't think there was anything wrong with me. It was only after I had been home for a while that I told my parents about this incident. My mother said she wanted me to have a long life. She said, "The *tuurngait* are wanting you more and more. They are going after you. I don't want you to be an *angakkuq*." My father never talked much. Although my father seemed not to know as much as my mother, when I started telling him about the fox, he said that I had travelled, counter-clockwise, opposite the path of the sun. He said that it was my uncle Qimuksiraaq's[38] *tuurngaq* that I saw. Afterwards, when the now deceased Arnaluk was coming home for the last time and came to visit us, she started telling stories. She has always called me her *attak*, her aunt. She said, "*Attak*, there are two who want you. Neither of them is bad. But if it is possible, follow Christianity instead. If you can leave the other behind, your life will be longer." I said, "Because I did not know this, I needed to be told." She said, "There are two people behind you. One is a female and one is a male." My hair just stood on end when she said that. I am trying to talk about this but it is hard. She said, "I don't know who they are. I don't know anything much about this

> but I know that this will end." At the time, I did not believe her when she said it would end, but after that, I did not have any scary feelings. Even afterwards when I went out alone, I never experienced fear and I was never forced to flee.[39]

The image of the *qamutiik* flying through the air is well known in Inuit stories of the trip to the moon. In Iluittuq's account, it takes shape in a modern setting where skidoo and *qamutiik* apparently fly through the air and the miraculous nature of the flight is corroborated by the small amounts of gasoline required for the trip. The trip culminates in a confrontation with the helping spirits of the famous *angakkuq* Qimuksiraaq. Iluittuq's mother and an old woman who called him her aunt both try to convince him that he should not heed the call. The final sentence suggests a relationship between the two figures standing beside him and his never experiencing fear and never having to flee.

Maree Kakkik from Iqaluit explained to Dorothee Komangapik (1999, 66–9) how, after being unconscious, she almost became a shaman through a dream and a vision of a polar bear:

> I nearly turned into a shaman when I was living with my in-laws … My big sister told me that we were to pick some bushes tomorrow. As I passed by her she said she was not going anymore … I went over [to] that place … As I got on the top of this hill, … I saw a polar bear lying in the snow. I just stood there for some time, thinking that I should just go back. Since I was being abused by the family, I did not want to go back … I went behind the bear, and it looked at me. The bear … gave out a big roar. At that, I fainted. This was in the morning on a fall day. When I woke up, the bear was gone … I was moaning. Was not sick or hurt, but I did not want to open my eyes … I decided to walk home. A couple of years later, we went to the same place to pick up bushes, and somebody was watching us … When I got there, my brother-in-law told me about this dream, about a bear and a person. He told me that he wanted to find out what it meant. That was when I got scared, because it was me that he dreamed about … I had no choice but to tell him the truth, which I said, maybe it was me in his dream … This was the time when I started to have a bear cub in my dreams, which belonged to me and [I] kept it right beside the tent to let it grow up. I found out that this was the thing that kept me able to do things I can do. With this, I thought that I started to see the lands and camps from above them … From there I had this knowledge that grew, day by day, week by week, and year by year … I grew up as I kept dreaming about it [the bear], and it gave me the ability to do anything I wanted to do. I used a lot of strength not to become a shaman because my father did not want me to turn into one of them, a shaman. Get this off me, get it off me, I thought

wishing this ability to be a shaman to let go of me. A year later I dreamt about this bear again. By this time it had really grown into an adult. I found that it was the last time I was to dream about it. The bear was not really white, but it was yellowish, and it was really poor. I knew this bear was not my pet anymore, and since then, I never dreamt about it again. If I had let it be my pet then, it would have remained my pet today. I have thought a lot about these things … I think it almost made me be a shaman.

In this story, Kakkik met a *tuurngaq* that was a polar bear. Her reference to the bear as her pet suggests the relationship between an *angakkuq* and a helping spirit. Her account also indicates how dreams are always ambiguous and have to be interpreted by other people. Non-human beings are supposed to communicate with human beings through their dreams.

DREAMS AND VISIONS

According to the Inuit, not only human beings dream. Mariano Aupilaarjuk from Kangiq&iniq (1999 interview) stated, "All animals dream; all that breathes has a right to these things like us humans."[40] Aupilaarjuk distinguished between dreams and visions: "*Takutitauniq* (vision) and *sinaktuumaniq* (dream) are not the same … Dreams sometimes can lie, although it seems to be real, but visions are very strong and real. In the Bible, John has a vision which is very real and many people in the old days had visions like that." He described a vision he once had: "I have had, at least one time, a real vision. I can say that people would not believe it as they did not see it. It was when I was with my father. The thing that I saw had wings like a bird and a body but no face. It had wings just like a bird, it was very big, very very big. I could not say what it was and when I told this to my father, he said that it was an angel. When it got close, it was an angel coming down. I said as a child, if it was an angel it would be very bright so I told him that it was not an angel. But it was the truth. I really saw it, that's what I told him."

A vision immediately raises questions with respect to its truth. Can something be an angel if it is not bright? In the same interview, Aupilaarjuk distinguished visions from hallucinations: "*Takutitauniit* (visions) and dreams are different from *haminnaarijut* (hallucinations). The first ones happen through the mind while the second ones only happen through the eyes. Sometimes we mix the two and that is why we have to be careful … If you hallucinate from sickness and say things and it happens, it might be through the mind as well."

According to Aupilaarjuk, the attitude towards dreams has changed: "When I used to teach children I would ask them if they had any dreams. I even asked my grandchildren who are now bigger than me if they dreamt. I told them they should tell me about their dreams but they never told me anything. When I was young, it was very important to our parents that we told them about our dreams. "Where was the dream coming from? Was there danger ahead?" They would take dreams very seriously. They used to ask us a lot about our dreams but nowadays dreams are not important anymore."[41]

Various terms for dreams are used. The word *sinaktuumaniq* (dream – literally, "he is dreaming during the night") refers to a vision one can have while asleep. The word *uqumangirniq*, often translated as "nightmare," does not refer to the visual aspect of the experience but to a feeling of paralysis during the dream. Hallendy (1985, 140–1) reports that Inuit at Kinngait (Cape Dorset) distinguished various types of dreams:

> There are many kinds of dreams … *Irkah-li-yuk* is when you dream of things which you know to be real. They are not special dreams and are close to, but not the same as, what you call daydreams. A daydream that allows you to see something that is about to happen or has happened is more impressive because it is certain. That very moment in the daydream when you see what is happening is called *iss-oh-rho*. There is another kind of dreaming called *nir-eu-zak-tuk*. These are dreams of things seen that have yet to happen. Most people have little dreams like those and some people have the power to dream often about things which are sure to happen in the future … (*Tikki-tu-siak-tuk* is a dream of someone coming back after a long absence) … There are two more kinds of dreams which are opposites to one another. The fearful dream is called *hunu-yak*. It is the dream of death, and it will surely come to the person the dreamer dreams of and to the dreamer, in the end. (*Ah-nay-ow-tuk* refers to someone dreaming of being seduced by a beautiful woman.)

Two elders from Iqaluit, Jaiku Pitsiulaaq and Aalasi Joamie distinguished between *qunujaaqtuq* (when a person dreams of something unpleasant, it is a sign that something bad will happen) and *niriujaaqtuq* (when a person dreams of something pleasant, it is a sign that something good will happen).[42] In the past, there seemed to be a distinction between nocturnal dreams (*sinaktuumaniq*) and daydreams (*qavvangniqsaujuq, isumannguarniq, ukijijuq*). According to Felix Pisuk from Kangiq&iniq, *qavvangniqsaujuq* means "dreaming while awake. Someone says they are dreaming about a person and bring up something the person is embarrassed about."[43]

Dreams are not necessarily significant, and elders vary in the importance they attribute to dreams. Aupilaarjuk stated, "I believe some of my dreams, others I don't believe."[44] Pisuk stated that he had just ordinary dreams, but in various workshops and courses he related some quite significant dreams, such as one that his son had:

> When my youngest son was old enough to have a wife, he got lost in a blizzard. He was travelling by Skidoo and had lost his *qamutiik*. He had an

idea where he was, but he wasn't sure. He didn't have his knife or his stove because he had left his *qamutiik* behind. This was in January when it was quite cold. He should have known where home was when he ran out of fuel, but the blizzard was quite strong.

He had been told by his grandfather to try to get to the coast if he was lost. He dug himself a hole and lay down against a piece of ice. He was lost for three days. My father had said that my son, who is named after him, was not to be searched for if he became lost, because the next time he was lost he would be even more lost.

My oldest son who was still alive at that time said, "My brother is going to get weaker and weaker." I told him his grandfather had said his brother was not to be searched for when he was lost. I told him that his grandfather did not want me to go looking for him so I didn't go out searching. When my son was found by my son-in-law, he was in shock. I blew in his ears and patted him on his shoulders. I told him his grandfather had said that he was going to be okay after this. When he was lost I was very emotional, but I remembered his grandfather's words so I didn't go to search for him.

His mitts were all covered with ice. They had totally frosted over but his hands weren't frozen. His wrists were red but he was okay. One custom that Inuit used to follow was that if a man came back from being lost his mother would put her nipple in his mouth even after he was an adult. After my wife put her nipple in my son's mouth, he seemed to come out of his shock. He said, "How am I?" He said his ears were beginning to *ivulaaq*, to thrum. When he got back to himself he was full of joy. I said he was probably very thirsty, so his mother gave him a cup of water and he felt better.

He had quite a story to tell afterwards. My son said that after he had sought his third shelter someone came to him and gave him a knife. He recognized it was mine. He was told, "I have brought this to you to use for your comfort." When he woke him up he said, "You are too young. It is not time for you to leave your life. Your children are young and you still have to live."

My son had been woken up by his grandfather. He told him he had to go back home. That's when he was given the knife. He told him he should start walking before he got too cold. His grandfather wanted him to get home that day.

Our adopted child was quite small then. He asked whether or not to bring my knife to him and I said, "Never mind about it for now." Maybe if my adopted child had taken the knife something might have happened to one of my grandchildren instead. I was very thankful.[45]

In this case, the life of Pisuk's son was saved by his deceased grandfather, who provided him with a knife and told him what to do. A person may receive advice or warnings in a dream, but the source is not always known. Ollie Itinnuaq from Kangiq&iniq told of a snowmobile accident in which a cousin lost his life:

> We had built an *iglu* and had put a cover over the top of the bombardier. We were going to close up the bombardier but I wanted to drink a cup of tea in a warm place so I started it up. My cousin was at the doorway. I had closed the bombardier tight. I started smelling something. I had two other companions so I went to locate them. I was going to tell them there was a strange smell, when everything went dark. I blacked out.
>
> It was winter so there was not much daylight. We had seen caribou tracks and were going to follow the tracks the next day. We were waiting for daylight. We had stopped to stay the night because we did not want to lose our way in the dark and there were no caribou there.
>
> We had all lost consciousness in the snow. When I regained consciousness, when I opened my eyes, I had my *kamiik* on, but I had no parka. I started dreaming that the bombardier was pointing at me. Something woke me up. I couldn't see what woke me up, and I was going to try to say something when I fell back asleep. The thing that woke me up, woke me up two more times. When I woke up again, I was lying on my side facing the bombardier. I was trying to stop the sound I was hearing. I was thinking, "I thought we were going to go caribou hunting." Then I passed out again. It was daylight when I regained consciousness and I wanted to look at my watch. That was all I was concentrating on. I could not see my watch because of the strap. I was trying to take my watch off, but I could not grasp it with my fingers. They couldn't grasp anything so I used my thumbs. I dropped it and picked it up with my thumbs. I recall this very clearly. It was again four in the afternoon. We had stopped for the day around four, because the days were short and it was going to get dark soon. I started wondering where my two companions were. I started to look around. The bombardier entrance was open and I saw a foot. We were on a lake and my cousin was there lying on the ground on his back. He had opened up his jacket. His hands were at his sides and they were very, very white. He had foam in his mouth and his face was very white also. This startled me, and I became more clear-headed. I tried to get up. I was unable to, so I rolled over. I was unaware I was up high, and I rolled down and almost fell on him. I went to touch him. His stomach and his hands were frozen. He had foam around his mouth, which was also frozen. The bombardier was not running. Then I thought of our other companion. The front door of the bombardier was open. I tried to get there but it was difficult for me to move. I finally managed to get to the door. It was ajar but not fully open. There was a blanket there. When I noticed that my second companion was breathing, I was really relieved. Then I lost consciousness

again. When I regained consciousness, I was woken up by something or someone. I went over to my companion and I tried to wake him up. I told him something had happened to us and that one of our companions had frozen to death. He sat up and put his arms around me. When he got up, I started retching inside the bombardier. After I had finished throwing up, I looked around. Finally I was really aware of our surroundings. I was unable to stand because my feet had frozen. I crawled around in there. The bombardier had two tanks and one of the tanks was empty. That's why it had stopped while the engine was still running. It had become very hot in there. I tried to run the engine, and it started right away. I thought we needed to take the body home. My other companion was fine. We were unable to load my cousin into the bombardier because he was frozen. We checked, but we knew he was dead so we wrapped him in a tarp. We went around the bombardier to the *iglu* and we headed home. We were going to follow our tracks home. While we were travelling, I was afraid we would pass out. Although I would almost fall asleep I managed to stay awake. I kept my companion awake as well, because I was afraid he was going to die. He too wanted to sleep. I kept on saying, "Don't go to sleep. Don't fall asleep." We got to where we had stopped to eat the previous day. Because I was thirsty, I wanted to stop but I thought if I stopped and had a drink, I would not be able to continue. Then we came across a person from Tikirarjuaq at Qamanaarjuk. Uqaqtialaaq [Norman Voisey] was there. I told him, "One of my companions is dead and wrapped in a tarp, and the other is falling asleep. I want to be taken home." He said, "Go home. I'm going home by dogteam." I got angry because he did not agree to take us home. I had stopped for quite a while but I did not feel I had stopped at all. When I arrived, I was not able to walk. I recall being dragged to the hospital by my arms. I am telling you about this incident because I dreamed someone was waking me up.[46]

Itinnuaq did not indicate who woke him up and thus saved his life.

COMMUNICATION WITH THE DECEASED

In the dream related by Pisuk, his deceased father intervened to save his grandson. In the case of Itinnuaq, the warning may also have come from a deceased relative or namesake. According to Rasmussen (1929, 93; see also 1931, 213), the *angakkuq* Ava pointed out that we often see the deceased in our dreams: "We believe that men live on after death here on earth, for we often see the dead in our dreams fully alive … 'Old folk' declare that when a man sleeps, his soul is turned upside down, so that the soul hangs head downwards, only clinging to the body by its big toe. For this reason we believe that death and sleep are nearly allied; for otherwise, the soul would not be held by so frail a bond when we sleep. But the Spirit of Sleep is also very fond of the dead, for when we sacrifice meat to him, he gives the souls of the dead meat from our offerings."

Dreams often refer to the wish of the deceased to be reborn or to live on in a name. Turner (1979, 36) reported the case of a woman who had heard someone knocking on the door. An elder told her "that it was the rapping of her brother, who had died suddenly some two years before. She must go home and prepare a cup of tea, with a slice of bread, and give it to the nurse, as her brother, Nakvak (the one who died), was hungry and wanted food. She especially enjoined upon the woman that the girl must now be known as Nakvak (meaning 'found') and that through her the dead would procure the food which, although it subserves a good purpose in nourishing the living, tends, by its accompanying spirit, to allay the pangs of hunger in the dead."

Tipuula Qaapik Ataguttiaq from Ikpiarjuk recalled:

> It seemed to me that my child returned to me in my dreams. I lost a child who was about nine months old. I dreamed about holding and hugging him. He was wearing clothing that was all white that was different from the clothing we wear. I dreamed about this baby who was quite big and chubby while we were still living the traditional way. I dreamed that I was kissing him on his cheek. I was told from above that the child would return in the near future and that I should expect this. I was told the child was concerned that I was worrying about him. Shortly after this I became pregnant. Some dreams have a meaning. They happen every few years or so. I have never had a dream like that again. I was told that he was in the kingdom of God and after that, I felt healed.[47]

Salumi Mitiarjuk Nappaaluk (1994, 79), from Kangiqsujuaq, relates, "If a woman dreams often about someone, or if she is afraid of this person in her dreams, she will know that this person, even though dead, wants to have a namesake. If she dreams often of a living person, she will give [him] also a namesake when she gives birth to a child." The deceased person may express his desire in different ways; the woman "dreams that this person arrives, or that she is shaking their hand, or that she is caring for them. So it appears this person wants a namesake."

Ataguttiaq confirmed this: "When the mother dreams of a dead person, I believe that this person wants the baby to be named after him. When the dead person is asking for water in the dreams of a mother-to-be, it is seen as a sign that the baby must be named after him. So when the baby was born, he was named after the deceased."[48]

Alexina Kublu from Iglulik told a similar story involving her brother Nanauq:

> He carries the name of our uncle Arnarjuaq's mother-in-law Qannakuttuk. Shortly after he was born my mother had woken up and recognized Qannakuttuk sitting at the *qariaq* (guest bed) of the *qarmaq* in which my brother was born. She woke up my father and said: "Takkuuraalunguna" (Look at this awful thing here). My father had said to her: "*Anialugi*"' (Get out you awful thing). They both knew that she was not there in person. Qannakuttuk's apparition said: "Anigiaruma ningaukuluga naksarniaqtara najuruma&&arakku" (On my way out I'm going to bring with me my *ningaukuluk* [dear son-in-law] as I really want to stay by him). At that point my father said to my mother that Qannakuttuk wanted my brother to carry her name. If she so badly wanted to be with my sister Arnarjuaq let her do so. Even though it was not stated explicitly it was understood that my sister would have died if Qannakuttuk had taken her *ningaukuluk* with her.[49]

Relations between the deceased and their descendants are not always straightforward. At the Kugaaruk workshop in 2004, Nilaulaq from Talurjuaq (Spence Bay) recalled that even though her father did not want to be reborn or live on in another name, she dreamt of recognizing him in a child she had adopted:

> My father used to say that he didn't want me to have any children. But after he died, I became pregnant. He didn't want his name repeated. He didn't want his name passed on to anybody. In my dreams, I would look down and I would see my father's face. When I came to Uqsuqtuuq I told people about this dream. In Uqsuqtuuq after somebody named someone after my father, I saw his face in my dream because he didn't want his name passed on to another person. Just before going to sleep, I usually look at my Bible and mark something. My father used to tell me to try to believe in the Bible, and do my best to live right. I adopted a child in May. Then the next month, in June, after I woke up, I could see my father's face in the baby's face. It was not a pretty sight to see, so I grabbed my Bible. I lay him down. He was just a baby. It was a very sad thing to see. I covered his face, and when I uncovered him, he was a baby again. My father didn't want to be born again after this life. He didn't want anybody to be named after him. I could feel this sometimes in my sleep.

Elders agree that dreams provide an opportunity for the deceased to contact their descendants and express their wishes to them, but such communications should not be excessive. Ilisapi Uuttuvak from Mittimatalik reminded her audience, "If we are constantly thinking about a close deceased relative, we can let our grief get the better of us. It can even affect our sleep. Even if we feel a lot of grief, we have to tell ourselves that that is in the past and his life is finished.

Some people can make themselves sick or age prematurely from grieving too much over a deceased relative."[50] Peter Suvaksiuq from Arviat related, "When my mother was about to die, she told me not to cry for her because I was going to dream about her. When she died, I tried to cry but I was unable to. They say that when you don't express your grief over a person through tears, you tend to dream about them a lot."[51] Felix Pisuk and Salome Qalasiq from Kangiq&iniq emphasized that it might be necessary to end a relationship with a deceased person: "If a person such as my son or daughter or I started dreaming about my deceased father or mother coming to get us, we would realize that there was something bad about this person. We would *qinugijuq*, order the person to leave."[52] The most efficient way to end such a relationship was to communicate the dream to another person. George Kappianaq from Iglulik explained that this was how his first wife stopped an invisible lover from harassing her in her dreams.

UQUMANGIRNIQ

Elders explain that a person enters a state of *uqumangirniq* when he feels threatened. It manifests itself in a state of complete paralysis and a person does not know whether he is asleep or awake.[53] Pisuk described such an experience of *uqumangirniq* (or *aqtuqsittuq*):[54]

> Some people don't just have ordinary *aqtuqsinniit*. I think some people are made to *aqtuqsittuq* by a*ngakkuit* and they don't wake up at all. My grandmother told me when I was experiencing an *aqtuqsinniq* that I was to hold up my middle finger. There was one time I was in bed with my wife and I couldn't wake up at all. There was an old man wearing caribou clothing. My wife and I have a double bed. This old man was standing between us and was smiling at me and reaching towards me. His face was healthy and handsome but it started to become older. He became ugly and he seemed to have lots of hair. Because I remembered what my grandmother had told me to do, I stuck my finger up at him. I seemed to feel him, and then he fell backwards and disappeared. I thought this had come from someone and I didn't want to die. I started wondering, "Why are Tautunngi and Qabluittuq's son doing this to me." Then I thought, "I have hit his *tarniq*. Maybe he won't live."
>
> Later on when the days started getting longer there was something like a balloon above his house. My middle son saw this. It looked like a balloon but it wasn't because it was a complete bubble. It started coming towards the house and then it burst. During the night that man hung himself. When something bounces back to the one who sent it this is called *utirviujuq*. That's why I have to tell you about this. Some people just don't experience *aqtuqsinniq*. Some people end up not being able to move because someone is going after them.[55]

The *uqumangirniq* described by Pisuk was clearly experienced as an attack. Pisuk knew who was attacking him and was able to defend himself. In dreams, people interact on the level of the *tarniq*. Pisuk killed the *tarniq* of his opponent by pointing towards it, and as consequence the bubble burst and his enemy died. He overcame his enemy because he remembered his grandmother's advice and applied it.

The *uqumangirniq* can also imply a completely different type of relationship, as related by Pisuk:

> In some ways *aqtuqsinniit* can be helpful. If you were to *aqtuqsittuq* you could see a nice looking man or woman that perhaps was a *tarniq*. If it came to you and you were unable to move, it had sex with you [and] then you could end up with an unseen lover. If you enjoyed it and you wanted to keep this unseen lover, you didn't tell anyone about it. You would have found yourself something pleasurable. Even if you didn't tell an *angakkuq* about it, an *angakkuq* would eventually find out. I was not handsome and I did not show off. When girls started teasing me, I asked them if they wanted to get an unseen lover. They would say no, and would stop teasing me. I think some of them should have just said yes.[56]

Usually, elders interpret an *uqumangirniq* as an attack, and they suggest various means of defence, such as changing the position of the body. Aalasi Joamie from Iqaluit and Tipuula Ataguttiaq from Ikpiarjuk advised placing a weapon such as a knife or even better a Bible under the pillow.[57] Pisuk suggested defending oneself by spitting, by pointing a finger, or by turning the big toe.[58]

In the workshop in Kangiq&iniq in 2002, a young woman from Kangiq&iniq, Rosalie Pisuk, related a dream in which she felt she was being attacked by a knife:

> In 1995, there were two houses. We had a house with two bedrooms and we were moved into a house with three bedrooms while our house was being renovated. We were next door to Saumik and Noah Tittaq. While we were in that three bedroom house, we were given other people's discards and we would be pleased with them. While we were going through these discards, we came across a little knife that had strings attached to it. It seemed like something I knew about from one of the stories but I wasn't sure. The kitchen table was high up so we put it up high so it didn't get lost. Then we hung it up. My older son who was here was five years old. My daughter was four years old at the time. We hung it up high because we didn't want to lose it. It was important to us. It would give me the shivers.
>
> When my two daughters were comfortable to go to the bathroom on their own, we would keep their bedroom lit and the bathroom lit so they would be able to go the washroom at night. We went to sleep. In my sleep

I was dreaming, and in my dream I went to the bathroom. Even before I got to the bathroom – I was near where the washing machine was – I was yanked by my neck. When I dream, I can see everything clearly in my dreams. When I am awake, I can hardly see anything at all. When I was yanked, I looked to see what was yanking me. When I looked upwards, it was something very, very dark. You couldn't see the end and it was very dismal. It frightened me. Then I became aware of what I had seen. It was something that was made to not break. I also noticed that it was made of ivory and bone and it was square. Also the top was shorter than the bottom and the sides were the same length. It was not going to be removed and it was not going to break at all. I saw around my neck a skin rope that was not going to break. I tried to see where it was from. It went past the washing machine and it was attached to the little knife that we had hung up on the wall. I was losing my strength. I was becoming unable to move and my breathing was becoming laboured and I was being pulled. It seemed like I was hearing a ringing. I was losing my strength and heard ringing in my ears. I was getting cold. I seemed to be awake and I was frightened. I wondered what was going to happen. I was so frightened I wasn't able to cry out. There were no tears, and I was trying to keep aware of what was going on.

I heard my son. Being older he was playing around and laughing. He wanted to play with his sister. They were playing and running around and laughing. Then I thought, "How can I get back to my children. I still want to be with them." That crossed my mind. I couldn't see what was pulling me because whenever I looked that way there was nothing but darkness, and it was cold. My breathing was becoming more laboured. In my dream one of my children went to the washroom and when they saw me, they started laughing. My son took my right hand and my daughter took my left hand. Being children they were laughing. They said I should be asleep and when they said that, what was above me disappeared. Then I was on the floor and nothing at all was wrong with me. I was going towards the washroom and there were windows and when I looked out, there was a great big piece of ice over the window and it was very dismal. The house I was in was very dark and dismal. My two children were having fun as usual. After looking out the window I looked towards the door. There was a woman sewing with my sewing machine and she was laughing. My two children took me to my bedroom and put me to bed and after I went to bed, I woke up. I still had the same feeling.

I often wanted to ask an elder about my dream but I have kept myself from asking because I don't like to ask elders questions very often. I always wanted to know about my dream. That little knife disappeared. Maybe we dropped it when we were moving houses. It was just before or after I had this dream that my father's cousin Barry who is an orphan was visiting us in this same house. We were just chatting and there was nothing wrong with me at all. I walked into the kitchen because I was going to make myself a cup of coffee. Even now I try to remember if this happened before or after my dream. I seemed to be suddenly pulled very hard and I was not able to breathe. When I became unable to breathe, I was also unable to see anything. I was hitting the counter. My husband came to me right away and asked me what was wrong with me. His cousin was further away and came to see what was wrong with me. I said I was unable to take a breath and I couldn't see anything. My husband asked me if I wanted a glass of water, and I said. "Yes," but I couldn't swallow anything. I was losing my strength. I was about to fall on the floor. He told me I was becoming very pale. I tried to keep myself from blacking out. My children being children were not aware. My son who was looking after me said that I was getting very pale. I couldn't take a breath in at all. I tried to prevent myself from blacking out. I had to go to Winnipeg to find out what was wrong with me and they did numerous tests but they have never been able to find out the cause.

In Inuit society, objects embody relationships, and when the former owner of an object is not known, a person cannot be sure which relationships are evoked by it. People are therefore reluctant to accept an object without knowing something about its former owner. In the case of Rosalie Pisuk, it never became clear who the former owner of the knife was who might have been suggested in the events in the dream. Pisuk said she did not remember what happened to the knife.

In the 2004 Kugaaruk workshop, Nilaulaq from Talurjuaq told of being attacked by a *tuurngaq* in her dreams:

Another dream I had was that I was sick in Talurjuaq. I was a teacher there. I remembered seeing this old woman when I was a child. I saw her coming after me. It was dark. I was in an *iglu*. I couldn't breathe out of fear. I was afraid, because she was fearsome. I tried to pray, but I couldn't pray at all. I fell asleep again, and I had the same dream. I had never seen a *tupilaq* or a *tuurngaq* in my dream before. Still today I think about it. It was a bad thing. I got angry at it, and I tried to go after it, I grabbed it outside. After I grabbed it, it burst. When it burst it was full of blood. There was blood all over. I looked for the bones but there were none. After I woke up, I started to think that this thing was after me. I told my father and my aunt about this dream. They told me that I would get help. After that, I woke up feeling a little better. I was sick before, but I got better. In Talurjuaq there was still an *angakkuq*. He was always helpful to me. I told him about my dream, about that ball, and said when it burst it was full of blood. Somebody sent a *tupilaq* through my dream. I'm not ashamed to tell you this. There were other dreams I had before, but I will stop here for now.

In the same workshop, Jose Angutinngurniq from Kugaaruk recalled how he was attacked and had to defend himself in a dream:

> Sometimes you have bad dreams even if you are an *angakkuq*. I have had two dreams that came true, but they were not as strong, because I wasn't an *angakkuq*. I don't like dreams when they come true. I visited my sister's mother-in-law in the daytime, in the middle of the day. One of my sister's husband's brothers had his own little knife that he made. I joked with him. He started to get uncomfortable when I said something to him. After that, I knew by the look on his face that he was not happy. You can tell when people are not happy by the look on their face. Every time I saw him he was unhappy, because of the joke I had made. I knew he didn't like me anymore. That night when we went to sleep I dreamed that Qipingajuq was crawling inside, trying not to make any noise. He wanted to harm me, because of the joke I had made. In the dream, he was getting closer and closer. I started to think that if he moved first to attack me, something would happen to me. I went to him and grabbed his hand at the wrist, and then bit his throat. This was all in my dream. We are not *angakkuit*. We all have a soul. I went up to him and attacked him, and bit him on the throat. I seemed to hear myself making an animal-like sound. I knew my wife was beside me but I couldn't get up in my dream. When you hear a polar bear, it has a roaring sound. My voice was like that in my dream. I could hear myself. When he surrendered I let him go. When he started to go I came to. My wife was trying to wake me up. I was like a different person, not really aware. My wife couldn't wake me up. She was shaking and shaking me. Later that morning, I said I had had a dream about Qipingajuq. I dreamed that I was fighting him. Somebody came by a little while later and said that Qipingajuq had died. I dreamed I was fighting him, but he actually died.
>
> Another dream I had was that Aggagak had died. That was on our way back to the community after my wife and I had been out camping. I dreamed about Aggagak. He became a black bear. I attacked that black bear in my dream. I had a bad feeling about it. In my dream I bit it in the throat. My wife was trying to wake me up. I could feel my wife trying to wake me up, but I couldn't wake up. In my dream Aggagak went down. The next thing I heard was that Aggagak had died. It's a bad feeling to have that kind of dream. It seems like you killed a person through your dream.

Lucassie Nutaraaluk from Iqaluit told how his son, a very successful hunter, had been killed by an *angakkuq* out of jealousy. Then that same *angakkuq* had tried to go for Nutaraaluk, but he succeeded in defending himself. He described a dream that represented his struggle:

> I had a dream in which it seemed that I was awake not asleep. I seemed to be seeing the form of a lion through the walls of an *iglu*. The lion was growling and started coming towards me. I thought to myself, the sword of God is my only weapon. When I thought that, it seemed that the Holy Spirit was with me as a sword and it seemed to be moving towards the lion. Then the lion seemed to disintegrate into dust. After that incident I knew that that *angakkuq* had tried to go after me. Later he became so sick he had to go to the hospital down south. I think that image of the lion was the *angakkuq's tuurngaq* … A person can defeat an *angakkuq* as long as they have firm beliefs. We can use our Saviour to defeat them. Even though, I was defeated in regards to my son.[59]

Nutaraaluk's dream shows that dreams constitute an arena where conflicts can be decided. They are a matter of life and death.

Dreams might also predict what would happen. Paul Kunuk from Iglulik (IE 116) told a story about his father, who dreamt that an Indian pursued him. The next day he hunted a caribou that suddenly began to behave most peculiarly, sniffing at his traces and coming after him. When he shot at it, he missed several times and only managed to kill it with his last shot. After he had cached the caribou, one of his dogs began to behave very strangely; it didn't want to leave the place, so he tied it on the spot and left. When he looked back, he saw the Indian he had dreamt of leaving the place. He hurried home and lay down beside his wife. He heard sounds outside all night. In the morning he and his wife had an *aqtussittut* (dream of feeling paralysed) and thought the tent had collapsed on top of them. When they awoke, the sun was shining and the tent was completely intact. The actual experiences of Kunuk's father are embedded in his first dream as well as in the one he shared with this wife. It seems that the Indian was connected to both the caribou and the dog.

The association between a dream and the actual events that follow is not always easy to understand. Alain Ijiraq from Iglulik (IE 231) related:

> At the time when we had to sleep at the bottom of the fiord at Avvajaq before we went back to our tent, I had a disturbing dream. The dream I had was about a bee that had come to us. This particular bee was different from any other bees that I have seen. It had a real mouth and it was after me. I had a knife in my hand and hacked it with it into two. As it turned out there was another bee which went right to the one that I hacked and it immediately proceeded to lick the downed bee. Both bees had real eyes. As soon as the other started to lick it, the other started to get back together and regain its full size, at once they started for me again but I woke up. The

dream was short but I woke up my partner and told him about this strange dream that I dreamed and I told him that I had lost hope. As it turned out ... in the very near future I was going to fall into the water through the ice.

Ijiraq was convinced that his dream of the bees was connected to his falling into the water through the ice.

Felix Pisuk believed that his dreams of being attacked by a mosquito might mean that someone was going to die: "Another dream I have that I don't enjoy very much is about a mosquito that is coming towards me. If I swat it, it means that whoever is trying to do things against me is going to die."[60] He (Kolb and Law 2001, 91) also believed that his dreams could predict his hunting fortunes: "If I dreamed about a man with terrible skin that was brown, and the man looked fat, then I would know that a walrus would be killed. I'm not a good walrus hunter. I don't catch that many. If I had a dream about a woman who was beautiful, who didn't smile, sitting down at the floe edge, then I would know that I would get an *ugjuk*."

Angutinngurniq from Kugaaruk also had dreams that predicted a successful hunt: "A *niriujaarniq* is a good thing, especially the one I have about the woman, as I told you before. I know I will catch a caribou or another animal if I have that *niriujaarniq*. If I dream I am next to a woman, when I wake up the next morning I know I will have a good hunt."[61] A successful hunt is often represented by a beautiful woman appearing to the hunter in a dream.

Elders sometimes discuss the symbolism in dreams. Pisuk (1999 interview) recalled, "When the foxes were tradable, if I would dream of rainbows then I would know there would be animals and foxes available. That is why I was good at catching foxes. But when my father was dying he told me to stop trying to dream because there are now other means like machines and airplanes. Perhaps he stopped me because he wanted me to have a long life, I should not cut my life somewhat."

Rasmussen (1932, 23) reports that a rainbow (*kataujak*, "the entrance to an igloo") represents life and joy if high in the sky and death if low on the earth. Thus, the entrance to a trap may correspond to the entrance to the igloo. According to Pisuk, dreaming of two people fighting indicates the death of several people. Salome Qalasiq from Kangiq&iniq said that dreaming of dancing persons predicts there will be a contagious epidemics.[62] Elisapee Ootoova from Mittimatalik stated that losing a tooth signifies the death of a close relative.[63]

MacDonald (1998, 186–7) records the testimony of Aipilik Innuksuk, an Anglican who got lost between Iglulik and Nirliviktuuq. He was saved by a dream.

I heard someone say to me [in my sleep], "Iglusi takanna uqussinniitiappuq! Uqummuttiaq ingiraguvit iglusinnut angirarunnapputit!" (The direction of your camp is right on your lee side; if you just go downwind you can get home!) I could not see the person who told me this nor did I know who or what it was ... When I awoke it was dark. I thought about the words that had been spoken to me but I did not act on them immediately because of my doubts. I went back to sleep. It was getting light when I woke up again. Standing up I saw that the weather had cleared ... and there, not very far away, was our camp, downwind from where I stood! ... This was not the only time I was given directions in my sleep. Should other people have similar experiences I would advise them to do as they are told.

Dreams could also predict accidents, as illustrated in this account from Pisuk:

This summer I had a dream about four men in a boat. In this dream the boat had tipped over and it was resting on its mast. The wind blew it upright again, but it then once more tipped over. The first time it tipped over the four men managed to stay aboard but the second time it tipped over it was smashed against the rocks and the boat started to break apart. Two of the men were pushed ashore by the waves, but the other two were lost. As soon as I woke up I told my family about the dream I had. I told them not to talk about my dream with others, but I felt that there was probably going to be a boating accident that summer and two of the bodies would be found, but that the bodies of the two younger ones would not. Although I knew I was not going to be the one to cause the accident, I still knew that because some of my dreams came true, this accident was a real possibility. When you come to understand your dreams, you feel as though you are making predictions.[64]

Pisuk had more dreams about boating accidents:

One time I had a dream about a boat. This is not something new I am going to talk about. The top of the boat had holes punctured in it. I was going to go to the floe edge. I told my mother about my dream and she said, "You are going to have a bad accident. Don't go." I disobeyed her and I went down to the floe edge. My cousin Simiuni heard that I was going so he accompanied me. The water was calm. This was around May. It was high tide. We went down to the floe edge and we started making tea. We had some tea, and then the wind started blowing from the water. We got to the edge of the water, and the moving ice started getting closer. We started making more tea, and while we were doing this, the moving ice started breaking the ice we were on. The wind started getting stronger. The ice around us started pulling us. The stove was still burning. That is when the companion I was with drowned. My mother had warned me. She had said that there was going to be a bad accident and told me not to go. She told me to wait for another day. I want to learn more about my dreams. I did not pay attention to that dream and that's why I lost my hunting companion.[65]

Niviuvaq from Uqsuqtuuq reminded her audience at the 2004 Kugaaruk workshop that you should always warn people if you have a dream that predicts an accident so that they can take precautions. She recounted her own experience:

> I have forgotten some of my dreams. I never pay much attention to them. Last year during the winter I went to sleep, and then got up again. It was dark. There was a black spot on the floor. It was in the middle, inside, on the floor. I couldn't see clearly because it was dark. That was the night before somebody accidentally drowned. I could see it, but because it was dark I could just make out a picture of the spot. I tried to look at it. It was a bad sign. This is what I wanted to tell you. This is my experience of seeing trouble ahead of time. That person usually went out hunting or went to other places. This death was indicated when I saw that dark spot on the floor that winter. That happened just last year. I think about that dream now and then. Sometimes I have this dream. I'm thankful other people are telling me things they don't normally talk about. I warn children about dangerous places, and warn them about bad things. If you have a vision or a dream like the one I had, make sure you tell your children about it so the danger can be avoided. If you should have a dream like that about your child or anybody else, make sure you tell them.

Ignoring a warning is very dangerous, as Pisuk discovered: "Another time I was out walrus hunting with three of my sons and two of my grandsons and nephews down at the floe edge. I knew there was going to be an accident but I did not know the details. Somebody else had had a dream. I did not have it myself. I said we would be fine and nothing was going to happen. My three sons and I ended up in the water."[66] Pisuk himself almost drowned, and his son William only barely managed to save him.

TRANSITIONS

Dreams connect the past with the present. Salome Qalasiq from Kangiq&iniq (1999 interview) related a dream that evoked a shamanic descent to the sea woman:

> We were here [in Kangiq&iniq] when I dreamt of Chesterfield Inlet. I went into the Hudson's Bay Company store and there was a hole in the floor and there were steps leading up the hole. I was descending on the steps and got quite wet going down to my waist. I started thinking, "My children, I should go back to them," so I turned around and went back up into the store. Then I was told to look out the window. When I looked out there was the sea with a beautiful bottom and it looked like a beautiful land with beautiful animals. When I told the story to my cousin she told me that the

spirit of the sea made me dream. She told me that my dream forecast right. Qimuksiraaq had the sea spirit for a *tuurngaq*. Apparently the *tuurngaq* told Qimuksiraaq that the floor of the sea was a beautiful land and told him to go with her. Qimuksiraaq said, "No," but she repeated that it was very nice so she wanted him to go. She wanted him to go into the deep because it was beautiful and had a lot of animals.

Dreams are associated with the shamanic domain, but they remain very present in the Christian context as well. At the Kugaaruk workshop in 2004, Levi Iluittuq from Kugaaruk described various visions, some of them having a Christian perspective, others evoking shamanism. He had his first vision as a child: "We were outside one day in the summer time, getting ready to go out on the land for the winter. My parents went to sleep at night time. There were two black things just beside the tent. They were small, not big. They were medium sized. I cried very hard because I was afraid. One of my parents woke up. I think it was my mother, who said it was a vision, to get it to go away. I don't think it was a vision. I really did see those black things when I was outside. The two of them were right on the doorway, completely black. Still today I think about them. I saw them."

Later Iluittuq had visions of Jesus. The first vision he shared with his wife:

Once in the fall, when there was hardly any snow, my wife and I were in a place called Ukpik, a place not far from here. It was close to Ukpik. We travelled through there. I was carrying a *pukiq*, the white part of a caribou skin. I had the caribou skin on my back. We looked over that way. We saw a cross out there. It was big. There were two people who were the size of that one, a little ways off the ground. My wife saw this, too. We both saw it. We started to look at it. There was a picture of Jesus hanging on the cross, just like the picture of Jesus we have seen. The cross seemed to be made of a cloud. It seems that way. Something picked it up, and then it disappeared completely.

He had another vision of Jesus on his own: "Just last year, I saw something else. I was out smoking in a porch. I thought I was in a porch. Yes, it was in a porch. I told you about this. I saw the face of Jesus, just the face. I turned around and every time I turned back to look at it, it would still be there, just the face. I could see the branches around his head. He was wearing the crown of thorns. It was exactly like that, right around his head."

Iluittuq doubted that these experiences were visions, as they seemed so real. He added, "I hear things that are not there. I hear things. I think my wife and I hear things. Whenever there is death coming, we hear a noise. Just as you can hear sounds on the tape recorder, we hear a noise, like music in the middle of the night. There is a bell at the church. The bell at the church started to ring by itself, because somebody was going to die soon. It started by itself. My wife and

I could hear it." Most of Iluittuq's visions focus on Christianity, but some also deal with other domains. He chooses to be a Christian, but he is still torn between the old traditions and Christianity. In the same workshop, Otto Apsauqtaun from Kugaaruk related a vision he had had during Christmas celebrations:

> One Sunday, we had our service at the old stone church down there on the beach. It was Christmas time. I saw this with my own eyes. I saw the priest. He had a light green light just above his head. It was a little cross. He was praying. The light would go farther up, go down, and move a little ways, just above him. It was right there. I saw it with my own eyes. Just before the service ended, it went up and disappeared. I was going to tell Ataata Vinnivi[67] about it right away. I thought to myself, I need to tell him. People started to go. I was near the doorway. As the last person went out, he closed the door. Ataata Vinnivi came and I said, "How are you?" I told Ataata Vinnivi that just a few minutes ago there was something above his head. He said, "Don't say anything." I didn't say anything more, but he knew that something had happened. I saw it with my own eyes. I think he felt it. After that I went to church. Ataata Vinnivi had a light on. There was an old dog. I don't know whose dog it was. In the porch, there was a platform made of snow. I made sure I could see the dog outside. It moved. I could see it clearly. It was not a vision. I saw it with my own eyes. I looked hard at it. It started to look. It had been partly eaten, but it was still standing. The back of that dog had not been eaten. It was standing. I went to the second porch. Just before I went out it disappeared. I thought to myself, "What happened?" I don't think it was a vision. I saw it.

Apphia Agalakti Siqpaapik Awa from Mittimatalik described a vision she had had when her mother was slowly dying from a lung infection. In the middle of the night she and her relatives had gone outside to pray for the sick woman:

> We went outside to the side of the house, and my father started to pray. We closed our eyes as we were praying, and through my eyelids I saw a bright light. I opened my eyes and looked up, and there was a light so bright I couldn't look at it. The bright light went into the *qarmaq*, and my father said to me, "Utagannaakulu, it has come for your mother." Then he started to cry, and he went inside. I followed him and listened to everyone crying very hard. Then somebody pulled him over to the bed, and he went to his wife to try and bring her back to life. He couldn't bring her back to life. That light came at the right time. The reason that it came was because my mother used to pray a lot. She used to pray that she would be saved by the faith she had in God. She used to pray to God that she wanted to go to heaven and follow her son.[68]

Dreams might lead to religious conversion, as observed by Richling 1989 and Stuckenberger 2005 (89). In Nunavut, Rose Iqallijuq from Iglulik spoke about the conversion of her family in Igluligaarjuk:

> When I was growing up, I used to go to church and as I came home, my mother used to tell me never to go to church. I used to say no, no. But my mother was saying that we were praying for nothing. But later, my mother dreamt about something, maybe about herself. She heard a voice but she had never seen anything. The voice was wearing white clothing, and was saying: "He made all these people to become Christians and He even made a land, somewhere up there so they can go there after they died." My mother got really scared and she did not know what to say. She went to visit the priest about her dreaming and the priest thanked her. That's how she became a Christian and started to go to church. Then, my mother told me to go to church very often in order that she would not have another dream like this.[69]

Stuckenberger (2005, 87–8) records a dream that Sami Qappik from Qikiqtarjuaq (Broughton Island) related about his conversion:

> In my life I used to do drugs, alcohol, little bit of gambling, sometimes break and enter. I used to do all sorts of stuff, but it is gone. I used to see dreams. They were about dead stuff. Sin is dead stuff. These were not regular dreams. My mother was a lay-reader. I told her I had these dreams to commit suicide and to pray to Satan, all sorts of stuff. When I did all sorts of drugs, my life was not happy. When you are not happy, your room seems to be very dark. There is no joy and happiness. Your body feels down, the whole house is fuzzy and grey. The house follows that person.
>
> I said let someone go and pray to my house. There were three people, besides my mother: two lay-readers and a reverend [Loasie Kunilusie]. They prayed for me first. I prayed with them. Loasie told me that after he prayed for me, my house would be prayed for. Something unusual came out from me. I heard a noise coming out from me very fast. Like "wwwrrrmm." The people praying didn't hear it, but I heard it. Maybe an angel took it away from me. I never experienced something like it. That was unspeakable. There was warmth all around my body, a warmth, which made me happy. My underarms were warm. It was not me. It was different, unspeakable. My heart was warm. A small little light was going through the room, entering my heart. My heart was burning. I started crying, sitting on the couch. I rarely cried before. They started to pray on the house. Making crosses on the walls, using tap water which they spoke prayers about.

The effects of these rituals were immediately perceptible to all those present: "After finishing praying for the house, my mother told me to see my room. The lights were on, but it was brighter than normal. It seems there were no shadows, that bright. That was the glory of God in my room. My mother told me to go to the other room, which was lit only by one bulb that was not very bright. This room was also brighter. The glory of God shone in the whole house. The same in the living room."

In Qappik's vision, there was a connection between his state of mind and the state of the house – "The glory of God shone in the whole house." This image evokes Ava's experience of *qaumaniq*: "When it came to me, it was as if the passage and roof of the house were lifted up, and I felt such a power of vision, that I could see right through the house, in through the earth and up into the sky."[70]

CONCLUSION

The detailed accounts of shamanic initiation that we have indicate that the ordeals the *angakkuit* went through to become shamans could be arduous. These accounts, however, vary considerably. Ujarak's account of his father's initiation, for example, is completely different from the one Ava gave to Rasmussen of his experience. Neither did Suvaksiuq's description of Igjugarjuk's initiation agree with that of Rasmussen. For elders, these discrepancies did not constitute a problem, as they are well aware of the great variation in oral traditions. All these varying accounts contribute to the prestige of these *angakkuit* of the past and give evidence of their remarkable powers. Rasmussen comments that he never witnessed a shamanic séance that really impressed him and that contemporary shamanic séances do no match the splendid accounts of the séances of the past. The *angakkuit*'s verbal accounts of their experiences add an important extra dimension to the events that are actually taking place and show how important the verbal discourse is to the shamanic tradition. Here shamanic actions acquire their meaning and are elevated to another level.

Shamanic visions enabled the *angakkuit* to see *tarniit*, *tuurngait,* and other beings that were not perceived by other people. Most people would have encounters with non-human beings such as *ijirait*, but they would not be able to see the *tuurngait* and *tupilait*. Shamanic vision was part of the shamanic calling, and if people stopped their shamanic training, they would lose that capacity. Thus, Pisuk was no longer able to see *tupilait* after his uncle stopped his training. The nature of an *angakkuq*'s initiation was usually decided by spirits that appeared in dreams and visions.[71]

Today, visions and dreams provide contexts in which Inuit can be in touch with the various agencies and beings that populate their universe, including the deceased. Dreams and visions are not conceived of as just products of the human mind; rather they are seen as allowing people to communicate with spirits or the deceased. Dreams are a medium that the deceased can use to assist their namesakes and descendants in times of need or to communicate their wish to be renamed. Dreams and visions might also constitute an arena where rivals can fight and compete with one another. The outcome in a dream may determine the outcome of the actual conflicts.

The dream operates on the level of the *tarniq*. What happens in a dream will decide what happens in ordinary life. Many elders showed themselves quite able to defend themselves in their dreams against attacks. Dreams also predict good hunting, usually alluding to a metaphoric relationship between prey and women, but they may also predict death and disaster. Such a dream has to be communicated to others just as a meeting with a non-human being had to be.

After the adoption of Christianity, Inuit began to experience visions of angels, Jesus, God, or Satan. But in these visions and dreams, old patterns were retained. Thus Apphia Agalakti Siqpaapik Awa tells the story of a woman who, after hearing the dogs barking, darting, and jumping around, went out of her tent and started shooting at what she thought was Satan.[72]

Dreams and visions indicate whether or not the dreamer or visionary has a connection to non-human agencies such as God, spirits, and the deceased, and knows how to handle it. Elders would deny that they are *angakkuit* or had any shamanic powers. Yet their dreams and visions showed that they had the ability to handle encounters with non-human agencies and were capable of defending themselves against those that attacked them.

8

Healing as a Socio-cosmic Process

INTRODUCTION

In the past, illness could be caused by various things: transgression of *pittailiniit*, loss of *tarniq*, attacks by *tupilait* (evil spirits), or *ilisitsut* (evil *angakkuit*). Elders indicated that healing had been the major task of the *angakkuit*. According to Boas (1964 [1888], 592–3), it was their principal office:

> The principal office of the angakut is to find out the reason of sickness and death or of any other misfortune visiting the natives. The Eskimo believes that he is obliged to answer the angakoq's questions truthfully. The lamps being lowered, the angakoq strips off his outer jacket, pulls the hood over his head, and sits down in the back part of the hut facing the wall. He claps his hands, which are covered with mittens, and, shaking his whole body, utters sounds which one would hardly recognize as human. Thus he invokes his tornaq, singing and shouting alternately, the listeners, who sit on the edge of the bed, joining the chorus and answering his questions. Then he asks the sick person, "Did you work when it was forbidden?" "Did you eat when you were not allowed to eat?" And if the poor fellow happens to remember any transgression of such laws, he cries, "Yes, I have worked." "Yes, I have eaten." And the angakoq rejoins, "I thought so" and issues his commands as to the manner of atonement.

When an *angakkuq* went to treat a patient, he would receive a gift, such as a kayak or a dog. Often the patient would attach a small object to the belt of the *angakkuq*. The *angakkuq* would not hunt when he was treating the patient, so he would not kill an animal in which the *tarniq* of the patient might have taken refuge. A patient could only be healed if he confessed all his transgressions. The confessions should be made in public so that other people, as well as non-human agencies, would be able to hear them.

Health was never primarily a personal matter, but rather implied a socio-cosmic order in which the individual person was integrated into an encompassing social, temporal, spiritual, and non-empirical environment. Names (*atiit*) inherited from the deceased, for instance, played an essential role in one's personal identity, destiny, and health.[1] According to Saladin d'Anglure (2001, 193), shamans often gave the names of their *tuurngait* (helping spirits) to children in order to save them from danger or sickness.

In Inuit perceptions of health and illness, body and mind were closely interrelated, since every person was linked to a broader physical and social environment. People's relationships to animals and the land were connected to their mental and physical health. Biological disorders were often interpreted as expressions of socio-cosmic relationships. Reconnecting with the land and animals through hunting and eating strong country food – seal blood, for example – not only healed the body but also the mind.[2] Sickness was often thought to come from outside and to travel through the body.[3] The treatment of sickness might imply that a foreign element had to come out.[4]

Healing involved social as well a cosmic relationships. These relationships were interdependent, and people could only preserve their health if they maintained correct relationships with other people as well as with non-human agencies. If these relationships went wrong, they had to be corrected by an *angakkuq* or another healer; otherwise a person might die. In many cases of illness, the cause was a transgression that had never been acknowledged and had to be confessed to an *angakkuq*. In the workshops, elders often emphasized the importance of the confession and the need to reintegrate the sick person back into the community and restore his or her relationships with ancestors, animals, and other non-human agencies.[5] The health and autonomy of the subject were always subordinated to his or her membership in society at large and connections with the many spiritual agencies inhabiting the universe. Today, some of these causes of illness still apply, but new problems have emerged due to alcohol, suicides, and drugs. Many Inuit do not believe that doctors are capable of dealing with all these problems. They think that their own traditions should receive more respect in their communities and be practised more extensively.

In this chapter, we will first examine shamanic healing processes and then turn to a discussion of the non-human agencies involved in these processes, notably, *tuurngait, tupilait* (evil spirits), angels, and God, all of whom play important roles in sickness and health as well as in near death experiences. Finally, we will discuss the healing circles that have recently emerged in Nunavik and Nunavut.

HEALING AND CONFESSION

For any of the healing processes, it was essential that the cause of the disease was established. The illness could be the result of *ilisiq* (witchcraft, sorcery), or it

Felix Pisuk demonstrates the technique of *qilaniq* in Itinnuaq's hunting camp in Kangiq&iniq, 2002. *Left to right:* Gino Akkak, Jose Angutinngurniq, Felix Kupak, Ollie Itinnuaq, Lizzie Itinnuaq, Bernadette Saumik, and a child. Photograph by F. Laugrand.

could have a physical cause; but most often, the cause was thought to be a transgression. Healing practices varied, but they usually involved the enforcement of specific rules. Sometimes specific techniques were used. Boas (1964 [1888], 593) writes, "Sometimes their cure for sickness is laying a piece of burning wick upon the diseased part of the body and blowing it up into the air or merely blowing upon it."[6]

A healing administered by an *angakkuq* could be perceived as miraculous. Peter Suvaksiuq from Arviat recalled, "I saw Atauhilik at the Magoose River lose his fingers driving a tractor. The blood came out of his fingers right away. His wife was a very strong *angakkuq* and she was able to heal his fingers. He lost four fingers but as soon as that woman touched his bleeding fingers, the bleeding stopped. Atauhilik was just looking at his fingers, laughing at them, not in pain at all. This happened at Magoose River."[7] In assessing the causes of an illness, an *angakkuq* might take recourse to such divination techniques as *qilaniq* (head lifting) to get to the root of the problem.[8] In most cases he would invoke his *tuurngait* to assist him in the process.

Peck reports with respect to Cumberland Sound, "When a man is sick the sufferer gives pay to the conjuror, and the conjuror thus being paid commences with a loud voice to carry on his incantations. As often as he (the conj.) looks, gazes upon his spirit (tongak) he obtains (sees) revelations regarding the sufferer, and it is said (revealed) by the conjuror's spirit that the sick man did not do that which was commanded by the conjuror although such was spoken about (viz. the food, work, etc. to be abstained from) and so it has come to pass that he is sick (no longer able to do his usual work)."[9]

The *angakkuq* passed on to the patient and the other participants in the healing session the information provided by the *tuurngaq* so that it could be confirmed. The complex interaction between the *angakkuq*, the patient, and other participants is well described by Rasmussen (1929, 133–41), who based his text on extracts from Mathiassen's diary. It appears that in the winter of 1922–23 *angakkuit* on Salliq (Southampton Island) engaged almost daily in shamanic performances and healing sessions, procuring game, and protecting the community against evil spirits. The healing usually involved head lifting and confession of transgressions. Rasmussen provides an extensive description of a shamanic healing by Angutingmarik on 24 January 1923. Nanoraq, the wife of Makkik, was so ill she could hardly stand upright. All the members of the community were present. The *angakkuq* walked up and down, "talking in groans and sighs, in varying tones, sometimes breathing deeply as under extreme pressure." Then he asked his helping spirit Aksharquarnilik whether the illness was due to a wrongdoing that the *angakkuq* himself, Angutingmarik, had committed, or was it caused by a wrongdoing committed by Nanoraq or by Makkik. The patient answered that it was all her fault: "My thoughts have been bad and my actions evil." The *angakkuq* then began to explore the causes of the illness. The *angakkuq* would see a specific object, and either the patient or the other participants were to connect it to a transgression. "It looks like peat and yet it is not really peat. Is it that which is behind this ear, something that looks like the cartilage of the ear? There is something that gleams white. Is it the edge of a pipe, or what can it be?" The listeners all cried at once, "She has smoked a pipe that she ought not to have smoked. But never mind. We will not take any notice of that. Let her be forgiven, tauva!" Then the *angakkuq* continued with other items (hair, blood, etc.) that evoked confessions of other transgressions.

In this way the *angakkuq* identified many causes of the woman's illness. Mathiassen counted forty-four. Some were slight, others quite serious. After a number of causes had been revealed, the *angakkuq* said, "She is not released. It may perhaps prove impossible to release her from these burdens. What is it that I begin to see now? It must be blood, unless it is human filth. But it is also outside the house, on the ground. It looks like blood. It is frozen, and covered with loose snow. Someone has tried to hide it." The patient answered, "Yes, that was in the autumn. I had a miscarriage, and tried to conceal it. I tried to keep it secret to avoid the taboo." The audience reacted: "This is certainly a great and serious transgression to commit. But let her be released from it. Let her be released, *tauva*." In this way the performance proceeded. The *angakkuq* discerned the causes of the illness through his shamanic vision, the patient admitted all her wrongdoings, and the spectators pleaded on her behalf that she should be released from their consequences. The session lasted several hours. Once it was completed, the patient was exhausted, but everybody was convinced that now she would soon be well again. And indeed, several days later Mathiassen recorded in his diary that she was feeling better.

Afterwards, various interpretations of the illness were provided. Angutingmarik and his wife told Mathiassen, "Nanoraq had become ill in her right arm and hand (they were very swollen), because she had thrashed her little adoptive daughter Uklasilaq so much; when she ceased doing so it got better; but as she had again started to beat her, the arm turned bad again and she could not sew again."[10] Nanoraq herself had quite another explanation for her illness. "Nanôraq says that since the bear was shot she had been afraid more and more each day that passed and at last she fell ill. The skin, head and legs of a bear must not be taken home at once, but must first be cached; the result of this is that half of the bear's skin has now been eaten by dogs."[11] Nanoraq's name means "polar bear skin," and it is clear she felt abused because of the way the skin was treated. Angutingmarik and his wife put the blame on Nanoraq, while the woman herself blamed others. During the shamanic performance, however, the woman took the blame herself, while the other participants attempted to free her of the negative consequences of her transgressions.[12] In a discussion of the session by Inuit elders in Iglulik in 1971–72, Rose Iqallijuq from Iglulik explained, "She had been sick in the past but she had never fully disclosed her wrongdoings. It was only when she thought she was going to die that she fully disclosed them."[13]

Victor Tungilik from Naujaat remembered how he used to heal people when he was practising as an *angakkuq*. He would look for the causes of illness with his eyes closed. "Even though some people did not disclose what they had done, the *angakkuq* would find out the reason why a person was sick. A person would have to say, 'This is why I am sick. This is what I have done.' Then the person would start getting better."[14] It might also happen that people refused to admit their wrongdoings. "The most difficult people to heal were the ones who did not want to talk about why they were sick. Not about their pain, but about the kinds of things they had done, the kind of wrongdoings they had done. The ones who did not want to disclose anything were the hardest ones to deal with."[15]

Armand Tagoona explained that confession was so essential that even murderers were supposed to confess: "The Inuit used to say that a murderer has a person in him, the person that he killed is in his murderer, unless before the murderer dies he confesses what he has done. They call this confession *anitat*, meaning 'bring out,' or sometimes *miriaq*, meaning 'vomit.'"[16]

When *angakkuit* performed to heal a person, they would be given a gift. According to Tungilik, the giver could never ask for the gift back. He explained how this related to his giving up shamanism. "This is what happened. I was given a very nice rifle and a sewing machine by a couple. I'm not going to say who they were. After they were healed, I returned these things to them because they wanted their rifle back. I started thinking I'm not a doctor. I don't heal people through operations. I should not be a healer anymore. Once I started thinking about this I returned the rifle and the sewing machine and I sent away my helpers." Some time later the couple died. Tungilik explained that this was because "they went back to the cause of their sickness. They died because they had requested that those items be returned."[17] Tungilik's experience shows the importance of the gift in shamanic healing. What is given cannot be taken back. When the movement of the exchanges is inverted and objects are returned, patients as well as *angakkuit* are at risk.

TUURNGAIT

Angakkuit invoked their *tuurngait* whenever they needed their help. *Tuurngait* encompassed a wide range of beings: deceased people, animals, non-human beings, and owners of objects and places. Virtually anything other than a living human being could serve as a *tuurngaq* to an *angakkuq*. Nutaraaluk from Iqaluit explained, "The *angakkuit* used everything for their *tuurngait*, from insects to animals to Qallunaat, even before anyone had ever seen a Qallunaat up here. They used everything including things you would find down at the tidal flats such as shrimps, krill and seaweed."[18] *Tuurngait* could be referred to as *apiqsait* or *ikajuqtit* (helpers) when they supported someone or as *miqqiijuut* when they were not telling the truth. Evil *tuurngait* could be referred to as *tupilait* or *paijjaat* (especially in the Kivalliq). *Tuurngait* did not constitute a separate category of non-human beings, but encompassed all beings that might assist an *angakkuq*. The missionary Peck compiled a list of 347 *tuurngait* on South Baffin Island between 1894 and 1905.[19] The list presents an instructive overview of the features of the *tuurngait* on South Baffin at the beginning of the twentieth century.

Tuurngait could be identified and addressed as individual beings, and people could be named after them. They were thought to use a special language with a special vocabulary, sometimes referred to as the shamanic language. Most of the words are considered archaic and difficult to grasp: *angakkuq* was *takreoot* (*tarriut* in modern spelling), Inuk was *tau* ("shade"), and dogs were *pungoet* (*punnguit* in modern spelling). Rasmussen (1931, 122) notes that this vocabulary was not the exclusive property of the shamans. It could be used by anyone who wanted to communicate with the spirits. Spiritual beings, specific objects, and places were referred to by metaphors, images, analogies, and so on. An object or living being was only referred to obliquely, such as by a property, a form of behaviour, or an essential aspect. An *angakkuq* could be referred to as a *tarejumaq*, linking an *angakkuq* to the concept of *tarniq* (image, shade), which played an important part in the shamanic complex. Tungilik stated, "For instance, in the language of the *tuurngait*, an *inuk* is *tau*. A *qallunaaq* is *tauja*. Because Rachel is an old woman, she would be called *tulluq*. I would be called *sanilliaq*, because I am an old man now. You are young so you would be called *paliliaq*. A child was *quattiaq*. Animals were *qilujaksat*, which means those which are to be pulled.

Kumaruaq qilujaksat is a caribou. The word for seal is *qajuaq qilujaksat*. Their blubber is *uqsuliaq*. A polar bear is *tulurialik qilujaksat ... Qamutiik* is *ikinniq*. Dogs are *punnguit*, which is also the word for warts."[20]

When a being is referred to obliquely, it is not addressed directly, but an important feature of that being is nevertheless brought to the foreground. When an Inuk is referred to as *tau* (shadow), the level of the *tarniq* is brought into play. When a caribou is referred to as *kumarjuaq* (the big louse), its relation to the earth is evoked: they are the louses of the earth.

The names of *tuurngait* usually derive from the language of *tuurngait*. They often refer to physical appearance (shape, colour, clothing), sounds, movements, or objects (such as weapons). In Peck's list, Aupaluktãlik ("has something red") is a polar bear; Tuktwak ("stove pipe") looks very thin and long like a stove pipe; and Siggook ("beak") has a head like a crow and a body like a human being.

According to Peck's list, the most important functions of the *tuurngait* were to provide game or food and to give joy and light. Other functions, such as healing, improving the weather, divination, and killing evil spirits, are mentioned less frequently. However, Peck also refers to *tuurngait* as soul destroyers, such as when he comments on the *tuurngaq* Mekkoalak: "It is said that the torngak kills the souls of the seals etc. and thus causes them to be easily caught by the Eskimo, because the soul is the life of the body. The soul of a man, however, can never be destroyed, but a creature's body being used for food its soul can be killed."[21] After the souls of the game were destroyed, the animals could no longer resist the hunter and were easily killed. But the killing of souls was an issue of debate among the Inuit themselves, as indicated by one of Peck's informants, Qoojessie: "The spirits of animals are not destroyed, no spirit can be destroyed. The tongat are said to simply take out (separate) the souls of the creatures from their bodies, ... making the mere bodies inactive, having lost the vital part (the living powers), the soul."[22]

Many *tuurngait* gave light and provided joy. Peck relates light to goodness and associated the *tuurngait* with angels in a way rarely done by Inuit themselves. Clearly there was debate on the nature of the *tuurngait*, as reflected in Qoojessie's comments on the killing of souls. However, we should not stress the difference between shared views and idiosyncratic perspectives too much. Most in-depth information on shamanism reflects the individual views of particular *angakkuit*. *Angakkuit* were expected to develop their knowledge on the basis of their own experiences and perceptions. They built on existing traditions that show remarkable similarities in their basic patterns in different areas.

Tuurngait also assisted *angakkuit* in shamanic competition and rivalry. Etuangat Aksaajuq from Panniqtuuq (1995 interview) recalled: "I know that when the shaman got too many animals, the other shamans would try to find out how he is doing it. So if he is getting too much, he would try to slow it down as much as possible because they would try to compare each other through the *tuurngait*. They used the *tuurngait* to find how the other shamans are doing, like a competition in a way."

In the North Baffin and the Kivalliq areas, the shape and form of the *tuurngait* varied. Tungilik described their appearance: "Some of them would have twigs for hair. Some of them would have pelvic bones for a face, and they would seem to be dripping … [O]thers would have fire. It varied. Some of them would be animals such as polar bears or *nanurluit*, very big bears. There were different kinds of worms, and all kinds of animals from the land, from the sea, and birds that fly. They varied."[23]

Different *tuurngait* could be used for different purposes. Iqallijuq from Iglulik (1995 interview) related: "For example, walrus, polar bear and wolf *tuurngait* were used to kill people. These animal *tuurngait* would make a person sick or kill the person. On the other hand, the *tuurngait* of deceased people and of birds were used to heal the sick. The *angakkuq* would perform a ritual to heal a sick person."

Avalaaqiaq from Qamanittuaq recalled being healed by a *tuurngaq* who had the form of a dog: "When I was sick of measles as a child, I wasn't fully conscious and I don't really know what was wrong with me. I was being licked. It was a dog that was licking me. It was his spirit. I went back to sleep and woke up again and the dog was gone. I saw his spirit in dog form and it was really a skinny dog. It seemed to have a white harness on."[24]

Rasmussen (1929, 145 193) compiled lists and collected representations of *tuurngait* in the Kivalliq and the North Baffin area. Many of these resemble spirits described in Peck's list in name, appearance, or characteristics. But there are also important differences. Among the helping spirits in the Nattilik and Iglulik areas we find a high proportion of deceased people but no owners of places or owners of game. The *angakkuit* in the North Baffin area and the Kivalliq usually had between five and ten helping *tuurngait*. Balikci (1963, 382), for instance, mentions that Iksivalitaq, a famous Nattilik *angakkuq*, had seven helping spirits. Therefore, the 347 *tuurngait* in Peck's list surprised elders from other areas. Mariano Aupilaarjuk from Kangiq&iniq (1999 interview) did not believe that an *angakkuq* could have so many helping spirits. Too much *qaumaniq* (shamanic vision) or too many *tuurngait* shortened the life of an *angakkuq*.

Rasmussen observes that the moon man and the sea woman could be used as *tuurngait*. He recorded that the Nattilik *angakkuq* Unarâluk had among his helping spirits the sun, and the *angakkuq* Iksivalitaq had among his three helping spirits the moon man. Salome Qalasiq from Kangiq&iniq (1999 interview) related that the *angakkuq* Qimuksiraaq of Igluligaarjuk had the sea woman as a helping spirit.

In the Nattilik area there was a belief that *tuurngait* themselves were hunters. Balikci (1963, 384) relates that "seals could be killed by [*tuurngait*] in the open sea and be brought ashore, under the guidance of the shaman." But this notion was not as prevalent in the North Baffin area. Iqallijuq (2000 interview), in fact, found the idea of *tuurngait* as hunters quite funny.

Most of the elders from the Kivalliq area saw healing and the killing of evil *tupilait* as the most important activities of the *angakkuit*. Elders from the Iglulik area felt that the procuring of game had an important place in the shamanic complex. In Peck's list, the main emphasis is on procuring game, notably seals and caribou. Many of the *tuurngait* on the list are effectively described as owners of game. This may imply a different relationship between the *angakkuit* and their *tuurngait*, in which the *tuurngait* were not so much helpers of the *angakkuit* as owners, hunters, and givers – to *angakkuit* – of game.

The relationship between the *angakkuit* and the *tuurngait* was ambiguous. When asked who was in control, the *tuurngaq* or the *angakkuq*, Tungilik answered, "I was not in control of them, and they were not in control of me … we just helped each other."[25] According to Balikci (1963, 383), the relationship between the *angakkuq* and his *tuurngaq* would change over time: "Initially the *tunraq* was the master of the novice, and only gradually did the young *angatkok* learn to control it. Eventually, the novice became a full-fledged shaman, possessing a competence and strength apparently equal to that of his master."

Tungilik described how an *angakkuq* could give a voice to the *tuurngait:*

> Whenever we started singing the song of the *tuurngaq*, it would enter us. We would be told the cause of the sickness. We were also told what wrongdoings the person had committed. The *tuurngaq* would tell us what it saw. The *angakkuq*, who was the agent, would tell about that. This was called *sakaniq* … All those who were present could hear it. All those who were together would hear the song as they were present … I was singing it, but it was coming from the *tuurngaq*. The *tuurngaq* would express what it saw through the *angakkuq*. It would make the *angakkuq* put into words what it could see. When it was put into song it was *sakaniq*.[26]

The *angakkuit* put into words what the *tuurngaq* saw. According to Rasmussen (1929, 122–3), every *angakkuq* had his own songs for invoking his *tuurngait*. *Angakkuit* would sing when the *tuurngait* entered their body and would speak with the voices of the *tuurngait*. Iqallijuq (2000 interview) spoke of the songs of the *tuurngait:* "If this person had a *tuurngaq* which was a dog, the dog would start singing, 'I am a dog. I am a wart. I used to live in an old den. When they are gone, when they go out hunting, I think about you when I want to eat.' That is how they would talk when they wanted to communicate because they did not want to scare them. I imitated what the *angakkuq* sang. He sang with his hat and his mitts on."

George Kappianaq from Iglulik explained how the *tuurngait* expressed themselves through the voice of the *angakkuq*: "*Angakkuit* were able to imitate birds and bears and all kinds of noises. The voice that they use is the voice of their *tuurngaq*, which comes into them. At times, some of them would seem to be just telling a story. When they have a *tuurngaq* in them it seems like you can visualize what they were saying. Others would just be making sounds that seemed to be noises with their head down."[27]

The *tuurngait* might request things. Tungilik recalled, "I would make something. It could be very small. It did not have to be large. Sometimes I would make it into an animal, or into a knife, or a beating stick. Whatever the *tuurngaq* requested I would make."[28] He also provided some *tuurngait* with meat: "*Tuurngait* who were good would not hunt people. Those that were bad would hunt people. The *tuurngait* that would heal were not hunters. Some of them would need meat, but they would only require a small amount. This I know. If they needed some meat, you would throw it into an area with freshly fallen snow that had not had footprints on it ... I would throw them whatever they had requested."[29]

Tuurngait could be sent to attack people. Iqallijuq (IE 091) described the practice: "Sometimes the *angakkuq* may have got mad with someone and holds a grudge against the individual. Without other means of getting back at the individual he will resort to his shamanistic helping spirit to get back at him, usually killing him. This is known as *tarningirsiyuq* (to deprive one of one's soul). The soul is like a bubble, one can pop it by squeezing it, no one can see it, but it can be popped by hand squeezing it. That's the way some shamans use to kill."

Kappianaq said that *angakkuit,* not *tuurngait,* could take a soul:

> I have never heard of a *tuurngaq* taking a *tarniq*. But I have heard about an *angakkuq* who almost killed four people by removing their *tarniit*. His step-brother caught him. After his step-brother arrived, he didn't unload his sled. He just rushed into the *iglu* and caught him. He wanted to get there before the bodies died. The *angakkuq* was unable to walk, so he was just sitting there on the bed. He asked him, "What are you doing with them?" The *angakkuq* answered, "With these?" He had taken the *tarniit* of the children who were staying with them. Their bodies were there as casings, because they didn't have their *tarniit*. After he had been caught, the disabled *angakkuq* sent the *tarniit* back to the bodies. But I have never heard of *tarniit* being taken away permanently.[30]

But Kappianaq believed that *tuurngait* would attack people and told of how his granddaughter had been attacked by a *tuurngaq* at Maniituq in 1972:

> We lived there for quite a long while. It was a good place for procuring game daily, both for humans and for dogs. My granddaughter was devoured by something that appeared to be a wolverine there. The remains of her clothing were found just recently. They were torn to shreds ... They never found her body. No bones were found. I think they were all chewed up. There was just a pile of tattered clothing that was gathered, no bones

were ever found, probably because she was young and her bones were still soft. They said that it was while she was playing just out of sight of the tent that she was dragged away by that wolverine-like thing.[31]

The *tuurngaq* Kappianaq described might have been an *iqtuut*. Felix Pisuk from Kangiq&iniq described *iqtuut* as being fatter than wolverines but as big. Its feet are turned backwards.

Tuurngait may attack people in other ways. Rasmussen (1931, 198) relates, "It also happens that to·nrät seek sexual satisfaction with solitary men or women who while wandering have fallen asleep in the open. One never experiences this literally, but dreams of it. Afterwards one usually comes out in a rash and has stinking boils over the whole body." He also gives several examples of *tuurngait* attacking *angakkuit*.

Tuurngait inspired fear. According to Rasmussen (1931, 295), the Nattilik woman Tiagssaq, "the wife of Samik, was a shaman in her younger days, but abandoned the cult when she began to have children. Her expressed reason was that she could not sleep at night for fear of her helping spirits." Balikci (1963, 382) mentions that a spirit called Orpingalik in the Nattilik area "used to attack his master Anaidjuq suddenly from behind and pull out his genitals; the unfortunate shaman, after much yelling, could recover these during a trance."

Tuurngait could also make people ill. Tungilik related, "Whenever a person did something that displeased a *tuurngaq* the person would become sick. There were some *tuurngait* that would make a person sick because they had the desire to kill."[32] *Angakkuit* could use their *tuurngait* against human beings. Elisapee Ootoova from Mittimatalik recalled, "They would also use their *tuurngait,* their helping spirits, to attack animals. Once the *tuurngait* had done this they wanted to do it over and over again. My in-law's father had a *tuurngaq* that was like that. When he was out caribou hunting, one got away and he told his *tuurngaq* to go and get it. He did not just use this *tuurngaq* against animals, he used it against humans."[33]

After their conversion to Christianity, *angakkuit* often sent their *tuurngait* away or gave them to their relatives. Today, in both Nunavut and Nunavik, elders as well as many young people still assume that *tuurngait* are around, and once in a while hunters tell stories about their experiences with them out on the land. Saladin d'Anglure and Morin (1998, 67–9) and Ouellette (2002) record several of these stories from the Hudson Bay area.

TUPILAIT

Illness could also be caused by *tupilait* (evil spirits). A *tupilaq* is usually an evil *tuurngaq* or the *tarniq* (image or shade) of a deceased person. A *tupilaq* could also be created by an *angakkuq*. Rasmussen usually translates *tupilaq* as "evil spirit." He indicates that Inuit were well aware "that men had once possessed the power of making tupilait, but the art was now lost to them."[34] Kublu (2004, 151) glosses the meaning of the word as follows: "An evil spirit under human form, only visible to the *angakkuit*. It is like a pouch full of blood. For some people it is an evil *tuurngaq*, for others it is the unsatisfied soul of a deceased person; a lost, roaming spirit of the dead who frightens people which can be sent away by the power of *aarnguat*, amulets [Iglulik]."

Elders at the workshop in Kangiq&iniq in 2000 agreed that *tupilait* have no bones. Peck thought they were *tarniit* that had been rejected by Sedna: "1. They the (Tupelat) are the souls of the unforgiven ones who are rejected by Sedna and sent back to have their sins taken away. 2. The Tupelats are said to go to the dwellings of the Eskimos and try to do them harm by making them sick. 3. Those whose sins are pardoned do not return in this form. 4 The Tupelats are said to be killed only by the conjurors who just open their eyes a little and shoot or stab them. The Tupelats are said to call out (having a cry of as pain) when they are stabbed … 5. Tupelats are said to be easily killed when they first arrive from Sedna's abode, but are not easily killed if allowed to remain rushing about."[35]

Boas described the *tupilait* as the spirits of the evil dead who attacked the community in the fall in his description of the Sedna feast in Cumberland Sound. Aksaajuq from Panniqtuuq (1995 interview) recalled, "I heard that when people died, if they were so bad and did evil, their souls couldn't go up, so the shamans would find out those spirits around. Shamans would go after it and try to poke and hit it. When they would hit the *tupilait*, the evil part would die, and the soul would go up through the air. Sometimes the *tupilait* would run away from them and touch the tent and they would be stabbed by two shamans. It means that the person died a long time ago. When killing the *tupilait* they would hear a noise that would be the voice from that person who died a long time ago and they could recognize that voice."

Today, in the context of Christianity, *tupilait* are sometimes identified with ghosts or demons and said to be afraid of certain objects. Malaija Papatsie from Pangnirtuuq related, "My mother told us that people placed a wooden cross on the outside of the door if they were going to go after *tupilait*. They put the cross up and they called it an *aarnguaq*, an amulet. They hung it on the outside of the door. They did that so the *tupilait* would not be able to come in."[36]

Killing *tupilait* required special techniques or special tools. Rasmussen (1929, 144) observes, "An evil spirit must never be attacked with the right hand or arm, but only with the left. They are also called torngraluit, in contradistinction to torngrait, which are the helping spirits of the shaman. When a shaman strikes an evil spirit with his knife he says: 'to·rngra·lukpunga': 'I have caught a to·rngra·luk.'" Silas Putumiraqtuq from Qamanittuaq recalled hearing about a shaman killing *tupilait* in the porch of an *iglu*: "When shamans are fighting with evil spirits in an iglu porch they make a lot of noise … his/her hands become so bloody."[37] During the fifth Thule expedition, Jacob Olsen recorded a performance of the killing of *tupilait* on Salliq (Southampton Island). People assembled in the largest hut and the *angakkuq* Angutingmarik opened the proceedings by invoking the helping spirit Tipjarse. Then the *angakkuq* picked the evil from each participant, one by one. While the audience sang, "Let all that kind of evil be driven out of them," the *angakkuit* took turns and their helping spirits pointed out the culprits. Everyone had to confess. Rasmussen (1929, 145) describes in detail the posture and manner of speaking of the *angakkuit:* "A shaman driving out any form of evil must stand with his head towards the sky, his eyes closed, and his hands together. He must wear mittens. He must cough with every word he speaks, and frequently change his voice; whenever he does so, the listeners must cry: 'ade· – ade·: 'keep on, keep on!'"

After all confessions had been made, the *angakkuit* announced that the evil spirits had reappeared in the village. The people asked the *angakkuit* to go out again and the people inside cried for the helping spirit Tipjarse to help them: "TipjArse tipjArse, tauva!" When the *angakkuit* returned, they sat down on men's breeches spread out before them. The lamps were extinguished and all present closed their eyes. According to Rasmussen, if the people had kept their eyes open, they would have become blind. Then the *angakkuit* invoked the *tuurngait*.[38] They spoke in unrecognizable voices, breathed deeply, and finally asked someone to light the lamps. Then they declared that they had driven away the evil spirits.

These proceedings illustrate the complexity of the interaction of voice, coughing, breathing, and other sounds in the performance. The *angakkuit*'s intricate songs were interspersed with heavy breathing and various other sounds. The songs and sounds expressed the voices of the *tuurngait* as well as those of the *angakkuit*. The audience participated actively by joining in the invocations, such as invoking the *tuurngaq* Tipjarse. The interaction was entirely shaped by voices and sounds, and nobody, on pain of blindness, was allowed to see what was happening.

Barnabas Peryouar from Qamanittuaq recalled how people had to keep their eyes closed in these séances:

> I remember one incident that happened, where I was as frightened as I've ever been in my life … Niuqtuq was asked or told to do a ritual, so everyone was gathered at his tent, except women and children … The shaman placed a caribou-skin outer parka in the middle of the tent floor, then he was ready. He was standing on, or near, the caribou parka, and before he started his ritual he told us, "If the light goes out, let not even one person have his eyes open!" I could see him standing on the tent floor, and we could hear him speaking clearly. He had told us not to open our eyes after the light has been put out, and I complained in my head, "If we are not going to watch, and have to keep our eyes closed, then I won't be able to find out how he goes under something." Since I didn't know what he was going to do I was kind of scared, but he told us all to keep our eyes closed and not to open them. The lights were out and we all had our eyes closed,

> sitting on the edge of the bedding, and that man was standing in front of us, close to us. I was getting suspicious because he was being talked to. I had sat down near him wanting to get a good view, and yet I wasn't going to be watching. We just sat there with our eyes closed, listening to him while someone unknown talked to him. When the shaman answered or talked, his voice was starting to change, although he was speaking in Inuktitut that we know, and his breathing started to change. While he was talking, his voice seemed to be getting higher and higher, and it was starting to echo – I was getting so frightened. We had been told not to open our eyes or we would get blinded … I tried so hard not to open my eyes … I was just terrified. That shaman, with his voice changing and his breathing changing, answering whenever he was asked a question – he was the one I was terrified of, although I didn't see him because we all had our eyes closed.[39]

Mary-Rousselière reports that after the killing of a *tupilaq* gifts and exchanges of goods were required so that the *tupilaq* would not know where to go to bother other human beings.[40] Apparently the relations between human beings and *tupilait* could be changed by modifying relations between human beings and objects.

The elders of today still remember the killing of *tupilait,* and in a workshop in Kangiq&iniq in 2002, Luke Anautalik and Peter Suvaksiuq from Arviat gave a demonstration of this practice. Jose Angutinngurniq from Kugaaruk recalled how his uncle Iksivalitaq would kill *tupilait:* "My uncle was given something to heal someone. He was trying to kill a *tupilaq*. Others saw it, but being a child, I searched for it but could not see it. They said it was big but I could not see it at all. My uncle was down on the floor, and suddenly his hands were very bloody."[41] Later he added, "I remember this. I heard a snap and then the floor was all bloody. His hands were all bloody too. I remember him jumping on it. He seemed to be in a trance when he was doing this." Angutinngurniq continued, "He washed his hands in the urine pot, and his hands became clean. When I woke up the next day, we could see the shapes of a dog and a human on the floor. We were told that they were the images of the *tupilaak* that had been killed. We children were told to kill those *tupilait* so we started beating at those images. I remember this as a child. They were the images of the *tupilaak* that had been killed the day before. Maybe they were what had made the person sick."[42]

Ollie Itinnuaq from Kangiq&iniq also recalled the practice of killing *tupilait:*

> I have seen *tupilattuq* very often, ever since I was a child. It was after I became an adult that I no longer saw it. This was something that *angakkuit* did a lot. Even after Christianity arrived, you still saw *tupilattuq*. I saw Nagjuk, the *angakkuq* that Pisuk was talking about, do this numerous times. I also saw my father Anaqqaaq *tupilattuq* more than once. Their hands would become bloody, and they would clean them with urine.

> Maybe their hands did not become better smelling. Some *angakkuit* would allow others to see *tupilait* if they were able to do so. You could actually see the *tupilait*. The *angakkuit* were on the floor with them. The *tupilaq* was just a *tarniq*. When they were ready to kill it, you could not see it at all. You could only observe the *angakkuq*. If you were not an *angakkuq*, all you would see was the *angakkuq* moving about. I don't know how they did it, but when you saw it, it seemed like they were all alone fighting. Their hands would become all bloody but their clothing never did. It was only their skin. Maybe *tarniit* have blood and that's why they would become bloody too. There was nothing visible at all, and yet they would become bloody.[43]

Itinnuaq's account illustrates why one should avoid making essentialist distinctions between concepts. *Tarniit, tuurngait,* and *tupilait* cannot always be clearly distinguished. *Tarniit* are generally considered to have neither bones nor blood, but if a *tarniq* does have blood, then elders would infer that it is probably a *tupilaq*.

Although only *angakkuit* were supposed to be able to see *tupilait,* Rose Iqallijuq from Iglulik (2000 interview) saw one and remembered how an *angakkuq* had killed it:

> *Angakkuit* used to kill *tupilait*. They would kill them with a *savuujaq* that had a sharp tip. The *angakkuit* would stab the *tupilait*. I saw a *tupilaq* once. It was a *tuurngaq*. It looked like a very tiny person wearing a hat. As I was walking into the *iglu,* I realized that there was a tiny person trying to hide. As I went inside I stepped over it. People said there were *tupilait* around. The *angakkuq* went outside with a *savuujaq* when the lights were still on. When he re-entered, there was some blood on the *savuujaq*. He said that he killed the *tupilaq* by stabbing it. The blood was then licked off. That *tupilaq* was a very small black person wearing a hood. I walked over to where the *tupilaq* had been hiding at the entrance of the porch. But it had been stabbed. *Tupilait* used to frighten people because they could kill people. The one I saw did not make me ill because I stepped over it. The *angakkuit* would kill the *tupilait* when there was a sickness.

People would take precautions to prevent the deceased from becoming *tupilait*. Angutinngurniq related, "If a person who was going to die had said bad things to their family, a *situraut* [implement for sliding] was placed on their grave after their death. This was to prevent the person from going after others. This *situraut* in the grave would take up all their attention and they would only think of sliding. They would not be able to go after the people around them."[44]

Elders emphasize that *tarniit* are still around. Itinnuaq stated, "I think that after people die, sometimes their *tarniit* are still around. Probably some go up to heaven, but not all of them go."[45] According to Itinnuaq, a *tupilaq* is a *tarniq* that has turned bad.[46] He related, "I only know what my father recounted to me. He said the skin is very thin. It has a very thin covering. The moment it is touched it is cut and it bleeds right away. There are some *tarniit* that will become good if they are made to bleed more than once."[47] His statement suggests that the killing of a *tupilaq* is at the same time a healing process. This, according to Aksaajuq, might explain why a *tupilaq*'s final cry of anguish as it is being killed can be recognized as the voice of a deceased relative. In the cry at the moment of the stabbing, the social identity of the deceased is returned to him or her.

POSSESSION AND EXORCISM

Evil spirits could manifest themselves in sounds and voices. Lucassie Nutaraaluk from Iqaluit related how his kinsman Miqqualaaq killed his relatives because of the voices he was hearing:

> I remember when Miqqualaaq committed murder. In those days, even though they were not intoxicated, they tried to be fearsome …
>
> My father's mother and Miqqualaaq's father's mother were sisters. I don't know which one was older. Miqqualaaq committed three murders; he killed both his parents and my *aana*, grandmother. He'd run back and forth from the tents shooting at them. He was obeying the voices he was hearing …
>
> He started to believe the voices that he was hearing and as a result he started killing people. They say that people do things like that when they are hearing voices. Even today there are people like that, who hear voices …
>
> Miqqualaaq was taken to a place where the water didn't freeze because of the current. As they were about to push him, he jumped in. He disappeared under the water and bobbed up right away. Even though the current was very strong he wasn't moving with it. His hands had been tied behind his back with rope but when he came back up his hands were untied.[48]

The voices were never identified, but elders cautioned people to be careful when they heard voices. In giving an account about dangerous places, Kappianaq referred to the voices in those places. People had to be cautious in dealing with voices that did not come from human beings.[49] Voices have always played a crucial role in Inuit shamanism. Victor Tungilik from Naujaat compared speaking with the voice of a *tuurngaq* to *ilummiqtaujuq*, becoming possessed: "It would use me as an agent. It would have me start saying what it could see. These weren't my words. These were the words of my *tuurngaq*. You've heard of people being possessed. It is something like a person being possessed. This *tuurngaq* would enter me. If you've ever heard of a person becoming *ilummiqtaujuq*, possessed, it was the same kind of thing. The *tuurngaq* would have me say what it was seeing. We would be told to sing, but the songs would be different from those of humans."[50]

When a *tuurngaq* entered a person, his directions had to be followed. Winnie Putumiraqtuq from Qamanittuaq recalled, "I had Heeturat inside the *atigi* and sitting on the bed, then all of a sudden my father started going into trance. He started looking at me, and he started pointing all around, as though he wanted someone to come in. He was trying to tell me he wanted people to come to our iglu, because when Qinalugaq [his helping spirit] went inside him he couldn't say anything or do anything anymore. I didn't understand what he wanted … I finally understood and I knew that Qinalugaq had to be obeyed at all times."[51]

With the introduction of Christianity, *tuurngait* and *tupilait* were easily identified with devils and demons, and the presence of a *tuurngaq* in a human being could be seen as possession. A study by Fletcher and Kirmayer (1997) shows how such an idiom of possession developed in Inuit discourses.[52] The change of voice was now seen as a sign of possession: "In a demon possessed case, that person can't even talk on their own. They don't have their own voice anymore. They don't talk on their own."[53] Fletcher and Kirmayer (1997, 196) present a case of possession, quoting a friend of a girl in Nunavik who was thought to be possessed by a demon: "It's pretty hard to describe. My best girlfriend, she was kind of strange when she died. She told me that when you are, when you have something like this, you're the last person to know. Meaning that when she had demon inside her, she did not know that she had a demon inside her. And I wondered about that. She was kind of strange too – the way she used to think. Well, I remember what she used to do at one time she went, the truck was moving along and she just stopped right in front of it like she wanted to be killed or something. And she was very scared of a certain person."

Uuttuluttaq literally means "the one who is tried," and refers to the entrance of a spirit into a person's body. According to Fletcher and Kirmayer (1997, 197), this entity can reside in a person for years, having no effect on his or her outward appearance, and then suddenly manifest itself as the person unexpectedly begins to act "crazy." Fletcher and Kirmayer quote an informant from Nunavik: "Sometimes it takes some time to get into that thing. A person may be possessed for many years and not be, there may not be any indication whatsoever that he is possessed unless he actually goes crazy. If this person has never been sick, has never had a mental illness, and then he starts acting crazy, that's what I would call demon possessed. That's what I also believe in."

Stuckenberger (2005, 89–90) notes that possession is now a recognized problem in Qiqiqtarjuaq on South Baffin Island and that Anglican and evangelical church leaders have taken charge of exorcisms.

> The practice of expelling demons is called *anirnilumianitititu q*. Usually, specific church leaders are approached for help by the victim. One or more counselors might either visit the afflicted house or person or deal with a demon-possessed person during evening church services or at a prayer meeting. The counselors start with identifying the harming demon, each of whom is believed to have its own personality and features. Then, prayers

are spoken and additional measures are employed depending on the kind of demon one is dealing with. Prayer is one measure employed either for houses or persons. In dealing with demons through prayer, success is thought to increase with strong faith, the gift of discernment conveyed by the Holy Spirit, and ample experience in dealing with demons. Though most people tend to approach a religious leader for assistance, dealing with bad spirits was not exclusively a matter for experts. Loie Mike and Billy Arnaquq emphasized that, although some people may have special abilities to deal with demons, every person could be his/her own master in dealing with the evil spirits, provided that s/he is strong in faith. Loie Mike told me that she tried to reduce her requests for help in Pangnirtung by attending only to those people who were actually possessed and could, therefore, not help themselves very well.

In an article in the *Nunatsiaq News* (19 March 1999), journalist Jane George described a case of possession that occurred in the small village of Akulivik in Nunavik in 1999.

> Sources in the community, who agreed to speak to *Nunatsiaq News*, confirmed that not long after a visit from two southern evangelists, the local Anglican Church committee singled out one local woman as "possessed." One participant in the Akulivik exorcism, the woman's future brother-in-law, had reportedly told several others they should "repent their sins." Then, in a gruesome turn of events, the man later attempted to cut off his penis. He is now making a good recovery in Montreal from self inflicted wounds … Eli Aullaluk, who describes himself as a municipal councilor and a Christian, said that the woman's family first noticed that she was disturbed on February 19.
>
> "She was not being normal," he said. "Her mother asked her, 'who are you?' and her answer was, 'I'm a bad spider, a devil, a demon.' She knew right away that she wasn't well." … The woman, aged 30, was brought to the Anglican Church where the church committee spoke with her. "They decided she was possessed," said Aullaluk. "She was very disturbed. Naturally we would know that she was evilly possessed. We believe in this."
>
> A rite of exorcism followed. It was held in a room usually occupied by the community's social services, on the suggestion of the social worker, also a member of the church committee. The woman occasionally had to be restrained during the proceedings. "They had to hold down her arms and legs or tie her arms to her wrists sometimes to prevent her from hurting herself," said Aullaluk …
>
> The exorcism came to an end when the woman injured her hands by trying to grab at a window blind, according to Aullaluk. She was taken for medical treatment and then transferred to another location.

> The medical personnel wanted to remove the woman from Akulivik for medical treatment, against the wishes of her family and a well-respected healer from Puvirnituq, Eli Qinuayuaq, who had come to assist in her healing.
>
> "The reason why we wanted to deal with it is that she wasn't medically sick, but she was spiritually sick. There were people who were capable of working with her," said Aullaluk. "It was definitely a spiritual problem" ... Aullaluk said that such spiritual possession is not a regular situation, but one that other Inuit communities have seen recently and also a long time ago. "This community here strongly believes that it is very possible to believe that people can be possessed by evil spirits," he said.

Later on, Aullaluk defended the handling of the case in the *Nunatsiaq News*: "As Inuit, the undertakings we took here in our community of Akulivik were completely in relation to our way of life, belief and religion. According to our belief, the person, a female born in March 1969, had evil spirits in her since February 19, 1999. Our way of handling of this situation was, as it always is, when there is a situation such as this, that the person with evil spirits is treated by people with confidence of the Saviour (The Lord). We also know that when someone is in this situation, they are not usually capable of being treated, medically or socially."

Immediately after the adoption of Christianity, angels and God began to be involved in the healing process. Prayer replaced the *irinaliutiit* (powerful words), which we will discuss in chapter 9. The final decision about life and death was placed in the hands of God, as was made particularly evident in the various near-death experiences related by elders.

NEAR-DEATH EXPERIENCES

Several elders related near-death experiences. Both Peter Suvaksiuq from Arviat and Felix Kupak from Naujaat experienced coming back to life after dying. Mary Anautalik of Arviat related how her baby was revived by a missionary. In all their accounts, the interplay of old traditions and Christian ones is clear. At the 2003 workshop in Arviat, Suvaksiuq described two such experiences, separated by many years:

> I died one time. They were getting ready to bury me. Because Kiqpaq was an *angakkuq* she brought me back. She called me her grandchild. She said my grandchild is not going to be buried and she brought my body back and brought me back to life. Somehow I started to breathe again so here I am. She was a very strong *angakkuq*. I never really told you about the work that she used to do. It is hard to believe but it really did happen. When people were sick, I too was sick, she had a piece of wood she had carved that she

> would use to make us well. I remember we would go back to that rock and lick it so we had good health. When I died my throat closed up. My mother had put me beside the bed. My grandmother came in and she was wondering why everyone was crying. She said, "What happened to my grandson? My grandson is going to live." My grandmother gave my body to my mother and I came back to life.

In Suvaksiuq's second near-death experience, he died in an accident and was taken up to heaven:

> This happened a long time ago. A wolf bit me on my legs. There are black marks there from its front teeth. My leg was broken on my right. I died in Itiguviak when I had an accident one time. There were angels who grabbed me. They told me when those two spots disappeared I would die. After I died in this accident they grabbed me and took me to heaven, to the boss of the unwise, perhaps it was God. It was a beautiful place in heaven. There is a God up there and I was placed in front of this God. I was asked whether I wanted to stay in heaven or go back. I said I wanted to go back to the earth because my children were still very small. I was very sick. I went on the HF radio and called in an emergency. Ten skidoos came. Thomas Kadlak and Unik came by dogteam to get me after I had this accident. I was breathing like this, "huh huh huh." I was very sick. One of my ribs was broken and my leg. My arm just dropped. It was out of the joint. I didn't know that the shape right here has a very sharp edge so when you drop your arm it just hangs on your body. The RCMP and an ambulance were waiting for me near the Arviapaluk radio station. The nurse told me if the blood hadn't been coming out of me I would have died. I was hit in the back by three two by fours. They broke when they hit me. It was a really big *qamutiik*. I found an HF radio. I took five HF radios with me because I was working for the wildlife officers. I couldn't move my arm so I wrapped myself with a rope and turned myself. My right arm could move but my left arm couldn't. I died. I had a big *qamutiik*. The *qamutiik* was turned over on a hill like this. There was a really big ditch. The skidoo landed on my back. The skis on the skidoo were bent from hitting me. I was able to live that time. When I shook hands with my mother, my grandfather and other family members in heaven they had no bones. When you are in heaven there was no sickness anymore. There were crowds of people in this place. The people were very happy. After their time on earth some people will go to heaven and some people will go to hell. Our bones leave our bodies when we die. There are two people in me, my body and my soul. These marks on me remind me that something did happen to me. This really happened during my accident. I have found dead bodies of people who have frozen to death and I am used to it, but it was a very hard time to sit

in front of God. I was able to read the track in my life. Some of the things I did were bad, some were good, the hardships I went through, everything; I could see my tracks looking back. I could go on and on but I want other people to be able to speak. I am repeating this story about the time I died. I have a wolf bite on my left leg and two white spots that the angels gave me. They are getting smaller and smaller. They told me that when they disappear I will die. They are like marks on my body that tell me how long my life will be. My life is marked. That is the way I understand it. I can remember this incident like it was yesterday. Every time I have to walk I remember this incident and the marks on both my legs. It is a reminder that something did happen to me.[54]

Suvaksiuq emphasized that he had really died. He returned from heaven with marks on his body. In his near-death experience there were no *tuurngait,* only angels.

Kupak had this experience:

It was in the fall, just getting cold. There was no ice on the lakes yet that fall. You can see a spot right here. You can see a long scar right here. My step-father was there and my step-brother Silisita who was just a young man. We could see buildings, a tent which was not far. They were over there. That evening my step-father was cooking something with a fire outside. It was getting dark outside. It wasn't windy but there was a draft, a soft breeze. They had to walk towards that tent by a lake. I don't know why but I told him to walk towards that tent on the side of the lake. I told him to walk just north of that lake. I wasn't sick. I was going to eat. I was happy because someone was cooking so I didn't have any reason to tell them to walk in that direction. After we had eaten my father said whenever the storm comes I will wake you up. Our tent was around this size. It ripped in the middle. He woke me up. I was partly aware that he was waking me up. I was deep in sleep. I later found out that I had been hit by one of the tent beams at the side of the head like I showed you. I spent three nights and four days unconscious. I told you it would take a long time to tell this story. When we humans go through a near death experience we are like this. There are three things we have to go through as tests. Two of the tests are on the surface of the earth. They are not hard to follow, but the third one is very hard. You get very serious on the third test. It could be very scary. For example there is a rocky area that is curved. When you are in that state you would have to lie down, not face down when you are passing through these tests. In that stage there is a very big chasm that goes way down. It is very dark. It seems like it is an endless hole. I was able to look down there and see a person spread out. His leg was on fire. That person down there was on fire. It was something that had a human form that was on fire. If you fell in that chasm you would have no choice but to land on that being who was on fire. There was a rocky place with a deep chasm. Without feeling it, I could feel something behind me and a voice said, "Get up, go up." I replied, "No I can't do it." The voice told me I wouldn't fall down. It told me to climb up. I replied, "Then take my hand and help me up." I was very very scared and afraid. He said he wasn't going to take my hand and that I would have to get up myself. It was my responsibility to get up myself. I had to try myself. I was right there ready to fall. I put my hand towards that rock and my hand stuck to the rocks and I was able to climb up on my belly. I was able to climb up one rock at a time because my hands were sticking to the rocks. I was able to get up. I didn't know I had gone back to the place around the height of this. It was a little way up. It was like the form of a cloud. I went up again. There was another man on my right. He pointed to my right. I looked down where he was pointing. It was a terrible thing to see. Our land seemed to be beautiful but the land that we lived in seemed to be dirty, to be evil. Then I was unconscious again. Then I went further up to the next step. I stood up again on the same ledge where I had been unconscious and then without saying anything he was pointing to my right. It seems like I am lying but I am telling you the truth about the experience I had. I was able to see everybody in the world when I stepped up further. It seemed like they were hanging up on a piece of string. There were people from all around the world on this one string everywhere I looked. Another person told me he was going to ask his boss for permission about something and he told me to stay right there. He said not to go anywhere and to wait for him right there. He said he was going to ask his boss for something. He went to talk to his boss and he opened this door a little bit. It was amazing when he opened the door a little bit. It was very bright. There was wonder in that place. There was a big chair. I saw that someone was sitting on that throne. Then he came back. He said that his boss wanted me to go back to earth because there was something that I had to do on earth. I was still young so he asked me to go back where I came from. He told me to tell the world about what I experienced. I went back to my old life again in my life with my body. I didn't realize when I went back to my body. I have heard people talking about seeing their bodies, but not me I didn't have that experience. I was right here. The next thing I knew I received my strength back. I tried to sleep. My clothes were frozen. I was trying to put my coat on but I was unable to because my clothes were frozen solid. I was thirsty and I wanted to drink some water. I looked around for water, for lakes. There was no water all around me. I looked around. I wanted to drink some water. I remembered there was a river down there not too far from me. There was another river this way and I thought maybe I could make it there. I was walking through a dry lake carrying a pail to where we used to get water. I was very thirsty but I couldn't drink because there was no water. I was all alone. Right here someone touched me on my left shoulder. I looked back. It was my mother Mary and she was wearing a Rosary. She was wearing white clothing and she had no socks or boots on, just bare feet. She pointed to something right beside me. She didn't say anything; she just pointed. It was a pot like you bought from the store. I was trying to understand where that pot of water came from but I couldn't understand. I bent down to drink. She stopped me and said, "The people are coming and will be able to see this water. Wait for a minute because there are people coming in." Ajaruaq and others were going to bury me. They came to bury me. I got out of my unconsciousness. Even though I was unconscious at times I started realizing my surroundings and I came back. When you come back to this life again it is not very pleasant because you want to stay in the time you just experienced. I was sleeping. I was a very heavy sleeper. They came looking for me. It was early in the fall. This is my brief recollection. This will be the end of my story.[55]

In Kupak's experience, as in Suvaksiuq's, there were no *tuurngait*, but there were people who told him what he had to do. The dangers and the tests Kupak referred to evoke the dangers of the shamanic trips to the sea woman. The Christian symbolism takes shape in the rosary and in the name of his mother, Mary. In an interview in Kangiq&iniq in 2001, Kupak explained that his mother committed suicide when he was four years old and that Mary was his spiritual mother. She stopped him from drinking, and we may infer that if he had drunk the water, he would not have returned to life. Kupak explained that he was a changed man. It was like going through a confession. That fall, animals were scarce, but after he had the near-death experience and changed his life, it took him only a few days to catch one. His prayers were answered.

In the new context of Christianity, not only an *angakkuq*, but also a missionary could bring a person back to life. Mary Anautalik from Arviat described her experience:

One time we lived in Whale Cove. I lost one of my children and then had another baby. Her name was Martha. It was in the fall and it was very stormy and very windy. My baby never told me she was sick. We had no doctors or medical help. There was a child that had died before her. There were two of us, just the two of us. We didn't have an Anglican priest; there was just a Roman Catholic priest in Whale Cove. My baby was sick. We would put the baby on the bed. The Roman Catholic priest was our only source for medical help. Almost all night the baby just lay on the bed. I am a mother. I told you I had already lost a baby before her. The priest told me that there was no hope for the baby and that tomorrow we would make a casket. He said he would come back then. We usually put a flag on the grave, on the casket. He covered it with an ordinary blanket. After three or four hours I fell asleep. I heard him come in. He came in with a flag. He could speak Inuktitut very well. He told me how people prayed. He told me what he would do. He would do this. He would make a cross as a sign.

He put the baby on the flag and covered her. I was tired. I thought I saw something move, a movement. There was a shiny object that seemed to be moving. It kept moving. I was so tired. At the end of my bed my baby had died. He prayed over the grave and the baby moved. She started crying. He removed the flag. "I don't want to take her back. She was dead," I said in a loud voice. "I said take her! Take her! Adopt her! I don't want to have anything to do with her." I was afraid to touch her because she had come back to life. She was my own child, but she had come back to life. I asked the priest to keep her. The priest kept telling me this was a gift to me. She had died. She was already dead but today she is married now with children. Her name is Martha Iqquq. It is amazing that this happened. I have not had any other experiences with any other spiritual things but I couldn't understand how Ataata Papion's prayer was answered.[56]

In a Christian context, Suvaksiuq and Kupak were able to return from the dead because of their wish to continue living and the decisions of angels or even God himself. In the case of Mary Anautalik, her baby came back to life through the intervention of the missionary and the power of prayer.

HEALING CIRCLES

Healing circles, known as *mamisarnit* in Inuktitut,[57] were first introduced in Nunavik. In a paper published in *Inuktitut*, Eva Lapage (1997, 46–52), originally from Salluit, discusses her decision to start up these sessions and traces how the healing circles caught on in the Nunavik communities: "It was approximately 5–6 years ago that I initiated the healing circles ... With my job at the cultural centre, I was travelling to communities already, and on a trial basis, to see whether the healing circles would benefit others. I started up the healing circles in the outlying communities of Kuujjuaq."

At first, there was considerable resistance. Lapage came to understand that it was important to emphasize that the active agency was not the healer, but a higher power. "Others thought I was a healer, as we called the gatherings healing circles. We know as Christians that there is a higher power who helps us to heal, it is not us who heal ourselves. Because healing circles were initially misunderstood, it made it much harder to communicate to the people in denial of what healing circles are about."

Lapage had undertaken the challenge in Nunavik after she herself had experienced a healing session down south:

Using myself as an example, having had many hurts in my life, wanting no more pain, no longer wanting to despise others, and wanting to get rid of my past painful experiences I have inflicted upon myself and from relatives. Recognizing the pain and having lost several loved ones at close intervals, having gone through those experiences, I went through feelings

> that others need to go through, which is said to be a healing process. I took part in the healing cycle which has been thoroughly aspiring for me for all its worth. Forgiveness surfaced and I no longer had resentments towards them as a result of the healing circles. Having arrived at this understanding, I knew others could come to achieve this healing process and that allowed me to work even harder. I even resigned from my job to give more time to the people who needed help the most, who were struggling much with their lives.

Beginning with her own pain, Lapage moved to forgiveness as a means of healing. She emphasizes that, in contrast to what often happened in Amerindian communities, these healing circles should be open to anybody who wishes to take part in them. The church provides an ideal setting for these activities, but they can also be practised in other places. An important aspect of a healing circle is that all that happens during the sessions should remain private. "We make it clear that whatever is said and heard is to be kept confidential and to leave everything said at the healing circle site." She describes the process in some detail:

> For beginners we all sit around in a circle on the floor facing each other with some water and some Kleenex readily available. People are open to cry with all their might as pains carried can be extremely heavy if kept to oneself much too long, locked up inside the heart with no one to confide in. At the healing circle, people cry as loud as they want to for it is up to the individual and we are not allowed to respond to the person, or to ask any questions – they speak from within themselves only. Once they are done, they have to make it known that they are done by saying they are done. I freely ask, "What has hurt you in your life?" Whoever wants to reply, replies. Then I ask the same question over again.

She emphasizes the importance of prayer:

> A prerequisite to the healing circle is a prayer. We all have to pray first for I am only human like any other. I take part in the healing circle but I do not have the will to heal people, I am not the speaker, I am not about to be, I cannot heal anybody – I am just ordinary. Sometimes throughout the healing process, I go and pat people on the back at times as some people are unable to talk to their pains as their pains are much too unbearable to reveal even when they feel like talking ... This touching, it conveys a lot, it says, "I am supporting you, you are not alone" ... Prayers are much a part of the healing circle, for that reason I place my vows on the Lord and it is evident that the bad spirits roam around us wearing down our wellbeing. The love that arises from the healing circle is just paramount. The closed walls seem to caper away and when that happens, we come to a more

understanding realm of life, we come to understand that others have problems too. A helping environment is more visible and an understanding that we are not alone with our problems.

The healing circle provides a context where people can express their pain and anguish and be protected from the bad spirits that roam about. As in the shamanic tradition, there is a strong conviction that if people do not come out with what is burdening them, they cannot be healed. Therefore, Eva moves around the group, giving support to people who are unable to talk. Whereas in the context of shamanic healing the emphasis was on the confession of transgressions and wrongdoings, the healing circle focuses on the afflictions that have hurt the participants. In the small camps of old, all the adults might witness the confession. It was believed that nothing should be kept inside a person; everything should be taken out and made visible and shared with other people. In the large settlements of today, the healing session provides a social setting that guarantees safety and confidence to each participant. The prayer and the love that are generated in the circles protect people against bad spirits.

Radio communication played an important part in the spreading of the healing circle movement to neighbouring communities. Lapage writes, "All the communities have radio stations so I would make announcements on radio or post notices as to what a healing circle is and where they will be held. Today people involved in healing circles are able to announce the gatherings and I do not have to give it a lot of publicity to inform the people. The CBC was most helpful by broadcasting a round of a healing circle. From that broadcast, I accepted an invitation to go to Labrador, assisting them in starting up healing circles. Here, in Nunavik, I have visited all the communities to conduct healing circles."

Lapage explains how she took her inspiration from Amerindian practices:

> The first healing circle I attended was in Thunder Bay, Ontario. I travelled there with another Inuk; she did not take part in the healing circles though. The rest who took part to the healing circles were all Indian … Not knowing a thing about healing circles I decided to attend one of their evening gatherings. I was dumbstruck to see people crying their hearts out, vomiting and whatnot. When my turn came around, I would say I have no pains to tell, I do not need any healing. I did not feel the pressure within me to release my fears. The whole week passed and I still did not take part in the healing circles. I went home without having taken part. When I got home I started thinking as to what had been going on at the healing circles, asking myself, "What were they doing at the healing circles? What was the point of the healing circles? What does it mean?" I asked around about the concept of healing circles. Then it all flushed down upon me, all the pains that had affected me in my life started rolling into my being, I was all alone too. All the pain, the hatred I felt within me boiled into one all at once. As

I came to recognize them, it seemed that I had no one to confide in about my situation, I felt stuck with the burden churning within me with no place to go.

Openness to other cultures has always been a distinctive feature of Inuit traditions. Even in the oldest traditions of shamanism we see white people and Indians among the helping spirits of the *angakkuit*. It took Eva Lapage a little while to relate to the Indian healing circles, despite their similarity to the confession that lies at the core of Inuit healing traditions.

Originally from the Keewatin area, the Reverend Armand Tagoona was writing extensively about the practice of confession known as *aniartuq* (to bring a thing out in the open) in the 1970s. According to Tagoona, this practice consisted in confessing your wrongdoings before your death: "Nearly all Inuit in the olden days, just before they died, confessed everything they could remember that made them sick inside. Some still do this"[58] The context *par excellence* for *aniartuq* was provided by shamanism.

Other features of the healing circles also evoke shamanic practices. The gifts to the person in charge of the ceremony, for example, suggest the *tunijuti* practice when the *angakkuq* received a gift from a patient.[59] Lapage (1997, 55) relates, "I have been praised with many gifts from people who have acknowledged the support of the healing circles." A healer from Ikpijarjuk, Tipuula Ataguttiaq, referred to these gifts in her discussion of prayer: "Some people were good *angakkuit*. Today, you might say, 'I wish that person might pray for me. There could be some change if he prayed for me.' Sometimes when one person prays for you, you feel better and yet if another person prays for you, you feel worse. Even today there can be good *angakkuit*. You had to give a gift to the *angakkuit* if you wanted them to help you."[60]

Healing circles appeared at the end of the 1990s, first in the Pangnirtuuq area and then throughout Nunavut. Meeka Arnakaq, a social worker, born in the Panniqtuuq area in May 1942, had been active within the Anglican Church before she began to organize healing workshops in different South Baffin communities. In a paper published in Inuktitut, Arnakaq (1999, 33–7) explains why she and her husband Abraham feel that this new format is particularly well suited to helping solve the problems that affect modern Inuit society: "It helps to ease and release your innermost feelings of hurt. People with emotional, life, and personality traumas need to heal from within. Problems like these cannot be cured by medical doctors, psychologists, or psychiatrists. Emotional pain is not easily fixed through discussions. These have their benefits, but participating in healing circles will get to the heart of the matter … The reason why there are healing circles today is because there are problems today that weigh heavier on the mind than in the old days."

Arnakaq presents a long list of problems that can be solved through these new practices: "Being orphaned, or the least loved child; having been molested as a child; being a victim of rape; having deep emotional scars; losing a loved one;

suffering malice at home; having an unfaithful spouse; losing a loved one to murder; divorce, with its effects on children; alcoholism; violence; living away from the place one loves most; being imprisoned or having a loved one in jail; surviving a suicide attempt; the effects of residential school."

These problems deeply affect modern Nunavut society, and Inuit consider neither modern psychiatry nor social services capable of dealing with them. Healing circles can provide serenity, internal peace, compassion, forgiveness, patience, joy, discernment, humility, and gratitude – qualities essential for the healing process. Arnakaq insists that healing circles must be organized on a regular basis to be effective: "One session in a healing circle is not enough. It takes more than a year of participating, but not every day. The experience of unveiling your deepest sorrows can be emotionally exhausting, and you need some days in between to recuperate and make healing work. Taking part in a healing circle once a week, if it is available, is the best method."

Arnakaq connects the development of healing circles to the growth of the population and emphasizes the need for strong and wise leadership, suggesting by implication that participation in healing circles might be a requisite for such leadership: "Our population is growing and our communities are developing, and so we will continue to need strong and wise leadership. Leaders require inner strength. Ongoing healing circles are desirable because they help us to understand our identity, which in turn nurtures our culture and strengthens us in all we do."

Nowadays, healing circles are organized in many northern communities. Local or regional associations and institutions promote these activities.[61] Imported from outside Nunavut towards the end of the twentieth century, the format of healing circles has been very successful among Inuit. Healing circles seem to match well with Inuit perspectives. They are intended to help people overcome the problems that have caused them so much pain, either individually, such as in terms of alcoholism or drugs or sexual abuse, or collectively, such as in cases of relocation. Although the circles may derive their origin in part from outside the Inuit culture, they evoke important Inuit traditions. An example presented by Pauktuutit (Inuit Women of Canada) shows how crucial this connection to Inuit traditions is to the success of healing circles.

> Inuit men sit quietly in a circle around a qulliq (an oil lamp carved from stone). They are two thousand miles away from the shores of Canada's Arctic Ocean where, for centuries, lamps like this one have meant light, warmth and survival to the Inuit who thrived in perhaps the harshest environment on earth … The qulliq's light provides a glimmer of hope … The healers who lead the circle have traveled from Pangnirtung to this prison in Muskoka. They are steeped in their culture, articulate in their language and bring forth the best of Inuit values … Abraham Arnakaq sings softly an ancient song about the burden of pain and the joy of letting it go. His wife, Meeka, slowly beats a drum and then, when the old song fades,

speaks in a hushed voice to describe the courage, fortitude, and tenacity of Inuit, of how struggle and adaptability is as much a part of the culture as legends, caribou hunting and seal skin tents. She is speaking in metaphors … the men don't miss a word.[62]

The Inuktitut language, as well as the *qulliq* and the drum, seems to offer a way to connect the past to the present, and the healing process is thought to be facilitated by the circle model. According to the Greenlandic healer Angaangaq,[63] The circle makes communication among the participants easier, as it "does not have a beginning and an ending."[64] People do not pay for help but bring gifts instead. Angaangaq explains, "Inuit pay with seal meat, liver, caribou meat, they bring their stuff like fish, and I do not think about money but they come with a gift."[65]

Many of the Inuit identified as "traditional healers" can accept the designation of helper or facilitator, but they do not wish to be associated with shamans.[66] They remain firmly attached to Christian churches. Mariano Aupilaarjuk from Kangiq&iniq and Celestin Erkidjuk from Iqaluit are actively involved in the Catholic Church, and Elisapee Ootoova from Mittimatalik and Meeka Arnakaq from Panniqtuuq are fervent Anglican believers. Aupilaarjuk emphasizes how the old Inuit traditions can be combined with Christianity: "Today, our belief in God is no longer visible; it seems to be only about the appearance of belief. When we die we will know that in fact we had God in us. We will always believe in God … What I am trying to do is to follow our old spiritual beliefs and the religious beliefs as well, to have these two belief system co-exist, it will be better off for us."[67]

Alashuak from Puvirnituq, firmly places the healing circles in a Christian context: "I believe in God. I have God and Jesus in me. For me, this is my first priority. To believe and to be religious and healing is very beneficial. First, religious belief, spiritual belief, and then, second, healing. Spiritual belief is stronger. In the Bible, or what God tells us, is that we must speak to each other … If you believe in God, it is also a part of healing."[68]

A connection to shamanic practices is usually not valued by participants in healing circles. They tend to reject any connection to shamanic traditions, which are often associated with the devil. This very opposition appears to be necessary to create a context that allows people to share their pain and anguish with the community.

In recent years the residential school system has become a controversial issue. Much suffering is attributed to the system. In an article published in the *Nunatsiaq News* on 29 October 2004, Greg Younger-Lewis reports that healing circles are particularly useful in helping people deal with the pain left by the schools. Monica Ittusardjuat from Iglulik, a fifty-two-year-old woman well known for her active role in organizing healing circles, blames the residential school system for many of today's problems. She has travelled to many Nunavut communities in the context of the Qauma Mobile Treatment Project, a program that organizes healing circles and trips out on the land for former residential school students and their families, accompanied by counsellors, sex abuse therapists, and traditional healers. According to the *Nunatsiaq News,* the program receives considerable support.[69]

Healing circles present a way to reconnect with the traditional culture in a Christian context. By singing *ayaya* songs, lighting the *qulliq*, drum dancing, praying, confessing, and going out on the land, participants can heal the wounds inflicted by modern life. The connection to shamanism can only remain implicit, since the healing circles reject shamanism completely. Yet, a connection is often perceived, notably in the work by Inuit weaver Salea Nakashuk from Panniqtuuq, who commented, "The Storyteller, from a drawing by Joel Maniapik, is one of my favourites because it reminds me of the healing circles we have now. We don't use drums, but we sing the old rhymes, which have a calming effect. When I wove that piece, I thought I depicted a shaman expelling a demon."[70]

CONCLUSION

Healing is embedded in a socio-cosmic moral order. The well-being of an individual depends on his or her social and cosmic relationships with human and non-human agencies. This basic framework was retained when the shamanic discourse, which focused on the *tarniq, tirugusuusiit, tuurngait,* and *tupilait,* was replaced by a Christian one, which integrated many features of the old traditions. Confession and forgiveness have had a central place in the shamanic context as well as in the healing circles. In a shamanic performance, the audience would ask that the transgressions be forgiven and the non-human agents would acknowledge the confession by healing the patient or returning the game animals. In the healing circle, people support each other and forgiveness is granted by God.

Many Inuit assume that *tuurngait* and *tupilait* are still around, but today they are usually referred to as ghosts or demons or even Satan. Many Inuit claim to have encountered such beings. They play an important part in popular imagination and are often represented in art. Practices such as exorcism replaced the killing of *tupilait.* In the healing process, God and angels might communicate with people in very much the same way that *tuurngait* did in the past. A Christian context has provided a framework for near-death experiences, such as those of Suvaksiuq and Kupak, evoking accounts of shamanic initiations and shamanic trips. These experiences also have the connotations of spiritual rebirth.

Confession and prayer continue to be important in healing rituals. They confirm that healing today, as in the past, is effected through the correction of social and cosmological relationships. In a Christian context, a patient should confess to other people as well as to God. The leaders of the healing circles often refuse to be called healers, as only God can heal. But they are prepared to accept gifts, being well aware that gifts embody relationships. Gift exchanges organize social as well as cosmic relationships, and therefore they cannot easily be returned, as we saw in the case of Tungilik. In the next chapter, we will discuss the significance of objects in more detail.

9

Powerful Objects and Words

INTRODUCTION

In the past, objects and words constituted privileged means of connecting to ancestors and non-human beings. Christianization introduced new objects and new words, but strong continuities are obvious in their use and application. In the first part of this chapter, we will examine the many uses of *aarnguat* (amulets) and *qalugiujait* (miniature objects attached to a *tapsi,* a shamanic belt) in Inuit culture. We will then explore the powerful symbolism of miniatures; these operated on the same level as the *tarniq* and are still very popular among the Inuit today. Miniatures were given as burial gifts and played an important role in traditional funerary customs. We will show that the tradition of burial gifts is still very much alive in some communities of Nunavut.

In the second part of the chapter, we will explore the *irinaliutiit* (powerful words) that were used in Inuit traditions, and see how, with the coming of Christianity, they were replaced by prayers and hymns, which were often used for the same purpose.

POWERFUL OBJECTS: *AARNGUAT, TAPSIIT,* AND *QALUGIUJAIT*

In the past, protection was provided to the Inuit by powerful objects such as *aarnguat* (amulets), *tapsiit* (shamanic belts, also known as *angaluit*), and *qalugiujait* (miniature knives). The story of the first amulet was first recorded by Rasmussen (1929, 110):

> There were no shamans in those days, and men were ignorant of all those rules of life which have since taught them to be on their guard against danger and wickedness. The first amulet that ever existed was the shell portion of a sea-urchin. It has a hole through it, and is hence called iteq (anus) and the fact of its being made the first amulet was due to its being associated with a particular power of healing. When a man fell ill, one

> would go and sit by him, and, pointing to the diseased part, break wind behind. Then one went outside, while another held one hand hollowed over the diseased part, breathing at the same time out over the palm of his other hand in a direction away from the person to be cured. It was then believed that wind and breath together combined all the power emanating from within the human body, a power so mysterious and strong that it was able to cure disease. In that way everyone was a physician, and there was no need of any shamans.[1]

Women started to wear *aarnguat* to protect and strengthen their child when they were pregnant. Rasmussen (1929, 170) writes concerning the Iglulingmiut, "A pregnant woman must make two small dolls from a sako·t (iron scraper for softening skins) which has belonged to someone since dead; these dolls are to be placed as amulets in her inner jacket, one under each armpit. Such amulets, which are called imnarmin (let it be an adult) render the foetus light for the mother to carry." By establishing a relationship between a dead person (the deceased owner of the scraper) and the mother (who wore these amulets under her armpits), these amulets ensured that the child would grow up to become an adult.

According to Boas (1901 143–4), the mother would wear the *aarnguat* to protect the *tarniq* of the child until it got stronger. When the child could walk, the *aarnguat* would be sown to its clothes. Boas writes, "Akkolookjo and Oomernitoq[2] gave advice to the people saying, that when they should become numerous they would have to obey certain customs." In a workshop in Kangiq&iniq in 2000, several elders recalled how they used to have *aarnguat* as children.[3] Ollie Itinnuaq from Kangiq&iniq remembered having to wear them: "I used to be embarrassed about them. I had an ermine stitched on my shoulder. I don't know what the purpose of it was. It was always embarrassing when we were going visiting to be wearing this. I was also given the skin of a seal that had died in the winter. The outer claws had been tied together. I was told it would protect me and that I would not be struck whenever there was lightning."

The purpose of *aarnguat* was usually not explained to the children. Peter Suvaksiuq from Arviat recalled, "When I caught my first fish, my grandmother took the dorsal fin and placed it on my back. That's all I remember. She did not tell me why she had done this." Because of this lack of explanation elders today are not always sure whether or not they had worn *aarnguat* as children. Luke Nuliajuk from Uqsuqtuuq remembered, "I was not given any abilities by my mother. I don't remember this, but the skin of an owl head … was put on my head so I did not get grey hair quickly. Maybe this was an *aarnguaq*. It was also placed there so I would look at people. This was another reason it was placed on my head."[4]

Several elders at the 2000 workshop recalled that senior male relatives would put a stop to their wearing amulets. Felix Pisuk from Kangiq&iniq related, "I think I had an *aarnguaq*. The fore-claws and the eye teeth of a *siksik* were pierced and beaded into a necklace for me. My grandmother said that they were my protection, and no bear would chase after me. I am not a bear hunter at all. They say that *siksiit* can be used as a protection from ferocious animals such as walrus, and polar bears. When I was born, they must have known that I was going to be afraid of fierce animals because I was given this as a protection against them. I think my father's older brother cut them off and threw them away."

The adoption of Christianity induced some people to get rid of amulets. At the same workshop Mariano Aupilaarjuk from Kangiq&iniq recalled, "I, too, had an *aarnguaq*. It was a *qutjau'naq*, an eel-like sea creature. My grandfather Qimirluk, who was also called Uyarasuk, who I never knew, was a good seal hunter. I had his *uqsiut*, a thong used for dragging seal, as an *aarnguaq* placed on my hood. My father threw it away when we became Christian. He said we did not need those things any more. If then was now, I would have kept it. Maybe these weren't *aarnguat* but I was also given part of a ptarmigan and the fangs of a wolverine. I also wore the penis of an old squaw duck around my wrist. I don't know what they were used for, but these were what I wore."

Most adults had a belt (*tapsi*) to which *aarnguat* were attached, and certain situations required the use of a belt. Boas (1964, 206) reports that in the mourning ritual in Cumberland Sound, "[a]ll male relatives of the deceased wore a belt around the waist, besides which they constantly wore mittens." Belts had to be worn for protection in dangerous periods of transition. The use of *aarnguat* belts is well documented in the Kivalliq and Nattilik areas. Rasmussen (1930, 92) writes, "Atqaralaq's amulet belt … not only shields her from illness and other dangers but also enables her to break various taboo customs with impunity, for instance sewing the skin of the bearded seal. Besides ermine skins, ptarmigan and owl feet with the claws, the belt is composed of various kinds of insects sewn into small skin bags." Thus, the belt not only bestowed specific qualities on its wearer, but allowed the wearer to "break various taboo customs," *tirigususiit*.[5]

Photographs of several Nattilik amulet belts are reproduced in books by Rasmussen (1931, 270a). The caption under the photograph of the amulet belt of a Nattilik boy reads: "Amulet belt worn by Itqilik's son Tugaq from Eqornángerfik, North Somerset Island. The belt itself is of the thick neck skin of a musk-ox killed by his father. It is decorated with objects found at a Tuneq settlement, including a snow knife of whale bone and pieces of bone for use as skin stretchers. There are also bear, seal, and caribou teeth, all killed by his father. The belt is intended to protect the boy against danger and make him a clever hunter."

The *aarnguat* connected the boy to the *tuniit*, predecessors of the Inuit who were strong and capable hunters, and to his father. The father's skill as a hunter was shown by the teeth of the animals he killed, hanging from the belt. These objects showed that a man became a good hunter through his relationships to ancestors.

Birket-Smith (1929, 2:86; see also 1929, 206) holds that the shamanic belt was the most important and distinctive feature of *angakkuit* among the Inuit of the Kivalliq area: "Even the shamans do not distinguish themselves by any other peculiarity than their shaman's belt, which, like their staff … is necessary to the performance of their rites." Female as well as male shamans wore shamanic belts. Birket-Smith (1929, 1:218) described the belt of a female *angakkuq:* "It is therefore, like the belts of the male shamans, thickly trimmed with rags of cloth of various colours, some small pieces of skin representing bear paws – one of her familiar spirits was a bear – a few strings of beads, a twig, etc." Rasmussen (1930, 56–7) describes in great detail the shamanic belt of the Padlirmiut *angakkuq* Kinalik, a young woman of about thirty years of age:

> She had a good reputation as a shaman woman and, like her male colleagues, had a special shaman belt, to which were fastened the following:
>
> A piece of a gun butt, which she had to carry because she had become a shaman through "death visions," i.e. death by shooting.
> A piece of sinew thread which had held two tent poles fast and had been used for qilanEq.
> A ribbon that had once been tied round a piece of tobacco she had been presented with; she was welcome to smoke the tobacco itself, but the ribbon that had been round the gift acquired miraculous powers, when placed on the shaman belt.
> A piece of the cap of qaluhEra^{u}t, her dead brother.
> hErmErzihiut's feet, a polar bear that was her helping spirit.
> An ordinary piece of white caribou skin, which had received magical powers because it was a gift.
> A piece of knitted vest that had belonged to a white man.
> A caribou tooth.
> Mittens of caribou skin.
> A piece of skin from a seal flipper.
>
> All the components of the belt were gifts. These never need be large or costly, but the circumstance that they have been given as presents imparts power to them.

This shamanic belt provided information about the shaman's initiation. Each of its elements had its own explanation or history. The power of the objects attached to the belt stemmed from the fact that they were gifts; this illustrates the great significance of the gift of objects in Inuit society. The belt and the objects attached to it represented the social relations between the *angakkuq* and the people on whose behalf he or she worked. The belt of Kinalik also embodied the *angakkuq*'s relationships with dead people, helping spirits, and foreigners.

Belts could be used to transfer shamanic powers from one person to another. The Nattilik woman Utsugpaglaq wore various *aarnguat* for her little son, who would some day take them over: "Owl's foot, gives powerful fists. The boy's first stocking: will protect his soul later in life. The forehead skin of a caribou, used for wiping him clean when he was born, is an effective charm when hunting caribou. Piece of a shaman belt with strips of caribou skin, to give the boy powers as a shaman. His first cap will make his soul strong and shelter him from sickness."[6] Amulet belts connected the past to both the present and the future through objects handed down from the past worn on behalf of future generations, especially by mothers for their sons.

Felix Pisuk's father, an *angakkuq*, possessed *angaluit* that his wife had made for him. When Pisuk was a child, it was intended that he too would become an *angakkuq*, but his paternal uncle interfered. After his father's death, Pisuk's mother wanted him to hang on to these *angaluit*, telling him, "You're going to keep these. Don't show them to anyone at all." However, as Pisuk explained, when his father died in Churchill, Pisuk's brother Victor Alurniq searched for the *angaluit* and burned them. Thus Pisuk did not have the *angaluit*. Pisuk added, "The *angaluit* were worn by the *angakkuit*. Sometimes they were worn across the shoulder, sometimes they were worn as a belt and sometimes they were worn over the neck."[7]

Victor Tungilik from Naujaat told an interesting story about how he was perceived when he wore the *angaluk:*

> I went to the trader who had been impossible, and when he saw me wearing this, his face became very red, and I could see he was scared. He said to me, "You have been an *angakkuq*." He had been a trader around Kinngarjualik and he had learned to speak Inuktitut among the Arviarmiut. He spoke in that dialect and said, "What is it that you want?" I said to him, "You knew what I wanted yesterday." He said we would go into the store in a little while. I was able to get the food that I wanted. He gave me all that I wanted. As he was giving me so many things, I thought to myself, "This is a lot of food! I'm going to end up with a great big debt." So I told him to stop. It turned out that I didn't have to pay him back for this. Because I was not charged for this, I thought perhaps he put it against government social assistance. I got a lot of food from that.[8]

The number of objects on an *angaluk* gradually increased over the lifetime of an *angakkuq* as he continued to receive gifts from the people he cured. The *angaluk*, or *tapsi*, was a social construction made of the gifts from the people on whose behalf the shaman acted. In this respect, a comparison with the "amulet boys" in the Nattilik area is relevant, as these children wore their *aarnguat* on

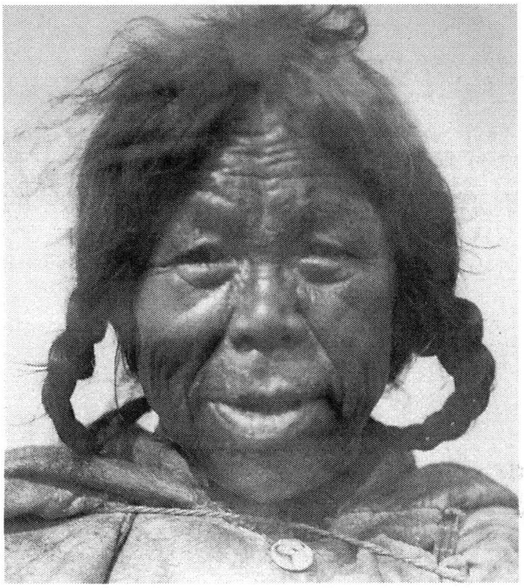

Inuk woman wearing a Christian medal.
Courtesy of Archives Deschâtelets.

behalf of the whole community. The notion of representation is important in both cases, as it was the amulet children and the shamans who represented the community and protected it against external dangers and malevolent spirits.

MINIATURES

Qalugiujait were the miniature objects attached to the belt. According to Tungilik, "When people found out that I was an *angakkuq*, the belt was made for me out of white caribou skin. I would be given little things, for that was what the *tuurngaq* wanted. I would tie these little things onto the fringe. There would be a little string attached to tie them to the fringe. It was called a *qalugiujaq*. They looked like little toys and were tied to the fringe. These were called *qalugiujait*."[9]

Pisuk provided detailed information on the shamanic objects or *qalugiujait* attached to the *tapsi* that his mother made for his father: "*Qalugiujait* were very tiny little knives made of antler. Because my father did not like using his hands to fight *tuurngait* either, he took a tiny knife to an area that had no footprints. Again, although it was at a distance, you could see blood. His little knife would be covered in blood. It would kill what was causing the sickness." Pisuk described the *qalugiujait* as "the weapons of the *tuurngait*. To a regular person they seem like tiny little toys." He explained, "*Qalugiujait,* such as little knives, were made from bones found on the land, especially from graves. Those have real *tuurngait*. *Angakkuit* that wore those on the *angaluk*, whether at their neck or at their waist, were able to make *tuurngait* visible when they were fighting them. Other *angakkuit* were unable to equal them. The *angaluit* are very powerful. *Angakkuit* that were very powerful would wear *angaluit* around their neck, or across

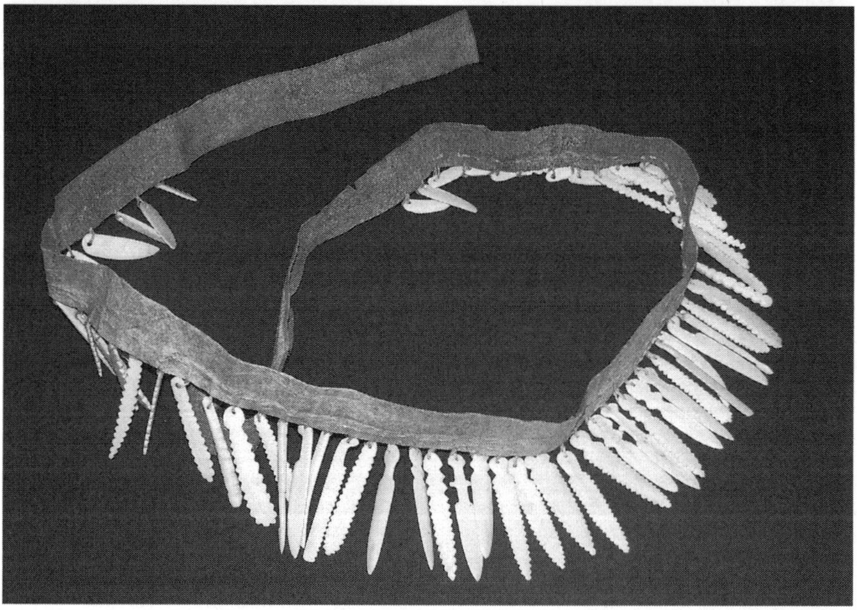

(above left) Miniature knife traditionally tied to a shamanic belt; (above right) Carving of the Madonna by Irene Katak Anguititaq from Naujaat. Courtesy of Eskimo Museum in Churchill; (below) Shamanic belt. Courtesy of Eskimo Museum in Churchill. Photographs by F. Laugrand.

Miniature carvings by Mark Tungilik from Naujaat. The artist presented these to Bishop Robidoux in 1983. Courtesy of Eskimo Museum in Churchill. Photograph by F. Laugrand.

their chest or as a belt. They would not be overpowered by a *tuurngaq* because of their *angaluit*. Silajuaq, the spirit of the universe, would always protect those *angakkuit*. They would always be helped."[10] Jose Angutinngurniq from Kugaaruk added, "I have seen an *angakkuq*'s *qalugiujait*. They belonged to my uncle Iksivalitaq. There were a number of small knives attached to a seal skin with sinew."[11] According to Pisuk, the *qalugiujait* were attached to the shamanic belt by sinews so that they could be hidden. They were not intended to be seen by everyone.

With the adoption of Christianity, new powerful objects were introduced, such as crosses, medals, scapulars, crucifixes, and religious images. In the 1920s, for example, Inuit refused to sell a small crucifix to Mathiassen; this object had been used by Umik "as a very powerful amulet" and thus could not be given away.[12] Many small Christian objects were circulating at that time. Medals and scapulars, for instance, were widely distributed by the Roman Catholic missionaries and used by the Inuit. In Iglulik in 1932, Father Bazin applied a small image of Guy de Fontgalland to a patient's body to heal a lung infection.[13]

In 2003 Laugrand received some miniatures made by the famous *angakkuq* Qimuksiraaq from the Grey Nuns of Nicolet. It is unclear whether these miniatures were ever used, but when Laugrand showed them to the elders in Kugaaruk, they clearly perceived them as objects of great power and would only touch them with their left hand.

A miniature could not only replace the object it represented, but in some cases could precede it. Rasmussen (1929, 183) relates that among Iglulingmiut, "when a piece of soapstone has been broken off to make a lamp, some small object must first be made from a fragment of the same block that is to be used for [the] lamp or cooking pot, as for instance a miniature lamp or pot; this will prevent the actual object when in use from being easily broken." A similar observation was made by Hawkes (1916, 90–1) in Nunavik: "The Labrador Eskimo make miniature models of their lamps and kettles ... which they preserve carefully. They say that as long as the models do not break or crack the originals will not." Thus, the fate of the object depends on the miniature that precedes it very much like the fate of a living being depends on that of its miniature image, the *tarniq*.

Hall (1864, 522–3) describes an interesting gift he received from an Inuk woman on South Baffin Island: "[She] had been nearly a week without eating, and was very hungry. I gave her what little I had of pemmican. She insisted on my taking something for it, thrusting into my hands twelve miniature ducks and other sea-birds, carved in walrus ivory. These I retain as mementoes of the occasion." Apparently the miniatures would guarantee abundant game for Hall in the future.

While most Inuit carvings are made for an external market, miniature objects remain a very popular Inuit art form within Inuit communities. Inuit are fond of these miniatures and often wear them as earrings (especially *kamiit* and *ulus*) or pins. Today, they are seen as ornaments and not as objects of power, but they have lost nothing of their attraction.

BURIAL GIFTS

Miniature objects were often deposited in burial places in the eastern Canadian Arctic.[14] In 1912–13, German anthropologist C. Leden collected a few of these objects during his trip in the Kivalliq area. As an anthropologist, Leden (1912, 198) was well aware of the value of these objects and the importance of such a tradition: "It is the Eskimo custom to bury the dead with all their belongings. What is not deposited in the grave is left leaning against the burial mound. It is a grievous sin to appropriate any of such articles or even to make use of them."

Nowadays, many museums preserve Inuit miniatures that were originally made for the deceased. Inuit artist Minnie Freeman points out the role of this tradition in the development of contemporary art: "A lot of traditional art was made for burial purposes."[15] Visitors to the Kugaaruk cemetery can still see miniatures near the graves. Simon Tookoome (2000, 35), originally from Qamanittuaq, explains that depositing miniatures on a grave, especially small pieces of meat, remains a valuable practice today: "Sometimes I give small gifts when I pass a grave; even if it is just a bit of food, I drop it on the ground near the grave."

(left) Postcards on a grave in Kugaaruk; (right) Cigarette on a grave in Kugaaruk. Photographs by C. Remie.

Sharing food with the deceased was quite common in the past. Hall (1864, 427–8) heard about the practice during his stay on South Baffin Island:

> Some time after I was informed that the grave of Nukertou had been visited by Innuits, according to another of their singular customs. They took down small pieces of tuktoo skin with the fur on, and of toodnoo. When there, they stood around her grave, upon which they placed the articles they had brought. Then one of them stepped up, took a piece of the tuktoo, cut a slice and ate it, at the same time cutting off another slice and placing it under a stone by the grave. Then the knife was passed from one hand to the other, both hands being thrown behind the person. This form of shifting the implement was continued for perhaps a minute, the motions being accompanied by constant talk with the dead. Then a piece of tuktoo fur and some toodnoo were placed under the stone, with an exclamation signifying, "Here, Nukertou, is something to eat and something to keep you warm." Each of the Innuits also went through the same forms. I was told by Tookoolito that this strange custom was invariably practised among the Innuits.[16]

According to Rasmussen (1929, 199),

> Apart from the implements proper, various articles in miniature are made for men, such as kayak, sledge, harpoon, bow and arrows, cup, these miniature objects being placed at the feet of the corpse. For women, a small lamp, meat fork, pot, cup and real needles and thimble are made; these are likewise laid at the feet. These things are made on the day before the na·ce·vik, or the stricter death taboo, comes to an end, and are placed

(left) Flowers and the end of a hockey stick on a grave in Kugaaruk. Photograph by C. Remie; (right) Handbag placed on a grave in Kugaaruk. Photograph by J. Oosten.

> in position on the day it ends. This is said to be done in order that the deceased may possess something. With these miniature objects the soul passes to Takanaluk as soon as the death taboo ceases.

The miniature gifts were on the same scale as the *tarniq*, which became separated from the corpse at death. The corpse was usually taken out of the settlement and placed on the earth. It was devoured by wildlife or dogs, while the *tarniq* remained on the spot for some time. Objects were supposed to facilitate its trip to the lands of the dead. People might be separated from their relatives at death, but not from their personal objects that identified them as a man or a woman. A person had to be complete on burial. The corpse as well as the objects belonging to the person constituted a whole that was not supposed to be broken. Neither bones nor objects were to be removed from the burial place. If an object had to be removed, it had to be replaced by another object. Indeed, Inuit would sometimes replace real objects with small ones. Rasmussen (1927, 134–5) describes a burial place where items were replaced by miniatures: "The body is never buried or enclosed in a cairn, but simply laid out on the earth at the chosen spot, with a few loose stones placed at head, shoulders and feet. In winter, a small snow shelter may be built above the corpse. Models in miniature of implements used by the dead, suitable for man or woman as the case may be, are fashioned and placed beside the corpse for use 'on the other side.'"

According to Rasmussen (1931, 46), miniatures were often used by the Innunait in the Western Canadian Arctic

> The dead must always be buried with his iŋelrutit: the things by means of which he makes his "life wandering." This means his unerat: harpoons,

(left) Miniature images of the Virgin Mary and an angel on a grave in Kugaaruk; (right) Miniature images deposited on a grave in Arviat. Photographs by J. Oosten.

> hâvgut: knives, pitithe: bow, qa·rjut: arrows. If among the deceased's weapons there are especially valuable objects they may be substituted by less costly ones. Some implements may also be replaced by miniature imitations carved in wood. The clothing of the dead is usually laid beside the ilofra, and, in addition to the objects mentioned, miniature sledges and kayaks as well, and often a whole cross-slat of a sledge, in order that the soul may have a supply of wood. Real articles such as ulos or cooking pots are never laid by a woman's grave, miniatures being used instead. All these grave offerings are called ilijät: that which is far away, and usually they are laid up along a stone and covered with small stones.

In the tradition of the Innuinait of the Western Canadian Arctic, miniatures might even be placed beside a bear or a wolf that was killed: "According to Milukkattak the usual custom is to lay a miniature bow and arrow beside only the male bear or wolf; beside the female the hunter places a strip of sealskin or deerskin which the shade of the animal can use as a needle-holder. They are like human beings, Milukkattak went on to say, and have need of the same things, the male of his hunting weapons, and the female of her needle-case."[17]

Boas (1964 [1888], 501) describes a similar hunting practice:

> After a polar bear has been killed, it is cut up on the spot, the intestines are thrown to the dogs, and the rest of the body is taken home. A piece of the tongue and other small parts are hung up in the hut; and knives, saws, drills, and other small objects, are attached to them as presents to the bear's soul. It is believed that then the soul will go to the other bears and tell them how well it has been treated, so that the others may be willing

Graveyard at Qamanittuaq. Photograph by J. Oosten.

> to be caught. At the end of three days, the man who killed the bear takes down the objects, carries them out into the passage-way, and then throws them into the house, where the boys stand ready to get what they can. This symbolizes the bear spirit presenting these objects to the people. The boys must return the objects to their owners. During these three days, the women are not allowed to comb their hair.

The bear becomes the owner of the objects and ends up being the giver of the objects to the boys through the mediation of the man who killed it.[18] Thus, the bear is transformed into a social partner by gifts. Whereas human beings after their death are supposed to become givers of meat, the dead bear becomes a giver of cultural objects – more precisely, miniatures. These burial gifts transform the deceased animal into a social being who can provide food or other gifts in abundance in exchange for small gifts.

Among the Nattilingmiut, the property of the deceased could not be used any more unless they had given it away before their death. In that case, miniature representations of the things they had given away should be placed with the corpse at the burial site.[19] Jenness (1922, 176) discusses a similar practice, but one that left the relatives more options:

> Often the relatives of a dead man will retain his more valuable property and place only miniature copies on his grave. This is done more particularly with the water-boots, but sometimes too with the bow and arrows. The dead man is able to enlarge the miniatures if he wants them, so there is no necessity to leave the genuine articles. Captain Bernard found a grave in Richardson bay on south-west Victoria Island where miniature water-boots had been substituted for the real ones. He described to us, too, a funeral in which the same substitution had taken place. A native named Ekkeahoak was stabbed by a companion near Lambert Island in the spring of 1913. His kinsmen wrapped the corpse in caribou skins and conveyed it by sled to the mainland, where they deposited it on the ground with its back to the north and its head to the east. They laid his possessions in a row by his side, piece by piece, the various tools, the bow and arrows, the sealing-harpoon broken into two pieces, and all his spare clothing, each garment neatly folded in a separate bundle; in place of the real water-boots, however, they left a miniature pair about an inch long. As soon as the corpse was thus disposed of all the people returned to their sealing-ground.

Replacement was clearly crucial. At the Kugaaruk workshop in 2004, Guy Kakkianiun from Kugaaruk spoke of how his family observed this practice: "My father used to say if I wanted something from a grave, I was to replace it with something else. I was not to take it freely. I was to replace it with something else, if I really need something that was on a grave. My son took something from a grave. Because he was only a child, he gave me something from a grave, but I had to return it. I told him that we were not to take anything from the dead." And Iqugaqtuq from Kugaaruk remembered:

> You should never take anything from a grave. When I was a child, we started to look around after we put up the tent. We went to get some water. We didn't think seriously about graves when we were children. We went to get water. We would try to walk fast and not waste any time. There was a cup. I picked it up and took it home. We lived in a tent. I said, "Look at this cup. It's beautiful!" My mother smiled and said, "Did this come from a grave? How did you get it? Put it back where you got it from." So I put it back where I had picked it up. This happened when I still lived with my mother. There was a cup I saw. It was beautiful. I took it home and gave it to my mother. My father said that it belonged to a grave. He said, "There was a grave out there. Put it back!" It was a very beautiful cup, but I had to return it.

Rasmussen (1999, 255–7) relates an interesting incident that happened when he was travelling with the Umingmaktormiutaq Netsit:

> Suddenly Netsit begged me to halt for a moment. I held in the dogs as well as I could, and he proceeded to climb the mass of rock.
>
> He stopped some distance up, and knelt down; there was barely light enough to make out what he was doing. I saw him digging a hole in the snow with his knife; then he took out the cigarette I had given him the night before, placed it, with a couple of matches, carefully in the hole and covered it all over with snow once more. Through the howling of the gale I could hear him reciting something, ending up with a few words to call attention to the valuable gift he had just deposited in the snow … Then he came running back to me and we continued our journey.
>
> What had happened, as I afterwards found, was this. He had been paying a visit to the grave of his father, Ilatsiaq, who had been a great wizard in his time. Netsit thought that the gift of so unusual a luxury as a cigarette would surely have power to call up the soul of the dead man, and secure his protection for us against the troublesome weather we were having …
>
> And certainly, in our case, it appeared as if the lamented Ilatsiaq had appreciated his cigarette. For on the following morning, on cutting a hole in the side of our hut to see what the weather was like, we found to our delight that it was a fine, calm, frosty day.

The tradition of depositing small objects on graves has been preserved to this day. In this respect, there is not much difference between Anglican and Catholic graveyards. In both, one will not only find plastic flowers beside the graves, but also small objects related to the deceased, sometimes personal possessions such as a cap, a bag, or even a cigarette or a newspaper clipping. Most graves consist of a cross with the name and the years of birth and death of the deceased, and their boundaries may be indicated by a row of stones. On several graves the authors noticed a small basket with round stones. Today, as in the past, the objects left by the graves should not be removed.[20]

IRINALIUTIIT, PRAYERS, AND HYMNS

According to Rasmussen (1929, 157), of all sources of power, *irinaliutiit* were the most difficult to obtain, but they were also the most effective. After all, it was *irinaliutiit* that created light. According to an Iglulik tradition, everything was dark until the raven and the fox met: "'Let us keep the dark and be without daylight,' said the fox. But the raven answered: 'May the light come and daylight alternate with the dark of night.' The raven kept on shrieking 'qau, qau.' (Thus the Eskimos interpret the cry of the raven, *qau*, roughly as *qauq*, which means dawn and light. The raven is thus born calling for light.) And at the raven's cry, light came, and day began to alternate with night."[21] Thus the *irinaliuti* that created light was the sound of the raven.[22] According to another Iglulik tradition, the first human beings lived on an island. They became so numerous that the island could not support them and began to slope down to the sea. Then an old woman shouted, "Let [it] be so ordered that human beings can die, for there will no longer be room for us on earth."[23] Thus the words of an elder created death.

The most powerful words were obtained in the solitude of the mountains. Rasmussen (1929, 114–15) describes one way this could be done:

> When one sees a raven fly past, one must follow it and keep on pursuing until one has caught it. If one shoots it with bow and arrow, one must run up to it the moment it falls to the ground, and standing over the bird as it flutters about in pain and fear, say out loud all that one intends to do, and mention everything that occupies the mind. The dying raven gives power to words and thoughts. The following magic words, which had great vitalising power, were obtained by Angutingmarik in the manner above stated:
>
> Earth, earth,
> Great earth,
> Round about on earth
> There are bones, bones, bones,
> Which are bleached by the great Sila
> By the weather, the sun, the air,
> So that all the flesh disappears,
> He – he – he.
>
> Spirit, spirit, spirit,
> And the day, the day,
> Go to my limbs
> Without drying them up,
> Without turning them to bones
> Uvai, uvai, uvai.

An *irinaliuti* is not necessarily an articulated sentence or even a word. Eva Muqyunniq from Arviat explained, "It is just a voice, a powerful command."[24] Rasmussen (1929, 278) points out that in stories about powerful words the words themselves are usually omitted, as the storytellers do not wish to share this knowledge and prefer to keep the words for their own use. *Irinaliutiit* can be passed on by a dying person or purchased. According to Rasmussen (1931, 278), among the Nattilingmiut *irinaliutiit* could be handed down from father to son or bought from a shaman. The price was high. A gun with an ample supply of ammunition was considered adequate payment. Rasmussen succeeded in obtaining *irinaliutiit* by trading *irinaliutiit* he had collected in Greenland for them.

> In this manner I obtained the following magic words from Aua, who had learned them from an old woman named Qiqertainaq. She was very old, and her family had handed down the words from generation to generation, right from the time of the first human beings. It was essential to remember them in the right order otherwise they had no value. In return for this valuable information, Aua had provided Qiqertainaq with food and clothing for the rest of her life. Every time he wished to make use of the magic words, he had first to utter her name; for only through her had the words any power. The words were to be uttered in jerks and repeated in a whisper, as secrets entrusted to Sila. Aua's method of referring to Qiqertainaq when using her magic words was, in his own language, as follows: "aivaluŋniarama" (a shaman's word for erinaliəriarama, meaning: "because I wish to utter an erinaliu·t") "qiqertain·aup qanianikqaŋErluŋa": "using as my mouth the mouth of Qiqertainaq."[25]

The payment Ava gave Qiqertainaq suggests that he took care of her as if she were his own mother; thus, a kinship relationship was created through gifts. Rasmussen (1931, 278) reports that, with respect to the Nattilingmiut, once *irinaliutiit* have been transferred to another person, they "only work for the benefit of the new owner, who must never utter them where others can hear them."

We discussed *irinaliutiit* in various workshops, but because these words lose their power when they are shared publicly, it was obviously difficult to collect them in the workshop setting. Elders gave examples of *irinaliutiit*, but only presented parts of them so that their usefulness would not be affected. *Irinaliutiit* are handed down from the ancestors to descendants, but people can also receive them in dreams or visions, as Job Muqyunniq from Arviat told the participants in the 2003 workshop in Arviat: "*Irinaliutiit* do not come from people. They come while you are sleeping. You dream about it or get an idea in your sleep from above."[26] Muqyunniq informed the other participants that he possessed an *irinaliuti* that had come to him in a dream:

> I have only used it twice. I was with Anoee and Ole. They asked me to perform it and to explain it so I did. I told them about this at bedtime when we were getting ready to sleep. They asked me about what kind of *irinaliut* I had. I told them it was a power I could use to make the caribou come closer. They were lying down when I told them. After I told them they got up. They kept asking me to perform. Everyone got up so I had no choice but to show them how my *irinaliut* worked … I told them they would have to give me what I wanted later on and they agreed with me. We went to sleep that night. Our minister got up first and made tea. He said, "Muqyunniq did his *irinaliut*" … That morning we had tea and Anoee went out. He said he couldn't wait to go out because Muqyunniq did his *irinaliut*. It was a beautiful day in the fall. He opened the tent and he said

there were caribou all around us. He said, "Get up. Get up. There are caribou all around. Get dressed. Go after them."[27]

Muqyunniq explained that he could exchange his *irinaliuti,* but specific conditions had to be met. His dream had told him that there had to be three people present at the transfer and that they would have to give him the front and hind legs of a caribou. Rasmussen (1929, 157), too, states that *irinaliutiit* could only be used under specific conditions: "On the day when a man seeks aid in magic words, he must not eat of the entrails of any beast, and a man when uttering such words must have his head covered with his hood; a woman must have the whole spread of the hood behind thrown forward over her face." He (1931, 278) also relates that *irinaliutiit* were addressed to the spirits of the air, to the souls of deceased humans or animals. They were used to heal sickness, to stop blizzards, or to procure game animals. Some *irinaliutiit* had their own melodies, always very monotonous, and had to be sung slowly, whereas others had to be spoken in a whisper and repeated again and again. Place and time were important: "They are sung or uttered according to subject and purpose, either inside a house in the early morning, before anyone has trodden the floor, or outside in the open air at a place, far from the beaten track, where there are no footprints of man."[28]

It was not easy to understand their meaning. Rasmussen (1929, 235) writes, "When I asked Ivaluardjuk about the power of words, he would smile shyly and answer that it was something no one could explain; for the rest, he would refer me to the old magic song I had already learned, and which made all difficult things easy. Or to the magic words which had power to stop the bleeding from a wound: 'This is blood, that flowed from a piece of wood.'"

Irinaliutiit were usually phrased in the language of the *tuurngait.* Rasmussen (1932, 113) collected seven *irinaliutiit* from the Umingamaktormiut that had been passed down to Tatilgäk by his grandfather. They could only be used inside the house early in the morning, before anybody had set foot on the floor. On rare occasions and under specific conditions they might be uttered under the open sky, but only in places where there were no tracks in the snow. Tatilgäk provided Rasmussen (1932, 117–18) with an *irinaliuti* to ensure his safe return. This *irinaliuti* was traditionally used to bring about the safe return to camp of people who had gone caribou hunting on their own and the sky had turned dark.

We rise from our bed
The great sky's, its enormous pillars
That keep it up, as we overturn them,
Down there and up there
They are upright as pillars – we overturn them
Rising from our bed
Big dwelling! Rest on your arms,
Hold fast!

Platform! Rest on your arms,
Hold fast!
I hold on to it, I faithfully hold on to it, to the island,
Like a gull, anxiously screaming for its young.

The *irinaliuti* clearly connects the universe, the house, and the human body.[29] An Iglulik *irinaliuti* refers to the catching of sea mammals:

Beast of the Sea,
Come and offer yourself in the dear early morning!
Beast of the plain!
Come and offer yourself in the dear morning![30]

In this *irinaliuti* the idea of the gift is clearly expressed. The animal is asked to offer itself to the hunter.

The Nattilik *angakkuq* Qaqurtingniq gave Rasmussen (1931, 286) an *irinaliuti* that ensured an easy delivery of the afterbirth.

What is this?
The after-birth here?
It comes to be set out for blow-flies.
What is this after-birth here?
It comes to be set out for bees.
You who usually come loose at the outer corner
You have always been chilly, you are chilly.

There is an association between the afterbirth and the blow-flies and bees that will feed on it. In Inuit culture, bees have a sexual symbolism and are a source of anxiety for Inuit women.

The elder Nicholas Irkotee recalled that in the Kivalliq *angakkuit* used songs to attract animals: "Some shamans used to try to communicate with the animals so there may be enough food for the other people they were living with. At times it was very difficult to find animals on land or at sea. People used to sing different songs for the animals; when the animals were scarce the people used to sing so that the animals would come close to the community and there would be enough food."[31]

Today's elders are still convinced of the efficacy of *irinaliutiit*. Lucassie Nutaraaluk from Iqaluit explained that an old lady called Tunukallak turned his father into an *angakkuq* simply by using words.[32] Rose Iqallijuq from Iglulik (2000 interview) related her own experience with an *irinaliuti:*

If a person could not eat anymore, and I wanted that person to eat, I would use my irinaliuti. I would say, "Arnaq˙quaksaaraarjuullu aippattauttaani situajumik kiviajumik iilugu iilugu." That is what the old person taught me. When my mother or my father were ill, and would vomit after they tried to eat, I was told to say those words, to irinaliuq. One time, Kunuk's wife Tulugaarjuk, who is now deceased, could not eat arctic char but kept craving for it. I was laughing about this and I said, "Let me say my irinaliuti for you." I went right in front of her and said, "Arnaq quaksaaraarjuullu aippattauttaani situajumik kiviajumik iilugu iilugu." I was pretending to irinaliuq and we were laughing. But I was told that she was able to eat arctic char after that. I did not believe in my irinaliuti. That is why I was laughing about it. But she was able to eat arctic char after that.

Noah Piugaattuk (IE 248) from Iglulik compared *irinaliutiit* to hymns: "Comparison can be made to our written hymns but in those days *irinaliutit* were known even though they were not written. They used to do *irinaliut* by following the words. These were usually short supplications, something that was not complicated, there were quite a few of these." He recalled that there were many kinds of *irinaliutiit:* "There were all kinds of *irinaliut* that one could offer. This was also done when the hunters were desperate to catch a game animal. When they were hunting they would watch a game animal that was not aware of the presence of the hunters. It was absolutely essential that the hunter catch this game animal. Once in a long while someone would offer a *irinaliut* so that the animal would not become aware of their presence thereby making it easy for the hunter to catch it. This type of *irinaliut* was known as *tirlisi.*"

Piugaattuk said that there was another type of *irinaliutiit* that was used to make people homesick:

> It is said that a person can offer a supplication for someone to show up sooner or return home sooner. In that way this person will make the next person homesick by offering an *irinaliut*. This is called *angiraummigaq*. I heard about a particular case. Nanuraq who lives in Kivalliq was single at the time. There was a woman who had two men and one of them was Nanuraq who was single so she was now in love with him, much more so than she was with her real husband. Nanuraq was trying not to get too serious with her because she was really trying to get him. Nanuraq went to another camp that was not too far in which he planned to spend the night in this camp. That night when he had settled he all of a sudden really got home sick, as it turn out his woman had offered an *angiraummigaq irinaliut*. It is said that these are very strong.

When asked whether *irinaliutiit* were whispered or spoken, Piugaattuk answered, "They said it according to what they were comfortable with, when they started out they would say, 'Wai! Wai!' With this they would start their *irinaliut*, after saying a few words they would again say 'Wai' which was followed by a sentence and again with 'Wai.' The words were well put together, they did not really whisper but they just use the tone that they were comfortable with." He recalled:

> [W]hen we first moved into an igloo in the autumn, when we have moved into this new snow dwelling my mother made an *irinaliut* by using *wai*, [these] were the words that would be used for this particular case just as the words that you would say when you are singing a particular hymn or a particular prayer. There were no written words for these but she just followed what she had learned. She was saying the words with *wai*. The reason was that she wanted us to pass the winter period without any adversities, she offered the *irinaliut* when we were now going to live in a snow dwelling. I remembered that when *irinaliut* were offered.

Jose Angutinngurniq from Kugaaruk possessed several *irinaliutiit*, but did not use them. One of them served to deflect bad thoughts. "I only know three. They have talked about the one that we are calling the deflector. I can deflect back bad thoughts. I can use this *irinaliuti*. I would use my grandfather Paksikkaq's *irinaliuti* as a deflector. I could deflect polar bears as well. I know these, but I have never used them." Another *irinaliutiit* could be used for healing. "I know another *irinaliuti* to heal someone who is ill. I have not used any of them" Angutinngurniq also knew an *irinalitiuti* that could surround an animal or human being: "If a polar bear is fleeing, there is an *irinaliuti* called an *avalaqsiut* which can be used to surround the bear. It could also be used to surround an adult or a child. That is where the danger lies with that *irinaliuti*. I would not use it because I have numerous children and grandchildren. It could also affect future generations." Angutinngurniq's mother taught him another one that he could use if he was lost in a dangerous area, but he never tried it.[33]

Victor Tungilik from Naujaat recounted a time when an *irinaliuti* was used on him:

> I only have adopted children left living. I had two sons from the woman that I didn't want to marry. The first one was adopted by his grandparents. When the second one was old enough to stand on its own, my father-in-law said to us, "People of your age have children of their own, you two should look after this one." It was in the Spring time. It was a beautiful day. There was no wind. We were out, because we were young. Those types of days are wonderful when you are young. My wife put the baby in her *amauti* and we went for a walk. There was a little grave we came upon, and there was a hole in the grave. I looked into it and saw that there was an *uviluq* [mussel]. It was an old, old grave. We went home and went to sleep. The baby was sleeping between us. When I woke up, it was no longer breathing. I woke

my wife up. I went to my father-in-law and he told me that we were no longer to have anymore children. That he was going to fix it, so we would not get any more children. I was wondering what was going to happen to us. He only said those words. He didn't do anything. He didn't touch us. He didn't raise hands or anything. He just said that we were no longer to have children, and we never had any more children after that. Because of that, we only had adopted children, and all the adopted children are alive to this day.[34]

Irinaliutiit could also be used to capture and kill a *tarniq*. Avalaaqiaq from Qamanittuaq remembered a technique that involved making a snowman and using it to capture the *tarniq* of a person. It required the use of *irinaliutiit:* "There is a special kind of innunguaq [imitation of a person] … made of snow. This was a fearsome snowman because it was made by a shaman. It was made to capture the spirit of the person that the shaman wished to harm. Secret words were spoken to it until it possessed the person's spirit. Then the shaman would take either a knife or a harpoon and kill the snowman. I have been told that the person, even if he was far away, would surely die."[35]

The use of *irinaliutiit* in sorcery was also reported by Felix Pisuk from Kangiq&iniq:

> My father's brother arranged for me to marry the daughter of his brother-in-law Kajjut. This had been arranged at birth but her father didn't want me as a *ningau*, a son-in-law, any more. He wanted somebody else. There was this young man who was very agile, who was very good at playing ball. He wanted him as a son-in-law instead. So he put an *ilisiiqsiniq* [hex] on me using an *irinaliuti*. I dreamed that he took a tube from an outboard motor and was blowing at me through it. I took the tube and bit on the end nearest to me and blocked it. I had teeth back then! I bent the tube and tied the end. I was in front of him. He was trying to continue to blow. After that he ended up with a bad leg because this bounced back to him. I told him that he was the cause of this. My knee became inflamed and I had difficulty walking for a while, but he became very sick from this and died about two years later.[36]

Irinaliutiit would rebound if they were not effective. Rasmussen (1931, 200–1) gives the example of the *angakkuq* Orpingalik, who lost his son and only just escaped death himself when an ice floe capsized: "This event, described in Orpingalik's own words, was later on commented upon by Qaqortingneq as follows: 'People say that the ice floe on which Orpingalik was crossing the river was so large that it ought not to have capsized in the current. But they say that it was as if the floe suddenly met with some resistance that forced it down under the waters of the river. Therefore it is believed that the cause of the disaster was magic words, bad magic words that rebounded upon their own master: erinalio.t utertoq inungminut.'"

Inugssaq, Orpingalik's drowned son, had been scolded by Captain Berthie from the Hudson's Bay Company, who was at Pelly Bay on a trading mission:

> Although he said nothing to Berthie, Orpingalik was offended at this and made evil magic words that were intended to kill Berthie before the year was over. Apparently they had not been powerful enough to kill him, however. He has been a greater shaman than Orpingalik, and the evil words have consequently turned against their source; as they were unable to kill Orpingalik either – he too was a great shaman – they killed his son. For a formula of wicked words like that must kill if there is any power in it; and if it does not kill the one it is made for, it turns against its creator, and if it cannot kill him either, one of his nearest must pay with his life.

The risk in using *irinaliutiit* was that they might affect one's wife, children, and grandchildren.[37]

Irinaliutiit were used for healing, hexing, hunting, facilitating birth, and making travel less onerous.[38] Some words, though, are still credited with a negative power. Inuit compare them to ammunition – words can destroy a person and even shorten an Inuk's life. Everyone has to be cautious; language, as an elder puts it, must not be abused.[39] Elders thought it was dangerous to use *irinaliutiit* without restraint. Aupilaarjuk explained:

> The term for procuring game is *manilirijuq*. I was told never to do this unless I was hungry, because they say the animals retaliate easily. If I was hungry, I could do this. I am going to say something that I heard. This is not something I have experienced personally. When I was young, I was not that capable. I had to try very hard to get animals. I was so desperate that I used to dream about them. Sometimes I thought I could see land that was far away. When you have a vision, it is not quite the same as reality, because it is not as bright, there is no sun. My father used to tell me that if I was not in need, I was not to go after game. I was told not to use *manilirijjutiit*. I was told there was danger in desiring game when you were not in need. He told me if I used *manilirijjutiit* when I didn't need to, I would not have any offspring.[40]

Pisuk was one of several elders who related that missionaries seemed to procure animals in very much the same way as Inuit did with *irinaliutiit:*

> I was told by my father that there was a priest named Father Thibert who was present when there was a famine around Qamanittuaq. Father Thibert

> told people not to constantly pray for animals. He said that just praying once would be enough. There is a place called Sattiumanittuaq. Father Thibert was waiting there to see if we got any caribou, and prayed for my father. He said that he hoped he would get enough. He said that when my father shot his rifle, none of the caribou would flee. It seemed as though it was the priest who was doing the *manilirijjuti*. During this time of hunger Iqqukti was camped at Nuvugusiq. We camped there although we were supposed to leave the next day to go caribou hunting. My father had started walking inland and came upon eighteen caribou that were gathered together grazing. They were in an area that was partly hidden from us. He thought that if he shot one, the others would flee. When he shot his rifle, they all looked up and moved slightly, but none of them fled. It seemed like the priest had made the *manilirijjuti* for him.
>
> My uncle also taught me that if I were ever in a situation where I thought I was going to starve to death or I would no longer be able to use this *manilirijjuti*, I was to give it to a person younger than myself. The only thing I heard from my father about this was about the time the priest said that *manilirijjuti* for him. My father died still being amazed over this incident.[41]

Such incidents explain why Inuit began to attribute great power to the missionaries and to prayer. Father Delalande (1958, 146) had a similar experience: "One day I had the misfortune to say to a woman who was going to visit the traps of her husband: Catch a wolverine. She caught one. Two weeks later she left again, but not after asking me to make the same wish. I said laughing: Catch a wolverine. And believe it or not, she caught another one. Such a coincidence, repeated twice, comes close to (borders on) mystery. How many times the relatives of a sick person that I visited asked me to wish that he became well."

When Inuit converted to Christianity, they could use hymns and prayers very much as they had used *irinaliutiit*. Oral and written ethnographical materials provide strong evidence of this. Victor Tungilik from Naujaat recalled:

> I remember once we were totally out of food. We had a bit of flour, but there was no more meat at all. We were told that our father wanted to pray. While he was in Iglulik, he had started to follow the Anglican religion. He wanted to pray to be given some food from God. The next day after we prayed, we went down to the floe-edge. I was a child back then, and my brother was still alive. There were a lot of seals. He killed a lot of seals. He even got a bearded seal. He came up by dog team to show us. It was only afterwards that I realized that his prayer had been answered by God. It was only later that I turned to God to give me what I needed. Before that time, I didn't think about God at all. I always remember the words that he prayed. They were not written down but I remember them to this day.[42]

Some of the elders – Noah Piugaattuk from Iglulik, for example, compared *irinaliutiit* with prayers. Pujuat Tapaqti from Kangiq&iniq recalled, "My grandmother taught me numerous *irinaliutit.* None of them were to be used against others. When she made a hole in the ice, she taught me the words to an *irinaliuti* to catch fish. Because we depended on catching fish, she taught me the words. I can't remember them though. She taught me so many. Also, if there was someone who was trying to do something against me, she taught me how to send back the bad thoughts. That seems to be the only one I remember. I don't want to use it here in front of so many people. She taught me that *irinaliutit* are a type of prayer for us Inuit."[43]

Ollie Itinnuaq from Kangiq&iniq stated, "Prayer is a form of *irinaliutit.* Our children have never learned these. Here I have this knowledge, it is within me, but my children don't know it. Maybe the reason why those of us who know them are not disclosing, is because nobody wants to talk about this. It is very difficult to believe an elder who says they don't know anything about these things."[44]

The written notes and diaries of the missionaries record how Inuit soon began using prayer in times of need. In 1895, for example, long before Peck made his first conversions, he wrote, "Men driven away on ice floe arrived quite safe. One of them in a very simple but sincere manner told me that he prayed to God four times, as follows: 'O God, save me, for I am in great danger.' On the morning these poor people noticed, to their great joy, that new ice had formed between them and Blacklead Island, and although this actually bent under their weight still as already stated, they succeeded in escaping from their perilous position."[45]

Inuit easily integrated their concept of the power of words into a new Christian perspective. Many examples of this can be found in the letters they sent to the missionaries. In a letter to Peck, Qillaapik writes, "I want to learn His good words, I want to have a good place in Him and in the Holy Spirit. I will follow them. I look at God's good words everyday and remember them. If we do that, we will have a better life."[46] In the Kivalliq and North Baffin regions, the power of prayer was also frequently mentioned.[47] Tuni from Igluligaarjuk told Father Turquetil that only prayer had saved him.[48] Rachel Uyarasuk from Iglulik recollected how prayer was used for healing as well as hunting:

> There were different kinds of prayers. This is true even today. There are different prayers used depending on the reason for the prayer. At the time we went through *siqqitiniq* [conversion ritual], there was a prayer used, but I can't remember the words. All of us who were present prayed. We prayed silently while our leaders prayed. I don't remember what the words were. It was only afterwards, when I became aware, that we were told that we had to gather together to pray. We were trying to follow what was in the Bible, what was in the prayer books, as we were becoming more religious. Whenever anyone was sick, we would have prayers for them in someone's house. Not a fatal sickness, but for instance, if somebody had a very bad cold or was not feeling well we would pray for this person. We had different

kinds of prayers, so I can't really say what the words of the prayers were. We would pray to be given meat. The hunters would pray to be given game for food in the morning before they went out hunting. Also, whenever people were experiencing difficulty dealing with something, they would pray in their dwellings. There wasn't a gathering. They would just pray in their dwelling. They would pray for what they would want. It was only on Sundays they gathered to pray and sing hymns. Also, if there was someone who had been sick for awhile, even though there were people in the household, others would come over to pray if this person was not getting better.[49]

A story told by Tipuula Ataguttiaq from Ikpiarjuk refers to the life-giving power of prayer:

I have revived a baby more than once. I guess it is not their time to die if they revive. The baby was completely lifeless. I held the baby's feet and folded and unfolded the baby at intervals so that the baby would be breathing. I was moving the stomach around and there was completely no pulse around the intestine area. I repeated the folding and unfolding and the baby got a pulse when I checked the tummy again. Then I said: "I do not know but let's say a prayer" and said what was in my mind. Then I did the Lord's Prayer. I said all the prayers I wanted. After that, I took the feet again, repeated the folding and unfolding and the tummy started to move. The baby started to breathe and cry more and more. He revived.[50]

Ataguttiaq then added, "I have heard from a former minister that some people recover from sickness, if they are prayed for before their *tarniq* has left them. Some do not recover even when they are prayed for, because their *tarniq* has left them while they are alive. That is the reason prayer does not revive them. That is what I have heard."

Victor Tungilik from Naujaat related that after he had sent his helping spirits away, he could only use prayer to help people: "I could heal only through prayer. I knew that I could only use prayer to help a person who was sick because I was not going to be using the powers of an *angakkuq* anymore. I was not going to be healing a person, God was. It seemed like the time I was an *angakkuq*, because it is a belief that God is all strength and God is love. We are all God's people, and a person belongs to God. If it is God's will that a person be healed, then he will be healed."[51]

Salome Qalasiq from Kangiq&iniq described how prayer had saved her when she fell into the water while jigging:

I remembered my father telling me that if I ever became desperate to think of him. I told myself I shouldn't think of him and instead I started to pray to Jesus. The surface of the lake seemed far away, but I started going upwards and got out of the hole I had fallen into. When I got to the surface, I started praying again. It seemed as though something underneath me had lifted me up. I ended up on top of the ice. It seemed as if I was very light, even though the clothing I wore was soaked which should have made me heavy, and I was wearing boots that were full of water. When I got out I was totally dry, even though I had been down at the bottom of the lake for a while. I was really amazed at this. I think my prayer was heard then. When I started going up from the bottom of the lake, it didn't take me any time at all. When I was at the bottom of the lake, I had no idea where I was supposed to surface, yet I managed to surface right at the hole.

I'm a bit fat, I'm not that light. It seemed that I was being pushed by something beneath me. As soon as I got out, I touched my clothing because I thought I was soaked, but my clothing was completely dry. This is an experience that I had personally that really amazed me ... After I talked about it I realized that I had been helped. To this day, I believe I was helped.[52]

But even when they became Christians, Inuit might take recourse to the old traditions in time of need. The old technique of *qinngaq* (praying by shouting) sometimes merged with the new traditions of Christian prayer. Rosie Iqallijuq from Iglulik explained the technique of *qinngaq*: "Each individual used his own words to *qinngaq*. A person would go to a place where there were no fresh tracks and would shout the *qinngaq*. A person did not have to be an *angakkuq* to *qinngaq* ... Anybody could do this except children. It was like they were praying. They would talk as if they were doing *saka* [call a helping spirit]; maybe they would *qinngaq* to a dead person ... *Qinngarniq* [a shouted prayer] was not *sakaniq*. It is similar to praying, but the person would be shouting."[53]

George Kappianaq from Iglulik described a time when he resorted to *qinngaq* even though he was a Christian:

We were out caribou hunting and became surrounded by ice. We were travelling by boat. Our boat was full of caribou meat and we were in dire straights. We were desperate. We had managed to get up on top of some nearby ice. All the ice that was around us was very close together and would break up as the pieces hit each other. I knew my grandchild thought we were lost. There was one piece of ice that was very very white. It wasn't old ice at all. We tried to pull the boat to that part but it was too heavy, so my grandson unloaded the boat and we carried it over. He carried the meat afterwards. The ice that we had climbed up on was ground up by the other ice and we lost some of the meat that had been in the boat. We were on a piece of ice that was higher up so we knew it wasn't going to break up right away. It was a fairly large piece of ice. My older son was with me. He thought we should pray. My grandson told his father the way he thought

> we should go. We tried to follow where there was the least ice. The ice was grinding and breaking up. Thoughts of my mother came to me. I had heard a *qinngarniq* … from her and I decided to *qinngaqtuq*. I shouted out to my mother. I remembered her words. I remembered her saying that if I became desperate to think of her. I thought of my own mother instead of thinking of the Virgin Mary. The ice that was all jumbled together parted, and there was space for us to continue our travels. When she was sick with the sickness that would cause her death, when she was no longer able to get up, she started seeing two people. When she told me she was seeing two people, because I was Christian I said, "Maybe you are seeing Satan." Maybe it wasn't Satan. Maybe they were my father's relatives. I remembered her words even though I thought I had forgotten them. A way seemed to be made for us and we were able to get to land … There were people who would use *qinngarniq* when they were in need, and they would be heard right away … If I were desperate, I would be said to *qinngaqtuq* if I were to yell aloud for help from someone. In my case I turned to my mother. Since she was my mother, I turned to her as if I were a child. As soon as we were passed the opening that had been created, the ice went back again.[54]

Another illustration of this form of prayer was given by Ujaraq from Iglulik, who reported doing a *qinngarniq* with his father in order to save his fellows hunters Nattar and Kublu after a boat accident:

> We went to the pressure-ice and climbed on to the highest piece and faced inland. We had our backs to them. We shouted with all our might, wanting the two to be carried towards the edge of the ice. Kublu had his pack with his bullets with him and that gave him additional weight. They clung to a paddle with one hand and paddled with the other. They managed to paddle to the ice in no time. This happened after we had stopped following *pittailiniq* [refrainings].
>
> Although my father had been an *angakkuq*, because he had now become a Christian he was no longer practising shamanism. My father said that since those two were young men they needed to live. He wanted to *qinngaq* and he wanted me to help. Because he was no longer an *angakkuq* and didn't have his *tuurngait* anymore, he was unable to use *sakaniq*. He said the only way he could save them was through *qinngarniq*.[55]

These examples show how Christian prayer fulfilled the same functions as *qinngarniq* did for those in need, and was used in similar circumstances. Qalasiq turned to Jesus instead of her father, Kappianaq to his mother instead of the Virgin Mary. Both were saved. In the workshop held in Churchill in 2008, Henri I&luarnik, Louis Angalik, and Donald Iluakluak, all from Arviat, said that they identified *qinngaqtuq* with praying. Today Christian prayer is considered to be the foundation of one's well-being. Noah Qaumagiaq from Arviat described how prayer had once helped him:

> I want to tell you something that happened to me through Christianity. One time I was sick and very ill. I couldn't move. This missionary came to me and prayed for me. I was able to get well again through prayer. I remember this for the rest of my life. I believe in my heart that I was healed through prayer. I was around nineteen years old when this happened. Ever since the time that this sickness disappeared, it never bothered me again. At the nursing station the nurses told me I didn't have much of a medical chart because I was really healthy after that. I went to the nursing station with a cold and that was about it after I was healed. I have been very healthy and had a very healthy life ever since that missionary prayed for me. I have not had to leave town for a medical problem or anything like that. I have had a very healthy life.[56]

Christian hymns are called *pisiit.* In many respects, they have replaced traditional and shamanic songs, but whereas traditional *pisiit* were personal and owned by a particular person,[57] hymns are collective and communal. Collections of hymns were spread by the missionaries in hymnbooks called *pisiliit.* They were introduced on North Baffin by people from the south. Rachel Uyarasuk from Iglulik recalled, "While we were living over there, there were people who arrived from the Panniqtuuq area. Only some people would get Bibles, because they didn't bring that many. We learned the hymns and prayers from these books. We started learning to read from these. It was the people in the Panniqtuuq area that brought the Bibles. The songs would be sung. That's how we learned to sing."[58]

The Christian hymns were frequently sung by Inuit. Elders recalled learning them as children. Uyarasuk remembered a hymn she learned as a child:

> During our time on earth
> We are in a place where we have to work.
> During our time on earth
> We are in a time of being saved.
> Just playing around is of no use.
> It is of use only for the worst thing.
> He doesn't want me playing around.
> Look at Jesus,
> Lamb, Son of God,
> Your only Savior.[59]

Hymns played an important part in rituals of departure and greeting. Rasmussen (1927, 118) visited Ava's camp just after the people had converted to Christianity:

Aua's hunting camp lay midway out in Lyon Inlet; I reached it late one afternoon, just as the setting sun was gilding the domes of the snow huts.

It was known that I was on the way, and above each hut waved a little white flag – a sign that the inmates had relinquished their old heathen faith and become Christians. As I drove up, men, women and children trooped out and formed up in line outside Aua's hut, and as soon as I had reined in my team, the whole party began singing a hymn. The tune was so unlike what they were accustomed to in their own pagan chants that they bungled it a little, but there was no mistaking the earnestness and pious feeling which inspired it. There was something very touching in such a greeting; these poor folk had plainly found in the new faith a refuge that meant a great deal in their lives.

Uyarasuk recalled:

After we became religious, we started shaking hands with people who had newly arrived to welcome them. Also, if there was someone arriving, even if they were related to us, we would all go outside and waiting for them to arrive. People would sing a hymn and when they got together, the dog team would stop and those who had been singing the hymn would go towards the *qamutiik* and shake hands with those who were arriving. That was what I saw. If people moved, or went to another camp, or were preparing to depart for a distance to go trading at a trading post, a few hymns were sung before the dog team would depart. That's what they would do. I think that's when religion was new. Afterwards this became less frequent.[60]

Hymns could also be used to obtain good hunting. Tungilik recalled a time when his family was completely out of food. His father sang a hymn to ask God for some food, and the next day his request seemed to be answered. They found lots of seals and even caught a bearded seal. This is the text of the hymn:

We sit on the highest throne,
With our father,
The ones who loves us, the one who gives us food,
The one who is good to us.
Praise our God.
Praise our God.
Food, clothing,
They come from him
They come from him.[61]

Tungilik said that his father was an *angakkuq* as well as a Christian: "My father would be given animals through the help of God. He did not think about the ministers or priests. My father would only make a request to God when we were out of food."[62]

Saullu Nakasuk from Panniqtuuq remembered that every time someone caught a bowhead they used to sing this song:

> When we catch something
> Holy, Holy, Holy
> We will see Jesus
> We say Holy
> Holy, Holy, Holy.[63]

Noah Piugaattuk from Iglulik (IE 315) recalled that the bishop always sang a hymn before flying on a plane to ensure safe travelling:

> However, for us that follow the Anglican denomination, when we are to travel by air, one must always say a prayer, at least that is what I do … It is said that when the Bishop gets on the plane and after he had settled down he will sing a short hymn … When one is to travel of a difficult journey, or a long journey, one must realize that if God did not create us we would not be alive today, indeed, there would be nothing. A short hymn needs to be sung so that we can have a safe journey. It does not matter where you may be, prayers must be offered to God, no matter where we may be … It does not matter where you are, if God had not created, there would be nothing. Indeed, we would not be alive, because he created us so this song must be sung when we are to take a long journey.
>
> > "Guuti qaumattainaruk akuttingnnik tamainnik tasiurtauniarputtillu naamanktuming." [Finally, know God in every way and you will be guided by the hand in the right direction.]
>
> This hymn is sung so that we can have a safe journey. The planes are now capable of journeying to long distance, so this prayer is offered so that we can stay alive and the people involved … be safe. That is what the hymn means. No matter where you may be, one must keep remembering God. That is what it means.

Eli Amaaq from Iglulik (IE 074) recalled how he had sung a hymn when he was spooked:

> As I started to climb a little hill before I reached the top I felt chills from head to my body, I could feel my hair raising, when that happened I got spooked, I was all alone and it was getting dark. I was getting closer to our tent. I would get chills from my head to my body with it came my help-

lessness, that time I almost had it, I even thought, it is also known that Uutukuttuk had starved to death near that place, it occurred to me then he had something to do with it. I could not run as I was walking on crutches as my other leg was useless. I could not think of anything that I should do so I had to say a prayer while I walked, as I reached the summit of the hill there were large stones so I sat down after having said my prayers. I was now more relaxed and not as spooked as before. When I sat down I started to sing a hymn which I have no recollection as to which hymn it was. As I started to sing my voice sounded exceptionally loud, but after awhile my voice became normal as my spook was dissipating, shortly thereafter it was completely gone. This was one experience that never had another.

CONCLUSION

Words and objects are powerful mediating elements that helped the Inuit deal with human and non-human agencies in either the shamanic or the Christian context. *Aarnguat* embodied relationships between people, deceased namesakes and relatives, animals, and other non-human agencies. They derived their power from these relationships. Miniatures were considered particularly powerful, as they were on the scale of the *tarniq*. The *qalugiujait,* the weapons attached to the shamanic belt, were miniatures, and so were many of the objects that were placed on the graves; these latter could not be removed without being replaced. The transfer and exchange of powerful objects was a delicate process because of the relationships and power they embodied. After the adoption of Christianity, *aarnguat* were often replaced by Christian symbols.

Words were often thought to be even more powerful, as they were able to effect changes. The *irinaliutiit*, powerful words, were often kept secret and could only be pronounced under specific conditions. They could be used for a wide variety of purposes. Piugaattuk from Iglulik (IE 248) provided several examples of different types of *irinaliutiit*. The elders participating in the workshops we organized preferred not to repeat them, and if they discussed them, they pronounced only a small part of the formula. Piugaattuk said that he had forgotten the words, although he also indicated that they were usually short texts so as to be easily remembered. In the past the transfer of these words was a sensitive exercise and required considerable gifts (note the case of Ava). In the workshop in Arviat in 2003, Job Muqyunniq offered to exchange an *irinaliuti* he knew, but his offer was rejected because of the risks involved if the transfer procedure was not done correctly. Elders explicitly compared the *irinaliutiit* to Christian hymns and prayers. These Christian texts are often used in much the same way as *irinaliutiit*, but they are not secret and can be used by anyone in any way. Using *irinaliutiit* was considered dangerous, as it was thought that the practice could shorten one's life. Moreover, they could be used to harm others.[64] Hymns and prayers, on the other hand, are thought to benefit a person.

Today, with the adoption of Christianity, elders point out that life has become easier. There are less *pitailiniit* to follow. Most of the non-human agencies that sanctioned human beings for transgressing these rules have receded to the background or disappeared altogether. God has taken their place. As Samson Quinangnaq from Qamanittuaq puts it, "God knows everything, sees everything."[65] Relating to God through hymns and prayers remains essential for a successful life. The elders' workshops always began and ended with prayer to ensure that the discussions would not be harmful in any way. As in the past, everything that is meaningful should be connected to a transcendent cosmic agency.

Part Four | Connecting to Ancestors and Land

10

Connecting to Ancestors: *Qilaniq* and *Qilauti*, Head Lifting and Drum Dancing

INTRODUCTION

In this chapter we will focus on techniques of divination and on the role of play in encounters with cosmological or human agencies. We will examine the connections between the *qilaniq* (head lifting) ritual and the *qilauti* (the drum, which played a central part in shamanic performances and drum dances). Divination was a central feature of many Inuit rituals. It allowed *angakkuit* to assess the true state of things in the past as well as in the present. Divination might reveal the cause of an illness or the reason for the absence of animals, as well as enable angakkuit to assess the hunting fortunes of the coming season. Techniques of divination were also integrated into rituals and games. The most famous divination technique is probably *qilaniq*. It involves lifting the head of a person or an object with a belt: if the head or object is heavy, the answer to a question is affirmative; if it is light, the answer is negative.

Rasmussen (1929, 228–9) suggests that there is a connection between the technique of *qilaniq* and the *qilauti*. In his description of Iglulik song festivals, he reports:

> The one who is to lead off with an original composition now steps forward, holding the large drum or tambourine, called qilaut, a term possibly related to the qilavoq previously mentioned: the art of getting into touch with spirits apart from the ordinary invocation. For qilaut means literally: "that by means of which the spirits are called up." This term for the drum, which with its mysterious rumbling dominates the general tone of the songs, is doubtless a reminiscence of the time when all song was sacred. For the old ones believe that song came to man from the souls in the Land of the Dead, brought thence by a shaman; spirit songs are therefore the beginning of all song. And the direct relation of the songs to the spirits is also explained by the fact that every Eskimo who under the influence of

powerful emotion loses control of himself, often breaks into song, whether the occasion be pleasurable or the reverse.

The Ahiarmiut refer to the stick they used in *qilaniq* as *qilauti*. The technique of *qilaniq* and the playing of the drum both call up the spirits, notably those of the dead.

The Role of the Deceased

We find no elaborate death or ancestor cult in Inuit society,[1] yet the deceased play an important part in the social life of Inuit and their descendants continue to depend on them. The significance of the dead is easily overlooked, for they rarely dominate in the context of ritual, but there is hardly a ritual in which they do not play a part. In chapter 4 we saw that visits to their graves are beneficial to their descendants and namesakes. Small gifts were given to the deceased in many situations, such as birth and death.[2] From the traditional death rituals it emerges that the dead were considered to be givers of game and that people shared drink and food with them at the graves so that they might continue to give.[3] In the naming system, the dead are represented in living people; these relationships are taken very seriously, since a deceased relative may be the only help a person can get in times of need.[4] Even today, Inuit women speak of how deceased relatives visited them in their dreams during their pregnancy, indicating that they wished to be renamed in the unborn child.[5]

The dead are always present in a dual way, as represented in their namesakes and as supporting their namesakes. The descendants are largely responsible for the fate of the deceased; the deceased can become benevolent ancestors who support their living namesakes or turn into evil *tupilait* intent on destroying those who did not respect them. Descendants and namesakes should honour the deceased by respecting them, observing the necessary rules, and renaming them in the children who are born.

But people should not become too attached to the deceased. Elders often emphasized that people should not grieve or mourn too much. Aalasi Joamie from Iqaluit stated, "You should not grieve for anyone you lose for too long. The deceased has a soul. The soul may end up roaming the earth if we grieve for them for too long." Akisu Joamie from Iqaluit agreed: "For that reason, we are advised to listen to the advice we are given. There is nothing more that we can do. When we don't let the deceased go, we just make ourselves suffer. Even if we feel hopeless, we have to listen to the advice we are given. We have to try to overcome our grief because if we don't it can overcome our body. The elders' minds are very powerful. We are always taught never to give an elder cause for concern. Even after death, an elder's thoughts may become reality."[6]

The names of the deceased should be remembered. *Inuit qaujimajatuqangit* helps to maintain people's connection to them. The deceased live on in the stories and songs that are told about them. Songs were even thought to come originally from the land of the dead. In this chapter we will discuss how *qilaniq*, as well as *qilauti*, address the deceased and allow people to connect to them.

The Drum

The cosmic dimensions of the drum are illustrated in the Nattilik myth of the origin of thunder and lightning. Rasmussen (1931, 378) relates how a brother and sister "turned themselves into spirits of the air and rushed across the sky, the sister striking sparks with her firestone, the brother striking his piece of dried skin like a drum, so that the heavens roared (*qilautErpalulErLune*), and in that way they rose up to the sky." Thus the heavens themselves resonated like a drum. The term *qilak* denotes heaven as well as the ceiling of a house and the palate of the mouth, thus connecting the various levels of the cosmos[7] – the universe, the house, and the human body.[8]

The *qilauti*, the drum, can be made of various materials, such as caribou skin or the bladder of a seal stretched over a frame. It played a central part in shamanic practices and song feasts. Today, drum dances are again an important feature of Inuit culture, especially in Kivalliq and the Western Arctic. They are integrated into cultural celebrations and feasts, such as the Inuit Summer Game Festival in Kivalliq and the Toonik Tyme Festival in Iqaluit.

In this chapter we will refer to various video recordings that were made of contemporary *qilaniq* séances and drum dances in the Kivalliq region. We will first explore the *qilaniq* technique and various other techniques of divination and then discuss the drum festivals as a means of communication between people and their deceased ancestors.

QILANIQ IN THE PAST AND IN CONTEMPORARY NUNAVUT

Descriptions of *qilaniq* go back as far as the sixteenth century. George Best, one of the naval officers who accompanied Martin Frobisher on the Northwest Passage voyages (1576–78), described the practice as he saw it done by the Inuit of Baffin Island: "These people are great enchaunters and use manye charmes of Witchcraft. For when their heads do ake, they tye a great stone with a string unto a sticke, and with certaine prayers & wordes done to the sticke, they lifte up the stone from the ground, which sometimes with all a mans force they cannot stir, & sometimes againe they lifte as easily as a feather, and hope thereby with certain ceremonious words to have ease and helpe."[9]

Best records that the technique was practised when people had a headache. As in many variants of the technique as described by later observers, the head itself was the object that was lifted, and thus there may have been a misunderstanding on his side. While it was usual for the head to be lifted, other objects, such as a leg, a stick, a snow beater, or a stone, could also be used. The power of rocks is a recurrent theme in accounts of *qilaniq*. Boas (1964 [1888]) had early on referred to the spirits of stones as powerful *tuurngait*. Stones could be consulted for the purpose of divination. Boas (1907, 511) writes, "When game has been scarce for some time, an angakok will address a boulder, as though speaking to Nuliayoq, asking why the game is scarce. Then the boulder will reply, stating what taboo has been violated. Meanwhile the earth will tremble. There is only one old man now living who is claimed to have this power." Thus, it seemed that rocks could mediate between the shaman and the earth as well as between the shaman and the sea woman.

The *qilaniq* technique usually involved the lifting of a person's head, but elders are aware of a great variety of techniques. Felix Kupak from Naujaat referred to some of these: "I could do *qilaniq*, too. There are different ways of doing *qilaniq*; there are little differences. Sometimes they used their leg, sometimes they used a heavy rock, and sometimes they put a stick inside a caribou parka, an *atigi*. They could do those too. Others used part of a person. There are many ways you can do *qilaniq* so there can be different demonstrations. If I realized that someone was trying to make fun of me or abuse me in some way I could take a piece of mud or rock and make it strong."[10]

Boas (1901, 135) describes the technique of head lifting:

> A thong is placed around the head of a person who lies down next to the patient. He is called the keleyak. The thong is attached to the end of a stick which is held in hand by the angakok, called in this case the keleyew. Then the latter summons the soul of a dead person. As soon as it appears, the head of the keleyak becomes so heavy that it cannot be lifted. Now he asks. Is the soul of so and so present? If he mentions the correct name, the head cannot be lifted. Then he continues to ask questions as to the nature and outcome of the disease, which are supposed to be answered by the soul of the dead person, which makes it impossible for the head to be lifted if the answer is affirmative, while the head is raised easily if the answer is negative. As soon as the soul of the departed leaves, the head can be moved without difficulty.

Even though Boas qualifies the technique as divination, it is often described as a healing technique. It involves the presence of the soul of a deceased person. As soon as that soul leaves the head of a person, the head can be moved without difficulty. In another description provided by Boas (1907, 492), relating to the Mittimatalik area, the dead person present in the patient is identified as the mother of the patient:

> A sick woman called in a man in whose power of curing by head-lifting she had faith. The man used a wand to the end of which a thong was fastened,

> which he slipped under the head of the patient, so that the nape of the neck rested on it. The patient lay stretched out flat. Then the person began to question the patient. "Are you this woman's mother's spirit?" When the answer was in the affirmative, the person felt a strain on the wand. (This is believed to be due to the fact that the spirit addressed is under the patient, and responds.) When a name of a spirit who was not present was mentioned, there was no response. After the performance, the head of the patient was pressed on both sides, as though it had to be pressed together.

In a *qilaniq* witnessed by the famous whaler Captain Comer, the spirit of a husband's grandfather had entered his wife:

> The strap used to raise the head was one worn by an angakok. There were attached to it a number of pieces or strips of skin, which show the number of diseases which the angakok has cured. The questions put generally referred to the transgression of taboos. For instance, Captain Comer said that the spirit possessing the woman was displeased because Captain Comer had cut off some hair from a ground-seal's skin without asking the consent of the woman who was in a trance. He was required to confess that he had done so by saying the words, "It is enough," and that then the evil effects of the transgression would be overcome.[11]

Peck describes *qilaniq* as a healing practice: "And if the (his) leg feels heavy, he accuses the sufferer of some guilty action (and says to him), because thou seest an evil country, perhaps has evil visions, therefore this [evil] sickness has come upon you, and so it (*is he brings*) him in guilty. Here in this neighborhood the conjurors also do the (same) to a sick person."[12] In this account, heaviness is associated with guilt. The cause of the disease is thought to be wrong vision, leading to wrong actions.

Rose Iqallijuq from Iglulik told Saladin d'Anglure (2001b, 133), "Even today, any one of us is capable of performing *qilaniq* even though we are not *angakkuit*, by lifting something using a thong." The technique could not be practised on a namesake, as was corroborated by Ujarak, Ava's son, with respect to a man named Arrak who used to practise *qilaniq*: "Even if one of his *avvait* (namesakes) were present, he never used them to perform *qilaniq*. This was probably because he considered them to be part of himself and thought that his *apiqsaq* [helping spirit] wouldn't go to them."[13] Clearly the *qilajuq* (the one who holds the stick in the *qilaniq* ritual) and the *qilajaq* (the one who is lying down in the *qilaniq* ritual) should not be too close. This was also expressed in clothing symbolism. Ujarak said that his mother, Orulo, always used the caribou socks of her husband or her son, never the head or clothing of the patient.[14] Rasmussen (1929, 141–3) recorded one case of *qilaniq* in considerable detail:

The object was to ascertain the cause of a particular illness. The *qilajəq* sat down beside the *qila·ŋa* and uttered the following words, tugging all the time at the strap, which was fastened to the head: "*kivfaqat·a·rta·rlaŋa, kivfaqat·a·rta·rlaŋa, kivfaqat·a·rta·la·rlaŋa. taiga kivfaqat·a·ri^{w}agit!*": "Let me try to lift your head a little. Let me try to lift your head a little. Let me try to lift your head. Now I am lifting your head."

The head becomes heavy, the *qilajəq* cannot lift it, the spirit is present, and the *qilajəq* says: "*taiga tagvun·arputit aŋerʃu·ta·nik un·ernialerputit*": "Now you have arrived. Tell us now what is the cause of the patient's sufferings."

Then again: "*tau^{w}iniuʃutit?*": "Are you a spirit that was once a human being?"

The head becomes heavy, the spirit answers: yes."

The *qilajəq* asks again: "*aipatiminik*?" This is shaman language, and means: "Is the illness due to forbidden food?"

The head grows lighter, the shaman lifts it with ease, and the listeners answer: "*a·k·agəq*": "No!"

"*isarajaŋnik*?": "Is the illness due the forbidden work?"

The spirit answers: "Yes!"

The next question is: "Is it because he has been working with iron?"

The spirit answers: "Yes!"

The patient must now himself state on what occasion he has committed a breach of taboo by working with iron. As soon as he has confessed, all present must lift up their hands and say: "*taiva·luk*": "Let it be; away with it."

Again the *qilajəq* asks: "*aipatiminik*?": "Has he worked with iron at a time when he was on a certain diet?"

The spirit answers: "Yes!"

The *qilajəq* asks: "*kaŋerzugʃamik*?": "Has he worked with iron at a time when he had also eaten the heads of animals killed?"

The spirit answers: "Yes!"

People in the house cry aloud: "*taiva·luk, taiva·luk*!": "Away with it! Let it be!"

If there is any suspicion that a woman with a newly born child has patched her clothing immediately after the capture of a bearded seal, or, in the case of a man, if it be suspected that his wife has patched or used her needle to his footgear while she was unclean, the question put is: "*aŋ·nərsaŋnik*?": "Is it clothing?"

Should the spirit answer "yes," then it remains to investigate further, with constant pulls at the line, what breach of taboo has taken place and under what circumstances. So the questioning goes on, letting the spirit answer all the time, until the presumable cause of the sickness has been ascertained.

When the *qilavəq* is at an end, the *qilajəq* who has interrogated the spirits lifts up the qilaˑŋa and says: "*kaxatˑiŋˑilagit, akaˑjəq kisiat*!": "I have done this not in order to hurt your head, but only for good."

According to Rasmussen, *qilaniq* was practised not only by *angakkuit*, but also by other people, especially women. In Rasmussen's account, the *qilajuq* first addresses the patient, announcing that he is going to lift the patient's head. When the head becomes heavy, it is a sign that the *apiqsaq* (helping spirit) has arrived. Then he asks the *apiqsaq* to reveal the cause of the disease, but before the healing can proceed, the *apiqsaq* has to be identified. As the *apiqsaq* can only respond by affirming or denying a question, the *qilajuq* has to frame the question in such a way that the spirit can respond. The *qilajuq* should be able to pose the right questions in the language of the *tuurngait,* and the helping spirit is identified as a deceased person. Apparently this is sufficient identification, and the *qilajuq* can proceed to ask questions relating to the cause of the illness. In Rasmussen's description, the role of other participants is limited. They respond to the revelations of the *apiqsaq* by exclaiming, "Away with it! Let it be!"

The structure of the session very much corresponds to the healing session recorded by Jacob Olsen (discussed in chapter 8),[15] although it was not a *qilaniq* session. The *angakkuq* walked up and down posing questions to the patient, and the questions were answered sometimes by the patient and sometimes by the audience. The audience repeatedly asked that the patient be released from her offences. The *angakkuq* was able to see the transgressions through his *qaumaniq,* whereas the *qilajuq* had to rely on the helping spirit for confirmation of his suggestions.

Rasmussen (1931, 295) provides some additional information on *qilaniq* among the Nattilingmiut: "The other method of getting into touch with one's apErʃat is the so-called qilanEq, which means that 'something happens by means of tying something fast.' It is just the same as the Iglulingmiut method. The shaman ties a line to one of his own legs or the head or leg of another; then he jerks the line to the continuous accompaniment of a monotonous repetition of: 'qilaⁱka nauk: where are those (spirits) I must bind fast to me?'"

An extensive description of the Nattilik *qilaniq* tradition, providing much information on the actions and objects used, was recorded by Father Van de Velde, who collected his information at Kugaaruk on 1 June 1957.[16] He explained that the technique was used in cases of illness, scarcity of game, and other difficult situations. The questions were asked in the language of the *tuurngait,* and the *tuurngaq* answered through signs (the object being lifted becoming heavy or light): "Everybody knew that Iksivalitaq was a sorcerer and that his protective spirit was 'Kanayok,' this demon Kanayok was thus his guardian spirit. He invoked him to get his help. Not only sorcerers had those protective spirits; everyone had them, but of varying quality and strength. From the Christian point of view, the *apirsait* could easily be replaced by our guardian angels. One day, an Eskimo told me *Inungnut ikajoteoyut, apersaoyut* (For Eskimos, they are guardians or *apirsait*)."[17]

Van de Velde describes the positions of the participants in some detail: "The Eskimo who wishes to have an answer to his questions lies down on the Eskimo platform (*iglerk*); he pulls down his hood and lies on his back with his feet turned to the rear of the igloo. The one in charge sits on the right side of the person lying down. He takes his mitten and covers that person's head so that the whole head is now completely covered. Then he makes a knot in a thong (made of the skin of an *ujuk*, bearded seal) tied around the head of the person lying down."[18]

Van de Velde points out that the *qilajaq* lies with his feet towards the back of the house. The *qilajuq* sits on his right side with his feet pointed to the entrance. Then the *qilajuq* pulls the thong with his two hands. He and the people attending remain silent until the head becomes heavy. Then they say, "*Okremangertok*"[19] ("it becomes heavy"). Then they start questioning the spirit. The *qilajuq*, the other people attending, and even the *qilajaq* can participate. The *qilajuq* continues to pull the thong, and if the head is heavy, the answer is affirmative.

> *Apersa?* Spirit (vocative)?
> *Unnerniarputit (okraniarputit)?* You will speak, won't you?
> *Tagva nalungilatit?* Therefore you will not deny us the knowledge we need?
> *Pidjutani nalungilatit?* Do you know what the issue is?
> *Taovinermik pipkrajaugam?* Did a deceased Eskimo do this to him?
> *Issarotararsluni?* Is it a man?
> *Saniliangoluni, issarotakrarani?* A woman sleeping beside her man?[20]

When the head is heavy, they say, "*nellautauyok*" (roughly, "he remains flat on the ground"); the *qilajuq* then has his answer, because the head is heavy (*okremangertok*). In this way, he can determine the reason for the problem – for example, the transgression of a rule or an action that is prohibited during menstruation. It sometimes happened that a person would not admit his transgressions out of shame. Then people would not believe him and would consider him a liar. If the head did not become heavy (*okremangertok*), they would say, "*kiongitok, nellautaungitok*." After the séance they blew on the spot where he had lain. Van de Velde notes that "sorcerers claim that to conquer a soul they only had to blow on it."[21] Thus, when the séance was finished and the patient had stood up again, the *qilajuq* would blow on the spot where he had lain.

Ujarak from Iglulik recalled seeing Arraq conduct a *qilaniq* performance in which he had lifted his own leg:

> My father and mother had gone to Naujaat shortly after the ice had frozen. Quite a while had passed and they still hadn't returned. Arraq began to get worried about them. Apparently, he thought that it was taking them too long to come back. One evening, when we had finished all our chores, he

decided to perform *qilaniq* using his leg to determine whether they were alright or not. The family I was staying with consisted of Arraq, his wife, his mother Nattiq, my brother Nataaq and I. Arraq decided to ask a helper to find out if anything was the matter with Ava and his wife. He tied up one of his legs and waited for his helper, which he called his *apiqsaq*, to come. He said when his *apiqsaq* came to his leg it would become heavy. When it became heavy he started asking whether or not the travellers were in danger. His leg would become very light when he would ask if they were in danger. When he ascertained that they were not in danger, he asked it when they would return. When he found out they would be coming back soon, and that they were not in any danger, then he concluded his *qilaniq*. He asked numerous questions to ascertain this information …

He tied the thong around the leg the same way he would have tied it around the head. Because he was wearing *kamiik* he didn't have to wear any padding as he would have done if it had been around the head. He used a short thong. He tried to have his leg totally relaxed. At times it would be very hard to lift and at other times it would be very light. Arraq would quite often perform *qilaniq* on the sleeping platform using his leg. When he was finished the *qilaniq*, he would untie the thong. Then he would shake his leg to get it back into shape and he would say, "*tauva*." I have never known him to use another person when performing *qilaniq*, only his leg.[22]

Qilaniq Session in Kangiq&iniq, 2000

In a workshop on Inuit Qaujimajatuqangit in Kangiq&iniq in 2000, Levi Iluittuq from Kugaaruk could only participate in the first half of the workshop, as he was on his way to Yellowknife to be treated in the hospital. He was worried about the condition of his hand, and after hearing the elders discuss *qilaniq*, he asked to have it performed on him. The elders agreed, although Mariano Aupilaarjuk from Kangiq&iniq made it clear that he would not participate himself: "The reason why I am not going to try to *qilajuq* is because I officiate in the church. That is the reason why I will not do it. I have seen it. I would recognize it being done. I am not going to do it, because I am not able to do it. I believe in it. I will not do it, but I am in agreement with it being done."

The *qilaniq* ritual for Iluittuq was conducted in the cabin Ollie Itinnuaq had prepared for the workshop, and it was recorded on both audiotape and videotape. Iluittuq lay down with his head towards the entrance and his face covered by a mitten. Luke Nuliajuk from Uqsuqtuuq acted as *qilajuq*. He tied a rope in a knot around the head and started to pull. The other elders were seated around Iluittuq and participated actively in the session. The following quotations are taken from the translation by Alexina Kublu of the video recording of the *qilaniq* session:

ITINNUAQ: We need an *apiqsaq*. You are the *apiqsaq* indicated to us, I wonder what it is.

PISUK: Maybe it is from me instead.

ITINNUAQ: It or she should be a good *qilaniq*. It should come from the *irq&uqquaq* direction (the path of the sun). It should be someone who is good with the *qilaniq*. I wonder what it is. I wonder where it is coming from, maybe it is coming from this person who is down, lying down there.

NULIAJUK: The head is very light.

PISUK: Maybe it is coming from me.

NULIAJUK: It is very easy to lift.

ITINNUAQ: I wonder what it is. It is very hard to find out. Maybe it is from the one who is being helped. When we can tell or show what it is it should let us know. Ask questions so we can find out where it is from.

PISUK: Maybe it is because I am the cause of discomfort to it.

ITINNUAQ: Maybe it is me that causes this discomfort.

ANGUTINNGURNIQ: Maybe it is from the one who is being helped that causes this discomfort.

ITINNUAQ: I wonder what it is. Maybe the one who is being helped, the one who is lying on the floor knows what it is?

In the first stage, the elders inquire about the cause of the problem. They suggest that they themselves may be responsible, evoking the healing session described by Olsen where Angutingmarik raised the same question with respect to his own role.[23] In the meantime, Nuliajuk keeps them informed about Iluittuq's head not being heavy.

ITINNUAQ: Maybe it is a dead person? I wonder what dead person it is. It is very hard to know. Maybe it is in the direction of the person who is down there. I wonder what it is. Maybe it was a grandchild. Maybe the dead person was a woman? Although I know how to ask questions I don't know what the cause is. This person might know because I don't know. I don't know what would be the possible *apiqsaq* of this person who is lying down. Maybe the person who is lying on the floor made the *apiqsaq* displeased? It is very hard to know …

ANGUTINNGURNIQ: Maybe it is the *atiq* (the name of the person). Maybe the cause is the *atiq* of the person who is lying on the floor?

ITINNUAQ: Iluittuq, if you have any idea of what it might be, let us know, tell us what.

ILUITTUQ: I have no idea what it could possibly be.

Itinnuaq indicates that even though he knows how to ask questions he cannot ascertain the cause. He suggests that the *apiqsaq* that has to make the head heavy is connected to Iluittuq, who is lying down. Jose Angutinngurniq from Kugaaruk suggests that a namesake relationship may be involved. Finally Itinnuaq addresses Iluittuq directly, but he cannot answer his question. Nuliajuk emphasizes that Iluittuq should not feel embarrassed about anything he has to bring out:

> NULIAJUK: There is no cause of embarrassment about any of this.
> ILUITTUQ: If I were to have done anything sinful, I would not hesitate to tell about it.
> AUPILAARJUK: Maybe it is because the person who is trying to be lifted had displeased the one that is to be the helper.

As Iluittuq is not coming up with any confession, Itinnuaq invites Peter Suvaksiuq from Arviat to take over the rope from Nuliajuk. Suvaksiuq feels the heaviness of the head, and some other participants do the same. In the meantime, suggestions continue to be made. Itinnuaq suggests that Iluittuq may have hurt someone. Pujuat Tapaqti from Kangiq&iniq proposes, "Maybe this person had had his clothes worn by someone who was not supposed to wear his clothing? Because that too could be a cause, a reason." Then one of the participants accidentally steps over the body of Iluittuq, and as a consequence the *apiqsaq* leaves and the head becomes light. Itinnuaq says, "The moment that someone went over them, over it, it went away right away. One is not supposed to go over the body ... you are supposed to go around the person." The session then focuses again on Iluittuq's problem. As the elders try to determine the cause of Iluittuq's problem, they raise the question of his passivity during the session and stimulate him to explore the causes of his discomfort himself:

> ITINNUAQ: Also, maybe if we had managed to find [it]. If we manage to hit upon the cause what the reason is. It is also much more difficult when Iluittuq himself is not saying anything.
> ANGUTINNGURNIQ: Yes it is much more difficult in that case for he, too, is supposed to ask questions to himself because he himself might know what the cause is. Yes, because in the past they used to ask questions to the *apiqsaq* themselves. That is the way they used to do it.

Angutinngurniq now directly addresses Iluittuq, who can no longer remain silent:

> ANGUTINNGURNIQ: Is there anything you are embarrassed about?
> ILUITTUQ: I have done things I have been embarrassed about.
> ANGUTINNGURNIQ: One is not supposed to be embarrassed about these things.
> ITINNUAQ: It is much better if what the cause [is] is dealt with so it can become part of the past.

Pisuk suggests Iluittuq's problem may be related to contacts with women, and Iluittuq acknowledges that this may be the case.

ILUITTUQ: That might be the cause. I have touched women I was not supposed to.

NULIAJUK: If you had been born into the time of our ancestors this would not have been embarrassing. We were not supposed to be embarrassed with these things.

The elders clearly are not convinced that this is the real cause of Iluittuq's trouble:

PISUK: Those that have strong power of *qilaniq* are able at times to even see what the cause is. It is very hard to know what the cause is. It is hard to know. We don't know.

ANGUTINNGURNIQ: Had he touched women that he was not supposed to touch? I wonder what the reason is. It is very difficult to know.

ITINNUAQ: It is extremely difficult to know.

ANGUTINNGURNIQ: It is because he has something he is embarrassed about that he does not want to disclose. That is the way it is.

Even though the session did not fully succeed in clarifying the cause of Iluittuq's damaged hand, the elders were quite happy with the demonstration. The session and the exchanges showed the strong commitment of the participants to the well-being and health of the one for whose benefit the ritual was performed. The elders believed that a health problem could be the result of past actions. After this demonstration of a *qilaniq* session, a series of other demonstrations followed. Various elders took turns either as *qilajuq* or *qilajaq*. Suvaksiuq in particular enjoyed the practice, for he succeeded in making the head of Angutinngurniq heavy, not an easy task, as Angutinngurniq explained: "I have had people experienced in performing *qilaniq* try to use me but I have never become heavy. The *tuurngait* are squeamish about me, even the ones that are not evil. This is the first time that I have ever become heavy, when Suvaksiuq used me to perform *qilaniq*. Those who have the capability of finding out the cause of sickness easily are *qilagiktut*. I feel that Suvaksiuq is *qilagiktuq*. Even though he was pulling hard, I could not feel the rope. This is the first time I have ever become heavy so I consider him to be *qilagiktuq*. Others have tried in the past but have not managed to make me reach heaviness."

Suvaksiuq responded to this acknowledgment of his ability by promising to give Angutinngurniq a small gift in acknowledgment: "Yesterday I thought if we did this, I would give someone a brand new pen. I did not voice this but I thought about it. I thought whoever reaches heaviness is the person I am going to give the pen to. I hadn't voiced that thought, but I am telling you about it in retrospect. I am going to go get a pen for Angutinngurniq when the store opens."[24]

Qilaniq Session in Arviat

In a workshop in Arviat in 2003, the Ahiarmiut technique of *qilaniq* was discussed and demonstrated. The Ahiarmiut practised *qilaniq* with a stick, as described in Rasmussen 1930 (61):

> Besides ordinary shamanizing, these people also know the usual qilaneq, only here they use a special qidlaut staff, an ordinary stick to which the shaman belt is tied. A piece of skin is then laid over the shaman belt itself, and the spirit comes up in the usual manner through the ground. When a spirit, for instance qaluheraut, was to be summoned, the charm for this form of qilaneq was: "qaijiniarmata qaijijuarartut qaluheraut qaut: you must now enlighten these people who wish to know what is hidden; come here, qaluheraut, come." This was repeated time after time until the staff became so heavy that one could no longer lift either it or the shaman belt, quite in the same manner as a qilaneq proceeds by lifting another person's head with a thong. As soon as the shaman staff becomes heavy, it means that the spirit is present and its advice may then be asked.

Eva Muqyunniq from Arviat recalled the *qilaut* (the staff) of her grandfather Aklaujuat:

> I've seen a *qilaut* too. Aklaujuat was my grandfather. He had a stick. There were all kinds of objects tied to this stick like pieces of weasel skin. If you could move this *qilaut*, this object, then you were not going to get well, but if it stuck to ground or wherever you placed it you would get well. If it didn't work you would not get well. If it worked, then you would get well. This was about *qilaut*. If it worked, it was like using medicine. You could make your body well. I used it myself. I know how it works. I remember how it works. It is not scary. We can play around with it. We can test it. The owner of that stick was not scary at all. He was very open to other people. We were not afraid of him at all because he was very open to us. We could play with that stick. Whenever a serious matter came up, like when someone was sick, they could use that *qilaut*. It really worked too. You could try with all your strength but it wouldn't move, not even one inch. A lot of us have seen this. It wouldn't move at all. We are here. We can see each other. We have seen people performing this. I have seen Aklaujuaq's performing this. When he died, we should have put it in his grave. It is still up there even though the owner has died. The question was about *qilaut*.

> We don't use it, but it is a story for others to hear. It is a wonder. There is awe in it.

Her husband, Job Muqyunniq, remembered that as children they used to play with Aklaujuaq's stick: "In Qamutalik just outside Arviat I've seen this. I've used it. Children used it and played with [it] whenever the children went out by skidoo or Honda. We, too, as children used to play with Aklaujuaq's *qilaut*. We were allowed to play with it. It was right there in the open for the children to play with and test it. When the children couldn't move it, they would just leave it out there."

Luke Anautalik from Arviat received a *qilaut* from Aklaujuaq:

> *Qilaut* was the weakest thing an *angakkuq* could use. It had the least power. I had a *qilaut* from Aklaujuaq. I was one of the people he gave a *qilaut* to. I received one. It was not very strong. You could just sit and practice it without really moving. The questions would come from around us. Only people who would be asking questions would be there. There would be simple questions and the answers you are seeking would be right there. You could ask if you would have good health or you were getting well. Sometimes it would not stick. I really don't understand this myself. Sometimes your questions would be answered with a "no." Maybe the question asked was not related to this. I don't know. When a question was answered with a "yes" it would stick. That is all I can tell you about this. The way I see it, it would start with *qilaut* and then other powers would be stronger and stronger. If you want to understand more, that's how it works, from the weakest and then they got stronger.

According to Eva Muqyunniq, people would tie something to the *qilaut:* "It was not decorated but people would tie things to it. This was the people's responsibility … You would give something to it, tie it around it." She said that the stick might also be covered with skin. Job Muqyunniq brought a *qilaut*, specially made for the occasion, to the Arviat workshop for a demonstration. It was about sixty centimetres long and three centimetres in diameter. It was decorated with strips of white and black caribou skin and red-coloured strips of paper. He placed the *qilaut* on a piece of caribou string on the table, pointing away from him. He grasped the stick with his left hand, which was close to his body, and then lifted or dropped it with his right. Thus, the left hand remained stable and the right hand applied force, just as in other *qilaniq* techniques.

Qilaniq Session in Kugaaruk, 2004

In 2004 elders demonstrated the technique of *qilaniq* in a meeting hall in the school in Kugaaruk. Specially constructed in the shape of an igloo, the hall was

Qilaut, staff for the divination practice of *qilaniq*, made by Job and Eva Muqyunniq for a demonstration of *qilaniq* performed by the Ahiarmiut. Fringes of *pukiq* (white caribou) are attached to the staff. Photograph by F. Laugrand.

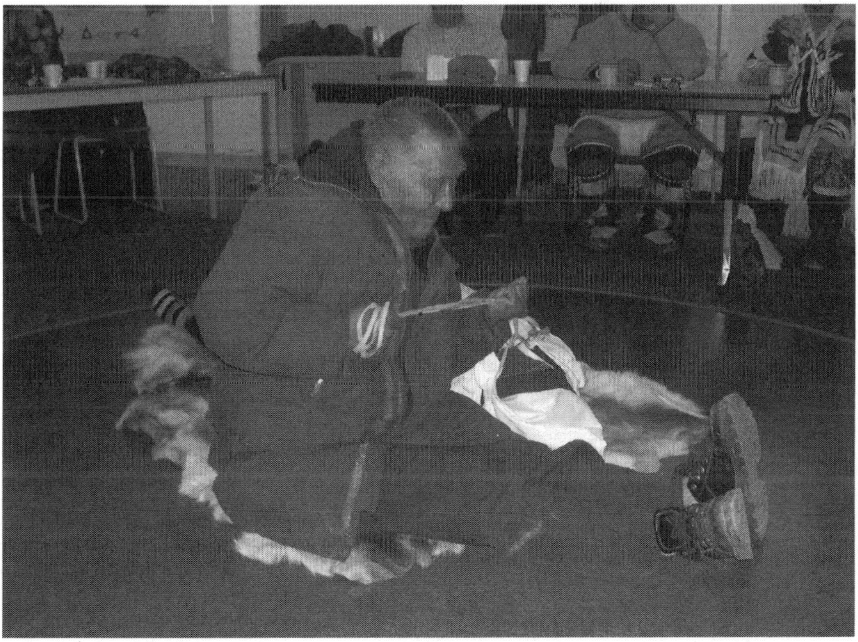

Luke Nuliajuk performing *qilaniq* in Kugaaruk, 2004. Photograph by C. Remie.

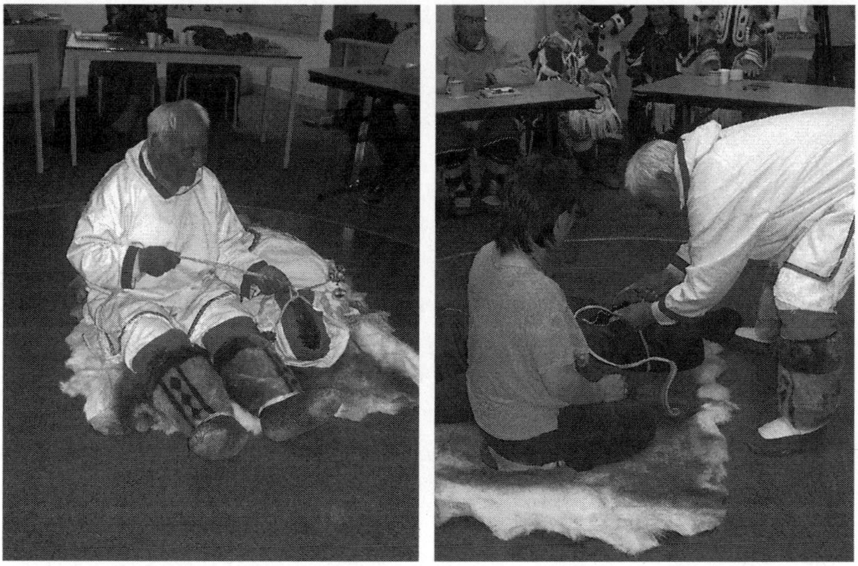

(left) Jose Angutinngurniq performing *qilaniq* in Kugaaruk, 2004; (right) Jose Angutinngurniq teaching a young woman how to perform *qilaniq* in the school of Kugaaruuk, 2004. Photographs by C. Remie.

usually used for meetings with elders and instruction in traditional skills, as well as other purposes. For the demonstration, it was decided that the windows should be covered in order to create a more intimate and traditional setting, comparable to that of a large igloo.

In Kangiq&iniq the demonstration was done in a cabin out on the land with no witnesses present, and in Arviat it was conducted in the presence of two young women. In Kugaaruk, it was decided that younger people should be present. The elders decided to wear traditional clothing during the demonstration. Felix Kupak from Naujaat began by showing how *qilaniq* could be conducted with a snow beater inside a caribou parka. Then the more common technique of lifting the head of another person was shown. After the elders had finished, the younger people were allowed to practise the technique. The distinction between a demonstration and a healing ritual began to blur when the younger people discovered how effective the technique was and started to raise their own personal problems. The elders offered their comments and counselled them if they could. Finally two youngsters were given a chance, but they did not find it easy going until Angutinngurniq took over and the head of the *qilajaq* immediately became heavy.

Qilaniq was generally considered a weak technique that could be used by anyone. However, it still required the ability to invoke an *apiqsaq* and to understand the language of the *tuurngait*. The actual pulling of the head or object was done with a *qillati*, a thong or rope. A *tapsi* or *angaluk* (shamanic belt) made of *pukiq* (white fur of the belly of the caribou) was often used. Strips of skin were usually attached to it. The staff made in Arviat was decorated in a similar way.

DRUMS AND DRUM DANCING

The close relationship between games and rituals and play in Inuit society was clearly perceived by Thalbitzer (1926) with respect to Greenlandic games. The Inuktitut word for play, *pinnguartuq*, means "to pretend not to do something," "to pretend, to play, to make believe." A *pinnguaq* is a "child's toy," and a *pinngua-rusiq* is a "game." The notion of pretence is central to the idea of play, expressing its paradoxical nature: it does not just refer to "pretending" but more subtly to "pretending not to do something that one is actually doing."

In the Jordan lectures of 1995, Roberte Hamayon pointed out that many of the terms for shaman or for performing a shamanic séance are derived from roots that mean "to play." Thus, the Yakuts of North Siberia refer to the shaman as *oyuun*, a word derived from *oy-*, "to play." Hamayon gives many examples of words referring to shamanism and of their relation to play. She explains that many features of shamanic behaviour in Siberian societies can be seen as play. A shaman, for example, has to take an animal spirit wife and imitates the behaviour of a rutting male animal copulating with its mate (Hamayon 1995, 13). By representing an animal, the shaman involves it in a game, a game that the animal is bound to lose. As Hamayon has shown, play is at the heart of the shamanic complex.

In play, people can represent spirits, animals, or deceased namesakes. In chapter 3 ("Inuit Winter Feasts"), we saw how play was always a structural feature of these feasts. In play, people can represent non-human agencies and pretend they are only playing, but thereby resolve conflicts and tensions. Play is central to drumming, which fulfils these very functions.

Drum dances and song feasts were usually celebrated in a large snow house (*qaggiq*) in the winter season.[25] According to Noah Piugaattuk (IE 189), an elder from Iglulik, "When they were assured that the days ahead would now be able to provide them with their food, and the fact that they had survived the worst, especially the period when there was much want of food throughout the period of scarcity, they would start to hold *qaggi*. When there were times when hunting was essential more so than other times, they will withhold *qaggi* until much later in the spring. Today, about this time would be the time when the people were no longer apprehensive about the days to come, so there would be times when *qaggi* would be held periodically."[26]

George Kappianaq from Iglulik (IE 155) recalled that the *qaggiq* was usually held when hunters and their families came to a central location, for instance when they made camp on the ice when seal hunting. When people who had been inland hunting caribou the preceding summer arrived at a central location and started to hunt seals by *maulliq* (hunting seals at their breathing holes), they would hold *qaggiq*. This could be in January or even earlier. The location was usually a place on the ice where the hunters would have easier access to the hunting grounds.

Rasmussen (1929, 227–8) relates that feasts were only celebrated if there was an abundance of blubber and meat. A feasting house would be built or the community would assemble in the largest igloo: "Those taking part in a song festival are called qag·iʃut; the poem recited is called piseq, the melody of a song iᵛŋerut: and to sing is iᵛŋerta·rneq; the combination of song, words and dance is expressed by the word mumerneq: 'changing about'; having reference to the fact that as soon as the leading singer has finished, another comes forward; he sings: mumerpəq, plural mumertut. The chorus, which must always accompany the leading singer, who beats time with his drum while dancing, is called iŋiərtut: those who accompany in song."

According to Rasmussen (1929, 240), people celebrated the feast in a circle, with the men inside and the women outside. The women supported and accompanied their men, who played the drum. "Every wife must know her husband's songs, for the woman is supposed to be the man's memory. The mumertəq will therefore often content himself with flinging out a few lines of the text, while his wife leads the chorus. A woman thus conducting the performance of her husband's productions is called iwŋertəq: the chorus being termed iŋiərtut. A man without a wife, in other words, a singer with no one to take this important part, simply stands erect and sings his words."

The men would act as hosts of the feast. Rasmussen (1931, 241) reports that among the Nattilingmiut, "[o]n the evening when any man of the village gives a banquet and festival in the qag·e, the following cry is used to call the people together: 'qag·iava·, qag·iava·,' this is shouted about the place until all have heard." Usually the men and women dressed up in their best clothes. Rasmussen (1932, 130) describes an Umingmaktormiut feast: "Everything is done to make the event as festive as possible; both men and women deck themselves out in special garments that gleam brightly with all the pretty inlays of white belly-skin, let in as patterns. Over back and shoulders the men have skins of white ermines that stream like pennants during their movements, and great pains have been taken in embroidering the boots of men and women with red and white strips of skin. On their heads they wear helmets of skin strips sewn together, with the beak of a loon sticking up like a spike at the top."

In Iglulik, before the song festival began, the drum had to be carefully tuned up. "The skin, which is stretched on a wooden frame, sometimes quite round, sometimes oval in shape, is made from the hide of a caribou cow or calf with the hair removed. This is called ija·, the 'eye' of the drum, and must be moistened with water and well stretched before use. Only thus will it give the true, mysterious rumbling and thundering sound."[27]

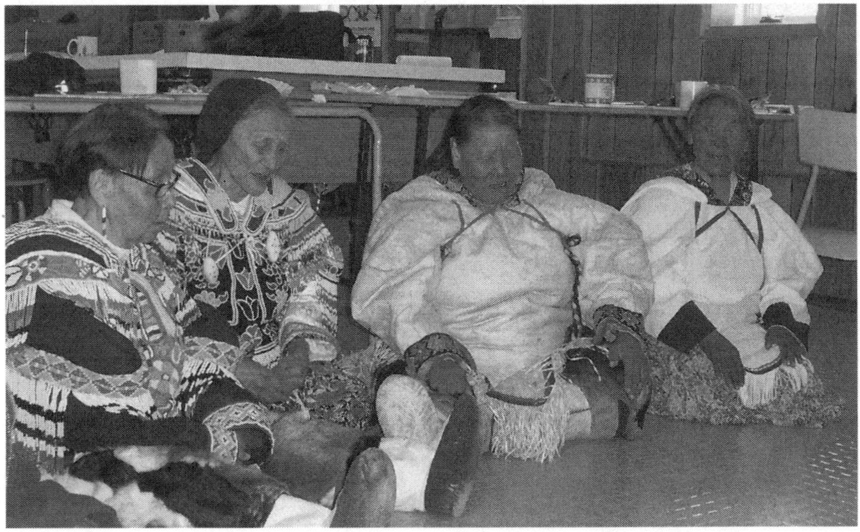

Elders Ilisapi Enowyak, Helen Konek, Margaret Hannah, and Martha Otokala Okutak singing at a drum dance in Arviat, 2006. Photograph by J. Oosten.

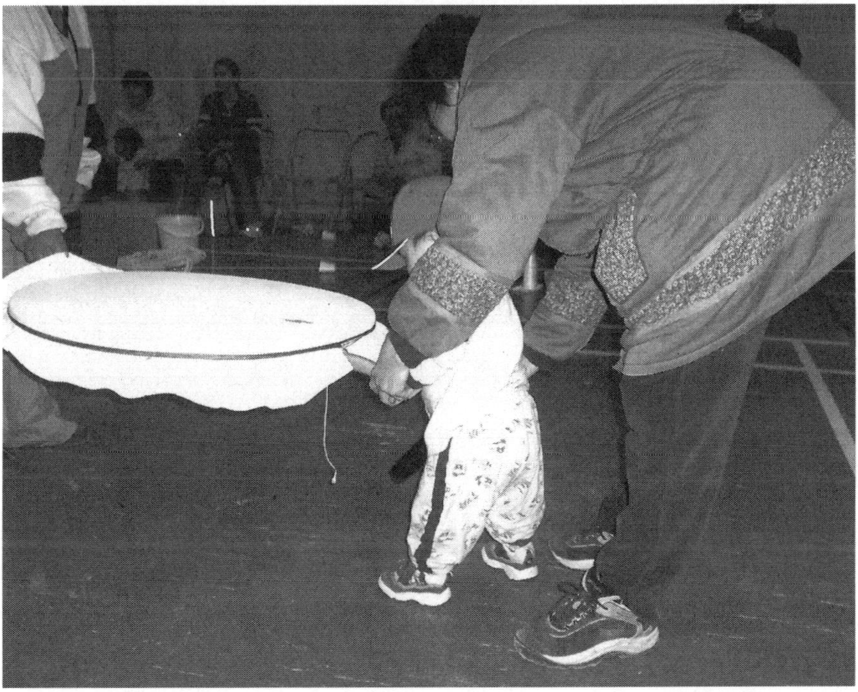

Inuk woman teaches drum dancing to her little boy in Kugaaruk, 2004. Photograph by J. Oosten.

Willie Niptayok drum dancing in Kugaaruk in the 1950s. Courtesy of Archives Deschâtelets.

Among the Umingmaktormiut, the drum had cosmological connotations:

> Sometimes a ring forms round the sun; it is called qilauta·: the drum of the sun; for it forms a figure round about the sun just like the drum used in the festival house. We do not quite know what this means; some believe that, simply because it resembles the drum we dance to, the sun drum is an omen of something pleasant that will happen.
>
> If it is not a ring, but only an arc that forms round the sun it is called nataineq, which is thought to mean a part of the wooden rim of the drum. This, then, means that somebody has died.[28]

Each person had his own personal style of drumming. Luke Arngna'naaq from Arviat discussed this feature: "Each has his own unique style of drum dancing movement. Why this is so, I cannot tell. Some don't do the knee-bending motion, they just stand still while they beat the drum. Some move around in a circle without ever uttering a sound. Some appear to struggle with the drum but eventually seem to overcome it while still in a drum dance procession … Some are so good in their motions that they move back and forth gracefully. Others run back and forth while some seem to jump from one place to another in successive moves."[29]

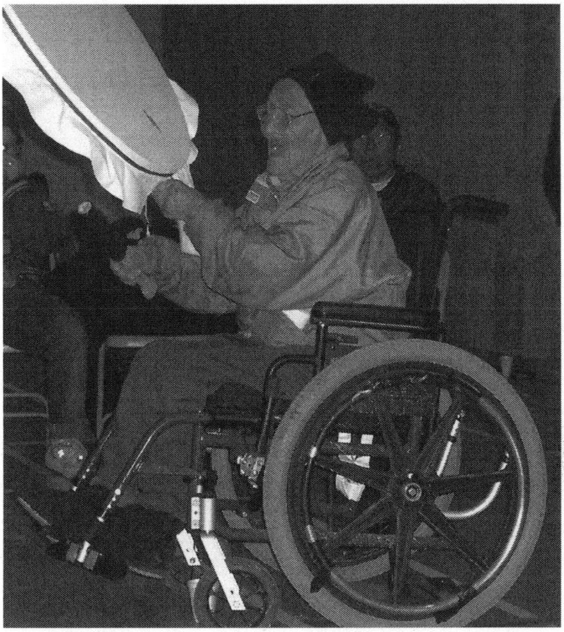

Niviuvaq, about a hundred years old, drum dancing in her wheelchair, 2004. She is one of the few women still living who has the traditional tattoos. Photograph by J. Oosten.

Rasmussen (1929, 230) describes the style of drumming among the Iglulingmiut: "The singer stands in the middle of the floor, with knees slightly bent, the upper part of the body bowed slightly forward, swaying from the hips, and rising and sinking from the knees with a rhythmic movement, keeping time throughout with his own beating of the drum. Then he begins to sing, keeping his eves shut all the time; for a singer and a poet must always look inward in thought, concentrating on his own emotion."

The closing of the eyes suggests that it is now the eye of the drum that matters. The vision generated by the drum now takes precedence over the individual vision. The skin of the drum, its eye, is never hit. According to Rasmussen (1929, 229–30), "There are very precise rules for the use of the *qilaut*. The skin of the drum itself is never struck, the edge of the wooden frame being beaten instead, with a short and rather thick stick. The drum is held in the left hand, by a short handle attached to the frame, and as it is fairly heavy, and has to be constantly moved to and fro, it requires not only skill, but also considerable muscular power, to keep this going sometimes for hours on end."

George Kappianaq from Iglulik (IE 190) also described the beating of the drum: "When striking the drum one should try to hit the rim opposite each other, one must not hold the handle too tightly, the beating of the drum is going to keep the drum in place. When you are holding the handle too tightly so that the drum is secured by your grip, you can get tired very easily. In those days the drums used to be bigger as the drum would have been used as a competing

Jose Angutinngurniq drum dancing in Kugaaruk, 2004. Photograph by F. Laugrand.

instrument, jovially. This would be the case between the '*avvariik*' [namesakes] or the '*illuriik* [song partners]' Each of these individuals must play the drum in competition." According to Ootooroot (Pallirmiut), a hierarchical order was followed: "The oldest man drums first, then the next oldest, and so on, with the young lads drumming last."[30]

It was necessary that the drum dance be completed. Donald Suluk from Arviat related, "Long ago, drum dancing was a very big part of the Inuit way of life. This is reflected by an extreme example: if a person died while dancing, others would take up the dance and continue until it ended; only then would mourning begin. The bereaved relatives of the dancer who had just died would be suffering, but they would continue dancing because that was the traditional law. If there weren't many relatives, others would help in the dance because the effort to be glad would always win out."[31]

According to Kleivan and Sonne (1985, 25), the drum was not part of the shamanic complex in Canada as it was in Greenland. In fact, we rarely find references to the drum. Boas (1901, 154), however, observes with respect to shamanic activities, "In these incantations a drum is used which is made of a large wooden hoop covered with deer-hide." Armand Tagoona from Kivalliq also connected the drum to shamanic performances: "Drum dancing … in the olden days was not just drum dancing. It always had something to do with the spirits. Oh yes, during the dance the dancer did it for fun and sang his own song or sang with

Felix Kupak from Naujaat drum dancing in Kugaaruk, 2004. Photograph by F. Laugrand.

others. But by doing this he was telling others through the song things he could not tell them just by talking. As long as he's moving around and hitting the drum and dancing on the snow floor his shyness cannot be seen, and usually the singers closed their eyes too. Most of the time, the dance took place because the *angakkuq* was going to do something for the good of the camp and for the Inuit in that camp."[32]

While *angakkuit* may have used the drum for some purposes, the ethnographic data suggest that the drum had special significance in the context of the feast. Here it allowed the drummer to connect to spirits, and this connection was strengthened by *pisiit* (songs), which could bring the drummer to a state of joy as he reached another dimension in time and space.

PISIIT, SONGS

According to Emile Imaruittuq from Iglulik, "There are three types of traditional songs, *pisiit*, *qilaujjarusiit*, which are *pisiit* sung with a drum, and *iviutiit*, which were used to embarrass people, to make fun of other people, to make fun of their weaknesses. They created songs to make fun of others. There are also *sakausiit*, used by *angakkuit*."[33]

Men and women and sometimes children would have their own songs, with appropriate melodies. Kappianaq (IE 155) related:

> Once they started to drum dance the snow in the *qaggi* would give from the heat created from the body heat. There would be a lot of people in the *qaggi*, in fact the whole surrounding at the floor level would have been made so that it could seat everyone. Once the dance started, only the women would sing to the dancer. They must sing the song that the dancer had composed; they will not sing a song that had been composed by someone else. The only time they could sing someone else's composition, which was rare, only if it was deemed that the dancer would borrow the composition and that the composer must not be present, he must be somewhere else. The composition would be sung by a woman who knew the song. The borrower of the song will dance to it.

In a song festival a man would not sing his own *pisiq*. He would be accompanied by his wife and would beat the drum while his wife or a group of women sang his *pisiq*. Men and women both had songs, but there was usually a division of tasks. Martha Tunnuq from Qamanittuaq related, "The men are the ones that make up their own songs. Their wives in turn would sing them. He would teach her how to sing the song after he makes it up. She would memorize it and remember it. This is the way we learn songs."[34]

According to Piugaattuk (IE 189), the women were in charge of the singing and decided which *pisiq* was to be sung:

> Yes, once the drummer had presented himself to the floor and grabbed hold of the *qilaut*, the women ... together will determine which song they will sing and who will lead in the singing ... So when the dancer had concluded his dance he will lay down the drum, at which time another dancer will present himself to the floor and take the drum.
>
> When that happens the women will discuss the *pisiq* among themselves and decide which one will lead on this particular *pisiq*. As soon as the leader sings out the rest of the woman will join in on the *pisiq*. It sounded really good when all of them sang in chorus, this is called; "ingiuttut." This term is used when they sing ayaa'ya to the drummer.

When the men were out on the land, the women could organize their own song feasts. According to Martha Paniaq (Arviligjuarmiut), "There have always been woman drum dancers. In the past when all the men would leave the camp to go hunting, sometimes all women would have a drum dance without men at all."[35] The songs and games of the women clearly represent an old tradition. Parry (1824, 2:538ff.) was reporting on them extensively early in the nineteenth century.

Rasmussen (1929, 231) reports that a person composing a song should "draw inspiration from the old spirit songs, which were the first songs mankind ever had; he must cry aloud to the empty air, shout incomprehensible, often meaningless words at the governing powers, yet withal words which are an attempt at a form of expression unlike that of everyday speech."

According to Mikitoq Bruce from Aivilik, "*Pihiit* were composed for others to hear. The lyrics told of the composer's accomplishments in life, especially those that deserved to be heard by other people. Some *pihiit* contained words that could help others to lead a better life. Some seemed to imply resentment to something and others seemed to portray a person's great abilities in many things. The lyrics were about all sorts of things because composers were free to develop songs of their choice that spoke of many things."[36]

Pisiit usually referred to personal experiences of the past. In a workshop in Churchill in 2008, Henri I&luarnik and Donald Uluakluak from Arviat said that *pisiit* would sometimes generate such strong emotions that the drummer would lose the drum beater if it was not properly carved. The songs were accompanied by a refrain – *aijaaja* – and thus are often referred to as *aijaaja* songs. Imaruittuq explained, "It is a way of expressing one's feelings and one's experiences. In the old days if they were longing to do something they would express themselves through *aijaaja* songs, either about wildlife or about experiences."[37]

The songs expressed the joy of the hunter on viewing the game animals. They were often based on inspiration received out on the land. The Nattilik *angakkuq* Orpingalik explained:

> Songs are thoughts, sung out with the breath when people are moved by great forces and ordinary speech no longer suffices. Man is moved just like the ice floe sailing here and there out in the current. His thoughts are driven by a flowing force when he feels joy, when he feels fear, when he feels sorrow. Thoughts can wash over him like a flood, making his breath come in gasps and his heart throb. Something, like an abatement in the weather, will keep him thawed up. And then it will happen that we, who always think we are small, will feel still smaller. And we will fear to use words. But it will happen that the words we need will come of themselves. When the words we want to use shoot up of themselves – we get a new song.[38]

Not only human beings had *pisiit*. Animals, too, had songs feasts and *pisiit*. Even *tuurngait* had *pisiit*. Peck collected several spirit songs on South Baffin.[39] Victor Tungilik from Naujaat said that one of his "*tuurngait* had a *pisiq*. The *pisiq* was talking about the reflection of a mirror":

> Me, myself
> He does not consider me as merely belonging among the shadows,
> I am happy.[40]

Thus, all beings – human beings, animals, and even *tuurngait* – had songs that could be sung in the feast house.

Many *pisiit* expressed values and feelings. Respect for animals, modesty, joy, and sadness were recurrent topics. A hunter would emphasize his shortcomings and his desire to be more successful at hunting, as in a *pisiq* by Imaruittuq:

> aajaa, as one of those hunting for food I envision myself
> aa, those that remain dear to me this is their land,
> how wonderful this looks, ijajaa
> ajajaa aijaa ajajaa ajajaajajaajaa
>
> aajaa, as one of those searching for a tent I envision myself
> aa, those that remain dear to me, this is their land,
> how wonderful this looks, ijajaa
> ajajaa aijaa ajajaa ajajaajajaajaa
>
> aajaa, that there are many polar bears to catch, I consider myself dirty
> aa, to be left behind, that there are many polar bears to catch,
> how wonderful this looks, ijajaa
> ajajaa aijaa ajajaa ajajaajajaajaa
>
> aajaa, as one of those searching for warmth I envision myself
> aa, that I continue to hold dear, that this tent is now experiencing summer,
> how wonderful this looks, ijajaa.[41]

People could also borrow the *pisiq* of another person. Donald Suluk explained, "The *pihiit* had rules to follow. For example, if you had not made up the *pihiq* you could not claim it for yourself. This was even more true if it was an old *pihiq* because everyone else had already learned it. But it was alright if you were just going to borrow it ... Children can dance to their father's *pihiq* if they don't have one themselves."[42]

People could allow other people to use their *pisiq*. Imaruittuq gave this example: "Piugaattuk's stepfather told his sons and stepsons to sing his *pisiq* when they were looking for tracks, so it would be easy for them to get an animal. The one named after Qaunaq, the one who passed away, used to go out caribou hunting and he started trying to sing his stepfather's song. He would practise this song when he was relaxing and he noticed it made a difference to his hunting."[43]

People could not only sing the *pisiit* of the ancestors, but also change them to suit themselves. Imaruittuq presented a song that had been changed by one of his relatives:

> Maniq was her name. She made changes to this song that I am going to sing. This is Maniq's song. Because there were made changes made to this *pisiq*. It is an *ikiaqtagaq*.[44]

Maniq's song, with her changes

aijaa ijajaajaajaa, let me sing slowly
let me sing slowly and search for a song
ijajaajaajaa

aijaa ijajaajaajaa, I have not acquired a song
I have not acquired a song because they have finished them on us
ijajaajaajaa

aijaa ijajaajaajaa, they have finished them on us
they have finished them on us, our ancestors of any song
ijajaajaajaa

aijaa ijajaajaajaa, removing incoming snow
are you removing snow from this that is becoming snow covered
ijajaajaajaa

aijaa ijajaajaajaa, I remember
I remember my difficulty in breathing
ijajaajaajaa

aijaa ijajaajaajaa, they have finished them on us
they have finished them on us, our ancestors of any song
ijajaajaajaa

aijaa ijajaajaajaa, it is about to come to an end
it is about to come to an end because they have no title
ijajaajaajaa

I'm just singing part of the song. There is a lot more to it and this is a revised song.[45]

Imaruittuq explained the meaning of the song,

In this song she said she was searching and searching for a song. She finally finds a song which she made changes to. Because she wanted to make changes to the song she asked the person who owned the song. He agreed. When she started to sing it, it had no title for our ancestors had used up all the titles. The part about having difficulty breathing had a lot of meaning to it. At that time there had been people buried in a blizzard. If they camped where a snowdrift was formed then they would be buried and so they were cautioned to be aware of what would be covered in a blizzard.

They were also told not to build an *iglu* under an *aluiqqaniq*, snow overhang. I have been told not to camp under an *aluiqqaniq* because it could be covered, and it is very difficult to breathe. The snow hole gets covered and you can't breathe. That is the meaning of the song.[46]

The ancestors have used up all the titles for *pisiit*. Descendants can only change and add. But through the *pisiit*, people still can pass on their experiences and knowledge to their descendants. By singing the songs of the ancestors, the descendants can keep their memory alive.

A special vocabulary was usually used in *pisiit*. Donald Suluk recalled that people's "hunting equipment and their other belongings had names in their songs and in their vocabulary. In song, a spear was called *tigumiaq*, but when speaking it was called *ipu*."[47] The words that were used might identify the singer. According to Luke Arngna'naaq from Arviat, "Traditional Inuit songs usually start off with compositional terms like *hammaijaa*, *pangmaijaa* or *ungmaijaa*. The term *hamma* implies the coastal area, while *pangma* refers to the inland area. The term *ungma* refers to something offshore while *ava* refers to something in the inland interior. The term *qangmaa* or *aninaa* implies that the *pihiq* is that of a woman who has five or more sons."[48]

Illuriik, Song Partners

Song feasts were hosted by men, but the men were not equally well positioned to act as host. Rasmussen (1929, 231) writes:

> Then again, every man who aspires to be considered one with any power of gathering his neighbours together must also have challenged some one else to a song contest … Two such opponents in song contests must be the very best of friends; they call themselves, indeed, iglurik, which means "song cousins," and must endeavour, not only in their verses but also in all manner of sport, each to outdo the other; when they meet, they must exchange costly gifts, here also endeavouring each to surpass the other in extravagant generosity. Song cousins regard themselves as so intimately associated that whenever they meet, they change wives for the duration of their stay. On first meeting after a prolonged absence, they must embrace and kiss each other by rubbing noses.
>
> Song cousins may very well expose each other in their respective songs, and thus deliver home truths, but it must always be done in a humorous form, and in words so chosen as to excite no feeling among the audience but that of merriment.

George Kappianaq (IE 190) explained that the partners in a song contest were called *avvariik* (namesakes) or *illuriik* (song partners). Namesakes were apparently well suited to act as each other's song partner in a song feast, and the term *illuriik* also refers to cross-cousins. Interestingly, in the *tivajuut* (winter feasts), the two masked men used this form of address when referring to each other. Competition and outdoing one's song partner were important features of the song feast. As Kappianaq related, the two opponents opened the song feast with a fist fight, and the one who lost would try to overcome the winner in drum dancing:

> It was by custom that the so called "cousins" (*illuriik*) would start the drum dancing, the two would try and outdo each other in anyway, possibly through fisticuffs to the shoulder or *irsattuutijuk*, so whichever loses out in this competition would try and get back at him through drum dancing. Once they had done this then the rest would start to participate in the drum dancing. That is what I have heard anyway. They first must *illuttulauqlutik*, that is to say that the two first must compete in the fisticuff, so one would give up before the other so he would submit to defeat in the fisticuff by not hitting back, then the one that had submitted will now try to get back at his opponent through the drum dance. Whichever can drum dance longer and by this he can show that he does not tire as easily therefore will be declared the winner of the competition.

Wife exchange marked the relationship between song partners, as Rasmussen (1931, 195) observes:

> Wife-exchanging for short periods often takes place, especially between men who are usually song-fellows at festivals in the qaχʃge. Husbands have almost always a certain man to whom they hand the drum when they have sung their song. 'l his man, who has to sing a song in reply, is called his iglua: his song-comrade or song-fellow. They say: "torlor&lugo iglormingnik tunivăk·ait: calling him his fellow he gives it him" (the drum). Two such men who usually follow one another at a song festival are considered to be so closely associated that not only after the ceremony but at all times when they feel inclined, they can exchange wives.

Wives were obliged to cooperate in these exchanges between *illuriik*. Rasmussen (1931, 196) relates a story he heard from the *angakkoq* Sâmik, who believed it would be contrary to the wishes of the spirits if the wives of *illuriik* refused to participate in the exchange.

> Two men, Oqortoq and Tinaoq, had one evening agreed to exchange wives. When night came and they were to retire to rest they each bade his wife to go to the tent of the man whose wife he awaited. But then the strange thing happened that both women, whose names were Arnangussaq and Tinôreq, declared that they would not sleep with any other than their

own husbands. Nevertheless the husbands compelled them to go out, but neither of them would go into the other tent; they remained standing outside. Then suddenly a spirit came over them, the spirit that is called Ivigtarssuaq, "the big bee." Ordinarily it is only a common bee; but when its anger is aroused it can turn into any form, become big and dangerous and frightful. In this case it came over these two disobedient women as an enormous and shapeless figure. Arnangussaq at once fell swooning outside the tent she should have been in, whereas Tinôreq fled out into the dark night. With great difficulty Arnangussaq was called to life again, after which they started to look for Tinôreq. At length she was found by Oqortoq, for he was a shaman. She lay like one dead, stretched out on the ground and chilled through and through, and her heart beat so faintly that it could scarcely be heard. She [He][49] succeeded in bringing her to life again.

So great can the anger of the spirits be when women refuse to do their duty. And it is said that after that these two women willingly lay with others whenever their husbands required them to do so.

The word *illuriik,* a dual form derived from *illuq,* refers to a cross-cousin or joking partner. Namesakes and cross-cousins were especially suitable song partners, but the term probably referred to any song partner with whom one exchanged wives. The exchange might take place in the context of ritual as well as in daily life.[50]

To what extent *illuriik* relationships connected different camps is not clear. As camps were constituted on the basis of close agnatic relationships, one might expect that cross-cousins would generally be members of different camps. Therefore, *illuriik* relations might have served to organize the relations between camps in a framework of exchange and competition. Joking relationships, rivalry, and competition were carefully balanced in the song feasts. Rasmussen contrasts the gentle exchanges between *illuriiik* with the quite harsh encounters between enemies in a song context. But both exchanges were fraught with danger. Ridiculing an opponent in public was not a thing to be taken lightly. The relationships involved were always ambiguous. In the context of a contest between cross-cousins or song partners with whom one exchanged wives, sexual and marital relationships came into play. In the case of namesakes, a shared identity was at stake, and in the case of enemies, peaceful social relations and finally life itself were threatened. The contests between song partners might involve the whole community.[51]

It was important for a man to learn to perform well in a song feast. Rasmussen (1929, 176) describes a ritual a mother could perform to ensure her son's success in song contests: "A mother who has a son must boil the head of a dog, and then pretend that the dog's head is the child's igloq or 'song-cousin,' that is, the man one likes most of all to sing with, or have as partner in athletic sports, compete with and sometimes sing abusive songs about. The mother must then let the child's little hands strike the head of the dog, pretending that the dog's head represents the song-cousin's head. This is supposed to give the boy 'a hard head against fisticuffs.' Afterwards, the mother herself eats the dog's head."

Songs intended to embarrass an opponent were called *iviutiit.* Imaruittuq from Iglulik explains the meaning of *iviq*: "It is singing about another person in an attempt to embarrass them. They would sing about a person's life and use that to ridicule them. Basically making fun of a person, trying to embarrass them."[52] Today's elders point out the negative connotations of songs intended to embarrass other people. Tungilik from Naujaat stated, "There are songs that are sung for joy, and songs that are not joyful. The kind of songs that are sung for joy are the ones that are danced to with a drum. I don't consider the ones that are sung against someone else as songs of joy. They were meant to hurt."[53]

In the past, people enjoyed these song contests. The elderly Aivilingmiutaq Ivaluardjuk recalled, "When I was young, every day was as a beginning of some new thing, and every evening ended with the glow of the next day's dawn. Now, I have only the old stories and songs to fall back upon, the songs that I sang myself in the days when I delighted to challenge my comrades to a song-contest in the feasting house."[54]

There are stories about people who enjoyed the contests so much that they left their children unattended in their houses, at risk of being killed or captured by spirits. Rasmussen (1929, 217) reports, "There are spirits which take care that human beings shall not become too devoted to songs and festivals; they also dislike to hear children making too much noise out in the open or in the houses when alone without adults." In one story, a spirit, using a live bearded seal as a whip, killed all the children in a settlement while the parents were in a feast house, but then the parents avenged themselves upon him. Similarly, a Nattilik story relates how the cannibal woman Amajorsuk stole a child while the parents were in the feasting house.[55]

In a song duel, the two opponents took the drum in turn, the one handing it to the other. First one man was given the opportunity to sing his song, supported by his family, then his opponent. Rasmussen gives many examples of these songs. Just as with the text of *pisiit,* the interpretation of these songs usually requires knowledge of their context. The songs would often refer to events obliquely, and the singer might limit himself to allusions that would only be obvious to those who are familiar with the events.

The song duel has sometimes been interpreted as being a legal procedure to solve a conflict between parties. However, the song duel allowed both adversaries to present their points of view, and there was no authority to decide the outcome. Thus, the adherents of both parties might feel that they had gained the upper hand. The central issue was not so much that a decision had to be made about who was right and who was wrong, but rather that the parties could express their grievances against, as well as their aggressiveness towards, each other so that these could become part of the past. In this respect, the song duel was much closer to confession, to *aniartuq* (to bring a thing out in the open), than to a legal procedure. The purpose of the song feasts and song duels was not to determine who was right or wrong, guilty or not guilty, but to ensure that conflicts were resolved.

By singing songs, the participants could not only address their opponent and the audience, but also their ancestors, notably the namesakes, as well as the spirits and animals that observe human behaviour. A story collected by Rasmussen (1929, 103–4) from Inugpasugjuk (originally a Nattilingmiutaq) shows that the deceased could be actively involved in a song festival. As the story goes, a man named Sereraut killed his companion when they were out hunting for seal because he wanted to have his wife. After killing him, Sereraut sent the body to the bottom of the sea with the seal his victim had caught. He did not marry the widow, however, who lived on in great poverty with her mother. The next winter, during a song festival, Sereraut saw the man he had killed together with the bearded seal, "shooting up through the floor and bearing in his body the harpoon head and line with which Sereraut had harpooned him. And now he, whom all knew to be dead, stood there and cried aloud: 'Sereraut killed me, tied me to a bearded seal I had caught, and sent me to the bottom of the sea.'" Then he disappeared, but after a moment's pause he returned with the same message. He returned for a third time and vanished again, but this time Sereraut himself disappeared through the same hole in the floor, suffering the same fate as his companion. Then the man whom Sereraut had killed came into the feasting house, but this time the line that had pulled him to the bottom of the sea was no longer fastened to his body. When his mother heard what had happened, she said, "This magic was spoken over my son, that he shall return to life if he dies." The young hunter returned to life and to his village, but Sereraut disappeared forever. He had kept his misdeed a secret and therefore could not come to life again. In this narrative, the crime of Sereraut was made public by his victim in the feast house and retaliation took place on the spot. This suggests that even conflicts between the living and the deceased might be resolved in the feast house.

THE DYNAMICS OF CHANGE

The drum appears to have been an instrument that could be used by everyone, men and women, to connect to the ancestors, spirits, and animals. The missionaries tended to associate the drum with the shamanic complex and tried to suppress its use, and as a consequence much of the knowledge of drumming techniques and of the *pisiit* involved has been lost.

Noah Piugaattuk (IE 189) observed, "As for my younger brother he was born almost at the same time when we were introduced to Christianity, so all of the traditional form of entertainment, in particular the drum dances, were discouraged as a result, these kinds of entertainment were no longer practiced, on account of that I would have to say that, to get him to help out in these traditional songs, I think it would be a waste of time to ask him to sing some of the traditional songs."

Especially on Baffin Island the tradition of drum dancing declined rapidly, while in the Iglulik area and particularly in the Kivalliq and Nattilik areas, it was retained much longer. Rachel Uyarasuk, who was born in the Kangigtugaapik area and later moved to the Iglulik area, recalled:

> When I was a small child, there was no *qillaujjarniq* [drum dancing]. It was only when I went to the Iglulingmiut area that I saw people drum dancing. While we were over there, when we got religion, we were told that whether they were *angakkuq*'s chants, or drumming, or singing *pisiit,* they were no longer to be practiced. It was when I became old enough to go visiting that I heard a person singing a *pisiq*. It would come into my head that my parents never sang that kind of song. It was when I would go visiting, that I would hear it. When my parents seemed to be asleep and I was old enough to go visiting on my own I would hear the song. At first, I would sing it in my head. Then, I would quietly start singing. My father would tell me we were not to sing those songs any more. These songs belonged to those who were not religious. Now that we had religion, we were not to sing those songs any more. I became quite embarrassed that time, and I stopped doing this. We did not *qilaujjaq* [drum dance] over there.[56]

The drum was gradually replaced by musical instruments newly introduced to the North (see Lutz 1978), and drum dancing was replaced by the square dancing introduced by the Scottish whalers. Rachel Uyarasuk recalled, "After we started celebrating Christmas, we started trying to learn how to dance. People would start practicing with the harmonica. Some people played the harmonica while others tried to dance. This was before any accordions were acquired. There were people who were able to play the harmonica, and around Christmas we would dance in an *iglu* to harmonica music. Of course we tried to use the largest *iglu*."[57]

Today, drum dancing has revived, especially in the Qitirmiut and Kivalliq regions, and many of the elders still posses the required skills. Modern drum dances are performed at celebratory occasions, often in community halls, gyms, or elders' centres. They are no longer connected to the song duels and wife exchanges of the past. The usual pattern is that a senior elder picks up the drum and a small group of women take care of the singing. We have seen many elders perform, and their performances are always impressive. A single dancer begins slowly, gradually building up a rhythm, until at the height of the dance he seems almost carried away by the music, expressing himself in short exclamations that have no meaning but seem to emerge from a great depth. Abe Okpik (2005, 230) writes of dancers who are especially skilled: "When Angutinngurniq drum dances, I think he goes into some kind of a trance; you could see it in his eyes."

But a man should never be lost in his song and the drum should be passed on. Everyone should have a chance to dance. The elder will put the drum on the floor and another elder will pick it up. Thus, each person will play the drum.

The drum appears to be an instrument that everyone should use, men and women, to connect to ancestors, spirits, and animals. Young people are taking up drum dancing, and at drum-dancing feasts even very young children are taught the techniques. Drumming provides a connection to the lifestyle of the *inummariit*, the true Inuit, and some young Inuit who have practised drum dancing said that they envisioned their ancestors watching them during the dance. Clearly, the drum dance seems to have retained or regained the crucial function of connecting people and ancestors.

And as for the old songs, the fact that they are difficult to understand has only contributed to their power. Margaret Uyauperk Aniksak from Arviat observed, "The words contained in the throat singing (*qiaqpaarniq*) tradition are words that were used by our remote ancestors. People have forgotten the meaning behind the words and that, I assume, adds to why people don't have any knowledge of their meaning ... They came from the mouths of the ancient."[58]

In the songs, people not only gave a voice to themselves, but also to their ancestors, to animals, and to *tuurngait*, allowing them to participate in the celebrations. The *pisiit* thus helped shaped the relations between the living and the non-human beings who observed human society and became participants through rituals such as these.

CONCLUSION

Qilaniq, head lifting, is a divinatory practice that requires the presence of a helper, usually a deceased relative. It is described as a technique that can be practised not only by *angakkuit*, but by everyone. It is a technique that allows one to connect to ancestors to get information about the causes of disease or the presence of game. But it is not without risk. Elders, for example, thought it dangerous to use one's own leg for *qilaniq*. One should not use it on namesakes, and various rules apply to its practice. *Qilaniq* requires knowledge, skill, and caution. In the demonstration by elders that we saw, it became clear to us that they possessed the skill and knowledge required to practise *qilaniq*, and thus we may surmise that its application has never really discontinued.

Drum dancing involved the complex interplay of husband and wife, the wife giving a voice to the man by singing the song he has composed, the man performing the drum dance. The *pisiq*, the personal song, will always be connected to the person, and after his death the song can only be used when his name is referred to. People live on in their songs as they do in their names. Guided by women, the drum dancer reaches a point where he expresses himself in his breath, without words. In the past, strict rules applied to the feast house. During menstruation, women could not enter a house where song feasts were held,[59] and song feasts were prohibited after a death.[60] The deceased and the animals were aware of the feasts and would retaliate if the rules were transgressed.

The song feast provided the social context *par excellence* for men as well as women to connect to agencies such as namesakes and ancestors, enabling them to participate in the feast of their namesakes and descendants. By singing the *pisiit* of their ancestors, people brought them to life again, just as they did in passing on the ancestors' names to their children.

Qilaut, *pisiit*, *sakajuq*, and even *ivijutiit* connected people to ancestors and non-human beings. With the exception of *sakajuq*, they were practised by all adults. Specific qualities, techniques, and skills were required. The practitioner had to know how to perform the technique and how to make and master the connection with ancestors and spirits. Relations between human beings, ancestors, and animals were by no means the prerogative of the *angakkuit*. Only the *sakajuq* technique was specifically considered a shamanic practice. All of these techniques involved the use of sounds or words and derived their efficacy from an original inspiration, handed down by an ancestor or, preferably, acquired out on the land. Because these sounds and words derived their strength from their connection to the agencies, they enabled people to make that connection again. But the preferred context for the expression of these words and sounds was play, play within in the context of a feast where the abundance of food testified to the generosity of the non-human agencies that provided it and the human participants who shared it. The visitor, the opponent, the rival, or song cousin was drawn into a competition that invited the participants to demonstrate their skills. Conflict and tension could not only be resolved, but their expression in play could become a source of enjoyment for the human and non-human participants in the feast. Competition benefited the players as well as the community. According to Rasmussen (1929, 244), "There is also an Eskimo proverb which says that those who know how to play can easily leap over the adversities of life. And one who can sing and laugh never brews mischief." The feast was the most important ritual expression of the well-being of the community. It established the people's relationships with strangers and visitors from other places whose arrival had triggered the feast. And through the songs, sounds, and dances at the feast, the people were connected to the ancestors who were represented in the songs, the music, and the names of the participants themselves, as well as to the animals and other non-human agencies that witness human life.

11

Reconnecting People and Healing the Land: Inuit Pentecostal and Evangelical Movements

INTRODUCTION

Since the early 1970s, the rapid development of Pentecostal and evangelical movements has given a new dynamic to Inuit Christianity.[1] In this chapter we will focus our analysis on these contemporary forms of Inuit religiosity. Although these modern movements claim to represent a break with the past, they shape both old and new features in a variety of ways. They advocate new forms of solidarity, integrating modern ideologies in a Christian perspective. They aspire to heal society by providing space and context for the preservation of local views, models, and practices within a Christian framework. We will see that relations to the land and the connection to shamanism remain central issues in contemporary Inuit discourses and take shape in new forms of evangelism and Pentecostalism. Although most of the new religious movements strongly oppose shamanic traditions, some of their practices evoke these very traditions, especially for elders who have witnessed shamanic practices in the past. Why are these practices perceived this way? How do these new movements integrate Christian and traditional beliefs?

We will begin this chapter by presenting a brief history of some of the most important religious movements in the North, as well as the views of some elders, such as Salome Qalasiq and Felix Pisuk from Kangiq&iniq and Felix Kupak from Naujaat. Next, in more detail, we will examine recent developments, notably the healing-the-land rituals developed by the Canada Awakening Ministries in collaboration with a Fijian Healing the Land team. Finally, we will discuss some of the basic characteristics of these new Christian movements, which in some areas of Nunavik and Nunavut have become as popular as the more traditional Anglican and Roman Catholic churches.

ANGLICAN, PENTECOSTAL, AND EVANGELICAL CHURCHES

Belief in the life-giving power of the Holy Spirit, now so marked in Pentecostalism, has always been part of the Anglican tradition. Thus, the first letters that

Inuit sent to the Anglican missionaries, Peck and others, at the end of the nineteenth century and the beginning of the twentieth, refer to the regenerative power of the Holy Spirit and Christian prayer. Maria Aaraniq, one of the first converts, writes, "I expect the Holy Spirit to stand by us and guide our hands, and give us life." The first native pastor on Baffin Island, Peter Tulugarjuaq, stated, "The Holy Ghost is in our souls, it is helping us to believe." And others added, "Jesus and the Holy Spirit will give us life ... God will ask the Holy Ghost to enter our souls. We want to do that because Jesus will come again."[2] The Anglican and evangelical churches were soon promoting a similar native ministry. Some of the modern evangelical movements are quite close to the nineteenth-century "Native Church Policy" introduced by the Church Missionary Society, which promoted the training of native pastors, and close as well to the Anglicanism preached by Reverend Turner in the North Baffin area in the first half of the twentieth century.[3] It is interesting to note that Reverend Turner is an important figure in the recent evangelical movie *Transformations II*.

In many respects, Inuit Pentecostalism shares important features with old Inuit shamanic traditions and with Christian traditions influenced by Methodist views. Inuit contemporary Pentecostalism is not just a new doctrine brought from the outside world, but also the further development of ideas already familiar to the Inuit. Like earlier Protestant traditions, evangelicalism and Pentecostalism stress the authority of the Scriptures and present conversion as an individual decision and a transformation that will have powerful effects on the body and the mind. Converted people are referred as "born again," and collective conversion movements as "a religious awakening."[4]

In the Eastern Arctic, the emergence of evangelical movements can be dated to the 1950s, but it was only in the 1970s that these movements became more structured. At first, many of the Pentecostal followers were disillusioned members of other churches. Pentecostalism cannot be considered to have been a substitute for Catholicism or mainstream Protestantism,[5] since the Pentecostal and evangelical movements have had their own dynamics and capacities to attract people.

In Nunavik, veteran aviator John Spillenaar and his wife, Tyyne, started one of the first evangelical movements in the North. In his website, Spillenaar states that he received his call to go north and preach the Gospel in 1936. In 1950 he and his wife started the Northland Mission. Since that time they "have founded two more ministries in the region, the latest of which is the Arctic Mission Outreach Trust Fund, which has built five churches in the last five years in the Arctic."[6]

A few Inuit pastors are actively involved in the evangelical movement, including James and Loie Arreak from Iqaluit, Peter Airo and Tommy Kudluk from Kangirsuk, Etulu Anminguiq from Panniqtuuq, Billy Arnaquq from Qikiqtarjuaq, and Eva and Bobby Deer from Quaqtaq, Nunavik.

For evangelicals, conversion is an experience of complete transformation, and miracles serve as proof of the power of the transformation. In the *Arctic Mission Outreach Trust Fund Newsletter* of spring 2006, David Ellyatt recalls the story of one of their pastors, Peter Airo, known as Niki: "Peter Airo was sent home to die with cancer in 1982, after which he received the Lord as his personal Savior and was healed. Last year he died twice in the hospital in Montreal and had a wonderful visitation in heaven which he is sharing across the North. Pastor Niki is 73 years old and going strong."

The first evangelical church was built on the west coast of Hudson Bay; this was the Alliance Church led by missionary Gleason Ledyard, who was affiliated to the Christian and Missionary Alliance, an American evangelical group close to the Billy Graham network. Ledyard became a pilot and began to visit the Inuit of Magoose River with his wife, Kathryn. He established a mission in Arviat in 1946. Travelling to far-flung Inuit camps in his small plane, Ledyard reached many Inuit, including groups located at Ennadai Lake, Padlei, and Southampton Island.[7] Kathryn and Gleason Ledyard spent about fifteen years in this area, from 1946 to 1961. They also visited Back River, Spence Bay, King William Island, and Iglulik. They opened a school on the tundra at Maguse River, with a class of about twenty-eight children. They played records produced in Alaska by Gospel Reading International and worked on translations of the Bible. They even produced their own recordings with the help of Eric Anoee, who later became a minister in Arviat.[8] Their work was carried on by Inuit such as Mark Kalluak, who translated the *New Life Testament* in 1984, and more recently by Luke Suluk,[9] a son of the famous and controversial religious leader Donald Suluk, who was considered a Christian preacher by some and a shaman by others. In a religious service we attended in the Arviat Alliance church in October 2005, Luke Suluk was very open, encouraging audience participation. He invited everyone to join in the singing and other activities or to take the floor if they so wished. The movement is in some respects very modern, yet descriptions of religious experiences may evoke shamanic traditions. An account of the conversion of Thomas Kutluk, a follower of that church, is quite instructive:

> One day in the spring of 1983 I went with a group of men and our dog teams out to the flow edge on the Hudson Bay. We came to a place where we had to detour around slushy ice along the edge … The dogs, lacking experience, ran directly into the open water, pulling the sleigh in behind them. I could not swim, but somehow I managed to get to the ice's edge where I hung on with my elbows. The water current was so strong that I was being pulled under the ice. With my body tilted and my face toward heaven I cried out to God. I had no words, just a voice from deep within me, a desperate cry to the Lord God. At that moment the Lord touched my heart. Suddenly I remembered my father telling me, "If you ever fall in the water, hang onto the ice and kick your feet." Just two strong kicks and I lay on top of the ice. I was so happy. I was thanking and praying to God. My dogs also made it onto the ice, and with a change of clothing from one of the other men I was able to make the one-hour trip back to the settlement

and home … I continue to rejoice in God's goodness in sparing my physical life but especially for His goodness in restoring my spiritual life.[10]

In this story, the immersion in the water and the call for help, as well as the voice Kutluk heard, are reminiscent of a shamanic initiation involving immersion.[11] The change of clothing is also symbolic. The story recalls the experience of Salome Qalasiq, a member of the Pentecostal group in Kangiq&iniq, who was saved by prayer when she fell into the water while jigging.[12] The fact that Qalasiq's clothing was dry when she came out of the water testifies to the miraculous nature of the event.

A young woman named Kavy Gordon started another evangelical movement on the west coast of Hudson Bay. In 1956, at the age of twenty-two, she opened the very first Glad Tidings Church in the Western Arctic, in Tuktoyaktuk. From there she travelled extensively in the Arctic, and during one of these trips she introduced her church's message to a few Kivalliq communities, particularly those in Arviat and Kangiq&iniq, where she was in charge of the Glad Tidings Church for some time. During the services we attended in Arviat in October 2005, the church was full of young people, couples, and elders. Prayers, hymns, conversion narratives, and music alternated, and the participants clearly enjoyed the service. The sermon was delivered by a minister from the south who had been working as a missionary in Africa, and it was enthusiastically translated by a local member of the church. The service raised much fervour and joy. At the end, the floor was offered to all those who wished to express their feelings or connect with the Holy Spirit. Quite a few people moved from the back of the church to the front, crying or falling down as they were touched by the Holy Spirit.

In 1974 Bill Prankard brought the Full Gospel Church to the North. Originally from Ontario, he was ordained as a minister of the Pentecostal Assemblies of Canada. On his website he states, "Bill Prankard Evangelistic Association provided literature, equipment, training and support, and built churches in several communities." Prankard focuses on the social problems affecting the northern communities. He emphasizes the effectiveness of his movement and its close collaboration with the Glad Tidings Arctic Missions in the Keewatin. His activities include annual "short-term Bible School in Kangiq&iniq," "missionary-evangelism journeys into the Arctic," and trips abroad, including to Russia.[13] The Bill Prankard Evangelistic Association operates in several northern Canadian communities, as well as in Siberia. In northern Canada, it supports the Full Gospel Church in Qikiqtarjuaq[14] and Nain (Labrador). The leader hosts a daily television teaching program seen in over 140 countries.

Roger Armbruster is another influential evangelical leader. Together with his wife, Marge, he developed the Canada Awakening Ministries, aimed at building an indigenous church in Canada's North. Founded in 1978, these ministries now support several churches in the North and organize many activities. They are based in the Maranatha Good News Centre in Niverville, Manitoba.[15]

The Northern Canada Evangelical Mission (NCEM) also turned to the Arctic, particularly the community of Puvirnituq in Nunavik. In 1980 the NCEM missionary Noriko Suzuki spent about three weeks in that community, and she returned to it in 1981. According to the NCEM website,[16] the movement is now about to expand its activities into the neighbouring community of Salluit. The NCEM enters this new field as "language-learners," to use one of their concepts. They present themselves as an interdenominational faith organization seeking to bring the Gospel of Jesus Christ to the native peoples of Canada. Organized since 1946 and strongly represented in Saskatchewan, the NCEM now has about 150 full-time missionaries on about fifty stations across the country. Like the Pentecostal churches, the movement wants "to establish indigenous churches that will propagate the Gospel in their own communities." According to its website, NCEM is a member of the Interdenominational Foreign Mission Association, and its doctrinal statement is contained in the Constitution of the Northern Canada Evangelical Mission.

Since the opening of the Anglican and Catholic missions in Nunavut, two main periods can be identified. From the 1950s to the 1990s, the Pentecostal and evangelical movements gradually emerged in various communities as new churches were opened.[17] At first they had little impact on the other churches. However, a second phase started in the early 1990s when the evangelical movements and churches began to attract many more followers. Several factors contributed to this process, notably the extensive development of Pentecostalism at the international level as well as the new socio-political context that took shape in the North with the creation of Nunavut and the ensuing "inuitization" of many Western institutions.

Many Inuit pastors and leaders – for example, Louie Bruce, Pasha Bruce, Kanayuk Bruce, Raymond Ningeocheak, Shavekok Ningeacheck, Tongola Sandy, Rosemary Sandy, Mani Thompson, Timothy Jar, and Sheosiak Jar – work within evangelical and Pentecostal movements. Former leaders of these movements include Annie Alogut, Peter Alogut, Matoo Matoo, and Mary Matoo.

Many Inuit evangelical leaders were once fervent members of the Anglican Church. They may have felt that the inuitization of the Anglican Church was insufficient and thus decided to distance themselves from the traditional and well-established churches. Evangelical and Pentecostal movements and churches provided a suitable environment for the expression of their views, emotions, and religious spontaneity.[18] In Nunavik and the North Baffin area, many Anglicans gradually turned to Pentecostalism and evangelism.

PRAYING IN THE POLITICAL ARENA: CONTEMPORARY NETWORKS

In Nunavik the Full Gospel churches expanded through local as well as regional networks.[19] Powerful families and leaders such as Annie and Mark Tertiluk were ardent followers of John Spillenaar and took an active part in the movement. Local leaders organized networks and exploited local opportunities to spread the message of the new movements. The central value of prayer in Inuit religious tradition was further developed in the new movements. Canada's Christian Community Online, for example, states that "Prayer and Unity precede Revival" and that fervent and regular prayer will lead to important changes. When Canadian Governor-General Adrienne Clarkson visited the community of Puvirnituq and asked the leader Harry Tulugak what the major factor was behind the change for the better in a community once fraught with suicides and other problems, Tulugak replied emphatically, "Prayer!"[20]

When Anglicans turned to Pentecostalism, the Anglican congregations began to adapt their beliefs and practices to Pentecostalism. Today, evangelical leaders note that the antagonism of the established churches to the new movements is disappearing. Missionary Kavy Gordon stated, "I don't think the animosity is there that once was." Anglican, Pentecostal, and evangelical churches work together to organize religious meetings in northern communities. Especially in the last five years, the size and frequency of Biblical conferences and religious meetings have increased considerably.[21] These Biblical conferences serve as venues where evangelical leaders from different communities can meet and exchange information. A network of influential leaders, some of them also active in political and economic networks, has gradually developed through participation in meetings such as the Arctic Pastors and Leaders Conference.

Tagak Curley, the member of the Legislative Assembly (MLA) from Kangiq&iniq, is among a number of well-known evangelical leaders in Nunavut. A prominent evangelical and political leader as well as a businessman, he founded the Inuit Tapirisat of Canada (ITC). After resigning from his ministerial post in 1987, he stayed out of the political arena for some time, but he returned in 2003 with a strong evangelical message. He was the main challenger of Paul Okalik in the 2004 election for premier of Nunavut, making a strong argument for the prohibition of same-sex marriages. Another prominent and charismatic leader is James Arreak, minister of the Iqaluit Christian Fellowship as well as an active political leader. Loie Mike and Billy Arnaquq are well-known South Baffin evangelical leaders, and Eva Lapage in Nunavik and Kavy Gordon in the Kivalliq figure prominently in various closely linked evangelical websites.

Most of the evangelical websites, such as Canada Awakening, Christian Outreach, Canadian Christianity, Three Cord Ministries, and Christianity Today, are based in the south of Canada or the United States. They are run by evangelical leaders such as Roger and Marge Armbruster, Bill Prankard, and John Spillenaar, who are strongly committed to the spread of the Full Gospel in the North. Like other Pentecostal and evangelical groups, the Inuit movements are marked by a lack of centralized authority. "A web-like structure of personal connections" allows members of the relevant networks to easily find financial and technical support down south when needed.[22] Today, Pentecostal and evangelical groups can no longer be considered as peripheral groups. Their influence can be seen at many different levels, from the political arena to the field of radio and telecommunications.

Since the late 1990s, Roger Armbruster's Canada Awakening Ministries have been a major influence in the development of evangelical and Pentecostal movements in the Canadian Arctic. Moreover, other movements tend to connect to these ministries. Therefore, we will pay special attention to the programs and activities of the Canada Awakening Ministries, which profess a strong interest in the connection between the religious and political arenas.

The institution of the Nunavut government in 1999 provided scope for a political debate on the responsibility of government with respect to religious and moral values. Journalist Bell (2004) quotes Armbruster's statement that in Nunavut "there is a real warfare over the government, as the enemy seeks to influence those in office to be controlled by deceptive thoughts or by humanistic thinking rather than by the Word of God."

On 21 June 2006 evangelical leaders signed a covenant on Parliament Hill, pledging to work together. Article 2 of the covenant reads, "The First Peoples of Canada, as a healed, restored and released people, hereby affirm to co-exist and co-labour as partners in transformation with one another and with the Church in Canada, nations and governments. We will walk together in peace, prosperity and freedom. We commit to the restoration, advancement and promotion of the moral and spiritual and political integrity of our society, and the release for all from a negative past. We declare healing for our land and revival in Canada; and Canada will be a banner of healing for all nations worldwide."[23] This document was signed by religious leaders Arreak, Deer, Tertiluk, Dewar, Arnaquq, among others. Clearly, the Pentecostal and evangelical movements see themselves as representing the First Nations.

In November 2003, the film *Broken Promises – The High Arctic Relocation*[24] provided an opportunity for Armbruster to write a text that fully supported the Inuit demands. Armbruster claimed that Inuit should receive official apologies and more financial support from the federal government.

Paul White reported on the Canada Awakening website how a "Healing Workshop" had been set up to heal the wounds associated with the relocating of Inuit to Qausuittuq (Resolute Bay) and Aujuittuq (Grise Fiord) in the 1950s. A "Cleansing the Land" exercise was performed in two stages. The first stage consisted in the people making a rock monument on the seashore where the relocated Inuit had first been dropped off. A general confession followed and then communion, in which wine was poured onto the ground. The second part of the ceremony was conducted at the abandoned Resolute military base; the bar at the base had led to serious problems of drunkenness and social violence. To cleanse the land, communion wine was poured onto the snow.

Pentecostal and evangelical movements promote Christianity and Christian rules but at the same time put forward Inuit models that fit well within the Nunavut agenda. Journalist Bob Weber (2004) quotes James Arreak:

"The creation of Nunavut is our opportunity to demonstrate the true calling of who God called us to be. The signs are indicating that we need to prepare ourselves for the Second Coming" …

Arreak preaches that hard-core Christian values are not only congruent with traditional Inuit ways, they are what the Inuit were meant to live by all along. The creation of Nunavut was simply a step along that path.

"We are a unique people, unique in almost every way," he says. Again and again, he repeats that the creation of Nunavut is a call from God for the Inuit to transform themselves.

He effortlessly brings the old-time shamans who guided the Inuit before Christianity under his spiritual tent.

"There are oral traditional stories that shamans were sent into the spirit world to investigate the reality of (the Christian) God. They came back saying 'Wow!'"

One of those shamans might feel right at home in Arreak's church. He talks casually of speaking in tongues, faith-healing and exorcisms.

"We do lots of them. A couple months ago, I did one in Iqaluit" …

The next step, says Arreak, will be to complete the joining together of separate congregations across Nunavut and northern Quebec into a single church.

These statements and references express the ambivalence of Inuit Pentecostal movements. On the one hand, these movements claim to break with past views in order to promote modernity, formal education, and political initiatives, all the while taking from the shamanic traditions whatever is needed, and on the other hand, they must deal with the victims of the same modern system, which brought alcohol and other social problems to the North. One cannot attribute the success of these movements over the last fifty years to disorganization and deprivation in Inuit communities in the same period. Cultural dimensions have to be taken into account, for it is clear that these movements have integrated important Inuit traditions into a new Christian framework.

EVANGELISM, PENTECOSTALISM, AND SHAMANISM

Many of today's elders see a connection between Pentecostalism and shamanism. They refer to the Pentecostal people as *qiajuit* – "those who cry" – and compare their rituals to the shamanic practices of the past. Felix Kupak from Naujaat (2001 interview) observed, "The people with the new faith are repenting and lifting their arms and saying 'Halaluya' very loud. The second time they say this it is a bit louder, and then on the third halaluya they act like *angakkuit*. I don't think it's the right kind of faith."

Felix Pisuk from Kangiq&iniq commented, "I started hearing Glad Tidings people in Kangiq&iniq saying that they could hear the souls going to heaven. When you know the people involved, you know that not all souls go to heaven. There are those that you envy, those that observe Sundays and go to church. Some might try to go up to heaven but they fall down the side of a cliff."[25] The image of falling off a cliff suggests the sort of obstacles *angakkuit* might meet on their trips to the lands of the dead. Qalasiq from Kangiq&iniq warned one should not become too religious:

> Now that we are Christian, there is a saying that if you become too fervently religious, He whom we believe in, will come and get you before you have committed a great sin. That's why some people die when they are young. If they became very religious and their extreme religiousness was going to become fanatical, then they were made to die before they were lost. My son, who drowned, was very religious. He became extremely religious. He started knowing things that nobody else knew about. I warned him that he might die prematurely. He died when he was still young. He was trying very hard to help other people.[26]

And Pisuk added, "What she has said is true. I have been told by two Catholic priests that even if I believed in religion, that I was not to become too fervently religious, as this might cost me my life. I was not to change my denomination and I was not to go overboard with religion either. To this day I can't forget this. I go and pray with others and go to funerals but I try not to go overboard. I was told I was to pray, but not to ignore everything else in order to do so."[27]

In the past, it was the parousial movements that were generally criticized for being too religious.[28] Following strict rules and prohibitions (no alcohol, no work on Sunday, etc.) was reminiscent of traditional prohibitions known as *tirigusuusiit*. What often attracts younger and middle-aged people in Pentecostalism (e.g., ecstatic experiences, visions, healings) worries elders, who connect these features to shamanism. In comparing Christian and shamanic experiences, however, elders point out that in shamanism one actually saw things, whereas in the church one sees nothing exceptional. Pisuk related:

> If I were to go to an Evangelical or Anglican or Catholic church service, even if I really wanted to be made to see something, I wouldn't see anything. I was able to see Qimuksiraaq's *tuurngaq*. It was in the shape of an Arctic hare. He would go and get it from outdoors after we heard the sound of it moving on the ground. He held it in his arms and brought it inside. It was alive. The tips of its ears weren't black at all, just like a Qallunaat rabbit. He would put it in his parka as though he was going to take it with him. Nowadays when I go to church and I want to see something, I don't see anything at all.
>
> I am Catholic, but if I wanted to see something in church, I wouldn't be able to. We had an *angakkuq* who was very powerful and had polar bear teeth and yet was a member of the Catholic Church. He wore a cross. He

> carried a rosary around his neck. He went to church on Sundays and in the early mornings, and he took communion. If shamanism was really bad, I don't think he would have been able to take communion. That's why I think that shamanism has some good to it.[29]

Pisuk thought the shamans were more effective healers than the new religious leaders: "The priests and ministers, and the leaders in the church are not like the *angakkuit*. None of them are able to help heal you. I have heard people from the Glad Tidings church go on the radio. They say, 'Let us pray for so and so who is sick.' If someone would say to a member of the Glad Tidings church, 'Let's go visit that person who has cancer,' they wouldn't be able to heal them. If the *angakkuit* were to deal with them, they would be healed."

Dorais (2001, 76), after studying the influence of the Four Gospels Church in Quaqtaq, Nunavik, concluded:

> At the same time as it is modern, Pentecostalism revives some very traditional Inuit religious attitudes. Like shamanism, it is based on a personal relation with the supernatural rather than on a corpus of doctrine, with the difference that Pentecostalism relies on a written guide, the Bible, to explain how to properly establish this relation. The similarity between both traditions is implicitly acknowledged by the Quaqtaq Pentecostals, when they assert that the shamans of old established relationships with the evil spirits (*tuurngait*), whereas they themselves prefer to turn away from the devils, to relate to Jesus and his angels.

Other Pentecostal rituals and beliefs – public confessions; the notion that God, Jesus, or evil spirits can enter a person's body and speak in tongues; the belief in the healing power of the Holy Spirit; the practice of exorcism – also evoke shamanic traditions.[30]

CONVERSION AND TRANSFORMATION

The new religious movements not only announce the imminent return of Christ, they also emphasize the potential and regenerative power of the Holy Spirit to solve the social problems that affect Arctic communities today. This perspective is well illustrated in the film *Transformations* produced by the Sentinel Group. Its founder, an American named George Otis, Jr, worked for a long time with the famous American evangelical leader Billy Graham. At first, the group set out to document spiritual transformations induced by Christian prayer, producing a few videos on the subject.[31] The group now actively proselytizes and puts an emphasis on the concept of "spiritual warfare." Its ideology is described on its website: "Our theological worldview is perhaps best defined as 'conservative charismatic' … We are convinced that prayer and spiritual warfare are an essential part of our mission to extend Christ's kingdom on the earth."[32] The Sentinel Group emphasizes the capacity of the Holy Ghost to transform people by giving them a direct contact with God through conversion.[33]

The first videotapes produced by the Sentinel Group dealt with people from many parts of the world, and they were well received in the northern communities. The new movements began to take root in the North at a time when many of the communities were facing severe social problems such as suicide, domestic violence, and alcoholism, and evangelical groups were well aware of these problems. Their video *Transformations II* began with various Inuit commenting on the social problems in northern communities. It ended with them talking of being "born again" and revived by the Lord, to use the expression of Reverend Elliasie Sallialuk from Puvirnituq.[34] Social workers (e.g., Eyuka Pinguatuq, Alasie Arngaq, Attasie Qarisaq), local teachers (Maggie Akpahatak), and even mayors (Johny Akpahatak in Aupaluk) and evangelical leaders (Annie and Mark Tertiluk in Kangirsujuaq) appear in the video, glorifying evangelical prayer and the healing power of the Holy Spirit.[35]

The video clearly illustrates the continuity between the old Anglican tradition and the new religious movements. It presents an interview with Joan Turner, the wife of the famous canon John Hudspith Turner, founder of the first Anglican mission in Mittimatalik in 1929.[36] Joan Turner relates a vision she had about Inuit singing hymns and gathering together for prayer.

The video refers to the ritual of *siqqitirniq*. At the beginning of the tape, the story of the conversion of Angutijjuaq from Mittimatalik is presented in detail by one of his descendants, the former RCMP agent Joanasie Benjamin Arreak. Arreak explains how, almost a hundred years ago, Angutijjuaq decided to convert after having a vision and a dream. He caught a seal at an *aglu* (the breathing hole of a seal) after a bright light and three winged beings appeared at the hole. The *aglu* always was a point of connection between the worlds of human beings, ancestors, and sea game.[37] Here the hunter killed the sea game that the camp needed for its survival. The appearance of the three angels at such a crucial place and in conjunction with the successful kill embedded the relationship between hunter and prey in a Christian framework.[38]

Part of this video was devoted to an extraordinary church service in Mittimatalik in 1999. According to those who had been present, Mittimatalik had been visited by the Holy Spirit. The rumour soon spread to neighbouring communities as a clear sign of an "Arctic revival." In an article published in the winter 2002, a journalist describes the event and its effects:

> It started like thunder, and at first no one knew what was happening. Moses Kyak, who was operating the sound system, turned the volume off but the noise kept getting louder. Then people began falling down without anyone touching them. James Arreak, who had been leading worship,

began to shake. The building began to shake. For about a minute the noise continued to fill the church, like a mighty, rushing wind. "It sounds like Niagara Falls," says Rev. Joshua Arreak, who was helping lead an afternoon service at St. Timothy's Anglican Church with his younger brother James. And then the sound went away. Along with the Arreak brothers, about 40 people were in attendance for the service in Pond Inlet … It was the conclusion of several days of Bible teaching and, as is common in northern church services, people were praying fervently for God's Spirit to come down on them. Some asked for deliverance from sins and others for healing from deep emotional wounds.

As James Arreak, a house church pastor in Iqaluit, was leading worship, Looee Arreak, now his wife, was praying for those who went forward. Rev. Joshua Arreak, rector at St. Timothy's, was praying for people at the back of the church, while another pastor, Moses Kyak, was watching the sound system.

"And suddenly," says Joshua Arreak, "without our expecting anything supernatural, there was a visitation. The noise started to happen."

At first, no one talked about it. It wasn't until later that day, Feb. 28, 1999, that people realized how powerfully they had been shaken by God's Spirit. In a service that evening, Arreak remembers, "I was up in the front leading the worship and I realized that something spectacular had happened earlier that afternoon."

Then someone realized the event had been taped. "I asked for the tape to be played to the congregation to let them know that this happened. That's when we realized that it was a very powerful visitation of God. As soon as that tape was on, people started praising God" …

Why did this happen in Pond Inlet? … All Joshua Arreak knows is that people had been praying for the community, especially for the young people, on a regular basis. A few years earlier, they had gotten together to destroy, in a huge bonfire, about $100,000 worth of heavy metal music, pornography and drugs. "That's may be partly why God was so gracious to us," says Arreak. "We've been really humbled by this."[39]

The Sentinel Group provided more details in its videotape. Bill Arnaquq added: "Something started to happen that was without our control … Everything was shaking in Pond Inlet. It sounds like a jet. This was another visitation of the Holy Spirit."[40] A central theme in the testimonies at the service was the contrast between the heavy metal music that is leading young people astray and religious music. The events illustrated how easily modern technology could be integrated into a perspective built on old traditions.

Matthew Akaralak, an elder from Arviat, related that he used to play evil music on his tape deck. One day, someone had apparently changed the tape and he heard Gospel music instead. He was deeply touched and decided to go to church.[41] Music plays a central part in modern evangelical services. Participants are encouraged to join in the singing and let the music help them connect to the Holy Spirit. Dance and bodily movements are thought to support this connection and to be evidence that a connection has been made that will bring healing joy and salvation to the believers. The importance of the connection is well illustrated by the name of the Taivititut Music Gospel Festival in Nunavik. *Taivititut* means giving praise as King David had praised God, and connects the performer to David, who was criticized by his wife Michal for dancing naked in honour of God (see 2 Samuel 6).

Events similar to those in Mittimatalik occurred in other communities. In Aupaluk, Kangirsujuaq, Puvirnituq, Quaqtaq, and Ikpiarjuk, people burned drugs, tapes of heavy metal music, and pornography out on the ice.[42] In the past as well as in the present, music plays a central part in the communication with transcendent and non-human agencies.

Stuckenberger (2005, 84) interviewed some people in Qikiqtarjuaq who had been involved in heavy metal in 1986 or 1987: "Some of these teenagers, now grown men, actually told me about practices of devil worship in which they felt inspired by the music and songs, but also motivated by their wish to gain power to change things and have them the way they wanted them to be. A young – and from all that I heard, well-respected – man killed himself in his room that was heavily decorated with Heavy Metal paraphernalia. This, as well as a number of subsequent suicides, was thought by many people to be related to the influence Heavy Metal had on the young people."

Stuckenberger (2005, 84) relates how tapes were burnt in Qikirtarjuaq:

> This initiative was adopted in Qikiqtarjuaq. Many young people, on their own initiative or persuaded by their parents and elders, piled their things up at the beach. Many people came to see when the bonfire was lighted. Some people reported that crying and talking came out of the tapes when they were burnt; an observation that justified for many of them the drastic measure of burning their property. One acquaintance, who informed me about the event, commented that Heavy Metal was interesting to him and his friends, and they liked to listen to it together while visiting each other. Though he perceived that his social demeanor changed, he pointed out that he wanted to provoke people to see how they would react to him. Having been persuaded by social pressure and the hope of doing something to end the suicides, to burn his things, he was very disappointed when the wave of suicides continued.

Pentecostal groups are successful in attracting people who want to heal and have a better life. For many new converts, Pentecostalism offers a new model and new rules to help them deal with the social and spiritual problems of today's northern communities.

THE CANADA AWAKENING MINISTRIES

One of the great lacunas in research on Pentecostalism and evangelism is the lack of good descriptions of rituals. Therefore, it is worthwhile to examine various new rituals that evangelical groups have developed in recent years. In the following section, we will examine some of the new practices of the Canada Awakening Ministries to see how they combine features from the past with more contemporary elements. We did not witness these rituals ourselves and base our descriptions on the detailed information provided on www.canadaawakening.com. All quotations and photographs in this section are from this website.[43]

Networks and Globalization: The Fijian Connection

Canada Awakening Ministries sponsored a few trips of new Inuit converts to Greenland (26 November–3 December 2002). In 2003, sixteen Inuit were brought to Israel (16–26 January 2003), and in 2004, twenty visited the same country (18–29 January). The Canada Awakening movement organized a visit to the Gypsy Cultural centre in Jerusalem and organized many meetings with the Domari Bedouins during the trip in Israel in 2004. In the participants' descriptions of these trips, Christian and Inuit traditions are effectively entwined. The Inuit drum, for example, is presented as "the heartbeat of life," and a bone carving of an Inuit drum dancer as "a symbol of peace, joy and celebration." In 2006 the ministries organized a ten-day trip, entitled "From the Land of the North Star to the Land of the Star of David" (23 January to 3 February 2006), as the 7th Annual Inuit Ministries Holy Land Pilgrimage to Israel, at a price of $2,799 for each participant.

In 2004, the ministries organized a fundraiser, inspired by Tagak Curley,[44] to help underprivileged and impoverished children in Israel – The North Wind for Israel Trust Fund – raising over $10,000. Tagak Curley explained that the ministries not only did work in Israel, but made commitments in other areas as well, including financially supporting the building of a new church in Nuuk, Greenland.[45]

An important value of the evangelical movements is represented by the participation of different cultures. The movements allow for the integration of local traditions and practices into a global evangelical framework. New rituals are developed that meet evangelical as well as local requirements.

a) Healing the Land

In emphasizing that the process of transformation not only involves a transformation of people, but also a transformation of the land, the Canada Awakening Ministries connect to the traditional Inuit belief that the health of people and that of the land are closely connected.[46]

Maggie Akpahatak, the pastor from Aupaluk, relates, "Many people, including our government leaders, don't see any connection between prayer and repentance with the healing of the land, but indigenous peoples have long understood the connection that there is between people and land. What people do in a particular area can either defile or pollute the land, or it can cleanse and bringing healing to it. How people speak and act can determine the productivity of the land on which they live."[47]

On the website of Canada Awakening, Armbruster discusses how ancient Thule sites at Resolute Bay were cleansed through prayer. He presents Thule people as "a very controlled, male-dominant people" who abused their women routinely:

> But the land can be cleansed and the website describes how Allie and Susan Salluviniq, respectively the town foreman and the mayor of Resolute Bay began to heal the land by praying prayers of repentance for the "sins of the fathers" that have been committed on this ancient site many years ago, but which was still affecting the area and the land itself today.
>
> ... When these legal "gatekeepers" begin to take responsibility for the sins that have defiled that part of the earth where they now have legal authority, you can be sure that something will happen to the land itself. The land will become healed so that the dry, barren desolate areas will begin to become productive, and will support the inhabitants that live there.[48]

The quotation shows the importance of the association between religion and politics in Armbruster's view. The legal gatekeepers are the dignitaries in the administrative system. Once they accept their responsibility to integrate their political and religious perspectives, the land can begin to heal. The healing will bear fruit in the reappearance of animals. In October 2005, Armbruster reports:

> It was my privilege to personally talk with big game hunters, Nathaniel and Martha Kalluk of Resolute Bay. They were very excited about the fact that when they were out on the land in the High Arctic in August and early September of 2005, that they found that every caribou cow had at least one calf, and that some had more than one. It is very unusual and uncommon to see a whole herd of caribou cows with even one calf, let alone some with more than one! The believers in the High Arctic see this as an answer to the prayers of God's people to heal the land, and as God's response to the prayers of repentance that have taken place for the ancestral and more recent sins that have brought defilement upon the land, and caused it to become barren and desolate for many years.

Mention of the return of game refers not only to caribou moving back but also to the return of narwhals and other animals. Armbruster quotes Inuit from

Nunavik: "Maggie Akpahatak, the pastor from Aupaluk, for example, told me in October of 2005, that since they have been praying for the land, they are not only seeing greater numbers of animals on the land, but a greater variety of animals, and of living creatures!"[49] Armbruster describes how the land around Kangiq&iniq was cleansed during Thanksgiving weekend (8–11 October) of 2005. At a traditional meeting place where game had become sparse, about ten miles north of Kangiq&iniq, people cleansed the land of its defilements by partaking of communion with one another and applying the power of the blood of Jesus to the land itself.

Again, the ritual is not perceived as just a religious act, for Armbruster recognizes that some "legal authority" had to be responsible for the transformation: "On the rock around which the small group gathered, there is a communion set. Communion was received, and the blood of Jesus applied, to our own lives, and to the land itself. I realize that there needs to be a legal authority to do this by the gatekeepers and people in authority where one is praying. In view of the fact that Veronica Dewar is a prominent leader among the Inuit, and the Past President of the Inuit Women's Association, I believe that her presence among us added to the legal authority to what we were doing."

The ritual proved effective. On Christmas day of 2005, Veronica Dewar informed Armbruster that there were many caribou around Kangiq&iniq. Not only animals but even trees and plants were returning to the once barren land at Qausuittuq.

> I am told that now in some places, even in the High Arctic, edible berries are beginning to grow as well … There has never been a berry season in the High Arctic – only desolate wilderness … Larry Audlaluk and Susan Salluviniq even shared with me how … trees are now starting to appear above the ground that were once buried and below the surface …
>
> Could it be that the treeless Arctic tundra was once covered with trees, and was once like a garden, and that it will once again be covered with trees, and become like a garden once again? This is definitely a vision that is worth praying into, and I believe that there is scriptural backing for it.

Prayer would have a positive effect on minerals and land resources as well. The Canada Awakening website concludes that we see on the earth the signs that God is healing the land in response to the prayers of his people. Thus, the transformation of the land becomes possible through prayer.

b) Reconciliation at Kangiq&iniq

The Canada Awakening Ministries decided to bring together indigenous people from the North as well as from the South, to represent the ends of the earth. In both Fiji and Nunavut, the evangelical movements are strongly represented in the political establishment. Fijian prime minister Laisena Qarase, like Tagak

Curley in Nunavut, strongly opposes same-sex marriages and supports the evangelical movements.

In 2003 a program was developed to connect Fiji, representing the South, and Nunavut, representing the North. A meeting held in Fiji to organize the program was attended by Otis of the Sentinel Group, Armbruster of the Canada Awakening Ministries, Curley from Nunavut, and various other dignitaries. The Fijian prime minister gave his political support to this initiative to bring Inuit and Fijians together. The Fijian "Healing the Land" team was set up to restore the natural resources in Fiji, and a visit to Israel by both Fijians and Inuit was planned for the beginning of 2006.

It was also decided that the Fijian Healing the Land team would travel to Nunavut in July 2006. When the team arrived in Nunavut on its healing mission, it travelled to various places. It developed ritual procedures to ensure the healing, but as its first step, it sought to diagnose the causes of the wounds of the land. According to Armbruster, the original inhabitants of the land were partly to blame but they also had a spiritual claim to the land: "Relations to the lands are not only disrupted by the sins of the ancestors, but also by the conflicts between the descendants of the original inhabitants of the land and newcomers." He continues: "The original inhabitants have a legitimate claim to a special relationship with the land, but often they hold resentments towards the later groups, and the types of changes that they have brought in building buildings and changing the landscape in ways that the originals did not approve." It is clear that Armbruster relates the problems of the land to the sins of the ancestors and to the tensions between descendants of original inhabitants and newcomers. In his perspective, the reconciliation of the land requires a reconciliation of the groups concerned:

> In Rankin Inlet, on the morning of Monday, July 10, some of the descendants of the original inhabitants of the area began to humble themselves, and to repent of the bitterness and anger that they held in their hearts towards the descendants of the later inhabitants. On that same morning of July 10 in Rankin Inlet, the later people and their descendants began to repent to the original inhabitants for not having observed proper protocol, of having simply come into the area, and doing their own thing without even asking for permission. Many tears were shed as representatives from both groups began to embrace one another …
>
> Some 30 believers showed up who wanted to bring cleansing to the land where it had become defiled through past conflicts and violence.
>
> Then a ritual of reconciliation was celebrated within a circle of stones marking the site of an ancient dwelling.
>
> The original inhabitants then did what had never been done many years previously, and that was to officially welcome the later groups to this area. They welcomed them to come and join them inside the circle where they were standing inside of one of the original dwellings.

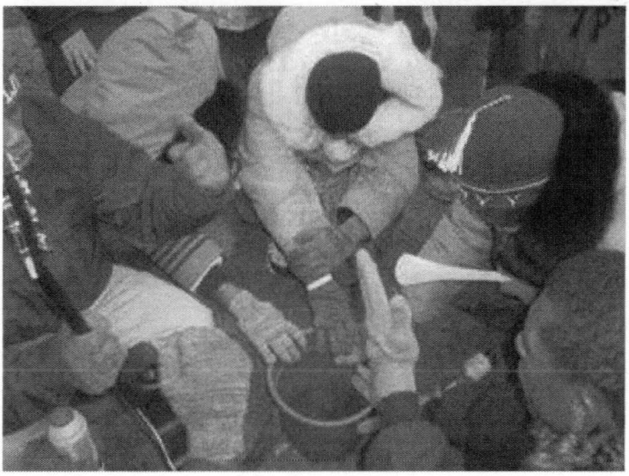

(above) David Aglukark, on behalf of the original habitants, and Tagak Curley, on behalf of the newcomers, apply the wine and bread representing the blood and body of Christ to the land; (below) A mixture of oil, salt, and water is blessed before it is applied to the land. Source: http://www.canada-awakening.com.

> This time, the later groups came into the circle with a legal authority and permission that would enable the two groups to enter into their inheritance together, to see the land cleansed and healed, and to produce enough to provide for all.

In this ritual the descendants of the original inhabitants were endowed with a "legal authority" to welcome the newcomers on the land. By standing in the stone circles, they represented their ancestors and nullified the tensions of the past. At the end of the ritual, the newcomers and the descendants of the original inhabitants embraced one another.

The reconciliation of the two parties, however, was not sufficient; a relationship between the land and Christ had to be made. Thus Communion was prepared with a specific division of tasks in which the two groups partook. Then, prayers were put into a hole and a stone memorial erected.

Water, oil, and salt were then applied to the land. The water speaks of "living water" (John 7:37, 38); the oil speaks of the anointing that destroys the yoke

(Isaiah 10:27); and the salt is to be a preservative agent against corruption and defilement (Matthew 5:13). The water, oil and salt had previously been spiritually cleansed through the word of God and prayer, and set apart as a healing agent to bring a cleansing of the land's defilements, and a healing to the land.

Thus, the reconciliation between newcomers and the original inhabitants was followed by a healing of the land that comprised four steps: (1) anointing the land with bread and wine, (2) putting prayers into a hole, (3) erecting a stone monument, and (4) applying a mixture of oil, water, and salt to the land as a healing agent. The first step required the cooperation of the aboriginal people and the newcomers who had just been reconciled. The second step built on the important tradition of prayer, with the participants making a physical connection between the land and prayer by putting written prayers into a hole. The third step followed the Inuit tradition of making *inuksuit* (stone markers) on the land, in this case creating an emblem of the healing of the land. The final step involved the Fijians situating the ritual in a global perspective encompassing North and South.

Within two days the land was abounding with caribou: "[A]ccording to the wildlife manager in Rankin Inlet, some 15,000 of them showed up right at the spot where the forgiveness and cleansing had taken place, and where the healing of the land had been prayed for. Local residents stated that the caribou in this number had not been seen in the area for some four years." A photograph on the website shows Armbruster and the Fijians touching the antlers of the first caribou shot after the ritual. There are no Inuit in the photo, but they probably did the shooting.

c) Healing at Panniqtuuq

The Fiji Healing the Land team flew to Panniqtuuq on 13 July 2006 for another healing-the-land conference. That same evening a group of believers drove through a place "where drug dealings are alleged to have taken place, and in an area near there, in previous generations, shamanistic practices had taken place, and in some cases, curses had been released that needed to be broken. Strong prayers and intercession was waged right from that very spot."

On Saturday evening, 15 July, the Fijian pastor Vuniani Nakauyaca invited the original inhabitants and people who arrived later (including Qallunaat) to come to the front and form two groups facing each other. Then he invited Armbruster to take over the meeting, and there followed a general repentance of all participants for their attitudes and behaviour towards members of the other group. Armbruster emphasized that even though some outsiders were present for the ritual (including twelve Greenlanders and one or two representatives from other communities on Baffin Island), "the people and leadership of Pangnirtung clearly saw this as their Conference. It was done under their authority, and with their blessing. They took ownership of both the Conference and the follow-up afterwards." As in Kangiq&iniq, the repentance was followed by the members of the two groups embracing each other.

Creating a healing circle to cleanse the land. Source: http://www.canadaawakening.com.

The following morning, Sunday, 16 July, the Anglican and Full Gospel churches joined together in a Communion led by the Anglican bishop Benjamin Arreak and the Anglican minister in Panniqtuuq, Reverend Darren McCartney. Then the Healing the Land team took the floor, and according to Armbruster, a miracle took place:

> Pastor Vuniani Nakauyaca repented on behalf of Pentecostal people towards those from different denominations ... He then called up the Healing the Land Team from Fiji to wash the feet of the spiritual leaders of Pangnirtung – both Full Gospel and Anglican leaders.
>
> In the evening a healing service took place and Vuni's son Save Nakauyaca preached about the crippled man at the pool of Bethesda, "Do you want to be healed?" (John 5:6).
>
> A man called Jeetaloo, who had been bound to a wheelchair for some four years, for the first time got out of his wheelchair and walked!

As in Kangiq&iniq, the land in Panniqtuuq was also cleansed with oil, water, and salt. Armbruster argues that the land already belongs to the Lord because he had created Panniqtuuq and the whole procedure of cleansing was therefore much less elaborate. It took place in the local gymnasium. Soil of the land was collected in a bucket and mixed with water, salt, and oil. It was "prayed over by the Fiji Healing the Land Team to be given back to the Lord while the leaders and elders of Pangnirtung gathered around to give their agreement and approval."

Apparently the defilement of the land was not seen in terms of long-term conflicts as in Kangiq&iniq, but in terms of the short-term problems in the community today. On July 17 Loie Mike writes, "Our land was defiled by you and me. Whenever you and I commit idolatry, adultery, shedding of innocent blood, breaking of covenants, and hold back our tithes and offerings, we defile the land, and it needs healing."

During the final evening service held with the Fiji team in Panniqtuuq, on Thursday, 20 July, a beautiful rainbow appeared over the whole community.

Vuniani pointed out that the rainbow was a sign of the covenant that God had made with man to remove the curse and never to let the earth suffer a great flood again.

THE NEED FOR MORAL REFORM

Solving social problems is high on the Pentecostal agenda. Members of the Full Gospel Church do not drink alcohol, they are discouraged from smoking tobacco, and they are not permitted to substitute marriage with common-law relationships. At Pentecostal and evangelical meetings, such as the meeting in Kangirsuk in April 2003, the topics discussed include gender relationships, intergenerational relationships, same-sex marriage, and reconciliation between generations.

Some political candidates, including Tagak Curley (elected in Kangiq&iniq), have campaigned against the inclusion of sexual orientation in the Nunavut Human Rights Act. Janice Tibbetts (2003) reports, "James Arreak said he was testifying on behalf of Inuit elders who oppose a 'gay tidal wave.' The Inuit, explained Mr. Arreak, strongly oppose same-sex marriage because it violates survival through procreation. Inuit values would say that gay people cannot create life, that they cannot produce a child."

For similar reasons, others, for example Norman Ishulutak in Iqaluit West and Rebekah Williams in Qurluktuq, have campaigned for the restoration of religious instruction in the schools (Bell 2004). In Nunavik, many people and at least three communities, notably Salluit, contested the teaching of Darwin's theory in local schools, arguing that this theory of evolution offends Inuit traditional beliefs.

During an event of the Promise Keepers (a Christian evangelical ministry dedicated to uniting men to become "godly influences" in the world),[50] held in Arviat on 27–29 August 2004, David Aglukark, Tagak Curley, James Arreak, and others discussed marriage and intergenerational relationships at length, emphasizing the value of protecting the institutions of marriage and family.

At the Promise Keepers event for the youth of Puvirnituq in 2004, pastors Eliyassie Sallualuk, Qalingo Tookaluk, and Jonas Alloloo addressed the young people. The meeting was described as follows:

> The youth were exhorted to become violent in the spirit against the evil spirits of suicide and lust that had been attacking them from without, and against the attitudes of bitterness and unforgiveness that had been attacking them from within …
>
> While youth were crying out to the Lord, one night, this young girl … came up to plead with her fellow youth to forgive their parents, to let the past go, to no longer hang on to the old resentments and bitterness.
>
> In between sobs, she spoke passionately and powerfully, and her words hit home with her fellow young people. Parents were also exhorted to reach

out to their youth and children, and to turn their hearts to their children, so that the hearts of the children would be restored to the fathers …

Many of the youth began to weep as they wondered what to do next, wondering if they should go to their parents to release forgiveness, and some of them no doubt wondering if they even wanted to let go of the past …

Then it happened. Many of the youth did not walk, but literally ran to their parents to fling themselves toward them as they were sitting in their chairs or standing. They were completely wholehearted to release forgiveness, and to hold nothing back. These are things that happen when the Spirit of God is outpoured.

At this gathering, a relative of a young man who had attempted to commit suicide that very night asked the people to pray for this youth. The next day he returned to say that the young man had not only survived, but had fully recovered.[51]

The Promise Keepers event held in Kangiq&iniq on Thanksgiving weekend, 7–9 October 2005, was dedicated to the topic of "Marriages of Integrity." Many people attended, including Tongola Sandy (director of the Kivalliq Inuit Association), Tagak Curley (founding member of ITK), and Raymond Ningeocheak (second vice-president of Nunavut Tunngavik Incorporated). One of the several social issues under discussion was the need to heal the gap between the generations. Fathers were encouraged to create bonds with their children, and a plea was made to parents to retain the wholeness of the family and avoid separation, which victimizes the children. "Each family member is unique and special, and yet each needs to be connected in order to achieve their own destiny and purpose in life. We cannot do it completely independently or in isolation from family and from community … This is how the world will be changed – one family at a time – as each comes into oneness, wholeness and healing rather than to normalize and legalize our promiscuity and disconnectedness and isolationism from one another."[52]

Beyond promoting the creation of regenerated family groups, Pentecostal and evangelical movements provide women with new opportunities to develop skills in public leadership, hence the good relationships between these groups and the Pauktuutit/Inuit Women of Canada. They very clearly intend to involve more women in religious activities. Since 2006, women leaders from across Canada have thus been invited to the Linking Hearts Annual Women's Conferences.[53] All these issues have been central in the Promise Keepers events organized since 2004.

REDEFINING CONNECTIONS TO THE PAST

Apart from dealing with present-day problems, the transformation of a community also implies redefining connections to the past. Such a perspective is congruent with Inuit conceptions. Inuit elders have always emphasized that one's wrongdoings would affect the life of children and grandchildren. Conversely, the misfortunes of people are often related to the misdeeds of their ancestors and namesakes.

The Pentecostal and evangelical movements reveal a similar perspective when they argue that many contemporary problems are linked to the sins of the previous generations: "Since those sins committed in previous generations are still affecting our generation today, this generation can break that curse and defilement by identifying with the sins of our fathers, and repenting for them. We might say, 'Well, I was not there when these things happened,' or that 'I didn't do those things personally.'"

Thus, transformation implies connecting with the past as well as redefining it. This ambiguity of the past is a structural feature of the modern discourse. The *inummariit*, the true Inuit of the past, represent a generation that was able to survive out on the land without modern technology, but they are also associated with taboos and superstitions that should be rejected.

Many of today's elders favour a revalorization of the past. The Nunavut government have followed suit in coining the phrase and promoting the notion of Inuit Qaujimajatuqangit. Inuit should reconnect with the *inummariit* and their ancestors' way of life. The Pentecostal and evangelical movements have addressed this problem of redefining the past, focusing not only on the *inummariit* but also on early newcomers, such as whalers and traders. The Fijian Healing the Land team visited two places with strong historical connotations: Uqsuriaq (Marble Island), northeast of Kangiq&iniq and associated with whalers and traditional practices, and Qiqirtat, where the Scottish whalers had their station, in Cumberland Sound.

a) Uqsuriaq, Marble Island

On 11 July 2006, some twenty-five Inuit from Kangiq&iniq, eleven members of the Fijian Healing the Land team, and Roger and Marge Armbruster travelled by boat from Kangiq&iniq to Uqsuriaq. The island was cleansed and healed the next day. Armbruster summarizes an origin myth of the island, quoting the words of an old woman, "'I wish, how I wish, that ice could turn into an island so I could live there.'" He continued, "Two years later, Uanik came back to the spot where he had left the old woman, but she wasn't anywhere on the island. He heard her voice say, 'Uanik, at last I got my wish; please don't worry anymore.' Uanik saw that the ice had turned to 'marble.' Then the old woman told him, 'My spirit lives on this marble island.'"

Armbruster does not question the existence of such a spirit, but wonders about its moral nature: "Clearly, we can see that this refers to some kind of an ancestral spirit that is alleged to live on this strange island of pure white rock which it is said to have first materialized as if by magic. The question needs to be asked, 'Is this spirit motivated by fear of by love?'"

Armbruster explains that people who visit the island are told to crawl a few feet out of respect for the old woman's spirit:[54] "In fact, some legends have it that if people do not bow down and 'crawl' to show respect for this ancestral spirit, that they will die within two years. I do not know if these myths were created by some of the original shamans, but I do know that not all of the shamans were plugged into the dark side of the spirit world. Some were true prophets of God who prepared the way for the coming of the gospel, and used their spiritual authority to encourage their people to accept the teachings of the Bible."

Clearly, Armbruster does not reject the shamanic past completely but instead integrates it into his Christian perspective, postulating that shamans prepared the way for the coming of the Gospel. Indeed, Uqsuriaq is a special place partly because of old Inuit traditions and partly because of the presence of white people. Armbruster refers to the James Knight expedition of 1719; its two ships were wrecked on the island and all members of the expedition died there. He lists many other disasters relating to Uqsuriaq and discusses how the whalers brought various forms of sickness and disease to the island and then took Inuit wives and begot many children: "As a result, as the children born to these relationships grew up, imagine their identity crisis, as the children were part Inuit and part non-Inuit. Without their non-Inuit fathers, not there to raise them and to love them, the children suffered, and many had to struggle to accept themselves, and to believe that they were just as valuable as children who had fathers, and whose parents were both Inuit. Further, the mothers could not have felt other than used, exploited and without self-esteem. There was no equality in the relationships."

Armbruster explains why the sins of the past still affect us today and need to be addressed; he identifies four particular areas "that bring defilement to the land, and that affect the environment in which we live today … 1. Idolatry, witchcraft, or the worship of ancestral spirits or the impersonal gods of nature; 2. Adultery, or any kind of sexual sin or perversion; 3. The shedding of innocent blood; 4. The breaking of treaties and covenants."

The pictures of the group's arrival on the island indicate that "nobody came onto the island crawling, or intimated that the spirit that controlled this island could bring a curse upon those who had come here, because they knew that the power of blessing is greater than the power of cursing." Armbruster identifies the participants in the "repentance and cleansing of the land" process that took place on Uqsuriaq:

1. The Fiji Healing the Land Team, led by Vuniani Nakauyaca, led the healing process, a process that they have seen work so effectively in village after village when they work under the legal authority of the indigenous tribal chiefs throughout Fiji.
2. There was one of the descendants of the original inhabitants of the land there, who represented those original peoples whom God had placed as stewards and as gatekeepers over this land.

3. There were those descendants whose fathers had practiced shamanism, who had entered the dark side of the spirit world, in such a way as to bring curses and defilement. The fact that some kind of a curse had existed on this island was evident by Marble Island's tragic history.
4. There were white people like Roger and Marge Armbruster, who could identify with the European and American forefathers, the whalers, who had added to the defilement of this land by exploiting both the sea resources and the people of this area.

The cleansing-of-the-land ritual is not described on the website of the Canada Awakening Ministries, but we may infer that it was done in very much the same way as in Kangiq&iniq, by applying the bread and wine representing the flesh and blood of Christ to the land. Armbruster explains, "Each of us could see our father's sin as our sin, and that we needed to identify with it, and apply the blood of Jesus to cleanse the land of its defilements and spiritual pollution. We praise God that the blood of Jesus speaks of better things than that of Abel's blood (Hebrews 12:24)." The land cannot be cleansed by money but only "by the shedding of blood, for life is in the blood." Armbruster explains that "[i]t will ultimately either be the blood of the family who sinned, or it will be the blood of Jesus which continually cleanses us from all sin whenever it is applied. Justice demands that sin be atoned by blood."

The Fijian Vuniani and an Inuk, one of the former announcers for CBC North, had a vision that a tarp of defilement that had covered the land was being lifted as the land was cleansed. Those participating in the cleansing gathered a pile of stones to make a monument. This memorial would serve for the next generation but also as a sign of God's blessing. In the caption under a photograph of the three religious leaders in the cleansing process, Armbruster explains how the cleansing of the land had required the cooperation of all of them: "These three leaders represent three spheres of influence who combined together to effect a healing of the land on Marble Island on that day. To the left is Vuniani Nakauyaca, who represented the Fiji Healing the Land Team. In the middle is Roger Armbruster, who represented his European and American forefathers, including the whalers. To the right is Tagak Curley, who represented his Inuit forefathers. I believe that this was a day that the land itself had been waiting for."

b) Qikiqtaq, Kekerten Island

When the Fijian team was in Panniqtuuq in July 2006, the issue was raised that some of the main problems in the community stemmed from the sins of adultery committed by the people who lived in Qikiqtaq in Cumberland Sound, some fifty kilometres south of Panniqtuuq. Many Inuit used to live on the island of Qikiqtaq in the heyday of the whalers. Present-day elders in Panniqtuuq acknowledge that during the days of the whalers many Inuit men would let the whalers have sexual intercourse with their wives in exchange for tobacco and cigarettes.

(above) A prayer is spoken, and two elders then explain what had happened on the island; (below) The male descendants of the men who allowed their wives to be used by the whalers kneel in front of the women and repent their sin and the sin of their fathers. Source: http://www.canada-awakening.com.

Armbruster relates that, according of Loie Mike, another source of present-day problems goes back to a curse a shaman made in 1970 when people exceeded their whale quota: "Local Inuit say that since that time, the number of whales diminished even more, and they have never since been as plentiful as they once were."

The trip to Kekerten Historic Park, on 19 July 2006, involved some forty people and eight boats. "The group included young believers but also elders and thus many descendants of the original inhabitants of the area. With the Healing the Land Team from Fiji consisting of three women … along with Cristina Maas from the International House of Prayer in Kansas City, Roger Armbruster of Canada Awakening Ministries and a group of local Inuit went out to Kekerten island. The whole group gathered together within the foundations of one of the original storehouses in a circle and the healing process was soon led by Savenaca Nakauyaca of the Fiji Healing the Land Team."

The group assembled in a circle around the original flagpole, which had been erected in 1857 beside the largest house in the station. "The Stories were told about how the Inuit women were used by the whalers for their own sexual gratification.

(above) A woman elder releases forgiveness to the men and repents on behalf of the women who had sinned as well; (below) After the men's repentance and the women's release of forgiveness, husbands and wives embrace one another. Source: http://www.canadaawakening.com.

However, the fault was not only with the whalers. The Inuit men realized that their fathers had allowed their wives to be exploited for sexual purposes by the whalers, sometimes in exchange only for something like tobacco."

The participants divided into two groups, a male one and a female one, and each group was asked to repent.[55] Armbruster explains: "It seems that misogyny, or the oppression of women, is a prominent sin through which the demonic finds an entrance into pretty much every culture, particularly through sexual exploitation which can be expressed in a myriad of ways internationally. Some of these include male dominance, marital subjection, buying and selling of brides, ritual deflowering of virgins, female circumcision, killing of baby girls, divorce, promiscuity of husbands, prostitution, pornography, discrimination of women in the family, education, leadership, the market place, and in the church."

In the first stage of the ritual, the men and women repented and apologised to each other on behalf of their ancestors. In the second stage, Armbruster, together with Darren McCartney, the Anglican minister from Panniqtuuq, repented "on behalf of the European and American whalers for their horrendous exploitation of the Inuit, for not having observed proper protocol and respect and for having

Monument erected in Qikiqtaq. Source: http://www.canadaawakening.com.

used their women. This was a horrific sin, and an abomination to God, who created every human being in his image and likeness to be treated with respect and dignity." After the collective repentance, husbands and wives spoke to one another one-on-one, discussing the issues they had between them and apologizing for their wrongdoings.

In the next stage of the ritual, the shamanic curse was reversed and transformed into a blessing: "Further, the Inuit identified with the sins of their fathers wherever they had put curses on the land, such as with the shaman who had cursed those government officials who charged an Inuk man for surpassing the quota on whales during the 1970s, resulting in a further depletion of the whales. That curse was changed into a blessing, so that the curse would be reversed, and transformed into a blessing, and a returning of the whales in greater number."

Finally, Vuniani Nakauyaca and the participants read aloud Deuteronomy 33:13–16a, 19, and Psalm 148:7–10, verses that stress the richness of the resources of the earth. As in the cleansings of the land conducted elsewhere, water, oil, and salt that had been prayed over and sanctified unto the Lord were applied to the land. In this case, they were poured onto a pile of rocks at the Kekerten Historical Site.

Now the curse was reversed. The water around Qikiqtaq changed to its original dark colour, and a new kind of fish was seen in the water.

CONCLUSION

Evangelical and Pentecostal movements in Nunavut have developed in close cooperation with religious leaders in the North and with Pentecostal and evangelical organizations down south. They have a strong social commitment and focus on solving the social problems in the North. The healing circles that developed in the 1990s (Lapage 1997; Arnakaq 1999) were closely connected to the new movements, and today their leaders play an important role in the expanding Pentecostal and evangelical movements. The healing circles focus on human suffering. They present the past as a source of wisdom as well as of suffering. By reconnecting to the old traditions, people can be healed of their pain and suffering. The causes of suffering are often attributed to the coming of white men and the institutions they introduced. Angaangaq, a healer originally from Greenland, recalled, "When the white men arrived, they made Inuit small." He stressed that the "complexity of social problems is deep and disturbing. Why are there so many? One of the greatest reasons is that Inuit are being put down by the people who came up north. They did not come to serve Inuit, they came to take over. And of course when someone takes over your life, you lose your own identity. You lose your own security. You lose your own traditions. We are clinging on to them."[56]

Pentecostal and evangelical churches have a similar reasoning and have developed similar concepts of regeneration. Many of their leaders are reborn and only became religious leaders after suffering from one or more of the severe social problems that beset modern Nunavut.[57]

Today a close network of political and religious leaders supports the evangelical movements and churches in local communities. Although evangelism has spread rapidly in the Arctic, its institutional basis remains weak. While many Inuit attend large-scale services and meetings, this does not imply that they have left or plan to leave their old churches. The evangelical and Pentecostal movements have a strong appeal, but they also evoke strong resistance. Elders associate certain aspects of these movements with shamanic traditions, but they also object to their being too religious.

Since the late 1990s, the Canada Awakening Ministries, supported by the Sentinel Group, has developed an ambitious program to connect North and South, the political and the religious realms, and to transform the land and society into a new religious and political order. The covenant signed at Parliament Hill on 21 June 2006 testifies to this ambition. It illustrates how evangelical leaders have come claim the role of representing Canada's first inhabitants. This ambition is clearly expressed in the rituals of healing the land. Armbruster tries to give legal foundation to these rituals by involving administrative authorities, but it is clear that the consent of the communities is not really required. The evangelical leaders themselves organize the rituals and decide how the various categories of people – aboriginal people, newcomers, men, and women – will be represented. These healing rituals evoke traditional rituals as well as Western traditions. Rituals of cleansing the land appear to have existed before the coming of Christianity. Peck, for example, reports that the *nunagiksaktut*[58] carried the confessions of the people to Sedna and in doing so prepared the land for hunting.[59] In the traditional rituals, people had to respect the land and adapt to it. They had to follow the rules of the location, crawl to Uqsuriaq, give pieces of meat at specific river crossings, avoid specific places, and so forth.

In the Pentecostal rituals, we find an inverse approach. The traditional rules are abolished, and the land is subordinated to the new religious and political order. In this respect, the Pentecostal rituals bring to mind the early explorers' tradition of claiming the land by hoisting the national flag on a pole inserted in the ground. In this way the land was subordinated to the political order that the newcomers represented, and the relations of the original inhabitants to the land were subordinated to this new order. Pentecostalism is a transcendent order that subordinates the land to Christ. The application to the land of bread and wine, representing the flesh and blood of Christ, and of water, salt, and oil effects this transformation, which is then objectified in the erection of a stone monument commemorating it.

Pentecostalism operates according to a modern ideology effecting transformation through a ritual of repentance. It is deemed that men and women, newcomers, and original inhabitants should become each other's equals and repent all actions that deviated from this course. The new transcendent moral order thus implies a cleansed land inhabited by individuals who respect each other as equals. The model fits perfectly into the modern ideology of the Canadian state, and thus these evangelical rituals can easily be perceived as a bridge from the present state of aboriginal suffering to a new political and religious order that harmoniously unifies modern Christian and political ideals. The rituals play on the old ideals of confession and repentance, the use of *inuksuit* as markers, and the close relationship between the health of society and that of the land. Thus, they provide a recognizable idiom that allows for the transition to a modern political structure. In their emphasis on global relationships, they connect Inuit to Fijians and Israelis, testifying to a new mobility that allows all nations to meet in the context of this new transcendent order.

A striking feature of Pentecostalism is its egalitarianism. No special place is allotted to the elders. The old Inuit traditions do not have an intrinsic value, but derive their value from an evangelical perspective. Younger people and politicians (e.g., Tagak Curley) seem to be more attracted to the evangelical movements than are the elders, who are still familiar with the old traditions. One can predict that the integration of Inuit Qaujimajatuqangit into the evangelical movements will become an important issue in the future.

12

Transitions and Transformations

Today, as in the past, many people wonder whether Inuit culture can survive in the modern world. Is the present interest in Inuit Qaujimajatuqangit a genuine attempt to preserve traditional Inuit culture, or does it signify the victory of modernity, objectifying and solidifying Inuit culture into a relic of the past? History shows that Inuit culture is tenacious and resilient. Inuit have managed to transform and reshape their culture continuously. Far from succumbing to the impact of Western culture and notwithstanding the incorporation of many new elements, Inuit have always refused to identify with Qallunaat, valorizing their own perspectives and traditions. When Inuit adopted Christianity, they did not value the new religion for its Qallunaat origin but soon viewed it as part of the Inuit cultural heritage. The shape of the cross could be recognized in the *inuksuk* represented on the Nunavut flag, and today we can find these flags in many churches. The syllabic system, which was introduced to the Inuit by Wesleyan and Anglican missionaries in the middle of the nineteenth century and was used for the translation of the Scriptures and hymns books, is now considered fully Inuit. The fact that most Westerners cannot read these texts only reinforces this perception. Similarly, the square dances introduced by the Scottish whalers are no longer associated with the days of the whalers, but are now considered part of Inuit tradition. Thus, the origins of objects and values do not really matter to the Inuit. They take a pragmatic approach, viewing the skills, ideas, and values that were adopted by the *inummariit*, "the true Inuit," as part of Inuit culture.

Early ethnographers saw no future for the Inuit. They believed that their culture was doomed once it came into contact with Western civilization. Inuit society would either disappear or be absorbed by Western civilisation. Early ethnographers, like many modern anthropologists, were caught in an ideology that considers the incorporation of foreign elements into Western culture as cultural enrichment and, conversely, the adoption of Western culture by other societies as a loss of authenticity. From this essentialist point of view, other cultures gradually disintegrate, losing their own traditions as they succumb to modernity,

The flag of Nunavut. The image of the *inuksuk* celebrates the stone monuments that guide the people on the land and mark sacred and other special places. The star is the Niqirtsuituq, the North Star, the traditional guide for navigation and the symbol of the unchanging leadership of the elders in the community. Source: http://www.assembly.nu.ca/english/about/flag.html.

whereas Western culture gradually increases in richness and cultural diversity as it absorbs other cultures. However, if we invert this ideological perspective, the development of Inuit culture in the last two hundred years can be viewed as a continuous process of enrichment, Western traditions becoming part and parcel of Inuit culture. Inuit culture did not disappear, but it has transformed as it had always done in the past.

PRE-CONTACT PERIOD

Archaeological evidence shows that in the pre-contact period Inuit continually refined their technologies and adapted them to the challenges of an ever-changing environment. We lack sufficient data about pre-contact beliefs and ritualistic practices to reconstruct them in any detail, but the archaeological evidence shows ample continuity in carvings, burial gifts, and ornaments. It suggests a gradual shift from a Thule lifestyle based mainly on sea mammal hunting to a more mixed orientation combining land animal hunting with sea mammal hunting. This probably affected Inuit beliefs and way of life, but we lack the data necessary to understand the process fully. There is no doubt that in pre-contact times Inuit were much more dispersed over the land than today, and population numbers may have been considerably higher before Inuit were afflicted by the contagious diseases imported by explorers and whalers.

We may infer that in the pre-contact cultures technology and religion were not separate as they are in Western culture or in contemporary Inuit culture. Religion did not exist as an autonomous domain. Beliefs and practices were related to hunting, birth, and death, and they could hardly be lumped together in a general category such as religion. The nomadic life required an extensive knowledge of the land that was not restricted to geographical knowledge but encompassed knowledge of the land's history and its non-human inhabitants.

Modern imagination tends to represent this period as a "timeless present."[1] The tendency to deny history to people without literate traditions, "people without history,"[2] is still strong in the fields of history and anthropology. Moreover, what is the point of speculating about a history without data? Yet archaeological data show that Inuit culture was always changing as it adapted to the environment and integrated external influences. Today, Inuit perceive the past as the world of the *inummariit*, the true ancestors, as it is described in *unikaaqtuat*, stories about the distant past. The Inuit film *Atanarjuat, the Fast Runner*, directed by Zacharias Kunuk, represents such a world as seen from the perspective of modern Inuit.

FIRST CONTACTS

For a long time Qallunaat mainly made contact with Inuit at the coast, and inland Inuit probably only heard rumours about these strange people, exclusively men, usually visiting the Inuit on their ships in the summer, and disappearing again before the sea froze over. Inuit inland in the southern Kivalliq likely profited from trade with the Hudson's Bay Company after the foundation of Fort Churchill in 1717. Some Inuit served as interpreters in the early 1800s. As long as the contacts with the Qallunaat were incidental, they probably had little effect on Inuit cultural traditions and migration patterns.

It is only for the period of first contacts that we have reliable information on Inuit religious beliefs and practices. Relations to land and animals, to ancestors, and between living people were integrated into the cosmological perspective of a hunting society valorizing the reproduction of animal and human life. These relations were safeguarded by *tirigusuusiit*, "traditional rules." Transgressions would result in retaliation by non-human agencies such as the weather, animals, ancestors, or non-human beings. Then the *angakkuq*, the shaman, would have to intervene to restore the relations between human society and these non-human agencies.

Parry, Lyon, Hall, Kumlien, and other early explorers reported on the nature of Inuit beliefs and practices. The nineteenth century was a period of transition, partly because the imported diseases greatly reduced the Inuit population, especially in areas such as South Baffin Island and the west coast of Hudson Bay where there was frequent contact with the whalers. In other areas, the effects of disease emerged more slowly, although imported diseases continued to plague the Inuit population until well into the twentieth century.

The Qallunaat ships also brought new goods, new opportunities, new ideas and technologies, and new values. Inuit rapidly integrated Western material goods and technologies into their way of life. They learned to appreciate the use of guns, knives, needles, and other goods. Inuit men sometimes sent their women to the ships to obtain tobacco, knives, and other useful things in exchange for sexual favours, but sometimes the whalers forced Inuit women to have sexual intercourse with them. The children of Inuit women and whalers were raised within the Inuit camps, and their status may have been similar to that of the children born from the pairings made at the Sedna feasts, who were considered the responsibility of the community.

Inuit also integrated the Qallunaat into their cosmological system. In the origin myth that depicts the Qallunaat as the offspring of the woman who did not want to have a husband and a dog, Inuit emphasized the skills of the Qallunaat in making tools. But the impact of Inuit relations with the Qallunaat is hard to assess. Birgitte Sonne (1990) argues that trade relationships with the whalers played an important part in the development of the myth of the girl who did not want to marry and the fulmar. Unfortunately, hard data are lacking. The connections she establishes between fingers and trade is not convincing when the complex symbolism of hands and fingers in Inuit cosmology is taken into account. The origin of Qallunaat is explained in the myth of the woman who married a dog, a mythical theme that appears to be very old. This story can be found across North America and Siberia, and the integration of the Qallunaat into the myth appears to be a minor adaptation that does not affect the basic structure of the narrative. Early sources (e.g., Lyon 1824) gave quite a complete account of the sea woman, her dwelling, and her companions (notably her father and her dog-husband), suggesting that at that time the complex of beliefs and practices relating to the sea woman was already fully developed.

In the second half of the nineteenth century, ancient traditions such as the tattooing of women and the celebration of the Sedna feast were already in decline. When new technologies were adopted, the associated rules and perceptions of life were also adapted. Thus, new rules were applied to the use of kettles by women (e.g., the cleaning of the soot) and to the use of guns by men. However, the shooting of animals with guns seemed to involve fewer rules than the killing of animals with bows and arrows.

Shamanism (*angakkuuniq*) appears to have been an arena of innovation. Shamans have always been in the vanguard of cultural development and were greatly interested in incorporating the beliefs and practices they learned from the Qallunaat into their own beliefs and practices. The list of *tuurngait* (helping spirits) compiled by Peck between 1894 and 1905 included many spirits that were inspired by Inuit images derived from Western culture, and testifies to the rapid integration of new perspectives into a shamanic framework. In the course of time, spirits in the shape of serpents, elephants, and telescopes were included in lists of shamanic helping spirits. Nineteenth-century celebrations of the Sedna feast may already have integrated some elements from the Christmas celebrations on the Qallunaat ships. Shamans such as Tuni in Igluligaarjuk played important roles in the adoption of Christianity. Tulugarjuaq, the first lay preacher in Baffin Island, may well have also been a shaman.

The shamanic world view was flexible and open, and the distinctions between the various categories of non-human beings and between different levels and scales of reality were always diffuse. Distinct categories (men and woman, people and animals, land and sea, seals and caribou, etc.) were part of the social world, which was organized by strict rules that kept these entities apart. As soon as we cross over into the non-social world of non-human agencies, these distinctions become problematic. This is particularly clear in the context of shamanism. A shaman could easily transform into an animal, interact with the dead, have both male and female features, and adopt any shape. The shaman operated on different levels and scales. When he made his shamanic journeys, it was an issue of debate among the Inuit themselves whether it was his *tarniq* or the *angakkuq* himself that made the trip. The different scales were also exemplified in the *qalugiujait* (the miniature weapons of the shaman) and the miniatures among the burial gifts and the *aarnguat* (amulets). The apparent lack of distinction in the Inuit categories of non-human beings was a structural feature of a cosmological system within which appearances deceive and transformations can take place in the world of non-human beings. The shaman had to be able to see through these appearances and transformations and make good use of them.

There is no doubt that Inuit beliefs and practices were changing considerably before the Inuit converted to Christianity, and the decline of old traditions may have facilitated the adoption of Christianity. We have to take into account that long before the arrival of the missionaries, Inuit were aware that the explorers and whalers practised Christianity. Some Inuit were given Bibles, witnessed Christian services, and received Christian instruction from whaling captains or explorers. In the middle of the nineteenth century, a few Inuit were even taken abroad to England and later returned to their native land to tell of their experiences.

People in the Nunavik region, in particular, would have known about the presence of Moravians in Labrador since 1765, long before the Church Missionary Society missionaries arrived in the area. Moravian missionary Matthias Warmow visited Cumberland Sound in 1857–58, and thus when Peck arrived in Uumanarjuaq in 1894, people may already have had some notions about the nature of Christianity and what to expect. In the Kivalliq, people became acquainted with Christianity through visits to Churchill, where the Anglican missionary Lofthouse resided in 1883.

The period of transition just preceding the adoption of Christianity is particularly rich in information. Boas and Peck in the South Baffin area and Rasmussen and the members of the Fifth Thule expedition in the Iglulik, Nattilik, and Kivalliq areas were remarkably successful in collecting detailed information on Inuit religious beliefs and practices. Yet, while Boas, Peck, and Rasmussen collected much information, they did not witness many rituals or ceremonies. Their descriptions suggest that these rituals were no longer practised (see Peck on the Sedna feast and Rasmussen on the Tivajuut in chapter 3). To what extent this was actually the case or to what extent Inuit just wanted to give this impression is hard to assess. Moreover, the early ethnographers avoided describing the new practices influenced by Qallunaat (see chapter 3 for Boas on the winter feast and chapter 2 for the lack of data in Rasmussen on Umik and the conversion rituals in Iglulik).

THE ADOPTION OF CHRISTIANITY

It took the missionaries in Uumanarjuaq and Igluligaarjuk many years before they made their first Inuit converts. The conversion process itself was initiated by the missionaries, but it could not succeed until Inuit shamans and leaders had decided that it was time to convert to the new religion. Thus, in most permanent mission posts, many former shamans played a leading role in the process, acting as preachers and lay readers.

The conversion process as practised in the areas of influence of the Roman Catholic and the Anglican churches diverged considerably. The Anglican missionaries spread Christianity through their famous red books; these were avidly read by Inuit and allowed Inuit leaders and shamans to develop their own versions of Christianity. The *siqqitirniq* ritual celebrated in the North Baffin area is a splendid example of a conversion ritual that elegantly combined Christian and shamanic traditions. Roman Catholic as well as Anglican missionaries rejected many of the new religious movements, especially those that developed in the Anglican sphere of influence, because they combined Christian and shamanic traditions.

The new movements were often led by shamans who included such different practices in their services as hand shaking, wife exchanges, Bible readings, and divination. Some practices had eschatological connotations, and religious leaders might identify with God or Christ. The movement started by Umik and his son Nuqallak in Iglulik played a major part in the transition to Christianity in that area. Whereas contemporary ethnographers emphasize that Nuqallak was a murderer, Inuit elders still speak of Umik with great respect. The movement stimulated the old *angakkuq* Ava to pass on his helping spirits to his sister, since he had now become a Christian and would no longer need them. It allowed him to speak freely about *angakkuuniq*, providing Rasmussen with a wealth of information, without endangering his shamanic abilities.

For a long time, the missionaries postulated that Christianity and *angakkuuniq* were incompatible, indicating that shamanism and Christian views should not be mixed. In some parousial movements, there were attempts to combine Christian and shamanic elements, but they did not succeed. The elders of today think that the founders of these movements sometimes went too far, and they stress the importance of moderation when it come to Christian beliefs and practices.

The Inuit's adoption of Christianity did not imply that they had lost their belief in shamanism; it only implied that they were no longer allowed to practise it. Moreover, some Qallunaat were considered potential *angakkuit*, and they (Van de Velde, for example) were usually well aware of it. Ethnographers and Oblate missionaries often took advantage of this opportunity to influence the spiritual lives of the Inuit. When missionaries claimed that their prayers and practices were more effective than those of the shamans, they placed themselves in the position of *angakkuit*. By accepting this role, they were in effect following the pattern of keeping one's identity as an *angakkuq* a secret. This may have been an old tradition. Qimuksiraaq's wife hid her shamanic abilities from her husband, and Takornaq informed Rasmussen (1929, 22) that most of the time she practised in secret.

After the adoption of Christianity, shamanism went underground and became invisible to Qallunaat. While it was no longer publicly performed, the recollections of the elders indicate that many shamanic practices continued and the missionary codices show that missionaries were perfectly aware of it. The skill with which the elders demonstrated *qilaniq* suggests that this form of divination has continued to be practised.

Certain central features of Inuit culture, such as shamanism and wife exchange, were targeted by the first missionaries as beliefs and practices that were wrong and immoral and should be abandoned. Other central elements, such as respect for animals, the naming system, and adoption, could be kept because the missionaries did not see them as falling within their religious domain. Biblical names were combined with Inuktitut names, connecting people to biblical figures as well as to Inuit ancestors. These practices are still very common today, even among the younger generations. Young people may change or abandon some traditions (such as selecting names only from their family), but they keep these ones alive. Thus, they bring their traditions up to date, adapting them to the conditions of modern social life.

Old rules (such as the prohibition against beginning the sea mammal hunt before the sewing of caribou skins was completed) were abolished and new rules (such as respecting Sundays) were introduced, but many of the old traditions were preserved to varying degrees in different areas. Traditions such as not having sex with a woman before hunting, of encouraging young women not to sit idle but remain active so that later they would have a quick delivery, of depositing tokens at specific places, and of not taking objects from graves and the land continued to be observed. These were no longer viewed as part of the traditional *pittailiniit* (refraining rules), as they were integrated within a Christian perspective. The celebration of Christmas introduced by the missionaries was quickly adopted by the Inuit, and Inuit games rapidly became an important feature of the celebrations. The practice of making gifts and giving presents became widespread.

For a long time, there existed fierce competition between Anglican and Roman Catholic missionaries. They represented not only different religious traditions but also different cultural traditions. Most of the Anglicans came from the British cultural tradition and espoused the Victorian moral values of the time. They abhorred the Inuit ritualistic practice of wife exchange and strongly opposed sexual relations between the whalers and Inuit women. They kept themselves aloof from the Inuit people in many respects and frowned upon any sexual relations between a missionary and an Inuk woman. Most Roman Catholic missionaries came from a French cultural tradition, although some had a Flemish background. They were much more prepared to accommodate and adapt to Inuit lifestyles. While their strict rule of celibacy might indicate that the Catholic missionaries did not have sexual relations with Inuit, the complaints about sexual abuse in residential schools suggest that they may have indulged in sexual activity with Inuit but kept it hidden from the public eye. Like the Anglicans, the Catholic missionaries remained aloof from their flocks. And on both sides, there was the expectation that the people would practise Christian sexual morality, namely monogamy. It may well be that the strong ban on sexual exchange may have contributed to the widespread popularity of adoption – that is, the exchange of children might have been seen as another means of connecting families.

Inuit were expected to be loyal to their creeds, Anglican or Catholic, and in their own lives reflect the antagonism that existed between the churches. Not all Inuit felt comfortable with this situation, and some Inuit preachers – Armand Tagoona, for example – switched their allegiance in the course of their careers.

LIFE IN PERMANENT SETTLEMENTS

In the years when Inuit first adopted Christianity, the churches took care not only of their religion but also of their education and health. Trade was dominated by the Hudson's Bay Company as well as some other private companies, while law and order was maintained by the Royal Canadian Mounted Police. All of these institutions played a role in assisting Inuit in times of need and starvation. However, in the attempt to develop policies that would address such difficult periods, the government came up with the idea of settling Inuit in permanent settlements and integrating them into the fabric of Canadian society. And this it proceeded to do. These experiences were very traumatic for Inuit, and the relocations in particular left deep scars. Many elders feel that white people deliberately severed their relation to the land in an attempt to destroy their culture.

In the permanent settlements that were developed in the 1950s and 1960s, education and medical care were no longer considered the responsibility of the churches. The government took over. The position of priests and ministers became less prominent. They were no longer the only ones to look out for the well-being of the Inuit; they now had to share this role with representatives of the government. Many viewed the development of these new settlements as a transition to modernity, and anthropologists have studied it from this perspective. There was little awareness among authorities and scholars that Inuit cultural life was still flourishing on its own terms. In the naming system, in the sharing of country food, in the practice of adoption, in visiting patterns, and in many other social dimensions, Inuit preserved their own traditions.

With respect to religion, the pattern was not altogether different. The hymns and prayers were used in much the same way as *irinaliutiit* were in the past; respect for animals remained a central feature of the value system; and perceptions of Sila (the weather) and the interactions with the land preserved and transformed old values. On the one hand, Inuit increasingly acted as ministers and lay readers, while on the other they continued to practise traditional healing and divination, though in secret – some even practised as *angakkuit*, notably in the Kivalliq. Elders believe that *tuurngait* are still around and can make contact with people, as in the case of Tungilik, who began to see a *tuurngaq* of his father, or that of Iluittuq, who saw a *tuurngaq* of the famous *angakkuq* Qimuksiraaq. Thus, the apparently modern communities, on the threshold of a new era, were integrating the past with the present, never completely relinquishing the fundamental values of Inuit society with respect to land and animals.

The era of the 1960s and 1970s was the heyday for community studies, particularly modern Inuit studies. The preservation of Inuit traditions and values had little priority and was left to specialists in the field, such as the Oblate Fathers, who faithfully preserved old traditions and songs on audiotape. In the 1970s and 1980s anthropologists began to realize that they were not dealing with a dead tradition. Various oral tradition projects involved the recording of the recollections of elders. The revalorization of the traditions of the past was closely connected to a new political consciousness, to the land claims, and to the wish for political autonomy that developed among the younger Inuit, especially those who had attended the residential schools. Their political activism played a major role in the establishment of Nunavut.

NUNAVUT

The creation of Nunavut in 1999 contributed greatly to political and cultural self-consciousness among the Inuit. The new government coined the notion of Inuit Qaujimajatuqangit – Inuit traditional knowledge – and actively began to encourage the preservation of this knowledge and its transfer to younger generations. Knowledge of the land and the animals was essential to a life on the land. This knowledge has diminished, since most Inuit no longer live out on the land but in permanent communities. They only go out on the land in spring or during the weekends, but they still identify as hunters. Whereas in the past Inuit travelled by foot and dogsled, today they more often use skidoos and ATVs (all-terrain vehicles) that allow them to travel faster and cover greater distances. As a result, their knowledge of the land and its history is much less detailed. The elders, however, have retained much knowledge of the land and its non-human inhabitants and are able to transmit this knowledge to the younger generations.

The various oral tradition projects and the ensuing publications, such as the Nunavut Arctic College Project and the Iglulik Oral History Project (see Bennett and Rowley 2004), revealed the richness of the recollections of the elders. Revalorization of the past is a continuing process. As one generation of elders succeeds another, perspectives of the past change. The elders Noah Piugaattuk and Rosie Iqallijuq clearly remembered life before the adoption of Christianity. We interviewed many elders born in the early 1920s. They grew up when Christianity was already around, but they witnessed many shamanic performances, especially in the Kivalliq. Many of the elders continued to observe old rules and precepts of life. Many of the elders who participated in our workshops had received training as *angakkuit* long ago, and some of them confirmed that they had passed on their knowledge to close relatives. However, not to be discussed publicly were such details as who is considered an *angakkuq* or to whom has been passed on his knowledge, powers, and helping spirits.

In modern-day Inuit culture, the notion of *ukpirniq* (religion) specifically applies to Christianity but not to the shamanic context associated with the many non-human beings that populate the tundra. As elsewhere, new notions have emerged. One of these is the concept Inuit spirituality, which is evident in healing circles and evangelical religious meetings.

Shamanism has become less visible in terms of practice, but it remains very much alive in the discourse. Elders prefer not to discuss their practices, but they take it for granted that people in desperate need will take recourse to the well-proven shamanic knowledge of the past. Except for a few isolated initiatives, neo-shamanism has not yet taken root in Inuit culture. We may assume that the old traditions are still too strong and that people should not fool around with neo-shamanism. The *angakkuq* Qimuksiraaq is reported to have said that shamanism would return through Christianity. In the past, preachers such as Tulugarjuaq, Qillaapik, and Nasook were deeply attached to the Christian models, but later, preachers such as Donald Suluk and Armand Tagoona integrated shamanic perspectives into their Christian beliefs and practices. Even today, elders maintain that shamanism continues and that each community will have its shamans "until the end of time," to use Kappianaq's expression. Most elders deny that they are *angakkuit*, but they openly admit to having some knowledge of it. The distinction between *angakkuit* and other people was never very clear, as everyone might have some powers. Today, there is plenty of room for speculation about who might have been (or still are) *angakkuit*. Even today's politicians in Nunavut might indicate that they have some shamanic knowledge. Peter Irniq taught a course on shamanism at Nunavut Arctic College in Iqaluit.

While from the modern perspective, *angakkuuniq* (shamanism) may tend to be presented in an idealized way, particularly in terms of wisdom and healing, the older generations know better. They know that *angakkuit* used their powers not only for the benefit of other people, but also for personal ends, which explains their resistance to teaching their shamanic knowledge to the younger people. Elders are aware that an *angakkuq* remains a dangerous enemy. In that respect, *angakkuuniq* always kept its ambiguity. Since *angakkuit* could heal as well as kill, hide as well as reveal, the danger of *ilisiq* (hexing) is always there. Inuit people today may feel grateful to Christianity for its message "to love one another," but when they or their relatives are in trouble, they may still turn to *angakkuuniq* for healing or protection. Interestingly, according to many Inuit, Christian prayers and hymns can be used for similar purposes. Despite some changes, shamanic views are thus still operating, though in a Christian context. The old tradition that an unsuccessful attack would turn against the attacker still seemed to work in the accounts of the dreams of Pisuk and Nutaraaluk. Evidently, even hymns and prayers could become instruments of death. The practice of *angakkuuniq* was restricted not so much because it was evil or non-Christian but because it shortened one's life and would affect the life of one's loved ones. The sufferings and even deaths of many people are still attributed to the actions of their ancestors.

Elders tend to be sceptical about the development of modern Nunavut, as well as about the lax attitude of many modern priests. In their old age, they have witnessed the rise of Pentecostalism, and many were reminded of the shamans. The Kivalliq elders often look back favourably on the work of the Grey Nuns and the residential schools. That generation is now rapidly disappearing, and younger elders are taking over. Soon the generation that went through the residential schools will be acknowledged as elders. They have a far less positive perspective on the residential schools and are much more positive about Nunavut, which they helped to create. There is clearly no such thing as an Inuit perspective or even an elders' perspective. Perspectives vary and they change rapidly.

The development of permanent communities in Nunavut and the consequent need to find ways to improve daily life in such communities could provide a new context for the revival of some views from the past. Inuit elders feel that life in these settlements is unhealthy, that there is overcrowding, and they advise that young people should be taken out on the land to help them reconnect to the land and the animals.

The rise of evangelical and Pentecostal movements is one of the most significant developments in modern Nunavut. These movements combine an effervescent Christianity with modern ideology. The Canada Awakening Ministries initiated the healing-the-land ritual in Panniqtuuq in which men apologized to women for sending them to the whalers and both outsiders and insiders apologized for their mutual lack of understanding. The ideals of the equality of the genders and of native people and newcomers were combined with traditional ideas about healing the land. The revalorization of the old Inuit culture has taken shape in the revival of drum dancing, new rituals for lighting the *qulliq* (seal oil lamp), courses in traditional skills (e.g., sewing and igloo building), the valorization of traditional clothing, and many other ways. However, the status of shamanism remains ambiguous. Some people feel that the good things about shamanism should be preserved; others feel they are better left behind.

REGIONAL COMPARISON

It is difficult to compare the various areas in the North because of the problem of uneven sources. Traditional beliefs and practices in the South Baffin area are described by Boas and Peck on the basis of data collected between 1882 and 1905. After the Inuit were converted to Christianity, ethnographic interest in their beliefs and practices dwindled. For the North Baffin area, the Nattilik area, and the Kivalliq, detailed information was provided a generation later by members of the Fifth Thule expedition (1921–24). The cult of the sea woman played a more important part on South Baffin Island than in the other area we have discussed. Boas and Peck refer to the great autumn feast as the Sedna feast. They might have exaggerated the importance of Sedna in light of their interest in identifying a supreme being in Inuit religion, but there is no doubt that Sedna was an important figure in Inuit culture. In North Baffin she seems to have been less conspicuous, and in the Tivajuut she does not appear to have played a role of any importance. In the Nattilik area, her role was even less significant, and in the Kivalliq, especially among inland people like the Ahiarmiut or Harvaqtormiut, she receded to the background, merging with Hila in the figure of Pinga.

There are other notable variations. Much more attention is given to Sila in the Kivalliq and the North Baffin sources, for example, than in the South Baffin sources. The importance of helping spirits also seems to have varied greatly in different regions. While there is an emphasis on the helping spirits as givers of game and bringers of joy in the data provided by Peck on Cumberland Sound, there is much more emphasis on *tupilattuq*, the killing of evil spirits, in the data from the Nattilik area and the Kivalliq. North and South Baffin both appear to have been marked by very elaborate systems of ritual rules, while this system seems to have been less marked in the Nattilik area and the Kivalliq. But in those areas the use of *aarnguat* (amulets) may have been much more prominent and the use of the drum and drum feasts more elaborate. We must, however, be cautious in assessing these regional differences. In many cases, the ethnographic data do not give conclusive evidence about the extent of these differences, and in some cases, they may be based on the idiosyncratic opinions of the Inuit informants of the early ethnographers in the nineteenth and twentieth centuries.

Baffin Island became predominantly Anglican, and the transition to the new religion there resulted in an abrupt break with the shamanic traditions of the past. Elders remember that these traditions were no longer discussed after their parents had converted. In the predominantly Catholic Nattilik and Kivalliq areas, however, the transition to the new religion seems to have been more gradual. Many elders relate that they or their parents combined traditional beliefs with Christianity. It is likely that these regional differences were to an important extent determined by the dominant religious affiliation of an area. Catholicism, it seems, gave more scope to combining aspects of two traditions than Anglicanism did. Anglicanism, however, was more successful in bringing Inuit into their church. Before long there were Inuit ministers, but no Inuk was ever ordained a priest. We find many parousial movements in the Anglican areas, but scarcely any in the Roman Catholic areas. The Anglican strategy of distributing the famous red books in syllabic writing may have played a part in enabling Inuit to develop their own versions of Christianity, but there were other regional factors as well. In our research we found that Baffin elders generally had less knowledge but also less interest in the shamanic traditions of the past. After the conversion to Christianity, shamanic performances were no longer practised and shamanic topics were no longer discussed. As a consequence, very little knowledge of shamanic traditions was preserved in the South Baffin area. Iglulik, on the boundary of Baffin Island and the Kivalliq, as well as the Roman Catholic and Anglican areas, takes an intermediate position in this respect. In the Kivalliq, not only have many Inuit elders preserved the knowledge about the shamanic traditions of their ancestors, but some still have the skills required for practices such as drum dancing and *qilaniq*.

For many years after the adoption of Christianity, the antagonism between Roman Catholicism and Anglicanism was traditionally quite strong in the northern communities, reinforcing the differences between those areas. Since the late 1990s, when this antagonism began to lose its strength, a new force appeared on the scene in the form of the evangelical and Pentecostal movements. These movements have their origin in Protestant traditions, and they initially developed largely in an Anglican context. They soon caught on strongly in the Kivalliq. Paradoxically, they seem to evoke to the elders' shamanism more than any other religious denomination. Speaking in tongues is one of several characteristics of evangelism and Pentecostalism that recalls shamanic behaviour. The Canada Awakening Ministries developed a religious and ideological perspective with a global orientation that in many respects fits Inuit beliefs and traditions perfectly. The rituals of confession and cleansing the land that Inuit, a Fijian delegation, and Qallunaat celebrated together evoked many traditional Inuit beliefs and practices relating to the land. Nevertheless, these movements strongly reject shamanism, and so it remains to be seen how the current increasing interest in *angakkuuniq* will affect the growth of the evangelical and Pentecostal movements in Nunavut. After initially opposing these movements, the Roman Catholic and the Anglican churches have now agreed to collaborate with them. Inuit attitudes towards these churches, which were once considered part of traditional Inuit culture itself by the elders, may change as the churches lose their grip on the population. Clearly, the continuing development of Nunavut and the rapid growth of the evangelical and Pentecostal movements will lead to further regional variation, to be explored in future research.

TRANSFORMATIONS

Ideas and values have shaped Inuit perceptions of both the past and the present. Their perceptions of continuities and discontinuities have very much depended on their points of view. Inuit value their connections with the past. They value the old skills, such as sewing traditional clothing, building igloos and kayaks, and handling the *qulliq*, and want them to be preserved. People enjoy wearing traditional clothing at festive occasions, as it allows them to identify with the *inummariit*. Drum dancing, now revived, enables Inuit to connect with their ancestors and has become an important feature of modern Inuit feasts. This connection with the ancestors has been greatly underestimated in ethnographic literature, but it played an important role in the conversion process. The first converts were called *majulajuit*, "those who want to go to heaven," and it seems that as soon as Inuit first heard about Christianity, they were fascinated by the idea of being able to meet their kin after death. Before Christianity, such connections with ancestors were only possible through the recycling of names, but with the Christian notion of heaven, connections were now possible at the level of the soul.

The institutionalization of respect for the elders also shaped Inuit valorization of the past. Whereas in the past relative age was always an important organizational feature in social relationships, today *innatuqait* (elders) have become an institutionalized category recognized by the Nunavut government. Special workshops and conferences are set up to record their recollections and views, and they are considered authorities on Inuit Qaujimajatuqangit. Obviously not all elders have the same degree of knowledge and understanding, and thus the idea of certifying elders has sometimes arisen; this, of course, would lead to further institutionalization of the position of the elders. This process can also be seen among other aboriginal populations. This trend to institutionalizing elders is part of a process that identifies traditional culture with the past, and it suggests that elders are the last representatives of that culture. When the last elder is gone, the old culture will have disappeared. Such a perspective risks obscuring our understanding of the dynamics of a culture that preserves its continuity by transforming and integrating new traditions all the time. Western technologies, syllabic writing, Christianity, square dancing – all became part of an Inuit cultural heritage. Many Inuit do not see why square dancing, practised by Inuit for generations, should be less a part of Inuit culture than drum dancing.

By integrating Western traditions into their own culture, Inuit transformed their own traditions as well as the new traditions. By transforming the *inuksuk* into a symbol of the cross, they have effectively made the cross an Inuit symbol, one that encourages people to follow the directions of their ancestors who built the *inuksuit*. By assuming that *qaumaniq* (shamanic enlightenment) does not come from this world but from God, as stated by Angutinngurniq and others,[3] Inuit embed their shamanic traditions in a Christian perspective. Such transformations always imply a double process, changing the perspective of the past as well as that of the present. There is thus no point in looking for authenticity. Inuit always knew how to adapt, and their culture has always changed over time.

In the past, health and well-being depended on observing the *pitailiniit* that governed the relationships between human beings, animals, and other non-human agencies. If people broke the social rules, hunting might fail, people might become sick, and thus the survival of society could be at risk. It was the task of the shamans to restore the balance between human beings and the non-human agencies that sanctioned behaviour. Inuit today still perceive a close connection between social and moral behaviour and the health and well-being of individuals and the community. The social problems of modern society are often attributed to lack of respect for the land, the animals, and social rules. Healing circles and evangelical movements make these connections in a Christian context, and the healing-the-land rituals of the Canada Awakening Ministries purport to heal people by connecting them to their ancestors and the land.

The transition from shamanism to Christianity took place over a long period, from the late nineteenth century until the middle of the twentieth. The missionaries expected that it was only a matter of time before the traditional beliefs and practices would abandoned, and they did not expect to see shamanic patterns reproduced in the Christian traditions or in other aspects of modern culture. But the missionaries themselves contributed considerably to this process when they began to collect oral accounts of the old traditions and encouraged the development of Inuit art.

Inuit art became an especially privileged field for the expression, representation, and transformation of shamanic traditions – replete with images of dancing bears, Sedna, non-human beings (especially animals with human features), *angakkuit*, and drum dancers. Inuit artists create miniatures of objects that used to have a complex symbolism in the shamanic context, such as *kamiit* (boots), knives, animals, and so on. Whereas in the past the *angakkuit* were the ones who could see the non-human beings and would describe to others what they looked like, now it is the prerogative of the artists to shape these representations. The artists are sometimes asked to explain to what extent their representations are based on their own experience, but most of them, in contrast to *angakkuit*, prefer to remain silent on that topic. But when we examine Inuit art in light of the oral traditions, it becomes obvious that encounters with non-human beings continue to play a central part in the discourse. Such encounters may occur out on the land or in dreams and visions. There is a vivid interest in these domains, as is illustrated in Inuit art, books, and films.

Discourses on non-human beings, souls, respect for the land and the weather, the power of animals to retaliate, the existence of *angakkuit* in the communities, and the causes of sickness and death are still very much engaged in. The question of to what extent living practices are related to these discourses, however, is not easy to answer. But here we should be cautious. Many elders were trained as *angakkuit* even if their parents had already converted to Christianity, and they continued to observe ritual rules despite being Christians themselves. But they did not easily acknowledge these practices, for they thought this was a sensitive issue. In the context of our workshops, we developed presentations and plays that allowed elders to demonstrate their skills in various practices without having to reveal whether they were being serious about it or not. In the demonstrations of *qilaniq*, it was immediately clear that many elders had great skill in these techniques and were familiar with the details of the procedure. In the play performed at the Kangiq&iniq workshop in 2002, Luke Anautalik from Arviat gave such a convincing demonstration of the killing of a *tupilait* that many spectators wondered whether this was the "real thing" and members of the Glad Tidings Church questioned the whole idea of such a play. Obviously it was just a play, and the elders would never have agreed to give these demonstrations if it had been anything else.

The elders are great players, and their demonstrations gave us insight into their capacities and abilities. They made it clear that they were not *angakkuit*, but in the workshops they also made it clear that they had the knowledge and skills to defend themselves and their families if necessary. Most elders are convinced that shamanism can be found in every community. Shamanism may have disappeared from the public eye, but the elders still pass on their knowledge to trusted relatives. As we have little information about how this is done, we prefer not to speculate, but we do assume that much knowledge as well as many practices are transferred to the following the generations.

The main element of the present interest in shamanism that we can record is the discourse. On one side we find the Pentecostals and the evangelists, both of whom totally reject shamanism, associating it with evil and the devil; on the other we have the elders, who argue that the good aspects of *angakkuuniq* should be retained, and the Nunavut government, which supports its study. But there is little to be observed in terms of shamanistic practice, since shamanism is no longer practised in public. Rasmussen complained that he did not witness truly impressive shamanic séances and that shamanism appeared to be on the decline. We receive impressive accounts of the initiations of great shamans such as Ava and Igjugaarjuk, but then are given completely different accounts of these initiations by elders such as Ujarak and Suvaksiuq. Moreover, the elders are perfectly aware that the terms of the discourse usually cannot be realized in practice. When Suvaksiuq decided to give a demonstration of initiation by immersion in water, he was not considering the period of five days he attributed to the initiation of Igjugaarjuk, but only a period of a few minutes. It is the very tension between the discourse and the practice that gives shamanism its meaning in the present day. Even though shamanic performances can be impressive in their own right, they can never match the feats of the shamans of the past. In chapter 1, we observed that the shamans of the past are usually reputed to have been more powerful than those of the present and that an *angakkuq* such as Qimuksiraaq from Kangiq&iniq acquired his great reputation only after death. This does not mean that we have to accept a model of decline, but we should acknowledge that the tension between discourse and practice has always been a structural feature of the shamanic complex.

There is a little sign that shamanism as an institution will return to Nunavut. Neo-shamanism has not yet taken root among the younger generations, and the transformations of shamanism seem to take shape within Christian context rather than outside it. The integration of shamanism into Christianity took place through the transformation of *irinaliutiit* into prayers and hymns, *aniartuq* into confession, *tarniit* into souls, and *angakkuit* into ministers and priests.

These transformations were usually acknowledged by the ministers and priests, but they nevertheless assumed that they had been instrumental in the ultimate victory of a complete transformation to Christianity. However, in more recent forms of Christianity, the shamanic dimensions seem stronger, not weaker, and this explains why some elders view Pentecostal and evangelical movements with suspicion. Although these movements take a strong position against shamanism, it seems that we can see some of its elements transformed in their notions of Satan, demons, rituals of cleansing the land, and the evil influence of hard rock and drugs. Modern categories are substituted for the evil spirits of the past, and accounts of being twice born through baptism sometimes evoke shamanic initiation. For these reasons, many elders reject Pentecostalism in favour of the more traditional forms of Anglicanism and Roman Catholicism.

Younger generations do not necessarily share the elders' perception that Christianity is part and parcel of Inuit culture. In the film *The Journals of Knud Rasmussen,* director Zacharias Kunuk focuses on the transition to Christianity. The *angakkuq* Ava appears as a true representative of the *inummariit* of the past. Despite his misgivings about the new religion, he sends his helping spirits away, while his daughter, tempted by the food to be had at Umik's camp, decides to join the new religion. The members of the Fifth Thule expedition represented in the film – Rasmussen, Freuchen, and Mathiassen – do not influence these developments in any way. The Inuit themselves make the transition to the new religion, although the influence of the white people is acknowledged in a dialogue between Nuqallaq and Ava. Nuqallaq states that he has opted for the ways of the white man, but Ava refuses to do so. The film provides an open ending. Ava sends his helping spirits away and becomes a Christian, but in the last shots of the film, we see Ava and his wife on his *qamutik* travelling across the land towards a group of people, but whether he will join Umik and his band, who have opted for the white man's way of life, remains an open question. Whereas the elders tend to represent the adoption of Christianity as an improvement, as freeing people from the restrictions of the traditional rules, the film presents a more modern perspective, suggesting that Umik's control of food played an significant part in the process of conversion and that conversion itself implied a deviation from fundamental Inuit values of sharing.

EPILOGUE

According to Inuit tradition, the words of the elders are very strong and must be heeded. In the introduction to this book, we quoted Saullu Nakasuk: "It is not possible to forget the words of our elders, when we had our elders as the ones who gave us instructions. Even so, what one heard as a child keeps on coming back even though it is not always on your mind." Elders may die, but their words will come to life again in the younger generations. Nunavut is a modern society, but Inuit culture is an old tradition. As long as the words of the elders keep coming back, Inuit will preserve their connection with their cultural heritage. Many of the elders quoted in this book have now passed away, but they have been replaced by younger people who now have the responsibility to speak with authority about the traditions of the past. As new generations of elders take over, the complex pattern of cultural resilience and cultural innovation will be retained. The cultural heritage of the Inuit will be reshaped to answer the challenges of modernization but will keep its connections with the past.

Appendix 1 | Glossary of Inuktitut Words

The Glossary is intended to facilitate reading. The spelling is not always consistent, as some words come from different areas. Moreover, different styles of transcription were used by different authors. For a more elaborate and detailed glossary that gives valuable information on local variations, we refer the reader to Kublu 2004.

Aagjuuk – Constellation comprising the stars Altair and Tarazed
Aakulugjuusi (also *Akkolookjo*) – First ancestor of the Inuit
aarnguaq, pl. *aarnguat* – Amulet
aglu – Breathing hole of a seal
aijaaja – Songs
Aivilingmio, pl. *Aivilingmiut* (also *Aivilingmiutaq*) – Inhabitants of Aivilik
aivirminiq – Walrus meat
Akkak – Father's brother
Akkuktujut – Orion's shoulder stars
Akudnirmiut, sg. *Akudnermio* – People living near Baffin Bay
alaq – Sole of a kamik (boot)
allaq, pl. *allait* (also *itqilît*) – Indian
aluk – Seal oil that is melted
Amajurjuk – Non-human being that carries human beings off in her *amauti*
amauti (also *amaut*) – Hood
Anaana – Mother
anautaq – Snow-beating stick
angak – Mother's brother, maternal uncle
angakkua – See *qaumaniq*
angakkuq, pl. *angakkuit* (also *angatquq*) – Shaman
angakkuuniq – Shamanism
angakok – See *angakkuq*
angakulaurtut – Shamanic power
angalik tingilik – "Has pubic hair"

angaluk – Shamanic belt. See also *tapsi*
angatquq – See *angakkuq*
angiaq – Undisclosed still-born child
angiraaliniq – The return of an animal once it has served humankind
angiraummigaq – Using an *irinaliuti* to make a person homesick
Anguta – Sedna's father
angutiqati – Paternal cousin
aniartuq – Confession, bringing things into the open
Anirnialuk – God (Christian)
anirnilumianitititituq – Practice of expelling demons (South Baffin)
anitat – Bring out
apiqsaq, pl. *apiqsait* – Helping spirit (Kivalliq). See also *tuurngaq*
apsait – Non-human beings who cause the earth to shake
aqsaq – Kickball
aqsarniit – Northern lights
aqtuqsinniq (also *aqtuqsittuq*) – A nightmare. See also *uqumangirniq*
ariserpoq – Ritual of eating a piece of intestine on behalf of your child
Arnakäp^{s}ha·luk – Sea woman
arnanait – Non-human beings, men carrying children in their *amauti*
Arviligjuarmiut – People from Pelly Bay
Ataata – Father
atigi – Inner caribou parka
atiq, pl. *atiit* – Name, namesake
avalaqsiut – *Irinaliuti* to surround a bear or a person
avatait – Sealskin floats
avvait (also *avvariik*) – Namesakes. See also *illuriik*
Ayurnarmat – Journal created by the Inuit Cultural Institute
Ekkos, sg. *Ekko* – Two spirits described by Boas
Ekkotow – See *Ekkos*
*ersigi*avut* – "Those we fear"
Guuti – God
haminnaarijut – Hallucinations
Harvaqtôrmiut – Inuit people in Kivalliq
havu·jaq – Knife with no iron edge inserted
i&urramut – Following the path of the sun
iglu, pl. *igluit* – Snow house
Iglulingmiutaq, *Iglulingmio*, pl. *Iglulingmiut* – Inhabitant of Iglulik
ijiraq, pl. *ijirait* – Invisible non-human being that can appear as a caribou
ikajuqti – Helping spirit. See also *apirsaq*, *tuurngaq*
iksirardjuaq – Catholic priest
ikuf.ifut – The one who hacks out something with an axe or knife. See also *ikujijut*
ikujijut – Part of frozen meat

ikuktaq – Part separated from a whole by a violent act
ikut·aujəq – Boas's term for the chosen woman in the Sedna feast
ilisiiqsiniq – Hexing someone
ilisiq – Sorcery, witchcraft
ilisitsut – Evil shamans
illuriik – Exchange partners, song partners, cross-cousins
ilummiqtaujuq – When a spirit enters a person's body
imuneq – A form of pack-ice
inaluat – Guts
ingillit – Angels
ingniriujaq, pl. *ingniriugjait* – Non-human being, shore spirit
inua – Its person, inhabitant, owner
inugarulligait – Non-human beings, dwarfs
Inuit Qaujimajatuqangit – Inuit knowledge that is still useful
inuk, pl. *inuit* – Person, owner, inhabitant
inukpak, pl. *inukpait* – Non-human being, giant
inuksuk, pl. *inuksuit* (also *inuksugaq*) – Stone marker in the shape of a human being
inummariit – True Inuit
inunguaq – Imitation of a person
inurajaq, pl. *inurajait* – Invisible being that has footprints
inurlak – Almost a person
inusia or *inusiq* – Appearance as a human being, identified with *tarniq* by Rasmussen
inuunngittut – Non-human beings
iqaaqtui – When an *angakkuq* questions someone
iqtuut – *Tuurngait:* Fatter than wolverines but as big. Their feet are turned backwards.
irinaliuti, pl. *irinaliutiit* or *irinaliut* – Powerful word, shamanic formula, incantation
irngutaq – Grandchild
irniq – Son
irsattuutijuk – Fist fight
Isarrataitsoq – Guardian of the Narrow Land
isuma – Reason, thought
isumannguarniq – Daydreaming
Isumasi – Journal created by the Inuit Cultural Institute
isumataq – The one with thought, intelligence; camp leader
itiqanngitut – Non-human beings, "people without an anus"
itqiliq, pl. *itqilît* – Indian. See *allaq*
ivik – Singing about another person to embarrass them
iviutiit – Songs that are used to embarrass people
ivulaaq – A thrumming sound

kaivitijung – The direction of the sun
Kajagsuk – Name of a mistreated orphan boy in an *unikaaqtuat*
kajait (also *ka'tut*) – Non-human beings, wolves
kamik; pair, *kamiik;* pl. *kamiit* – Boot
kanajuk – Sea scorpion
kataujak – Entrance of the *iglu*
kigluraq (also *kigjugaq*) – A little tattoo between the eyebrows
kinirvik – Special birth hut
kitingujaak – A river valley
kiversautit – Ritual consisting of a small offering to the sea woman
Kiviuq (also *Kivioq*) – Inuit traveller
komitik – See *qamutiik*
kukialuit – Fingernails
kukilingiattiat – Non-human beings, people with claws
lumajuut – Non-human beings living in the sea
majulajuit – "Those who want to go to heaven"
maktaaq – Whale blubber
maligaq – Rule, Canadian law
mamisarnit – Healing circle
manilirijuq – Procuring game
maturniit – Old campsites
*mianeri*avut* – "Those we keep away from and regard with caution"
Mikiniqsaq – Inuit name for Reverend J.H. Turner
mikittukuluk – Small pieces
miqqiijuut – Helpings spirits that are not telling the truth
miriaq – Vomit
na·ce·vəq – Period when men and women have to abstain from working, hunting, cutting meat, etc. See *nasivik*
nablut – Crossing places in the rivers used by caribou
nakasungnaikut – Those who have no calves, dangerous man-eaters
nakkaajuq – Descent of a shaman to the sea woman
nanurluit – Giant polar bears
narajait, sg. *narajaq* – Non-human beings, "people with the huge bellies"
narsiaq – Scarf
Narssuk (also *Nartsuk*, *Narshuk*, *Nârssuk*) – Spirit of the wind, child of a giant, often identified with Sila, the owner of the sky
nasivik – Period of observing rules especially after a death, funerary
Nattilingmiutaq, pl. *Nattilingmiut* (also *Netsilingmio*, pl. *Netsilingmiut*) – Inhabitants of Nattilik
niaqutait – Hillocks, tuft of moss
niksik (also *niksillu*) – Hook
ningauk or *ningau* – Son-in-law
niriujaaqtuq (also *niriujaarniq*) – Dreaming of something good

nirivigjuaq or *nirivijjuaq* – Big meal, Christmas
nugluktaq – Game consisting of pointing a stick into a hole
Nugumiut – People from South Baffin
nukak – Younger brother
Nuliajuk (also *Nuliayok*) – See *Sedna*
nuliaksaq – Man who has a non-human wife
nuliijaut – Wife sharing
nuna – Land
nunagiqsaktuq, *noonagekshown* (Boas), or *noonagêksaktuq* (Peck) – *Angakkuq* preparing the land for hunting.
nunajisartung – Boas's spelling of *nunagiqsaktuq*
Nunaliuqti – God
nunaluit – Evil spirits. See also *tupilaq*
nunaqqatigiit – "Those who share a piece of land"
Nunavut – "Our land"
nuqqavik – "Time to stop" (Christmas)
Nuqumiut – People from South Baffin
Okhamuk (also *Uqammaq*) – Inuit name for missionary E.J. Peck
okjuk (also *ukjuk*) – Bearded seal
Oqomiut – See *Uqqumiut*
Padlirmiutaq, pl. *Padlirmiut* (also pl. *Pallirmiut*) – People in the Kivalliq
paijjaat – Evil spirits. See also *tupilaq*
panik – Daughter
parlaniq – Scramble
pinguq – Ice hill
pinnguartuq – Play
piqujaq, pl. *piqujait* – Rule: "something that was requested to be done"
pisiliit – Hymns
pisiq, pl. *pisiit* (also *pihiq*, pl. *pihiit*) – Personal song
pitailiniq, pl. *pitailiniit* (also *pittailiniq*, pl. *pittailiniit*) – Rule: "refraining from doing something"
piusiq – Custom
pivijuaq – Christmas
puijiit – Sea mammals
pujartuq – Vapour emanating from the human body
Pukimma – Owner of the caribou
pukiq (also *pukeq*) – White parts of a caribou skin
pullalik (also *pullaalik*) – "He still has air"
pullaq – Bubble air containing the *tarniq*
Qaenermio (also *Qainirmiut*) – People in the Kivalliq
qaggilutit – Gathering in the ceremonial house
qaggiq (also *qage, qaggi*) – Big igloo where a feast is held
Qailertetang – See *qiluktelãk*

Qallunaat – White people
qallupilluit, sg. *qallupalik* – Non-human beings in the sea
qalugiujait – Miniature objects attached to a shamanic belt
qamutiik (also *komitik*) – Dogsled
qaqqialiq – Confession
qarisaq – Brain
qarmaq – House covered with skins
qau – Light
qaumaniq (also *angakkua*) – Shamanic light and vision
qavvangniqsaujuq – Dreaming while awake
qayaq (also *qajaq*) – Kayak, canoe
qiaqpaarniq – Throat singing
qilagiktut – Person able to do *qilaniq*
qilajaq (also *keleyak*) – The one who is lying down in the *qilaniq* ritual
qilajuq (also *keleyew*) – The one who holds the stick in the *qilaniq* ritual
qilak – Heaven, ceiling, palate
qilaniq – Head lifting
qilaujjarusiit – *Pisiit* sung with a drum
qilauti (also *qilaut*) – Drum, stick used in *qilaniq* by the Ahiarmiut
qilauta – Drum of the sun (i.e., the ring around the sun)
qillati – The rope or thong used in the *qilaniq* ritual
qillaujaq – Drum dance
qillaujjarniq – Drum dancing
qiluktelãk – Pair of *angakkuit* representing non-human beings at the Sedna feast
Qimiujarmiut (also *Atlet*) – People from the narrow land
qinngaq – Pray by shouting words
qinngarniq – Shouted prayer
qiqquat – Seaweed
qitinguq – "In the middle" (Christmas)
qiviutaq – Piece of feather used while hunting at a seal breathing hole
quaq – Frozen fish or meat
qulittaq – Caribou parka
qulliq – Seal oil lamp
qunujaaqtuq – Dreaming of something unpleasant
Quviasukvik – Christmas, time of joy
sakajuq – Calling a *tuurngaq*
sakaniq – Shamanic practice, when a *tuurngaq* enters the body of the *angakkuq*
sakausiit – Songs used by *angakkuit*
Sanah (also *Sanna*) – See *Sedna*
sanaji – Midwife
sanavoq – To work, to make
Satanasi – Satan

savuujaq – Knife with a sharp tip for killing *tupilait*

Sedna (also *Nuliajuk*, *Nuliayok*, *Sumna*, *Sanah*, *Sanna*, *Takanakapsaluk*, *Takannaaluk*, *Uinigumasuittuq*) – "The one down there," the sea woman

siksiit – Ground squirrels

Sila (also *Hila* [Kivalliq]) – Reason, weather

silagiqsaqtuq – Ritual consisting of cutting the wind

silaq, pl. *silaat* – Earth egg

silaup inua – The owner of Sila, weather spirit

silaqqatigiit – "Those who share a piece of Sila" (i.e., a piece of air, wind, weather)

sinaktuumaniq – Dreams

Siqiniq – Sun

siqqitiq (also *siqqitirniq*) – Conversion ritual involving the eating of forbidden meat

siturauti – Something used for sliding that was put on the grave of a person one thought was going to go after others, to prevent the person from doing so

sivullit – Ancestors, those who go in front

sunarlluk – When a man engages in sexual conduct with non-human beings

Takanakapsaluk (also *Takannaaluk*) – See *Sedna*

takutitauniq – Vision

taliillaajuuq, pl. *taliillajuut* – Non-human beings in the water, usually with a fishtail

tapsi, pl. *tapsiit* – Shamanic belt. See also *angaluk*

Taqqiq (also *Aninga* [lit. her brother], *Aningat*, *Tarqeq*, *Tatqiq*) – Moon

tarejumaq – "Shadowmaker," shaman

tarningirsiyuq – To deprive one of one's soul

tarniq, pl. *tarniit* (also *tarneq*, *tarninga*, *inusia*) – Miniature image of a being contained in a bubble of air, "soul"

tarriassuit (also *tallirait*, *talliqat*) – Invisible or shadow people

tau – Shade, human being

te^{g}*arut* – Short dog whip

Tikkertserktok – Name of the woman who owned the caribou

tinguq – Liver

tirigusuktuq – Abstaining from doing something

tirigusungniq – The fact that you have to refrain from something

tirigusuusiq, pl. *tirigusuusiit* – Rule: "refraining from something that is forbidden"

tiringnaqtuq – When a person has to follow certain rules, especially relating to clothing and food

tirlisi – Using an *irinaliuti* to keep an animal from being aware of the presence of the hunter

tivajuut – Inuit winter feast (North Baffin)

tonraq hiqloriqtuq – An evil spirit

tornarssuk – Big *tuurngaq*
Tugtut Igfianut – Name of the mother of the caribou
Tumivut – Journal created by the Avataq Cultural Institute
tunijjuti – A gift that is given to a *tuurngaq* through an *angakkuq* to enhance its power so that the task at hand will be completed successfully
tuniq, pl. *tuniit* (also *tunrit*) – People preceding the Inuit as inhabitants of the land
tunnituarruk – Non-human beings
tunuq – Caribou fat
tupilaq, pl. *tupilait* (also *tupelat*) – Evil spirit. See also *nunaluit*
tupilattuq – Killing an evil spirit
tuq&urausiq – Terms of address without mentioning the name of the person
tuurngaq, pl. *tuurngait* (also *torngaq, torngak*) – Helping spirit. See also *apirsaq, ikajuqti*
tuutaliit, sg. *tuutalik* – Non-human beings in the sea
Udlormiut (also *Ullormiut*) – Deceased people in the land of the day. See also *Ullurmiut*
ugjuk – Bearded seal
uilijauti – Husband sharing
Uinigumasuittuq – "She who did not want a husband," sea woman (North Baffin)
uiksaq – Woman who has a non-human husband
uissuit – Non-human beings living in the water
ukijijuq – Daydreaming
Ukjulingmiut – Inuit from Back River area
ukpiit – Non-human beings, people who changed from the shape of a bird to take human forms
ukpikarniq – Jump that allowed Inuit to rejuvenate themselves in the time before death existed
ukpirniq – Christian religion
ukpirtuit – Christian people
ukpirtuujuviniq – A religious person
Ulluriaqjuaq – Venus
Ullurmiut – Deceased people from the land of the day
ulu – Woman's knife
Ululiarnaq – Name of the woman with the *ulu* who eats the entrails of anyone who cannot resist her pranks
umiaq – A woman's boat
Umingmaktormiut – People in Qitirmiut
unalit – Indians, those who make war
ungirlaak – A bound-up bundle of walrus meat
unikaat – Stories referring to a recent past
unikkaaqtuat – Stories referring to a distant past

uqalaujau – When someone is told he or she is loved by the elders
uqalurait – Snowdrifts
uqaq – Tongue
Uqqumiut – People in South Baffin Island
uqsiut – Thong for dragging seal
uqumangirniq (also *aqtuqsittuq*) – The feeling of paralysis in a dream
Utkuhigjalingmiut – People in the Qitirmiut area
uujuq – Cooked meat
Uumaarniittuq (also *Omerneeto*) – First ancestor of the Inuit
uumajuit – Animals
uummati – Heart
uunarsiqunagu – The earth getting hot
uvivigtut – Non-human beings, "the fidgety ones"
uviluq – Mussel

Appendix 2 | Inuit Elders

Most of the elders in this list are identified by their place of residence when they were participating in our courses or workshops. While this information has helped us organize our regional perspective, the relation between an elder and a community is not always straightforward. Some elders may have grown up in another community, they may identify more with a specific category (e.g., Nattilingmiut) than with a specific community, and so forth. We have included in the list major Inuit informants of Rasmussen, Boas, and Peck, among whom are some renowned *angakkuit*.

Aaraniq, Maria: an informant of Peck, Cumberland Sound
Agalakti Siqpaapik Awa, Apphia: elder from Mittimatalik
Aglukkaq, Nilaulaq: elder from Talurjuaq
Akaralak, Matthew: elder from Arviat
Akkak, Gino: elder from Kugaaruk
Akpahatak, Maggie: Inuk from Aupaluk, Nunavik
Akpaliapik, Tategat: elder from Mittimatalik
Aksaajuq, Etuangat: elder from Panniqtuuq
Alasua Amittu, Davidialuk: elder from Povungnituk, Nunavik
Amaaq, Eli: elder from Iglulik
Amarualik, Eugene: elder from Iglulik
Amarualik, Jaypete: elder from Mittimatalik
Anarqaq: an informant of Rasmussen (Nattilingmiut)
Anautalik, Luke: elder from Arviat
Anautalik, Mary: elder from Arviat
Angalik, Louis: elder from Arviat
Angmalik, Pauloosie: elder from Panniqtuuq
Angugatiaq, Martha: elder from the Kivalliq
Anguti, Mary: elder from Kugaaruk
Angutinngurniq, Jose: elder from Kugaaruk
Aniksak, Neory: elder from Arviat

Anoee, Erik: Inuit pastor from the Kivalliq
Apsauqtaun, Otto: elder from Kugaaruk
Arnakak, Jay: Inuk from Kangiqtugaapik
Arnakallak, Samuel: elder from Mittimatalik
Arnatsiaq, Peter: elder from Iglulik
Arngna'naaq, Luke: elder from Arviat
Arngnasungaaq, Barnabas: elder from Qamanittuaq
Arngnasungaaq, Fanny: elder from Qamanittuaq
Arreak, Benjamin: elder from Mittimatalik
Ataguttiaq, Tipuula Qaapik: elder from Ikpiarjuk/Tununirusiq
Atsainak, Akeeshoo: Inuk from Iqaluit
Atuat (Mary Thompson): elder from Arviat
Atuat: elder from Ikpiarjuk/Tununirusiq
Aua. *See* Ava
Aullaluk, Eli: elder from Akulivik, Nunavik
Aupilaarjuk, Mariano: elder from Kangiq&iniq
Ava (also spelled "Aua"): an *angakkuq* and an Aivilingmiutaq informant of Rasmussen
Avaalaaqiaq: elder from Qamanittuaq
Bruce, Mikitok: elder from Aivilik
Enowyak, Ilisapi: elder from Arviat
Erkidjuk, Celestin: elder from Iqaluit
Hannah, Margaret: elder from Arviat
Haulli, Joe (also called Tasiuq): elder from Iglulik
Haulli, Sarah: elder from Iglulik
Igjugârjuk (also Igjugarjuk or Igjugaarjuk): famous *angakkuq* from the Kivalliq; informant of Rasmussen
Ijiraq, Alain: elder from Iglulik
Ijjangiaq, Teresi: elder from Iglulik
Ikilinik: from Back River; informant of Rasmussen
Iksivalitaq: famous *angakkuq* from Kugaaruk; informant of Rasmussen
I&luarnik, Henri: elder from Arviat
Iluakluak, Donald: elder from Arviat
Iluittuq, Levi: elder from Kugaaruk
Imaruittuq, Emile: elder from Iglulik
Inannerunasuaq: Inuk from Iglulik, probably originally from Nattilik
Ingniruniq: elder from Iglulik; father of Joe Haulli
Innuksuk, Aipilik: elder from Iglulik
Inugpasugjuk: from Nattilik; informant of Rasmussen
Inukjuarjuk: Inuk from Kinngait
Inuksaq, Simon: elder from Kugaaruk
Iqallijuq, Rose: elder from Iglulik
Iqalujjuup, Levi: from the Kivalliq

Iqijjuk, Celestine: elder from the Kivalliq
Iqugaqtuq: elder from Kugaaruk
Irkotee, Nicholas: elder from the Kivalliq
Irniq, Peter: elder from Naujaat
Irqugaqtuq, Bernard: elder from Kugaaruk
Itinnuaq, Ollie: elder from Kangiq&iniq
Ivaluardjuk: Aivilingmiutaq informant of Rasmussen
Ivaluarjuk, Henri: elder from Iglulik
Joamie, Akisu: elder from Iqaluit
Joamie, Aalasi: elder from Iqaluit
Kadloo, Timothy: elder from Mittimatalik
Kakkianiun, Guy: elder from Kugaaruk
Kakkik, Maaki: Inuk from Panniqtuuq
Kalluk, Silas: elder from Qamanittuaq
Kappianaq, George Agiaq: elder from Iglulik
Keenainak, Tapea: Inuk from Iqaluit
Kibkarjut: Inuk from the Pallirmiut group
Kigusiutnak, Philip: elder from Arviat
Konek, Helen: elder from Arviat
Kopanuak, Monique: elder from Arviat
Kublu, Alexina: Inuk from Iglulik
Kunuk, Paul: elder from Iglulik
Kupaaq, Michel: elder from Iglulik
Kupak, Felix: elder from Naujaat
Kuptana, William: elder from Kugluqtuq
Kutluk, Thomas: Inuk from Arviat
Makitgaq, John: elder from Qamanittuaq
Makpah, Jimmy: elder from Arviat
Mamgark, Andy: elder from Arviat
Manelaq: Nattilik elder; informant of Rasmussen
Mitiarjuk Nappaaluk, Salome: elder from Kangiqsujuaq (Nunavik)
Muqyunniq, Eva: elder from Arviat
Muqyunniq, Job: elder from Arviat
Nakasuk, Saullu: elder from Panniqtuuq
Nakasuk: Nattilik informant of Rasmussen
Nalungiaq: Nattilik informant of Rasmussen
Nanauk, Pelagie: elder from Arviat
Nasook, Martha: elder from Iglulik
Nasuk, Noah: Inuit pastor from Iglulik
Niviuvaq: elder from Talurjuaq
Nuliajuk, Luke: elder from Uqsuqtuuq
Nutaraaluk, Lucassie: elder from Iqaluit
Nuvalingaq, Moses: elder from Sanikiluaq

Okpik, Abe: elder living in Iqaluit
Okutak, Martha: elder from Arviat
Oosotapik: an informant of Peck's from Cumberland Sound
Ootooroot: elder from Arviat
Ootoova, Elisapee: elder from Mittimatalik
Orpingalik: Nattilik informant of Rasmussen
Orulo: Iglulik informant of Rasmussen
Paniaq, Herve: elder from Iglulik
Paniaq, Martha: elder from Kugaaruk
Papatsie, July: Inuk from Panniqtuuq
Papatsie, Malaija: elder from Panniqtuuq
Paungat, Helen: elder from Kivalliq
Peryouar, Barnabas: elder from Qamanittuaq
Peter, Aaju: Inuk originally from Greenland, living in Iqaluit
Pisuk, Felix: elder from Kangiq&iniq
Pitseolak, Peter: elder from Kinngait
Pitsiulaaq, Jaiku: elder from Iqaluit
Pitsiulak, Kudlu: elder from Panniqtuuq
Piugaattuq, Noah: elder from Iglulik
Putumiraqtuq, Silas: elder from Qamanittuaq
Qalasiq, Salome: elder from Kangiq&iniq
Qanguq, Isapie: Inuk from Iglulik
Qappik, Sami: elder from Qikiqtarjuaq
Qaqurtungniq: Nattilik informant of Rasmussen
Qasaluaq, Dominic: elder from Igluligaarjuk
Qaumagiaq, Noah: elder from Arviat
Qƒvigarssuaq: Kitlinermiut informant of Rasmussen
Qillaapik, Luke: South Baffin informant of Peck
Qimuksiraaq: famous *angakkuq* from Nattilik
Qinuayuaq, Eli: elder from Puvirnituq, Nunavik
Qitsualik, Rachel: Inuk from Iqaluit
Qojessie: South Baffin informant of Peck
Quassa, François: elder from Iglulik
Quinangnaq, Samson: elder from Qamanittuaq
Qulaut, Elise: elder from Iglulik
Qumangaapik: elder from Mittimatalik
Qumaq, Taamusi: elder from Nunavik
Sâmik: Nattilik informant of Rasmussen
Saumik, Bernadette: elder from Kangiq&iniq
Shamaiyuk, Julia: Inuk from Panniqtuuq
Shamaiyuk, Simon: elder from Panniqtuuq
Suluk, Donald: elder from Arviat
Suluk, Luke: elder from Arviat

Suvaksiuq, Peter: elder from Arviat
Tagoona, Armand: Inuit Christian leader from Kivalliq
Takornaq: Iglulik informant of Mathiassen
Taliriktuq: famous *angakkuq* from Igluligaarjuk
Tapaqti, Pujuat: elder from Kangiq&iniq
Tarqiapik, Sakariasi: elder from Nunavik
Tatilgäk: Inunnait informant of Rasmussen
Tirisikuluk, Niaqulluk: Inuk from Kivalliq
Tooloakjuak. *See* Tulugarjuaq
Tooloogakjuak. *See* Tulugarjuaq
Tulimaq: from Iglulik; informant of Lyon
Tulugaq, Julie: elder from Qamanittuaq
Tulugarjuaq, Peter: lay preacher; South Baffin informant of Peck
Tungilik, Victor: elder from Naujaat
Tuni, Joseph: catechist from Igluligaarjuk
Tunnuq, Elizabeth: elder from Qamanittuaq
Tunnuq, Martha: elder from Qamanittuaq
Tuttu, Miali: elder from Iqaluit
Ubluriak, Thomas: elder from Arviat
Ugpik: Nattilik informant of Rasmussen
Ujaraq: elder from Iglulik
Ujaraq, Hannah: elder from Iglulik
Uluakluak, Donald: elder from Arviat
Umik (also Uming): religious leader in Iglulik in the 1920s
Unaliq (also Unaleq): informant of Rasmussen in Iglulik
Uqayuituq, Janet: elder from Qamanittuaq
Uuttuvak, Ilisapi. *See* Ootoova
Uyarasuk, Rachel: elder from Iglulik
Uyauperk Aniksak, Margaret: elder from Arviat

Notes

Introduction

1 Oosten and Laugrand 1999b, 84.

Chapter One

1 Ross 1835, 25.
2 Quoted in Kekerten Historic Park, 14–15.
3 Ross 1997, 200. When Warmow (1858, 91) discussed the impact of his work, a rather different picture emerged and the continuity of Inuit traditions appeared much stronger: "Ready as they were to listen to me, superstition was deeply rooted in their minds, and they continued to lay the blame of sickness on the angakok."
4 See Ross 1975, 1977; Eber 1989; and Stevenson 1993.
5 See Boas 1964 [1888], 425–6: "the population has diminished at a terrible rate … The reason for the rapid diminution in the population of this country is undoubtedly to be found in the diseases which have been taken thither by the whalers. Of all these, syphilis has made the greatest ravages among the natives." See also Stevenson 1993 on the decline of the population in Cumberland Sound. He calculated that the population declined from 1250 to 380 and only reached the number of 1250 again in 2001. Similar processes of demographic reduction and cultural change occurred in the Kivalliq and North Baffin. Csonka (1995, 152) estimates the decline of the caribou Inuit from 1890 to 1923 to be from 1,375 to 630, and Mathiassen (1928, 208, 239–40) attributes the decline of the Iglulik population to exploitation, alcoholic, and disease.
6 National Archives of Canada (NAC)/Church Missionary Society (CMS), Reel A, 119, Letter from Peck to Mr Baring-Gould, 12/03/1897.
7 NAC/CMS/G1 C1/0, files 3 and 4, p. 13, Journal from J.W. Bilby for the year 1900.
8 See Kumlien 1879, 26; and Mathiassen 1928, 199.
9 Cole and Müller-Wille 1983, 50.
10 See Boas 1907 on the shooting of the snow-men (chap. 3; Müller Wille 1998, 137–8) and Mathiassen on Umik's Christian movement (chap. 2; 1928, 235).
11 For the impact of the whalers, see Sabo and Sabo 1985; Eber 1989; and Stevenson 1993.
12 To be discussed in chapter 2.
13 Mathiassen 1928, 236.

14 See, for instance, Father Van de Velde in the Codex Historicus of the Kugaaruk Mission of 26 October 1959.

15 See Thibert 1958. The story of Mitiarjuk from Kangirsujuaq was published 2002 by B. Saladin d'Anglure (see Mitiarjuk Nappaaluk 2002). In 1978 Cor Remie defended a PhD thesis on the diary of Bernard Irqugaqtuq from Pelly Bay/Kugaaruk. In consultation with the family of Bernard Irqugaqtuq, he is now preparing the manuscript for publication.

16 See Cowan and Innuksuk 1976.

17 The Inuit Cultural Institute organized three Inuit elders conferences, in 1982, 1983, and 1985; published a few life stories (e.g., *Recollections of Martha Angugatiaq, Helen Paungat, Levi Iqalujjuup*); and created two journals, *Isumasi* and *Ayurnarmat*. In Nunavik, the Avataq Cultural Institute was created in 1980 on the same model. Avataq organized six elders conferences; published two life stories; started a journal, *Tumivut* (more than twelve issues have been published to date); and published a cultural encyclopaedia written by T. Qumaq (see Laugrand 2002b and Csonka 2005).

18 The Iglulik Oral History Project, started in 1986, now consists of about 450 interviews that are accessible to the community and academic researchers. The files are preserved in a computer located at the Department of CLEY (Culture, Language, Elders and Youth). Much of the information published by Rasing (1994), by MacDonald (1998), and later on by Bennett and Rowley (2004) comes from these files.

19 The Iqaluit Oral History Project was initiated in 1994 and involved the cooperation of elders, Inuit youths, and facilitators in various sessions of about three weeks each. The project resulted in the production of a few life stories and in the publication of about twenty books in English, Inuktitut, and French within four different series: Interviewing Inuit Elders; Inuit Perspectives on the XXth Century; Memory and History in Nunavut; and Life Stories of Northern Leaders. The last series includes biographies of Abe Okpik (McComber 2005), John Amaroalik (McComber 2007), Paul Quassa (McComber 2008), Peter Freuchen Itinnuaq (Rodon 2008), and James Arvaluk (McDermott 2008).

20 During the fall of 2005, the Nunavut Arctic College offered a second course on shamanism (the first one being facilitated by B. Saladin d'Anglure), taught by the famous leader and former Nunavut commissioner Peter Irniq.

21 Rasmussen 1931, 120.

22 Iqallijuq interview, 1995. On the presence of Rasmussen among the Canadian Inuit, see Oosten 1988; Saladin d'Anglure 1988c; Remie 1988; Burch 1988; Damas 1988; and Hastrup 2004–5. See also Eber 2008.

23 Rasmussen 1931, 499–500.

24 See Michéa 1949.

25 In this respect, we derive inspiration from the medieval historians Le Goff, Schmitt, Le Roy Ladurie, and especially Kantorowicz (1957), who showed how the notion of kingship became embodied in the individual king and how the temporary identification of the physical body and the political body ensured the continuity of kingship. Thus, medieval people were well aware of how social categories need to be embodied in individuals to ensure the continuity of the society.

26 Durkheim 1920 (1912), 603–4, quoted in de Coppet 1992, 3.

27 See Therrien 2002a.

28 See Oosten and Laugrand 2002.

29 See Oosten and Laugrand 1999a, 5–6.

30 Many early ethnographers were not trained as anthropologists and lacked a clear theoretical perspective. Mauss produced one of the major theoretical contributions to the study of Inuit societies in 1904–5, but the value of his work for Inuit studies was only acknowledged much later by most ethnographers. For the debate on theory in ethnography of the Inuit, see Balikci 1978 and Riches 1991.
31 Oosten, Laugrand, and Rasing 1999, 27.
32 Oosten and Laugrand 1999b, 104.
33 Oosten and Laugrand 2001, 101.
34 See http://www.nac.nu.ca/publication/index.html and various books edited by Oosten and Laugrand, Briggs, Therrien and Laugrand, and Saladin d'Anglure.
35 See Douglas 1998.
36 Oosten and Laugrand 1999a, 26.
37 Our present research project, *The School of the Tundra* (L'école de la toundra), financed by SSHRC, focuses on this perspective.
38 See Oosten and Laugrand 2002, 2004, for more details about the participants' final recommendations.
39 Oosten, Laugrand, and Rasing 1999, 103.
40 Oosten and Laugrand 2002, 26.
41 Ibid., 15.
42 Ibid., 45.
43 Oosten and Laugrand 2002.
44 See Oosten and Laugrand 1999a.
45 Rasmussen 1931, 50.
46 See also Stevenson 1993 on warfare.
47 See also the Qitdlarssuaq story reconstructed by Father Mary-Rousselière (1991) that relates the nineteenth-century journey of a few Inuit families that followed their leader who had been involved in a killing incident. The group left South Baffin Island and reached Greenland after a difficult trip.
48 Oosten and Laugrand 1999a, 188.
49 See Oosten 2006 for a more extended discussion of Mauss and the field of anthropological study approach.
50 See Appendix 2 for a list of elders from the different communities.
51 Damas 2002, 195.
52 For an excellent introduction to shamanism and overview of the relevant literature, see Perrin 1995.
53 For example, Eliade 1970. See Hamayon 1993 for a critical review of the notion of trance in shamanism.
54 For example, Findeisen 1957; Lommel 1967.
55 Haases's book is probably the most comprehensive survey of Inuit shamanism, but as it is written in German, it is not accessible to many readers in the Canadian Arctic. Merkur also conducted a survey from a theoretical perspective, emphasizing the esoteric nature of shamanism. Saladin d'Anglure (2001) made important contributions to the debate and edited a volume on shamanism and cosmology.
56 Saladin d'Anglure 2001, 3–4.
57 Oosten and Laugrand 2002b.
58 See Oosten 1984.

59 See Rasmussen 1999, 124.
60 Oosten and Laugrand 1999b, 119–20.
61 On S. Frederiksen's archival material, see Saladin d'Anglure and Hansen 1997.

Chapter Two

1 Before 1912 Christian ideas were already circulating in the Kivalliq. In the 1860s Oblate missionaries established a mission post near Lac Brochet, and Anglican missionaries were evangelizing Inuit at their mission opened in Churchill in 1886 by Joseph Lofthouse. For more details on the history of the missions, see Laugrand 2002c; Brandson 1996; and Trott 1998.
2 We examine the role of Pentecostal churches in the North in chapter 11.
3 NAC/CMS, Reel A, 119, Journal from E.J. Peck, 1894–95, 26/12/1894 and 29/01-03/02/1895.
4 NAC/CMS, Reel A, 119, Journal from E.J. Peck, 1895–96, 26/04/1896.
5 For more detail on the Uumanarjuaq mission and context, see Laugrand, Oosten, and Kakkik 2003; Laugrand, Oosten, and Trudel 2006; Stevenson 1997; and Payment 1996.
6 Pitseolak and Eber 1993, 40–3.
7 See Oosten 1984; and Blaisel and Arnakak 1993.
8 Pitseolak and Eber 1993, 40.
9 Anglican Church of Canada (ACC)/General Synod Archives (GSA)/Peck Papers, M56-1, Series 38, no. 4, Journal from E.J. Peck, 1900–01, 28/01/1901.
10 Annie Atterngouyak died the day after, on June 13 (ACC/GSA/Peck Papers, M56-1, Series 37, no. 4, Journal from E.J. Peck, 1900–01, 13/05/1901).
11 Peck 1922, 21. ACC/GSA/Peck Papers, M56-1, Series 37, no. 4, Journal from E.J. Peck, 1900–01, 28/04 and 4–7/05/1901.
12 ACC/GSA/Peck Papers, M56-1, Series 37, no. 4, Journal from E.J. Peck, 1900–01, 14–15/01/1901.
13 ACC/GSA/Peck Papers, M56-1, Series 37, no. 4, Journal from E.J. Peck, 1900–01, 20 and 26/05/1901.
14 NAC/CMS/G1 C1/0, 1902, file no. 3, Letter from J.W. Bilby to Mr Baring-Gould, p. 2.
15 Lewis 1908, 319.
16 Eevik, quoted in *Stories from Pangnirtung*, 1976, 78–9.
17 See Blaisel, Laugrand, and Oosten 1999.
18 Laugrand, Oosten, and Trudel 2006, 193; ACC/GSA/Peck Papers, M56-1, Series 37, no. 5, Journal by E.J. Peck, 1903–04, 23/11/1903.
19 Such a movement of collective conversions can also be documented in Labrador, where historians refer to "a religious awakening." According to Jenness (1965, 14) and more contemporary historians (Hiller 1971, 852; Kennedy 1977, 268), Inuit shamans (e.g., Tuglavina and Kingminguse) started a Christian religious movement in Hopedale that soon reached Nain and Okak, where other shamans (e.g., Kapik and Siksigak) took over the conversion process.
20 Laugrand, Oosten, and Trudel 2006, 17–18; NAC/CMS/G1 C1/0, 1902, file no. 3, Letter from J.W. Bilby to Mr Baring-Gould, p. 2.
21 See chapter 3.
22 Laugrand, Oosten, and Trudel 2000.
23 NAC/CMS, Reel A, 119, Journal from E.J. Peck, 1895–96, 18/09/1896.
24 NAC, An Arctic Diary, 10 September 1910.

25 NAC, An Arctic Diary, Letter from Greenshield to his mother and father, 28/08/1911.
26 NAC/G1 C1/0 1991, no. 2, Letter from Greenshield to Mr Baring-Gould, 29/08/1911.
27 Oosten, Laugrand, and Rasing 1999, 114.
28 See Harper 1985 for the development of syllabic orthography and Laugrand, Oosten, and Kakkik 2003 for literacy among the early Anglican converts.
29 Mathiassen 1928, 235.
30 Ibid., 236.
31 See Saladin d'Anglure 1991, 15.
32 RCMP 1924, 36.
33 Rasmussen 1926, 22.
34 Ibid., 226 (our translation).
35 Rasmussen 1927, 127.
36 Laugrand 2002c, 205.
37 Qanguq and Mary-Rousselière 1985–86, 7.
38 White 1975, 41.
39 RCMP 1923, 35.
40 Ruskin 1972, 33.
41 RCMP 1924, 37.
42 Ruskin 1972, 33.
43 RCMP 1924, 37.
44 See Grant 2002, 216–17.
45 See Blaisel, Laugrand, and Oosten 1999.
46 Oosten, Laugrand, and Rasing 1999, 126.
47 See chapter 7 for a discussion of shamanic initiation.
48 Rasmussen 1931, 215.
49 NAC/RG 85, vol. 1017, file 18101.
50 Flint 1949, 49.
51 Schneider n.d., 116.
52 Father Rio was one of the founders of the mission at Qamanittuaq in 1927.
53 See Rio 1995, 52.
54 Thérèse was declared a saint in 1924.
55 Turquetil 1954, 320.
56 For more details on the history of the Catholic mission and the conversion process in Igluligaarjuk, see Turquetil 1954 and Laugrand 2002c.
57 For more information on the history of the Kugaaruk mission, see Van de Velde 1956b; Remie 1983; and Remie and Oosten 2002.
58 Laugrand 2002c, 162.
59 Ibid., 418.
60 For additional information on the Tirisikuluk story as related by the Oblate missionaries, see Fafard 1934, 1986, 1987.
61 See chapter 4 for a discussion of this practice.
62 Oosten and Laugrand 2007, 210.
63 Laugrand 2002c, 168 (our translation).
64 Ibid., 418 (our translation).
65 Oosten and Laugrand, eds, 1999a, 137.
66 Oosten, Laugrand, and Rasing 1999, 22–3.
67 Journal entry for 7 January 1898, in Laugrand, Oosten, and Trudel 2006, 91.

68 Oosten and Laugrand 2002, 46–7.
69 Ibid., 47–8.
70 Remie and Oosten 2002, 136.
71 See the Codex Historicus of Igluligaarjuk (January and July 1944); see also the Codex Historicus of Mittimatalik (20-06-1952) referring to the case of Kautainum. Inuit and missionaries attributed about six murders to him.
72 See Remie and Oosten 2002, 133.
73 Archives Deschâtelets (AD)/HEB 1933 J83C 10b, Journal du père Joseph Buliard, 17 octobre 1945 au 20 juillet 1949.
74 Ibid.
75 Oosten and Laugrand, eds, 1999b, 89.
76 Ibid., 94–5.
77 Ibid., 11.
78 Ibid., 109.
79 Ibid., 75.
80 Ibid.
81 Oosten and Laugrand 1999b, 126.
82 See Laugrand 2002c.
83 The tradition of electing Inuit pastors continued for a long time. Erik Anoee, Armand Tagoona, and Noah Nasuk are other well-known pastors. It is only since the 1960s that new leaders, such as Benjamin Arreak, have been trained at the Arthur Turner Training School in Panniqtuuq.
84 See Fafard 1967a.
85 This is particularly obvious in the attitude of missionaries towards clothing. See Geller 1998 and Trott 2001.
86 Parousial and prophetical movements are widespread in the Arctic, especially in areas under the influence of Protestant churches. In Nunavik a few cases are summarily mentioned by Balikci (1960) and Saladin d'Anglure (1984, 1991): in the 1920s a local messiah named Qituraaluk on the eastern coast of Hudson Bay announced the end of the world and the departure of the Inuit to Heaven; in another movement, in Kangirsuk in 1920, Inuit prepared themselves for the end of the world (see Grant 1997); in the 1940s a woman on Milliit Island announced the return of Jesus; and in Nain, Labrador (1873–74), Inuit imitated the descent of the Holy Ghost at Pentecost and decided to kill a woman accused of being possessed by the devil. For information about religious upheavals outside Canada's Eastern Arctic area, see Holland 1979 and Laugrand 2002c.
87 Codex Historicus de la mission d'Igloolik 1941, 106.
88 The concepts of time and space (*-vik*) are closely related in Inuktitut.
89 See Atuat's comments in Innuksuk and Cowan 1976, 23–4.
90 On negotiation, see Fienup-Riordan (1990, 1997), who developed this approach with respect to Alaska.
91 See Stuckenberger 2005.

Chapter Three

1 See Boas 1864, 607–8: "Inasmuch as Hall did not see the feast himself, but had only a description by an Eskimo, into which he introduced points of similarity with Christian feasts, it may be looked upon as fairly agreeing with the feast of the Oqomiut."

2 Boas 1964, 606.

3 Quoted in Boas 1907, 489–90.

4 See Knötsch 1991, 75–6.

5 Boas 1964, 195–8.

6 Müller-Wille 1998, 137–8. Boas (1907, 512) writes: "Sometimes after the meetings of angakut, snow-men will be made. After they are finished, the men rush out and cut them to pieces, and then run back to the house in a great hurry, apparently in fear of the spirits of the snow-men." Elsewhere he explains the dangers of the *tupilait*: "Some Netchillik Eskimo, when leaving a village, made a couple of snow-men, which were cut to pieces by one of the natives, who was afraid of them. After returning home, this man became unwell; and it was believed that, if the snow-men had been left, they would have caused trouble of some kind in the village. If an angakok had cut them down, he would not have felt any ill effects."

7 See also Bilby 1923, 210–24.

8 For the role of play in Inuit winter feasts, see Oosten 2001; and for the exchanges in feasts, see Blaisel and Oosten 1997; and Saladin d'Anglure 1989.

9 Quoted in Boas 1901, 139–40.

10 Laugrand, Oosten, and Trudel 2006, chap. 13; see also Bilby 1923, 210.

11 Boas 1901, 140–1.

12 Laugrand, Oosten, and Trudel 2006, 333.

13 See also Amarualik (IE 287) and Kappianaq (IE 174), both from Iglulik, in MacDonald 1998, 48, for similar practices in the North Baffin area.

14 Laugrand, Oosten, and Trudel 2006, 321–2.

15 See Rasmussen 1929, 231–2, 241–3. See also the testimonies from Atuat and Ujaraq collected by B. Saladin d'Anglure (1989). The etymology of *tivajuut* is unclear. Duncan Pryde points out that in the Western Arctic the word refers to a foot movement in a drum dance (John MacDonald, oral communication, May 2001). Thalbitzer (1925, 249) relates, "On the northerly section of the west coast tiwaneq 'to dance with writhings of the body, drum in hand,' and tiwasoq 'the one who dances' corresponds to E. Gr. Tiwaneq and tiwaleq. Several other words belonging to the old dance terminology are preserved on the west coast, mumerneq for instance, whereas the E. Gr. uaajeerneq 'mimic dancing' is unknown in West Greenland. North of Disko Bay (70° N. lat.) I saw the old fashioned tiwaneq combined with a round dance in which the dancers joined hands and circled from right to left. That dance form is perhaps still preserved there. The tiwasoq dancer stood in the center of the circle and led the singing, those in the circle joining in the chorus."

16 MacDonald 1998, 40.

17 Ibid., 120–3.

18 See Oosten 1986 for a discussion of this practice.

19 Oral communication, 17 August 1998.

20 According to Trott, "this song is the very well known 'Alianaiλaqpuq inuunialirama' or 'Quviaksukpunga inuunialirama' (which has now almost become a national song). The interpretation of the song comes from Arnaujumajuq of Ikpiarjuk. The interpretation differs from that given by Qanguq of Mittimatalik as recorded by Nattiez (and following Nattiez, Conlon) and also from the interpretation provided by Susan Aglukark in Mittimatalik."

21 *Aagjuuk* is a constellation comprising the stars Altair and Tarazed and possibly in some regions Alshain. These stars form part of the European constellation Aquila (MacDonald 1998, 44; Oosten and Laugrand 2001, glossary).

22 An excellent survey of Christmas celebrations, especially of the older sources, is provided by Kenn Harper's book *Christmas in the Big Igloo: True Tales from the Canadian Arctic.* For the descriptions of Christmas in the 1930s and 1940s, we rely on accounts published in journals such as the *Beaver, Eskimo, North, Inuit Monthly, Inuktitut,* and *Inuit Today,* as well as on oral information provided by Inuit elders.

23 National Library of Canada Bulletin, January/February 2002, vol. 34, no. 1.

24 See, for example, a description of a Christmas celebration in 1819–20 by Captain Parry (quoted in Harper 1983, 1).

25 Oosten and Laugrand 1999a, 197.

26 Burant 1998, 83.

27 Christmas celebrations in Labrador could be fruitfully compared to similar festivities in Greenland. See Laugrand and Oosten 2002b for more details and additional references. "In West Greenland in the days about the 1 January it was the custom, not so very long ago, to celebrate the so called beggars' feast (*qinusaqattaaufik*[,] 'the begging time')" (Thalbitzer 1925, 246). In Nunavik, more recent Christmas celebrations have been described by Lapage (1976), Metcalfe (1978), and Dorais (2000). See also Anonymous 1981. Games emerged as particularly important elsewhere. In Alaska, Christmas celebrations were marked by games, competition, and communal feasting (see Bodenhorn 1993).

28 Hall 1864, 1,193.

29 Laugrand, Oosten, and Trudel 2006, 70–1; NAC/CMS, Reel A, 119, Journal from E.J. Peck, 1895–96, 24/12/1895.

30 See Hantzsch 1977, 37–8.

31 See Fleming's description of a Christmas celebration in 1913 (in Harper 1983, 17–18).

32 Ducharme, "Christmas in the land of Santa Claus. Christmas in the far north," Archives Deschâtelets, Ottawa.

33 See also accounts given by Captain H.T. Munn (1932, 252).

34 J-E. Bernier, "Christmas in Arctic Bay, Baffin Island" (1909) (in Harper 1983, 10–12).

35 For the 1930s and 1940s period, other accounts of Christmas can be found in the Oblate missionary archives: see "Christmas in Iglulik" (AD/LCB 421 C56R 4); "Noël Esquimau" (AD/HEB 3335 L93C 19); and "Noël fiévreux" (AD/HEB 3335 L93C 20).

36 See Harper 1983, 36–9.

37 Ibid., 28.

38 See Laugrand and Oosten 2002a.

39 The year she moved to Aggu Bay she could no longer see Venus at Christmas: "I thought it might be a sign that [the] world would end" (MacDonald 1998, 93).

40 Oosten and Laugrand 1999b, 130–1.

41 Laugrand 1997a; Blaisel, Laugrand, and Oosten 1999.

42 Oosten and Laugrand 1999b, 81.

43 See the film *Light in the Darkness* by G. Mary-Rousselière.

44 See also the account of Christmas celebrations in Pelly Bay in Van de Velde 1956b.

45 See, for example, "Noël Esquimau" (AD/HEB 3335 L93C 19). The Oblate missionary observes that the first thing visiting people did when they used to gather for Christmas, was to buy new clothing for all of them (including children) at the Hudson's Bay Company post.

46 NAC/CMS, Reel A, 121, Journal of Julian Bilby 1898–1899.

47 Quoted in Harper 1983, 18.
48 See also "Noël Esquimau" (AD/HEB 3335 L93C 19). The Oblate missionary stated that Catholics as well as Anglicans attended the Midnight Mass.
49 See Dorais 2000 and Stuckenberger 2004.
50 See chapter 4 for a discussion of the notion of owner.

Chapter Four

1 Much of the material on human origins comes from Iglulik sources. For an excellent study of these mythological data and present views, see Saladin d'Anglure 2006.
2 See also the version told by Unaliq's wife, Tuglik (Rasmussen 1929, 252–3).
3 This myth is well known on Baffin Island (see Boas 1901, 143–4, 178; 1907, 483–5; Bilby 1926, 206; Rasmussen 1929, 252; Saladin d'Anglure 1977, 88; 1986, 48–9, 51; 1988b, 21; 1990, 84–8; 2006, 64–9), as well as among the Nattilingmiut (see Rasmussen 1931, 209).
4 Oosten, Laugrand, and Rasing 1999, 199.
5 See Kappianaq IE 358 and Laugrand 1999a.
6 Rasmussen 1929, 235; 1931, 108.
7 On the arctic night, see Bordin 2002, 2008.
8 Rasmussen 1929, 92.
9 Ibid., 253.
10 Ibid., 254.
11 Saladin d'Anglure 1977.
12 See Saladin d'Anglure 2006, 69.
13 With the coming of Christianity, the myth of Aakulukjjusi and Uumanirtuq tended to merge with the story of Adam and Eve. Thus, Jaypete Amarualik from Mittimatalik stated, "Aakulukjjusi and Uumanirtuq are the first two Inuit ancestors. They were husband and wife in the life before us. I think they are Adam and Eve like it is written in the Bibl." (Amarualik, 1995 interview; see also Eevik in *Stories from Pangnirtung*, 1976, 87. The adoption of rules remained a central point. Ujaraq from Iglulik related, "Because Adam was the only man on earth he couldn't bear children, so God gave Eve to him and they had children. When the people started to grow the evil spirit came out and gave them evil minds … Now this is why there is a lot of forbidden things, like, why women were not supposed to smoke anything from the ground when they had their babies" (Thérien 1978, Interview 1, 25/07/1978).
14 Boas 1901, 143.
15 Arviat workshop, 2007.
16 Ibid.
17 Ibid.
18 Ibid.
19 Bennett and Rowley 2004, 31.
20 Oosten, Laugrand, and Rasing 1999, 40.
21 See chapter 6.
22 See also Rasmussen 1929, 257–9.
23 Rasmussen 1929, 287–90; 1931, 364 ff. See Oosten 2002 for a study of variants of the Kiviuq myth.
24 Oosten and Laugrand 1999a, 152.
25 Oosten and Laugrand 1999b, 67–8.

26 Kugaaruk workshop, 2004.
27 See chapter 7 for a discussion of this kind of dream.
28 Kolb and Law 2001, 36.
29 Schneider 1985, 267.
30 Kolb and Law 2001, 39.
31 Ibid., 35.
32 Rasmussen 1929, 97–8.
33 Laugrand, Oosten, and Trudel 2006, 370.
34 See Guemple 1994.
35 See Blaisel and Arnakak 1993.
36 Boas 1901, 323. In relating the experiences of the soul in its various modes of existence, this story constitutes an interesting variant of the story of the boy and the seal recorded and extensively discussed by Ann Fienup-Riordan (2000) in her work on the Yupik of Alaska.
37 Rasmussen 1931, 215.
38 See also Thalbitzer 1930.
39 Laugrand, Oosten, and Trudel 2006, 383–4.
40 Rasmussen 1929, 57.
41 Ibid., 56–7. According to Rasmussen (1929, 57–8), "The nablut were the water crossings where the caribou were lanced from kayaks. At these sacred places bones were not to be cracked with stones for the marrow. An Iglulik narrative recounts that the earth suddenly closed over a woman who broke this injunction, as the powerful souls of the caribou killed her."
42 See Mannik 1998, 177–8.
43 Ibid., 156; 205.
44 Ibid., 188.
45 See Kublu 2004.
46 Oosten and Laugrand 1999a, 58.
47 Rasmussen 1929, 199.
48 Ibid., 184.
49 Ibid., 183.
50 Bennett and Rowley 2004, 44.
51 See Laugrand 1999, 2002c.
52 Oosten and Laugrand 1999b, 3.
53 See Galatians 2:1–14 for Saint Paul's discussion of how Mosaic law relates to the freedom of Christ.
54 Oosten and Laugrand 1999b, 34–5. The Anglicans and, to a lesser extent, the Catholics strongly supported abstaining from work on Sundays (see Laugrand 2002c, 349, on new Christian rules).
55 Oosten and Laugrand 2002, 173.
56 Kugaaruk workshop, 2004.
57 Ibid.
58 Oosten and Laugrand 2002, 26.
59 On the role of insects in Inuit shamanism, see Laugrand and Oosten n.d.
60 Oosten, Laugrand, and Rasing 1999, 37–8.
61 Ibid., 34.
62 Ibid.

63 Ibid., 36.
64 See *Nunatsiaq News,* 14 March 2008 on the number of bowhead whales.
65 Mannik 1998, 177–8.
66 See Laugrand and Oosten 2002a.
67 Turquetil 1968, 43.
68 Rasmussen 1931, 220.
69 Mannik 1998, 70–1.
70 Rasmussen 1929, 148.
71 Ibid., 59.
72 Boas 1907, 239.
73 Rasmussen 1929, 178. On terms of addresses (*tuq&urausiq*), see Kublu and Oosten 1999.
74 Bennett and Rowley 2004, 7.
75 See Damas 1972, 48–9; and Guemple 1972, 63.
76 Kublu and Oosten 1999, 69–70.
77 Through names and words, the elders would be able to shape the identity of the baby. Elizabeth Tunnuq from Baker Lake explained, "When people are going to make a baby with words, they tell the baby to be what the adult wants it to be. Sometimes the adult tells the baby to be a certain way because the adult couldn't be the way s/he to be, so s/he would tell the child to be as s/he said, like to be a great hunter, or good in sewing (Mannik 1998, 246).
78 Bennett and Rowley 2004, 4; see also Mannik 1998, 174.
79 On government names and "Project Surname" in the early 1970s, see Alia 1994.
80 Kublu and Oosten 1999, 70.
81 Quoted in Scheffer 1950, 97. According to Soby 1997, Inuit in Greenland took many names from the missionaries, thinking these names would protect them. Pitseolak and Eber (1993, 61) mention similar practises in the South Baffin area. On the naming system in contemporary Inuit society, see also Saladin d'Anglure 1998a; and Nuttall 1994.
82 Kublu and Oosten 1999, 80.
83 Ibid., 68.
84 On the reincarnation of *tarniit,* see Guemple 1994 and Blaisel and Arnakak 1993.
85 See Fienup-Riordan (1990, 167–91) Original Ecologists, The relationship between Yup'ik Eskimos and animals.
86 Peter et al. 2002, 170.
87 Ibid., 167.
88 See Laugrand and Oosten 2007 on the relationships between bears and human beings.

Chapter Five

1 See Thalbitzer 1926.
2 Oosten, Laugrand, and Rasing 1999, 5. Today, Pentecostal groups and other religious people fear that God may retaliate by bringing the world to an end through storms and other ecological disasters.
3 Bennett and Rowley 2004, 119.
4 Carpenter (1955, 71), for instance, writes, "Today there is a recognition of the existence of a god superior to and more powerful than Sumna [Sanna]; and there is recognition of Jesus as the Son of God who came to save the world from sin … there is no acceptance of the idea that Sumna and the old spirits do not exist. The missionary says they are false,

and the Aivilik accept this as meaning that they are evil and deceitful or simply outworn and inefficient. But the Aivilik still believe that the ancient spirits exist and can interfere in the affairs of men if allowed to do so … It is thought that she [Sumna] is restrained from further revenge only by the powers of the new deity. Christianity then does not stand alone in the new spiritual order … [it has] merely enlarged the native pantheon."

5 Various versions of the myth of Aakulujjuusi and Uumarnituq exist. Rasmussen (1929, 252) writes, "There was once a world before this, and in it lived people who were not of our tribe. But the pillars of the earth collapsed, and all was destroyed. And the world was emptiness. Then two men grew up from a hummock of earth. They were born and fully grown all at once. And they wished to have children. A magic song changed one of them into a woman, and they had children. These were our earliest forefathers, and from their offspring all the lands were peopled."

6 Rasmussen 1929, 254; 1929, 110.

7 Oosten, Laugrand, and Rasing 1999, 199.

8 Rasmussen 1931, 212. The early ethnographers often refer to this language as the shamanic language.

9 Ibid., 265.

10 Rasmussen 1929, 98.

11 See also Kappianaq, "There is another island just north of it called Avvajja that was left behind to 'cool,'" in Oosten and Laugrand 2001, 63.

12 See Saladin d'Anglure 2001b, 142–4.

13 Ibid., 143.

14 Saladin d'Anglure 2006, 75.

15 Kugaaruk workshop, 2004; see also Bennett and Rowley 2004, 122.

16 Bennett and Rowley 2004, 122.

17 Ibid., 123.

18 Oosten and Laugrand 2001, 81.

19 Bennett and Rowley 2004, 124.

20 Ibid., 123.

21 Ibid., 122.

22 Ibid.

23 Ibid.

24 Ibid., 5.

25 Ibid., 224.

26 See Rasmussen 1929, 115.

27 See Oosten, Laugrand, and Rasing 1999, 34.

28 For discussions of Sila, see Saladin d'Anglure 1980a, 1990, 2006.

29 Saladin d'Anglure 2001b, 90.

30 Ibid.

31 See also Rasmussen 1931, 210, 229–30.

32 Rasmussen 1929, 230.

33 Rasmussen 1931, 230.

34 Ibid., 230–1.

35 Oosten and Laugrand 2007, 180–1.

36 Oosten, Laugrand, and Rasing 2000, 124.

37 See Ijituuq and Ujaraq in Saladin d'Anglure 2001b, 183.

38 See also Boas 1901, 493.

39 Rasmussen 1931, 265.
40 Oosten and Laugrand 2002, 96–7.
41 Ibid., 98.
42 See Saladin d'Anglure 1980a; 1989; 2006, 84–105; and Oosten 1989.
43 See also Saladin d'Anglure 2001b, 182–3.
44 See MacDonald 1998 for extensive discussions of Inuit astronomy.
45 Rasmussen 1931, 232.
46 See also Rasmussen 1931, 232–6; Oosten 1983; Kublu, quoted in Oosten and Laugrand 1999s, 161–82; and Saladin d'Anglure 2006, 106–41.
47 See Oosten 1983 and Saladin d'Anglure 1990.
48 Oosten, Laugrand, and Rasing 1999, 187.
49 Rasmussen 1929, 74.
50 Rasmussen 1931, 231; see also Rasmussen 1929, 74.
51 Akatsiaq, quoted in MacDonald 1998, 133.
52 Rasmussen 1929, 612.
53 See Saladin d'Anglure 1989 and MacDonald 1998 for more details about the arctic sky and related stories.
54 Swinton 1980 (13) presents a survey of the various names in different areas. It is not always clear whether we are dealing with distinct names or with dialectical variations (e.g., Nuliajuk, Nuliaqok, Nualiayok). Lyon, who wintered in the Iglulik area in the early 1820s, called the sea woman Ay-willi-ay-oo (Aiviliajuq), or Nooli-ay-oo (Nuliajuk), "the ever copulating one" (Thalbitzer 1926, 378). Aiviliajuq is glossed by Thalbitzer 1926, 378 (see also 1928, 401), as "the one who easily (and always) divorces, who does not want to be married."
55 Oosten and Laugrand 1999b, 99.
56 Laugrand, Oosten, and Trudel 2006, 401.
57 See discussion of Sumna among the Aivilingmiut in Carpenter 1955, 72.
58 Laugrand, Oosten, and Trudel 2006, 368,
59 Rasmussen 1932, 172.
60 See also Boas 1901, 167, for other versions of the myth.
61 Rasmussen 1929, 193. For the Nattilingmiut ritual, see Boas 1907, 502, which contains Captain Comer's report: "After the new caribou-skin clothing has been made for the winter, and when the men are ready to go sealing for the first time, the whole of their clothing and hunting-implements are hung over a smudge made of dry seaweed. The Netchillik use nests of small birds for making the smudge. It is supposed that the smoke takes away the smell of the caribou, which would offend the sea-mammals." See also Rasmussen 1931, 242.
62 Laugrand, Oosten, and Trudel 2006, 369.
63 See Laugrand and Oosten 2006 for a discussion of the significance of these small gifts.
64 Oosten and Laugrand 2002, 114.
65 Oosten and Laugrand 1999a, 152–61; see also the version by Kupaaq in Saladin d'Anglure 1992a, 2006, 142–69.
66 See Sonne 1990 for an extensive discussion of variants; see also Swinton 1980. Rasmussen (1929, 63–6) collected an extensive version of the story in Iglulik in the early 1920s from Orulo, the wife of the *angakkuq* Ava. Although a seventy-five-year gap separates the two versions, the texts of Orulo and Kupaaq are quite close, testifying to the strength of the oral tradition in this area.

67 See chapter 6 for a discussion of these various beings.
68 See also Rasmussen 1931, 380–2.
69 Oosten and Laugrand 1999a, 152.
70 Rasmussen 1931, 498.
71 This substitution is problematic. Many rituals require a person to cover the hands and to wear mittens (e.g., an *angakkuq* during a shamanic performance).
72 See Laugrand and Oosten 2003.
73 Rasmussen 1929, 173.
74 Rasmussen 1929, 253. The narrative of the sea woman suggests that the fulmar was robbed of the fingers of his wife by her father, who transformed them into sea mammals. In that respect, the connection between fingers and light is intriguing, as the theft of light by the raven in Alaskan mythology constitutes a very old theme.
75 Rasmussen 1929, 127.
76 Oosten, Laugrand, and Rasing 1999, 190.
77 Tape 6 IV C – 12 TIV – C 15TI, preserved in the Canadian Museum of Civilization in Ottawa.
78 See Boas 1907, 483: "It is believed that Sedna's father is sitting beside the door in her hut. His head is covered with a blanket, and his hand is ever ready to take hold of the soul that enters the house. His hand is always raised, and, as soon as he takes hold of a soul, he draws it under his blanket into his bed."
79 Rasmussen 1932, 24.
80 Bennett and Rowley 2004, 186.
81 Boas 1901, 145.
82 See also Lyon 1824, 363: "a very large and fierce dog, which has no tail, and whose hinder quarters are black." According to Boas (1964 [1888], 588), the dog had only one eye, like her father, and he never moved from his place while in the house.
83 Rasmussen 1931, 226.
84 See Lyon 1824, 364.
85 See Thalbitzer 1926, 381; and Jenness 1922, 188–9.
86 See Kroeber 1900, 317.
87 Pentekainen (1968, 335–52) examined the *angiaq* complex. The word *angiaq* means something hidden or concealed and often refers specifically to hidden miscarriages and stillborn babies. In Greenland a miscarriage resulted in the transformation of the miscarried fetus into an evil spirit. Glahn, quoted in Pentekainen 1968, 337, reports: "When a woman conceals and refuses to reveal her periods to others or delivers her child in secret without telling others that she has made an abortion, both the aborted fetus and the menstrual blood change into an *angiaq*" that has to be killed by an *angakkuq* in very much the same way a *tupilaq* is killed. Pentekainen assumes that this phenomenon only occurs in the Eastern Arctic and is due to Viking influence. The belief that a miscarriage should never be hidden is widespread among Inuit, and it is unlikely that it can be explained by Norse influences.
88 Oosten, Laugrand, and Rasing 1999, 189. According to Rasmussen (1929, 197), caribou hair could also be used to protect oneself. Anyone dressing a corpse for burial must stop up his or her nostrils with caribou hair (see also Boas 1901, 516). Rasmussen (1929, 181) relates that when leaving a house, one can prevent others who use it from having successful hunting by sweeping caribou hairs – which are always left behind on the sleeping platform – in towards the inner side of the platform. All game will then leave the

immediate neighbourhood. This method of making a snow hut unlucky is called *piŋuserluineq*.

89 Rasmussen 1932, 27.

90 Boas 1964 [1888], 504.

91 The prohibition to smile evokes the prohibition to smile at the *tivajuut* (see pp. 78–9), as well as the prohibition to smile in the presence of Aukjuk, who lives in the land of the moon man and cuts out the entrails of those who laugh at her pranks.

92 See Boas 1907, 504–5.

93 Oosten and Laugrand 2002, 113.

94 Rasmussen 1929, 100.

95 Ibid., 100–2.

96 Bennett and Rowley 2004, 185.

97 Oosten and Laugrand 1999b, 98.

98 Oosten and Laugrand 2002, 114. See Rasmussen 1930, 51, for the harpooning of the sea woman as described by Qalaseq from Igluligaarjuk.

99 Kugaaruk workshop, 2004.

100 Ibid.

101 Arviat workshop, 2003.

102 The name of the mother of the moon spirit.

103 Oosten and Laugrand, 1999b, 126.

104 Oosten and Laugrand 2002, 39.

105 See chapter 6.

106 See Laugrand and Oosten 2008a.

Chapter Six

1 Saladin d'Anglure, ed., 2001, 64.

2 Oosten and Laugrand 2001, 71–4.

3 See Laugrand, Oosten, and Trudel 2000; and Ouellette 2002.

4 See also Merkur 1985.

5 See Balikci 1963.

6 Saladin d'Anglure 2001, 248.

7 See Sonne 1990 for a survey and analysis of various versions of the myth.

8 Rasmussen 1929, 256.

9 Ibid., 66.

10 Rasmussen 1931, 121–2.

11 Rasmussen 1929; 1931, 122. See Holtved 1943 for a discussion of the versions of the myth.

12 See, for example, a myth collected by Boas (1901, 171–3, 203–9) about the origin of *allait*, according to which a woman was transformed into an *allaq* (a hairy monster) that killed her parents; and several stories about *allait* attacks on Inuit (Boas 1907, 522–5; 529–32).

13 See Kalluak 1974.

14 See also Sonne 1996, 241–2.

15 Rasmussen 1929, 195.

16 See Boas 1964 [1888], 634–6; 1901, 210–13; 1907, 541–2; and Brody in Freeman 1976 for various traditions on *tuniit*. Hawkes (1916, 143–7) and Nungak and Arima (1988, 31) describe the *tuniit* in Nunavik as giant people who live in stone houses.

17 Rasmussen 1931, 113.

18 Mannik 1998, 134.
19 This detail is consistent with what Nunavik Inuit indicated to Saladin d'Anglure (2006, 154), that the *tuniit* fled to Greenland through northern Labrador.
20 Rasmussen 1931, 117.
21 Rasmussen 1929, 256.
22 Ibid., 195.
23 Rasmussen 1931, 115.
24 Ibid., 114.
25 Rasmussen 1929, 256–7.
26 Rasmussen 1931, 116.
27 See Brody in Freeman 1976, 186.
28 Ibid., 117–18.
29 See Holtved 1943 for an extensive discussion of the Navaranaq myths.
30 Oosten and Laugrand 2001, 96.
31 See also Boas 1964 [1888], 232; 1901, 213–14.
32 Oosten and Laugrand 2002, 132.
33 Nasby 2002, 51. Many stories about *ijirait* can be found in the ethnographic literature: see the experiences of Makitgaq in Mannik 1998, 139–40; those of Amarualik and others in Saladin d'Anglure 1983 and Saladin d'Anglure and Morin 1998; or those of Kupak (2003 interview).
34 See Kappianaq's representation of an *ijiraq* in Saladin d'Anglure 2006, 156, fig. 18.
35 Rasmussen 1929, 204–5.
36 Ibid., 197.
37 Saladin d'Anglure 2001, 54–7; see also Saladin d'Anglure 1983.
38 See Rasmussen 1930, 104–5; 1931, 244; Oosten and Laugrand 2002, 132–6; and Evic-Twerdin 1991, 17.
39 Oosten and Laugrand 2002, 132–4.
40 Saladin d'Anglure 2001, 60, 62.
41 Oosten and Laugrand 2001, 71–4.
42 See also Boas 1907, 509–10; Saladin d'Anglure 1983; and Oosten 1995.
43 See also the story in Holtved 1943 about a woman called Javaranaaq or Navanaraq who had relatives among the *ijirait*.
44 Saladin d'Anglure 2001b, 217.
45 See also Boas 1901, 214–16; and Rasmussen 1931, 245.
46 Rasmussen 1931, 245–6.
47 Saladin d'Anglure 2001b, 218.
48 According to Mary-Rousselière, they protect and assist *angakkuit* in seal hunting. Okumaluk, an elder from Iglulik, related an event when an *angakkuq* was bitten by the game he desired, probably an *ingneriujaq* in the guise of a seal. Mary-Rousselière, Archives Dechâtelets (AD)/HR 3068 E77R 3C.
49 Rasmussen 1929; 1931, 244–5.
50 Boas 1901, 197–202; 1907, 521–2, 540–1.
51 Oosten, Laugrand, and Rasing 1999, 127.
52 Oosten and Laugrand 2001, 74.
53 Oosten and Laugrand 2007, 173.
54 Ibid., 164.
55 Arviat workshop, 2003.

56 Oosten and Laugrand 2007, 163.
57 Mannik 1998, 22.
58 McComber 2005, 65.
59 Ibid., 67.
60 Rasmussen 1931, 252; Boas 1964 [888], 636; 1901, 173, 196). See also Koodlowetto, quoted in Boas 1901, 195; and Alainang, quoted in Boas 1907, 520–1.
61 See also Rasmussen 1930, 114; and Boas 1901, 196–7. Stories about giants can also be found in works by Saladin d'Anglure (1992a, 2006) who introduced the notion of varying scales as a key element in understanding Inuit mythology.
62 Rasmussen 1931, 252.
63 Oosten and Laugrand 2007, 162–3.
64 Rasmussen 1931, 246–7.
65 Saladin d'Anglure 2001b, 65.
66 Oosten and Laugrand 2007, 168.
67 Ibid.
68 Bennett and Rowley 2004, 155; see also Oosten and Laugrand 2007, 177.
69 Saladin d'Anglure 2001b, 65, summarized in Kublu 2004.
70 Laugrand, Oosten, and Trudel 2000, 124–6.
71 Oosten and Laugrand 2007, 177.
72 Evic-Twerdin 1991, 47.
73 Therrien and Laugrand 2001, 151.
74 Oosten and Laugrand 2001, 75–6.
75 Rasmussen 1931, 248; see also Boas 1901, 197; and Rasmussen 1929, 212.
76 Oosten and Laugrand 1999b, 119.
77 Oosten and Laugrand 2001, 76–7.
78 Pitseolak and Eber 1993, 94.
79 Oosten and Laugrand 1999a, 194–200.
80 Von Finckenstein 2002, 148.
81 Oosten and Laugrand 1999a, 201.
82 Oosten and Laugrand 1999a, 204.
83 Pitseolak and Eber 1993, 94–5.
84 Nungak and Arima 1969, 53. See also Jackson and Nasby 1987, 49; and Wight 1991, 118–19, for representations of this woman.
85 Nungak and Arima 1988, 93.
86 See, for example, Swinton 1980, 40.
87 Oosten and Laugrand, 2002, 39.
88 Arviat workshop, 2003.
89 Ibid.
90 See the *aggajaat* spirit drawn by Malaija Papatsie in Laugrand, Oosten, and Trudel 2000, 119. The relationship between *kukilingiattiat* and *aggajaat* needs further exploration.
91 Evic-Twerdin 1991, 51.
92 Rasmussen 1929, 217; see also Rasmussen 1931, 247; and Boas 1907, 497.
93 Rasmussen 1929, 216.
94 Ibid.
95 Rasmussen 1931, 245.
96 Ibid., 250.
97 Mannik 1998, 220–1.

98 Rasmussen (1931, 266) relates, "The animals have taboos just like humans, and a raven must not eat of human flesh on the same day that it has eaten caribou. If it does, it will be sick. Now its neighbours had gone away hunting and it was left behind, but the shaman cured it. Then the raven thought over what to give in return, and gave the shaman a dog's turd. I suppose it was hard for it to find a proper game animal." We have to take into account that the raven has a special position and itself should not be eaten. See Oosten and Laugrand 2006 on the special position of the raven.

99 Blodgett 1986, 46.

100 Saladin d'Anglure 2001b, 61.

101 See Fletcher and Kirmayer 1997 for Nunavik.

102 Saladin d'Anglure 2001b, 218.

103 Oosten and Laugrand 1999b, 53.

104 MacDonald 1998, 204.

105 Ibid., 205. See also the story related by Helen Pownuk about the death of her little son: "I hate myself for sewing an *atigi* on a Sunday as it resulted in the accident of the little one" (Kalluak 1974, 75).

106 Dogs are named and participate to some extent in social life and the cycle of names (see Laugrand and Oosten 2002a). *Tuurngait* also have individual names, often given to human beings. Shamans have close personal relationships with their helping spirits (see Laugrand, Oosten, and Trudel 2000).

107 Kublu and Oosten 1999.

Chapter Seven

1 Blodgett (1979) presents a classic vision of the shaman when he sees himself as a skeleton. On initiation in a structural and comparative perspective, see Oosten 1976; and for a detailed analysis of the various sequences in initiation, see Blaisel 1993a, 1993b. See also Sonne 2007, which discusses the polysemy of *pooq* and connects the *puulik* initiation to the symbolism of rebirth in life, time, and space. *Pooq* refers to a bag but also to clothing and the skin of animals (Sonne 2007, 18).

2 See chapter 9 for a discussion of these objects.

3 Kugaaruk workshop, 2004.

4 Rasmussen 1929, 1930.

5 Laugrand, Oosten, and Trudel 2006, 328.

6 Bilby 1923, 198.

7 See Laugrand, Oosten, and Trudel 2006, 414–15.

8 Rasmussen 1929, 113.

9 The origin of *qaumaniq* remains a controversial issue among present-day elders. Peter Suvaksiuq from Arviat distinguished the *qaumaniq* of *angakkuuniq* from the *qaumaniq* of prayer. Mariano Aupilaarjuk from Kangiq&iniq and Jose Angutinngurniq from Kugaaruk stated that *qaumaniq* came from "The Most Powerful One" or from God, but not "from this world." Ollie Itinnuaq from Kangiq&iniq related it to shamanism, adding that an *angakkuq* was only able to see when the *qaumaniq* came to him (Oosten and Laugrand 2002, 81–3).

10 See Boas 1964, 591–2, for the acquisition of *tuurngait*, especially stones and bears, in Cumberland Sound.

11 According to Boas (1907, 511), "The angakok wears a strap to which is attached a number of strips of skin, which show the number of diseases which he has cured or warded off. Ultimately this strap is placed under a stone as an offering to the angakok's guardian spirit."
12 Rasmussen 1929, 114.
13 Ibid. 118.
14 Ibid., 118–19.
15 Ibid., 120–1.
16 Ibid., 123.
17 Thérien 1978, interview 1.
18 Ibid., interview 8.
19 Ibid., interview 6.
20 Ibid., interview 8.
21 Rasmussen 1930, 51.
22 Ibid., 52–4.
23 Oosten and Laugrand 2002, 74.
24 Rasmussen 1930, 57–8.
25 Ibid., 58.
26 See also Rasmussen 1931, 296–7.
27 Oosten, Laugrand, and Rasing 1999, 18.
28 Rasmussen 1931, 296–7.
29 Oosten and Laugrand 1999b, 89.
30 Ibid., 90.
31 Oosten and Laugrand 2002, 69.
32 To kill an evil spirit.
33 Oosten and Laugrand 2002, 70.
34 Midwife – shapes the baby by giving him or her specific qualities.
35 The one shaped by the midwife.
36 Oosten and Laugrand 2002, 77–8.
37 Bennett and Rowley 2004, 177.
38 Qimuksiraaq was a renowned *angakkuq* from Igluligaarjuk.
39 Oosten and Laugrand 2002, 31–4.
40 Hallendy (1985, 140) reports a similar phenomenon: "All things that breathe have dreams. I do not know what dogs and ravens dream, but they do dream." In the Canadian Arctic, dreams have been studied extensively in recent years: Richling (1989) explored the role of dream in the eighteenth century among Labrador Inuit; Kolb and Law (2001) collected many dreams among young Inuit and adults living in Iqaluit; and Mitiarjuk Nappaaluk (1997), Laugrand (2001), and Saladin d'Anglure (2001b) provide additional material on the role of spirits and deceased. See also Therrien 2002b and Bordin 2008.
41 Oosten, Laugrand, and Rasing 1999, 24–5.
42 Therrien and Laugrand 2001, 223–4.
43 Kolb and Law 2001, 88.
44 Oosten and Laugrand 2001, 116.
45 Kolb and Law 2001, 92–3.
46 Oosten and Laugrand 2002, 119–21.
47 Therrien and Laugrand 2001, 129.

48 Ataguttiaq, quoted in ibid. See also Bennett and Rowley 2004, 4–5.
49 Kublu and Oosten 1999, 70.
50 Therrien and Laugrand 2001, 132.
51 Oosten and Laugrand 2002, 118.
52 Kolb and Law 2001, 159.
53 Oosten, Laugrand, and Rasing 1999, 232. See also Bloom and Gelardin 1976, 21–2.
54 The terms are usually taken to mean the same thing, although some elders distinguish between them (e.g., Tipuula Ataguttiaq in Therrien and Laugrand 2001, 130–2.
55 Kolb and Law 2001, 189.
56 Ibid., 190.
57 In the past, people used to sleep with a knife close by when someone had died.
58 According to Rasmussen (1929, 92–4), the *tarniq* was connected to the body by the big toe.
59 Oosten, Laugrand, and Rasing 1999, 132.
60 Oosten and Laugrand 2007, 112.
61 Kugaaruk workshop, 2004.
62 Kolb and Law 2001, 86.
63 Therrien and Laugrand 2001, 143.
64 Kolb and Law 2001, 84.
65 Oosten and Laugrand 2002, 116–17.
66 Oosten and Laugrand 2001, 117.
67 Father Van de Velde.
68 Wachowich 1999, 25.
69 Laugrand 1997a, 660.
70 Rasmussen 1929, 119.
71 Ibid., 113.
72 Wachowich 1999, 81.

Chapter Eight

1 See Kublu and Oosten 1999.
2 For the power associated with seal blood, see Borré 1994 and Aaju and al. 1999).
3 See Therrien 1995a.
4 The following description, provided by William Kuptana from Coppermine, is instructive: "Anyone who was ill was cured quickly by a momentous action as if the disease itself was a substance to be taken out [of the body]. If that ill person breached, then they knew they were infringing upon the disease. Then it was bitten out of the ill person, so it seemed. But when a cure was not in sight, more shamans were called to cast out whatever vice was still in the ill person. Caribou mitts or caribou mukluks were given in return for a cure. For instance, shamans would take a knife and slice up a caribou mitt. The sliced up mitt would then be eaten by the participating shamans. When they had eaten the whole thing, one of them would grab a parka and shake it until a mitt dropped out" (Condon 1996, 88).
5 Therrien and Laugrand 2001, 2.
6 See also Therrien and Laugrand 2001 for various healing techniques.
7 Arviat workshop, 2003.
8 We will discuss this technique and the role of the deceased in the process in chapter 11.

9 Laugrand, Oosten, and Trudel 2006, 314–15.
10 Rasmussen 1930, 111.
11 Ibid., 108.
12 For a discussion of this session, see Oosten 1984, and for a discussion of the session by Iglulik elders, see Saladin d'Anglure 2001b, 103–30.
13 Saladin d'Anglure 2001b, 129; see also ibid., 110.
14 Oosten and Laugrand 1999b, 99.
15 Ibid., 103.
16 Tagoona 1975, n.p.
17 Oosten and Laugrand 1999b, 109.
18 Oosten, Laugrand, and Rasing 1999, 122.
19 See Laugrand, Oosten, and Trudel 2006, chaps 17 and 18.
20 Oosten and Laugrand 1999b, 100–1.
21 ACC/GSA/Peck Papers M56-1, Series 32, no. 1, Eskimo Mythology and Customs.
22 See Laugrand, Oosten, and Trudel 2006, 383–4; ACC/GSA/Peck Papers M56-1, Series 32, no. 3, Box 4, untitled document, p. 58.
23 Oosten and Laugrand 1999b, 96.
24 Nasby 2002, 50–1.
25 Oosten and Laugrand 1999b, 109.
26 Ibid., 108.
27 Oosten and Laugrand 2001, 21.
28 Oosten and Laugrand 1999b, 103.
29 Ibid., 110.
30 Kolb and Law 2001, 117–18.
31 Oosten and Laugrand 2001, 31–3.
32 Oosten and Laugrand 1999b, 99.
33 Therrien and Laugrand 2001, 127.
34 Rasmussen 1929, 143.
35 Laugrand, Oosten and Trudel 2006, 371–2.
36 Therrien and Laugrand 2001, 283.
37 Mannik 1998, 21.
38 Rasmussen 1929, 146–7.
39 Bennett and Rowley 2004, 192–3.
40 HR 3068 E77R 3C.
41 Oosten and Laugrand 2002, 77.
42 Ibid., 132.
43 Ibid., 131–2.
44 Ibid., 116.
45 Ibid., 44.
46 Ibid., 48.
47 Ibid., 50.
48 Oosten, Laugrand, and Rasing 1999, 157–9.
49 Oosten and Laugrand 2001, 80.
50 Oosten and Laugrand 1999b, 107.
51 Mannik 1998, 9–10.
52 See also Saladin d'Anglure 1997 and Laugrand, n.d.
53 Fletcher and Kirmayer 1997, 196.

54 Arviat workshop, 2003.

55 Ibid.

56 Ibid.

57 The Inuktitut term *mamisarnit* refers to a deep wound as well as to complete restoration. According to M. Therrien (personal communication, 2007), *mami* (or *mamik*) refers to the hypodermis that is visible once the upper layers of skin have been removed, and thus indicates that the psychological wounds of the person run very deep. But the notion of *mamisimajuq* also suggests a successful sewing operation.

58 Tagoona 1975, n.p.

59 Saladin d'Anglure 1997, 64–5.

60 Therrien and Laugrand 2001, 127–8.

61 The Nunavut Brighter Futures report (1999–2000) produced by the Nunavut Department of Health and Social Services (http://healthbehaviorchange.org/Doc/January05/BFutures.pdf – no longer available) refers to the presence of healing circles in many programs. In Iqaluit, the Qivitoo and Pudlooping program (Healing Reunion) offered healing circles organized by Inuit from Panniqtuuq. Leaders such as Reverend Daniel Aupalu sought to help those who had suffered from relocations in the past. Between 1998 and 1999, Inuit from Pond Inlet, Clyde River, Qikiqtarjuaq, Panniqtuuq, Ottawa, and Iqaluit met in the places where they were born to start a process of healing. In Kimmirut, the Grieving and Healing Program of Nunavut Arctic College organized healing circles led by Abraham Arnakaq and his wife Meeka Arnakaq. In Sanikiluaq, the Community Healing Circles offered help to victims of sexual abuse through meetings and healing circles that were organized once a week by the Suyurglingiituq to improve relations between elders and youths. In Coral Harbour, healing circles were organized by the Nuvvitiit Healing Group for people needing to heal from traumas and past painful experiences. In Talojoak, the Healing and Grieving Session program organized healing circles in the community and even at the local school. In the Nuluaq Project (National Inuit Strategy for Abuse Prevention) report entitled *Abuse Prevention Services in Inuit Communities* (2004), the association Pauktuutit (Inuit Women's Association) describes the available resources in terms of healing circles: the healing project of Meeka Arnakaq, based in Panniqtuuq, often visits other communities; Meeka and her husband travel extensively to neighbouring communities, within the network of Nunavut Arctic College campus, or to jails through the Tupiq program; healing circles organized by social worker Alashuak Kenuajuaq are based in Puvirnituq, in Nunavik; the healing program of the Qikiqtani Inuit Association (QIA, based in Iqaluit, provides financial support to healing activities by paying airline tickets to healing circle leaders; the Cape Dorset Healing and Harmony Team organizes workshops and healing circles on demand; the Labrador Inuit Health Commission program, directed by Sarah Ponniuk, though based in Nain, sometimes organizes healing sessions in other communities.

Pauktuutit also identifies resources that are available to people living outside northern communities, particularly to Inuit living in Ottawa. The Inuit Women's Healing Circle project of the Tungasuvvingat Inuit Association, based in Ottawa, organizes (through the healer Teresa Hughes) healing and counselling sessions in Inuktitut for those who live far from their home communities. The Living a Healthier Lifestyle project directed by Kanayuk Salamonie, an Inuk woman from Cape Dorset, organizes healing sessions in Cape Dorset and other communities through the Tupiq program. The Tupiq program aims to help the wrongdoers in the Fenbrook Penitentiary and was launched by the federal government in March 2001. A project started by Angaangaq, originally from Greenland, is based in Iqaluit. Having been a victim of sexual abuse, he created the Society for Northern Renewal.

62 Nuluaq Project 2004, 10.

63 The Nuluaq website states, "Angaangaq is a traditional healer specializing in Inuit specific trauma recovery for Inuit adult survivors of child sexual abuse. He also provides healing services in federal prisons and participates in national and international meetings on native spirituality, healing and culture. He is originally from Greenland but has lived in Nunavut and southern Canada. Currently, he resides in Ottawa but travels frequently in the North" (http://www.pauktuutit.ca/nuluaq/agency).

64 Nuluaq Project 2004, 32.

65 Ibid., 33.

66 Pitsula Akavak, who works at the Tukisiniarvik Centre in Iqaluit, stated clearly in her interview, "I don't know if I am a healer. I don't like that word in English ... What I can do is to help or facilitate another person's healing ... If you call someone a healer in Inuktitut it would be like saying they were a magic person who used their magic to heal or fix someone. We can't do that as people. We can't fix another person" (Nuluaq Project 2004, 25).

67 Nuluaq Project 2004, 50, 55.

68 Ibid., 92.

69 "After next month's trip to Chesterfield Inlet, the committee overseeing the Qauma project will choose the next four communities to be visited. The $4-million program, funded by the Aboriginal Healing Foundation, will continue for the next three years, covering 16 communities in total."

70 Von Finckenstein 2002, 178.

Chapter Nine

1 See also Boas 1901, 133; and Saladin d'Anglure 2006, 288–300, who recorded the myth of Itijjuaq from Iqallijuq and Kupaaq in Iglulik.

2 Usually considered by the Inuit as the first people but later on identified with Adam and Eve.

3 Oosten and Laugrand 2002, 123–4.

4 Ibid., 124.

5 See Bennett and Rowley 2004, 184. On *aarnguat*, see Oosten 1997; Saladin d'Anglure 2001b, 144–5; and Pollick 2003.

6 Rasmussen 1931, 274a.

7 Oosten and Laugrand 2002, 28.

8 Oosten and Laugrand 1999b, 89.

9 Ibid., 90–1.

10 Oosten and Laugrand 2002, 27–8.

11 Ibid., 28.

12 Mathiassen 1928, 235.

13 Laugrand 2002c, 339.

14 For examples pertaining to South Baffin traditions, see Bilby 1923, 232.

15 In Leroux, Jackson, and Freeman 1996.

16 See also Waldmann 1909–10 (439), which notes that, in Killinek (Labrador), if a person needed help from a deceased to avoid starvation, small pieces of meat could be retrieved: "L'Esquimau sacrifie aux mânes des défunts. Ceux-ci jouent encore, pendant un temps, un certain rôle au sein de leurs familles, lesquelles célèbrent souvent des repas auprès du monceau de pierres qui recouvre le mort. S'il y a un homonyme parmi les convives il faut que celui-ci dépose un morceau de viande ou du poisson sur le tombeau pour empêcher le défunt d'inquiéter les survivants. Il arrive aussi qu'une personne isolée apporte de la nourriture sur le tombeau, mais elle a le droit de la reprendre dans le cas où elle n'aurait plus rien à manger elle-même. C'est ainsi que l'on signale à un défunt le fait que sa parenté est dans le besoin et que son devoir est de lui venir en aide." ["The Eskimo sacrifices to the shades of the deceased. For some time the shades still play a specific role at the heart of their families that often celebrate with a meal close to the pile of stones that covers the deceased. If there is namesake among them, the namesake should depose a piece of meat or fish on the grave to prevent the deceased from disturbing the people. It also happens that a sole woman brings food to a grave, but she is entitled to take it back, when she has nothing to eat herself. In this way the deceased is informed that his relatives are in need and that it is his duty to come to their aid."] Our translation.

17 Jenness 1922, 181.

18 See Laugrand and Oosten 2007.

19 Rasmussen 1929, 264.

20 On the role of miniatures, see Laugrand and Oosten 2008b.

21 Rasmussen 1929, 253.

22 On the raven symbolism, see Randa 1994; and Oosten and Laugrand 2006.

23 Rasmussen 1929, 92.

24 Arviat workshop, 2003.

25 Rasmussen 1929, 165.

26 Arviat workshop, 2003.

27 Ibid.

28 Rasmussen 1931, 278.

29 See Therrien 1987 for linguistic connections between these categories. On forbidden words, see Therrien 2008.

30 Rasmussen 1929, 168.

31 Bennett and Rowley 2004, 190.

32 Saladin d'Anglure 2001b, 86.

33 Oosten and Laugrand 2002, 105.

34 Oosten and Laugrand 1999b, 59.

35 Nasby 2002, 66–7.

36 Kolb and Law 2001, 165.

37 Rasmussen (1931, 201) describes a case where a man's wife died because he had used an *irinaliuti*.

38 Rasmussen 1929, 165–6.

39 Therrien and Laugrand 2001, 5.

40 Oosten and Laugrand 2002, 108–9.

41 Ibid., 109–10.

42 Oosten and Laugrand 1999b, 61.

43 Oosten and Laugrand 2002, 104.

44 Ibid., 106.
45 Laugrand, Oosten, and Trudel 2006, 54–5.
46 ACC/GSA/PP, M56-1, Series 26, Eskimo letters, C6. The power of words is mentioned in few more letters published in Laugrand, Oosten, and Kakkik 2003 (A9, A13, A14, B1, B4, B9, B14, C1, D, D7, D9, D11, and D13).
47 Mannik 1998, 101.
48 Turquetil, *L'Ami du Foyer*, August 1919, in Morice 1935, 123.
49 Oosten and Laugrand 1999b, 149.
50 Therrien and Laugrand 2001, 5.
51 Oosten and Laugrand 1999b, 95.
52 Kolb and Law 2001, 96–7.
53 Saladin d'Anglure 2001b, 142–3.
54 Kolb and Law 2001, 96. On *qinngarniq*, see Saladin d'Anglure 2001, 48, 141–4. See also Aupilaarjuk from Kangiq&iniq (quoted in Saladin d'Anglure 2001b, 48), who uses the notion of *qinngaqtauti*, shouted prayers. According to Aupilaarjuk, *qinngaqtauti* and *irinaliutiit* are similar but not identical, both actions being oral requests.
55 Saladin d'Anglure 2001b, 143.
56 Arviat workshop, 2003.
57 See chapter 10 on *pisiit*.
58 Oosten and Laugrand 1999b, 136.
59 Ibid., 132.
60 Ibid., 136.
61 Oosten and Laugrand 1999b, 61–2).
62 Ibid., 75.
63 Oosten and Laugrand 1999a, 137.
64 Elders usually avoided the topic of *ilisiq*, so we received little information about it.
65 Mannik 1998, 122.

Chapter Ten

1 Some anthropologists (e.g., Rasmussen), as well as some Inuit, use the term "ancestors." Inuit use the term *sivullit* (those who go ahead or in front) when referring to the *inummariit* ("true" Inuit) of the past.
2 See Rasmussen 1929, 173: "Hanging beside her lamp, the mother must have a small skin bag (*mi*ulErtEqutEqArfia*). Whenever she is about to eat, she must cut off a small piece of meat, rub it on the child's mouth, and place it in the bag, before commencing her meal. This is called *mi*ulErtEri**q*, and is regarded as a sacred rite – a sacrifice in effigy to the spirits, the dead, and the holy meat. This act protects the child against hunger, and renders it skillful in hunting later on, bringing abundance of game. Another interpretation says that it is *nutAra*lu*p ati*e nErErqublugit*: in order that the child's namesake soul may have something to eat."
3 See, for example, Boas (1907, 486), who relates that at the third night after death the mourners visit the grave and take some food for the deceased, saying to the *tarniq*, "You were kind to the people when you had plenty of caribou-meat, plenty of seal, walrus, and salmon, and your soul shall send us plenty of game."
4 See Kolb and Law 2001, 96.
5 See chapter 4.

6 Therrien and Laugrand 2001, 245.

7 The cosmos itself has the connotations of a house. The universe rests on pillars that will be destroyed by Sila at the end of time (see Rasmussen 1929, 37, 252; 1931, 230–1).

8 See Therrien 1987.

9 Best, quoted in Stefansson 1938, 127.

10 Arviat workshop, 2003.

11 Boas 1907, 512.

12 Laugrand, Oosten, and Trudel 2006, 318.

13 Saladin d'Anglure 2001b, 136.

14 Ibid., 136–7.

15 See Rasmussen 1929, 133–40.

16 Notes sur les Esquimaux: sorcellerie: *krelayut*, Pelly Bay, 1er juin 1957 (Archives Deschâtelets, HEF 3244.F82C 1). We present Van de Velde's information in English (our translation) and the original French text in endnotes 17–21.

17 Tout le monde sait que Iksiwalitark était sorcier et que son esprit protecteur était "Kanayok," ce démon Kanayok était donc son esprit protecteur; il l'invoquait et s'en faisait soi-disant aider. Pas seulement les sorciers avaient ces esprits protecteurs; tous en avaient, mais de qualité et de force différentes. Les *Apersait*, sous le point de vue chrétien, pourraient être remplacés éminemment par nos anges gardiens. Un esquimau me dit un jour: *Inungnut ikajoteoyut, apersaoyut* (Pour les esquimaux ils sont gardiens ou *apersait*).

18 L'Esquimau qui veut recevoir une réponse se met sur le lit esquimau (*iglerk*), il retire son capuchon et se couche sur le dos, les pieds tournés vers le fond de l'iglu. Celui qui va faire le manège s'assied à la droite du sujet couché. Il prend sa mitaine, lui couvre le visage de façon que toute la tête soit enveloppée maintenant. Puis, avec une corde d'*udjuk* (phoque barbu) il fait un nœud autour de la tête de celui qui est couché.

19 *Okremangetok – iktariksiyok*: il est lourd: le mot okremangetok par ailleurs est employé avec la signification de: "à l'état de cauchemar" par exemple: un enfant qui dort et se lève en sursaut, pleurant, se levant en criant, il parle, mais ne se rappelle de rien par la suite; on pourrait presque dire somnanbule (*itiblertok*).

20 *Apersa*?: esprit (au vocatif)?
Unnerniarputit (okraniarputit)? : tu vas parler n'est-ce pas?
Tagva nalungilatit? : voilà que tu n'ignores pas ce que nous voulons savoir?
Pidjutani nalungilatit? : connais-tu cette affaire?
Taovinermik pipkrajaugami? : Est-ce un ancien Esquimau qui lui a fait cela?
Issarotararsluni? : est-ce un mâle?
Saniliangoluni, issarotakrarani? : une femme couchée à côté de son mari?

21 Les sorciers se réclamaient de leur pouvoir pour remporter une victoire sur une âme, rien qu'en soufflant dessus.

22 Saladin d'Anglure 2001b, 135–6.

23 Rasmussen 1929, 141ff.

24 Oosten and Laugrand 2002, 139–40.

25 *Qaggiq* or *qaggi*. Rasmussen uses the word *qagse*. The institution of the feast house is widespread across the Arctic. In Alaska it was a place where men lived and rituals and festivals took place. In the Canadian Arctic the feast house was usually a temporary construction for feasts and festivals. Whereas the *kinirvik*, the birth hut, was exclusively a female domain and the igloo was shared by men and women, the feast house may have

been a male domain, as suggested by a story about the spirit of the feast house related by Rasmussen (1929, 224–5), as well as by the narrative of the origin of the sun and moon. Noah Piugaattuk (IE 189) explained, "There were taboos that had to be respected, so there were times when woman were barred from participating in any of the large gatherings such as the *qaggi*. These included the women that had just given birth or [had] advanced pregnancies, or for those who might have had a recent miscarriage. These were usually the women that had to abide by the taboos with many restrictions."

26 See also Rasmussen 1929, 228.

27 Ibid., 230.

28 Rasmussen 1932, 23.

29 Bennett and Rowley 2004, 109.

30 Ibid.

31 Ibid., 110.

32 Tagoona 1975, n.p.

33 Oosten, Laugrand, and Rasing 1999, 199.

34 Bennett and Rowley 2004, 108.

35 Ibid., 109.

36 Ibid., 107.

37 Oosten, Laugrand, and Rasing 1999, 219.

38 Rasmussen 1931, 321.

39 See Laugrand, Oosten, and Trudel 2006.

40 Oosten and Laugrand 1999b, 106.

41 Oosten, Laugrand, and Rasing 1999, 201–2.

42 Bennett and Rowley 2004, 110.

43 Oosten, Laugrand, and Rasing 1999, 206.

44 *Ikiaqtagaq*, a *pisiq* that had had changes made to it.

45 Oosten, Laugrand, and Rasing 1999, 203–4.

46 Ibid., 204–5.

47 Bennett and Rowley 2004, 108.

48 Ibid.

49 Since Oqortoq was a man, we assume there is a mistake in the text.

50 Rasmussen (1931, 195) observes, "Some religious appraisement undoubtedly lies behind this fellowship. It involves both advantages and obligations; for instance, if a man is about to set out on a long journey – perhaps to trade – and his wife is with child, sick or in some other manner unfit to go with him, he can borrow the wife of his *igloq* to accompany him, giving his own in exchange. This form of wife-exchange is necessary in a community living the nomad life of Eskimos."

51 See also Rasmussen 1929, 243–4, for an extensive description of a feast organized on the basis of a contest between *illuriik*.

52 Oosten, Laugrand, and Rasing 1999, 208.

53 Oosten and Laugrand 1999b, 107.

54 Rasmussen 1929, 17.

55 Rasmussen 1931, 248–9.

56 Oosten and Laugrand 1999b, 131.

57 Ibid., 134.

58 Bennett and Rowley 2004, 108.

59 Rasmussen 1929, 179.

60 Rasmussen 1929, 199; 1931, 265.

Chapter Eleven

1 Studies of Inuit Pentecostalism in Nunavik are rare; see Dorais 1996, 1997; and Fletcher and Kirmayer 1997. Stuckenberger (2005, 2007) presents a case study of the Pentecostal movement on Broughton Island.
2 Laugrand, Oosten, and Kakkik 2003, 42, 76, 114.
3 The Reverend John Turner came to Mittimatalik in 1929 and worked as a missionary in the Arctic until his death in 1947.
4 In the Arctic, the notion of "religious awakening" had already appeared among Moravian missionaries in Labrador in the eighteenth century.
5 In Iglulik, for instance, the first followers of the Pentecostal church were mainly former Catholics (Saladin d'Anglure 1991). In Quaqtaq, they came from the Anglican Church.
6 http://www.arcticmissions.com.
7 They also visited various places in Nunavik, for example Sugluk, Ivujivik, Povungnituk, and Inukjuak.
8 See Curwin 1988, 25–31.
9 The Alliance Church also has a presence in Churchill.
10 Kutluk 1985, 7.
11 See also Rasmussen 1929, 120.
12 See chapter 9.
13 See http://www.kintera.org/site/c.irKSIYPAIoE/b.2027387/k.87A1/Canadian_Arctic.htm.
14 Stuckenberger 2005, 66.
15 See http://www.canadaawakening.com/pages/aboutus/aboutus.html.
16 See http://www.ncem.ca/.
17 Full Gospel churches opened in Kangirsuk in 1970 and from there expanded to communities such as Quaqtaq and Kangirsujuaq in 1978 (Dorais 2001, 76), as well as to Aupaluk, Puvirnituq, Ivujivik, Salluit, and Tasiujaq. In Nunavut, Full Gospel churches opened in Ikpiarjuk, Mittimatalik, Panniqtuuq, and finally, in 1999–2000, Kinngait. Glad Tidings churches were opened in Arviat in 1969, Iqaluktuuttiaq (Cambridge Bay) in 1971, Salliq (Coral Harbour) in 1971, and Qamanittuaq. More recently, a Glad Tidings Bible school was opened in Kangiq&iniq.
18 See the case of Pauloosie Kunilusie, leader of the Glad Tidings Church in Qikiqtarjuaq, in Stuckenberger 2005, 67.
19 See Dorais 1997, 76.
20 http://www.christianity.ca/church/outreach/2003/06.001.htm.
21 The first Bible conference was organized by John Spillenaar in Ikpiarjuk in 1984, with twenty people attending. From 1992 to 1998, there were Bible conferences every year, and in 2006 the 22nd Arctic Annual Bible Conference was held in Kuujjuaq. Some of these conferences have brought hundreds of people together. Eight hundred people gathered in Baker Lake in 2003. According to Armbruster, the cost of the airplane charters exceeded $300,000. In 2005 more than five hundred people attended the Bible Conference in Salliq, a community of seven hundred.
22 See Coleman 2000.
23 http://spiritalive.org.

24 National Film Board, Montreal, 1994.
25 Kolb and Law 2001, 86.
26 Ibid., 46.
27 Ibid.
28 See Blaisel, Laugrand, and Oosten 1999.
29 Kolb and Law 2001, 79.
30 See Fletcher and Kirmayer 1997. Another Pentecostal practice consists in having a visitor choose a card from a selection of cards with a good word written on them. The visitor must then read their card's message aloud to the other people. This game is congruent with many divination practices of the past, in which much allowance was given to the spirit world. See Stuckenberger 2005 for more details on games in a Pentecostal community.
31 See the videotapes *Transformations* I, II, III, produced by the Sentinel Group (www.sentinelgroup.org).
32 http://www.transformations.com.
33 See Otis 2001.
34 Stuckenberger 2007 examines Pentecostal baptism and the process of being "reborn Christian," showing that religious transformation and social restoration are closely interconnected.
35 In contrast to other Pentecostal communities elsewhere in the world, the local elite plays a major role in the spread of the movement. Dorais (1997, 78) points out that in Quaqtaq in 1990, the principal and six out of seven Inuit teachers of the school were Pentecostals.
36 Turner died after an accident in 1947 but is still well known among the Inuit as Mikiniqsaq (see Trott 1997).
37 See Rasmussen 1929, 125.
38 See also Laugrand 2002, 448–9, for a similar description of Angutijjuaq's conversion.
39 *Faith Today,* 2002, http://www.christianity.ca/church/outreach/2003/06.001.html.
40 Otis 2001.
41 Arviat workshop 2007.
42 See Otis 2001. The location out on the ice is significant, since sea ice was a privileged place for making contact with God (see "*Siqqitiq*" in chapter 4), as indicated by events on the Belcher Islands in 1941: "At the camp Mina's zeal increased. 'Jesus is coming,' she prophesied to the women and children, 'Take off your clothes and go out on the sea ice to meet him'" (RCMP 1941, 156).
43 Unfortunately, the website is no longer available.
44 http://www.canadaawakening.com/northwinds/northwindhome.html.
45 Canada Awakening is not the only group active in this way. Bill Prankard's association sent a team of nine Inuit leaders to Siberia to spread the Gospel. The team was transported by helicopter to different villages over a period of nine months. According to its report, the team was welcomed and spent most its the time praying with the local people (see http://www.sendrevival.com/testimonies/antarctica/revival_russian_inuit.htm).
46 See chapter 5.
47 http://www.canadaawakening.com.
48 Ibid.
49 Ibid.
50 According to their website, the Promise Keepers' mission is to ignite and unite men to become passionate followers of Jesus Christ through the effective communication of

seven promises to God, their fellow men, family, church, and the world. The Promise Keepers' vision is simply put in three words: "Men Transformed Worldwide."

51 http://www.canadaawakening.com/pages/Fall%202004%20Reports/PuvirnituqYouth.html.

52 http://www.canadaawakening.com/2005%20Reports/December%2005/genderandgenerations.htm.

53 Linking Hearts is a Christian support network founded by Veronica de War and Wanda Frost in 2004. It identifies itself as a charitable organization that aims to further the Gospel of Jesus Christ. Its purposes are to link the circumpolar nations of the world in prayer, to provide training in prayer, to strengthen and equip and to teach the precepts of Christianity, and to minister to the spiritual needs of all individuals. In 2006 the Linking Hearts Second Annual Women's Conference was organized in Kangiq&iniq.

54 See chapter 5.

55 This division is reminiscent of *qaggilutit* (gathering in the ceremonial house), an old shamanic practice described by Jaikku Pitseolak from Iqaluit: "They played games. People from different camps gathered into one place. The adults danced by having the men in line on one side and the women on the other side. They slowly walked towards each other. When they met, the men who liked the women had to kiss them. Even though the man did not look too good to kiss, the woman had to let him kiss her or people would call her *qunujuq*. My grandmother used to say that she let a man kiss her even though she did not like him. That was their tradition. That was the way they played. Our ancestors had different games they played too. I cannot remember now. I think that there was more to it" (Therrien and Laugrand 2001, 285). However, whereas in the evangelical context the husband-wife relation is emphasized, the shamanic tradition focuses on the extramarital relationship.

56 Nuluaq Project 2004, 37.

57 See the cases of Alashuaq Kenuajuaq from Puvirnituq, Angaangaq from Iqaluit, and Lucy Dillon from Tuktoyaktuk. See Nuluaq Project 2004.

58 See the discussion of winter feasts in chapter 3.

59 See chapter 3.

Chapter Twelve

1 See Carpenter 1968a.

2 See Wolf 1982.

3 Oosten and Laugrand 2002, 82.

References

Aaju, Peter, et al. 2002. "The Seal: An Integral Part of Our Culture." *Études Inuit Studies* 26 (1): 167–74.

Akeeshoo, Atsaina. 1974. "Christmas in a Hunting Camp." *Inukshuk* 23 (December): 8.

Alia, Valeria. 1994. *Names, Numbers, and Northern Policy.* Halifax: Fernwood Publishing.

Anonymous. 1981. "Les fêtes de Noël au Nouveau Québec." *Inuktitut* 48:28–33.

– 2006. "Darwin Put on Ice in Northern Quebec Community." *CBC News.* 19 May 2006 (from cbc.ca).

Arnakaq Allattangit, M. 1999. "Healing Circles. Mamisarniup missanut nalunaijaijuq." *Inuktitut* 85: 33–9.

Balikci, Asen. 1960. "Some Acculturative Trends among the Eastern Canadian Eskimos." *Anthropologica* 2 (2): 139–53.

– 1962. "Missionary and Shaman among the Netsilik Eskimo." Paper presented at the sixty-first annual meeting of the American Anthropological Association, Chicago, November 1962.

– 1963. "Shamanistic Behavior among the Netsilik Eskimos." *Southwestern Journal of Anthropology* 19:380–96.

– 1970. *The Netsilik Eskimo.* New York: Garden City.

– 1978. "The Netsilik Inuit Today." *Études Inuit Studies* 2 (1): 111–19.

Bartholomew's Notes on Religion (from the Canadian *Leader-Post*). 2006. "Neo-Pentecostal Revival Suspected for Destruction of Ancient Arctic Art." Posted 29 August.

Bell, Jim. 2004. "Fundamentalists Seek Foothold in Legislature." *Nunatsiaq News*, 13 February.

Ben-Dor, Shmuel. 1969. "The 'Naluyuks' of Northern Labrador: A Mechanism of Social Control." In H. Halpert and G.M. Story, eds, *Christmas Mumming in Newfoundland*, 76–103. Toronto: University of Toronto Press.

Bennett, John, and Susan Rowley, eds. 2004. *Uqalurait: An Oral History of Nunavut.* Montreal and Kingston: McGill University Press.

Berger, Peter L., and Thomas Luckmann. 1966. *The Social Construction of Reality: A Treatise in the Sociology of Knowledge.* Garden City, NY: Doubleday.

Bernier, Joseph-Elzear. 1909. *Report on the Dominion Government Expedition to Arctic Islands and the Hudson Strait on Board the C.G.S. "Arctic" 1906–1907.* Ottawa: King's Printer.

– n.d. *Report on the Dominion Government Expedition to Arctic Islands and the Hudson Strait on Board the C.G.S. "Arctic" 1910*. Ottawa: King's Printer.
Bilby, Julian W. 1923. *Among Unknown Eskimos: An Account of Twelve Years Intimate Relations with the Primitive Eskimo of Ice Bound Baffin Land, with a Description of Their Ways of Living, Hunting Customs and Beliefs*. London: Seeley Service.
– 1927. *Nanook of the North*. London: George Newness.
Birket-Smith, Kaj. 1929. *The Caribou Eskimos: Material and Social Life and Their Cultural Position*. Vol. 5 (1–2) of *Report of the Fifth Thule Expedition 1921–24*. Copenhagen: Gyldendalske Boghandel.
– 1937. *Moeurs et coutumes des esquimaux*. Paris: Payot.
– 1940. *Anthropological Observations on the Central Eskimos*. Vol. 3 (2) of *Report of the Fifth Thule Expedition 1921–24*. Copenhagen: Gyldendalske Boghandel.
Blaisel, Xavier. 1993a. "Du sacrifice des hommes aux esprits selon la règle des initiations chamaniques chez les Inuit." *L'Ethnographie* 89 (1): 113–48.
– 1993b. "La chair et l'os: Espace cérémoniel et temps universel chez les Inuit du Nunavut (Canada), les valeurs coutumières inuit et les rapports rituels entre humains, gibiers, esprits et forces de l'univers." PhD thesis, École des hautes études en sciences sociales, Paris.
Blaisel, Xavier, and Jay Arnakak. 1993. "Trajet rituel: Du harponnage à la naissance dans le mythe d'Arnaqtaaqtuq." *Études Inuit Studies* 17:15–46.
Blaisel, Xavier, Frédéric Laugrand, and Jarich Oosten. 1999. "Shamans and Leaders: Parousial Movements among the Inuit of Northeast Canada." *Numen* 46:370–411.
Blaisel, Xavier, and Jarich G. Oosten. 1997. "La logique des échanges des fêtes d'hiver inuit." *Anthropologie et Sociétés* 21 (2–3): 19–44.
Blodgett, Jean. 1979. *The Coming and the Going of the Shaman: Eskimo Shamanism and Art*. Winnipeg: Winnipeg Art Gallery.
– 1985. *Kenojuak*. Toronto: Firefly Books.
– 1986. *North Baffin Drawings*. Collected by Terry Ryan on North Baffin Island in 1964. Ontario: Art Gallery of Ontario.
Bloom, Joseph D., and Richard D. Gelardin. 1976. "Uqamairineq and Uqumanigianiq: Eskimo Sleep Paralysis." *Arctic* 29 (1): 20–6.
Boas, Franz. 1885. "Cumberland Sound and Its Eskimos." *Popular Science Monthly* 26 (1): 768–79.
– 1887. "Unter den Eskimos." *Deutsch-Amerikanisches Magasin* 1:613–23.
– 1901. "The Eskimo of Baffin Land and Hudson Bay. From Notes Collected by Capt. George Comer, Capt. James S. Mutch, and Rev. E.J. Peck." *Bulletin of the American Museum of Natural History* 15 (1): 1–370.
– 1907. "Second Report on the Eskimo of Baffin Land and Hudson Bay. From Notes Collected by Captain George Comer, Captain James S. Mutch, and Rev. E.J. Peck." *Bulletin of the American Museum of Natural History* 15 (2): 371–570.
– 1964 [1888]. *The Central Eskimo*. Lincoln: University of Nebraska Press.
– 1966. "The Folk-lore of the Eskimo (1904)." In *Race, Language and Culture*, 503–16. New York: Free Press.
– 1974. "A Year among the Eskimo." In G.W. Stocking, ed., *The Shaping of American Anthropology 1883–1911. A Franz Boas Reader*, 44–55. New York: Basic Books.
Bodenhorn, Barbara. 1993. "Christmas Present: Christmas Public." In D. Miller, ed., *Unwrapping Christmas*, 193–216. Oxford: Clarendon Press.

Bogoras, William. 1904. *The Chukchee*. Leiden: E.J. Brill.

Boisclair, J.B. 1950. "Christmas in the Far North." *Eskimo* 19:13–14.

Bordin, Guy. 2002. "La nuit inuit: Éléments de réflexion." *Études Inuit Studies* 26 (1): 45–70.

– 2003. *Lexique analytique de l'anatomie humaine*. Collection Arctique no. 6. Paris: Peeters, Selaf.

– 2008. "La nuit Inuit. Vécu et représentation de la nuit chez les Inuit du nord de la Terre de Baffin (Nunavut, Arctique Canadien)." PhD thesis. Paris: Nanterre University.

Borré, Kristen. 1994. "The Healing Power of the Seal: The Meaning of Inuit Health Practice and Belief." *Arctic Anthropology* 31 (1): 1–15.

Bourdieu, Pierre. 1985. "Structure and the Habitus." In *Outline of a Theory of Practice*, 72–95. Cambridge: Cambridge University Press.

Brandson, Lorraine E. 1996. "Les croyances spirituelles des Inuit et l'introduction du christianisme." *Eskimo* 51:17–25.

Briggs, Jean L. 1970. *Never in Anger*. Cambridge, MA: Harvard University Press.

– 1979. *Aspects of Inuit Value Organization*. Mercury series, no. 56. Ottawa: National Museum of Man.

– 1998. *Inuit Morality Play*. St Johns: Institute for Social and Economic Research.

Briggs Jean L., ed. 2000. *Childrearing practices*. Interviewing Inuit Elders 3. Iqaluit: Nunavut Arctic College.

Brody, Hugh. 1979. "Inummariit: The Real Eskimo." In M.R. Freeman, ed., *Inuit Land Use and Occupancy Project*. Vol. 2. Ottawa: Department of Indian Affairs and Northern Development.

– 1987. *Living Arctic: Hunters of the Canadian North*. London: Faber and Faber.

Buijs, Cunera, ed. 1993. *Continuity and Discontinuity in Arctic Cultures*. Leiden: Centre of Non-Western Studies.

Buijs, Cunera, and Jarich Oosten, eds. 1997. *Braving the Cold: Continuity and Change in Arctic Clothing*. Leiden: Centre of Non-Western Studies.

Burant, Jim. 1998. "Using Photography to Assert Canadian Sovereignty in the Arctic: The A.P. Low Expedition of 1903–4 Aboard the CGS *Neptune*." In J.C.H. King and H. Lidchi, *Imaging the Arctic*, 77–87. London: British Museum.

Burch, Ernst, Jr. 1971. "The Nonempirical Environment of the Arctic Alaskan Eskimos." *Southwestern Journal of Anthropology* 27 (2): 148–65.

– 1988. "Knud Rasmussen and the 'Original' Inland Eskimos of Southern Keewatin." *Études Inuit Studies* 12 (1–2): 81–100.

– 1994. "The Inupiat and the Christianization of Arctic Alaska." *Études Inuit Studies* 18 (1–2): 81–108.

Carpenter, Samuel. 1955. "Changes in the Sedna Myth among the Aivilik." *Anthropological Papers of the University of Alaska* 3 (1): 69–73.

– 1968a. "The Timeless Present in the Mythology of the Aivilik Eskimos." In V.F. Valentine and F.G. Vallee, eds, *Eskimo of the Canadian Arctic*. Toronto: McClelland & Stewart.

– 1968b. "Witch-Fear among the Aivilik Eskimos." In V.F. Valentine and F.G. Vallee, eds, *Eskimo of the Canadian Arctic*. Toronto: McClelland & Stewart.

Cavanagh, Beverley. 1982. *Music of the Netsilik Eskimo: A Study of Stability and Change*. 2 vols. Ottawa: National Museums of Canada.

Choque, Father Charles. 1985. *Kajualuk. Pierre Henri. Missionary Oblate of Mary Immaculate. Apostle of the Inuit.* Diocese of Churchill, Hudson Bay.
– 1987. *75th Anniversary of the First Catholic Mission to the Hudson Bay Inuit.* Diocese of Churchill, Hudson Bay.
Clabaut, Armand. 1932. "Noël chez les Esquimaux." *L'Apostolat* 11:8–19.
Codex Historicus de la mission d'Igloolik. Iglulik, Nunavut.
Codex Historicus de la mission de Pelly Bay. Kugaaruk, Nunavut.
Cole, Douglas, and Ludger Müller-Wille. 1983. "The Value of a Person Lies in His *Herzensbildung*: Franz Boas Baffin Island Letter Diary, 1883–1885." In G.W. Stocking, ed., *Observers Observed: Essays on Ethnographic Fieldwork.* History of Ethnography 1. Madison: University of Wisconsin Press.
– 1984. "Franz Boas' Expedition to Baffin Island, 1883–1884." *Études Inuit Studies* 8 (1): 37–64.
Coleman, Simon. 2000. *The Globalization of Charismatic Christianity: Spreading the Gospel of Prosperity.* Cambridge: Cambridge University Press.
Collignon, Béatrice. 1996. *Les Inuit: Ce qu'ils savent du territoire.* Paris: L'Harmattan.
Condon, Richard G. 1996. *The Northern Copper Inuit: A History.* Norman and London: University of Oklahoma Press.
Conlon, Paula T. 1992. "Drum-dance Songs of the Iglulik Inuit in the Northern Baffin Island Area: A Study of Their Structures." PhD thesis, Université de Montréal, Montreal.
Cowan, R., and Rhoda Innuksuk. 1976. *We Don't Live in Snow Houses Now.* Ottawa: Canadian Arctic Producers.
Crantz, David. 1767. *The History of Greenland.* 2 vols. London: Brethren's Society.
Crowe, K.J. 1969. *A Cultural Geography of Northern Foxe Basin N.W.T.* Ottawa: Department of Indian Affairs and Northern Development.
Csonka, Yvon. 1995. *Les Ahiarmiut: A l'écart des Inuit Caribous.* Neuchâtel: Victor Attinger.
– 2005. "Les sens inuit de l'histoire et leurs divergences au Groenland de l'Ouest et au Nunavut." *Études Inuit Studies* 29 (1–2): 47–66.
Curwin, Kelly. 1988. "Life at Maguse River during the 50s: An Interview with Gleason and Kathryn Ledyard." *Isumasi* 1 (3): 25–31.
Damas, David. 1963. *Igluligmiut Kinship and Local Groupings: A Structural Approach.* National Museums of Canada Bulletin.
– 1969. "Environment, History, and Central Eskimo Societies." *National Museums of Canada Bulletin,* no. 230: 40–64.
– 1972. "The Structure of Central Eskimo Associations." In L. Guemple, ed., *Alliance in Eskimo Society,* 40–55. Seattle: University of Washington Press.
–, ed. 1984. *Arctic.* Vol. 5 of *Handbook of North American Indians.* Washington: Smithsonian Institution.
– 1988. "Journey at the Threshold: Knud Rasmussen's Study of the Copper Eskimos, 1923–24." *Études Inuit Studies* 12 (1–2): 129–50.
– 2002. *Arctic Migrants/Arctic Villagers: The Transformation of Inuit Settlement in the Central Arctic.* Montreal and Kingston: McGill-Queen's University Press.
Daniélo, Étienne. 1949. "'Ke-na-owet ?' (What is your name?)." *Eskimo* 14:13–15.
D'Argencourt, Leah. 1976. "Christmas at Aulatsivik." *Inuit Today* 5 (11): 28–40.
de Coppet, Daniel. 1992. *Understanding Rituals.* London: Routledge.

de Josselin de Jong, Jan P.B. 1977. "The Malay Archipelago as a Field of Ethnological Study." In P.E. de Josselin de Jong, ed., *Structural Anthropology in the Netherlands*, 166–82. The Hague: Nijhoff.

de Josselin de Jong, Patrick E. 1956. "De visie der participanten op hun cultuur." *Bijdragen to de Taal-, Land-, en Volkenkunde* 112 (12): 149–68.

– 1977. "The Participants' View of Their Culture." In P.E. de Josselin de Jong, ed., *Structural Anthropology in the Netherlands*, 233–52. The Hague: Nijhoff.

– 1984. *Unity in Diversity: Indonesia as a Field of Anthropological Study*. Dordrecht: Foris Publications.

Delalande, Father. 1958. *Sous le soleil de minuit*. Montreal: Rayonnement.

Descola, Philippe. 2005. *Par-delà nature culture*. Paris: Gallimard.

Désveaux, Emmanuel. 2001. *Quadratura Americana: Essai d'anthropologie lévi-straussienne*. Genève: Georg Editeur.

– 2007. *Spectres de l'anthropologie*. Paris: Au Lieu d'être.

Dewar, Patricia. 1990. "A Historical and Interpretive Study of Inuit Drum Dance in the Central Canadian Arctic: The Meaning Expressed in Dance, Culture and Performance." PhD thesis, University of Alberta, Edmonton.

Dick, L. 1995. "Pibloktoq (Arctic Hysteria): A Construction of European-Inuit Relations." *Arctic Anthropology* 32 (2): 1–42.

Dorais, Louis-Jacques. 1997a. *Quaqtaq: Modernity and Identity in an Inuit Community*. Toronto: University of Toronto Press.

– 1997b. "Pratiques et sentiments religieux à Quaqtaq: Continuité et modernité." *Études Inuit Studies* 21 (1–2): 255–67.

– 2000. "Le temps des Fêtes à Quaqtaq." *Études Inuit Studies* 24 (2): 139–50.

Douglas, Anne S. 1998. "'There's Life and Then There's School': School and Community as Contradictory Contexts for Inuit Self/Knowledge." PhD thesis, McGill University, Montreal.

Douglas, Mary. 1970. *Natural Symbols*. New York: Pantheon Books.

Driscoll, Bernadette. 1982. *Inuit Myths, Legends and Songs*. Winnipeg: Winnipeg Art Gallery.

Ducharme, Lionel. 1954. "A sorcier … sorcier et demi." *Eskimo* 33 (September): 7, 10.

Dufour, Rose. 1977. *Les noms de personnes chez les Inuit d'Iglulik*. MA thesis, Université Laval, Quebec City.

– 1988. *Femme et enfantement: Sagesse dans la culture Inuit*. Quebec City: Les éditions Papyrus.

Eber, Dorothy Harley. 1989. *When the Whalers Were Up North: Inuit Memories from the Eastern Arctic*. Montreal and Kingston: McGill-Queen's University Press.

– 1997. *Images of Justice*. Montreal and Kingston: McGill-Queen's University Press.

– 2008. *Encounters on the Passage: Inuit Meet Explorers*. Toronto: University of Toronto Press.

Eckert, P., and R. Newmark. 1980. "Central Eskimo Song Duels: A Contextual Analysis of Ritual Ambiguity." *Ethnology* 19 (2): 191–211.

Egede, Hans. 1818. *A Description of Greenland*. London: T. and J. Allman.

Eliade, M. 1970. *Shamanism: Archaic Techniques of Ecstasy*. London: Routledge & Kegan Paul. (1951. *Le chamanisme et les techniques archaïques de l'extase*. Paris: Payot.)

Ellyatt, David. 2005. "Arctic Mission Outreach Trust Fund." Newsletter, spring 2005.

– 2006. "Arctic Mission Outreach Trust Fund." Newsletter, spring 2006.

Evans-Pritchard, Edward E. 1962. *Essays in Social Anthropology*. London: Faber and Faber.
Evic-Twerdin, Leena. 1991. *Traditional Inuit Beliefs in Stories and Legends*. Iqaluit: Nortext/Baffin Divisional Board of Education.
Fafard, Eugène. 1934. "La petite Thérèse esquimaude." *L'Apostolat* 30 (5): 53–5.
– 1944. "Les Ténèbres protestantes." *L'Apostolat* 15:10–12.
– 1967a. "Rôle de la Bible et des catéchistes dans l'évangélisation des Esquimaux." *Kerygma* 1 (1): 23–6.
– 1967b. "Aurions nous formé des chrétiens de thé? Paternalisme d'hier et d'aujourd'hui." *Kerygma* 1 (4): 156–61.
– 1986–88. "Tirisikuluk, petite fleur … " *Eskimo*, no. 32 (1986): 3–7; no. 33 (1987): 28–31; no. 34 (autumn 1987–winter 1988): 10–14; no. 35: 21–4.
Fieguth, Debra. 2000. "Fire and Ice." *Christianity Today*, 23 October.
– 2002. "Arctic Revival." *Faith Today*, January–February.
Fienup-Riordan, Ann. 1983. *The Nelson Island Eskimo: Social Structure and Ritual Distribution*. Anchorage: Alaska Pacific University Press.
– 1986. "The Real People: The Concept of Personhood among the Yup'ik Eskimos of Western Alaska." *Études Inuit Studies* 10 (1–2): 261–70.
– 1987. "The Mask: The Eye of the Dance." *Arctic Anthropology* 24 (2): 40–55.
– 1988. *The Yup'ik Eskimos as described in the Travel Journals and Ethnographic Accounts of John and Edith Kilbuck 1885–1900*. Kingston, ON: Limestone Press.
– 1990a. *Eskimo Essays*. New Brunswick: Rutgers University Press.
– 1990b. *The Real People and the Children of the Thunder: The Yup'ik Eskimo Encounter with Moravian Missionaries John and Edith Kilbuck*. Norman: University of Oklahoma Press.
– 1994. *Boundaries and Passages: Rule and Ritual in Yup'ik Eskimo Oral Tradition*. Norman: University of Oklahoma Press.
– 1996. *The Living Tradition of Yupik Masks*. Seattle: University of Washington Press.
– 1997. "Metaphors of Conversion, Metaphors of Change." *Arctic Anthropology* 34 (1): 102–16.
– 2000. *Hunting Tradition in a Changing World*. New Brunswick, NJ: Rutgers University Press.
Findeisen, H. 1957. *Schamanentum, dargestellt am beispiel der Besessenheitspriester Nordeurasiatischer Völker*. Stuttgart: Kohlhammer Verlag.
Finnie, Richard. 1940. *Lure of the North*. Philadelphia: David McKay Company.
Fischer, John F. 1975. "An Analysis of the Central Eskimo Sedna Myth." *Temenos* 2:27–42.
Fleming, Archibald Lang. 1956. *Archibald the Arctic*. New York: Appleton-Century-Crofts, Inc.
Fletcher, Christopher M., and Laurence Kirmayer. 1997. "Spirit Work: Nunavimmiut Experiences of Affliction and Healing." *Études Inuit Studies* 21 (1–2): 189–208.
Flint, Maurice. 1949. *Operation Canon: A Short Account of the Life and Witness of the Rev. John Hudspith Turner … Missionary of the Bible Churchmen's Missionary Society in Its Eskimo Field*. London: Bible Churchmen's Missionary Society.
Fortescue, Michael, S. Jacobson, and Larry Kaplan. 1994. *Comparative Eskimo Dictionary: With Aleut Cognates*. Fairbanks: Alaska Native Language Center.

Frederiksen, Svend. 1964. "Some Preliminaries on the Soul Complex in Eskimo Shamanistic Belief." *Journal of the Washington Academy of Sciences* 54: 109–12.

– 1967. "Shaman Language as a Key to an Understanding of Eskimo Culture." In H. Findeisen, dir., *Rundschau Fur Menschen und Menschheitskunde,* 8–12. Vol. 1. Oosterhout, Netherlands: Anthropological Publications.

Freeman, Milton R. 1976. *Inuit Land Use and Occupancy Project.* 3 vols. Ottawa: Department of Indian and Northern Affairs.

Freuchen, Peter. 1939 *Aventure arctique, ma vie dans les glaces du nord.* Paris: Albin Michel.

– 1961. *Book of the Eskimos.* Cleveland and New York: World Publishing Co.

Gabus, Jean. 1940. *Iglous, vie des Esquimaux-caribou.* Neuchatel and Paris: Attinger.

– 1944. *Vie et coutumes des Esquimaux Caribous.* Lausanne: Payot.

Gasté, Alphonse. 1869. "Father Gasté Meets the Inland Eskimos: Ninety-Two Years Ago." *Eskimo* 57 (1960): 3–17.

Geller, Peter. 1998. "Pictures of the Arctic Night: Archibald Lang Flemming and the Representation of the Canadian Inuit." In J.C.H. King and H. Lidchi, eds, *Imaging the Arctic,* 60–8. London: British Museum.

Gessain, R., and P.E. Victor. 1973. "Le tambour chez les Ammassalimiut." *Objets et mondes* 13 (3): 129–60.

Giddens, Anthony. 1984. *The Constitution of Society: Outline of the Theory of Structuration.* Cambridge: Polity Press.

Gonda, Frank S. 1963. "Christmas in the Big Igloo." *North* 10 (6): 28–9.

Graburn, Nelson H.H. 1969. *Eskimos without Igloos: Social and Economic Development in Sugluk.* Boston: Little Brown.

– 1980. "Man, Beast, and Transformation in Canadian Inuit Art and Culture." In Marjorie M. Halpin and Michael M. Ames, eds, *Manlike Monsters on Trial: Early Records and Modern Evidence,* 193–210. Vancouver: University of British Columbia Press.

Grant, Shelah. 1997. "Religious Fanaticism in Northern Ungava." *Études Inuit Studies* 21 (1–2): 159–88.

– 2002. *Arctic Justice: On Trial for Murder, Pond Inlet, 1923.* Montreal and Kingston: McGill-Queen's University Press.

Greer, Darrell. 1999. "Teaching the Word of God: Inuit Evangelists Reach Out to Northern Youth." Northern News Services, 31 March 1999.

Guemple, Lee. 1972. *Alliance in Eskimo Society.* Seattle: University of Washington Press.

– 1994. "Born-Again Pagans: The Inuit Cycle of Spirits." In A. Mills and R. Slobodin, eds, *Amerindian Rebirth: Reincarnation Belief among North American Indians and Inuit,* 107–22. Toronto: University of Toronto Press.

Haase, Evelyn. 1987. *Der Schamanismus der Eskimo.* Aachen: Rader Verlag.

Haberland, W. 1975. *Nordamerika. Indianer. Eskimo. Westindien.* Baden-Baden: Holle Verlag.

Hall, Charles F. 1864. *Life with the Esquimaux.* Vols 1 and 2. London: Sampson, Low, Son, and Marston.

Hallendy, Norman. 1985. "Reflections, Shades and Shadows." In M. Patterson, R. Janes, and C. Arnold, eds, *Collected Papers on the Human History of the Northwest Territories,* 125–67. Occasional Paper no. 1. Yellowknife: Prince of Wales Northern Heritage Centre.

Halpert, H., and G.M. Story, eds. 1969. *Christmas Mumming in Newfoundland*. Toronto: University of Toronto Press.

Hamayon, Roberte. 1993. "Are 'Trance,' 'Ecstasy' and Similar Concepts Appropriate in the Study of Shamanism?" *Shaman* 1 (2): 3–25.

– 1995. "Why Do Ritual Games Please Shamanic Spirits and Displease Transcendent Gods? An Essay on 'Playing' as a Basic Type of Ritual Behaviour." *The Louis H. Jordan Lectures in Comparative Religion 1995*. London: School of Oriental and African Studies.

Hantzsch, Bernhard Adolph. 1977. *My Life among the Eskimos: The Baffinland Journals of Bernhard Adolph Hantzsch 1909–1911*. Saskatoon: University of Saskatchewan.

Harper, Kenn. 1983. *Christmas in the Big Igloo: True Tales from the Canadian Arctic*. Yellowknife: Outcrop, Northern Publishers.

– 1985. "The Early Development of Inuktitut Syllabic Orthography." *Inuit Studies* 9:141–62.

– 2004. Letter to the Editor, "Harper Challenges Irniq, Anawak on Sedna." *Nunavut News North*, 1 April.

Hastrup, Kirsten. 2004–5. "Knud Rasmussen (1879–1933): The Anthropologist as Explorer, Hunter, and Narrator." *Folk* 46/47:159–80.

Hawkes, Edward W. 1916. "The Labrador Eskimo." *Geological Survey Memoir 91*. Anthropological series 14. Ottawa: Department of Mines.

– 1973. *The Inviting-In Feast of the Alaskan Eskimo*. Ottawa: National Museum of Man.

Hessel, Ingo. 1998. *Inuit Art: An Introduction*. London: British Museum Press.

Hiller, James K. 1971. "The Moravians in Labrador 1771–1805." *Polar Record* 15 (99): 839–54.

Himmelheber, Hans. 1953. *Eskimokünstler*. Eisenach: Erich Roth-Verlag.

– 1993. *Eskimo Artists*. University of Alaska Press.

Hoebel, Edward A. 1964. *The Law of Primitive Man*. Cambridge, MA: Harvard University Press.

Holland, Paula Lee. 1979. "Seven Eskimo Religious Movements: Description and Analysis." MA thesis, Department of Anthropology, University of Manitoba.

Holtved, Erik. 1943. *The Eskimo Legend of Navaranaq*. Copenhagen: Acta Artica Fascicule no. 1.

– 1951. *The Polar Eskimo: Language and Folklore*. 2 vols. Copenhagen: Meddelelser om Gronland.

– 1963. "Tôrnârssuk, an Eskimo Deity." *Folk* 5:157–71.

– 1966. "The Eskimo Myth about the Sea Woman." *Folk* 8/9: 145–53.

Houston, John, ed. 1976. *Pangnirtung 1976: Prints*. Toronto.

Hutchinson, Elisabeth. 1977. "Order and Chaos in the Cosmology of the Baffin Island Eskimo." *Anthropology* 1 (2): 120–38.

Iglulik Oral History database. IE-interviews. Consulted in Iglulik, Nunavut.

Inuaraq, Susan. 1995. "Traditional Justice among the Inuit." In A.V. Charrin, J.M. Lacroix, and M. Therrien, eds, *Peuples des Grands Nords: Traditions et transitions*, 255–62. Paris: Presses de la Sorbonne Nouvelle/INALCO.

Innuksuk, R., and S. Cowan. 1976. *We Don't Live in Snow Houses Now: Reflections of Arctic Bay*. Canadian Arctic Producers.

Ipellie, Alooktook. 1972. "Community Christmas." *North* 19 (6): 24–7.

– 1974. "Christmas Is for Everyone." *Inuit Monthly* 3 (9): 36–9.

Irimoto, T., and T. Yamada. 1994. *Circumpolar Religion and Ecology: An Anthropology of the North*. Tokyo: University of Tokyo Press.

Irniq, Peter. 2008. "One Bone at a Time." *Cahiers du CIÉRA*, no. 2: 45–8.

Issenman, Betty. 1997. *Sinews of Survival: The Living Legacy of Inuit Clothing*. Vancouver: University of British Columbia Press.

Issenman, Betty, and Catherine Rankin. 1988. *Ivalu: Traditions of Inuit Clothing*. Montreal: McCord Museum of Canadian History.

Jackson, Marion E., and Judith M. Nasby. 1987. *Contemporary Inuit Drawings*. Guelph, ON: Macdonald Stewart Art Centre.

Jakobsen, M.D. 1996. *Shamanism: Traditional and Contemporary Approaches to the Mastery of Spirits and Healing*. New York: Berghahn Books.

Jenness, Diamond. 1922. *The Life of the Copper Eskimos*. Vol. 12 (A) of *Report of the Canadian Arctic Expedition, 1913–1918*. Ottawa: F.A. Acland.

– 1959. *The People of the Twilight*. Chicago: University of Chicago Press.

– 1965. *Eskimo Administration, III: Labrador*. Technical Paper 16. Montreal: Institute of North America.

– 1986. *The Indians of Canada*. Ottawa: University of Toronto Press.

Johnstone, Meg. 2001. "'Wind of God' Blowing through Northern Communities." *BC Christian News* 21 (1). Read on canadianchristianity.com.

Juel, Erik. 1945. "Notes on Seal-Hunting Ceremonialism in the Arctic." *Ethnos* 10 (2–3): 143–64.

Kalluak, Mark. 1974. *How Kabloonat Became and Other Inuit Legends*. Yellowknife: Department of Education.

Kantorowicz, Ernst H. 1957. *The King's Two Bodies: A Study in Medieval Political Theology*. Princeton: Princeton University Press.

Kekerten Historic Park. N.d. Northwest Territories Historic Parks.

Kennedy, John. 1977. "Northern Labrador: An Ethnohistorical Account." In R. Paine, ed., *The White Arctic: Anthropological Essays on Tutelage and Ethnicity*, 264–306. Newfoundland Social and Economic Studies, no. 27. St John's: Memorial University of Newfoundland.

Kennedy Michael P.J. 1997. "The Sea Goddess Sedna: An Enduring Pan-Arctic Legend from Traditional Orature to the New Narratives of the Late Twentieth Century." In J. Moss, ed., *Echoing Silence: Essays on Arctic Narrative*, 211–30. Ottawa: University of Ottawa.

Kishigami, Nobuhiro. 1994. "Why Become Christian? Hypotheses on the Christianization of the Canadian Inuit." In T. Irimoto and T. Yamada, eds, *Circumpolar Religion and Ecology*, 221–36. Tokyo: University of Tokyo Press.

Kleivan, Inge. 1960. "Mitârtut, Vestiges of the Eskimo Sea-Woman Cult in West Greenland." *Med. Om Grönland* 161 (5): 1–30.

– 1978. "'Lamb of God' = 'Seal of God'? Some Semantic Problems in Translating the Animal Names of the New Testament into Greenlandic." In *Papers from the 4th Scandinavian Conference of Linguistics*, 339–45. Hindsgavl, 7–8 January.

Kleivan, Inge, and Birgitte Sonne. 1985. *Eskimos: Greenland and Canada*. Leiden: Brill.

Klutschak, H. 1987. *Overland to Starvation Cove: With the Inuit in Search of Franklin*. Toronto: University of Toronto Press.

Knötsch, Kathleen. 1991. *Franz Boas bei den kanadischen Inuit im Jahre 1883–1884*. Bonn: Holos Verlag.

Kolb, Stéphane, and Samuel Law, eds. 2001. *Dreams and Dream Interpretation*. Inuit Perspectives on the 20th Century 4. Iqaluit: Nunavut Arctic College.

Komangapik, Dorothee, ed. 1999. *Iqaluit Elders in the Museum Project 1997–1998: Memories and Stories*. Iqaluit: Nunatta Sunakkutaangit Museum Society.

Kretschmar, Freda. 1938. *Hundestammvater und Kerberos*. Stuttgart: Strecker und Schroder Verlag.

Kroeber, Alfred L. 1900. "The Eskimo of Smith Sound." *Bulletin of the American Museum of Natural History* 12 (21): 256–327.

Kublu, Alexina. 2004. *Edited Elders Glossary*. Iqaluit: Nunavut Arctic College.

Kublu, Alexina, and Jarich Oosten. 1999. "Changing Perspectives of Name and Identity among the Inuit of Northeast Canada." In J. Oosten and C. Remie, eds, *Arctic Identities: Continuity and Change in Inuit and Saami Societies*, 57–85. Leiden: Centre of Non-Western Studies.

Kulchyski, Peter, Don McCaskill, and David Newhouse, eds. 2003. *In the Words of Elders*. Toronto: University of Toronto Press.

Kumlien, Ludvig. 1879. *Contributions to the Natural History of Arctic America*. Bulletin of the United States National Museum, no. 15. Washington: United States Printing Office.

Kuper, Adam J. 1982. *Wives for Cattle*. London: Routledge & Kegan Paul.

Kutluk, Thomas. 1985. "Breakthrough at Eskimo Point: God Used an Icy Plunge to Redirect This Eskimo's Life Testimony." *Alliance Witness* 120 (1) (2 January).

Lantis, Margaret. 1950. "The Religion of the Eskimos." In Vergilius Fern, ed., *Forgotten Religions*, 311–39. New York: Philosophical Library.

– 1966. *Alaskan Eskimo Ceremonialism*. Seattle and London: University of Washington Press.

Lapage, Eva. 1976. "Christmas Time in Sugluk." *Inuit Today* 5 (11): 44–7.

– 1997. "Healing Circles in Nunavik." *Inuktitut* 81:45–58.

Laugrand, Frédéric. 1997a. "Siqqitiqpuq: Conversion et réception du christianisme par les Inuit de l'Arctique de l'Est canadien (1894–1940)." PhD, Département d'anthropologie, Université Laval, Quebec City.

– 1997b. "Le siqqitiq: Renouvellement religieux et premier rituel de conversion chez les Inuit du nord de la Terre de Baffin." *Études Inuit Studies* 21 (1–2): 101–40.

– 1999a. "Le mythe comme instrument de mémoire: Remémoration et interprétation d'un extrait de Genèse par un aîné inuit de l'île de Baffin." *Études Inuit Studies* 23: (1–2): 91–115.

– 1999b. "Mourir et renaître: La conversion au christianisme des Inuit de l'Arctique de l'Est." *L'Homme* 152:115–42.

– 2001. "Des humains, des ancêtres et des esprits: L'hétéronomie du rêve chez les aînés inuit de l'Arctique canadien." *Études Inuit Studies* 25 (1–2): 73–100.

– 2002a. "Les onze 'apôtres' du Rév. E.J. Peck: Les premières conversions inuit de Little Whale River (1876–1885)." *Recherches amérindiennes au Québec* 32 (2): 83–98.

– 2002b. "Écrire pour prendre parole: Conscience historique, mémoires d'aînés et régimes d'historicité au Nunavut." *Anthropologie et Société* 26 (2–3): 91–116.

– 2002c. *Mourir et renaître: La réception du christianisme par les Inuit de l'Arctique de l'Est (1890–1940)*. Quebec City: Presses de l'Université Laval; Leiden: Centre of Non-Western Studies.

– n.d. "Contact direct avec les esprits et incorporations: Réflexions critiques sur les notions de chamanisme et de possession à partir du cas des Inuit de l'Arctique canadien." In R. Crépeau, ed., *Chamanisme et possession*. Montreal: Presses de l'Université de Montréal, forthcoming.

Laugrand, Frédéric, and Jarich Oosten. 2002a. "Canicide and Healing. The Social Position of the Dog in the Canadian Arctic." *Anthropos* 97 (1): 89–105.

– 2002b. "Quviasukvik: The Celebration of an Inuit Winter Feast in the Central Arctic." *Journal de la Société des Américanistes* 88:203–26.

– 2003. "Le pouvoir de transformation des miniatures." In *Miniatures inuit*, 25–45. Catalogue. Musée de la miniature de Montélimar (France), Imprimerie Bayle.

– 2006. "Connecting and Protecting: Lines and Belts in the Canadian Arctic." *Anthropological Papers of the University of Alaska* 4 (1): 133–47.

– 2007. "Bears and Dogs in Canadian Inuit Cosmology." In F. Laugrand and J. Oosten, eds, *La nature des esprits dans les cosmologies autochtones / Spirits of Nature in Aboriginal Cosmologies*, 353–86. Quebec City: Presses de l'Université Laval.

– 2008a. *The Sea Woman: Sedna in Inuit Shamanism and Art in the Eastern Arctic*. Fairbanks: Alaska University Press.

–2008b. "'When toys and ornaments come into play': The Transformative Power of Miniatures in Canadian Inuit Cosmology." *Museum Anthropology* 31 (2): 69–84.

– n.d. "*Qupirruit,* Insects and Worms in Inuit Shamanic Traditions." Forthcoming, *Arctic Anthropology*.

Laugrand, Frédéric, Jarich Oosten, and Maaki Kakkik. 2003. *Keeping the Faith*. Memory and History in Nunavut 3. Iqaluit: Nunavut Arctic College.

Laugrand, Frédéric, Jarich Oosten, and Francois Trudel. 2000. *Representing Tuurngait*. Memory and History in Nunavut 1. Iqaluit: Nunavut Arctic College.

– 2002. "Hunters, Owners and Givers of Light: The *Tuurngait* of South Baffin Island." *Arctic Anthropology* 39 (1–2): 27–50.

– 2006. *Apostle to the Inuit: The Journals and Ethnographic Notes of Edmund James Peck. The Baffin Years: 1894–1905*. Toronto: University of Toronto Press.

Laugrand, Frédéric, and Gilles Routhier. 2001. "Réception et enracinement de Vatican II en milieu inuit." In G. Routhier, ed., *Enracinement et réception de Vatican II*, 327–53. Montreal: Fides.

Leden, C. 1912. *Across the Keewatin Icefields*. Winnipeg: Watson and Wyer Publishing.

Leroux, Odette, Marion E. Jackson, and Minnie Aodla Freeman, eds. 1994. *Inuit Women Artists*. San Francisco: Chronicle Books.

Lewis, Arthur. 1908 [1904]. *The Life and Work of the Rev. E.J. Peck among the Eskimo*. London: Hodder and Stroughton.

Lommel, A. 1967 [1965]. *The World of the Early Hunters*. London: Evelyn, Adams & Mackay.

Low, Albert L. 1906. *Cruise of the Neptune, 1903–1904: Report on the Dominion Government Expedition to Hudson Bay and the Arctic Islands on Board the D.G.S. Neptune*. Ottawa: Government Printing Bureau.

Lutz, Maija M. 1978. *The Effects of Acculturation on Eskimo Music of Cumberland Peninsula*. Ottawa. National Museum of Man. Mercure Collection, Canadian Ethnology Service.

Lyon, George F. 1824. *The Private Journal of Captain G.F. Lyon of H.M.S. Hecla, During the Recent Voyage of Discovery under Captain Parry*. London: John Murray.

– 1970 [1824]. *The Private Journal of Captain G.F. Lyon of H.M.S. Hecla, During the Recent Voyage of Discovery under Captain Parry*. Barre, MA: Imprint Society.

McComber, Louis, ed. 2005. *We Call It Survival: Abraham Okpik*. Life Stories of Northern Leaders 1. Iqaluit: Nunavut Arctic College.
– 2007. *Changing the Face of Canada: John Amagoalik*. Life Stories of Northern Leaders 2. Iqaluit: Nunavut Arctic College.
– 2008. *Paul Quassa: We Need to Know Who We Are*. Life Stories of Northern Leaders 3. Iqaluit: Nunavut Arctic College.
McDermott, Noel, ed. 2008. *James Arvaluk: That's My Vision*. Life Stories of Northern Leaders 4. Iqaluit: Nunavut Arctic College.
MacDonald, John. 1998. *The Arctic Sky: Inuit Astronomy, Star Lore and Legend*. Toronto: Royal Ontario Museum/Nunavut Research Institute.
McGhee, Robert. 1990. "Ivory for the Sea Woman: The Symbolic Attributes of a Prehistoric Technology." *Canadian Journal of Archaeology* 1:141–9.
– 1996. *Ancient People of the Arctic*. Vancouver: University of British Columbia Press.
Malaurie, Jean, and Jacques Rousseau, eds. 1961. *Le Nouveau-Québec: Contribution à l'étude de l'occupation humaine*. Paris: Mouton.
Mannik, Hattie. 1998. *Inuit Nunamiut: Inland Inuit*. Altona, MB: Friesen Corporation.
Maranda, Pierre. 2001. *The Double Twist: From Ethnography to Morphodynamics*. Toronto: University of Toronto Press.
Mary-Rousselière, Guy. 1949. "Pastor of the North Pole." *Eskimo* 15:11–15.
– 1991. *Qitdlarssuaq: The Story of a Polar Migration*. Winnipeg: Wuerz.
Mathiassen, Therkel. 1927. *Archaeology of the Central Eskimo*. Vol. 4 (1–2) of *Report of the Fifth Thule Expedition 1921–24*. Copenhagen: Gyldendalske Boghandel.
– 1928. *Material Culture of the Iglulik Eskimos*. Vol. 6 of *Report of the Fifth Thule Expedition*. Copenhagen: Gyldendalske Boghandel.
– 1930a. *Archaeological Collections from the Western Eskimos*. Vol. 6 (1) of *Report of the Fifth Thule Expedition, 1921–24*. Copenhagen: Gyldendalske Boghandel.
– 1930b. Diary extracts. In K. Rasmussen, ed., *Intellectual Culture of the Caribou Eskimos. Iglulik and Caribou Eskimo Texts*. Vol. 7 (2–3) of *Report of the Fifth Thule Expedition*. Copenhagen: Gyldendalske Boghandel.
Matthiason, John S. 1996. *Living on the Land: Change among the Inuit of Baffin Land*. Peterborough, ON: Broadview Press.
Mauss, Marcel, and Henri Beuchat. 1985 [1904]. "Essai sur les variations saisonnières des sociétés Eskimo. Étude de morphologie sociale." In M. Mauss, *Sociologie et anthropologie*. Paris: PUF.
Mauss, Marcel, in collaboration with Henri Beuchat. 1979. *Seasonal Variations of the Eskimo*. London: Routledge & Kegan Paul.
Merkur, Daniel. 1985. *Becoming Half Hidden: Shamanism and Initiation among the Inuit*. Stockholm: Almquist and Wiksell International.
– 1991. *Powers Which We Do Not Know: The Gods and Spirits of the Inuit*. Moscow, ID: University of Idaho Press.
Métayer, Maurice. 1970. *Tales from the Igloo*. Edmonton: Hurtig Publishers.
– 1973. *Unikpat*. Centre d'Études Nordiques. Quebec City: Université Laval.
Metcalfe, Sam. 1978. "Christmas Time in Northern Labrador." *Inuktitut*, winter, 18–26.
Michéa, Jean. 1949. *Terre stérile: Six mois chez les Esquimaux Caribous*. Paris: Bloud et Gay.
Mills, Antonia, and Slobodin, Richard, eds. 1994. *Amerindian Rebirth: Reincarnation Belief among North American Indians and Inuit*. Toronto: University of Toronto Press.

Mitiarjuk Nappaaluk, Salumi. 1994. "The Inuit Encyclopedia of Mitiarjuk." *Tumivut* 5:73–80.
– 1997. "Un témoignage inédit de Mitiarjuk sur les *mumitsimajut* de Baie aux Feuilles, et sur les *uirsaliit* et *nuliarsaliit* du Nunavik." *Études Inuit Studies* 21 (1–2): 249–54.
– 2002. *Sanaaq*. Transliterated and translated from Inuktitut by B. Saladin d'Anglure. Montreal: Stanké.
Morice, Gabriel. 1935. *Mgr Turquetil Omi, apôtre des Esquimaux et le miracle de ses missions.* Winnipeg/St-Boniface: Chez l'auteur/Juniorat des omi.
Morrow, Phillis. 1984. "It Is Time for Drumming: A Summary of Recent Research on Yup'ik Ceremonialism." *Études Inuit Studies* 8:113–40.
Mousalimas, Soterio A. 1995. *The Transition from Shamanism to Russian Orthodoxy in Alaska*. Oxford: Berghahn Books.
Mowat, Farley. 1954. *People of the Deer*. London: Readers Union and Michael Joseph.
Müller, G.F. 1967. *Voyages from Asia to America*. Amsterdam: N. Israel.
– 1986. *Bering's Voyages: The Reports from Russia*. Fairbanks: University of Alaska Press.
Müller-Wille, Ludger. 1998. *Franz Boas among the Inuit of Baffin Island 1883–188: Journals and Letters*. Toronto: University of Toronto Press.
Munn, Capt. Henry Toke. 1932. *Prairie Trails and Arctic By-ways*. London: Hurst and Blackett.
Murphy, Jane M. 1969. "Psychotherapeutic Aspects of Shamanism on St. Lawrence Island, Alaska." In A. Kiev, ed., *Magic, Faith and Healing*, 53–84. New York: Free Press of Glencoe.
Nasby, Judith. 2002. *Irene Avaalaaqiaq: Myth and Reality*. Montreal and Kingston: McGill-Queen's University Press; Seattle: University of Washington Press.
Nattiez, Jean-Jacques. 1988. "La danse à tambour chez les Inuit Igloolik (nord de la Terre de Baffin)." *Recherches amérindiennes au Québec* 18 (4): 37–48.
Nellemann, Georg. 1960. "Mitârneq, a West Greenland Winter Ceremony." *Folk* 2: 99–113.
Nelson, Edward W. 1980. *The Eskimo about Bering Strait (1899)*. Washington, DC: Smithsonian Institution Press.
Nickels, Scot Jamal Shirley, and Gital Laider, eds. 2006. *Negotiating Research Relationships with Inuit Communities: A Guide for Researchers*. Ottawa and Iqaluit: Inuit Tapiriit Kanatami and Nunavut Research Institute.
Nooter, Gert. 1975. "Mitârtut, Winter Feast In Greenland." *Objets et Mondes* 15 (2): 159–68.
Nuluaq Project. 2004. *Analysis Report: Inuit Healing in Contemporary Inuit Society.* 31 March. http://www.pauktuutit.ca/pdf/publications/abuse/AHFNuluaqInuitHealing_e.pdf.
Nunavut Social Development Council, n.d. "A Discussion Paper: Towards an Inuit Qaujimajatuqangit (IQ). Policy for Nunavut."
– 1998. "Towards Justice That Brings Peace." NSDC Justice Retreat and Conference, Rankin Inlet, Nunavut, 1–3 September 1998.
Nungak, Zebedee, and Eugene Arima. 1988. Inuit Stories / Légendes inuit / Unikkatuat: Povungnituk. Bulletin no. 235. Quebec: Canadian Museum of Civilization.
Nuttall, Mark. 1994. "The Name Never Dies: Greenland Inuit Ideas of the Persons." In A. Mills and R. Slobodin, eds, *Amerindian Rebirth: Reincarnation Belief among North American Indians and Inuit*, 123–35. Toronto: University of Toronto Press.

Oakes, Jill, and Rick Riewe. 1991. *Our Boots: An Inuit Women's Art.* London: Thames and Hudson.

Oosten, Jarich G. 1976. *The Theoretical Structure of the Religion of the Netsilik and Iglulik.* Meppel: Krips Repro.

– 1981. "The Structure of the Shamanistic Complex among the Netsilik and Iglulik." *Études Inuit Studies* 5 (1): 83–98.

– 1982. "The Symbolism of the Body in Inuit Culture." In H.G. Kippenberg, ed., *Commemorative Figures*, 98–112. Leiden: Brill.

– 1983. "The Incest of Sun and Moon." *Études Inuit Studies* 7 (1): 43–51.

– 1984. "The Diary of Therkel Mathiassen: An Examination of the Practice of Inuit Shamanism on Southampton Island (1922–1923)." In M. Hoppál, ed., *Shamanism in Eurasia.* Vol. 2, 377–90. Göttingen: Edition Herodot.

– 1985. *The War of the Gods. The Social Code in Indo-European Mythology.* London: Routledge & Kegan Paul.

– 1986. "Male and Female in Inuit Shamanism." *Études Inuit Studies* 10 (1–2): 115–31.

– 1988. "The Prime Mover and Fear in Inuit Religion." In Maarten Jansen, Peter van der Loo, and Roswitha Manning, eds., *Continuity and Identity in Native America: Essays in Honour of Benedikt Hartmann*, 69–83. Leiden: Brill.

– 1989. "Theoretical Problems in the Study of Inuit Shamanism." In Mihaly Hoppal and Otto von Sadovsky, eds, *Shamanism Past and Present,* 2:331–42. Budapest: International Society for Trans-Oceanic Research Books.

– 1992. "Representing the Spirits: The Masks of the Alaskan Inuit." In Jeremy Coote and Anthony Shelton, eds, *Anthropology Art and Aesthetics,* 113–34. Oxford: Clarendon Press.

– 1994. "Violent Words and Evil Actions Populate the Sky: The Creation Myths of the Inuit of North-East Canada." In Jarich G. Oosten, ed., *Text and Tales: Studies in Oral Traditions,* 116–31. Leiden: Centre of Non-Western Studies.

– 1995. "Inuit Cosmology and the Problem of the Third Sex." *Études mongoles et sibériennes* 26:83–106.

– 1996. "Dynamiques des principes socio-cosmiques de la personne." In N. Tersis and Michèle Therrien, eds, *La dynamique dans la langue et la culture inuit*, 177–95. Paris: Peeters.

– 1997. "Amulets, Shamanic Clothes and Paraphernalia in Inuit culture." In C. Buijs and J. Oosten, eds, *Braving the Cold: Continuity and Change in Arctic Clothing,* 105–30. Leiden: Centre of Non-Western Studies.

– 2000. "The Concept of Inua and the Dynamics of Inuit Knowledge." In *Inuit inuunerup tunngaaviinik paasinninnerat/Inuit Philosophy,* 114–36. Nuuk: Ilismatusarfik, University of Greenland.

– 2001. "Ritual Play at an Inuit Winter Feast." *North Atlantic Studies* 4 (1–2): 17–24.

– 2002. "Kiviuq: An Epic in the Making?" *Anthropologie et Sociétés* 26 (2–3): 71–90.

– 2005. "Ideals and Values in the Participants' View of Their Culture: A View from the Inuit Field." *Social Anthropology* 13 (2): 185–98.

– 2006. "A Privileged Field of Study: Marcel Mauss and Structural Anthropology in Leiden." *Etudes Inuit Studies* 30 (2): 51–72.

Oosten, Jarich, and Frédéric Laugrand. 2006a. "The Bringer of Light: The Raven in Inuit Traditions." *Polar Record* 42 (3): 187–204.

– 2006b. "Time and Space in the Perception of Non-Human Beings in Northeast Canada." *Folk* 46/47:85–120.

Oosten, Jarich, and Frédéric Laugrand, eds. 1999a. *Introduction.* Interviewing Inuit Elders 1. Iqaluit: Nunavut Arctic College.

– 1999b. *The Transition to Christianity.* Inuit Perspectives on the 20th Century 1. Iqaluit: Nunavut Arctic College.

– 2001. *Travelling and Surviving on Our Land.* Inuit Perspectives on the 20th Century. Iqaluit: Nunavut Arctic College.

– 2002. *Inuit Qaujimajatuqangit: Shamanism and Reintegrating Wrongdoers.* Inuit Perspectives on the 20th Century 2. Iqaluit: Nunavut Arctic College.

– 2007. *Surviving in Different Worlds: Transferring Inuit Traditions from Elders to Youths.* Iqaluit: Nunatta-Campus/Arctic College.

Oosten, Jarich, Frédéric Laugrand, and Wim Rasing, eds, 1999. *Perspectives on Traditional Law.* Interviewing Inuit Elders 2. Iqaluit: Nunavut Arctic College.

Oosten, Jarich, Frederic Laugrand, and Cor Remie. 2006. "Perceptions of Decline: Inuit Shamanism in the Canadian Arctic." *Ethnohistory* 53 (3): 455–77.

Oosten, Jarich, and Cor Remie. 1997. "*Angakkut* and Reproduction. Social and Symbolic Aspects of Netsilik Symbolism." *Études Inuit Studies* 21 (1–2): 75–100.

– 1999. *Arctic Identities: Continuity and Change in Inuit and Saami Societies.* Leiden: Centre of Non-Western Studies.

Otis, George, Jr. 2001. *Transformations II.* The Glory Spreads. Videotape. Sentinel Group.

Ouellette, Nathalie. 2002. "Les *tuurngait* dans le Nunavik occidental contemporain." *Études Inuit Studies* 26 (2): 107–32.

Parry, William E. 1821. *Journal of a Voyage for the Discovery of a North-West Passage.* London: John Murray.

– 1824. *Journal of a Second Voyage for the Discovery of a North-West Passage from the Atlantic to the Pacific: performed in the years 1821–22–23, in His Majesty's Ships Fury and Hecla.* London: John Murray.

Payment, Diane. 1996. "Persistence and Change in the Spiritual Traditions of the Inuit of Pangnirtung and Qikiqtarjuaq (Broughton Island) since the 1980." In R. Huel, ed., *Études oblates de l'Ouest 4 / Western Oblate Studies 4*, 143–160. Winnipeg. Saint-Boniface: Presses universitaires de Saint-Boniface.

Peck, Edmund James. 1922. *The Eskimo, Our Brethren of the Arctic.* Toronto: Missionary Society of the Church of England in Canada.

Pelinski, Ramón. 1981. *La musique des Inuit du Caribou: Cinq perspectives méthodologiques.* Montreal: Presses de l'Université de Montréal.

Pelinski, Ramón, et al. 1979. *Inuit Songs from Eskimo Point.* Ottawa.

Pentekainen, Juha. 1965. *The Nordic Dead-Child Beings.* Helsinki: FF Communications.

Perrin, Michel. 1995. *Le chamanisme.* Paris: PUF.

Philippe, Jean. 1948. "Eskimo Psychology: Marriage." *Eskimo* 10:2–7, 14.

– 1952. "Christmas." *Eskimo* 27:2–4.

– 1956. "Noël chez les Esquimaux." *Eskimo*, 31 December, 6–7.

Pitseolak, Peter, and Dorothy Harley Eber. 1993. *People from Our Side: A Life Story with Photographs and Oral Biography.* Montreal and Kingston: McGill-Queen's University Press.

– 2003 [1978]. *Pitseolak: Pictures out of My Life.* Montreal and Kingston: McGill-Queen's University Press.

Pollick, Jason. 2003. "Anguaks in Copper and Netsilik Inuit Spirituality." MA thesis, Université Laval, Quebec City.

Platenkamp, Jos D.M. 1991. "Het samenwerkingsverband CASA-ERASME en de relatie Parijs-Leiden." In H.F. Vermeulen, ed., *Recente ontwikkelingen in de Leidse antropologie*, 41–8. ICA Publicaties 91. Leiden: Vakgroep Culturele Antropologie en Sociologie der Niet-Westerse Samenlevingen.

Qanguq, Isapie, and Guy Mary-Rousselière. 1985–86. "Aspirant *angakkuq* frustré." *Eskimo*, autumn 1985–winter 1986 (30): 6–8.

Qitsualik, Rachel. 1999. "The Problem with Sedna," pt 4. *Nunatsiaq News*, 26 March, 12.

Radcliffe-Brown, A.R. 1930–31. "The Social Organization of Australian Tribes." *Oceania* 1:34–63, 206–56, 322–41, 426–56.

Randa, Vladimir. 1986. *L'ours polaire et les Inuit*. Paris: Selaf.

– 1994. "*Inuillu uumajuillu*: Les animaux dans les savoirs, les représentations et la langue des Iglulingmiut (Arctique oriental canadien)." PhD thesis, École des hautes études en sciences sociales, Paris.

Rasing, Wim. 1994. *Too Many People: Order and Non-conformity in Iglulingmiut Social Process*. Nijmegen: Katholieke Universiteit Faculteit der Rechtsgeleerdheid. Recht and Samenleving.

Rasmussen, Knud. 1908. *The People of the Polar North*. London: K. Paul, Trench, Trübner.

– 1922a. *Grönlandsagen*. Berlin: Gyldendal.

– 1922b. *In der Heimat des Polarmenschen. Die zweite Thule-Expedition 1916–1918*. Leipzig: Brockhaus.

– 1926. *Rasmussens Thulefahrt*. Bearbeitet und übersetzt von Friedrich Sieburg. Frankfurt am Main: Frankfurter Societäts-Druckerei GBMH.

– 1927. *Across Arctic America*. New York and London: G.P. Putnam's Sons.

– 1929. *Intellectual Culture of the Iglulik Eskimos*. Vol. 7 (1) of *Report of the Fifth Thule Expedition 1921–24*. Copenhagen: Gyldendalske Boghandel.

– 1930. *Observations on the Intellectual Culture of the Caribou Eskimos: Iglulik and Caribou Eskimo Texts*. Vol. 12 (2–3) of *Report of the Fifth Thule Expedition 1921–24*. Copenhagen: Gyldendalske Boghandel.

– 1931. *The Netsilik Eskimos: Social Life and Spiritual Culture*. Vol. 8 (1–2) of *Report of the Fifth Thule Expedition 1921–24*. Copenhagen: Gyldendalske Boghandel.

– 1932. *Intellectual Culture of the Copper Eskimos*. Vol. 9 of *Report of the Fifth Thule Expedition 1921–24*. Copenhagen: Gyldendalske Boghandel.

– 1999 [1927]. *Across Arctic America*. Fairbanks: University of Alaska Press.

RCMP (Royal Canadian Mounted Police). 1921–43. *Annual Reports*. Ottawa: King's Printer.

– 1941. "The Law Goes North." *RCMP Quarterly* 9 (2): 152–60.

Recollections of Martha Angugatiaq Ungalaaq. 1985. Eskimo Point: Inuit Cultural Institute.

Recollections of Inuit Elders. 1986. Eskimo Point: Inuit Cultural Institute.

Recollections of Levi Iqalujjuup. 1988. Eskimo Point: Inuit Cultural Institute.

Recollections of Helen Paungat. 1988. Eskimo Point: Inuit Cultural Institute.

Remie, Cor H.W. 1982. *Culture Change and the Persistence of Traditional Religious Beliefs and Practices: Notes on the Oblate Mission on a Community of Hunters and Gatherers 1953–1963*. Nijmegen: Vakgroep Sociale Antropologie.

– 1983. "Culture Change and Religious Continuity among the Arviligdjuarmiut of Pelly Bay, NWT, 1935–1963." *Études Inuit Studies* 7 (2): 53–77.
– 1987. "The Struggle for Land among the Inuit of the Canadian Arctic." In G. Peperkamp and C.H.W. Remie, eds., *The Struggle for Land World-Wide*, 19–29. Saarbrücken: Breitenbach.
– 1988. "Flying like a Butterfly, or Knud Rasmussen among the Netsilingmiut." *Études Inuit Studies* 12 (1–2): 101–28.
Remie, Cor, ed. 1999. *Facing the Future: Inughuit Youth of Qanaaq. Report of the 1898 University of Nijmegen Expedition to Qanaaq, Thule District, Northern Greenland*. Nijmegen: Nijmegen University Press.
Remie, Cor, and Jarich Oosten. 2002. "The Birth of a Catholic Inuit Community: The Transition to Christianity in Pelly Bay, Nunavut, 1935–1950." *Études Inuit Studies* 26 (1–2): 109–42.
Riches, David. 1991. "The Force of Tradition in Eskimology." In R. Fardon, ed., *Localizing Strategies, Regional Traditions of Ethnographic Writing*, 71–89. Washington, DC: Smithsonian Institution Press.
Richling, Barnett. 1983. "Labrador Naluyuk: The Transformation of an Aboriginal Ritual Complex in a Post-Contact Setting." In N. Ross Crumrine and M. Halpin, eds, *The Power of Symbols: Mask and Masquerade in the Americas*, 21–9. Vancouver: University of British Columbia Press.
– 1989. "'Very Serious Reflections': Inuit Dreams about Salvation and Loss in Eighteenth-Century Labrador." *Ethnohistory* 36 (2): 148–69.
Rink, Henry. 1875. *Tales and Traditions of the Eskimo with a sketch of their habits, religion, language and other peculiarities*. Edinburgh: Wm Blackwood and Sons.
Rio, Marcel. 1995. *Un vrai Inuk. M. Rio: Itinéraire d'un homme de foi*. Outremont, QC: Novalis.
Rodon, Thierry, ed. 2008. *Peter Freuchen Ittinuar: Teach an Eskimo How to Read*. Life Stories of Northern Leaders 5. Iqaluit: Nunavut Arctic College.
Roheim, Geza. 1924. "Die Sednasage." *Imago* (Leipzig) 10:159–77.
– 1927. "Mond Mythologie und Mond Religion." *Imago* (Leipzig) 13:442–537.
Ross, John. 1819. *Voyage of discovery made under the orders of the admiralty, in his majesty's ships Isabella and Alexander, for the purpose of Exploring Baffin's Bay and inquiring into the probability of a North-West Passage*. London: John Murray.
– 1835. *Narrative of a Second Voyage in Search of a North-West Passage and of a Residence in the Arctic Regions during the years 1829, 1830, 1831, 1832, 1833*. London: A.W. Webster.
Ross, W. Gillies. 1975. *Whaling and Eskimos: Hudson Bay 1860–1915*. Ottawa: National Museums of Canada.
– 1977. "Whaling and the Decline of Native Populations." *Arctic Anthropology* 14 (2): 1–8.
– 1984a. *An Arctic Whaling Diary: The Journal of Captain George Comer in Hudson Bay 1903–1905*. Toronto: University of Toronto Press.
– 1984b. "George Comer, Franz Boas, and the American Museum of Natural History." *Études Inuit Studies* 8 (1): 145–64.
– 1997. *This Distant and Unsurveyed Country: A Woman's Winter at Baffin Island, 1857–1858*. Montreal and Kingston: McGill-Queen's University Press.
Ruskin, Olga. 1972. "Pangnirtung Adventures." *North* 19 (5): 29–33; (6): 32–5.

Sabo, George, and Deborah Sabo. 1985. "Belief System and the Ecology of Sea Mammal Hunting among the Baffin Island Eskimo." *Arctic Anthropology* 22 (2): 77–86.
Saladin d'Anglure, Bernard. 1977. "Iqallijuq, ou les reminiscences d'une âme-nom Inuit." *Études Inuit Studies* 1 (1): 33–63.
– 1978a. "L'Homme (angut), le fils (irniq) et la lumière (qau) ou le cercle du pouvoir masculin chez les Inuit de l'Arctique Central Canadien." *Anthropologica* 20 (1–2): 104–44.
– 1978b. *Vie et oeuvre de Davidialuk Alasuaq, artiste inuit du Québec arctique.* Gouvernement du Québec. Ministère des Affaires culturelles. Direction générale du patrimoine.
– 1980a. "Petit-ventre, l'enfant-géant du cosmos inuit (Ethnographie de l'enfant et enfance de l'ethnographie dans l'Arctique central inuit)." *L'Homme* 20 (1): 7–46.
– 1980b. "Nanuq super-mâle: L'ours blanc dans l'espace imaginaire et le temps social des Inuit." *Études Mongoles et Sibériennes* 11:63–94.
– 1981. "Esquimaux. La mythologie des Inuit de l'Arctique central nord-américain." In Y. Bonnefoy, gen. ed., *Dictionnaire des mythologies.* Vol. 1, 379–86. Paris: Flammarion.
– 1983. "Ijjiqat: Voyage au pays de l'invisible inuit." *Études Inuit Studies* 7 (1): 67–83.
– 1984. "Inuit of Nouveau-Québec." In D. Damas, ed., *Arctic,* 476–508. Vol. 5 of W.C. Sturtevant, gen. ed., *Handbook of North American Indians.* Washington: Smithsonian Institution.
– 1986. "Du foetus au chamane: La construction d'un 'troisième sexe' inuit." *Études Inuit Studies* 10 (1–2): 25–113.
– 1987. "Du projet 'PARADI' au sexe des anges: Notes et débats autour d'un 'troisième sexe.'" *Anthropologie et Sociétés* 9 (3): 139–76.
– 1988a. "Enfants nomades au pays des Inuit Iglulik." *Anthropologie et Sociétés* 12 (2): 125–66.
– 1988b. "Penser le 'féminin' chamanique, ou le 'tiers-sexe' des chamanes inuit." *Recherches amérindiennes au Québec* 18 (2–3): 19–50.
– 1988c. "Kunut et les *angakkut* iglulik." *Études Inuit Studies* 12 (1–2): 57–80.
– 1989. "La part du chamane ou le communisme sexuel inuit revisité dans l'arctique central canadien." *Journal de la Société des Américanistes* 85:133–71.
– 1990. "Frère-lune (Taqqiq), soeur-soleil (Siqiniq) et l'intelligence du monde (Sila)." *Études Inuit Studies* 14 (2): 75–140.
– 1991. "Chamanisme et christianisme dans l'Arctique central canadien." In *Encyclopaedia Italiana.* Milan.
– 1992a. "Pygmées arctiques et géants lubriques ou les avatars de l'image de l'autre lors des premières rencontres entre Inuit et Blancs." *Recherches amérindiennes au Québec* 22 (2–3): 73–88.
– 1992b. "Le 'troisième' sexe." *La Recherche* 245 (23): 836–44.
– 1992c. "Au clair de la lune circumpolaire, la cosmologie des Inuit." *Interface* 13 (6): 14–28.
– 1997. "Pour un nouveau regard ethnographique sur le chamanisme, la possession et la christianisation." *Études Inuit Studies* 21 (1–2): 5–20.
– 1998a. "La parenté élective chez les Inuit du Canada, fiction empirique ou réalité virtuelle." In A. Fine, ed., *Adoptions, la parenté choisie,* 121–50. Paris: Éditions MSH.
– 1998b. "Entre forces létales et forces vitales: Les tribulations du fœtus et de l'enfant inuit." In F. Zonabend and C. Le Grand Sébille, ed., *Le fœtus, le nourrisson et la mort,* 55–76. Paris: L'Harmattan.

– 2000. "'Pijariuniq': Performances et rituels inuit de la première fois." *Études Inuit Studies* 24 (2): 89–113.
– 2001a. "La construction de l'identité chamanique chez les Inuit du Nunavut et du Nunavik." *Études Inuit Studies* 25 (1–2): 191–215.
– 2001b. "Erotic Dreams, Mystical Kinship, and Shamanism." *North Atlantic Studies* 4 (1–2): 512.
– 2004. "La toponymie religieuse et l'appropriation symbolique du territoire par les Inuit du Nunavik et du Nunavut." *Études Inuit Studies* 28 (2): 107–32.
– 2006. *Être et renaître inuit: Homme, femme ou chamane*. Paris: Gallimard.
Saladin d'Anglure, Bernard, ed. 2001. *Cosmology and Shamanism*. Interviewing Inuit Elders 4. Iqaluit: Nunavut Arctic College.
Saladin d'Anglure, Bernard, and Klauss G. Hansen. 1997. "Svend Frederiksen et le chamanisme inuit ou la circulation des noms (*atiit*), des âmes (*tarniit*), des dons (*tunijjutiit*) et des esprits." *Études Inuit Studies* 21 (1–2): 37–74.
Saladin d'Anglure, Bernard, and Françoise Morin. 1998. "Mariages mystiques et pouvoir chamanique chez les Shipibo-Conibo d'Amazonie péruvienne et les Inuit du Nunavut canadien." *Anthropologie et Sociétés* 22 (2): 49–74.
Savard, Remi. 1970. "La déesse sous-marine des Eskimo." In *Échanges et Communications*, 1331–55. Mélanges offerts à Lévi-Strauss 2. The Hague: Mouton.
Scheffer, Lionel. 1950. "La valeur religieuse des religions païennes." In *L'Union missionnaire du Clergé*, 91–8. Quebec City.
Schefold, Reimar. 1994. "Cultural Anthropology, Future Tasks for *Bijdragen*, and the Indonesian Field of Anthropological Study: Some Developments in a Research Programme." *Bijdragen tot de Taal-, Land- en Volkenkunde* 150 (4): 805–24.
Schneider, Lucien. 1983. "La vie à Tavani … il y a 40 ans." *Eskimo* 25:10–18.
– 1985. *Ulirnaisigutiit. An Inuktitut-English Dictionary of Northern Québec: Labrador and Eastern Arctic Dialects*. Quebec City: Presses de l'Université Laval.
– n.d. "Grandeur et misère d'une épopée." Unpublished manuscript. Archives Deschâtelets, Ottawa.
Soby, Regitze Margarethe. 1969–70. "The Eskimo Animal Cult." *Folk* 11–12:43–78.
– 1997. "Naming and Christianity." *Études Inuit Studies* 21 (1–2): 293–302.
Sonne, Birgitte. 1978. "Ritual Bonds between the Living and the Dead in Yukon Eskimo Society." *Temenos* 14:127–83.
– 1980. *The Happy Family: Myths, Ritual, and Society on Nunivak*. Kobenhavns Universitet: Institut for Religionssociologi.
– 1986. "Toornaarsuk: An Historical Protheus." *Arctic Anthropology* 23 (1–2): 199–220.
– 1988. *Agayut: Nunivak Eskimo Masks and Drawings from the 5th Thule Expedition 1921–24, Collected by Knud Rasmussen*. Copenhagen: Gyldendal.
– 1990. "The Acculturative Role of Sea Woman: Early Contact Relations between Inuit and Whites as Revealed in the Origin Myth of Sea Woman." *Man and Society* 13:1–34.
– 1996. "Genuine Humans and 'Others': Criteria of 'Otherness' at the Beginning of Colonization in Greenland." In *Cultural and Social Research in Greenland 95/96: Essays in Honour of Robert Petersen*, 241–52. Nuuk: Ilisimatusarfik/Atuakkiorfik.
– 2000. "Heaven Negotiated: The Realms of Death in Early Colonial West Greenland." *Études Inuit Studies* 24 (2): 65–88.
– 2007. "La vie est un sac rempli d'air. Polysémie de pooq et autres notions associées." *Anthropologie et Sociétés* 31 (3): 15–36.

Spalding, Alex. 1998. *Inuktitut: A Multidialectical Outline*. Iqaluit: Nunavut Arctic College.
Spencer, Robert F. 1977 [1957]. *The North Alaskan Eskimo: A Study in Ecology and Society*. New York: Dover Publications.
Steenhoven, Geert van den. 1959. "Legal Concepts among the Netsilik Eskimos of Pelly Bay." In *Northern Coordination and Research Centre Report* 3. Ottawa: Department of Northern Affairs and National Resources.
– 1967. *The Eskimos*. Bruxelles: Université Libre de Bruxelles and Éditions de l'Institut de Sociologie.
Stefansson, Viljamur. 1913. *My Life with the Eskimo*. New York: Macmillan.
– 1922. *The Friendly Arctic: The Story of Five Years in Polar Regions*. New York: MacMillan Company.
– 1938. *The Three Voyages of Martin Frobisher in Search of a Passage to Cathay and India by the North-west, A.D. 1576–8. From the Original 1578 Text of George Best*. London: Argonaut Press.
Stevenson, Alex. 1965. "Quviasukvik. The Time for Rejoicing. Arctic Christmas Thirty Years Ago." *North* 12 (6): 28–31.
Stevenson, Marc. 1997. *Inuit Whalers and Cultural Persistence: Structure in Cumberland Sound and Central Inuit Social Organization*. Oxford: Oxford University Press.
Stirk, Frank. 2004. "Revival comes to the Arctic." *Christian Week*, 22 June 2004, vol. 18, issue 7.
Stories from Pangnirtung. 1976. Edmonton: Hurtig Publishers.
Stories from Sanikiluaq. 1991. Iqaluit: Nunavut Arctic College.
Stuckenberger, Nicole. 2005. *Community at Play: Social and Religious Dynamics in the Modern Inuit Community of Qikiqtarjuaq*. Utrecht: Rien Rabbers.
– 2007. "Transformation pentecôtiste et restauration sociale chez les Inuit." *Anthropologie et Sociétés* 31 (3): 37–64.
Sturtevant, William C. 1977. "The First Inuit Depiction by Europeans." *Études Inuit Studies* 4 (1–2): 47–9.
Suluk, Donald. 1983. "Some Thoughts on Traditional Inuit Music." *Inuktitut* 54:24–30.
Sutherland, P.C. 1856. "On the Esquimaux." *Ethnological Society of London Journal* 4: 193–214.
Suvaguuq. 2004. "The Nuluaq Project: Bringing People Together to Heal the Hurt." *Suvaguuq, National Newsletter on Inuit Social and Cultural Issues* 15 (2): 4 pages.
Swinton, Nelda. 1980. *The Inuit Sea Goddess*. Montreal: Montreal Museum of Fine Arts.
Szala-Meneok, Karen. 1994. "Christmas Janneying and Easter Drinking: Symbolic Inversion, Contingency, and Ritual Time in Coastal Labrador." *Arctic Anthropology* 31 (1): 103–16.
Tagoona, Armand. 1975. *Shadows*. Toronto: Oberon Press.
Taylor, John G. 1993. "Canicide in Labrador: Function and Meaning." *Études Inuit Studies* 17 (1): 7–21.
– 1997. "Deconstructing Deities: Tuurngatsuak and Tuurngaatsuk in Labrador Inuit Religion." *Études Inuit Studies* 21 (1–2): 141–58.
Thalbitzer, William. 1908. "The Heathen Priests of East Greenland (Angakut)." In *Verhandlungen des XV internationalen Amerikanistenkongresses*, 447–564. Reprint. Nendeln/Liechtenstein: Klauss.
– 1921. "Language and Folklore 1921." In *The Ammasalik Eskimo*. Pt 2, 113–564.

– 1925. "Cultic Games and Festivals in Greenland." In Congrès international des Américanistes, *Compte-Rendu de la XIIe Session. Deuxième partie tenue à Göteborg en 1924*, 236–55. Göteborg.
– 1926. "The Cultic Deities of the Inuit (Eskimo)." In *Atti del XXII Congresso Internazionale degli Americanisti Roma* 2:367–93.
– 1928. "Die Kultische Gottheiten der Eskimos." *Archiv für Religionswissenschaft* (Leipzig) 26 (3/4): 364–430.
– 1930. "Les magiciens esquimaux, leurs conceptions du monde, de l'âme et de la vie." *Journal de la Société des Américanistes* (Paris), n.s., 22:71–106.
Thalbitzer, William, ed. 1914. *The Ammasalik Eskimo.* Pt 1. Copenhagen: C.A. Reitzel.
–, ed. 1923. *The Ammasalik Eskimo.* Pt 2. Copenhagen: C.A. Reitzel.
Thérien, François. 1978. "Recherches sur le chamanisme inuit dans la région d'Igloolik." Unpublished manuscript. GÉTIC, Université Laval, Quebec City.
Therrien, Michèle. 1987. *Le Corps inuit (Québec arctique).* Paris: SELAF.
– 1995a. "Corps sain, corps malade chez les Inuit: Une tension entre l'intérieur et l'extérieur." *Recherches amérindiennes au Québec* 25 (1): 71–84.
– 1995b. "Tradition et transition: La notion de dynamique chez les Inuit." In A.V. Charrin, J.M. Lacroix, and M. Therrien, eds, *Peuples des Grands Nords: Traditions et transitions*, 245–54. Paris: Presses de la Sorbonne Nouvelle/ Institut National des Langues et Civilisations Orientales.
– 1996a. "Expériences premières et dynamique généralisée dans la culture inuit." In N. Tersis and M. Therrien, eds, *La dynamique dans la langue et la culture inuit*, 23–41. Paris: Selaf/Peeters.
– 1999. *Printemps inuit: Naissance du Nunavut.* Montpellier: Indigènes éditions.
– 2002a. "How Semantic Information Can Contribute to Shed Light on Concepts We Want to Investigate." In M. Therrien, ed., *Dynamics and Shifting Perspectives: Arctic Societies and Research*, 241–53. Proceedings of the First IPSSAS Seminar, Nuuk: Greenland: Ilisimatusarfik.
– 2002b. "Rêves d'une apprentie chamane inuit." *Cahiers de littérature orale* 51:169–83.
– 2008. "Tout révéler et rester discret chez les Inuit de l'Arctique canadien." In M. Therrien, ed., *Paroles interdites*, 251–86. Paris: Karthala.
Therrien, Michèle, and Frédéric Laugrand, eds. 2001. *Perspectives on Traditional Health.* Interviewing Inuit Elders 5. Iqaluit: Nunavut Arctic College.
Thibert, Arthur. 1958. *25 Folklore Eskimo Tales Written in Syllabics by the Eskimos Themselves.* Trans. A. Thibert. 3rd ed. Ottawa: Research Centre for Amerindian Anthropology.
Tibbetts, Janice. 2003. "Same-Sex Marriage 'alien to us,' Inuit Tell Commons Committee." *National Post*, 1 May 2003.
Tookoome, Simon. 2000. *The Shaman's Nephew: A Life in the Far North.* Toronto: Stoddart Kids.
Trott, Christopher G. 1988. "Structure and Pragmatics: Social Relations among the Tununirrusirmiut." PhD thesis, University of Toronto, Toronto.
– 1997. "The Rapture and the Rupture: Religious Change amongst the Inuit of North Baffin Island." *Études Inuit Studies* 21 (1–2): 209–28.
– 1998. "Mission and Opposition in North Baffin Island." *Journal of Canadian Church Historical Society* 30:31–55.

– 2000. "Structure into Practice: A Theory of Inuit Music." In K. Ralls-Macleod and G. Harvey, *Indigenous Religious Musics*, 183–97. Aldershot, Ashgate Publishing.
– 2001. "The Dialectics of 'Us' and 'Other': Anglican Missionary Photographs of the Inuit." *American Review of Canadian Studies* 22 (3): 171–90.
Turner, Edith. 1994. "The Effect of Contact on the Religion of Inupiat Eskimos." In T. Irimoto and T. Yamada, eds, *Circumpolar Religion and Ecology*, 143–62. Tokyo: University of Tokyo Press.
Turner, Lucien. 1979 [1894]. *Indians and Eskimos in the Quebec-Labrador Peninsula*. Quebec City: Coméditex.
Turquetil, Arsène. 1954. "Chez les Esquimaux." *Prêtre et Missions* 12 (7–8): 300–2.
– 1968. "Religious Rituals and Beliefs." In V.F. Valentine and F.G. Vallee, eds, *Eskimo of the Canadian Arctic*, 43–8. Toronto: McClelland & Stewart.
Valentine, V.F., and Frank G. Vallee. 1968. *Eskimo of the Canadian Arctic*. Carleton Library 41. Toronto: McClelland & Stewart.
Vallee, Frank G. 1962. *Kabloona and Eskimo in the Central Keewatin*. Northern Coordination and Research Centre. Ottawa: Department of Northern Affairs and National Resources.
– 1966. "Eskimo Theories of Mental Illness in the Hudson Bay Region." *Anthropologica* 8 (1): 53–83.
– 1968. "Differentiation among the Eskimo in Some Canadian Arctic Settlements." In V.F. Valentine and F.G. Vallee, eds, *Eskimo of the Canadian Arctic*, 109–26. Toronto: McClelland & Stewart.
Vallee, F.G., D.G Smith, and J.D. Cooper. 1984. "Contemporary Canadian Inuit." In D. Damas, ed., *Arctic*, 666–75. Vol. 5 of *Handbook of North American Indians*. Washington: Smithsonian Institution.
Van de Velde, Franz. 1956a. "Les règles du partage des phoques pris par la chasse aux aglus." *Anthropologica* 3:5–15.
– 1956b. "Religion and Morals among the Pelly Bay Eskimos." *Eskimo* 39:7–8, 14–16.
Vézinet, Monique. 1980. *Les Nunamiut: Inuit au coeur des terres*. Quebec City: Ministère des affaires culturelles.
Von Finckenstein, Maria, ed. 2002. *Nuvisavik: "Là où nous tissons."* Ottawa: Canadian Museum of Civilization.
Wachowich, Nancy. 1999. *Sagiyuq: Stories from the Lives of Three Inuit Women*. Montreal and Kingston: McGill-Queen's University Press.
Wachtel, Nathan. 1971. *La vision des vaincus*. Paris: Gallimard.
Wachtmeister, A. 1956. "Naming and Reincarnation among the Eskimos." *Ethnos* 21 (1–2): 130–42.
Waldmann, 1909–10. "Les Esquimaux du nord du Labrador." *Bulletin de la Société Neuchateloise de Géographie* 20:430–44.
Wallis, W.D. 1943. *Messiahs, Their Role in Civilization*. Washington, DC: American Council on Public Affairs.
Wardle, H.N. 1900. "The Sedna Cycle." *American Anthropologist* 2:568–80.
Warmow, Mathias. 1858. Extracts from Br. Mathias Warmow's journal of his residence in Cumberland Inlet, during the winter of 1857–58. *Periodical Accounts Relating to the Missions of the Church of the United Brethren, established among the Heathen*. Vol. 23, 1858–1860.

Weber, Bob. 2004. "Nunavut Church to Combine Religion, Cultural Pride" (CP, 29 February). Worldwide Religious News (WWRN).

Wenzel, George. 1997. "Animal Rights, Human Rights: Ecology, Economy and Ideology in the Canadian Arctic." Toronto: University of Toronto Press.

Weyer, Edward M. 1932. *The Eskimos, Their Environment and Folkways*. New Haven: Yale University Press.

White, Gavin. 1975. "Missionaries and Traders in Baffin Island 1894–1913." *Journal of the Canadian Church Historical Society* 17 (1): 2–10.

Wight, Darlene Coward. 1991. *The First Passionate Collector: The Ian Lindsay Collection of Inuit Art*. Winnipeg: Winnipeg Art Gallery.

Williamson, Robert G. 1974. *Eskimo Underground: Socio-cultural Change in Canadian Central Arctic*. Occasional Papers 2. Uppsala: Almqvist and Wiksell.

– 1988. "Some Aspects of the History of the Eskimo Naming System, Name-Change and Network Loss." *Folk* 30:245–64.

Wolf, E.R. 1982. *Europe and the People without History*. Berkeley: University of California Press.

Younger-Lewis, Greg. 2004. "Teaching Males 'How to Be a Man.'" *Nunatsiaq News*, 3 September 2004.

Zumwalt, Rosemary. 1982. "The Sea Spirit of the Central Eskimo and Her Relationship to the Living: A Delicate Balance." In G. Calame-Griaule, V. Görög-Karady, and M. Chiche, eds., *Le conte pourquoi? Comment / Folktales, Why and How?* 277–91. Paris: Centre National de Recherches Scientifiques.

Index

Note: This index includes Inuit elders, Christian missionaries, and the most important Inuit and Qallunaat concepts discussed in the book.